# MUSIC BUSINESS AGREEMENTS

# MUSIC BUSINESS AGREEMENTS

by

RICHARD BAGEHOT
*Solicitor of the Supreme Court*
**Partner in Field Fisher Waterhouse**

LONDON
SWEET & MAXWELL

First edition 1989 (Waterlow Publishers)
Reprinted 1990
Reprinted 1994 (Sweet & Maxwell)

Published by Sweet & Maxwell Limited of
South Quay Plaza, 183 Marsh Wall, London E14 9FT.



ISBN 0 08 036905 7

**British Library Cataloguing in Publication Data**

Bagehot, Richard
Music business agreement.—(Waterlow practitioner's library)
1. Great Britain. Music industries. Legal aspects
I. Title
344.103'7878

*Printed and bound in Great Britain by*
*Hartnolls Ltd, Bodmin, Cornwall*

# *Foreword*

The world record business in retail value in 1987 is estimated to have reached a size of nearly $16m; if one adds to that the income generated by music publishing (and associated activities of public performance and broadcasting revenues), and other copyright based industries, the IFPI have estimated that in aggregate this accounts for 2–3% of GDP in most major countries.

Supporting this impressive edifice of intangible property is national copyright legislation, national laws, international conventions and a myriad of industry agreements necessitated by the collision of the exigencies of practice and the almost immutable nature of copyright statutes and conventions.

To a novice, layman or lawyer, the need for practical guides to the curious world of the music business is obvious. Fulfilling it is a most difficult task. There have been some excellent American attempts (*This Business of Music* by Shemel and Krasilovsky) and the British Phonographic Industry, the Record Industry Association of America and the Performing Right Society publish year books which are models of their kind. Even so, having worked in one of the world's largest record groups since 1975, and having spent several of them as General Counsel, I realise that I know very little of the whole picture. That, of course, is wisdom of a kind—Montaigne, I believe it was, whose motto was "Que sais-je?"

So I am delighted at this attempt to explain music business agreements to the non-expert. It is a brave man who sets off along this path, but I am sure the author will see this work through many editions and gradually I hope it will become the universally acknowledged place to advise people to start in finding out about one of the greatest and most fascinating of industries.

*Michael Kuhn*
*Senior Vice President PolyGram International*
*CEO New Business Division*
*London 1989*

# *Contents*

# *Introduction*

Over the years there has been an increasing pace in the production of records of every musical taste, and technology has been achieved to create newer and better means of recording and reproducing sound and vision. This is only one aspect of the musical entertainment industry, but is the primary means of promoting an artiste, and is the basis from which his performances earn money for the artiste, his record company, publisher and manager. Like most commercial enterprises, a lot of money and hard work needs to be invested in any artiste to give him a good chance of success. When he is at the top, an artiste will have a high earning capacity. However, the likelihood of getting there is remote.

Managers are aware that most of the pop idols of today were struggling to earn a pittance only a short time prior to being "discovered". But for a lucky break accorded to only a few, such impecunious anonymity would still be theirs. Therefore a manager sometimes feels justified in binding an artiste by a contract with terms giving the manager a substantial share of the artiste's earnings, and control over his career, consistent with the time, effort and expense laid out by him on the artiste's behalf. In many instances, what might at first appear to be oppressive to the artiste is shown to be fair in all the circumstances.

All music business contracts, relating as they do to personal services, have the inherent weakness of requiring continued confidence, trust and good-will between the contracting parties to enable the venture to be successful. There is a greater element of security for a record company or music publisher, as the end product of performance of the contract is something tangible or permanent, with potentially valuable rights which survive after the services which created those products has ceased.

The music industry has grown to gigantic proportions, and the level of investment in it is such that financial influences tend to have an overriding effect upon the attitude of promoters and artistes to legal obligations contained in agreements.

Music industry agreements have become detailed and complicated, due to the various sources of potential income, and the granting of, and protection of, the rights to those sources. Agreements are frequently entered into by artistes without thinking of the possible consequences. The oft-heard cry is "I did not know what I was signing". With that utterance in mind, this book is intended to be a general guide in layman's language through the structure of, and the normal problems relating to, music industry contracts. This should be of use to those not experienced in the business, but there are few situations to which a mere set of rules can be applied to find a practical solution.

No agreement can cater for every possible contingency; there is no such thing as a perfect agreement. It can only be drafted on the basis of the facts known at the time, and the specific points of agreement between the parties. It can take into account reasonably foreseeable events, but difficulties created in the future by unexpected circumstances must be dealt with at the time. The outcome will depend upon the stability of the relationship between the parties at the time the crisis occurs, and upon the interpretation of the legal obligations contained in the contract.

Examples of clauses in the text, and sample agreements in Appendix II are only illustrative. All legal advisers have their own opinions on what constitutes a good clause or agreement, ultimately each one is the result of negotiated compromise.

Appendix III contains a selection of interesting music industry cases to illustrate some of the principles on which contracts seem to be litigated most often. The judgments in each case are lengthy, and should be studied.

The questions and answers set out in Appendix I are meant to give practical answers to the most common questions which are asked by people not familiar with how the music business works.

For much the same reason Chapter 11 contains a simplified explanation of the principles of various factors which are commonly faced in practical dealings, but which have a legal basis. The law can be complicated, the object is to point out that it need not be a complete mystery.

CHAPTER 1

# *Management Agreements*

## SECTION 1: GENERAL CONSIDERATIONS

### 1 Fundamental basis of a management agreement

**1.1** Most artistes do not have the time, inclination or experience to manage the promotion of their careers and the administration of their business activities. They appoint a manager to do so for them. Some managers are substantial, experienced and honest, and some are not. The choice of management can make or break an artiste. Some managers are professional and will if necessary invest risk capital in getting the artiste established; and some who are involved on the fringes of music think that it is a side line which is a bit of a doddle. For all these reasons an artiste must choose his management carefully, and must ensure that the management agreement gives him reasonable protection against a bad experience.

**1.2** Management means different things to rock artistes, philharmonic orchestras and jazz musicians, as their career needs are not the same. The emphasis in this book is on the rock or pop artiste as a means of focusing on broad principles and relevant items of detail. For all of the others, the principles will be much the same, but their specific requirements may be different. As the artiste is employing the manager, he should establish the management terms according to his requirements.

**1.3** Implied in any management agreement are three things:

(a) the essence of mutual trust and confidence between manager and artiste;

(b) the manager's obligation to use his best endeavours to further the career of the artiste;

(c) the doing of all things by both parties in relation to each other in good faith.

A management agreement may be terminable if it is proved that any of these vital aspects has been so substantially broken or disregarded as to constitute a fundamental breach of contract.

**1.4** Nobody, not even the court, can make an artiste sing, record or perform. Refusal to do so by an artiste, if caused by the dishonest, antagonistic or prejudicial behaviour of the manager, should not operate unfairly against the artiste. On the other hand a manager must have adequate protection against an artiste who himself dishonestly, and in total disregard of his contractual obligations, makes wild or unfounded allegations against the manager to provide a basis for termination of their agreement.

**1.5.1** Mutual trust and confidence are not part of the legal aspects of the management contract. The artiste depends on the manager to make him a success, using his skill, experience and contacts to do so. If the artiste believes that the manager is no longer capable of fulfilling his obligations, or is no longer willing to do so, he is concerned that his career and earning prospects will suffer. Management is a personal relationship, and cannot work if the parties are antagonistic.

**1.5.2** What constitutes best endeavours depends on the circumstances. Whenever the artiste is not satisfied with progress, the question is whether the manager is still doing his best for the artiste. A manager who loses interest in the artiste will not continue to act enthusiastically or with as much diligence for him. The measure of best endeavours is a personal judgement, so a dissatisfied artiste should take careful notes on what proposals the manager makes, or what activities he initiates, to demonstrate (if necessary) to an impartial judge that the manager has failed to promote the artiste in the manner which could reasonably be expected from him. The artiste must also be receptive to management ideas and projects; if he consistently ignores them or turns them down, there will come a time when the manager gives up trying.

**1.6** The exercise of good faith is a subjective test in the course of acting within the spirit of an agreement. The use of bad faith is, for example, where one party to the agreement deliberately:

(a) does something prejudicial to the interests of the other party, or does not disclose a conflict of interest;
(b) fails in his duty of care resulting in a loss to the other party;
(c) does a deal less advantageous than he could have got, in return for retaining an undisclosed benefit.

## 2 Contract of employment

*Example*

"Subject to and upon the terms and conditions herein contained the Artiste hereby appoints the Manager as his manager and representative."

**2.1.1** A management agreement is a contract of employment for services, so who is to be the employer? In most cases the artiste appoints the manager, and so employs him. In certain circumstances it may be more convenient to have the manager as employer and the artiste as employee. An example will be where, for tax purposes, there is a company which employs the artiste, and provides his services to third parties. The income from recording, songwriting and performance contracts entered into by it belongs to the company, which pays the artiste a substantial salary plus bonuses. The total remuneration of the artiste will be the balance after the company has retained the equivalent of the management commission plus a carefully calculated corporate operating profit, so that it is seen to be a commercial entity in its own right. There can be benefits in operating through a company, but if the structure is a sham with no commercial purpose of a real nature, the Inland Revenue may attempt to disregard it when it comes to charge tax on the artiste's income. The company can be the management vehicle, or it can wholly relate to the artiste, and itself appoint the manager.

**2.1.2** In the latter case the freedom of the artiste within the terms of the employment agreement will be rather more restricted. It must look like and genuinely work as an employment on a commercial *bona fide* basis, so the employment contract must contain the matters customarily relating to top executives. The agreement must also observe the statutory regulations governing employers. When the artiste appoints a manager, it is not strictly an employment situation in the same sense, as the manager is technically an independent contractor providing services to the artiste.

**2.2** The obligations involved in the management of an artiste tend to overlap those pertinent to agency. The two sides of representation will be distinguished by separate agreements between the artiste and each of the manager and the agent; although a comprehensive management agreement will include many matters relevant to an agency agreement. An agent represents the artiste for certain limited purposes only, whereas a manager will represent the artiste in the whole promotion of his musical career.

**2.3** A manager must ensure that his agreement with the artiste is fair and reasonable, and that, from the artiste's point of view, all contracts entered into by him with third parties meet the same criteria. Each contract must contain the best terms available, and adequate safeguards for the artiste. The artiste must be guided by the manager through the proper fulfilment of each contract, and must be advised upon all business matters under his supervision. He is not bound to accept or comply with the advice he receives, but he should give it proper consideration.

## 3 Choice of manager

**3.1** An artiste must choose carefully who is to manage him. Because it sounds like a glamorous occupation there are many part-time and semi-serious "managers" who do not have the skill, contacts and experience necessary to do a good job. They might not be prepared to spend money on supporting the artiste, and on promotion and publicity for his career—even if they have it.

**3.2** Inexperienced managers hope to make a favourable impression by using the popularity of the artiste, and by using their association with him to build up a name for themselves, and from that to establish a business. The manager may not really know what he is doing, which can be dangerous when the manager negotiates long-term or other agreements for the artiste's services. He will not always have the facilities for extensive representation, or proper accounting and administration. For an unknown artiste with nothing to lose except the stardom he might otherwise have reached, such a manager relies upon the fact that the artiste must start somewhere. There is also a tendency for him to require a "one way contract" in his favour, through greed or inexperience.

**3.3** The first choice for an artiste with potential will be an established and successful manager with a good reputation. The strength of a manager is only as great as the popularity of the acts he represents. A well-respected manager who is temporarily in the doldrums, having lost a top act and before finding the next one, will have a "credibility bank" with the right people in power in the right places. The manager will put the whole of his effort into the next act he finds, as his ability to open the right doors to display unproven talent will fade with the passage of time.

**3.4** To a new artiste, the disadvantages of approaching a top manager are that he will be selective in who he manages, and his existing acts will take up most of his time. His top acts are also likely to have priority of choice where deals are available. A good manager will use the power of the top acts to help the new artiste to get enough of the right work to prove his ability and quality.

**3.5** A top manager will want to be associated only with successful artistes. His earning power and reputation depend on the level of that success. What is there to manage? Initially an artist depends almost entirely on having an active recording deal. Without record releases, personal appearances for an unknown artiste will be difficult to obtain. With an active recording and touring schedule, the making of video recordings and other avenues of promotion open up. If the artiste is also a songwriter and/or a record producer, successful records are necessary to promote those activities. However talented the artiste may be, "making it" is extremely difficult. Good and effective management is therefore crucial.

## 4 Prior agreements

*Example*

"(a) Subject as disclosed in the First Schedule hereto the Artiste warrants that he is not a party to any written or oral agreement or commitment current or contingent (including those which have any options yet to be exercised) which relate to or which may detract from any of the rights granted to the Manager under this Agreement and that the Artiste is fully entitled to enter into this Agreement and that his doing so is not in breach of any third party rights.

(b) The Artiste undertakes to indemnify the Manager from any damage cost loss or liability incurred by him as a direct result of a breach by the Artiste of the Warranty set out in (a) above."

**4.1** An artiste may have a prior existing management agreement with some time still to run, although (for example) it may be dormant because either he has left the group to which the management agreement related, or because the manager has temporarily ceased to operate. The artiste cannot grant the same rights at the same time to two separate managers, so any further management agreement he signs during that period can only become effective immediately upon the termination of the prior agreement. He must immediately take all the necessary steps to terminate, or to get confirmation from the prior manager of termination of, the dormant agreement. If the artiste gets no response from the prior manager, he cannot legally assume that the management agreement has terminated. If it can reasonably be deduced that the prior manager has no intention of returning to the artiste, and as he is therefore not fulfilling his obligations, the artiste will have no alternative but to terminate the management agreement by sending written notice to the prior manager. There is a risk that he would promptly surface, but that risk will have to be taken. This termination right would not arise if the artiste knows full well that the prior manager has only taken a long holiday, or if for any other reason it is evident that his absence is only temporary, and he has no intention of abandoning the artiste.

**4.2.1** All prior agreements of whatever nature relating to the artiste should be investigated to confirm that they are not currently valid, including checking upon the existence of options. This avoids the possibility of injunctions being granted against the artiste and the new manager to preserve third party rights. An injunction would be sought, for example, to prevent the artiste from signing any agreement elsewhere for unauthorised performances or to prevent the unauthorised recording, manufacture, distribution and release of records containing his performances. An injunction may be granted unless its effect would be to give specific enforcement to a contract for personal services, or where in all the circumstances damages would be the appropriate remedy. It also minimises the risk of a court order being sought to freeze the earnings of the artiste until the resolution of any claim made by the prior manager. If the artiste has been in and out of several groups before appointing the manager, he may not realise that he has legal obligations, or that he is subject to restrictions remainng effective from the past.

**4.2.2** The termination of, or the release of a member of a group individually from, all existing agreements should be fully documented, as written agreements cannot safely be cancelled orally.

**4.3** Where compensation is required by the manager for releasing the artiste by premature termination of his existing agreement, it ought to be negotiated and concluded by a signed agreement before a new management agreement is signed—before then he is not entitled to appoint the new manager. If compensation is already being paid by a member of a group to yet another previous manager, such as by means of deductions from his share of the present group income, this should not be allowed to affect the current settlement negotiations on behalf of the group as a whole. This would be an ideal time for all past obligations to be rationalised.

**4.4.1** All existing contracts to which the artiste is a party, and which affect the management contract which he is about to sign, should be scheduled to it, or clearly referred to and identified in it. This prevents any subsequent claim of their non-disclosure resulting in allegations by the manager of misrepresentation or breach of warranty by the artiste.

**4.4.2** If there is a potential conflict between the various agreements, or if an existing agreement is sufficiently wide as possibly to restrict the proper exercise of the new management agreement, the artiste must indemnify the manager from the results of any successful claim against him arising from breach of the earlier contracts. If the manager is fully aware of the existing contractual problems, and the risks in being appointed by the artiste, arguably it should be a *caveat emptor* position, and the artiste should not give him an indemnity.

**4.5** Before a manager is appointed, part of his brief should be to get copies of all of the artiste's existing contracts, to identify all of his outstanding legal obligations, and to ensure that the management appointment will not be in breach of any third party rights.

## 5 Exclusivity of territory

*Example*

> "The Manager shall be the sole and exlusive manager of the Artiste within [ ] (hereinafter called the Territory) in respect of the following activities of the Artiste within the entertainment industry:" (see Paragraph **15**).

**5.1** To have any value to the manager, a management agreement must be a sole and exclusive appointment. It should cover the whole of the music and entertainment industry within which the manager is capable of undertaking his obligations, and throughout so many countries as the manager can cover effectively.

**5.2** An artiste who is also an actor may also have a separate theatrical stage manager. Wherever there is multiple management representation within separate areas of music and show business, the different contracts should accurately state and distinguish between the legal rights of each party. Each contract should be negotiated with consideration for what other contracts may be needed in the future. Multiple representation will create a clash of ideas and personalities, and is not recommended.

**5.3** If the manager cannot cover the whole world effectively, separate representation in different continental territories can be agreed. The separate managers for different territories should co-ordinate their efforts so as not to confuse promotion of the artiste by independently entering into conflicting commitments for him without having consulted him and each other first. Worthwhile management will require worldwide exclusive representation of the artiste. The manager can delegate his responsibilities in territories which he cannot fully supervise himself, provided he is contractually entitled to do so.

**5.4** Exclusivity ensures an orderly basis of management administration. Where the artiste is successful, exclusive rights are valuable assets for the manager. The artiste looks for efficient, honest and forceful management.

**5.5** During the exclusive period the artiste cannot appoint another manager to take over from an unsatisfactory manager, so the termination provisions in any management agreement should refer to any special concern of the artiste, failure of which by the manager will be a termination event.

## 6 Written agreements

**6.1.1** As the manager and the artiste should treat the business side of their personal relationship as a commercial transaction, an agreement in writing is necessary for the benefit of both of them. This will enable their professional advisers to negotiate a fair and reasonable contract, and to explain clearly to them the meaning and effect of each entitlement, obligation or restriction. There may also be tax or other financial considerations which can be effected for the artiste's benefit.

**6.1.2** The agreement will be disputed if one party feels strongly either that he could do better elsewhere, or that the other party is not doing his best. At least a written memorandum, if not a detailed agreement, confirms what basic terms were originally negotiated, but it should be sufficiently detailed to enable the rights of the parties to be ascertained. A rambling incomprehensible agreement may be worse than not having one at all.

**6.2** It is practical and prudent to draft the management agreement with a view to proving its validity and enforceability in a dispute. To negotiate an agreement in detail means that many of the common causes of contention will be considered and discussed, so that the agreement can be sensibly drafted, and the parties will know how they stand upon the happening of those events. The outlook of the person drafting the agreement is influenced by whether he is acting for the manager, or for the artiste, hence the benefit of expert negotiation by professionals.

**6.3.1** Enforcement of a management contract is intended to obtain for the manager compensation for loss on its breach by the artiste. Specific performance will not be granted by the court to compel the artiste to retain the manager, damages are deemed to be an adequate remedy for a claim which would in any event revolve around monetary considerations.

**6.3.2** In the assessment of proper compensation, there is a distinction between a case where loss, liability, or expense is incurred by the manager through no fault of his own; and where no real monetary damage has been incurred, but the manager wants to punish an errant artiste for having broken his contract. The first purpose is to compensate the manager financially, whereas the other purpose is motivated by malice or thoughts of revenge. This distinction is relevant, for example, in the case of an infant, (a person under 18 years), who successfully challenges his contract where the manager has not stinted himself on his behalf in good faith, notwithstanding the risks inherent in dealing with youngsters.

**6.3.3** The music industry is one in which, with luck and the right contacts, large sums of money can be made in a time and with an effort disproportionately small to the size of the possible ultimate reward.

**6.4** Contracts relating to personal services come under close scrutiny, and are subject to severe testing in the course of litigation. Management contracts are amongst the most vulnerable types of contract, as their essence is personal performance by the artiste where no physical asset is thereby acquired—such as records or copyrights. A manager does not have the same negotiating strength, or "give and take", as a record company or a publisher when discussing the extension of his contract, as he has little to give other than a reduction of his commission rate.

**6.5.1** A manager may be inclined to bias the strength and the profit element of the agreement unreasonably in his favour. A philosophy sometimes applied by a manager with a "high risk" artiste is that he should try to get what he can out of the artiste while he can. The manager knows that if the agreement continues on a long term basis, eliminating the initial risk, the financial arrangements in the future can be modified voluntarily by him more to the artiste's benefit to make up for the previous disparity.

**6.5.2** The manager should make the management agreement fair and reasonable to the artiste from the beginning. No artiste should expect anything less than strict safeguards to be taken by the manager, especially if the artiste is known to be in the habit of treating his contractual liabilities with frivolity.

**6.6.1** If the artiste's services are promoted through a management/record production company, which manages the artiste, and owns the mechanical copyrights in the artiste's recordings, the management agreement should not contain provisions unnecessarily protective to the company. An example of an unacceptable clause would be where, if the company is entitled to terminate the management agreement upon a substantial breach by the artiste, the artiste will no longer be entitled to receive any income from any source of promotion which remains within the control of the company. In theory this would be claimed to be justified on the basis that when an employee leaves, he would not expect to continue to be remunerated. That limitation is not acceptable in any circumstances. Following the reference in paragraph **2.1.1** to commercial validity, the same point can be made here. Where else does an employee continue to get "full pay" indefinitely after the employment is terminated?

**6.6.2** Unless there are extraordinary circumstances which make the provision reasonable in an individual case, it is a penalty which attempts to give to the manager a right to damages in a sum which never stops being paid. This can hardly be a genuine pre-estimation of proper compensation, and the artiste should never sign an agreement with such a clause.

**6.6.3** Normally such a clause will be considered to be unenforceable, as, despite the employee point, an artiste's royalty should always be due to him, subject to recoupment of advances. The court would take a hard look at the genuineness of the employment contract, and this example highlights one of the differences between a contract for services, and a service contract. It is reasonable for the company to retain a genuine estimated amount for which the artiste may reasonably be liable to the manager as a result of its claim for damages and compensation. When the total ascertained liability has been extinguished by retaining his royalties, the artiste should receive any excess balance withheld, and all royalties due to him in the future.

## 7 Personal and corporate management

*Example*

"Upon giving written notice to the Artiste the Manager shall be entitled to assign the benefit and obligations of this Agreement to a limited liability company which he controls [define] provided that:

(a) he will continue to provide his personal services to the Artiste through the Company;

(b) such assignment will be without prejudice to any existing claims against the manager;
(c) upon the manager becoming permanently in breach of (a) above the Artiste will be entitled to give written notice to the company of termination of this Agreement."

**7.1** A prospective manager must consider whether the management should be by him personally, or by means of a company of which he has effective control. The choice should be made with tax savings and commercial liabilities in mind. The use of a company by the manager will minimise his personal financial liability, and can give greater flexibility to his management activities if he advises several artistes.

**7.2.1** If the artiste will be the only act represented by the manager with his recording, publishing and other earning activities going through the company, he can be given a stake in his own future, by allotting him shares in the management company and making him a director of it. This would be unusual, and would represent a form of business partnership between them not within the normal manager/artiste relationship. Instead of a management agreement, the artiste would have a service agreement with the company with the same terms, and with the same protections for both parties, which the management agreement would have had. In doing so they must address the question of what happens if they have an irreconcilable dispute.

**7.2.2.** Both the manager and the artiste should obtain advice on the tax implications of a jointly owned company, particularly if the artiste wishes to obtain tax relief on earnings from work undertaken overseas. Before entering into any commitment to such a proposal, the artiste should obtain independent advice upon how the proposal affects his rights and obligations in comparison with those applying to an ordinary management situation. A management structure which is best for the manager may not be suitable for the artiste.

**7.2.3** The artiste is less likely to breach the service agreement, as by doing so he would be injuring himself in proportion to his holding in the company, particularly if it owns his copyrights and his recordings. Should he be sued by the company for breach of contract, to some extent he will be suing himself. An explanation of this potential conflict of interest should be part of the independent legal advice.

**7.2.4** The greater the stake of the artiste in the capital of the company, the greater is his security and control over his own destiny, and the greater may be his reluctance to make alternative management arrangements. To be effective, the security would have to be incorporated into a shareholders' agreement and the articles of association of the company, whether or not he has less than 50% of the shares.

**7.3** A company is also useful for the management of more than one artiste, because of the great responsibility for the personal supervision of each of his artistes by a manager acting on his own. If more than one artiste is handled by the management company, it would not be practical to give each of the artistes shares in the company.

**7.4.1** A personal manager may decide to expand his business, or to reduce his personal liabilities, and for that purpose he can form a company and have assigned to it the benefit of the personal management agreement, if he has the right to do so. It would be reasonable for the artiste to stipulate that the continued personal supervision by the manager is a prior condition of assignment, and should be of the essence of the artiste's contract with the company. It would not necessarily matter if the manager does not retain legal control over the company, provided that he himself is employed by it on a satisfactory basis specifically to carry on his personal management of the artiste. This could happen if the management company goes public.

**7.4.2** Personal management may arise through friendship of the parties, or their mutual confidence in a stable business relationship. A reasonable condition for the protection of the artiste in a personal management contract is that it remains on a personal basis. Where that becomes impersonal, such as by the manager assigning the agreement to a company, the artiste should be able to terminate the contract if he reasonably considers that the promotion of his career will genuinely be prejudiced. Hence the pre-conditions for assignment. The consent provision should be qualified by the artiste having an absolute discretion to consent or not.

**7.5** If the management agreement is with a company initially, the artiste may request that some person of executive authority be made personally responsible for the supervision of his career. Within a large concern this is not always practical. The point usually arises where the artiste was attracted to a management company through confidence in a specific executive. He would be unlikely to sign the contract unless he thought that person, or some other suitable person acceptable to him, would continue to take an active interest in him as an artiste, rather than merely treating him as one object among many requiring promotion. In the absence of a nominated personal supervisor contact, the management company will manage generally through its executive staff.

**7.6** Management of an artiste in an effective and efficient manner cannot be done on a part-time basis. A practical motto for any manager is to keep the artiste happy within reason. It is generally the unhappy ones who tend to leave abruptly and untimely when circumstances suit them. Whether or not they were right in so doing depends on what caused the unhappiness. In this context "unhappiness" means having a genuine legal or contractual grievance, not simply becoming sulky, petulant or arrogant on the pretext of an excess of artistic temperament.

## 8 Initial financing

*Example*

"(a) The Artiste acknowledges that the Manager has spent the sum of [£ ] prior to the date hereof which the Artiste agrees shall be deemed to be recoupable as money spent under (b) below.
(b) The Artiste agrees that the Manager may spend money for his benefit provided that the artiste first approves the purpose and amount of any sum spent in excess of [£250].
(c) The Artiste authorises the Manager to retain by way of recoupment from moneys due to the Artiste such agreed or approved expenses under (a) and (b) above.
(d) On a [monthly] basis the Manager shall provide the Artiste with a detailed account of all of the Artiste's income received by the Manager and of all recoupable expense incurred by the Manager on behalf of the Artiste." (See also paragraphs **18**, **19** and **20**.)

**8.1** Where a manager is promoting an unknown artiste, money may need to be spent on promotion, publicity, instruments, stage clothes and many other items necessary to give the artiste a reasonable chance to show his talents to the right people in the right places at the right times. The manager's normal business operating expenses are not included within this category.

**8.2** These promotional expenses are normally speculative, and should only be recouped as a first charge on the artiste's share of earnings. The manager is spending his own money on the artiste as he thinks best. If the artiste has no control over the expenditure, he should not have to pay it back if it is not recouped through earnings. An experienced manager will not spend money unnecessarily in case it is not recovered, but an inexperienced one may rapidly run the artiste into substantial debt for no visible value. The artiste will usually leave it to the judgment of the manager as to what should sensibly be spent, but to protect himself he should always be consulted first on any significant expense with a strict limited budget laid down.

**8.3** The manager may have already spent money prior to the management agreement being signed, and which is agreed by the artiste to be recoupable. The agreement should have a clause identifying the agreed amount, and bringing it contractually within the context of recoupable expense. Alternatively the effective date of the management agreement can be made retrospective to a date prior to the expense having been incurred. In the absence of either provision, as the management agreement is effective after the expense has been incurred, the artiste would not be obliged to repay it.

**8.4.1** The expenditure is treated as an advance or loan to the artiste recoupable from his own personal share of earnings, and not as a "top-slice" recoupment out of gross profits. By this means the manager receives his commission on the gross income, but the artiste only receives his own share of the income after all deductions have been made, including management commission, and when the manager has been repaid his advances in full.

**8.4.2** But, if as a result the artiste receives nothing, what does he live on? The manager would have to make further advances to cover his living costs, and the debt to the manager increases. Therefore, while the artiste's income is at a low level, the manager might agree to recover his debt from an agreed proportion of income to prevent this happening. The artiste's first significant income may only come from recording or publishing advances, and there will be no more money due from those sources until they have each been fully recouped by the relevant company. Financial planning is essential in the early period of an artiste's career, as effectively, his first income tends to be borrowed money. Unless real income can be generated within a reasonable time, the level of debt can get out of control.

**8.4.3** Although the financial speculation on a new artiste may be a risk taken by the manager, during the period of recoupment out of the artiste's earnings the artiste must be given a reasonable allowance on which to live. What is reasonable will depend upon the frugal style which he is used to, or which, in consultation with the manager, he needs to adopt. His personal allowance will depend on who pays the artiste's major outgoings, such as rent, rates, gas, electricity, telephone and travelling. Both the artiste and the manager must be realistic when agreeing upon the allowance. This assumes that the artiste does not have a job or any other source of income during the initial period before professional earnings are received. If the artiste still has a job so that he can earn enough to live on until his entertainment career takes off, the manager should not be given the right to have speculative advances repaid from that income.

**8.5.1** If the manager has adjusted the commission rate disproportionately in his favour by agreement with the artiste during the period of recoupment, once the outlay has been recouped, the rate of commission should revert to the original figure. The reason given for such a proposal is that, as the manager is totally at risk, he should be compensated for taking that risk. This reason is not acceptable, and should never be agreed to, as such an arrangement has a serious adverse effect on the artiste. As recoupment of expenditure is from the artiste's share of income, there is less to recoup from. Therefore the recoupment period is increased, and during the whole of such increased period the manager continues to receive the uprated commission.

**8.5.2** The level of expenditure, and the inflated commission, when related to the artiste's net income, may mean that he will never be out of debt until his career really takes off, and therefore he will always pay a high commission. This would be compounded if the recoupable expenditure is increased disproportionately to the income generated in an effort to increase that income, however well meaning that effort may be. This is a circular argument, and this prospect can depress the artiste to the point where he feels compelled to repudiate his agreement to get away from it all. This unsatisfactory position should never arise, and is one to beware of.

**8.6** Where recoupment of initial expenditure looks unlikely, how should management advances be dealt with in the accounts of the manager, and of the artiste? To what extent will the loan/loss be tax deductible, and which of them should take that benefit?

**8.7** If the management is of a group, and one member has commissionable activities outside the group, eg being a record producer, unless it is specifically agreed, the manager should not take the member's share of such income after commission towards recoupment of his portion of group advances.

## 9 Enticement of an artiste

**9.1** A successful artiste may receive attractive offers from other managers. They will be aware of his existing contractual commitments, but they are prepared to "take-over" the supervision, promotion and management of his career. This is even more likely once the groundwork has been laid and the initial risks have been taken by the manager, and the preliminary finance has been expended in establishing the artiste.

**9.2** Enticement is a calculated risk upon whether the injured manager will take legal action if the artiste succumbs to the offer. The risk will be greater if the successful take-over was an active inducement to the artiste to breach his contract with the manager. There is less risk when the new manager is only responding to positive overtures by the artiste, who has already repudiated his agreement with the manager. The manager can claim against the artiste for breach of contract, and against the new manager for inducing that breach. The claim will be for damages in the usual manner.

The actionable damage caused to the manager as a direct result of the artiste's change of allegiance is diminished where the new manager limited his activities to only picking up the pieces after the artiste and the manager have already irretrievably fallen out. If it was the artiste who set up the new deal on his own initiative, and who only terminated the management agreement when he knew the alternative management was in place, the new manager would be justified in asking for an indemnity from the artiste against any claim made by the terminated manager.

## 10 Bankruptcy of artiste

**10.1** Where an unknown and insolvent group approaches a prospective manager, he should check whether each member is an undischarged bankrupt, or has creditors' court judgements outstanding against him. The most likely cause of bankruptcy is failure to pay tax, but it could come from other creditors, such as major credit card companies for significant unpaid accounts.

**10.2** If a bankrupt member is signatory to a group bank account, where gross earnings are received before apportionment to the individual members, there is a risk, until the legal rights of the other members have been ascertained, of attachment by his trustee in bankruptcy of the whole of the group's earnings. Attachments could be either against the source of the income, or upon the joint bank account of the group. As soon as such a situation arises it should be rectified, so that the bankrupt artiste has only his own share of money taken toward his creditors' claims.

**10.3** If a member is bankrupt, his trustee or creditors should be consulted prior to the management agreement being entered into, to see how the statutory restrictions imposed on the artiste can best be dealt with. Apart from the problems facing the manager when trying to promote the group, he may have difficulty in obtaining his management commission. The creditors will want the artiste to earn as much as possible for their benefit, so some arrangement should be reached.

**10.4** Because there are statutory restrictions upon an undischarged bankrupt carrying on business, the group structure may have to be modified accordingly. It is possible that, if the creditors can be reasonably satisfied that it would be in their interests to do so, they would not make the artiste bankrupt. He could then get on, and sources of his income can be directed to pay a proportion of it directly to a creditors' fund.

## 11 Termination

*Example*

"Either party shall be entitled to terminate this Agreement by giving written notice to the other party in the event of the other party:

(a) remaining in material breach of any obligation hereunder for more than [21] days after receipt of a written notice specifying the breach and requiring its remedy;

(b) becoming bankrupt or (being a company) being wound up otherwise than for amalgamation or reconstruction;

(c) threatening to permanently cease trading;

(d) compounding generally with his creditors."

**11.1** The agreement must have a means of identifying when it is to expire or terminate. If there is no expiry date, ie, it just goes on indefinitely, the law implies the right of either party to terminate it at any time by giving reasonable notice. If the agreement is to extend for a minimum period then it must say so. Whatever the proposed expiry date, either party should be entitled to terminate the management agreement upon the happening of certain events. Apart from breaches of contract, these should relate to the capacity or ability of the other party to fulfil his obligations, and should also take into account his willingness to do so. A manager is not likely to terminate his agreement with an artiste unless, for example, he has a conflict of interest, or in his opinion the artiste is an endless investment and expense with no potential future, despite all his efforts.

**11.2** Some management agreements include as terminable acts breaches of social etiquette, such as drug taking or being extremely objectionable as a way of life, or having criminal convictions. Apart from a drugs conviction, these may in no way physically impair the artiste's ability to pursue his career or to fulfil his obligations. An English court may consider the more frivolous of such terms to be unreasonable and unduly onerous, and at least unrealistic in the light of present day attitudes to personal freedom.

**11.3** If a conviction, such as for a drugs offence, results in a term of imprisonment, the artiste would not be able to fulfil his part of the contract, and termination by the manager would be reasonable. The artiste would have a similar right if a personal manager is imprisoned. If the conviction is for drugs or any other offence which results in major countries like the USA and Japan refusing work permits or entry visas, the prohibition would severely restrict the ability of the artiste to work internationally. That would inhibit the manager from carrying out his obligations if he has worldwide rights, but would not be a fundamental breach by the artiste.

**11.4** If an agreement is to run for a specified period, but contains no premature termination clause, the right to terminate will be implied by law upon the happening of substantial incapacitating events, which totally frustrate the carrying out of the contract. Examples are the permanent loss of voice of a singer, or a guitarist having one of his hands amputated. Legal frustration, such as refusal by a foreign country to allow work permits for a tour, will affect the viability of the tour promoter's contract, but will not fundamentally affect the management contract. If somehow the manager is the cause of the legal frustration, that may be a material breach by the manager of his obligations to the artiste. Automatic termination will only be implied upon impossibility of performance, such as upon the death of the artiste or a personal manager. Impossibility of performance of a specific job arising from human failing, such as the manager missing a plane, will not fall within this category.

**11.5** Fundamental breaches of contract should be caught by a well defined termination clause. If the parties agree that any unusual event or failure should be deemed to be a fundamental breach, that should be included in clear wording. Sometimes there is a distinction between an event which gives the right to terminate, (which might not be exercised), and an event on the happening of which the agreement is deemed to have terminated without any action being required by either party. If the latter is to apply, it will have to be clearly set out. All terminable events trigger the right to give a termination notice, so the affected party has time to consider how he wants to react. Re-negotiation of parts of the agreement may be more beneficial to him than terminating it.

**11.6** There can be breaches of contract which merit termination, but where the right of termination is not exercised. This may be because a compromise is agreed, or because a compensation payment is considered to be adequate. There is no obligation to terminate, but if the right is not exercised within a reasonable period of the party becoming aware of the breach, it may be deemed to be waived. For clarification there should be a clause stating that if the right is not exercised within [21] days after the occurrence or the discovery of the breach, whichever is the later, it shall be waived. There is a grey area between the statutory period within which legal rights can be exercised, (six years), and the legal presumption that if nothing is done to exercise that right within a reasonable time, it will be deemed to have been waived. When a terminable act or breach is committed, commercially the affected party must decide promptly whether to terminate or to continue. If he continues, there is an acceptance of the status, and shortly both parties will have proceeded to the point where it would be inequitable for the breach to be resurrected, and the agreement terminated. (See paragraph **14.8**).

**11.7** There are also breaches of contract which are not serious enough to merit termination. These need to be remedied where possible. Compensation can normally only be claimed where the party has actually suffered a loss or expense as a result of the breach, and not when the default is just an irritation or inconvenience. If the breach causes a potential liability to a third party, compensation or performance (as the case may be) will only be needed if and when that liability is activated. It is possible for the breach to be known, but the potential damages only to be ascertained at a later date. To protect the breach rights, the aggrieved party can either get an acceptance by the other party of liability on the basis that payment will be later, or if the liability is denied he will have to sue on the breach.

**11.8** A clause giving arbitrary and excessive compensation rights wholly unrealistic to the breach will be unenforceable as a penalty. A genuine realistically calculated pre-estimate of loss or damage should be enforceable, even though in the event it is not precisely correct. Compensation or damages are awarded to the extent necessary to rectify a loss, although that loss may not be capable of being quantified. A penalty is a financial threat with no basis for legal or commercial justification, although it will depend on what both the parties genuinely believed the potential damage or loss to be. Where a claim is made under a penalty clause, the court will not enforce it, even to awarding the valid amount only and disregarding the balance.

**11.9** The claiming party may be entitled to both a right of termination and a compensation payment arising from the same breach. The scope of this should be clarified if the parties wish to limit the possibility to specified circumstances. The compensation should be limited to actual loss or expense.

**11.10** Both parties must be careful that, despite emotional involvement or apparently unanswerable allegations, they do nothing to put themselves irreparably in the wrong if, in the light of subsequent analysis of the situation, the legal effects of the circumstances are not as they were assumed to be.

**11.11** What is the position where a manager, without good cause, and without being entitled to, simply terminates the management agreement? He is in breach of the agreement, but what compensation (if any) can the artiste claim against him? Can the artiste be said to be deprived of his earning sources? What is the immediate impact on his workload, is there any employment he has failed to get as a result? What damage has been done to his career? He may have to rely on general damages for breach, and an account for all money being dealt with by the manager, and a claim for any expense he reasonably has to incur in finding a new manager. As no manager is likely to release a profitable artiste, it may simply be because the manager considers he can do no more for him.

## SECTION II: TERMS TO BE CONSIDERED

### 12 General principles

**12.1** Every manager has his own idea of what should be contained in a management agreement, and how fair to be to an artiste who may be unreasonable later; and how tight the agreement can be made in his favour without making it unconscionable.

**12.2** There are industry norms of what is acceptable in practice within a range of variation, depending upon the circumstances. There are categories of clauses which will be familiar in all well drafted management agreements, but negotiation determines the details of their extent and application. Unusual individual contractual requirements can be included, but the preparation of a memorandum explaining the reasons for agreeing them may prevent future problems of explaining or justifying motive or reasonableness.

**12.3** The artiste should take independent advice to ensure that the manager is not insisting on unduly onerous or unfair terms. He must also accept that if he freely agrees, with full knowledge of the consequences, to terms which give an apparently unfair advantage to the manager, he cannot complain afterwards about them. If he does not take advice, and the manager grossly misrepresents the true effect of the terms, there would be a lack of good faith, and possibly a right of termination.

**12.4** If the artiste can afford to obtain legal and financial advice on the terms of the agreement, he should take it for his own protection. The cost of settling the wrongful termination of an unsatisfactory contract will probably be much greater than the cost of the advice. Apart from the overall legal implications, the artiste may not be aware of everything which should be in the agreement for his benefit and protection, and which has been omitted.

**12.5** It is impossible for either the manager or the artiste to take every contingency into account. The following aspects should be considered by both parties when negotiating the terms of the management agreement.

## 13 Who employs whom?

*Example*

> "The Artiste hereby appoints the Manager to be his Manager in accordance with the terms of this Agreement."

**13.1** An artiste employs a manager to administer his business affairs, and to promote his career. It is possible for a specific event, such as a charity concert or for a "manufactured" group, that a manager can employ an artiste to perform in accordance with his wishes and directions. This would be most unusual, but is discussed below.

**13.2** It is common for an artiste to be the employee of a company which provides his services to third parties. The reason is simple—reduction of tax liabilities. The employment must be genuine, not just a show. The artiste has to have implicit trust in the persons who own and control the company employing him, as it will be the beneficial recipient of all royalties and fees paid from the sources of his earnings.

**13.3.1** The form of agreement used for each approach differs in many material respects. The most practical one is to determine who makes the final decisions in all matters dealt with by the manager. If the artiste is the employer, the manager will receive a commission based on the artiste's earnings. If the manager is the employer, the artiste will only receive a salary, which will need to be calculated on a basis which will give the artiste the same income as he would have had otherwise.

**13.3.2** There are technical and legal differences between a contract "of service" and a contract "for services". The main distinction is that an ordinary employment of service is full time for a wage, and the employee is under the direction and control of the employer. In a contract for services, the other party is "employed" as an independent contractor. Ordinary employment is subject to the complicated employment legislation, such as for redundancy and unfair dismissal. An agreement with an independent contractor is outside the employment legislation, and is subject to the ordinary rules of contract law.

**13.4** Something seldom considered by an artiste is that if he commits to employing the manager for, say, five years, and wrongfully terminates the agreement after only six months, the measure of damages awarded to the manager may be greater than if the manager employed the artiste, who had left his employment giving no prior notice. Where the manager has been wrongfully dismissed, his claim for compensation is based initially upon the amount which he would have received had the agreement gone its full term. It is not possible to calculate in advance what he would have received, even if the artiste has great potential which has yet to be converted into earnings. The manager has a duty to mitigate his loss, such as by seeking other artistes, and allowance should be made for the manager not having to incur time, effort and expense for the artiste after termination.

**13.5** The style of agreement used will also determine:

(a) whether the artiste has prior approval rights in respect of material to be recorded, or of the time and places of personal appearances, and of photographs and personal details to be published;

(b) to what extent he will be subject to directions from the manager upon performance and style or mode of presentation; and

(c) whether or not he will be contractually entitled to any element of control over, or consultation upon, the planning and promotion of his professional career.

No artiste should sign an agreement which removes from him the ultimate right of controlling his career. It may be technically necessary in a true service contract, but that would be acceptable where the employer is, say, the artiste's own company.

**13.6** Confusion sometimes arises where under the management agreement, the manager is employed by the artiste, but the artiste is "granted" periods of holiday or other concessions, and has obligations normally relevant to an employee. These are not appropriate to a management agreement. The manager will insist upon his employment by the artiste being sole and exclusive, but he will not tie himself exclusively to the artiste.

**13.7** Whoever is the employer, the written consents required by the Copyright Designs and Patents Act 1988 must be granted by the artiste to authorise the creation and public use of his recorded or filmed performances. This grant should be contained in the management agreement, as well as in all other contracts where the consents are specifically needed. Termination of the management agreement will also act as revocation of the general consent contained in it. The revocation will not be retrospective, and will not affect the rights in any unreleased records or films existing at the termination date.

## 14 Joint and several

*Example*

". . . (hereinafter jointly and severally called the Artistes)".

**14.1** The artistes who comprise a group will normally execute the same management agreement, "jointly and severally". The "joint" refers to all of the members collectively, and the "several" refers to them individually. Any liability incurred by the group under the management agreement "jointly and severally" will make each of the members individually responsible to the manager for the whole of the liability. The claim would be made against them all, but if some can pay and some cannot, those who can will have to subsidise those who can't. This individual responsibility is notwithstanding any agreed apportionment of the liability between the members of the group as an internal arrangement. The manager can also choose just to claim against whoever has money, without bringing into the action any member who has no money, or who cannot be found.

**14.2** This wording represents acceptance of responsibility by each member of the group for the consequences of the defaults of the others. This helps the manager should litigation arise as a result of damage or loss caused to him through breach of contract by any one or more group members. Each artiste should realise that he is taking on responsibility for the consequences of something over which he may have no control, and for which he may not otherwise have been personally liable.

**14.3** Another effect of "joint and several" is that, although it is the group which is signing the management agreement, they are also committed to the manager as individual artistes. Therefore, having individually granted to the manager exclusive management rights, an artiste is not free of the management agreement after he leaves the group, unless it contains a clause specifically to that effect. The artiste should also check whether he has a continuing liability after leaving the group to contribute to the manager's unrecouped expense at that date. If so, does that include recoupment from any source outside his share of future earnings from the group in which he continues to participate? His only continuing group income will be record royalties, publishing royalties (if he was a writer) and merchandising income (which is not normally significant except for a "super group"). As the recoupment liability is joint and several over the whole group income, the remaining group members will be responsible for the whole of the departed artiste's share if he is released by the manager from his continuing personal liability. They can then claim from him his proportion. In most cases the group will have no specific agreement between them to cover these circumstances. The group should insist that if a departed member is released from his recoupment obligation, the amount to be recouped by the manager from the remaining members should be reduced accordingly.

**14.4** A member's personal liability under the joint and several principle should only come into effect where the point of contention is a group problem, rather than being a problem which is solely the personal responsibility of another individual member. This can only be achieved by having a clause in the management agreement to that effect. It may be difficult in some cases to distinguish between a group and an individual liability. The guitarist may be advanced money to buy a new instrument, but for accounting purposes it is treated as a group expense. The guitarist leaves the group, taking the instrument with him, and has no immediate earning prospects. Should the manager be able to recoup any outstanding balance of advance for the guitar against the group?

**14.5** With the exception of "recoupable" expense being retained by the manager only from group earnings, the risk of each member for any other liability to the manager, or any group liability to a third party, is to the extent of his personal assets. In the last resort those with more to their name are harder hit that those with nothing behind them. Where each member is struggling for a living, this point is academic. It becomes significant where one of the members is wealthy in his own right, or becomes successful independently of other members of the group, such as where he is the sole composer/writer of the songs they record, or he is a record producer.

**14.6** If one member has to pay the whole, or a disproportionate part of, a joint group liability, he will be entitled to claim reimbursement of their proportions of what he has paid from each of the other members. This will apply whether or not they were claimed against, and whether or not they are still members of the group at the time the original claim is made and settled, or when reimbursement is claimed from them. The member who settled the liability may be prevented from claiming reimbursement from the others if the liability arose solely due to his fault. Any artiste joining a group should make it clear in any group or management agreement that he does not accept liability for any claims made in the future in respect of any matter arising prior to his joining. If he replaces a leaving artiste, it should also be clear that the substitution does not mean he has taken over any of his predecessor's obligations or liabilities.

**14.7** The group should have an agreement whereby, notwithstanding their joint liability to the manager for group obligations, each member indemnifies the others in respect of his proportion of the joint expense or liability. Indemnifying the others, and actually paying up when the time comes, are two different matters. Ready cash may not be available, so it would be a matter of deducting each member's liability from his earnings to be received.

**14.8** Unless a leaving member is specifically released by the manager from his individual obligations under the management agreement, he is still bound by it for so long as it remains in force. In practice this will depend upon whether the manager has taken the same (or any) professional interest in the member after he leaves the group, and whether, in full knowledge, he has allowed the artiste to join a new band with another manager without asserting his rights. Even if the artiste does not join a new group, but is "resting" for a substantial period, if the manager does nothing for him and disregards him, there will come a time when he will be deemed to have waived his managerial rights. He will also be technically in breach of his "best endeavours" obligations, so after a reasonable interval the artiste could serve a breach notice followed by termination. The manager should not be able to treat the departure of the artiste as a tactical means of getting compensation from him if he has suffered no loss, and has no intention of continuing to manage him.

**14.9** When an option to renew the management agreement is subsequently exercised by the manager, the departed member must be served with notice in accordance with the option terms if the contract is to be kept alive against him. Most artistes assume that the management agreement applies only for so long as they remain a group member, so that is one item to check before it is signed. Even if the agreement makes no reference to the point, the manager will not be able to enforce his rights unless he can clearly demonstrate that he will be as active for that leaving member as he will be for the group he left. Except for a lead singer with a potential solo career, that is not likely. The courts take a hard look at any claim for enforcement of personal service contracts, and take into account the practical circumstances of the people involved.

**14.10** Whether the artiste has continuing obligations to the manager should depend on the circumstances in which he leaves the group. If he is not a star in his own right, and the group "fires" him so he has to look for other work, he should be free to accept whatever management applies to his new position. If he leaves voluntarily due to a genuine dispute within the group, and with no ready alternative, the same should apply. However, if he is a key member and is "poached" by another group or management, against the wishes of the group and the manager, it would be reasonable for him to have to negotiate a termination of his obligations to the manager. His obligations to the group are examined in chapter eight.

**14.11** There are other factors to consider if the leaving member is the light and soul of the group. What is to happen if it becomes clear that the group without that member is a shadow of its former self, and ceases to have commercial and popular appeal? The manager then finds that his investment is jeopardised, the remaining group is not viable or promotable, and a potentially profitable future has been destroyed. How can that be calculated, and should the leaving member bear any responsibility for this serious knock-on effect? What about the same effects upon the remaining members of the group? The leaving member could mitigate or eliminate any liability to the manager by inviting him to manage him as a solo artiste, or the whole of his new group. The management agreement may contain a clause to the effect that the manager is committed to the group as currently constituted when the agreement is signed, and may review his position in the event of any change in membership. The group, whether or not they are aware of it, normally constitute a partnership, so in the absence of a written agreement between themselves, the Partnership Act 1890 will apply. (See chapter 8 paragraph 30). This contains the right of partners to leave the partnership by giving written notice. The leaving member cannot be held responsible if the remaining group fails to prosper, he is not obliged to be their meal ticket for life. But he does have to comply with his contractual obligations.

**14.12** It is not practical to hold a departed member of a group to a management agreement which he cannot fulfil. If the member was expelled from the group, the court might hold that the group management agreement, so far as he is concerned, has been ended by an uncontrollable supervening event.

**14.3** If the members sign individual management contracts without reference in them to the group as an entity, the "joint" element may not have been created. The group can, by common working practices between themselves and with the manager, make it obvious that they accept a joint liability for all matters relating to the group as an entity. By having individual contracts, the behaviour of each member should only affect his own agreement, and on leaving the group he will still be contracted as an individual artiste to the manager. A "joint and several" agreement signed by all the group members which is found to be unenforceable or invalid as a whole, will release all of them from it, and enable them to appoint another manager.

## 15 Extent of representation

*Example*

"The exclusive rights of the Manager as set out herein shall be in respect of the following personal performances and activities of the Artiste:

(a) the making of audio and audio/visual recordings in every medium for commercial manufacture and sale and for promotional purposes;

(b) personal live appearances before an audience whether public or private, paying or not;

(c) personal recorded appearances for video and/or television recording and/or broadcast including, where applicable, performance as a TV programme presenter and in cinematograph filming;

(d) the writing of lyrics and/or the composing of music including (but not limited to) songs for recording, commercial jingles, TV or cinematograph film theme or background music and for any other use;

(e) acting as the engineer or producer or director of audio or audio/visual recordings of his own performances or the performances of others;

(f) merchandising and making commercial use of his name, likeness and reputation by way of licence or otherwise in connection with products or services and sponsorship, product endorsement or otherwise;

(g) any other activity service or performance by the Artiste in connection with any of the above as may be agreed between the parties from time to time."

**15.1** The above list should be amended or added to as agreed to suit the parties. The phrase "within the whole of the entertainment industry" without any clarification as to category or extent is too general to use on its own. If it is not qualified so as to identify the extent of representation rights of the manager, it may be treated as too vague and uncertain to be enforceable against the artiste. By custom some activities are obvious, but it is still a contractual matter. A management agreement should set out specifically the areas of representation to be covered. The artiste might be able to appoint another manager for those areas not specified, so the clause should contain "sweeping up" wording, such as (g) in the example, without having to list every conceivable area of activity. Certain areas may already be covered by existing long term agreements, such as for recording or publishing. By going through the list of activities when negotiating the management agreement, the artiste can avoid generalisations which may infringe existing rights, or which may contradict any warranties given to the manager, or which may extend his rights into activities which were not intended to come within the agreement.

**15.2** The artiste may, for example, wish to exclude straight dramatic acting and cinematograph film or TV representation. These are specialist activities, and an appropriate agency may be of greater value to the artiste. An artiste who is also a composer will enter into an agreement with a music publisher, either as an individual or (for tax or commercial reasons) through a company which he owns. The management agreement may exclude all publishing matters which are already in existence for a well established artiste. The manager would still want his commission on some publishing income, which can be related to songs written by the artiste during the management period, although the manager did not procure or negotiate the artiste's publishing deal.

**15.3** If the manager is not experienced, the artiste should think seriously about whether he can be effective on an all round basis. While all deals and contracts should first be approved by the artiste, he must have confidence that all is fully negotiated for the best by the time approval is sought. When the artiste is unknown, he depends upon the efforts of the manager to get him a "break". Once the artiste has become really successful, the role of the manager changes from having to be a hustler to having to plan and administer. The hope is that the manager can reduce the necessity to sell the artiste at all costs; and become busy assessing the offers which stack up on his desk. This is an over-simplification, but the manager must know what he is doing, and be completely familiar with up to date music industry standards, and have the right contacts.

## 16 Manager's commission

*Example*

"In consideration of the proper fulfilment of the obligations of the Manager and subject as set out below he shall be entitled to receive a commission of [20] per cent of the gross earnings of the Artiste received in respect of or arising from all of the activities of the Artiste as set out in clause [ ] provided that:

(a) "Gross earnings" means money or moneys worth received by the Artiste or on his behalf in the UK directly or indirectly from any such activity but excluding any genuine gift or presentation to him which is not in lieu of or in consideration of foregoing any proper fee. "Received" means whenever received including after the termination of this Agreement in respect of any event contracted during the period hereof and being performed before or after such termination.

(b) Commission will not be paid on any sums paid by third parties as support for tours or towards promotional video expenses or any other support or subsidy towards any business expenses which would otherwise have been incurred by the Artiste.

(c) In respect of live personal appearances at concerts or upon tours the commission will be paid on the net profit thereof where "net profit" shall mean the difference between gross fees received and the total costs incurred reasonably attributable to the staging of the event after deducting third party support.

(d) After termination of this Agreement in respect of recording and publishing income the commission will be due on accountings for the

> [two] half yearly accounting periods of the record company or the Publisher (as the case may be) in connection with records made or released during the period of this Agreement."

**16.1** Precisely what the commission is due on, particularly after termination of the agreement, must be agreed. The risk is that there may be a double commission on some income when the new manager is remunerated. This must be avoided, as it would be uneconomical, and could lead to serious cashflow difficulties. Therefore the new management agreement would have to take that into account.

**16.2** A fair and reasonable commission for a manager depends upon the extent of his obligations to the artiste, the period of the agreement; how the venture is to be financed initially, and how expenses are to be shared. Whether an unknown artiste will achieve significant earnings in the near future through the efforts of the manager is an unknown quantity.

**16.3** Where there are no unusual or complicated financial or commercial arrangements for the benefit of the artiste which would justify otherwise, the commission should not exceed twenty per cent of gross earnings. There may be different percentages for different sources of income, and some receipts of the artiste may not be commissionable at all. Although the manager should receive a reasonable remuneration, it is much more important for the artiste to ensure tht he will receive a reasonable proportion of his own net income (ie after tax and commission).

**16.4.1** The key word is "gross" for earnings upon which management commission is charged, with the exception of tour income. The manager's commission should not be affected by the artiste's own personal or business expenses, which are beyond the control of the manager. Even if the manager charges a modest commission, it is possible for him to receive in commission as much as a new artiste receives as net income after deducting his business expenses and agency and management commission. An artiste can find himself highly successful, which profits all those who take a slice of his income—but at the end of the day he is tight for spendable cash. If there could be a simple and accurate method of computing commission on net earnings, the true proportions of usable net income received by the artiste, and retained by the manager, could be seen. There should be no management commission on the proportion of record royalties earned by the artiste but which are retained by the record company in recoupment of recording costs, which are treated contractually as recoupable advances.

The same would apply to recoupable advances in connection with the making of any audiovisual recording for promotion or otherwise. Commission would be payable on retained royalties used to recoup general advances to the artiste, as those advances are only an accelerated receipt of income.

**16.4.2** The traditional calculation of commission on gross income for personal appearances may well change to being calculated on a form of net income, ie, after deducting specific categories only of expenses from gross income. Agents charge their commission on gross fees for what they book; but that is their only limited source of earnings from the artiste. The manager takes his (normally greater) commission on all the artiste's earnings. Therefore, on tour income, the artiste can pay his agent 10% and his manager 20% of gross. After all expenses there's nothing left for him. A fair method of achieving an equitable balance between management remuneration based on net income, and some profit being left for the artiste, must be possible.

**16.5** Most artistes have wondered at some time why they see apparently so little of what they are reputedly earning. Part of a manager's obligations should be to keep track of the artiste's earnings and expenses, and to provide regular statements of account. These are not statutory audited accounts, but are in the form of commercial management accounts to supervise cashflow and to help with planning forward commitments. For a major artiste this should be done in conjunction with his accountant, but a new artiste may not have one.

**16.6** There should be no commission on record royalties if they arise through a lease-tape or production company owned or controlled by the manager. The artiste's royalties may also be significantly lower than those reasonably obtainable on an arm's length basis from an independent record company. This may be either because account is being taken of what would have been management commission, or because the artiste has not negotiated his deal well. The manager's company will be making its own profit from the recording services of the artiste, and if he commissions the artiste's share as well, the manager will effectively be taking two slices out of the same earnings. There may be an acceptable reason for a low royalty, but the manager's primary duty is to do his best for the artiste in good faith, and to disclose any interest which may conflict with that duty.

**16.7** The same situation arises if the manager takes a commission on publishing royalties due to the composer/artiste, where the manager also owns the publishing company. Together with a double slice of earnings, the manager will also be accumulating a potentially valuable asset by way of a catalogue of copyrights. This conflict can be dealt with by the manager/publishing company giving the composer an advantageous percentage of earnings.

**16.8** Subject to exceptional circumstances upon which the artiste has taken professional advice, he should avoid any set up as described in paragraphs **16.6** and **16.7**.

**16.9** Managers should not take commission from the performance income of an artiste's compositions, which is received by him direct through PRS. If the manager sets up the deal for the artiste with the publisher, he should come to some arrangement with the publisher on performance income, provided that does not adversely affect the royalty rate offered to the composer.

**16.10** For a developing artiste, touring is an essential part of the promotion of his career. At that level, touring is not likely to be profitable, after all costs and agency commission have been paid. There may not be any money left to pay management commission as well. Commission should not be charged on any sum contributed by a third party as "tour support", ie to reduce the extent of a tour loss.

**16.11** Commission should only be due to the manager from earnings which are actually received, either by the artiste or by someone on his behalf. He could be authorised to collect his share locally from earnings deposited in a foreign country with currency restrictions, except where that money represents retained withholding tax. If commission is deducted from gross earnings without reference to actual receipts, no account is taken of bad debts on contracts, earnings never received, or balances adjusted at the end of any accounting period where recoupable advances have been made to the artiste.

**16.12** There is an interesting distinction between commission "due to" the manager only on receipts; and it being due on money not yet received, with payment to be made out of any receipts. It depends on whether "receipts" is limited to the relevant source of earnings. If commission is due on aggregate receipts, cash flow can be controlled—no receipts, no commission. If it is due on money not yet received, but is payable out of aggregate receipts from whatever source, the manager receives his share of unreceived money before the artiste does. The proportion of cash flow going to the manager to keep his commission up to date could be excessive. If the unreceived money actually never arrives (such as if it is a bad debt) the artiste loses out. It is part of the manager's job to ensure that all money due to the artiste is received, and it is an incentive for him if payment of his commission depends on it being received.

**16.13.1** The definition of gross earnings should include "money or money's worth". Part of the fee may be represented by payments in kind, eg foreign flights, accommodation, or equipment, where it is an advantage to the promoter for local tax or other reasons to substitute services or goods for part of the cash fee. The goods may be provided as an added incentive as well as a market value cash fee. If the goods are really part of the contract fee, commission will be due on their value, in the absence of anything to the contrary. The commissionable value will have to be agreed. Where the tour would have been profitable without the added value of the costs contribution, they should be treated in the same way as payments in kind, to be included in the definition of "gross earnings in money or money's worth" for the calculation of management commission. If a happy promoter after a sell-out tour presents the artiste with a Ferrari as a surprise "thank you", it's value will not be commissionable.

**16.13.2** Payments in kind will normally give the artiste a greater total benefit. If the manager is not entitled to commission on money's worth, it will be against his own interests to negotiate a deal for the artiste which includes such benefits, and the artiste will be the loser.

**16.14** The commission clause must refer to any agreed rights of the manager to receive commission after the management agreement has ended. This is a sensitive and potentially contentious issue. The manager would like to be paid forever on everything, but that is not reasonable. Opinions vary, but general rules for the artiste to consider are:

(a) If the manager has concluded the setting up of a tour, TV special or other personal appearance which will happen after termination, he should get his commission. If he only established a contact, and the deal was initiated and fully negotiated by a third party after termination, the manager may be due a proportion of his commission or he may get nothing at all. In practice the decision is likely to be all or nothing, it depends on the construction of the commission clause.

(b) If he got the artiste a recording contract during his period of management, he should receive commission on some income flowing after termination. He might get commission on royalties due to the artiste according to an agreed number of accounting statements after termination to allow for "pipeline" income, but only in respect of recordings made prior to termination. He would get no commission on recordings made after termination. If the record deal was already in place when he was appointed, there is no reason for him to get commission on income arising after termination. One additional accounting statement should sweep up commissionable income arising in the agreement period, but which is late in arriving.

(c) If he was getting commission on composer royalty income, then the same philosophy would apply as set out in (b), but to compositions written prior to termination.

(d) If the artiste terminated the management agreement because of the manager's fundamental breach, such as fraud, dishonesty or bad faith; or because the manager became bankrupt (or if a company) became insolvent, ceased to trade or wound up, the manager should not be entitled to any commission on income arising after termination from record or publishing deals. The reasoning behind such a limitation is a selfish one. If the manager is bust he is not going to do any more for the artiste, who considers he would have a better use for that money than the creditors of the defunct manager. On the contrary, the artiste may have a claim against the manager, especially for fraud or dishonesty.

**16.15** A manager's commission is on group earnings. If a new member joins the group during the management period, that new member should ensure that the manager does not get commission on earnings received by the new member from, for example, record sales of his previous group. The new member may be the drummer, and his income from his previous group has nothing to do with the new group. So the new member should check the wording of the new group's management agreement on this point.

## 17 Period of agreement

*Example*

"Subject to [termination clause] this Agreement shall commence [on the date hereof] [with effect from the—] and will continue for the period of [three] years and the Artiste hereby grants the Manager the option to extend the period for a further [one] year upon giving the Artiste written notice not later than [sixty] days prior to the expiry of the initial period provided that at that time the Manager is not in breach of any of its obligations hereunder."

**17.1** The period of the management agreement may be an initial short period so the artiste can see how things get on, with a longer secondary period once he is satisfied. The manager may demand the security of a substantial period of time from the outset for his investment in, and contribution to, the artiste's future. A disadvantage to the artiste of a yearly basis renewable by the manager is that he is insecure and cannot plan his future with any long term confidence. He will only know for certain that he can appoint another manager when the renewal option has not been exercised by the present manager. It is always open to either party to approach the other to see whether the contract can be ended by mutual consent, but that is rare.

**17.2** A manager who knows the artiste is in demand, and who is in current or potential contention with him, might renew the agreement with the intention of forcing either the artiste or the new prospective manager to negotiate terms to buy him out.

**17.3** Where the contract is for a period of years, the manager can plan the artiste's career on a more permanent basis. He will find it easier to deal with promoters, and with record companies which require long term contracts. The manager should not take on any long term commitments which he does not think he will have time to fulfil within his contract period.

**17.4** Renewal options in management agreements invariably are in favour of the manager. As the artiste employs the manager, it is the employee who has the option to renew his own term of employment, while the employer will have limited rights of dismissal of his employee. The options should not enable the manager to renew the agreement indefinitely, and should only be exercisable if the manager at that time is not in breach of any of his obligations. There may be other conditions for renewal, such as if the manager has procured a recording contract for the artiste, or if minimum earnings for the artiste have been achieved.

## 18 Effective date of agreement

*Example*

> "Notwithstanding the date hereof this Agreement shall be deemed to have taken effect on the [ ] and the Artiste confirms that all activity undertaken by the Manager and all contracts entered into by the Artiste after that date will be deemed to be subject to this Agreement."

**18.1** A management agreement should state the date from which it is to operate retrospectively if it is executed an appreciable time after the manager started to act for the artiste. Earnings received in the future, but arising from events brought about by the manager prior to the date of execution of the contract, may not otherwise strictly come within its scope. A distinction must be made between speculative preparatory work by the manager, and serious efforts producing income on which management commission is to be paid.

**18.2** Establishing the effective date of the agreement is necessary where the manager has spent money on, or for the benefit of, the artiste prior to signing it. Prior expenditure for the promotion of the artiste, or on instruments or other necessary items for the artiste, may not be recoupable by the manager unless specifically dealt with. The agreement should confirm in detail the amount of prior expense which the artiste agrees to authorise the manager to recoup. The manager should account for the sum claimed, so the artiste can be satisfied that it is correct.

**18.3** If the proposed management agreement is never signed but with the artiste's knowledge and approval the manager has acted positively for his benefit, then, in the absence of agreement for reimbursement, money reasonably spent by him in doing so may be recoverable from earnings of the artiste arising from those efforts on what is known as the "quantum meruit" principle. This is an equitable principle based upon what the job done so far is worth by way of reasonable compensation. That will depend upon why the agreement was not signed, and the type of expenditure incurred. Any new artiste is quite willing for a prospective manager to spend money on him, but he does not expect to have to repay it if no management agreement is signed. He should make that quite clear at the outset. On the other hand, the artiste must not deliberately encourage a prospective manager to spend significant sums of money where the artiste has no intention of signing a management agreement with him.

**18.4** Money spent by the manager will not be recoverable if it was spent by him specifically as risk capital on the basis of "no contract, no recoupment". Prior to the expenditure, the proposed manager should require the artiste to sign an agreement on how and when it is to be recouped if a management agreement is eventually entered into. This can be done by an exchange of letters, followed up by accounts for the expenditure, which will have to be agreed by the artiste.

**18.5** As negotiations with the manager may not result in an agreement, an artiste should never agree to the repayment of preliminary risk expense to the proposed manager unless he is appointed. The artiste has no control over how much the proposed manager spends, or upon what he spends it, so an open reimbursement commitment would not be safe. If the preliminary expenditure has been incurred on tangible items such as equipment, it should be returned if the manager is not appointed; failure of negotiations should not unjustly enrich an artiste.

## 19 Expenses during period of agreement

*Example*

> "The Manager shall be entitled to recover from the Artiste's earnings hereunder any money disbursed by him at the request of the Artiste or with his prior authority or with his subsequent approval provided that:
> (a) the Manager will consult with the Artiste on the reason for any substantial expense;
> (b) necessary expenses not exceeding [£250] for any one item may be incurred by the Manager providing that he accounts to the Artiste on a monthly basis;
> (c) the Manager in consultation with the Artiste's accountant will maintain up to date cashflow and management accounts to keep all expense under control."

**19.1.1** The artiste will normally be required to pay for all the expenses reasonably incurred on his behalf by the manager with his authority or approval, except for the cost to the manager of running his business.

**19.1.2** The management agreement should state what part of the manager's own business expenditure incurred while attending to the artiste's matters ought to be paid by the artiste. For example, when the manager flies abroad to do record deals, or to visit the artiste while he is recording, or to check on touring progress, who should pay for his travel, accommodation and living costs? Should it depend on whether the travel is strictly necessary to solve problems, or whether the manager is bored in his office? Should the artiste only pay if he requests the travel; and if he doesn't request it, would he complain that the manager never takes the trouble to go out to see him. If the manager travels to see the artiste abroad, or to conclude a foreign based deal for him, the manager should only charge the artiste with a proper proportion of expense if, while he is there, he transacts business for other people, stays longer than necessary, or takes a scenic world tour to get there, or even treats the trip as part of a holiday.

**19.2** The following points should be considered:

(a) The type of expense which the manager can incur for the artiste without previously obtaining his approval should be limited to reasonable expenses necessary for, and directly attributable to, the promotion of the artiste. There must be some discretion for the manager to use his best judgment, and to that extent he must be trusted.

(b) For money which is recoupable from the artiste, the manager should be restricted to a financial limit for expenditure at any one time, or to an accumulated total of expenditure in any accounting period, before having to obtain the consent of the artiste. It is not practical to have to obtain approval for minor sums. What is considered to be minor will depend on projected promotion, tour and other costs. If the manager does not obtain the artiste's consent to unusual or significant expenditure, he may have difficulty in recouping it from the artiste at a later date, if there is any doubt as to whether it was incurred wholly for the artiste's benefit.

(c) The manager should prepare, and discuss with the artiste, regular financial projections and budgets geared to proposed promotional activities, such as concerts, touring or recording. This will reduce the risk of the aggregate sum of the expenses and the management and agency commissions exceeding gross earnings, with the result that the artiste has no net earnings. This is a real risk until the artiste's earnings reach a reasonable level. Income generated in the early stages tends to be used immediately to repay outstanding debts, and to fund forthcoming activities. The tax aspects must also be considered, and those liabilities reserved for by depositing money for instant access when the tax bills come in.

## 20 Tax on advance payments

*Example*

"The Manager will maintain as part of his accounting system for the Artiste detailed management accounts of income and expense for the purpose of enabling the Artiste's accountant to provide proper tax planning for the Artiste and in particular the Manager shall in consultation with such accountant maintain adequate cash reserves for taxation on all income received or receivable by the Artiste and supervised by the Manager."

**20.1** A major hazard for an artiste is to disregard the fact that demands will be made in the future by the Inland Revenue on money earned and received now. When an artiste is not earning enough to cover all expenses, including all commissions and the recoupment by the manager of his advances to the artiste, the tax position can be confusing. Because of the pressures of promotional and development expenses, and living costs, any money coming in tends to be used immediately.

**20.2** The artiste's accountant will see that the maximum allowable expenses relating to the artiste's activities will be deductible from tax. If the manager retains all of the artiste's income in recoupment of advances to him, and in the meantime makes further advances to him to cover his living expenses, a vicious circle is created because:

(a) Not all the expenses for which the advances are made will be tax deductible.

(b) The manager can choose:

  (i) to allow the artiste to retain enough income to pay the tax, with the result that recoupment through retention of only a proportion of the income will increase the recoupment period; or

  (ii) to pay the tax on behalf of the artiste, and treat that payment as a further advance to him, which is certainly not deductible for tax purposes.

(c) The same expenditure cannot be deducted from two independent sets of income—those of both the manager and the artiste. If the manager feels that he may never recover the expenditure, he may prefer to get his own bad debt tax allowances on it. That does not necessarily relieve the artiste from the obligation to reimburse the manager should sufficient income flow in subsequently. The payments remain loans to the artiste, which, if waived by the manager, might be considered by the Inland Revenue as a form of deemed income to the artiste, depending on how it was dealt with, and what it was for.

**20.3** Record companies and music publishers are the first source of initial funding of an artiste, by way of advances on account of royalties, paid when the agreements are signed. To be safe, the artiste should reserve the likely tax element of the advances, and only spend the balance. In reality the artiste spends the lot on immediate requirements, on the basis that as and when a tax demand arrives there will be cash available at the time. When the advances are made they are loans, which are repaid from future accountings from the relevant company. The loans are converted into income at the time of the accounting, and they then become subject to tax. This may not be in the same tax year in which the advances were made. However, as the artiste develops, the demand on available cash increases. The end result is massive accumulated tax bills which cannot be met. Financial organisation is a major management obligation.

**20.4** The tax implications are seldom considered when an artiste receives tour support through third party financial contributions, or the provision directly of goods (such as lighting and stage equipment) and services (such as air fares and accommodation). The value of all these is a taxable benefit, together with any other goods or services which could be in lieu of cash fees. An example might be a three concert tour of Hawaii in return for no cash, but an all expenses paid holiday there for two weeks. The Inland Revenue may not bother, or may never find out, but they can go back six years to claim tax, or they can go back indefinitely in the case of fraud. The benefits in kind do not provide the cash from which to make any reserves, so tax claimed will have to be found out of other income.

## 21 Agents

*Example*

> "The Manager shall be entitled to appoint agents where necessary to obtain engagements for the Artiste provided that the terms of any agency agreement are first approved by the Artiste. The Manager shall supervise all activities of the Agent and shall consult with the Artiste on all proposed engagements submitted by the Agent and advise him thereon. The Agent will not be empowered to sign any engagement contract without the prior approval of the Artiste and the Manager."

**21.1** There is no absolute demarcation line separating the activities of management and those of agency, but management agreements should cover agency representation in general terms. Where the artiste does not already have an agent, the manager should be able to appoint one with his consent. A manager must promote the artiste, and should choose the most suitable agent for the artiste's potential market. All deals and offers obtained by the agent, or submitted by a promoter to the artiste personally, must be dealt with through the manager to avoid confusion over dates and commitments.

**21.2** An agency agreement is made directly between the agent and the artiste. The agent and the manager should decide their respective roles in relation to the collection of fees, and how between them they will deal with promoters and negotiate deals, although the manager ultimately controls the agent's activities. Where a manager concentrates full time on one artiste only, it might be decided not to appoint an agent except for special deals.

## 22 Manager's directions

*Example*

> "The Manager's obligations shall include (but shall not be limited to) advising the Artiste upon the following:
> (a) his professional presentation for the promotion of his career, including his wardrobe and other personal features to create or have continuity of beneficial publicity;
> (b) his musical style including compositions to be recorded, the choice of recording studios record producer and upon album sleeve design;
> (c) producing personal publicity and promotional material including photographs and biographical material and attending personally at events and cooperating with radio, television and press media for interviews."

**22.1** To maintain the discipline necessary to organise an effective working and promotional schedule, the artiste should take notice of the directions and advice of the manager. He must have confidence that the manager will guide his career with the right flair. Decisions by the manager on activities to be undertaken by the artiste should be made only after consultation, and must be reasonable, and capable of fulfilment by the artiste. They will generally relate to times, dates and manner of presentation and performance whether for live, filmed or recorded performances.

**22.2** The choice of material to be performed by the artiste for his recordings should be chosen for its commerciality, as well as upon the more subjective view of artistic merit. Significant advance payments on account of future royalties may be received from a record company calculated upon its assessment or hope that whatever the artiste records will produce a much higher royalty return. This means keeping a commercial mercenary eye on what the fickle public wants to buy. Artistes who insist on "doing their own thing" do not always have a good objective opinion of what is best to perform, and how to arrange and produce it. Their own individual taste and style does not necessarily appeal to the record buying public. The manager should try to provide an objective view, even if that is not shared by the artiste.

**22.3** Once fame and fortune have "made" the artiste, the hope is that his fans will continue to accept whatever he records. This is the gamble which all artistes take when they change their established and accepted style, and branch out into different musical concepts.

## 23 Warranties

**23.1.1** The basic warranties normally required from an artiste under a management contract include the following:

(a) that he is entitled to enter into the agreement, and that there is no undisclosed hindrance to him doing so;

(b) that there are no existing contracts, other than those previously disclosed to the manager, concerning his career which adversely affect the present agreement;

(c) that he will do nothing during the period of the agreement to prejudice its fulfilment;

(d) where relevant, that all recorded performances given by him during the term of the agreement will be:

(i) original to him;

(ii) not in breach of the copyright or any other right of any other party;

(iii) not defamatory or obscene.

The manager may require other warranties to cover relevant matters upon which he has relied when signing the artiste.

**23.1.2** The basic warranties are reasonable, and are required by the manager to ensure that he is not incurring unexpected liabilities by signing the artiste to management. He should take all reasonable practical steps to check out the warranties, as most artistes never keep track of commitments made over the years. These have a habit of resurrecting themselves at awkward moments—mainly prompted by the discovery that money is in good supply.

**23.2** The artiste must be made aware that warranties or representations of a serious contractual nature, and upon which the manager will rely, are not to be given unless he is absolutely certain that they are correct and accurate. If they are not, the artiste should disclose all of the relevant facts and modify the warranty accordingly. He should not just hope for the best, Murphy's law is bound to operate.

The consequences of a breach of warranty can be significant and expensive, so if in doubt the artiste should obtain professional advice on them.

## 24 Indemnities

**24.1** An indemnity is a contractual obligation to reimburse the indemnified party against the consequences of the indemnified liability. Indemnities given by an artiste to a manager relate to any consequences arising from breach by the artiste of his warranties. The lack of an indemnity clause does not mean that the artiste has no liability for contract breach. The clause highlights the liability and defines its scope more clearly. It should focus the artiste's attention upon matters which he normally takes for granted, but which must be examined closely.

**24.2** The indemnity should be limited to reasonably direct consequences arising from the breach. Indemnity enforcement normally creates a debt payable, rather than treating the amount of liability as an addition to other money which is only recoupable by the manager from the artiste's earnings. If he has inadequate professional earnings to cover the liability, but has private wealth, the manager can claim against that in satisfaction of any indemnity liability. This distinction is not normally understood by artistes, who might assume that the manager will have to wait until some money comes in before he can claim payment.

**24.3** Indemnities are construed and enforced strictly according to their wording. The main headings of liability are expenses, losses generally, specific damages, and legal costs. Legal fees should be specifically on an "indemnity basis", as the court does not award the whole of the legal costs actually spent by the winner. The liability for legal costs should be made subject to the manager's claim being successful, to inhibit frivolous litigation.

**24.4** Where the manager incurs a liability to a third party through the act or default of the artiste, the manager should have the right to institute or defend any resultant court proceedings, which may have to be in the name of the artiste. Litigation can be lengthy and expensive, and according to his own legal advice the manager may have to settle in good faith claims made against him, upon payment of agreed compensation and costs. The manager should do his best in negotiation to minimise the extent of liability. Throughout the proceedings the artiste must make himself available to respond to the allegations, and to assist the manager in his defence. Prior to being committed by the manager to any settlement, the artiste must have the right to take legal advice on whether the settlement is reasonable. If the artiste's advice clashes with the manager's advice, the manager should agree to continue the litigation, subject to getting satisfactory security from the artiste for all legal costs and estimated damages (and the plaintiff's costs) if the manager loses the case.

**24.5** Indemnities are personal to the artiste, who cannot assign the liability to a third party. If the artiste has personal assets, he should protect them, especially if he has a wife and family to support. Reasonable precautions taken to limit personal liability are not the same as attempting to defraud potential creditors of security.

**24.6** The manager may accept a guarantor in special cases, but that would not relieve the artiste from primary liability. The guarantee should identify what event, liability or performance is to be guaranteed. It should state any monetary limit imposed by the guarantor, and the circumstances in which the manager can call upon the guarantor to fix the problem, or pay up under the guarantee. The guarantee will have to be in consideration of the manager undertaking the guaranteed event or risk, and should be carefully worded. Unless he is contractually entitled to do so in limited circumstances, a guarantor cannot just cancel his guarantee by giving notice to the manager. The guarantee can last indefinitely, and the manager does not have to exhaust all efforts against the artiste first before calling on the guarantee.

## 25 Incapacity of artiste

**25.1** Incapacity of a temporary nature (eg a broken leg or laryngitis) preventing an artiste from performing, as it is something beyond his control, should not be treated as a breach of the management agreement. If there is a substantial delay in the promotion of the artiste's career caused by his incapacity, the manager might like to be able to extend the term of the agreement, but such events are a normal risk. A possible exception would be where the incapacity is self-induced with the intention of prejudicing the manager or delaying a specific deal to take it outside his commissionable period. If, half way through the agreement period, the artiste genuinely decides to quit the music business, which is accepted by the manager, but the artiste returns to it two years later, should the manager be entitled to reinstate himself if his agreement expired during that period? In the absence of specific agreement when the artiste retired, the manager would not have such a right.

**25.2** If the artiste does agree to extension provisions in the management agreement, they should be sensible. Any right of extension should only apply after the period of the contract expires normally. If the extension rights arise during a contract year, where the period is of successive option years, only the relevant option year is extended. The date by which the next notice of an option exercise must be made is similarly postponed. The contract must also be clear as to how the period of the extension is calculated. This cannot be an exact science, and how is an extendable period to be identified? The purpose of extension is to protect the manager from losing useful time during which commissionable events are happening. If commissionable events have to be postponed due to incapacity, the manager would like still to benefit from them when the incapacity has ceased. But if the period of incapacity had nothing which would have happened in it, or if it did not prejudice any projected activity, a contract period extension is not appropriate.

**25.3** Medical evidence might be necessary to determine what is a permanent incapacity for ascertaining the right of extending, and whether the agreement should be terminable rather than extendable. Relevant factors would include a comparison of the probable period of incapacity in relation to the unexpired term of the agreement. If the manager can extend the period of the contract, the artiste cannot rely upon it ending on its due date, so forward planning may be difficult. An artiste would not be advised to include extension rights in the management agreement otherwise than for exceptional specified reasons.

## 26 Collection of and accounting for money

*Example*

"(a) The Manager shall use his best endeavours to collect or ensure the collection of all monies which may become due to the Artiste from whatever source connected with his activities under this Agreement. The Manager will notify the Artiste of any difficulty encountered in doing so, and appropriate steps will be agreed to enforce payment.

(b) If any income arises outside the UK which cannot be remitted to the UK due to exchange control regulations it will be paid into a local bank account in the name of the Artiste pending approval for remittance.

(c) The Manager will maintain separate full and accurate books of account for all income received and expense paid out by the Manager which is related to the Artiste. The Artiste or his qualified representative shall be entitled not more than once each year to inspect and take copies of all accounts and supporting documents by giving not less than 14 days prior written notice.

(d) The Manager will render accounts to the Artiste within 21 days after each quarter day for all the financial transactions within that quarter."

**26.1.1** A management obligation should be to collect and receive on behalf of the artiste the earnings arising from all sources promoted under the management agreement. "Receipt" includes ensuring that payment is made from the source of the income. After deducting loans, advances, proper expenses and commission from all money received by the manager, he must account to the artiste for the balance.

**26.1.2** While the artiste's money is held by the manager in his own bank account, although it belongs to the artiste, until it is handed over to him it may be treated legally as being the manager's own money by his creditors. If the manager compounds with his creditors, or becomes bankrupt, while retaining in his general bank account money which belongs to the artiste, payment to the artiste at that time, or even just before, may be set aside as a fraudulent preference over other creditors. The artiste is only an unsecured creditor of the manager, and is in the same position as everyone else to whom he owes money.

**26.1.3** The risk can be minimised by separating the manager's money from the artiste's money at all times. This is achieved by the manager opening an independent interest earning trust account in the name of the artiste, although operated by the manager. All of the artiste's money received by the manager is paid into this account, without first going through the managers bank account. If the trust account is properly identified and maintained, the money in it will be safe from any claims against the manager from his creditors. The manager should be prohibited from borrowing any money from that account, however temporarily. The only payments from it should be for the artiste's expenses, and for recoupment of advances and commission due to the manager. The balance from time to time should be paid to the artiste or his accountant.

**26.2.1** No manager can guarantee to the artiste payment in the United Kingdom of his earnings arising abroad, because of possible local exchange control restrictions or withholding tax regulations. Adverse rates of exchange may make it uneconomical to transfer funds for the time being. The manager should try to ensure that the artiste does not forego or lose the value of such earnings unnecessarily. It is also in the manager's financial interest, because of his commission on it.

**26.2.2** To minimise adverse cash flow and inconvenience to the artiste in respect of foreign earnings:

(a) As much as possible of all fees due should be deposited in advance in a free currency. The deposit can be held in escrow pending satisfactory performance by the artiste.

(b) There may be a means of settling local withholding tax by prior arrangement to speed up the process. Tax deduction certificates must be obtained, to enable the relevent double taxation convention to be applied.

**26.2.3** In any country where transfer restrictions cannot be avoided, the manager should open an account with a reputable local bank in the name of the artiste, and have paid into it all earnings arising in that country which cannot be remitted to the United Kingdom. The account should be a deposit account, as the artiste may not be able to make use of the restricted funds immediately. Locally retained funds and any withholding tax should be declared on the artiste's tax return.

**26.3.1** The manager must keep separate detailed accounting records for the artiste's earnings over which he has management control, and for expenditure by him of the artiste's money, including the manager's money spent which has been recouped from the artiste. The style of accounts is immaterial, provided it is effective and accurate, and they must be made easy for the artiste to check.

**26.3.2** The artiste, or his authorised representative, must be entitled to inspect the accounts and to take copies of entries. This should be done during normal office hours by appointment, upon giving reasonable prior notice in writing. It should not be necessary for the artiste to inspect the accounts more than once a year, unless he has good grounds to suspect that he is being cheated. An accounts audit is seldom done at all, let alone on an annual basis, but the right to do so must still be there.

**26.3.3** If the right of inspection is not contained in the management contract, it is inherent in common law. The practical means of forcing an inspection of the books is to apply to the court for an order for an account of money from the manager. The artiste may agree in advance to accept without question accounting statements certified by the manager's auditor as being complete and correct. That should only be accepted if the auditors are a substantial firm, but it is a limitation which is not recommended. To maintain confidentiality, and to ensure that the audit is properly done, the agreement may state that the manager's accounts are only to be audited by a professionally qualified accountant. This is a sensible provision, as neither the artiste nor his manager would be capable of doing so in any meaningful manner.

**26.3.4** The Inland Revenue is also interested in accounts dealing with the artiste's earnings, for the purpose of confirming the manager's income as well as that of the artiste.

**26.4.1** The dates upon which different managers account to their artistes vary. They depend upon the set-up of their computerised accounts administration, and upon the dates for accounting in the recording, publishing or other agreements from which the artiste receives his income. The accounting periods should ideally be monthly, but not less than quarterly, accounts being rendered to the artiste within (say) seven days after the close of a monthly accounting period. The use of standard computerised accounting systems for all of their artistes or composers in record or publishing companies means that they cannot accommodate different accounting date requirements requested by the artiste.

**26.4.2** Because of the frequency of the accounting periods, the accounts are not in a statutory form, they are for information required on a regular basis. Each accounting from the manager to the artiste should give details of his income and expenditure, deductions for money owed by him to the manager, tax reserves and money retained for future commitments. With the accounting must be the payment of any balance due to the artiste. The artiste should arrange for substantial recording or publishing royalty payments to be received by his accountant, who can notify the manager of them. The artiste may allow the manager to retain an adequate reserve of the artiste's money to enable him to meet payments becoming due within the next accounting period.

**26.4.3** It is not unusual to have a clause to the effect that all accountings are deemed to be accepted as correct and binding by the artiste unless objected to in writing within, say, one year after receipt of the statement. This period is too short, a reasonable compromise might be three years. The manager's accounting system must be adequate to deal with any investigation, as, together with supporting statements and vouchers, they should be retained for at least six years. This lesser period of limitation is designed to minimise the upheaval caused by having a detailed investigation and audit many years after the accounting periods have been closed. It might be reasonable to state that no audit may be undertaken of the manager's accounts after one year from the date the last accounts were submitted following termination of the management agreement. This would be subject to the artiste being entitled to audit the manager's accounts after that date if subsequent information points to fraud by the manager. Because of the expense, full auditing is rare, unless there are large sums of money involved, and fraud or dishonesty is reasonably suspected. Apart from administrative convenience, an honestly run management has no reason to fear an audit within a reasonable period.

## 27 Name, likeness and biography

*Example*

> "The manager shall be entitled to use the name, likeness and biographical details of the Artiste in the course of promoting his career provided that all of such material is approved by the Artiste prior to its initial use and that all promotional material referring to any career or personal matter is first checked with the artiste for accuracy and is in an agreed format."

**27.1** A manager must be entitled to use the name and image of the artiste in publicity and promotional material, in a suitable manner. The use of the name and any visual representations plus biographical material must be confined to those matters covered by the management agreement. The manager must be able to advertise that he represents the artiste. The artiste should co-operate with the manager in producing biographical material, as only he can give some of the necessary details. The artiste should approve the final material, as to its accuracy and the manner in which he is portrayed.

**27.2** The manager must use the name of the artiste in good faith, and not in a manner derogatory to the artiste, or in a defamatory manner, or for unauthorised endorsement of goods or services, or in circumstances which can amount to actionable misrepresentation. The latter is relevant to any advertisement or appeal where money is collected; whether for charity, or a fan club.

**27.3** Photographs, drawings or other graphic representations of the artiste for promotion and publicity should be used only if the artiste has first seen and approved them. Photographs used for record sleeves will be dealt with in the recording agreement, but the record company should first get the approval of the artiste.

**27.4** The artiste's consent should not be unreasonably withheld or delayed. This does not mean that every time the same picture is used the artiste must be consulted. When an album cover is being designed, or posters or advertisements are being prepared, the manager should agree with the artiste a selection of photographs to be used.

**27.5** Control over the use of a picture in the event of a dispute will depend upon who owns the copyright in it. This is different from attempting to prevent an unreasonable intrusion of privacy, or a derogatory distortion of the features of the artiste by trick photography or montage, or a use of photographs which show him in a bad light. Artistes choose to lead a public life, and will occasionally be caught in compromising or embarrassing situations.

**27.6** The right of the manager to use the artiste's name will cease upon termination of the management agreement, except to complete any venture, or to comply with any obligations entered into prior to termination.

## 28 Substitution of members of a group

*Example*

> "Upon any new member being brought into the Group the continuing members will procure that the new member signs a management agreement with the Manager in the same terms as herein set out prior to his membership becoming effective."

**28.1** The members of a group should agree to procure that any new member joining the group will enter into an identical agreement with the manager. This is to maintain the continuity of contract of the group as a whole. The new member's agreement should only be for a term as long as that remaining unexpired in the main agreement.

**28.2** The obligation to "procure" is a reasonable requirement in this context, instead of the members only being asked to use their "best endeavours". The group must ensure the execution of the management agreement by the new artiste as a prior condition to his membership. Management will become impossible if there is no contractual commitment between the manager and a new member.

**28.3** The manager should be consulted by the group whenever a member wishes to leave, or when the group wishes to substitute members, or increase the membership. The objective advice of the manager will be useful on whether the proposal will be beneficial. There may be legal or financial commitments to be cleared. The manager should not have the right to refuse a change in membership, or to impose unreasonable conditions upon a change. Neither should the manager have the right to alter the membership of the group.

**28.4** If it is appropriate, the management agreement should state whether the manager can terminate it if the change in members is so substantial that it ceases to be the group he wanted to manage. The following points are relevant:

(a) If the group consists of a star member supported by good musicians, what is to happen where the star decides to leave the group and start a solo career?

(b) A practical constraint on the manager terminating the agreement may be the amount of outstanding advances from him to be recouped. Recoupment can continue from long term deals done by the manager for the group, for so long as he is entitled to receive commissionable income.

(c) What would be the position of the manager where, due to a substantial membership change, he terminates the management agreement, and finds that after an interval of time the group re-forms with exactly the previous membership? The reasons could be purely coincidental, or they could have been a well executed plot to get out of a management agreement painlessly.

## 29 Merchandise

**29.1** Merchandising rights only become relevant and valuable when the artiste has reached such a prominence that his name and public image will sell products. The financing of a merchandising operation, and the administration of the initial market surveys, production orders, and manufacture and distribution, is a specialised business. For those reasons they are normally licensed out to specialist merchandising companies.

**29.2** A management agreement should cover merchandise rights, even if there is no immediate opportunity to exercise them. The manager hopes to build up the artiste, and should receive his share of the benefits of merchandising during the period of his agreement. Merchandising is discussed in detail in chapter nine.

## 30 Signing of contracts

*Example*

"The Manager shall ensure that all performance obligations of the Artiste shall be in writing and all agreements shall be approved and signed by the Artiste. The Artiste may authorise the Manager to sign concert and tour contracts on his behalf provided the Artiste has approved the terms thereof."

**30.1** Commitments for the artiste's services will be set out in a contract with the relevant promoter, which will be signed by the artiste. The manager may be authorised to sign them, but only after they have been approved by the artiste.

**30.2** The authority given to the manager is to act specifically as the agent of the artiste. By signing "for and on behalf of" the artiste with his authority and consent, and with the other party to the contract being aware of that authority, there is no liability on the manager if the artiste does not fulfil his obligations. If the manager does not have the artiste's authority, and the promoter is well aware of that fact, the artiste may not be bound by the contract. Customarily, the manager has the ostensible authority of the artiste, and if this has been exercised regularly without question to the promoter's knowledge, the artiste will be committed to the contract. The artiste will have allowed the promoter to believe the manager had the proper authority.

**30.3** The artiste should sign or countersign all significant contracts which affect him. By doing so he knows in advance what has been arranged for him, what his prospective earnings are, and how much effort the manager is exerting on his behalf. He can raise any query on a deal before he is committed, and he can keep track of his obligations.

## 31 Estimated damages

*Example*

> "In the event that the Artiste is liable to pay compensation of any description to the Manager under any warranty, undertaking or representation, and if the quantum is unknown but can reasonably be ascertained, the Manager shall be entitled to retain from money due to the Artiste an amount in respect of the minimum quantified liability to him to be held generally on account of the total to be ascertained."

**31.1** If the artiste incurs an absolute liability to the manager for damages, the manager may be entitled contractually to retain income of the Artiste in reduction of the damages. If the artiste agrees to such a clause it must differentiate between reimbursement of genuine monetary loss of the manager; and compensation claimed in an arbitrary amount for a breach of contract. The latter is not an acceptable reason for retention. The retention should not include an assessment of potential earnings which might never be received. If the claim is for a quantified sum, the earnings retained must not exceed that sum and a reasonable provision for costs. If the amount of the claim cannot be calculated until later, the amount retained should only be a reasonable assessment of damages and costs. If the claim fails, the artiste will receive the whole of the withheld money. The manager should place all withheld money on deposit. The right of the manager to retain any of the artiste's money for this reason should be made conditional upon him giving the artiste written notice specifying the breach, the claim, the damages, and the intended retention value. If the artiste believes that the retention is invalid in principle, or is excessive in amount, there will have to be a means of getting a quick and inexpensive adjudication on the matter.

**31.2** Retention provisions must be clear to avoid the possibility of a positive incentive for the manager to create an unintended retention situation for some ulterior motive. Examples might be where the manager and the artiste are in dispute, when it would suit the manager to keep the artiste short of money; or where the manager is in financial difficulties, and temporarily needs the money he tries to withhold from the artiste.

**31.3** An artiste would not be advised to authorise the manager to retain any of his money on these grounds—if he has a valid claim let him apply the usual rules of law.

## 32 Assignment by the manager

*Example*

> "The manager shall not be entitled to assign his benefit or obligations under this Agreement without the prior written consent of the Artiste, which may be withheld if the Artiste reasonably considers his interests would be damaged, or where (if applicable) the personal supervision of his career by a nominated individual will not be continued as a consequence of the assignment."

**32.1** If the manager's personal relationship with the artiste is an essential ingredient of their business relationship, then it is reasonable that he should be restricted from assigning the management agreement if that personal responsibility will cease. As a manager is responsible for developing the artiste's career, the artiste should have some control over who does the managing.

**32.2** Where the manager is a company, a change in the controlling shareholding does not constitute an assignment of the management agreement, as the legal party to the contract has not changed. If the shareholders sell out to a purchaser, the operation and control of the company will have changed. If the executives and personnel of the management company remain the same, the artiste should not be concerned with ownership. If ownership is a concern, such as where the management company is wholly owned by the persons doing the managing, a transfer of a controlling interest in the shares can be stated to be deemed to be an assignment for the purpose of review by the artiste of the agreement.

The benefit of the management agreement will be a factor in calculating the share value of the management company, so the purchaser may approach the artiste at an early stage to see whether he will object to the share disposal by the manager.

## 33 Confidentiality

*Example*

"The Manager undertakes to maintain confidentiality and not to disclose to unauthorised parties nor to make unauthorised use himself of any secret or confidential information relating to the Artiste or to his personal life or his business plans and activities. To maintain a proper balance between this restriction and the disclosure of information for the promotion of the career of the Artiste the Manager will first consult with him and get his approval for disclosure."

**33.1** The manager gets to know all about the artiste, his personal life and habits, and his business plans and activities, probably in greater depth than anyone else. The music press likes to have inside information on what is happening, and the Sunday papers like to have inside information on what is scandalous. If scandal is the main prop of the artiste's style of publicity, then confidentiality is not high in his priorities, and any complaint of breach of confidentiality may not be taken seriously. What is to be treated as confidential information needs a common sense approach. The existence of a recording contract is common knowledge, but not necessarily the amount of record advances or royalty points. If they (particularly advances) are spectacular, the artiste may publicise them to show how important he is commercially.

**33.2** Confidentiality is normally applied to sensitive information which could be of use to others to the detriment of the artiste, or because confidentiality was imposed as a condition of the deal, when it is a contractual obligation and not a matter of promotional judgment.

## 34 Undue influence

**34.1** There is repeated reference in various paragraphs of this chapter to the manager being fair to the artiste, disclosing to him any matter where a conflict of interest may arise, and ensuring, when appropriate, that he gets independent legal advice. As will be seen from the cases set out in Appendix III which relate to the repudiation by an artiste or composer of contracts he has signed, the court takes a strong view in the artiste's favour where he has relied on the manager, who has received a benefit which has acted as a disadvantage to the artiste. The two phrases to keep in mind are "fiduciary capacity" and "undue influence". A manager has strong fiduciary obligations to the artiste, and therefore owes him a duty of care to a high level. He cannot take any advantage over the artiste, which is not fully understood and agreed to by him. Because of the fiduciary relationship, the artiste places trust and confidence in the manager, and he is influenced by him. If, upon the advice of the manager, the artiste signs a contract which is not beneficial, and where the manager gets a benefit at the expense of the artiste and without his knowledge, the court may set it aside as not being binding on the artiste. It may be unenforceable, ie, it is terminated, or it is void, ie, it is treated as never having been entered into.

CHAPTER 2

# *Agency Agreements*

## 1 Agent and manager

**1.1** The responsibilities of a manager include most of those of an agent, ie, to get work for the artiste. For an agent, "work" has the narrow context of obtaining or negotiating personal appearances, such as tours, TV shows and concerts. For a manager the context is much wider, extending to all career activities of the artiste such as recording, writing and as a record producer, so all of these functions are contained in a management agreement. Upon the appointment of an agent, the personal live appearance work becomes his responsibility.

**1.2** Is it essential to have both a manager and an agent? Once things start to happen for the artiste the answer is "yes". They are each full time occupations but with different styles. The power of an agent depends largely on his roster of artiste clients, all of whom may come from different managements. An agency business must be independent from all management.

**1.3** A manager will spend a substantial part of his time with the artiste wherever he may be; an agent should be readily available to get work for the artiste and to deal with all such enquiries. One person acting as both manager and agent will not have time to take advantage of all the opportunities which can be generated through the broader contacts of a separate and independent agent.

## 2 Choice of agent

**2.1** The first choice of the artiste is an agent with a name and established reputation. It is difficult for an agent to become known and accepted by promoters as being reliable and consistently able to provide currently popular artistes. The choice of agent is important to the planning of an artiste's career.

**2.2** A big agency may not have the time or the inclination to develop a young unknown artiste, and generally prefers to take on only established acts. The only alternative may be a smaller more personal agent, who will spend the necessary time on the artiste. Once fame and fortune favour the artiste, a substantial established agency with international connections should be more beneficial to him.

**2.3** This philosophy is hard on the small agent who has worked hard to promote the artiste locally in the UK, and who should therefore share in the ultimate rewards if he can be as efficient internationally as his bigger competitors. An upwardly mobile artiste must face the decision squarely, but within his contractual commitments. The conflict is between what is best for the artiste and what is best for the agent. As the agent should act in the best interests of the artiste, should he on that ground alone release him from his agreement where not to do so would clearly restrict his progress? No—that would negate the purpose of having legal agreements, so each party knows where it stands.

## 3 Agent's responsibilities

*Example*

> "The Artiste hereby appoints the Agent and the Agent agrees to act as the Agent of the Artiste to represent him and to promote his career in connection with his live personal appearances and to obtain for him concert, tour and other engagements within the Territory [as defined] upon the best terms available which shall have first been approved by the Artiste prior to any commitment being made on his behalf."

**3.1** The agent is always employed by the artiste, although he may be chosen and appointed by his manager. An artiste has an agent to take advantage of his specialised knowledge and contacts. Employment is obtained by him for the artiste, in return for a commission, being a percentage of the gross earnings of the artiste arising from all personal appearances of the artiste during the agent's exclusive contract period, and within the agent's exclusive territory, whether or not generated by the agent's efforts.

**3.2** The agent's main responsibility is to seek out and negotiate contracts for personal appearances. No contract should be committed to without the artiste's approval. The agent should negotiate the highest fee which represents the market value of the artiste at that time. Market values may change, such as where the booking and its fee are confirmed for a date some way into the future, and in the meanwhile a record by the artiste gets into the charts. An experienced agent who has studied the development of the artiste, and who is fully informed of his record release schedule, can judge his future to take advantage of potential increases in his market value. If the artiste was once great but is now in decline, the agent's job is to cash in on the popularity of the artiste while it lasts.

**3.3** The scope of the agent's authority to act on his own initiative depends on his agreement. An agent cannot commit the artiste to fulfil any engagement unless he has the authority to do so. The artiste may get an adverse reputation with promoters, unless the agent is able to act wth some authority to negotiate contracts with a minimum of delay.

**3.4** The artiste should be fully consulted, and should see and sign each performance contract prior to being committed. The more successful the artiste is, the more impractical that may become due to the lack of his availability while touring, recording or holidaying abroad. The artiste may delegate the signing of appearance contracts to his agent, subject to prior approval by the artiste's manager.

## 4 Sole and exclusive

*Example*

> "The appointment of the Agent shall be on a sole and exclusive basis within [the United Kingdom and Europe] and during the period of this Agreement the Artiste undertakes not to appoint or utilise the services of any other party to obtain live performance engagements (as defined herein) and that he will refer to the Agent all offers he receives directly for any such engagement."

**4.1** No agent is prepared to act on behalf of an artiste except on a sole and exclusive basis. Different agents competing for the same market would be chaotic. An agent may obtain a good booking at a good fee, only to find that the artiste already has firm commitments elsewhere procured through another agent, or even by the artiste himself. This would make unprofitable the time and effort spent by the agent, and would damage his reputation.

**4.2** Bookings for even minor artistes may be made for dates months ahead. Unless the agent has the sole and exclusive representation of the artiste, he will have to obtain the artiste's clearance for each booking before he can confirm it to the promoter. If there is unreasonable delay in so doing, the promoter will not wait indefinitely for a decision, and will obtain another act for the performance.

**4.3** Exclusivity is essential to an agent who is negotiating a deal for the artiste, especially if the promoter is anxious to clinch it. If there is no exclusivity to the agent, there would be nothing to prevent the promoter from dealing direct with the artiste, if he is available and has the time to spend on negotiations. The promoter could also find out who else represents the artiste, such as his manager, to see whether more favourable terms to himself can be arranged without further reference to the agent.

**4.4** An artiste may want to develop several separate facets of his career, such as being a pop star, having a TV career and being a record producer. As they don't conflict, he could appoint an exclusive agent to represent him in each area, but they must be co-ordinated to ensure an uninterrupted career. Normally all of these career aspects would be dealt with by his manager.

**4.5** Under an exclusive agreement the artiste will be obliged to refer all offers for personal appearances direct to the agent for negotiation, and, to avoid confusion, the artiste should be restricted from acting on his own behalf. If the artiste does act for himself (such as for a one-off guest appearance), and if he receives the fees direct, he should account to the agent for his commission. If the artiste, by dealing direct with promoters in contravention of his agency agreement, prejudices other commitments properly entered into by his agent on his behalf, the artiste alone should be responsible for the consequences.

**4.6** While exclusivity is essential to the agent, it is also desirable for the artiste. In theory a sole agent is more likely to work harder, because he has strength in negotiations. As the agent is running a business, and is not a philanthropic society, his level of effort is influenced by the market forces.

## 5 Best endeavours

*Example*

> "The Agent undertakes that he will use his best endeavours in good faith to obtain personal appearance engagements for the Artiste upon the best terms reasonably obtainable and that he will consult with the Artiste upon available opportunities and all reasonable means of promoting the Artiste accordingly."

**5.1** An agent must be contractually committed to use his best endeavours to obtain as much of the right kind of work for the artiste upon the best financial terms. The success of the agent in doing so will depend upon the popularity of the artiste, and his ability to reproduce favourably at a live performance a quality and appeal comparable to that contained in his recordings. With existing technology, an expert sound engineer and a good record producer between them can do almost anything to improve upon an inadequate (or even non-existent!) vocal or instrumental performance which has been recorded. A concert audience expects much the same level of perfection and excitement. A hairy chest and designer stubble beard may be mandatory (except for ladies), but some stage ability is useful.

**5.2** The level of success, and the financial viability of doing live shows, depends largely upon having a record in the charts. Personal appearances, be they single concerts or extended tours, are a carefully organised promotional tool. They make money for mega-stars, but are likely to do no more than break even for a new artiste. Due to the power and influence of the broadcasting media over popular music, the agent must do his best to ensure that the success of the artiste's records sales and radio performances reflect in the status and earning power of his personal appearances.

**5.3** The agent cannot be an alchemist to the artiste, he cannot make a silk purse out of a sow's ear. The artiste has to use his best endeavours too, it is only he who can rehearse and perfect his performance to match up to the inevitable public relations hype.

It is not uncommon for an artiste who has received a whiff of success to suffer from delusions of grandeur. It can be damaging to the artiste for the agent to get prestige bookings if he cannot live up to what is expected of him by his audience and the promoter.

## 6 Good faith

**6.1** In a business in which its word is seldom its bond, it is possible (although most unlikely) for an agent to do a little deal "on the side", which by its nature is not likely to be in the best interests of the artiste. An example would be an engagement for a successful artiste at a fee which is substantially less than his proper rate, to encourage the promoter to take an unknown artiste who is also represented by the agent. The side deal may be "under the counter" money, or anything else of a dubious nature. None of these activities would be done by a reputable agent, they are just to illustrate the point.

**6.2** An agent must act in all respects in good faith for the artiste. If, for a booking, the agent is instructed by the promoter to provide only one artiste, or more than one but with differing styles of music or presentation, the choice will be in his absolute discretion. The fact that he chooses from those he represents one artiste and not another does not of itself mean he is not doing his best for that other, or that he is not using good faith.

**6.3** Should the agent receive any unusual requests for the artiste's services, the artiste should be consulted and advised by the agent to ensure that the request is acceptable to him. For example, an offer of an engagement at a "top spot" but for no fee, such as for charity, may be in his best interests for the publicity, although he will not earn anything from it—but neither will the agent.

**6.4** The element of good faith is intangible, and it can be difficult to decide whether it is lacking entirely, or whether it was used but with bad judgment. The motivation is what counts. If honourable intentions bring about disastrous consequences, that is not of itself bad faith. If an agent, acting in his own opinion in the best interests of the artiste, declines on his behalf an ostensibly marvellous offer without consulting him, because he considers the artiste incapable of fulfilling its requirements, the implication of bad faith may be difficult to refute. The agent would have to justify his actions, and his opinion would have to be reasonably founded if, on the face of it, the decision was wrong.

## 7 Administration

**7.1** The agent must co-ordinate local and overseas offers of work for the artiste, consulting with the artiste's manager to ensure continuity within long term or projected commitments, such as for his recording schedule. An example is where personal appearances in any major country should be geared to forthcoming record releases. These create fresh publicity and demand for the artiste, and provide new subject matter for interviews and promotional material. Ultimately the agent advises on opportunities, but the decisions of what to do and where to go are basically managerial.

**7.2** Any potentially lucrative "spin-off" market related to personal appearances should be investigated and analysed prior to incurring any expense for promotion and publicity. How far the agent would participate in the planning and presentation of any "spin-off" activity will depend upon the manager. A "spin-off" activity in this context means a promotion or opportunity such as merchandising, which has arisen through whatever the agent has done, but which is not within his contractual terms of reference. Ordinarily these activities should be dealt with by the manager, or whoever else has control over the relevant rights. If the spin-off activity would not have arisen but for the agent, he should have a reasonable remuneration from its exploitation.

**7.3** The artiste should have as uncomplicated a control over the promotion of his career as possible, because the pace at which the music business moves is such that opportunities must be seized as and when they arise—second chances seldom occur.

## 8 Extent of represeentation

**8.1** The artiste must decide whether to appoint the agent for limited representation, or for all his personal appearance activities. This decision will depend upon whether the artiste wishes to be only a pop singer, or whether he is trying to build up a serious film, or stage acting career as well. The agency should not cover specialist matters such as serious literary writing, or any independent commercial activity or interest of the artiste not directly connected with entertainment. Agents are normally limited to live personal appearances, except perhaps where the artiste does not have a manager.

**8.2** The area of effective representation by a smaller agent (ie having only a UK operation) will be limited. A large agency with international connections is more capable of dealing with, for example, the USA, Japan and Europe. A smaller agent would have to do a deal with an American, Japanese or European agent for the representation of the artiste abroad—which may not always be in the best interests of the artiste. If a small agent cannot represent the artiste effectively abroad, the artiste may be better off to deal direct with the foreign agent. A small agent may not have the staff to deal with a large clientele, but may compensate by providing a personal service.

## 9 Appointment of foreign agents

**9.1** If the artiste is contemplating the appointment of an agent in a foreign country for limited representation, the following should be resolved before any commitment is made:

(a) Is the purpose of the agreement for specified events, or is it for a period of time?
(b) Make sure the artiste is not breaching any other contractual commitment by signing it.
(c) As the events will be abroad, to whom will any deposits be paid, when and to whom will final fees be paid, and how can the artiste

secure accurate payment in full of what becomes due to him?

(d) Put in termination provisions suitable to the purpose of the agreement. Do not allow automatic extensions of the contract period for any reason.

(e) State upon what events and what sources of earning the agent will be entitled to receive commission, with specific reference to re-bookings, or other events contracted for but which will be performed after the agreement ends.

(f) Make the contract under English law, unless there is no alternative, in which case take competent local legal advice.

(g) If the concert will be recorded or televised, so that potential spin-off packages would include an album of the concert, a TV special programme and a TV cassette, be careful to limit agency commission to income arising from the concert ticket sales, and other appearance fees, only.

(h) Define the territorial limits carefully if the agreement is for a period of time.

(i) If the foreign country operates a withholding tax system on income received by the artiste, make it the agent's responsibility to get the tax deduction certificate, and to sort out effectively the tax authority formalities.

## 10 Period of contract

*Example*

"Subject to the termination provisions of Clause [ ] this Agreement shall commence on the date hereof [be deemed to have commenced with effect from the — —] and shall continue for [two] years certain and thereafter shall be terminable [by either party giving to the other not less than (six) months prior written notice] [on an annual basis by either party giving to the other not less than (three) months prior written notice expiring on the anniversary date] Provided that if within the first year the Agent does not obtain engagements for the Artiste which produce not less than [£ ] gross fees the Artiste may terminate this Agreement by written notice at the end of that year."

*Example*

". . . continue for one year and subject to [specify conditions] the Agent shall be entitled to extend the period of this Agreement annually for a further [three] years by giving the Artiste written notice no later than sixty days prior to the expiry of the then current contract year."

**10.1** If the artiste shows potential, the agent will want a long term contract, such as three years. The artiste would prefer a short term compatible with reasonable continuity of service by the agent, so that he can judge his performance and ability. The artiste can then decide, depending upon results, whether or not to extend the contract period. An extensive international tour may cover between two and four months including rest and holiday periods, and will normally be planned around projected album releases. Therefore a major artiste's personal appearance schedule may cover eighteen months ahead, so the agent needs a contract period to enable him to keep such a schedule going.

**10.2** An agent wants a reasonable period after the artiste has become successful within which to enhance his reputation, and to profit from the artiste's increased earning power. If the agency agreement is annual, for a new artiste, it may include yearly options in favour of the agent up to an agreed maximum period. In this case, although the agent is appointed by the artiste, it is the "employee" who has the right to extend his own term of service.

**10.3** If the agent wants a significant period of exclusivity, there must be a commitment in real terms to the artiste. The agent of a star spends his time sorting out a steady stream of offers, or at least has his own proposals to promoters taken seriously. The agent of an unknown artiste has to push against closed doors to get him a foothold. He may eventually get frustrated or bored, and cease to be active. One safeguard for the artiste is to state in the agency agreement that if his earnings through the efforts of the agent have not exceeded a minimum sum in any year the artiste may terminate the agreement. It should be clear whether the earnings are those only received, or whether they will include what will be paid under events which have been contracted for in this contract year, but which will be performed in the next contract year.

## 11 Commission

*Example*

> "The Agent shall be entitled to a commission of [15%] of the gross receipts of the Artiste arising from any engagement as defined herein whether or not procured by the Agent including engagements introduced or contracted for during the period hereof but to be performed after the termination of this Agreement. In the absence of specific agreement by the Artiste the Agent will be responsible for payment of any fee or commission due to any sub-agent or other party in connection with the securing or performance of any such engagement."

**11.1** Commission rates vary from 10% to 15%, but can be higher if agreed, and are calculated upon the gross earnings of the artiste from events contracted through the agent, or during the period of the agency agreement, including where the performance of the engagement occurs after termination of the agency agreement.

**11.2** The principle of commission being charged on payments in kind, or upon costs of the artiste which are paid by the promotor, was dealt with in paragraph **16** of chapter one, and applies equally to agent's commission.

**11.3** Sole and exclusive agency contracts usually state that the commission is payable on the earnings from all engagements of the artiste contracted for during the period of the agreement, whether or not procured by the agent. If the artiste obtains, or accepts, offers of employment negotiated and dealt with either by himself or through a third party (whether or not that party receives commission), the exclusive agent is entitled to his own commission, because that work should have been channelled through him. The fact that the other party is paid a commission in no way affects the agent's rights, it is just an expensive venue for the artiste in commission terms. If the agent waives all or some of his own commission entitlement, that is a voluntary concession to the artiste, and should not set a precedent.

**11.4** A manager who is acting also as an agent because one has not yet been appointed cannot charge the artiste with additional agency commission in recognition of his "two hat" position. Some areas of operation of a manager and an agent overlap, to the extent that appointment as "manager and agent" is the usual wording in a management contract. For so long as no agent is appointed, the manager must try to get work for the artiste as part of his management activities.

**11.5** An unusual possibility is where the manager and the agent of the artiste are two limited companies, each owned or controlled by the same persons, who are acting as managers and as agents as the executives of each of the companies. The same reasoning against a double commission charge applies, but the counter argument would be that, as the management and the agency are two distinct businesses, the transactions must be kept separate, each earning its own profit. In theory it is for the artiste to agree or disagree with that arrangement, and to accept or reject the contracts accordingly. In practice the artiste, when negotiating any agreement with his management or agency or any modification to it, should take professional advice. The manager/agent is not capable of giving him independent advice for obvious reasons. (See paragraph **34** of chapter one.)

**11.6** If, from the impression given to him, the artiste genuinely assumed that the management and agency companies were independent, he would have a strong claim for termination or rescission of the agreements based upon the exercise of undue influence by the manager, and for breach of his fiduciary obligations to the artiste. If he was not informed of the full facts, he had no reasonable means of finding them out. He could do a company search, but the shareholders and directors may be nominees. The two companies might argue that their association is irrelevant, as the artiste would not pay less commission if the manager and agent were separate concerns. That may be true, but it is not the point. The manager acting as agent, or the agent acting as manager, will do no more for the artiste than he would have done without the artificial separation. Independent managers and agents are bound to have different ideas, contacts and methods of doing business. Those are the benefits the artiste should have, and what he is paying for.

**11.7** If the agent has to obtain a certain booking through another agent, who acts exclusively for the promoter of the proposed venue, the artiste's agent may have to share his commission with the other agent. Alternatively, the other agent's fee may be charged to the artiste with his prior agreement, where the venue is of special value to the artiste and cannot be obtained in any other way. He should then negotiate a reduction of the commission paid to his own agent.

**11.8** The double commission contingency must be included in the agency agreement if the agent wants the right to apply it where necessary. There must be safeguards for the artiste to prevent the agent from charging a double commission fraudulently, and no such commitment should be made without the artiste's approval. If the agent gets a "rebate" on any third party fee or commission payable by the artiste, he should account for it and reduce the artiste's overall costs accordingly. Not to do so would be theft of that money, a serious offence.

The agent must not merely delegate his responsibility to others at the expense of the artiste. The basic principle is that the commission payable to the agent, whatever the circumstances, will not exceed the rate set out in the agency agreement. Any other factor must first be approved by the artiste, who may choose to pay a higher commission for something special.

**11.9** Disputes can arise from loose wording in the agency agreement, such as "extensions and renewals" of engagements or tours, and "follow-up" return visits, which are to be performed after the expiry of the agency agreement, upon which commission is to be charged. The agreement must define clearly what the terms mean, and in exactly what circumstances the agent will be due his commission. If a commissionable two week series of appearances, which starts in the agency period, but which is extended to four weeks, the last two of which are outside the period, the whole four week period would be commissionable. Commission should not be paid to the agent on any re-engagement which is not connected directly with the original performance contract, and which is a newly negotiated and contracted event all of which happened after the agency agreement has expired. It has been known for the "commission trap" to extend to a period of time after expiry of the agreement, however or whenever the re-engagement occurred. The claim becomes even more unfair, for example, if the artiste had already appeared at that venue prior to appointing the agent, as any re-engagement is not the result of the agent's initial introduction of the artiste to that venue.

**11.10** If the artiste is a success with the venue on the original appearance, or if he is a well known artiste, he may be approached by the venue promoters direct or through his new agent to appear there again. It may be true that, but for the original introduction by the first agent, a new artiste may not have become known to the venue at all, but that is his job.

**11.11** The danger in any exclusive agency agreement is to include unintentionally within the source of income on which the agent claims commission those matters, such as merchandise rights and publishing and recording agreements, which have a long term income potential. These are managerial responsibilities. The position may be different where the agent actually initiates and procures the contract which is accepted by the artiste, when he should be entitled to some reasonable remuneration for having done so. In those circumstances the artiste and his manager will negotiate a special rate or deal with the agent, who may never in practice have anything to do with the operation of the long term agreement. The artiste should ensure that he does not pay a double commission on long term income. Where an agency agreement is for a specific purpose only, commission is only payable on the artiste's earnings from the completion of that purpose.

**11.12** If a recording contract should be procured and negotiated by an agent, in the absence of anything to the contrary, he would be entitled to receive his commission on the royalties due to the artiste for the whole period of the recording contract. This is only likely to happen where the artiste does not have a manager. As the royalties can be substantial, and as the recording contract can extend over many years, the artiste should consider a different arrangement with the agent, before authorising him to contact any record companies.

**11.13** Another consideration is that, whatever the length of the term of a recording contract, royalties are paid to the artiste for so long as his records are sold. Therefore the agent's ordinary deal may not be fair to the artiste, even though the agent may have an exclusive contract with the artiste covering the whole of the period of the recording contract. The same applies to the earnings of an artiste/composer under a music publishing contract. In the same way as management commission, there has to be a compromise between a reasonable reward for the agent's effort, and excessive combined commissions on the artiste's earnings. The practical answer is to limit commission to a number of records made, or a period of time after expiry of the agency agreement.

**11.14** If commission on income from long term contracts is to be paid to the originating agent, irrespective of the length of the term of the agency contract, the artiste may be strongly tempted to "reorganise" his affairs so as to terminate that particular long term contract, and to substitute a new contract in its place. This activity cannot be condoned merely for the sake of sidestepping legal obligations, and may well not succeed, due to the distinction between the form and the substance of the transaction. Essentially, the record company will retain its continuity of rights to the same level irrespective of any contractual convolutions, which will be treated as an artificial device if it has no real commercial sense.

**11.15** If an agent receives commission on the artiste's earnings from a recording contract, the artiste must make certain that payments to the agent are consistent with the principles of calculation on which the artiste receives his payments. As the agent's commission will be on the gross royalties due to the artiste, it is vital to define "gross". For example, if the manager owns the production company through which the artiste's recordings are passed to the major record company, the artiste's royalty is that payable to him by the manager/production company. Where the record producer is paid his royalty directly from the record company, does the artiste pay all or part of it by way of reduction of his own royalty rates? The gross for this purpose should not include third party deductions of fees or royalties from the artiste's share. Recouped record company recording costs and promotion advances to cover specific expenditure should be excluded from gross for this purpose.

**11.16** Unless the agency agreement qualifies the basis of calculation, all commissions payable by the artiste are calculated on gross earnings, and not on what the artiste may finally receive net after deduction of all fees, commissions, and out of pocket expenses. The living, travelling, entertaining and incidental expenses of the artiste can, when tax liabilities and third party commissions are fully reserved for, reach or exceed his net earnings. That depends on his life style and how efficiently his business cash flow is managed, but there can be a significant risk of total expense exceeding total income after tax.

## 12 Accounting

*Example*

"(a) The Agent will maintain separate full and accurate books of account of all monies received by the Agent on behalf of the Artiste and paid out whether for the commission due to the agent or otherwise.

(b) All such monies shall be maintained at all times in a separate bank account designated "[Artiste] Trust Account" which shall be operated by the Agent.

(c) The Agent will deliver to the Artiste once each [Quarter] a detailed written statement of all financial transactions occuring within that [Quarter] together with copies of the relevant bank statements and once each year will provide an annual account certified as being correct by the Agent's auditors.

(alternative (c)) The Agent will account fully to the Artiste for all income and expense within [14] days after the completion of each tour or single concert.

(d) Not more than once each year upon giving 14 days prior notice the Artiste or his qualified representative will be entitled to inspect and take copies of such books of account."

**12.1** With the exception of well known artistes and venues, or by special arrangement, in respect of a "one night stand" an unknown artiste without an agent is usually paid after the performance, either in cash or by cheque. Where the artiste is sufficiently well known, and has an agent who has made the arrangements, the venue promoter will account direct to the agent with the authority of the artiste.

**12.2** For substantial dates or tours booked ahead, the agent may receive a proportion of the fee in advance as security, and towards compensation if the promoter fails to fulfil his obligations. If the artiste breaches the agreement or fails to appear, the promoter will want his deposit back. The agent will usually keep the deposit pending completion of the event or tour, and if the amount is significant the artiste should get the interest accrued on the deposit account.

It should be clear as to whether the agent is holding the deposit as stakeholder, as agent for the artiste, or as agent for the promoter. It will not be the last alternative. The distinction would become vital if the artiste breaches the promoter's agreement and fails to appear, but demands that the agent hands over the deposit notwithstanding. The agent will not want to do so, as he may be sued by the promoter, who will also be demanding its return. If the agent is holding the deposit as agent for the artiste, he would have to hand it to him, however reluctantly.

**12.3** Where the agent does not receive the performance fee, the artiste or his manager will have to account to him for his commission. The accounting from the agent to the artiste will be within so many days after completion of the event, or upon receipt of the money by the agent, whichever is the later. The artiste's share of all monies received by the agent will normally be paid to the manager. If the agent has been appointed by the manager to work with him, rather than to represent the artiste independently, the manager will pay the agent his commission out of the manager's share of the artiste's earnings. This is only likely to happen in a one-off situation.

**12.4** Subject to the recoupment of any advances made by the promoter to the artiste to cover day to day foreign touring expenses, the promoter will pay tour income direct to the agent. The advances are because the artiste or his tour manager does not want to carry unnecessarily large sums of money for tour crew "per diems" and incidental expenses. The agent must supervise the collection and payment of fees wherever he is responsible for receiving them. He can make whatever arrangements suit him best, provided the terms of the agency agreement are adhered to, and the interests of the artiste are not adversely affected.

**12.5** If there is a dispute with the venue promoter over the fee after the performance has taken place the agent may have to expend time and money in its recovery. A common cause of dispute is where the promoter decides to retain the whole or part of the outstanding balance of the fee as security for payment by the artiste for property damaged or removed by the artiste's entourage. The effort to obtain payment of the money must be made unless the artiste does not wish to, or unless to do so would clearly be uneconomic.

**12.6** If the agent fails to collect fees from the promoter for whatever reason, whether he will be entitled to his commission on the uncollected fee will depend upon the wording of his contract. Commission should only be payable on money received by the artiste, or by a third party on his behalf. However, the agent could reasonably claim that he had done his job, and he should not have to share in any business risk incurred by the artiste. It is a matter of negotiation. (See also paragraph **16.9**.) Where the failure is entirely the fault of the agent, the artiste may well be able to recover uncollected fees from him, by way of compensation for breach of his obligations.

**12.7** The agent must keep separate adequate and accurate books of account in respect of an artiste's earnings received by him, to enable the artiste and his accountants to verify the figures. Failure to do so invites accusations of incorrect accounting, or worse. Without sufficient evidence of all the transactions, the agent will not be in a position to prove otherwise. Running a close second to the charge of incompetence of the agent as a favourite ground for terminating an agency contract, is that of incorrect accounting. This charge is best rebutted by detailed and accurate book-keeping, and prompt payment.

**12.8** A separate trust account in the name of the artiste should be opened by the agent at his bank into which goes only the artiste's money, and from which the agent can draw his commission. This is used to identify and distinguish their respective money, so that if the agent gets into financial difficulties the money of the artiste is safe from the agent's creditors. If the agent uses his own account for receiving the artiste's money, in the event of disaster the artiste is only an unsecured creditor of the agent, together with all others. This precaution will not be necessary for a solid reputable agent, it only applies where, for example, a new artiste is using a small or new agency. The agent may consider the request to be offensive, and in fact the precaution is seldom taken.

**12.9** An agent should not ask for a contribution to his ordinary business expenses, except to cover any specific expense authorised by the artiste and which is not customarily an agent's responsibility. If the agent is negotiating an extensive foreign tour, he is likely to spend on international phone calls, faxes and telexes far more than normally anticipated in the ordinary course of business. These expenses may be difficult to monitor and cost accurately, but the agent may ask for a reasonable contribution. If the anticipated gross tour income is high enough to give the agent a handsome commission, the telecommunications costs may be acceptable and, in perspective, should remain the cost of the agent.

**12.10** If the agent receives income of the artiste which arises otherwise than from live personal performances, his own accounting to the artiste will be governed as to dates and amount by when the paying company itself accounts to the agent. The artiste must receive detailed statements clearly indicating how his gross income is made up, and showing all deductions for commission, and other payments made to the artiste or on his behalf. The artiste or his acountant must be empowered to inspect the agent's books at least once in every year. If the accounting is deficient by more than (say) 5%, the agent should pay the artiste's audit costs. Whatever the deficiency, interest should be paid on it calculated from the due date to the date of payment. There is no right to charge interest unless it is specified in the agency agreement.

## 13 Promoter's agreements

*Example*

> "The Agent will promptly submit to the Artiste details of all proposed engagement offers and if they are accepted in principle the Agent will produce the engagement contract for the Artiste to sign. If in future the Artiste authorises the Agent to sign engagement contracts on his behalf the authority must be in writing and will be conditional on the Artiste first accepting the engagement terms."

**13.1** A new artiste needs any reasonable booking to have the fee, and to get known; a star is in a position to pick and choose his engagements. In the former case the agent will have no substantial influence to exert when negotiating a fee with the promoter, or special terms such as the artiste's prominence in the billing. The artiste will have to accept the promoter's standard terms. In the latter case the agent will be in a position of strength to negotiate the most favourable terms available.

**13.2** The agent should submit to the artiste the terms of any proposed deal for approval before committing him, so the agent must not mislead the promoter when discussing them initially. Whether negotiation with the promoter "subject to the artiste's approval" is always practical depends upon the artiste or his manager being readily available to make the decisions. Some artistes cannot stand being left out of decision-making, whereas others leave everything to their agent, and only want to be kept informed of what has been fixed for them.

**13.3** All negotiations by the agent for the artiste must be in good faith, and he must genuinely do his best for the artiste by way of fee and terms. He must ensure that any provision for re-booking or extension of the engagement will fit in with the existing arrangements of the artiste for other appearances or his personal commitments, and that the fee will reflect the value of the artiste at that time.

**13.4** In a package deal with a promoter involving several artistes, the agent must do the best he can for all the artistes he represents. If the promoter will only offer terms which may suit some of the artistes, the agent may have to accept them or lose the booking. An agent in this dilemma should consult the artistes for their views. Career development is as important as fee levels, so any decision upon imperfect terms is a matter of commercial judgment.

**13.5** When a booking is confirmed by an agent on behalf of the artiste, he will be bound by the agreed terms governing that booking. This means that he must appear on time, for the length of the "spot" booked, and he must give a performance of the quality expected from him.

**13.6.1** If all goes well the audience and the promoter are happy, and the artiste is paid. However, the artiste may be late, or he may not arrive at all. He may give a bad performance, he may arrive and refuse to perform unless he is paid first, or he may make insulting remarks about the venue to the audience in his "warm up". He may be drunk; anything can, and does, happen. The artiste may even incite the audience to wreck the hall.

**13.6.2** It is only when such problems arise that the promoter, the agent and the artiste each take legal advice upon who should be liable for losses or damages. That will depend upon whether there was in fact any loss or damage, and if so its apparent cause: and upon the terms of the contracts and who signed them in what capacity. Any loss usually falls first upon the promoter, whether he owns or has hired the hall. Apart from the cost of physical damage to the hall, the promoter may even have to refund admission charges and lose future custom. His right of action is normally against the artiste, whether the artiste signed the booking agreement himself, or whether the agent did so for and on behalf of the artiste within his ostensible authority to do so. If the artiste is providing his services through a company, the company will be the contracting party, and so will be primarily liable to the promoter.

**13.7** If the agent signed the contract, and acted throughout in good faith within the terms of his appointment by the artiste, the agent will not be liable to the promoter for any breach or other actionable activity of the artiste, or third party activity for which he is responsible. Should the promoter take action against the agent as the signing party, the agent will plead agency and will bring in the artiste as the third party principal, so that the artiste and the promoter can fight it out directly between them themselves.

**13.8** The agent may himself be liable to some extent to the promoter if knowingly he made false or misleading representations to him about the ability or the availability of the artiste, or if he did anything which could be considered in law to be the act of a principal. If the false representations about the artiste's ability substantially influenced the promoter to book him, and his disastrous performance caused loss to the promoter, the agent may be liable for those misrepresentations.

**13.9** If the agent, by signing the promoter's contract, committed the artiste to the terms of a booking without fulfilling the relevant conditions of his agency contract, such as having to submit the terms of all engagements to the artiste for his prior approval, what is the legal position? Possibilities are:

(a) If the agent has always put himself out to promoters as being authorised to sign contracts on behalf of the artiste, and the artiste has never denied that the agent had the ostensible authority, the contract will commit the artiste whether he likes it or not. He has knowingly let the promoter assume the agent had the appropriate authority. He could notify the promoter that the agent's ostensible authority has been revoked, but that would not act retrospectively.

(b) If the promoter is aware that the artiste always signs his own contracts, and does not query the authority of the agent to do so on this occasion, the artiste might be able to claim that the contract did not commit him. Where there is a reasonable doubt in the promoter mind he should take all reasonable steps to verify the position.

The purpose of having an agent is to enable him to act on behalf of the artiste, and on balance it would be difficult for the artiste to repudiate an obligation to appear. This obligation may be confirmed by the artiste ratifying the agreement subsequently, such as by accepting the advance fee, or by becoming involved in the planning of the tour or concert. To be able to reject the deal, he would have to do so immediately he heard about it, without doing anything which could be deemed to be acceptance or part performance of it, and with reasonable grounds for rejecting it.

**13.10** Where the agent is at fault, he may still be bound contractually to the promoter to provide the artiste; and as he could not make the artiste fulfil the booking, the agent may be liable to the promoter for any resultant loss. This would not be a *force majeure* event, ie, frustration due to an event beyond his control. Neither would the agent have any claim against the artiste, if he was legally entitled to decide not to appear. If the artiste is obliged to fulfil a booking to which he is not legally committed, either to preserve his reputation or because he is legally advised to do so, the agent will be liable to the artiste for any adverse consequences. There may be none, and as he will have been paid the fee, there will have been a benefit. For all these reasons the agent should get the artiste either to sign each booking contract, or to countersign it as a confirmation of his approval of it.

**13.11** The agent should get approval from the artiste to agree with the promoter return visits, or to give options to the promoter for future priority of any booking which may take place after the expiry date of the agency agreement. It is a matter of expediency. The artiste should have sufficient work during any transition period after the expiry of the agency agreement, but his new agent would like to start off with his own contacts as soon as possible. If the artiste is happy with his agent, the relationship will continue past the contractual expiry date. If he has terminated the agency, he may not want to have anything further to do with the agent.

**13.12** If the promoter refuses to pay the fee negotiated by the agent, the artiste will have to make a claim against the promoter if the agent fails to get results. But if the promoter pays the agent, who does not account to the artiste for the balance due to him, the promoter will have discharged his liability. An exception may be where he knew prior to making the payment that the artiste had revoked the authority of the agent to act for him or to collect money on his behalf. This would be difficult to prove in the absence of the artiste having given the promoter specific written notice to that effect.

## 14 Delegation

*Example*

> "The Agent shall not be entitled to delegate any of his material obligations to any other party but he may be authorised by the Artiste to delegate specific matters from time to time provided that the Agent shall remain fully liable to the Artiste for the acts or defaults of that other party and that the Agent shall if reasonably requested by the Artiste revoke all instructions to that party and resume performance of the obligation."

**14.1** An agent trading as an individual, and who has contracted personally with the artiste, cannot delegate his obligations unless the agency agreement has a clear authority for him to do so. It is acceptable for his assistant, or his office, to deal with minor administrative matters under his supervision, but he must remain the primary contact with the artiste.

**14.2** Where the agent is a company, any of its executives may carry out its functions for the artiste. The agency agreement may be conditional upon one named person, or a substitute agreed by the artiste within the agency, representing the artiste at all times on a personal level.

**14.3** The agent should be entitled to appoint a sub-agent where necessary, such as for a foreign country within his territory, or for a specialised deal within the agent's authority. The agent will remain primarily responsible to the artiste for the acts, omissions and defaults of the sub-agent. In the absence of anything to the contrary in the agency agreement, the agent is responsible for the sub-agent's commission, ie it will come out of his own commission. A sub-agent will normally only be appointed for a specific event, so can be controlled and directed within the confines of that purpose.

## 15 Assignment

*Example*

"The Agent shall not be entitled to assign all or any part of his rights and obligations hereunder to any party without the prior written consent of the Artiste. If the Agent wishes to assign his personal obligations to a limited liability company such consent may be withheld if the Agent does not own or control the company and/or if his continued personal supervision of the Artiste will not be included in the assigned agency agreement."

**15.1** For the protection of the artiste, an agency agreement should contain a prohibition against assignment by the agent of the benefit of the agreement without his prior written consent. If the assignment represents a partial delegation only, it should be given or withheld subject to the assigning agent remaining liable for the acts, omissions and defaults of the assignee. The consent of the artiste should be in his absolute discretion, as he must have full approval of the choice of who will be his agent. The choice of an agent is both a personal and a commercial decision, and the artiste is not a commodity to be bought and sold.

**15.2** An agent is the employee of the artiste; he is appointed to carry out a certain function. If there is no exclusive agreement in writing, the agent will have nothing to assign. If a personal agent, acting within his rights, irrevocably delegates his obligations to a third party, in a practical sense he is assigning his part of the agreement. Where there is no actual assignment, and it is still the agent who ostensibly deals with the artiste, it may become evident that the agent is not doing his job properly. The question is whether the agent has any intention of continuing to represent the artiste, and if so, any delegation should cease.

**15.3** If the agent does not have the necessary experience, office back-up and ability to fulfil his obligations, and has another person effectively doing his job for him, the artiste may be able to terminate the agreement for breach of the delegation or assignment restrictions. The artiste may not complain if the system is working to his satisfaction. He may do so if he thinks he can do better elsewhere, and is looking for any reasonable excuse to terminate the agency agreement.

## 16 Termination

**16.1** An agent never guarantees to obtain employment for the artiste, he only undertakes to use his best endeavours to do so. It can be difficult to determine whether the agent is using his best endeavours, or whether he only does just enough to keep the artiste happy. The question arises where the artiste thinks he is not getting enough work, or that his booking fees are not realistic, and he is looking for a good reason to end the agency contract.

**16.2** The agent, in good faith, may be doing all for the artiste that he can reasonably be expected to do, but the work is just not available. The demonstrable fact that he is using his best endeavours, however unsuccessfully, should be a reasonable defence to a claim for termination of the contract for lack of activity by the agent. There may be exceptions, such as where there is a minimum earnings commitment, when failed best endeavours is no defence to termination.

**16.3** The normal grounds for contract termination should be included, such as substantial or persistent breach of contract by the agent, or his bankruptcy, or its winding up if it is a company, or upon the agent ceasing to trade. If any of the terms of the contract, such as the accounting provisions or a minimum earnings clause, is agreed to be "of the essence" of the agreement, a breach should be specified to be sufficient grounds for termination. This must be the clear intention of both parties stated in the agreement to be effective.

**16.4** The agency agreement may be subject to the successful conclusion of a trial period. The terms are usually that if the agent fails to obtain employment giving the artiste a stated minimum earning over the trial period, the artiste may terminate the contract at the end of the period. The wording of the clause may be sufficiently loose to enable the agent to make up any shortfall of earnings by the end of the trial period by a cash payment, thus preventing such termination. This might happen where the artiste shows great potential for the next period, although progress may well have been slow initially. In reality the relationship is either working, or it is not. If it is, it will continue. The agency agreement should state whether it will continue automatically into the main contract period unless written notice of termination is given by the artiste to the agent on the expiry of the trial period, or whether it will simply terminate without any notice being required. The first alternative favours the agent, as artistes tend to forget to give written notices.

**16.5** The agent may require the right to terminate the agreement at any time by giving to the artiste, say, three month's prior notice in writing. A similar term is seldom available to the artiste, who will usually be on an annual basis. All termination provisions should be reciprocal to be fair to both sides. An agent may need this right where he has an opportunity to represent a major artiste, but which would create a conflict of interest with an existing client, and a choice has to be made between them.

**16.6** The great advantage any artiste has over any agent is that the agent, despite his contract with the artiste, must always rely upon goodwill for the services of that artiste continuing to be provided. A successful artiste will always be able to find an agent who will act for him. It is the commercial attraction offered by others to the artiste, and the possiblity put before him of vast earnings to be made, which seem to make the breach by him of his contract worth risking. Therefore there is a tendency for contracts to be drafted with future court proceedings for compensation in mind.

**16.7** With broken agency contracts it can be difficult to determine the right compensation due to the agent. Apart from damages for the breach of contract, what has the agent lost for which he should be compensated? His financial loss includes the commission due to him from the earnings of the artiste coming within the scope of his agreement. The artiste has an obligation to pay commission due to the agent as at the date of the wrongful termination of the agreement for completed appearances not yet accounted for, and also for future appearances contracted for.

**16.8** Prospective commission on future work which he might have obtained for the artiste had the agreement remained in existence can only be speculative. If the court upholds the validity of the agent's agreement, it will not grant an injunction to prevent the breach or wrongful termination, but a reasonably calculated measure of compensation will be the commission upon what the artiste actually earns for that period from events which would have come within the agency agreement.

**16.9** Non-performance by an artiste of any engagement he is contractually committed to will be a breach of the promoter's contract. Such a breach should not have any adverse consequences upon the agent, if he acted correctly. The result is a claim made against the artiste, and non-payment of the fee by the promoter, which affects the agent as he does not get his commission. As the agent is not a party to the promoter's contract, he does not have any rights under it. The agent will have lost his earnings too, but whether he has any redress against the artiste for deprivation of commission will depend upon the terms of their contract, which normally will be silent on the point.

## 17 Confidentiality

**17.1** The agent will become aware of a significant amount of confidential information relating to the artiste, his management, career plans, financial status and the like, although he will not have the same depth of information as the artiste's manager. The agent must agree to keep confidential any such information, and not to make any unauthorised use of it in any way. Neither should he make exaggerated boasts about the artiste's earning capacity or lifestyle, as that can have unfortunate repercussions. Scandal is the lifeblood of some newspapers, and however incorrect any allegation may be, it can be hard to live down or deny convincingly. The special entertainers unit of the Inland Revenue takes seriously for possible investigation any plausible sounding "leak" of what might be an undeclared or underdeclared source of income or taxable benefits which may have been received by the artiste. They may also be interested in finding out how he can appear to live so far beyond his visible means of support.

CHAPTER 3

# *Personal Appearance Contracts*

## 1 General considerations

**1.1** The manager does not often have to negotiate a recording or music publishing contract for the artiste, as they are long term contracts. The routine of these agreements relates to songs to be recorded, or imminent record releases, with promotion and advertising to be agreed upon and set up. The artiste may record two albums within every 18 months, but the planning and organisation take a lot of time. The bulk of the regular contract negotiation which a manager does for his artiste is on personal appearances, and the rest of his time is spent on general career planning and administration. Personal appearances can be concerts or tours, TV shows, media interviews, and anything else which helps to promote the artiste, sell his records, or produce an income. Being an artiste is a business which needs publicity. Concerts and tours are expensive to stage, but the artiste must be available and retain a high profile. This also helps to sell records, without which the artiste will not have a major international career.

**1.2** The basic terms for a personal appearance contract will be:

(a) the fee;
(b) the date, place and time of performance;
(c) the priority of billing and order of performance, where there are several artistes performing at the same venue;
(d) the preparation of a schedule dealing with all practical points such as stage size and configuration, sound equipment, power sources, all the way down to drinks off stage.

It is the agent's job to negotiate with the promoter all the requirements of the artiste which are to be included in the contract. The more famous the artiste, the greater will be his demands, and this chapter deals with the most important items. From experience some artistes will have prepared their own detailed contract schedule containing their requirements. If they are taking all their own light show as well as sound equipment the promoter would not otherwise know what the venue must supply.

## SECTION I: FINANCIAL CONSIDERATIONS

### 2 Negotiation of fees

*Example*

"(a) The promoter will pay the fee of [$ ] as a minimum guarantee against [sixty] percent of gross ticket sales revenue and other receipts in connection with the concert after deducting the above fee from such gross receipts. 'Gross Receipts' shall include but shall not be limited to ticket sales, on site merchandise stall fees and all other payments made to the Promoter or as it directs, or from which the Promoter receives a benefit directly connected with the concert.

(b) The Promoter will ensure that the venue is registered with the [Performing Right Society Limited] for the public performances of copyright works and will ensure that the [PRS] receives an accurate cue sheet of all compositions performed and that all due copyright performance payments will be made.

(c) The Promoter will pay to the Artiste's Agent [fifty] per cent of the minimum guarantee fee on the signing of this Agreement which the Agent is irrevocably authorised to release to the Artiste immediately upon the performance by him of the concert.

(d) On completion of the concert the Promoter will forthwith pay the Artiste's Agent the balance of the fee calculated as in (a) above in cash, banker's draft or as may otherwise be agreed.

(e) Where the fee includes a percentage of gross receipts, the Promoter will give the Agent all reasonable access to the box office ticket sales and other records on the night of the concert, and will also enable him to verify the submitted statement within [21] days after submission. (See paragraph **4.6**.)

(f) If the Promoter cancels or breaches this Agreement the Artiste shall be entitled to retain any deposit made under (c) above as partial compensation without prejudice to any other rights the Artiste may have against the Promoter and upon cancellation by the Promoter the Artiste's Agent is hereby irrevocably authorised by the Promoter to release the deposit to the Artiste unconditionally. If the Artiste cancels or fails to appear at the concert the Artiste's agent is hereby irrevocably authorised to return the deposit to the Promoter unless he receives a written notice from the Artiste stating that such cancellation or failure was with due contractual cause when he will retain it pending settlement of the dispute.

[(g) The Promoter undertakes to pay for all the travel accommodation and other facilities to be provided by the Promoter under Clause [ ] of this Agreement in addition to all fees referred to above.]"

**2.1** The fee should be the highest negotiable cash figure, taking into account whether the promoter is also paying for travel and accommodation costs. The customary currency of payment is US dollars, whatever the country of the performance, except for an English artiste performing at an English concert, when sterling is used. In practice, payment made in or remitted to the United Kingdom may be the sterling equivalent. Payments will be made in local currency where cash is required during a foreign tour. When negotiating the fee, the agent must have prepared in conjunction with the artiste's manager a detailed budget for the tour. The fees should cover the tour costs at least, taking into account all commissions which will be taken from the fees. The fees will also depend on the "pulling power" of the artiste, and the size of halls to be played.

**2.2** If the total payments by the promoter will include prepaid air fares, and the cost of accommodation, local transportation, local lighting equipment or other services, they should be referred to in the contract. Their value may have to be added onto the fee for the calculation of local withholding tax, a point which needs to be checked. If that is the case then a higher proportion of the cash fee will be retained to cover the tax on benefits which have only a cash value. All benefits in kind must be declared in defining the taxable income of the Artiste. The Inland Revenue is well aware of the system, and an in-depth tax investigation is something to avoid. The provision of services may help to reduce any local withholding tax on cash fees. Their attributed value is a compromise between their real cost to the promoter, and what they would have cost the artiste on an arm's length basis.

## 3 Cancellation by artiste

**3.1** Any cancellation costs resulting from the non-appearance by the artiste will initially be borne by the promoter, although they may be included in his claim against the artiste where the non-appearance is a breach of contract. The non-appearance may be due to no fault, such as where he is incapacitated, or where there is an air strike or some other reason beyond his control. The artiste should ensure that there is a *force majeure* clause in his contract with the promoter. The promoter should insure himself against this kind of contingency. Prepaid airline tickets provided to the artiste in anticipation of his travelling to the concert must be cancelled or returned to the promoter. If they have been used, despite the non-appearance which is a breach of contract, that would be dishonest, and the promoter's claim will be increased accordingly.

**3.2** The contract may be conditional on specific substantial services being provided by the Promoter, failure of which will entitle the artiste to terminate the agreement (see paragraph **15**). The booking or provision of services by the promoter must be confirmed to the artiste within a sufficient time prior to the event to enable him to cancel for failure with the least inconvenience or expense. This may not be practical, so if the timing is likely to be tight, the relevant contract clause must be carefully worded.

**3.3** The artiste's agent will have received a non-returnable deposit from the promoter. The "non-returnable" refers to cancellation not caused by the artiste. It should be returned to the promoter if the cancellation is caused by the artiste's default, or where it is a *force majeure* cause, unless the promotion contract specifies otherwise.

## 4 Advance fee deposit

**4.1** A non-returnable deposit of a substantial part of the fee should be deposited by the promoter with the agent on exchange of the signed copies of the promoter's contract. This ensures that if the contract is broken by the promoter the artiste has some compensation immediately. Retention of the deposit will not preclude the artiste from suing the promoter for the balance of what the fee would have been, unless the deposit is so high that it can be treated as adequate compensation in full and final settlement of any claim against the promoter. Two points should be noted:

(a) The signed contracts should not be exchanged until the deposit is paid. If they are exchanged before, then the clause should make the contract fundamentally conditional on the deposit being received by a stated date, ie, it is of the essence of the contract.

(b) Where compensation is claimed for a fee balance which was to be based on a percentage of box office receipts, and if no tickets were put on sale, secondary evidence would be needed to show a reasonable estimate of what the ticket sales would have been.

**4.2.** If the promoter is operating from an awkward country, politically, geographically or financially, where there is a real risk that any balance of the fee will not be paid, he should be required to deposit the whole fee. Where the fee is a guaranteed minimum payment against a percentage of gross box office receipts, the risk is that the artiste does not receive any excess which becomes due. There may be genuine exchange control restrictions, or a shortage of hard currency in a developing country. The local legal system may make it impractical or uneconomical to consider suing for non-payment.

**4.3** Unless he is dealing with an agent he trusts absolutely, the promoter may ask for a reasonable safeguard against not being repaid the deposit if the concert is not performed by the artiste. If cancellation by the artiste is close to the date of the concert, the promoter will already have incurred expenses, such as payment to secure the hall, advertising and publicity, any backing musicians or an orchestra, and other relevant costs. All those expenses will be a loss to the promoter unless he is reimbursed by the artiste. The promoter will also have lost the opportunity to make money, and if the concert was a sell-out, or undeniably would have been so, he will have a firm basis for calculating his loss of net profit. If the promoter and the tour are both outside the UK, the possibility of compensation claims shows the necessity for the artiste to make the promoters contract subject to English law.

**4.4** The promoter may argue that if the deposit goes into a bank account in the joint names of the promoter and the artiste or the agent, with the bank mandate requiring both signatures for a withdrawal, it protects both parties. But by refusing to sign the withdrawal authority, the promoter can arbitrarily prevent withdrawal of the money by the agent, even if the artiste performs as agreed. The agent could do the same to the promoter should the artiste fail to perform as agreed. In the last resort the unpaid party will have to take legal action under the terms of the contract. Except in special circumstances this deposit alternative should not be agreed by the artiste. Where the proposal is agreed, the terms of the joint bank deposit, and all conditions surrounding its withdrawal, must be clear and cover every reasonable eventuality. For example, what alternative signatory arrangements will apply if either the agent or the promoter dies before the deposit is withdrawn?

**4.5** If the deposit is only a proportion of the fee, the balance will usually be payable immediately after the performance of the concert. If the reputation of the promoter, or the circumstances surrounding the concert, create a high risk of non-payment of the balance, it should be payable no later than a stated period prior to the performance taking place—usually when the artiste and all the equipment has turned up. This request will not be able to cover a percentage fee, unless the venue is already sold out. Payment should at this time be specified as being of the essence of the contract, enabling the artiste to cancel his performance even at that late hour if payment is not made. In many cases, that decision depends on whether it is physically safe for the artiste to do so.

**4.6** If the balance of the fee depends on box office receipts, the agent should inspect the ticket sales records as soon as possible after the last ticket has been sold. An experienced agent will also have a good idea by a visual estimate of the total audience whether the box office official returns are reasonably accurate. Where the concert is in a sports stadium, the seat ticket sales statement may be correct, but there may be an undeclared number of unofficial or unidentifiable "standing tickets" sold. These can only be discovered by checking individual members of the audience, which is not practical.

**4.7** To enable the agent to quote a fee to the promoter, the following provisions should also be in the contract, although the agent may be familiar with the venue. Outside the UK all on-site checking and sorting things out will be the responsibility of the tour manager, but reference is made to the agent for convenience.

(a) That not later than a specified time prior to the concert the promoter will verify in writing details of the audience capacity, an analysis of seat pricings, and the gross receipt on a full house. When the agent is negotiating the fee with the promoter, there must be a reasonable balance between the fee and the promoter's potential gross income from which he pays his expenses. The promoter must also have a potential profit. If that profit is not realised due to costs he had not catered for, or because the concert is not a sell-out, that is the risk of being a promoter.

If the promoter excludes from his calculations any seating capacity which is declared to be lost due to the siting of staging, the mixing desk or the public address system, the agent should verify the facts by inspecting the hall when the equipment is being set up.

Where the fee is a fixed sum calculated on the box office potential, there should be a clause entitling the agent to charge an additional fee if it is subsequently discovered that the seating capacity has been significantly understated, or the permitted number of standing audience has been omitted, or if the promoter is found to be charging a ticket price in excess of that stated to the agent.

(b) That the correct number and pricing of the free tickets delivered to or on behalf of the artiste, or given free to press, record company executives and the like, are excluded for the percentage calculation. The number of free tickets may be overstated, or may not actually be free. (See paragraph **14.1**.)

The next three caveats only relate to "dodgy" venues or promoters, generally in exotic countries.

(c) That the agent or his representative can be present at the box office and theatre door on the day of the performance. In countries where the national pastime is to "get away with it" this right is essential for those concerts where there are no seats provided, or where the seating accommodation is only a proportion of the available audience space. Where the box office percentage payable to the artiste for a hall with a large potential standing audience is substantial (such as a sports stadium) all entrances to the hall, authorised and unorthodox, should be policed by members of the road crew with push button counting machines, giving an accurate estimate of the total audience. These figures can be compared with the official total audience figure declared by the promoter. If there is a high prospect of being cheated by the promoter challenging the artiste's own audience count, the best way of verifying the audience figures is to have a promoter's representative counting alongside the artiste's road crew member. This level of checking may not be practical, the leeway being regarded as the promoter's profit contingency.

(d) That the box office gross percentage payment shall be certified as correct jointly by the promoter and by the hall management where possible. All ticket stubs and unsold tickets must be retained by the promoter or (preferably) the hall management for the period within which the artiste's representatives are entitled to audit the box office accountings. The promoter will put a time limit on the right of the artiste to make such an audit. All other accounting records which are relevant for calculating or confirming box office income must also be made available for inspection.

(e) Any loss of revenue due to forged tickets or gate-crashing must be the promoter's loss. This gives an incentive to the promoter to prevent these abuses. It also makes it unprofitable for the promoter to plan by rigging such devices a reduction of the fee payable to the artiste.

Basically either the promoter is honest, or he is not. If not, he will be experienced enough to hide any sidelines effectively.

**4.8** The balance of the fee can be paid in the same way as the deposit was paid by the promoter, or at the concert hall after the concert. If the fee is fixed, the balance can be paid in cash or by a bank certified cheque. If the artiste is due a percentage of the box office receipts, he should receive an immediate settlement of the balance after a single concert, for a tour an overall settlement will be made after the last concert.

**4.9** Detailed receipts showing the amount paid, and the promoter's and the recipient's signatures, must be made out for a fee in cash paid by the promoter after a concert, to avoid a dispute as to whether or not the money was really paid, or whether the amount paid was the amount stated on the receipt.

## 5 Income tax on performance fee

*Example*

> "The promoter shall notify the Agent forthwith in writing of any Revenue Authority requirement to deduct from the fee any withholding income tax. The promoter shall be entitled to retain the appropriate tax from the fee provided that he will procure an official tax deduction certificate from the Revenue Authority and shall forthwith pay to such Authority the whole of the tax charged. If any tax deducted is rebated or reduced subsequently the Promoter will forthwith collect it and pay it over to the Agent in full."

**5.1** The liability for local income tax or withholding tax in a foreign country must be dealt with in the promoter's contract. Local regulations differ in each country. Depending upon the financial arrangements with the artiste, either the promoter will withhold the appropriate tax and pay it to the Revenue Authorities, or the promoter will bear the liability for the local tax himself, and will not deduct it from the fee paid to the artiste. This would mean that the value of the fee to the artiste is increased by that amount. (See paragraph **5.4**.)

**5.2** If the promoter withholds the applicable local tax from the fee, the agent must check whether payment to the local Revenue Authority is the legal liability of the promoter or of the artiste. The liability to pay the tax is that of the artiste as the recipient of the income, but the liability of the promoter is to withhold that tax from money due to the artiste.

If the promoter withholds the tax but does not pay it to the local Revenue Authority, the artiste could possibly end up by paying twice. The promoter is treated as representing the artiste, not the Inland Revenue, in the collection of the tax. The liability for the tax is not satisfied until the tax is paid. If the promoter retains the amount withheld, the artiste still has an outstanding liability to the Inland Revenue. If subsequently the artiste has to pay the same tax direct to the Revenue Authorities because the promoter failed to do so, the artiste can reclaim from the promoter the amount he withheld. There may be other claims for fraud or technical theft against the promoter. What if the promoter goes bust before he pays the Inland Revenue the withheld tax? As he holds the money for the artiste, then (subject to the local laws) presumably the usual rules will apply, and the artiste will be an unsecured creditor for that amount. He will still have the tax liability.

**5.3** If the promoter does not account, or accounts incorrectly, to the tax authorities, and the discrepancy is not rectified when it is discovered, as well as still having the liability to the Inland Revenue, a charge of tax evasion may be made against the artiste. The problem may not be discovered by the artiste until he subsequently enters that country, only to find he is arrested at the airport because the immigration department has his name in its "black book". When the artiste's liability for local tax is settled, the promoter must ensure the artiste gets a tax deduction certificate issued by the local tax authority. He will need the certificate to take advantage of any double tax convention between England and the country in which he performed. He can check the tax deducted against the amount on the certificate, and will spot any discrepancy.

**5.4** If the promoter covers the cost of the tax which is technically the artiste's liability, can the artiste's agent or manager treat the amount of tax paid as representing an increase of the total fee for commission purposes? It is, in essence, an increase in the fee by way of a payment in kind, in exactly the same way as payments by the promoter of the costs of any services, which otherwise would have been incurred by the artiste from his cash fee. It would depend on the wording of the contract, but normally no such claim would be made. The promoter is not likely to be so generous, unless the combined fee and tax is an acceptable cost, and unless he can get the combined amount set off against tax in his accounts.

## SECTION II: PRACTICAL CONTRACTUAL MATTERS

### 6 Travel arrangements

*Route planning*

**6.1** The promoter's contract must describe accurately the starting time of the performance, and its minimum performance time. If the contract is for a tour, the manager must ensure that the spacing of the dates, and the sequence of their geographical locations, are compatible with proper travel facilities, vehicle and airflight routing, and allow for a reasonable time table of working days and rest days. This is most important when the artiste is flying between concerts because of the distances involved, and the equipment is going by road because of its bulk and weight.

**6.2** For a European tour, allowances must be made for rough weather and other delays if sea ferries are involved, and where, for commercial vehicles, travel restrictions may be imposed in some countries on Sundays and bank holidays. Heavy goods vehicles may be restricted to certain major routes, not necessarily the shortest or the most convenient, and this knowledge is critical when planning a tight time schedule between concerts. There may also be border customs delays for commercial vehicles, and for thorough customs examination of the equipment against the carnet.

The vehicles must comply in all respects with the Common Market vehicle regulations for loading, lights, licences and the tachometer recording equipment.

## 7 International carnets

**7.1** International Customs and Excise carnet requirements must be complied with strictly for foreign touring. The artiste's manager is responsible for organising the carnet.

**7.2** The carnet is issued by the London Chamber of Comerce, and consists of a complete detailed list of all equipment and instruments to be taken on tour, with their values and serial numbers. It's validity is limited to the countries stated upon it, and allows a temporary importation of the listed equipment duty-free, provided it is exported with the carnet on leaving the country. It is a facility to enable equipment which is exported temporarily from the UK to be re-imported without further duty being paid, and to ensure that equipment bought abroad will have duty paid on it when imported to the United Kingdom after a tour as a permanent acquisition. If equipment is exported without being subject to a valid carnet, upon its re-importation there may be difficulty in proving that it was purchased here and not liable to duty again. The same problem will arise for each country visited on the tour, hence the practical value of a carnet. The 1992 opening of all borders may make a carnet unnecessary throughout the European Comunity.

**7.3** A carnet is only issued after the documentation has been completed and a bank has provided written confirmation to the Chamber of Commerce that the current proportionate amount of the carnet equipment value (specified by the Chamber of Commerce) has been deposited with the bank by the carnet holder. This will be the top equivalent value of import duty rates applicable to the countries for which the carnet is valid. The deposit will be applied to any valid duty claim by such a country for any part of the carnet equipment if it was imported into that country, but cannot be shown to have been exported on the carnet.

**7.4** The equipment set out on a carnet must always travel across borders together, as a carnet cannot be "split". Every piece of equipment set out in the carnet must be re-imported into England, otherwise the carnet will not be accepted and stamped by the Customs at the port of re-entry. Unless the carnet is stamped by the Customs on re-entry to the UK, and discharged by the Chamber of Comerce, the bank cannot release the deposit money for such time as is laid down by the Chamber of Commerce. For incorrectly completed documents that can mean many months to allow for a possible duty claim to come in.

**7.5** Equipment listed on the carnet must not be sold, or part exchanged for new equipment, or otherwise disposed of during the tour. If equipment is broken or destroyed, all the bits must come back, to prove that it was not sold. Where equipment is stolen, a detailed local Police report on the theft, and any independent corroboration of the facts should be obtained, for the Customs and for the insurance claim.

## 8 Tour expenses

*Example*

> "The Promoter is not authorised to provide any funds or to make any payment out of the fee except to persons to be agreed between the Promoter and the Agent and all sums so paid by the Promoter may be retained from the final fee accounting provided that he has paid it only to an authorised person and has a legibly signed receipt therefor and provided that no payment shall exceed [$ ] without the express prior written approval of the Agent."

**8.1** The budget of income and expenditure for the tour must be realistic, and should cover unlikely contingencies as well as common risk factors. If the tour is throughout Europe and Scandinavia, the constant exchange of large sums of money from one currency into another can be expensive. Planning the amount required in each country is essential, especially if "cash after concert" money is being relied on to finance the everyday tour expenses.

**8.2** The promoter advances cash to the artiste during the progress of a tour, to be accounted for against the ultimate balance of the fee. This method of tour financing reduces the need to carry large sums of money, especially at the beginning of the tour.

The recipient of cash from a promoter must be authorised in writing by the agent, to prevent a stranger from stealing the money by claiming to be a member of the artiste's road crew, and conning a cash payment from the promoter. It also prevents the promoter from cheating the artiste by producing a receipt for money he claims to have paid in good faith to a "road crew member" who has an illegible signature, and deducting that amount from the balance of the fee due to the artiste.

**8.3** A tour manager must have internationally accepted credit cards to deal with emergencies, such as unexpected air flights, or where money is needed out of banking hours, or where cancellation of a concert deprives the tour manager of funds he was relying upon for the next stage of the tour.

## 9 Approval of support act

*Example*

> "The Artiste will be the headlining Artiste performing at the venue on each of the dates set out in the Schedule hereto and the Artiste has the approval right of any support act to perform before the Artiste. The right of approval is absolute and is of the essence of this Agreement."

**9.1** A successful artiste can insist on having the approval of any "warm-up" support artiste whose function is to get a good atmosphere going in the hall. As it is the artiste who the audience are paying to see, he wants to ensure that:

(a) The support act's music is compatible with his, to get the audience into a receptive mood.

(b) The support act is not seriously competitive with the artiste in its popular appeal, musical ability and visual stage show.

(c) The duration of the support act's performance is relatively short. If more than one support act is used, the sequence in which they perform, and the overall performance time, must be approved.

**9.2** For a tour, the following should be agreed between the artiste and the support act:

(a) The comparative prominence of credits, and the performance times, where different support acts may be used on tour sections. The artiste will naturally have top billing on all promotional material. There will be limitations on the prominence, size and placing of the credit of the support act on all advertisements and promotional material.

(b) The promoter will agree a separate fee with the support act. The artiste may ask the support act for a contribution towards his hire costs for any equipment, transportation or other facilities which are shared by the support act, as the sharing of such facilities reduces the support act's costs. It can take most of a day to set up a complicated sound and light system, which cannot be changed during the interval. Unknown artistes or their record companies may be prepared to pay for the privilege of getting them a "showcase" support group status, which can be the shared equipment contribution.

(c) Any limitation on the amount of lighting and other stage effects which can be used by the support act. Major artistes are famous for the cost and effect of spectacular sound and light systems, specially built stages and laser or video shows. These will not be made available to a support act, which will have to rely on the standard venue lights and their own stage presentation.

## 10 Personal interviews

**10.1** For foreign appearances the promoter's contract should contain restrictions upon him being able to commit the artiste to local radio, TV and press interviews. These can best be set up by the artiste's manager, or co-ordinated by the artiste's record company's local representative, especially if the artiste has a record newly released in the countries where he is performing.

**10.2** It is in the artiste's interest for his personal appearances and his recordings to be well publicised, provided that interviews are properly organised. All the possibilities should be investigated by the artiste's manager well in advance of the concert dates.

## 11 Merchandise rights

*Example*

"The Promoter will make available at each venue on the tour reasonable facilities to enable the Artiste's authorised merchandising licensee to publicise and sell his products and (if necessary) the Promoter will obtain the consent of the venue proprietor. It will be the responsibility of the Licensee to obtain any other permits required by him. The Promoter shall be entitled to charge the Licensee a reasonable fee for such facilities. The Artiste is not connected with the Licensee who is an independent contractor and the Artiste will not be liable for any act or default of the Licensee. The Licensee has no authority to make any statement or representation on behalf of the Artiste, or to pledge his credit or enter into any commitment on his behalf."

**11.1** Wherever a popular artiste performs, the merchandise sellers make the most of a limited but concentrated market of fans around the concert hall, as well as using local record shops, or other sales pitches. This is useful publicity for the artiste, from which he also earns money if the merchandiser is an authorised licensee.

**11.2** Where the artiste has already committed the overall exclusive merchandise rights to his name and image to a professional merchandise company, the promoter must be prohibited in his contract from being involved in unauthorised merchandise operations, whether directly or indirectly. The merchandiser and the promoter should co-operate to make the most of the available opportunities. If the artiste is free to grant merchandise rights to the promoter, his contract will include the terms upon which he does so.

**11.3** The promoter may get a professional merchandiser involved. The main points relating to a promoter's merchandising agreement will be:

(a) A list of the types of merchandise he can deal with. These will usually be "T" shirts, badges and posters. The artwork must be first approved by the artiste.
(b) The rate of royalty or fee per item sold.
(c) A clear definition of the geographical areas within which the sales can take place. The project may not be viable for only one concert.
(d) The dates between which the merchandise can be sold, if not limited to sale in and around the concert hall on the concert date.
(e) What is to happen to his excess stocks when his rights expire. The quantities are not likely to be significant, so any left over should not be a major concern to the artiste.
(f) The right given to the promoter must be non-exclusive, because the artiste's record company may also be promoting the artiste by distributing free small quantities of similar merchandise items to promote his records.

## 12 Unauthorised recordings of concerts

*Example*

"(a) The Promoter shall ensure that no facility is given to any party (except as set out in (b) below) which would enable him to make any audio or audio/visual recording of the artiste's performance. The Promoter will take every reasonable precaution to ensure that no such recording may be made.
(b) The Promoter agrees that the Artiste may make an audio or

audio/visual recording of the Concert provided that arrangements for equipment and any consent required by the Venue Proprietor are established in good time for prior access to the venue and any technical matters to be dealt with and provided that the sound/film crew comply with normal venue regulations.

(c) While the Promoter will give all reasonable assistance, he will not be responsible for "out of Venue" matters such as studio truck parking, external power requirements and recording or filming equipment safety."

**12.1** A major problem facing artistes and record companies is the making of unauthorised recordings of live concerts, from which records and tapes are made and sold. Apart from the non-payment of royalties, the sound quality is usually poor.

**12.2** The promoter must be prohibited from enabling or allowing unauthorised recordings of the concert to be made, whether audio or audio/visual. Security at many concert hall entrances is not strict except for ticket collection. Due to background noise and audience participation, trying to record from a spot within the auditorium on a personal basis does not work. If the concert hall used to be a cinema, or has projection room facilities, it is possible for long-range cameras to be mounted in the projection room, where they would be hidden from view as well as being soundproofed, and with an adequate power supply.

**12.3** If the artiste intends to record a live album of the concert, or to film it, the promoter must obtain the consent of the hall proprietors and any other necessary permission. There is no reason for the promoter to demand any consideration for doing so. Any applicable local authority regulations must be complied with, as well as any local musicians' union and film union rules. If the artiste is English, and the film is being made abroad, unless the English Musicians Union rules are strictly complied with, the union can prevent the exhibition of the film in the UK. This includes TV programmes which use video versions of the record for entertainment or promotional purposes. The regulations are not always practical, such as where the decision to make the film is taken shortly before the performance of the concert.

**12.4** The recording restriction will extend to the production of a recorded radio broadcast of the concert, unless there is an approved agreement with a local radio station. The radio station will use its professional equipment to record the concert, so the sound quality will be good. Assurance should be given for the security of the tape, to prevent subsequent unauthorised broadcasting, or use of it to produce unauthorised recordings. There should be a contractual prohibition against releasing a copy of any part of the tape to any other party. The recording should be mixed to a sound quality acceptable to the artiste before a broadcast is approved. Acceptance or approval should not be unreasonably withheld or delayed. The agreement with the radio station should give the artiste the right to a copy of the tape. If it is possible, the artiste should acquire the legal ownership of the master tape itself, so that it can be used in the future, for example, to release a "live album" of that concert, or to be able to use tracks from it commercially. Credit would be given to the radio station. Alternatively, as part of the consent to the recording, the artiste should obtain an unconditional licence to use the recording commercially as he sees fit.

**12.5** The same applies for the security of the sound track on a film made of the concert. The artiste's exclusive recording contract will contain an obligation on the artiste not to authorise the making of any sound recording which could be used by a third party for manufacturing records in breach of the record company's exclusive rights. The agreement for the radio or film sound track recording must be consistent with those obligations, and if there is any doubt, it would be wise to get the consent of the record company to the proposal.

## 13 Local regulations

**13.1** The promoter must inform the agent of any unusual local regulations which apply to the concert. These will include the maximum permitted audience, the fire and public safety regulations, opening and closing times for the bars, and the latest time for ending the concert. The last item will include details of any sanction which can be imposed for over-running the time of the concert, such as switching on the house lights during the artiste's performance, or terminating the performance prematurely. This information is essential in a country with a foreign language, to avoid confusion and misunderstanding creating chaos at a critical moment. Another local regulation dealt with under "travel" to be checked is any restriction on the travel of the equipment trucks for route scheduling purposes.

## 14 Free tickets and backstage passes

**14.1** The promoter should provide the artiste with a reasonable number of free tickets for the best seats. The number of free tickets and their price level should be specified in the promoter's contract. The artiste should also have priority in the purchasing of more tickets such as for record company executives and press.

**14.2** The artiste's management will also need back stage passes for the artiste and all authorised personnel. Apart from limiting the number of people back-stage, the pass system prevents unauthorised persons from getting into the security area, and minimises the risk of theft of equipment, and of valuables and personal belongings from dressing rooms. For a tour, the back-stage passes must be sufficiently security proof to prevent "length of tour" permanent passes from being confused with passes which are limited to each individual concert. An efficient back-stage pass list system should be maintained, with each pass being forgery proof, numbered and signed by the promoter, and (for permanent passes) having a photograph of the authorised holder. This prevents valid but not individually identifiable passes from being used by persons not entitled to hold them.

**14.3** It is a common practice to have a list at the backstage door, containing the names of those who have been invited backstage after the concert, but who do not have passes. Experienced backstage gate crashers find out the names on the list, pick one, and get in claiming to have that name. If in doubt, the door security should ask the guest to produce some identification to connect him with the name he claims to have.

There might be a distinction between a backstage pass and an onstage pass. Although there may be many people backstage, only minimal essential personnel should be allowed near the stage. This system may be used if the concert is being filmed, or if certain photographers are to be given preferential treatment, when they need access to the stage itself.

*Venue security*

**14.4.1** The promoter must provide adequate and secure dressing room facilities for the artiste, and security at the concert hall for the equipment. Specific security measures should be identified in the promoter's contract. Local public safety and crowd control regulations may require that all security arrangements must be approved by the police and fire departments. These arrangements should be cleared by the necessary authorities well in advance, especially in countries notorious for emotive audiences, or which are not familiar with the problems of staging such an event. Failure to get clearance may jeopardise the concert taking place. Regularly used venues are not a problem. There might be concern for a major outdoor festival, where security, crowd control and facilities may not be adequate for what might be an enormous audience.

**14.4.2** Whether the hall management provides security men at the promoter's cost, or whether the promoter provides security, the major concerns are audience control and the policing of the backstage entrances. Nobody without a valid backstage pass should get in or out of the security area, and no equipment should leave the backstage area or the hall unless the person taking it is well known to have that authority, or has a valid written authority to do so. Anyone leaving the area without a back stage pass is suspect if he is not known to the door security, and should be stopped. If he is not a road crew member, and has no valid explanation for being in the venue, he may be searched.

**14.4.3** Security is a delicate problem, because excessive security too strictly enforced can turn a good-humoured audience into an angry uncontrollable mass of people. Security must have a discreet high profile. The greatest danger in an uncontrolled mass of people is to themselves, from being either trampled or crushed. In an emergency, such as a fire, an organised speedy dispersal to safety of a chaotic crowd of people is not possible.

## 15 Cancellation of promoter's contract

**15.1** The promoter's contract must set out any circumstances in which it is agreed that either of the promoter or the artiste will be able to cancel the concert. These will normally relate to the failure of the other party to fulfil conditions considered to be so important that they are made "of the essence" of the agreement.

**15.2** If the promoter cancels the concert in breach of the agreement, the artiste's main claim will be for the fee he would have received, plus reinbursement of any relevant expense incurred or an indemnity and compensation for a commitment he cannot get out of. If cancellation by the promoter is at the last minute, the claim may extend to other losses suffered by the artiste, such as having refused another offer for the same date, which could have been accepted if the cancellation had been notified earlier. The claim will be limited to those losses and expenses directly attributable to the cancellation.

**15.3** If the artiste cancels the concert well in advance, but agrees a substitute date, the promoter may be able to mitigate his loss by booking another act. If the substitute concert is more profitable to the promoter then the cancelled one would have been, he may have no claim against the artiste at all. If the cancellation is at the last minute, apart from the loss of ticket sales revenue, the direct costs and losses incurred by the promoter could be considerable. These will include wasted advertising and ticket printing, as well as the hall hire, insurance, and the cost of making ticket refunds.

**15.4** The artiste may turn up at the venue well in advance to install the sound and lighting equipment and to run a sound check, only to find that, for either or both of the reasons set out below his manager advises against proceeding with the concert. To justify that decision, the matter complained of will have to be so bad, and incapable of remedy in time, that it constitutes a fundamental breach of contract. Termination at this state is so drastic that every reasonable effort should be made to remedy the deficiencies complained of, which may include:

(a) The security provided being so inadequate, that there is a real danger of personal injury to the artiste or to members of the audience. Before refusing to perform, the artiste should, if possible, consult the local police and the owner of the hall, who will be the first to complain if the concert takes place and there is a dangerous and damaging riot as a result of inadequate or inefficient security. There will be greater concern with a large standing audience which is not protected by barriers from potential injury from the equipment or electrical installations on and surrounding the stage.

(b) The hall, or its facilities, being so dangerous or inadequate that there is a genuine fear of personal injury, or substantial damage to or loss of essential equipment. Despite all warranties to the contrary, the available space in the hall may not be enough to install the equipment according to the contract. This can happen in halls not usually used for concerts, where the public safety precautions and security facilities are minimal, or where the hall is structurally inadequate for the well-known consequences of a mass of rhythmic stamping feet; or where the power supply cannot cope with the demands to be made upon it. This can cause a short-circuit resulting in a fire or electrocution. A complete failure of the power and lighting system may make it impossible to use the equipment and to perform the concert, and is also a safety hazard.

The above examples are not common, as a well known artiste would not normally agree to a venue which does not have a good track record for security and safety, and all the necessary facilities and space to set up and run all the lighting and PA system.

**15.5.1** Illness of the artiste causing cancellation of a concert will have to be supported by a doctor's certificate. The illness must be sufficiently serious to be a good reason for cancellation, and the doctor's certificate must be strong enough to justify the artiste's decision, in a court of law if necessary. If the illness occurs some time before the concert date the artiste would not have good reason to cancel it unless the medical opinions confirm that the anticipated period of incapacity will cover the date of the concert, or that recovery will not be sufficiently advanced to enable the artiste to perform without seriously damaging his health.

**15.5.2** The promoter may insist on having a right of independent medical inspection of the artiste where the concert is a major financial risk to the promoter if it is not performed, or where it will be a major money earner if it is performed. It is not unknown for an artiste to suddenly contract some disability of a vague but "incapacitating" nature if it suits him better not to perform. If medical inspection rights are not agreed, for his protection the promoter must be able to satisfy himself reasonably that the medical opinion given on the health of the artiste has been sought from a competent medical practitioner, and is not exaggerated. If the promoter has insured the event against cancellation on a *force majeure* basis, for either of expense wasted or loss of profit to a stated level, his insurance company may also demand to inspect the artiste for a medical opinion if it has any doubt that the cancellation was justifiable. (See paragraph **16**.)

**15.5.3** If the disability is self-inflicted and not accidental, or is prolonged unnecessarily by the unreasonable refusal of the artiste to seek or accept proper medical treatment, or to comply with doctor's orders, it would be inequitable for the artiste to cancel the performance without compensating the promoter.

**15.6** Upon a legitimate cancellation by the artiste for incapacity, where possible, both the promoter and the artiste should minimise their loss and inconvenience. For example, airline tickets already provided by the promoter to the artiste in advance should be returned, and so should any deposit money held by the artiste. Part of the settlement may be a new contract for a concert in substitution for the cancelled one. The promoter may be able to fill the cancelled date with another act.

## 16 Insurance

The special conditions section of the contract should set out the responsibility of the promoter and/or the artiste in the event of:

(a) loss of the artiste's equipment through theft, or damage to the equipment caused by the promoter's or the hall's employees or independent contractors;

(b) injury or death caused to anyone through bad crowd control, faulty equipment belonging to the hall or the artiste, or through the actions of any person connected with the promoter or the hall or the artiste;

(c) damage to the concert hall, by the audience or other persons where the artiste or his personnel are not the cause of it.

**16.1** Adequate insurance cover must be provided by the party who will be liable for any loss or injury sustained, a subject not always fully appreciated or covered thoroughly by promoters or artistes. The consequences can be extensive by way of damages payable, such as in the case of personal injuries. If the artiste is relying on the insurance cover held by the promoter or the venue itself, he should positively check whether there are any limits or exceptions which could cause a problem. The artiste may have to cancel subsequent engagements, such as for a tight schedule tour, if he loses the use of essential equipment through theft or damage. All tour or concert contracts should have a *force majeure* clause wide enough to protect the artiste in these circumstances. The cost of insuring against "loss of profits" may not be economical, except possibly in specific narrow circumstances.

**16.2** Third party liability for personal injury or death occurring within, or in the immediate confines of, the concert hall should be covered by insurance taken out by the hall owner or the promoter. This should be warranted in the promoter's contract. Where they and the artiste carry insurance, the primary liability in each case must be ascertained, because the upper limits and other terms and conditions of the insurance policies may be different.

**16.3** Where the promoter is providing the use of a chartered plane, a condition of charter may be that the hirer shall be liable for third party insurance beyond the normal cover included in the hire charges. The extent of cover should be checked. The promoter's contract must make it clear that he is the hirer, and that he is not hiring it as an agent for the artiste or his manager. Nevertheless, the artiste should have adequate contingency insurance cover wherever possible. A chartered plane is more likely to be hired by the artiste, as all the concert dates on a tour may not be for the same promoter, and the promoter is not responsible for getting the artiste to and from the concerts. The artiste may also need the plane to travel to some quiet spot to recover during rest periods set out in the itinerary of a long tour.

**16.4** The artiste must at all times be properly insured against liabilities which may arise at any time and anywhere in the world from the acts or defaults of any employee, or anyone else for whom the artiste is responsible. This responsibility extends to road crew, and might also extend to hired contractors while they are under the artiste's control. If an employee commits a crime or injures anybody (such as in a fight or a car crash) while he is not working, ie, he is acting in his personal capacity, he should bear the whole liability and responsibility. However, it may be claimed successfully that, while on tour, road crew are permanently working or on stand by, so that the artiste can be sued as well.

## 17 Auditorium and stage requirements

**17.1** Set out below are major points to be dealt with in relation to the stage and the hall to enable the concert to be performed to everyone's satisfaction.

**17.1.1** Depending on the size and complexity of the public address system used by the artiste, the promoter's contract must specify the minimum stage size and shape needed to accommodate it all. If the equipment is deployed in an unusual structure, support wings adjacent to the stage might be required, as might sky hooks for slung speakers. The promoter should ensure that the hall structure is capable of coping with all the equipment. It would be essential to know what facilities are already available at the hall, which may avoid duplication and unnecessary transportation, if those facilities will be used.

**17.1.2** The artiste's equipment will be set up at the sound-check held in the hall after the equipment has been installed, to ensure that it is all working and accoustically correct. There it will stay until the artiste performs, so the support act either uses that equipment, or sections of it, or brings its own—in which case the promoter must ensure that the stage size is adequate for both sets of equipment.

**17.1.3** The stage size is also critical where the artiste is providing his own special on-stage lighting which is suspended on a collapsible rig. The feet of the rig must not interfere with access to the stage or the equipment on it, and the stage roof must not be so low as to obscure the lighting effect, or to prevent the rig being used at all.

**17.2.1** Part of the public address sound system is the mixer desk. This is a compact "mini studio" through which all the sound channels from the microphones on the stage and from the electrical instruments are fed to enable the sound engineer to "mix" the sound. The effects of the sound mix go from the mixer desk to the public address system, and that determines how the audience hears what is actually played on stage. Most of the musical instruments are electrically amplified, and the sound mixer with an experienced operator, who knows exactly what will happen on stage and when, is essential to the success of the concert. The group will also have on stage a compact sound system by which they can monitor the sounds produced by each of them.

**17.2.2** For the sound engineer to use the mixing desk properly, he must be in the best accoustic area in the hall. Seats may have to be removed to accommodate the mixer, and the lost income from these seats, and from those behind it if unsaleable due to a blocked view, will be the loss of the promoter. The space and power cable requirements of the mixer must be in the promoter's contract. If the amount of room it requires, or its height, is excessive by normal standards, resulting in an unusually high loss of ticket sales on unusable seats, the promoter may want to take that into account when negotiating the fee for that concert.

**17.3.1** The hall must be made available by the promoter for the time required for the artiste's stage equipment and public address system to be unloaded from its trucks, and erected on stage in readiness for the sound-check prior to the performance. If this means overtime payments to the hall employees, or if other consents have to be obtained and payments have to be made as a result, these should be the responsibility of the promoter.

**17.3.2** The promoter should provide the artiste's road crew with any assistance they reasonably require to unload and set up the equipment. This will include electricians and maintenance men, who may be needed to move or dismantle property belonging to the hall, and to help with identifying and making ready the electrical power sources. If these people are not available, before using his own personnel or outsiders, the promoter should check that there are no local trade union rules on who can do what, which might cause a problem.

Using hall employees who are familiar with the hall equipment which is used, and its state of repair prior to the concert, may prevent subsequent erroneous claims by the hall proprietor alleging damage to or theft of his property by the artiste's road crew. This precaution may only be needed if a "posh" venue is used. The usual rock and roll venue has seen better days, and has a high level of tolerance within the concept of fair wear and tear.

**17.4** If the artiste needs a piece of equipment for the performance which the promoter has agreed to provide, such as a good piano, the promoter's contract must say so. For a piano, the state of tune required by the artiste should be specified. If the artiste is a solo performer, ie, a singer, and is provided with backing musicians by the promoter, the artiste must satisfy himself that they are competent, and he must have sufficient rehearsal time with them to get the act right. This would only apply to a singer of middle of the road music, any other artiste will provide his own musicians.

**17.5.1** Full details of the electrical supply circuits required by the artiste's equipment should be in the promoter's contract. Modern concert halls, and stadiums designed or modified for such entertainment, should have an adequate and conveniently placed power supply. In less well known or older places, which may have been built as live theatres or as cinemas, that may not be the case unless they are frequently used for this style of entertainment.

**17.5.2** If, for example, the concert will be held in a third world country, or wherever else power cuts or voltage reduction is common, the promoter should provide back-up generator facilities. If generators are used, there must be no operating noise affecting the show, or any static interference with the performance of the electrical equipment and instruments, or coming through the public address system. The generators must also be frequency-stabilised to make sure that fluctuations in their power output do not damage sensitive equipment.

**17.5.3** The power sources provided by the hall must be sufficient to deal with:

(a) the public address system;
(b) the house lights and the additional lighting used by the artiste, situated both in the auditorium and on the stage;
(c) the cables from the stage to the sound mixer, and back through the public address system;
(d) any electrical special effects used by the artiste.

**17.6** Although the artiste will usually have his own on stage lighting system, the promoter's contract must state any additional requirements for spot lights and fixed house lighting. To ensure smooth lighting continuity, the artiste may use his own lighting crew on house-provided spot lights, unless local union regulations make that difficult.

**17.7** The promoter should provide at each hall an internal personnel communication system, so that lighting cues can be given, and people can be contacted easily at key points in the auditorium and backstage. A well equipped artiste's road crew will have walkie-talkies for this purpose. The artiste must have control over the positioning of all equipment, lights and instruments, including the sound mixer, subject only to maintaining the hall's structural safety, and to observing other practical and legal limitations and restrictions, such as fire regulations and crowd safety requirements.

## 18 Law of the promoter's contract

**18.1** Where the artiste resides in England, and (for example) the concert tour covers most of Europe, and the promoter resides outside England, the contract should state which legal system will govern any conflict between the promoter and the artiste. In the absence of a stated legal system to apply to the contract, and with one party and the contract performance to be abroad, a foreign system is likely to be applied—either that of the promoter's country, or the country of performance. Uncertainty can only be avoided by stating which is to apply. Unless there is a compelling advantage in choosing any other legal system, a major artiste should insist that the law of the promoter's contract should be the law with which the artiste and his advisers are familiar. For an English artiste English law should apply. If the promoter is entitled to take action against the artiste outside England, the legal concepts of contract law in that country and in England may be radically different.

**18.2** The contract should also state that the court of competent jurisdiction is the English High Court. This prevents the promoter from taking action in his own country's courts, although the principles of English law could be applied by that court.

**18.3** Where a local liability arises in a foreign country, such as where a claim is made by a venue management for damage done to it by the audience or by the artiste's road crew, there should be no direct right of action against the artiste, as obviously the venue would sue in its own court. There is normally no privity of contract between the artiste and the venue owner, unless he is the promoter. As the promoter contracts directly with the venue any such claim will be his primary responsibility. Any right of indemnity the promoter has against the artiste as a result will be dealt with in accordance with their contract.

## 19 Work permits and visas

**19.1** Foreign artistes performing in England, or English artistes performing abroad, must have any necessary work permits and entry visas required by the relevant country. It should be the promoter's responsibility, together with the agent, to ensure that the work permits and visas are available well in advance of travel dates. The promoter's contract should be conditional upon visas and permits being issued in good time, otherwise failure to obtain them will cause the artiste to be in breach of the contract. It is doubtful whether such failure will come within the definition of *force majeure.*

**19.2** The issue of work permits will depend on the existence of signed performance contracts, the promoter complying with any local governmental requirements, co-operation with the local tax authorities, and clearance by the local musicians' union. Valid work permits will enable the artiste to get entry visas from the relevant embassy or consulate for the country to which he is travelling, which will be granted only for the time which is reasonably required to perform the concerts. Entry visas will be required for the road crew tour manager, and all other personnel travelling with the artiste.

**19.3** Many countries will not grant work permits or entry visas to people who have been convicted of drug offences, or what that country considers to be serious criminal acts. The artiste must keep copies of all applications for permits and visas for each country which he has signed, or which have been submitted for him, so that in any subsequent applications the documents will be consistent in their information. Non-disclosure of material information, or false information given, is treated severely. Most countries' embassies have computerised files which can be consulted rapidly by computer by an embassy anywhere in the world, so discrepancies in suspect application forms can be discovered easily.

## 20 Change of venue

**20.1** The venue will be stipulated in the promoter's contract, and he should be prohibited from switching the concert from that venue to any other one. Some of the reasons are:

(a) the agreed venue will be approved by the agent as suitable for the artiste before the contract is signed;

(b) the seating capacity and seat prices may have been relevant for calculating the fee;

(c) accommodation and other arrangements will have been made for convenience, and for easy access to the venue.

**20.2** The venue may have to be changed (or the concert cancelled) where, for example:

(a) the venue has had a fire or suffered other major structural damage;

(b) local authorities close the venue or make substantial restrictions on allowed audience capacity for safety reasons, or because the venue is in breach of local regulations applying to places of entertainment.

If demand for tickets to the concert exceeds expectations, the venue could always be changed to a bigger one by mutual consent to accommodate a greater audience, if the promoter can find one which is suitable.

CHAPTER 4

# *Artistes' Recording Agreements*

## 1 General aspects

**1.1** Under Part II of the Copyright Designs and Patents Act 1988 a performer has statutory rights in his performance, which can be protected from unauthorised recording, broadcast, or other exploitation. There is also, for the first time in the UK, a statutory perception of an "exclusive recording contract", and that, for example, record companies, will have statutory rights under them to the exclusive performance rights of their artistes. The 1988 Act is dealt with in chapter ten. The basis of all recording contracts is that the artiste has the ability to grant his performance rights to the record company, which will then have the exclusive right to them. This does not detract from the existing legal concept that contracts for personal performances will not be enforced by an order of the court. The record company protection is against third parties who make or sell unauthorised recordings of the artiste's performance.

**1.2** For an artiste a recording contract is the ultimate goal, and one which must be reached at all costs. Being a commercially attractive artiste does not necessarily mean that he will be offered a recording contract somewhere, it is very difficult to persuade a record company to take the plunge. This chapter assumes there is no such difficulty for the purpose of discussing recording contracts. There are good and bad contracts, enthusiastic and lethargic recording companies, and a considerable variation in the contractual terms they impose. Being given a recording contract and making successful records are two different things. So are making successful records and getting a fair deal and correct payment on their sales.

**1.3** Where there is a choice, the reputation of each record company, and the strength of its current roster of successful artistes, are major influences on the decision. Some companies are good in certain territories, and some have better international connections than others. These factors are important to the artiste, who will be giving his exclusive recording services to the record company for anything up to five years.

**1.4** The artiste must also make sure that he can terminate the contract cleanly should his recording career be seriously jeopardised or left redundant by the record company. For example, will the failure of the record company to enable the artiste to make records, or the failure by it to release the records, constitute a breach of contract? The relationship between the artiste and his record company should be such that both sides benefit from the deal. This chapter deals with the major factors to be discussed during the negotiation of a recording contract direct between an artiste and a record company. Chapter five deals with production company agreements, ie, where the artiste is not signed directly to the record company.

## 2 Choice of record company

**2.1** Before the artiste thinks about what should be in his contract, he must consider what sort of record company he would like to represent him. It is not easy to get a record deal, so the artiste may find he has to make compromise decisions to get one.

**2.2** Where one worldwide exclusive deal is anticipated, the first choice usually to be made is between English and American record companies. If the artiste is to live and record primarily in England, there are many disadvantages in having an exclusive contract with an American record company for the whole world, to be construed and enforced in accordance with the laws of an American state. There would be no objection to contracting with the English subsidiary of an American company, provided that the contract is in accordance with and subject to English law. It can be financially beneficial to have independent and non cross-collateralised contracts whereby an American company has exclusive rights for (say) the USA, Canada, and Japan, and an English company has exclusive rights for the rest of the world.

**2.3** Investing in making records is a form of gambling, as no matter what is spent on making and promoting them, there is no guarantee of success. The chances of success can be improved greatly by imaginative promotion, aggressive selling and a realistic appraisal of the quality of a record. These attitudes will be determined by the ability and enthusiasm of key personnel, who are vital to a record company. Impressive sounding royalty percentages are meaningless if that record company has been proved consistently incapable of selling records, or if it has an established reputation for not making accurate royalty payments, or if the basis of calculating the percentage figure is disproportionately loaded in favour of the record company.

## 3 Mechanical copyright

**3.1** There is a copyright, known as the mechanical copyright, in recorded performances. This gives the owner of the recorded performance the sole right of reproduction of that performance. Anyone who, without the consent of the mechanical copyright owner, reproduces that recorded performance is committing a breach of copyright. The mechanical copyright in a recorded work is not to be confused with the copyright of the composition which has been performed and recorded.

**3.2** The mechanical copyright (called in the Act the sound recording copyright) is the copyright in the specific recording itself, as issued by the record company. For example, an album might be first released in 1970, when the copyright credit will be "P 1970 XYZ Record Company Ltd". If a compilation album is released in 1989 containing a variety of previously released material, each of them in different years, nevertheless the phonographic copyright credit for the compilation album will be "P 1989 XYZ Record Company Ltd". The distinction is that the mechanical copyright belongs to the source owner of the recording itself, who may licence any number of third parties to reproduce that recording on their own compilation album. The mechanical copyright is created when the recording is first made, and that date (or the subsequent release date) will be the date from which the copyright period for the recording is calculated. Individual phonographic copyright dates are not relevant for the copyright period of the recorded work itself. The fact that a phonographic copyright owner has the rights in his own pressings does not confer on him the right to extract from the compilation album any individual track and release that as a single record. The licence he will have been granted to include the track on his compilation album will be solely for that limited use.

**3.3** The recording contract should identify the ownership of the mechanical copyright in the recordings to be made, as the definition of some of the rights will depend on it. If the artiste signs a contract direct with a major record company, invariably it will own the mechanical copyright in all the recordings he makes. The same will apply to a contract which an artiste signs with a production company, although the production company will licence the use of the mechanical copyright on to the record company as the basis of the production agreement.

**3.4** There is also an income to be derived from the public performance of the recordings themselves, being the phonographic performance income. This is independent of the public performance income attributable to the recorded composition, which is collected by PRS. The owner of the mechanical copyright in the recording is the legal recipient of phonographic performance income. Despite the similarity in the description, it does not belong to any third party who has made a licensed use of the mechanical copyright, whereby his compilation album has a "phonographic copyright" of its own. It is the source owner of the recording who receives this income. It is usually paid to the record company as the manufacturer of the records, as the agreement will confirm that the record company has the exclusive right to authorise the public performance of the artiste's recordings.

**3.5** Phonographic performance income collection is only calculated by broadcasters precisely according to the performances of each individual artiste's recordings. The major record companies will receive an allocation of the overall income, and will have the means of distinguishing how much is applicable to any particular recording.

## 4 Assessing contracts with record companies

**4.1** Recording agreements can be made in either of two ways. A contract may be entered into direct between the artiste and a major record company, or the artiste may contract with a record production company. The latter provides the artiste's services to the record company for each recording by means of a complete master tape together with album artwork and all copyright information. The contract between a production company and a record company is examined in chapter five.

**4.2** Advantages to an artiste of contracting direct with a successful and reputable record company include the availability of worldwide sales coverage through its international subsidiaries or licensees, and the probability of more money being made available by them more readily for a successful artiste to cover the cost of producing and promoting his records. While the availability may be there, the reality is that, except for major artistes of international stature, not that many territories outside the UK actually release the recordings of an artiste whose success may still only be in the UK, or within Europe. Wherever territorial rights are discussed, the main question should be in which territories is the record company likely to release the artistes records. For a relatively new artiste, the record company does not know whether in two years time he will be an international star, and so wants worldwide rights just in case he is.

**4.3** The benefits to a record company of signing an artiste direct include the close contractual relationship (including the ownership of the recordings), and the record company having total control over the choice, quality and timing of recordings for which it is paying. It is also able to use its own judgement on releases and promotion, according to its opinion of the potential of the recording.

**4.4** There is no "middleman" where the artiste contracts direct with the record company, so the artiste can benefit from receiving the whole of the artiste's royalty offered by it. A production company to which the artiste is contracted will take a proportion of the royalty paid to it by the record company, the level depending upon the success of the artiste, and his relationship with the production company. As the production company pays for all recording and other costs, and takes a commercial risk, it will generally receive a higher royalty rate from the record company than the artiste would have been offered on a direct signing. The whole of the recording costs will be recoupable from the artiste's share of royalties payable out of the royalties received by the production company from the record company.

**4.5** Direct payment to the artiste by the record company of the royalties due to him also removes any fear of the artiste who is contracted through a production company that he will not always be fully or promptly accounted to in respect of the share of record royalties due to him, such as when the production company has financial difficulties, ceases to trade, or winds up.

**4.6** A record company may favour releasing a record made by one of its own artistes, rather than a record delivered to it as part of the record delivery commitment of a production company. The decision in most cases where a choice has to be made, subject to any overriding contractual commitment, will be in favour of the artiste who has the greatest record sales potential. A choice may be necessary at busy times, such as at Christmas, when the factory pressing capacity is insufficient to deal with all of the new records, and when the release schedule is tight.

**4.7** One disadvantage of contracting direct with a record company is that the artiste becomes one of many artistes, each trying hard to get an allocation of production money and studio time for records to be produced. Only when there is a completed recording can it be given a date in the record production programme, and the release schedule of the record company is normally fixed for months ahead.

**4.8** The record company will have a "standard" form of contract for artistes to sign. It will be reluctant to deviate from it in any basic concept, unless the value of the artiste to the record company, or the complexity of the deal, is such that negotiation upon the major terms is conducted regardless of the standard form.

**4.9** The royalty rate is likely to be low for an unknown artiste, with a contract term which gives minimum commitment to the artiste and maximum security for the record company. Most artistes start by being unknown, and by the time they are successful they may be only half way through the potential period of their recording contract. At that stage the artiste is irritated by a royalty rate which may not be consistent with his then current earning capacity for the record company, and his status as a performer. Re-negotiation of the financial terms in favour of the artiste in consideration of his granting to the record company an extended period of the agreement is the usual method of recognising the change of the artiste's circumstances. Escalating royalty rates will automatically benefit the artiste for high selling albums, and so is another means of rewarding success, but without the aggravation of having to negotiate the uplift.

**4.10** Some record companies are less likely to spend substantial production and promotion costs on an album to be recorded by an unknown artiste. There is also the time and expense of finding the right song to suit the non-composer artiste, assigning a producer, fixing musical arrangements, doing all rehearsals and booking studio time well in advance.

**4.11** Because the record company will be taking the whole financial risk on a directly signed artiste, it will not usually pay a new artiste a substantial advance on account of royalties, unless it is satisfied either that it will sell enough records for the artiste's royalty to cover the advance within a reasonable period, or that the artiste shows great potential, but needs money to buy equipment or to settle debts, or to cover living costs in the meantime. Recording costs will be treated as an advance an account of royalties.

## 5 Artiste's previous contracts

**5.1** When negotiating a recording contract, the artiste should remember that on its termination he may start a new contract with a different record company. Therefore, together with all the usual items to be negotiated in a recording contract, he must make sure that there are no surprise skeletons which can emerge from his previous recording contracts which would put him in breach of his new contract.

**5.2** A record company about to sign a contract with an artiste needs to know whether he is subject to any existing contractual restrictions or obligations which might affect its complete freedom to sell recordings made for it by him. The artiste will have to warrant that there are no such restrictions, or that if there are, he will have disclosed them to the record company with all relevant details, prior to the recording contract being signed. If any disclosed matter concerns the record company so much that it would not want to sign the artiste until the matter had been resolved, clearly it is better to make the disclosure before, rather than after, the contract is signed. If the restrictions are unusual or significant in extent, they might affect the viability of the new agreement, or only some of the terms which are being negotiated. By identifying any existing problem, the record company can consider whether to resolve it by negotiation with the other party. A payment, credit, or over ride royalty payment may be required. The cost will be the artiste's liability, unless otherwise agreed.

**5.3** The record company should check whether there are any recordings made by the artiste during his previous contract, but never delivered to the previous record company, and if any recordings delivered to it were not released commercially during that contract period. It has been known for test tracks, or excess or rejected tracks, to be left in the studio archive store and wholly forgotten until one day they are discovered. At the height of the popularity of an artiste, the release for the first time of recordings made by him a long time ago for a previous record company can have the following effects:

(a) The previous record company can damage the reputation of the artiste by marketing an old album, which was not released when it was made because it lacked musical or technical quality or commercial appeal. The album could be made up from a selection of old studio or live concert tracks recorded through the years, but in each case rejected at the time as not being good enough to be released.

(b) The royalty payable to the artiste under the previous contract will not be as good as his current royalty rate. That is the previous record company's good fortune, and the artiste has no legal grounds of complaint on that score alone.

(c) The release of an old recording, not being in consultation with the present record company, may coincide with the release of a new album. This could prejudice the success of the marketing and promotion campaign of the new album, although the previous record company could benefit greatly from marketing the old album in a manner which is complementary to that campaign.

(d) The old recording may have been made so long ago that the musical style of the artiste has changed completely in the meantime. If the artiste is a group, the membership may also have changed, and it would be possible for a record company, which had a long term agreement with the group, to have unreleased tracks made by different versions of the group.

The artiste may be able to prevent such a damaging release by a court injunction, if it can be shown that whoever wants to release the album does not own the mechanical copyrights in it, and/or that the statutory artistes consents required under the 1988 Copyright Act (or the previous Performers Protection Acts) have never been obtained. Release might also be prevented where the recorded material is so bad as to content or quality that the reputation of the artiste would be damaged, and that the proposed release does not represent a *bona fide* reasonable commercial decision.

**5.4** As the record company will own the mechanical copyright in the recordings, its only restrictions or positive obligations will be contained in the agreement with the artiste. The artiste should try to negotiate that the subsequent release of previously unreleased recordings proposed, say, more than two years after the termination of his recording contract, will only be with his consent. This is not likely to happen for complete albums recorded in the studio, but there is considerable scope for the existence of unreleased live recordings, or excess or rejected studio tracks, complete or not, and mixed or not. Most major record companies would not agree to this restriction, so the artiste should maintain a check on what recordings are being shelved, and why.

When the artiste's contract expires, if the record company has in its possession unreleased recordings free of any contractual restriction, it can release them in any combination at any time in the future. This happens, for example, where the artiste records more tracks than necessary each time he goes into the studio, so that there is a choice of suitable tracks for the single or the album. In this case the unreleased tracks are of good acceptable quality, the excess was deliberate so as to have a choice.

**5.5** Some of the recordings may be incomplete, such as where an instrumental track is missing. In the absence of anything in the artiste's contract prohibiting it from doing so, in the case of a solo artiste, the record company may be free to complete the recording with musicians of its own choice, and to release the recording subject only to the terms of its expired contract with the artiste. This may be possible where the additional recorded material is incidental to the overall musical effect of the recording, and does not detract from the performance of the artiste, or (where the artiste is a group) does not wrongly attribute the additional performance, or give unauthorised credit to the additional performer.

**5.6** The recording contract should prohibit that being done, and should also prohibit the record company from adding to, deleting from, editing or re-mixing any existing complete recording without the prior consent of the artiste. The consent may be conditional on the artiste participating in, or supervising the completion of, the recording. Account would have to be taken of what is to happen if the artiste is not available, or refuses to be involved, or demands unreasonable remuneration for doing so, or (not having the right to do so) tries to exercise artistic control over the recording.

**5.7** The 1988 Copyright Act brought into English law for the first time the concept of "moral rights". These include the right of a composer to be associated with the work, and limits what can be done to change the work without his authority.

**5.8** Where a record company manufactures records under a licence, it does not own the mechanical copyright in the recordings, and can only do to them what is authorised under the contract. There should be an obligation on the record company to release at least in the UK all recordings delivered to it, and to return to the licensor unconditionally all recordings not released prior to the last date stated in the contract by which it is entitled to release all unreleased recordings in its possession. The record company would lose any advance payment already made to the production company in respect of the recordings to be returned. This would prevent any previously unreleased material turning up as a surprise at a later date.

## 6 Exclusivity

**6.1** All recording contracts are exclusive. The concern of an artiste with a record company in which he does not have complete confidence is that it will not release his recordings or promote his records to his reasonable satisfaction throughout the major markets within its exclusive territory. If the efforts of the record company are minimal by any reasonable standard, the artiste does not have the right to find another company which will do more for him, unless things are so bad that he is entitled to terminate his recording contract for fundamental breach. All record company contracts state that the company may, in its absolute discretion, decide how and when and where to market the records, and that inactivity will not be a culpable event. The record company will only spend what it considers to be sufficient for any record. It can make them, market and promote them, but it cannot make people buy them. Neither is there any commercial sense in heavily promoting a record which is generally recognised as dead.

**6.2** The record company is granted within the contract territory the sole right to the recorded performances of the artiste during the exclusive period of the contract for the purpose of making and selling his records. The wording of the contract will state that the record company has exclusive rights to every recording made by the artiste during the exclusive period of the contract, even if they are not released by the record company. The contract should refer to any recordings made by the artiste prior to the contract which are free from any other record company commitment, so which may give the record company the possibility of doing re-recordings of the artistes previous hit material.

**6.3** What is included within the recording contract should be well defined, as modern technology is opening up so many possibilities not previously thought of. An example is the progress from a sound recording all the way through to laser and compact discs and video recordings. If the record company's rights are not clearly defined, its general wording may not include newly invented or developed means of recording which were not thought of when the contract was signed. The wording must not include developments which may in the future form a completely separate industry and source of income for the artiste, and which would not be competitive with the activities of record companies in their normal course of business. Major record companies tend to be divisions of international corporate conglomerates, which altogether cover all of the industries coming within leisure and entertainment.

**6.4** The exlusivity clauses in recording contracts are drawn as wide as possible, but they must take into account any other professional activities of the artiste. If the artiste, being a singer, is a member of the cast of a theatrical stage show, he must be able to record his part on a "stage show album", even though the rights in that album do not belong to his record company. An accommodation would be agreed with his record company for an override royalty for "lending" the artiste for the recording. The record company's terms would have to be negotiated at the preliminary stages of setting up the caste album and financing of the show. The income from a successful caste album will be a major feature in preparing budgets for financing the live show.

**6.5** Possible conflict of exclusivity is not a problem if the artiste is starting out in the music business with no prior contracts or commitments. If he has been in the music business for some years, and he has worked in and out of groups and with different record companies, he must make certain that no previous contract can still catch him for potential exclusivity on the "joint and several" principle, or through any other latent commitment.

**6.6** The artiste should have cleared up all such matters by a letter of release or some other written confirmation each time he left a group or a record company, otherwise his right to enter into any new recording contract could be challenged. Members of a group will be required to sign an exclusive recording contract "jointly and severally". This means that each individual is contracted to the record company exclusively, whether recording as a member of the band, or as a solo artiste, or with anyone else during the exclusive period. Unless the contract limits the record company's rights to the artiste to only for so long as he is a member of the contracted group, a member leaving the group will have to obtain a written release from the record company.

**6.7** The record company might insist on the group recording as contracted, or having the right to terminate the recording agreement if the group refuses to do so. If the record company decides to risk an investment in the musical ability and appeal of the group members contracted to it as a unit, it will have a clause in the recording agreement to the effect that any change in membership will entitle it to terminate the agreement if it considers that it ceases to have what it originally contracted for. Depending on the clause wording, the group may also be in breach of contract if it decides arbitrarily to change its membership against the wishes of the record company. This might be a point where the heavy investment by the record company would be totally wasted if such a change takes place at that time. Its contractual rights are there to prevent, for example, a group signing the contract, taking the advance payments on account of royalties, and simply disbanding, believing that they have ripped off the record company successfully. In a blatant case, if deliberately no recordings are made by the group before disbanding, there could possibly be also a criminal charge of obtaining money by false pretences.

**6.8** If an artiste is invited to record jointly with others, whether or not contracted to the same record company, but on a "mention only" credit basis or anonymously, or if he wants to do session work which is credited but not featured, his rights to do so must be contained in his recording contract. Any recording he does outside his exclusive contract will be a breach of it, in the absence of either consent in the agreement or given specifically by the record company. The written consent of his record company will have to be obtained to avoid legal complications. Oral consent given, such as over the telephone, should be confirmed by the record company in writing before the recording takes place.

## 7 Definition of recordings

**7.1** A recording agreement must carefully define what is a record, so that the rights of the record company can be compared with other third party rights in, particularly, audiovisual films and the like. A recording is a device whereby sound has been "captured" permanently, by mechanical, electrical, electronic or any other means, whether or not together with vision, and from which the performance can be reproduced any number of times by activating the device. The artiste may make a promotional film for distribution to TV stations or cinema chains to promote either a hit recording or a forthcoming tour by the artiste. In this context a promotional film is not intended to be an audiovisual recording for commercial sale. If such an audiovisual recording is used for promotional purposes, these comments do not apply. Although a promotional film may be seen by a wide audience, it will not be shown as a regular feature over a long period of time, and copies of it will not be sold to the public, ie, they are not recordings intended for home consumption. Audio visual recordings are included in a recording contract, but the definition must exclude promotional films, and other audio visual devices not intended for commercial sale or for home consumption, allowing them to be freely used for their proper purpose. If the record company did not make the promotional film, it would protect its rights in the agreement enabling a third party to produce it.

**7.2** The definition of recordings will also include what a recording is intended to consist of. There will be a specified minimum playing time of music, or words and music together, but the playing time of words alone or music alone will be restricted. This prevents a reluctant artiste from fulfilling his minimum recording delivery commitment by recording an album of recited poetry, or by delivering an album's worth of musical backing tracks only. The words must have some genuine signifiance, and the music must be of a quality consistent with the usual standard of the artiste. If the artiste persists in spending £50,000 in wasted studio time recording "Colonel Bogey" backwards, he will eventually pay for it. If the recording agreement period is related to product delivery, he only injures himself, as such a recording will not be accepted towards the artiste's delivery commitment.

**7.3** The recording will have to be of "good commercial quality" in the reasonable opinion of the record company. This description should not be limited to the production of the recording, there should be some wording defining its contents, to ensure that the composition to be recorded is acceptable in the sense of being commercially attractive. Opinions may vary, and the recording agreement should have a statement as to whose decision is final. Commercial sound quality is not the same as the commercial appeal of the song. The content of the recording must not be defamatory or obscene, or in such bad taste that it becomes an unsaleable record because of public repugnance.

**7.4** Whether the song which has been recorded will be successful is a matter of personal opinion. The status of the artiste will be a reasonable guide to the prospect of success, but nothing is ever a certainty. Record companies seldom sign contracts with new artistes on the strength of hearing a demo recording of a few songs, and possibly with no idea of the artiste's stage presentation. As a distinctive combination of composing and performing is the basis of the decision to offer a contract, the record company might want the right to consider their position and the contract if the artiste so radically changes his musical style during the contract period that he has removed the musical basis upon which the business decision was made. Whatever was the original attraction to both record company and the record buying public may have disappeared. This can happen when an artiste decides he would like to do a "concept" album. The word "concept" gives record company executives nightmares, as it tends to mean a radical departure from an established format.

**7.5** The reconsideration by the record company would only take place after the new musical style has apparently been rejected by the public, indicated by lack of record sales. Therefore the record company needs an adequate time after the first release of the new musical style recording in which to measure public reaction, and to decide accordingly. It may be difficult to distinguish between a radical alteration in musical style, and the natural musical progression as the artiste matures.

## 8 Points distinctive to American contracts

**8.1** American recording contracts differ from Europen recording contracts in many substantial respects. This is due to the different ways in which American laws and Union regulations affect business transactions, and to the marketing techniques which have evolved to cater for an enormous territory to service. There is a greater scope for individuality of dealing with both the artiste and the public available to American companies on their home ground, and their contracts are not as conservative as those of the European record companies in the rights and protections they require.

**8.2** Comparisons where they occur in the relevant headings in this chapter will be pointed out, but general items relevant to American contracts include:

(a) The American Federation of Musicians (AFM) is the labour union in the USA to which all working musicians must belong. It has similar powers to those of the English Musicians Union for the protection of its members, and to ensure that all recordings made in the USA have been made in accordance with its regulations.

When recordings are made in the USA, the AFM is entitled to be paid by the company with the USA rights a royalty on each record manufactured and sold there. This explains the concern expressed in American contracts over any local labour union's regulations being fulfilled, and the negotiation over who is to pay the AFM royalty should that liability arise.

That factor, together with the USA legislation on mechanical copyright, makes it important to supply the American company which has the USA territorial rights with full details of when and where the recording took place.

(b) Some American record contracts include morality clauses, which state that the record company has rights of termination or extension of the contract period if the artiste is convicted of certain criminal offences, or if his personal behaviour adversely affects his standing or reputation as an artiste. If any activities of the artiste, outside his recording commitments, do not affect his ability to perform his obligations, the record company should not be concerned with them. If it is, then in an extreme case termination would be allowed, but not an extension of the contract period. These clauses should not be accepted, except possibly where the result of conviction would be to prevent the artiste from fulfilling his substantive obligations to the record company, in which case termination would be reasonable.

(c) American courts take a different view to that of English courts on when and in what circumstances the equitable relief of an injunction should be granted. American contracts have a clause whereby the artiste agrees that his personal services are of a unique nature, and that the record company should be entitled to an injunction against him if his recording services are wrongfully placed elsewhere. If an American court will take account of a contractual right of injunction where an English court may not, that highlights an important difference in the two legal systems. An English court will not apply the contractual right in circumstances where that is in conflict with established law. Such a clause should be struck out, and the record company left to rely on the ordinary course of law to protect its rights or to receive compensation.

There is a distinction between preventing an artiste from recording in breach of contract, and trying to make him record, and claiming ownership rights over recordings he makes in breach of his contract. An injunction in the UK will not normally be granted against an artiste to prevent him recording, the court will normally consider that an award of monetary compensation to the record company would be an adequate remedy. An injunction and/or an ownership claim may be made in respect of the recording itself.

(d) By their nature, American contracts contain a clause making the interpretation and enforcement of the contract to be undertaken in accordance with the laws of the State in which the record company is incorporated, and that the state court will be the venue of any litigation. The artiste should get the specialist advice of an American attorney in London upon the differences between that state law and English law, if he can afford to do so. The greater hazard and inconvenience is that he will have to take or defend any legal action in that state court, with the significant expense that will entail. Immediately in most cases the record company has a massive advantage over the artiste. If the artiste lives in the UK, and the recordings will be made in the UK, he should if possible contract in the UK with the subsidiary of the American company, with the contract being subject to English law.

## 9 Warranties by the artiste

**9.1** Record companies require from an artiste warranties which state that the record company will get his recordings free from any encumbrance or liability. The warranties will include the following:

(a) That he is entitled to use his professional name, and that use of it by the record company will not be in breach of any third party rights. This warranty can have serious practical repercussions where an unknown artiste with a novel name is not aware that another unknown artiste with an identical or similar name is establishing at the same time a reputation in another major country. These facts would not make the duplication a breach of the artiste's warranty where the law considers both artistes to be each entitled to use their novel names. The chances of this happening are not great.

(b) That there are no outstanding obligations under prior recording contracts, and that the artiste is entirely free to enter into this contract unconditionally, and to fulfil all of its terms and conditions. He should also confirm that the agreement represents his consent under the 1988 Act to the record company making, distributing and selling recordings containing his performances.

(c) That during the period of the contract the artiste will do nothing which might impair the record company's continuing rights to his recording services. This should be dependent upon the record company complying with all of its own obligations.

(d) That no performance of the artiste which is recorded during the contract will be in breach of any existing recording restriction.

(e) That no composition recorded by the artiste will be obscene, defamatory, or will breach any copyright or other third party rights giving rise to a claim against the record company.

(f) That the artiste will belong to a recognised musicians union, and that all his recordings will be made in accordance with its regulations.

(g) Where existing unreleased recordings are delivered to the record company by or at the request of the artiste, that all recording costs, union fees and musicians' payments have been paid; that all necessary statutory performers consents have been obtained, and that there are no claims, liens or other encumbrances on them or on the right of the record company to manufacture and sell records from them on a worldwide basis. This can happen where recordings are made by the artiste before contracting with any record company, or where a previous record company has unreleased material which it is prepared to sell and assign to the new record company.

## 10 Rights required by record companies

**10.1** Where the record company owns the mechanical copyright and all other rights in the recordings unconditionally, it can do what it likes with them. Where a production company licences the recording to the record company, it can only do what is specified in the contract, all other rights being retained by the production company.

**10.2** All recording contracts will set out the principal rights of the record company, including the following:

(a) The exclusive rights as set out in (b) to (f) below in the recordings made by the artiste during the exclusive period of the agreement with the record company. The record company will control the choice of the record producer, which (for a new artiste) together with the right of the record company to approve the songs to be recorded, gives the record company absolute control over the content and quality of the final recording. The artiste can have consultation rights, but the ultimate decision will be taken by the record company. An international artiste will have greater control over the recorded material, but the record company would still retain final control to guard against the possibility of the artiste being silly.

(b) The exclusive right throughout the world (or in the case of a licence deal throughout the contract territory) to manufacture, distribute and sell records derived from the recordings, or to refrain from doing so in its absolute discretion. Although there may be territorial release obligations, the record company knows better than the artiste how to run the company's business. The record company will decide where and when to release the records. That decision will be influenced by the personal appearance programme of the artiste, to maximise the marketing impact in a foreign country, if he will be touring there in the near future.

(c) The exclusive right to use the artiste's name, likeness and biographical material for the promotion and advertising of records. This clause should not prohibit the artiste from endorsing merchandise, such as musical instruments, independently of the recording contract. Neither should it entitle the record company to make use of his name and likeness outside the strict business of selling and promoting his records.

(d) The right to release the recordings on the label or trademark of the company's choice. This would only apply where no specific label identification has been agreed upon for the artiste's recordings. The choice of label will also depend upon any restrictions upon the record company issuing low price or budget albums, or upon recoupling with the recordings of other artistes.

(e) The exclusive right to perform the recordings publicly. The right creates no control over the recorded composition itself, only over the actual recording. This entitles the record company to receive all the phonographic performance income attributed to the recordings. The record company can also control public performance of the recordings by way of background music, such as by hotels, restaurants and airlines, or its inclusion in any film or TV soundtrack.

(f) The exclusive right to manufacture records from the soundtracks of TV spectaculars and the like consisting entirely of the artiste's musical performances. Where the film contains the performances of several artistes, each being exclusively contracted to a different record company, which company is to release the record, and what the other companies get paid for licensing their rights, should be agreed before any commitment is made by the artiste for the TV show which is being filmed.

## 11 Royalties

**11.1** The range of royalties available from record companies varies for each individual artiste. It depends largely on the sales potential of the artiste, and any previous success he may have had. What would be a fair royalty rate for any artiste will differ in the opinion of each record company, which for a new artiste may range from 8% to 12% for the full price UK market sales, and a successful artiste may warrant a higher rate.

**11.2** Some record companies will have in their contract with the artiste a fixed rate of royalty whatever the volume of record sales. Others will have a sliding scale, starting with a reasonable rate for low sales, and rising to a good figure on high sales. The artiste should press for a sliding scale, because if by chance a number of his records are high sellers, he will be a star, and the sliding scale will give him the proper return for his success having exceeded normal expectations, without having to negotiate it. It does no harm to the record company, because if the sales are low, so is the royalty. Other alternatives are to have the royalty rate increased by a certain amount in each successive year of the contract, or at those dates when options to renew the period of the agreement are exercised by the record company. These alternatives are not satisfactory to a record company, as they are arbitrary and take no account of record sales; which is what counts. There is no reason to pay increased royalty rates where the sales of albums made in those periods are not spectacular.

**11.3** Where the royalty rate increases in steps of volume of sales of each record, it should be clear whether the increased rate is only applicable to the sales of that record within the relevant sales band, or whether once the threshold of the royalty step has been reached, all sales of that record from the first sale retrospectively attract the increased rate. The second possibility would not normally be acceptable to a record company, unless the starting royalty rate is so low that, on an aggregated royalty calculation, the overall rate is economic. For example, where there is an escalating royalty on record sales, are the "qualifying sales" for calculating when the escalation should operate all of the sales of the record of whatever royalty category through the record company territory? If different licencees of the record company within the territory have different rates, is the escalation only to apply in each country as and when sales in that country exceed the sales steps? If that is the case, the sales steps in each country would have to be at different levels, because the sales expectations of each would be different. A UK record company with licensees in other countries will have mostly "catalogue deals", unless they appoint licensees on a one-off basis each time. Therefore the ability of the record company to agree escalations of royalties on foreign sales will depend on the royalty rate "profit" they have on the deal. Royalty escalation clauses need to be worded carefully.

**11.4** Where the royalty rate increases annually during the contract, it should be clear whether the increased rates apply only to sales of recordings released during that year whenever sold, or whether the increase applies to recordings made during that year, although released in a later year. It will normally be related to the date of release, which will encourage prompt release by the record company. If the timing is crucial, such as coming up to Christmas, the release date should be decided upon to maximise the impact of the album on the market. It would not be good commercial sense to delay the release into the next contract year, just to qualify for a higher royalty rate.

**11.5** It might be agreed that the royalty rate starting base for all future recordings will be increased once any one record has achieved a stated level of worldwide sales, or if it reaches a specified placing in the popularity charts in one of the major record selling countries. This would only apply to a new artiste, whose initial record royalty rate is low, but improvable by success. This proposal does not have any merit, as all future albums may turn out to be disasters.

**11.6** Where there are royalty rate differences according to different territories, the clause must make it clear whether any general royalty increase will relate to record sales in all territories, or only to record sales in the UK and major territories. This will depend on whether the record company has worldwide rights or limited territory rights. It should also be made clear whether the increase only relates to the top royalty rate, or whether lesser rates are included. All pro-rata royalty rates (eg, two thirds of the full rate for mail order sales) will automatically be adjusted.

**11.7** The royalty rate will normally differ between home sales of records, and sales in foreign countries. Which country will be "home" depends on where the record company is based. A successful artiste will be given top royalty rates within the major record selling countries of the world. The remaining countries will be divided into other levels of territorial rates, depending on their record selling potential. If there are any merchandising or special album releases where the record company's licensee pays to the record company a flat fee per record sold, or a fee calculated to cover up to a states sales level, the record company will pay to the artiste an agreed proportion of what it receives. This occurs, for example, where there are political or currency problems, such as with Eastern bloc countries, and the record company is only likely to be paid once. If the company has to make other proper third party payments from the gross fee, that will be deductible before calculating the artiste's payments.

**11.8** The royalty rate will also differ in respect of records sold through normal retail channels, depending upon the price at which they are sold, and those disposed of in any other way. Records can be sold or given away together with merchandise as sales incentives for the latter, or sold at a reduced price through a budget label, or sold by mail order and through record clubs. Sales to the armed forces through the NAFFI and PX can be significant in some countries, such as Germany.

**11.9** Bulk sales of records at a lower price, although providing a reduced profit per unit sold, can be as profitable overall to the company as lower sales only on the full price label. It can also mean extensive promotion through more people becoming aware of the artiste, reducing the high cost of promotion which might otherwise be required to encourage full price sales to the same extent.

All record companies reduce the royalty rate on less than full price sales of records, and each has its own formula for doing so. The artiste might expect that, as a royalty rate is proportional, the reduction in the monetary amount he receives per record sold at a reduced price should be only because the normal royalty rate would be calculated on a lower figure. For example, a 10% royalty on an £8 album will produce (leaving aside all deductions) 80p. If the royalty rate is retained at 10% for a low price version of the album, say £5, the royalty will produce 50p, ie, a pro rata reduction. But the reduced royalty clause will say, for example, that the royalty rate on budget sales will be 60% of the full rate, so producing an amount of 30p per album. At first sight, by reducing both the price of the record, and the royalty rate, the record company is taking two bites from the same cherry. This is not so, because although the price of the record is reduced, manufacturing, distribution and advertising costs, as well as record company overheads, are not reduced.

**11.10** The royalty rate reductions for less than full price sales will be by between one third and one half of the applicable full price royalty rate, and the categories of rock bottom price upon which no royalty is payable at all will also vary. When comparing the monetary value of different companies' calculations where the reduction in royalty rate is the same, the original basis of the full royalty calculation must also be compared.

Some record companies will reduce or eliminate an artiste's royalty if they propose to release "sampler" compilation albums which, according to the contract, are sold at or about cost price solely for the purpose of promoting the artistes on it. It is arguable that a sampler album should be treated as an ordinary compilation album, the artiste's royalty being proportional to either the numbers of tracks on the recording or its playing time, and at a full or reduced rate depending upon its retail price category. If the sampler is not produced in the normal commercial quantities, and is only sold to the appropriate recipients at or about cost price for economical purposes, no royalties should be payable. If the sampler is a thinly disguised compilation album aimed at the normal market, a royalty should be paid. In any event there should be a "favoured nations" clause in the contract whereby the artiste will be paid a royalty if any other artiste receives one, and at the same rate and upon the same conditions.

**11.11** Record companies reduce the royalty rate payable on albums in respect of which substantial promotion expense will be incurred, such as by TV advertising. This reduction is only justifiable where the TV advertising is national, or at least is not just in one limited and modest test area, with a minimal number of 15 second TV advertisements, in the cheap periods. The reduced rate should only apply to sales in the country where a substantial and serious TV advertising promotional campaign takes place. A properly organised classy TV advertisement set for showing in prime time for a decent period over a significant area will only be made for records which the record company is confident will be high sellers, to justify the expense. Certain restrictions on applying the reduced rate of royalty should be imposed. For example, it would not benefit the artiste if an already successful record is given the TV advertisement treatment, and his royalties on it are subsequently reduced. TV campaigns are short-lived, and so is their effect on sales. If the album is not specifically produced just for a TV promoted campaign, there may be a six month period during which the TV campaign does increase sales, but thereafter sales revert to their normal pattern. From that point onwards, what is the validity for a perpetually reduced artiste's royalty on sales of the album, apart from recovering the costs of the TV promotion?

**11.12** Record companies also need to make a profit. The royalty paid to the artiste is related directly to the volume of sales of his records, and is not a proportion of general record company profits. The company's profits also depend on the volume of sales of all of its artiste's records, so to that extent the fortune of the company and that of the artiste are linked. In the promotion of royalty-bearing sales of records by the artiste by whatever means, what is good for the company is good for the artiste.

**11.13** For the sale of audio tapes, CD recordings, audiovisual records and any other packaged device, if the packaging cost is correctly charged by the record company, there is no justification for paying less than a full royalty rate. One method of calculation is for the royalty rate for devices to be the same as that for records, with an appropriate packaging cost allowance. Alternatively, the record company can treat the sale of a device as being the same as the sale of a record, paying to the artiste the same monetary amount as would be paid on the sale of a record, disregarding the different retail selling price and packaging cost. Packaging costs can also be different for a double album, or a boxed album set, or for a one-off gimmick sleeve which is expensive to produce. As long as the packaging cost to be deducted for the royalty calculation is reasonable, it should be agreed.

**11.14** Technology has extended the "record" to a video disc, laser disc, compact disc, and will no doubt continue to develop and refine existing and future playback means. The calculation of royalty rates, packaging costs and other relevant criteria will follow the needs of the business, while providing a fair return to the artiste.

**11.15** Other royalties which may have to be dealt with in the artiste's recording contract are:

(a) The record producer's royalty, and whether the artiste or the record company pays it. Record producer's agreements are dealt with in chapter six. This will depend upon the level of the royalty rate paid to the artiste, and upon whether the artiste or the record company controls the record production. The producer will be paid his royalty from the sale of the first record onwards, with no deductions except for the recoupment of any advance payments made to him on account of his royalties. The record company will pay the artiste his royalty, although calculated from the sale of the first record onwards, only after recoupment of all advances paid to him, including recording costs, and third party payments made by the record company for which the artiste is responsible.

It may be agreed that the record company pays the producer his royalties, but deducts all or part of the payments (including any advances on account) from the artiste's royalties, as being his liability. If the artiste is on a relatively low royalty rate, he should not be paying any part of the producer's costs. If he does, and if all his recordings are modest sellers only, he may never become entitled to receive any further payment of royalties once the accumulated advances and production costs and the producer's royalties are all taken into account.

(b) AFM payments when recordings are made in the USA.

(c) Any override royalty payable to another record company for a guest artiste who has performed on the artistes recording.

**11.16** A record company might put a clause in its contract whereby if the artiste breaches the contract, the record company may stop paying him any royalties until the final settlement of the dispute. This is an understandable request, but it should be severely limited, to protect the artiste from an unreasonable record company. Adequate safeguards should be included, such as:

(a) Withholding of royalties should only occur where there will be a true monetary loss to the record company, or where damages will almost certainly be awarded against the artiste together with costs. The loss and/or damages must be directly caused by the breach. There should be no retention for a technical breach which causes no monetary loss.

(b) The amount withheld should ot exceed a reasonable estimate of the artiste's genuine liability.

(c) The amount withheld should be put on deposit, the interest to belong to the artiste. Withheld money belongs to the artiste until the court says otherwise, and the interest should be added into the retained amount. If the record company gets an award of less than the retention, the balance (as increased by the interest) is to be paid to the artiste.

(d) Processing the claim should be expedited, and the excess of the retention over any damages and costs awarded should be paid promptly to the artiste.

## 12 Basis for calculating royalties

**12.1** Royalties are calculated as a percentage of the recommended retail selling price of the record after making certain deductions. Some record companies have used a royalty rate which is based not on retail selling price, but on the wholesale price charged by the record company to its primary distributors, which may be wholly owned subsidiaries. The royalty rate tends to be between one and a half times and twice that which is calculated on the retail price of a record, but the whole basis of the royalty calculation is different. This is not a recommended basis, as a "distributor price" is not as impartial as a known public selling price. A record company's regular published wholesale price to retailers would be an acceptable basis providing the royalty rate is adjusted accordingly.

**12.2** The method of calculation of the royalty rate used by the record company does not concern the artiste, provided that he is assured of receiving in monetary terms per record sold what he thought he was contracting for. The main practical difference is that the recommended retail selling price of a record is readily ascertainable, whereas the company's wholesale distributor price is an arbitrary decision of the company, with a basis of calculation totally under its control. It would be impossible for royalty calculations to be based on actual retail selling prices in the shops, because of the discounts given from time to time at all regular price levels as a part of trade competition.

**12.3** The usual deductions from the retail selling price are:

(a) government taxes, such as sales tax and value added tax;

(b) the packaging cost of the album sleeve, tape cassette, or other container.

The deductions should not include payments to any third party, such as copyright royalty payments. Where the royalty is a proportion of net receipts, such as of a fee received by the record company from one of its licensees, genuine and justifiable payments to be made to third parties by the record company can be deducted from the gross fee before its division with the artiste. The artiste should be safeguarded from any such third party payments being due to any entity related to the record company, or otherwise not being on a genuine arm's length basis, as a deliberate means of artificially reducing the value to the artiste of his share of the fee.

**12.4** Record companies express the packaging cost deduction as a percentage of retail selling price. This disregards the true packaging cost, but the percentage is easier to calculate and administer, and is arrived at by experience on what their costings represent as a percentage. A record company might state that the deduction will be the same as that charged to all of its artistes, without specifying what that charge will be. There must be some identification of the charge, even if it is adjustable from time to time to take account of real cost factors. The charge is likely to be based on the true packaging costs, calculated over a period of time, although most contracts do not make that a condition.

**12.5** There will also be some deduction by the record company to account for records sold which are subsequently returned for credit, as it should not have to pay a royalty on a record which is not sold. Sale or return arrangements are common within the retail trade, and other returns will relate to defective goods, errors in shipment or in billing, and as a concession by record companies where necessary on records which have been sold, to maintain good will with the record retail trade. The cost of making individual calculations of actual returns would be excessive, and it would not be practical, so for convenience the royalty rate is based on an arbitrary percentage of gross sales, normally 90% or 95%, to make an allowance for returns. This means that an artiste with high sales and no returns loses slightly, but he gains where he has reasonable sales and high returns. The level of the actual returns is immaterial in calculating the royalty on this basis. The alternative is to make the calculations on 100% of net sales, where these are computed by deducting known returns from gross sales. The artiste should resist the calculation being less than 100% of net sales, as all returns would be allowed to arrive at "net sales", after which what further allowance is needed? The record company is covering its prospective deficiency twice. A record sold which is subsequently returned and then resold should bear a royalty, assuming that the stock return computerised system maintains such a close control on credits and invoicing.

**12.6** An American company's substantive business is on a sale or return basis, because it is dealing with an enormous country serviced by a tremendous and widely spread number of record shops, supermarket racking companies, mail order clubs and numerous other forms of record sales outlets. A record shipped out from the factory to a customer is a sale by the record company for royalty calculation purposes unless it is returned. Each record company has its own regulations setting out the time limits within which, and the reasons for which, the returns of a record will be accepted for crediting to an artiste's account.

**12.7** In the calculation of the level of returns to be deducted in a net record sale royalty deal, record companies should take account of the possibility of promotional, bonus and other royalty free records which are distributed free of charge by the record company finding their way back to the record company in the guise of returns of records sold. For a low-selling album this can create a negative sales figure, to the embarrassment of the record company and the anger of the artiste. Another anomaly can arise should the royalty ever be calculated on 100% of gross sales, ie where no returns are deducted in the calculation of royalties. Records returned and then resold will effectively have two royalty payments made on it by the record company. This system is never used by record companies, as it leaves no flexibility, is not realistic within the way the record business works, and will be unacceptably expensive in royalty payments.

**12.8** In any territory where there are no wide scale sale or return agreements with the record retailers, there is a timidity in pressing policy to avoid being caught with excessive redundant stocks of records. As a result, there may be no records available in the shops, and no stocks available to supply to them, should an unforeseen demand arise. By the time more records have been pressed, and stocks are available, the demand may have lessened. As the American record companies ensure that they are not penalised in their royalty calculation clauses for pressing optimistic numbers of records to be distributed on a sale or return basis, they are able to cover their market more effectively. The disadvantage is that the royalty accounting system has to be cautious to protect them from over paying royalties in respect of late returns. Whatever the circumstances in the market place, record companies will not press more copies of a record at any time in excess of their projected sales anticipation.

**12.9** Where there are several countries within the record company's territory, such as in Europe, the calculation of royalties becomes complicated because each country has its own factors which determine the retail selling price of a record, and each has its own sales or value added tax levels. To avoid confusion it must be agreed whether the royalty is to be based on the recommended retail selling price of the records in the country of their sale, or in the country of their manufacture.

Record companies only have manufacturing plants in those countries where it is economically sensible, and the record company's subsidiary or licensee in each non-manufacturing country imports its stocks of records. Even manufacturing countries import stocks when they need more records than they can press, or when they need an initial stock to satisfy a demand which has arisen before local pressing has begun.

**12.10** The recording contract will normally give the record company the right to choose whether the royalties paid to the artiste will be calculated according to the country of manufacture of the records, or their country of sale. The obvious choice would be the country of manufacture, as that has the readily ascertainable figures of price, tax cost and other financial considerations which come within the royalty calculation. If that were the universal rule, there would be no royalty accountings from countries which do not have manufacturing facilities, and they would have to buy their stocks from manufacturers "post royalty". The flexibility is needed by record companies to even out this potential anomaly, and to allow each record selling territory to make its profit and to pay its own way. Other factors are:

(a) A batch of records manufactured in one country may be exported to and sold in different countries. If this applies to records pressed by several factories, to the point where it is possible for records pressed in one country to be sold in another manufacturing country, the choice of country of manufacture or country of sale might sound confusing;

(b) Is the choice intended to be made to save accounting problems, or is it a device to enable the record company to take advantage of the difference in manufacturing cost, tax levied, and retail price within the countries in respect of which the record company can make a choice, to minimise the value of the royalty to the artiste?

**12.11** The choice of country of manufacture or sale also affects:

(a) The currency in which the royalty received in the UK by the record company for that record sale is calculated initially.

(b) The time lapse before the record company accounts to the artiste for foreign royalties. This depends upon whether a record made in one country and exported to another country for sale there is deemed to be sold for royalty purposes in the accounting period within which it was manufactured, or within which it was exported (where the royalty is calculated in the country of manufacture); or in the accounting period in which the local distributor of the imported record sells it to a consumer through the retail trade, (where the royalty is calculated in the country of sale).

## 13 Exchange rates for royalties

**13.1** As the dates upon which the record company receives foreign royalties, and the dates upon which the artiste is accounted to for his share of those royalties, will be different, the artiste's contract should state at which of the dates the rate of exchange for payment to the artiste will be calculated. Currency speculation is a hazardous occupation, so UK record companies calculate the conversion of foreign currency into sterling at the rate prevailing when it receives and converts the foreign royalties, and the artiste is accounted to at that rate. Inevitably the exchange rates at the date of receipt and the date at which the artiste is accounted to will be different. The artiste is paid in sterling, so the date when the record company itself received sterling is appropriate for the exchange rate calculation. It is no concern of the artiste whether the record company actually converts the foreign currency at the date of its receipt, so any speculation by the record company on the fluctuations of the exchange rates is its own affair.

**13.2** If the record company, at the request of the artiste, accounts to him in a foreign country for the actual amount of his royalties it receives in that currency, the benefit of profit or the risk of loss in exchange rates for sterling between the date of receipt by the record company and the date of payment to the artiste is that of the artiste. This may happen, for example, in a blocked currency country, or where the artiste needs a lot of dollars left for him in the USA, to avoid two lots of foreign exchange charges. An exception would be where the record company fails to pay the artiste by his contractual date, after which date, and prior to payment, the rate of exchange fluctuates so that the rate on the actual payment date is not as favourable as that prevailing on the contractual payment date. The artiste ought to be able to claim the difference from the record company if it paid the royalties late and on the less favourable exchange rate, as a deliberate means of obtaining an exchange rate benefit.

**13.3** The same point arises where royalties earned in an accounting period do not yet exceed advance payments already received by the artiste, and the rate of exchange on the date of receipt by the record company of foreign money from which the artistes royalty will be paid is different from the rate of exchange on the contractual date of accounting to the artiste. Although no part of these foreign money receipts will be paid to the artiste, according to which date is taken, there can be a significant difference in the calculation of by how much the artiste's advance has been recouped. The contractual exchange rate date is what counts.

## 14 Royalty reserves

**14.1** Royalty reserves should only be applied in respect of record sales on a sale or return basis of distribution and selling of records, to prevent the over-payment of royalties to the artiste in any accounting period, and it applies primarily to the USA. Shipments of records by the record company to record shops and other points of sale are treated in its books as being sales of those records, unless they are returned to the record company. Records returned may not be received by the record company for several months after their date of shipment, and the returns are not likely to be received within the accounting period in which the original sale was deemed to have been made.

**14.2** The record company retains as a reserve from royalties payable in respect of sales (ie shipments) in any accounting period that proportion of royalties which it thinks will be attributable to all the records which will be returned out of those sold in that period. The reserve provisions may be higher than the reasonably anticipated returns, to allow for misjudgement of the returns level, and for fluctuations covering several consecutive accounting periods of the contract. As there is no means of identifying individual copies of records, over a period of time it is not possible to distinguish within which accounting period any particular record returned was deemed to have been a sale.

**14.3** As a safety factor for the artiste the royalty reserve for any accounting period must be "liquidated" no more than, say, three quarterly accounting periods (or two half yearly accounting periods) after the end of the accounting period in which the reserve was made. This creates a rolling reserve which is maintained at a level consistent with the historic returns pattern for the artiste's recordings. Control is retained by the artiste over the royalty reserve retentions by including in the recording contract a maximum percentage which can be retained by the record company from the royalties due to the artiste in respect of each accounting period. The accounting period by which the reserve retained from a prior accounting statement is to be liquidated must be stated. When the accounting date has been reached at which the reserve held for a prior accounting period is to be liquidated, the balance of that reserve is released and added to the royalties now to be accounted for to the artiste.

**14.4** All records returned to the record company which have not previously been deducted in royalty statements are deducted in the current statement as a general debit. The wording of the royalty reserve clause should not be wide enough so that in an accounting statement the liquidated reserve figure is added to the royalty due for that period for the purpose of calculating the new reserve to be withheld. The reserve is calculated only on that accounting period's royalties, and the value of the liquidated reserve after deduction of returns is added to the payment to be made to the artiste.

Single records tend to be pressed more freely than albums, because the cost of doing so is less, the loss of profit on returns is less, and they are widely used for the promotion of the artiste's albums. Therefore the reserve percentage of royalties payable on singles will be higher than the percentage to be reserved from royalties on album sales.

In a perfect world interest should be payable on the released amount of the royalty reserve, as the artiste has not had the use of that money for some considerable period. The request would not normally be granted.

**14.5** Where the recordings are licensed to the record company, there must be a formula to liquidate the total royalty reserve at some specified date after the expiry of the non-exclusive stock sell-off period. After that time any credit given in respect of records returned will be at the cost of the record company.

**14.6** When the sales of one of the artiste's albums start to diminish, and shipments are therefore reduced accordingly, two things happen which tend to justify the apparently severe royalty reserve structure. As the sales in each accounting period reduce, so does the level of the royalty reserve for each of the accounting periods, as it is a percentage of royalties due on sales in that accounting period. At the same time, the reduction in confirmed sales is being aggravated by an increase in the level of returns in respect of higher shipments made within prior accounting periods. By close monitoring of the levels of records pressed, distributed and returned, at an appreciable time before returns reach an unacceptable level, the rate of pressing is reduced. The ideal situation for the record company is where the extinction of demand for the record matches the sell out of all stocks held of that record.

**14.7** The disadvantage to the artiste of royalties held in reserve is that he does not have the use in the meantime of that part of the royalty reserve which is ultimately released to him, although in times of fluctuation of exchange rates, the artiste might even make money through the delayed payment. Inflation is also disregarded in respect of royalty payments which are delayed for a substantial time due to the royalty reserve structure. In the meantime the record company has the use of the money.

## 15 Recording costs

**15.1** Where the artiste is contracted direct to the record company, it will pay for all the costs of producing and recording his records. The company will recoup all such costs incurred as a first charge to be deducted from the aggregate of all royalties payable to the artiste on the sales of records derived from all of the artiste's recordings. The investment risk of the record company is spread, so that the earnings from successful records subsidise those records the earnings from which never exceed their production costs, or which are much slower to do so. If recording costs were only to be treated as an advance against the royalties due on the sales of that album, it would encourage the record company to release it and promote it whenever reasonably possible. There would only be a problem if the artiste's royalties never exceeded the recording costs. But such a proposal would make record companies much more wary of incurring such costs, so on balance the artiste is better off under the present system.

**15.2** Although the recording costs are recouped wholly from the artiste's share of royalties, the artiste is not in a position to control the cost. As the record company is spending the money at its own risk, it wants the control over expenditure, and for its own benefit will want to reduce such costs to a minimum. If the final recording is not successful, the artiste may claim that the record company is responsible for wasted or excessive recording expenditure, or for not spending enough to enable the recording to be promoted properly, as the case may be. Promotion costs are not recoupable, but will influence the success of the record sales. If the artiste had control over the recording expenditure, because it is in effect being lent to him, he would have a conflict of interest between spending the least, and budgeting properly to obtain the best results. Some artistes would spend vast amounts, regardless of the consequences, given the opportunity.

## 16 Royalty advance payments

**16.1** A major artiste can sometimes receive from a record company a non-returnable and non-recoupable incentive payment to procure the signing of the contract. An inducement payment for the artiste's signature should be separated from the other financial terms of the contract, unless there are conditions in it to be fulfilled after signature relating solely to the inducement payment.

**16.2** It is usual for advances to be a non-returnable but recoupable payment on account of the artiste's royalties due to him under his contract with the record company. Apart from exceptional circumstances, by custom in the record industry advances are never returnable, ie they are not repayable otherwise than from royalties. The advance may be returnable, for example, if the artiste is fraudulent, or simply refuses to do anything for the company, where the record company is able to rescind the contract. Recording contracts do not envisage that the artiste might be so dishonest, so the claim by the record company would be made under the normal rules governing contracts.

**16.3** The amount advanced by the record company will depend upon the status of the artiste, and the chances of total recoupment by the record company from record sales within a reasonable time. The time it will take the record company to recoup advances will also depend upon the artiste's royalty rate. The lower the royalty rate, the longer will be the time before he receives any part of his own income in excess of advances. This is one good reason to argue for a high rate of royalty, although the logic may not be acceptable to a record company. Whether an advance payment made directly to the artiste was spent wisely on equipment he needs, or recklessly on an expensive motor car, will not affect the issue.

**16.4** The royalties expectant in any accounting period will be important to the artiste if he has no other source of income, and if he relies upon his record royalties to support his other career costs. If he also composes the songs he records, reasonable record sales levels would indicate a similarly reasonable flow of publishing income. If the artiste has a reasonable level of earnings from other sources, he should take his personal tax position into account when negotiating advance payments under his recording contract, and he should obtain an accountant's advice on the best strategy to adopt.

**16.5** Where a contract consisting of yearly periods with renewal options to be exercised by the record company contains modest album advances, the artiste should try to negotiate significant additional advance payments by the record company on the exercise of each option. Exercise of the option and payment of the advance by the record company will indicate that it considers the artiste to be a worthwhile investment for at least one more year. There is also a further incentive for it to promote the artiste seriously.

**16.6** All advances paid to the artiste by the record company for whatever reason, including deemed advances such as recording costs, will be cumulative for the purpose of recoupment. The artiste's royalties due in any accounting period from every record released and sold under his recording agreement will first be retained towards the recoupment by the record company of the whole of the then outstanding balance of advance payments which have been made to the artiste. If the accounting shows that there is money to be paid to the artiste because all prior advances have been recouped, then it is paid to the artiste. The record company cannot withhold any of the royalties in anticipation of an imminent advance payment due to be made to the artiste, such as where he is just about to deliver a new album. The record company should not be entitled to "be late" in paying the due accounting, so that it falls after the date of payment of the advance, on the principle that it can then deduct that advance from the royalties. Payment of the royalties must be made as if they had been made on the due date, and the advance will be recouped on the next accounting.

**16.7** It would be most unusual for the record company to agree to the recoupment of advances in respect of individual albums to be against only the royalties arising from the sales of the specific album, and any singles taken from it, and any track on it which is included in a compilation album. If it did so agree, the recoupment of general advances would have to be dealt with separately, and the amount of the advance committed to recordings not yet made would be at a much lower level, to reduce the risk of non-recoupment on isolated unsuccessful albums.

**16.8** When a group member leaves the group, the recoupment by the record company of advances made to the group before his departure will still be out of their total group royalty, including his future share of royalties, until the advances are cleared. The record company may give the group further advances after the member's departure, from which he receives no benefit. Recoupment of the new advance, and of all future advances made after he leaves the group, should be made from all royalties due to the group on recordings made before and after his departure. The departed member's share of royalties arising from records in which he participates should be exempt from any connection with future advances and should be paid to him, subject only to recoupment of his share of previous advances. A group should deal with that position when negotiating the recording agreement, to avoid confusion when the event happens. In any agreement between group members, (see chapter eight), there should be a clause to protect a departed member from never getting his future royalty payments because they are retained by the record company for the recoupment of future advances.

## 17 Promotion records, "freebies" and "sell-outs"

**17.1** At the lower end of the scale of records which rank for a reduced royalty rate, or no royalty at all, are those given away free, or distributed at or about cost price. Free promotion records are those given away to radio station and disc jockeys, record programme producers, reviewers in music publications, and any other person whose job it is to promote, plug, play and talk about records to a receptive public. The selling success of a record depends upon the public being made aware it exists by critical review, and by being broadcast. Favourable comment upon it, and the praises of those whose opinions are valued by record buyers, give any record an added chance of getting into the popularity charts. Inclusion in radio station play lists is essential to chart success.

**17.2** Those people in that side of the record business will not buy records just for the purpose of their job. Every record company will do its best, especially by providing free records to those who matter, to get their records selected for play on the radio programmes, out of all the new records released each week. The distribution of free records genuinely used for promotional purposes is beneficial to both the artiste and the record company. The number of records allocated within the USA for this purpose is so great that to prevent serious mis-use of the concession, mainly in respect of albums:

(a) The number of free promotion albums given away should be limited to a reasonable proportion of full price royalty sales. For singles the marketing strategy is different, as where possible they are used to promote the albums from which they are taken, or on which they are shortly to be released. The record company profitability level for singles may be less than for albums, so a higher rate of allowance for free promotion singles is acceptable. Although the objective in giving away free promotion records is clear, the artiste's recording contract should contain some limitation on the categories of people who will receive them. The ability to acquire from record company executives free albums of favourite artistes is widely used as a perk or a goodwill gesture, to maintain a connection with influential people, perhaps not even remotely connected with the record business.

(b) Promotion albums distributed free of charge should have some obvious and permanent feature whereby they can immediately be recognised for what they are, such as a sticker on the record label. Without such identification they can either be offered for sale to the public, or they can be returned to the record company for credit against delivery of records by other artistes. In each case the artiste is deprived of his royalty, and the record company loses money. There have been various attempts to do this in the past, for example by punching a hole in the album sleeve, thus branding it as a free promotion album, but it is not practical. Dealing in free promotional goods is seen as one of the perks of the business.

**17.3** Records distributed for a reduced or cost price, and on which no royalties are paid, may also be used as supermarket loss leaders, or as incentive gifts to go with services, or just to get rid of the records, which cannot otherwise be sold or used at a profit in merchandise promotion deals. While genuine promotion records are a calculated and accepted expense to the record company, the distribution of "freebies" sometimes is a desperate measure just to clear the space in the warehouse.

**17.4** When a record has reached the end of its useful selling life, and if there is little prospect of shifting the excess stock of records through the retail trade in economical quantities, the record company can exercise any "sell-out" rights it has to auction or junk the remaining stocks just to get rid of them. At worst they can be scrapped. A well organised record company will recognise the decline in sales of an album at an early date, and will reduce production levels accordingly. Should demand for the record arise in the future, they will be re-pressed and re-released for sale through appropriate retail channels. Storage space is money, and a realistic attitude must be taken to excess stocks where the record company has a large number of artistes which it records.

**17.5** Reasonable restrictions should be applied to the circumstances in which long-standing residual stocks of unsold records by the artiste can be off-loaded by the record company whereby no royalty is payable. For example, it would be reasonable where a record has been deleted from the company's current catalogue because of lack of sales. An important natural regulator is that the record company itself does not get a profit on such measures.

**17.6** If records of the artiste are of no selling value to the record company, it should be allowed to mitigate its production and pressing losses by disposing of stocks for other considerations which have some benefit to it. If the unrelated benefit is substantially in excess of the stock costs which would otherwise have been written off, the record company would consider that to be a windfall, which reduces its loss in that respect. The artiste's contract with the record company, when dealing with these sources of diminished revenue, must take into account his record company's normal practice.

## 18 Mail order sales

**18.1** There is a thriving direct mail order business in records, where the ordinary retail selling price can be undercut because of the saving in overhead costs, and the volume of potential sales. If the mail order company expands its turnover by offering free premium records as a purchase incentive for other albums, there will be no royalty on the premium record, and a reduced royalty on regular mail order sales. The premium record by the artiste may be used to promote recordings by other artistes through mail order, not necessarily his own. There should be a restriction on using his recordings in that manner, both as to quantity and as to timing—or at all except after being deleted from the current catalogue. It depends on whether, somewhere in the mail order scheme, the artiste also receives a worthwhile benefit. There is scope for a record company to juggle the proportion of low price albums against the free incentive albums whereby the record company reduces its royalty commitment on the combination of those records disposed of.

**18.2** Mail order sales can be considerable, and even with a reduced royalty rate the artiste's income can be substantial. There should be a time restriction on the record company providing stocks of records for mail order sales of an album which is bound to be a high seller through the full price retail trade, or which still has a long term full price selling potential. As mail order customers want either a re-issued popular catalogue album, or a current best seller if available through that source, it makes no sense to deprive the artiste or the record company of the benefit of the top royalty rate on full price retail sales until such time as it becomes more beneficial to take a reduced royalty rate of revived sales through mail order.

## 19 Record clubs

**19.1** Record clubs benefit their members and promote records by making cheap continuity purchase attractive. Through a record club it is possible to obtain records either at a much reduced price, or free in various promotion or bonus offers. It is a promotion method based on the appealing premise of purchasing a number of records to get one free, and of offering low price records to members. The difference between mail order and record clubs is that the former is based on impulse purchasing, whereas the latter is a commitment to purchase minimum quantities over a period of time to be eligible for the attractive reduced prices. Record clubs may also offer a wider choice of product. Clearly it would not pay record companies to dispose of all their stocks of records at somewhere just over cost price, even though no royalties, or royalties at a reduced rate, are paid to the artiste. Equally important is the promotion value through the bulk distribution of his records, which can make an artiste known, although demands through these outlets will usually be for established artistes or popular albums.

**19.2** The artiste's royalties on records disposed of through mail order, record clubs and budget line labels are reduced to either half or two thirds of the full royalty rate. The reasoning is that as record pressing costs and sleeve costs are the same as for full price label releases, and the mechanical royalty rate stays the same (if not based on record price), the reduced price to the purchaser means that there is less to be shared between the record company and the artiste. But the artiste's royalty has two bites taken out of it—the reduced royalty rate and the reduced price on which it is calculated—which is not a reduction on the same basis as that of the record company.

**19.3** The record company should ensure that the record club is *bona fide*, and the record company should not distribute through that medium more than a reasonable percentage of the number of the artiste's records sold to the public through the normal retail channels for so long as the retail demand is high. The recording agreement should specify that there should also be a minimum period of full price retail selling before any record club is given the right to include the record in its current catalogue. Subject only to contractual limits and obligations, record companies reserve the right to manufacture, distribute and sell records as they see fit in their absolute discretion, so decisions on these matters are made in accordance with normal company policy.

**19.4** The record company is doing its best through record sales to make money for itself, and in the process it also does so for the artiste. The more full price records which are sold, the higher will be the company's profit. If it uses merchandise promotions, mail order, budget line labels, and record clubs to maintain a satisfactory level of sales of records by the artiste, that is a commercial decision, and it does not do so just to pay the artiste a lower royalty.

## 20 Budget line labels

**20.1** Apart from giving preferential terms to record clubs, and giving away records as merchandise incentives, an effective means of selling more records is to lower the selling price. For full price records, on which the record company pays the full rate of royalties, the available margin of profit at the point of sale enables a retailer to give a reasonable price reduction to the purchaser. To make record buying more attractive there are budget line record labels, upon which both the record company and the artiste accept a reduced earnings for each record sold, to enable the retailer to give a competitive decreased retail price.

**20.2** The reason for different trade labels for budget line records is to create a separate identity for them, and to establish a consumer awareness that the original quality is not impaired by a lower price. As a marketing concept, a budget label is just a cheaper version of the regular label. The artiste should ensure that the first release of his records in any territory will be on a full price label, and that relegation of any recording to a budget label should only occur after a minimum period of time following it first release, or after sales of that recording at full price have peaked. Because of the popularity of budget line records, the increased sales helps to counteract the lower royalty received.

**20.3** Some budget labels are used for releasing cover records of the well known artiste's original recordings which are performed by other artistes, such as "hits in the style of", or "songs made famous by" albums. The packaging and advertising must not give the impression that the songs are the recordings originally made by the stars with whom they are closely associated. This side of the budget line market is aimed at those people who fancy the tune, and who are not fussy about who sings it. There are specialist budget line labels which acquire the use of popular original recordings from various record companies for inclusion in a compilation album. The tracks are chosen to be compatible within a limited type of music, such as nostalgia, rock, or teeny bop music. The budget label will negotiate a royalty rate direct with each track licensor, which will be agreed in the context of the proven sales potential of such compilations. These records tend to be nostalgic, and have the benefit of not incurring recording costs, and the required tracks are instantly available. It is a useful and profitable means of introducing to each new record buying generation the hits of yesteryear. The artiste's royalty will be within the "percentage of receipts" clause in his contract.

## 21 Copyright royalties

**21.1** On the sale of a record containing copyright musical works, the owner of the copyright in the song is entitled to be paid a royalty which the relevant law in each country specifies. These payments are made by the record companies direct to the copyright owners or to their collecting agents, such as the Mechanical Copyright Protection Society Ltd (MCPS). The payments do not affect, and are not connected with, the royalties or any other payments made by the record company to the artiste in respect of his performance. These payments are called mechanical royalties, which is confusing because they have no connection with the mechanical copyright in the record itself.

**21.2** The amounts of the mechanical royalty differ around the world, some countries charge a fixed rate per track, some adopt a percentage of retail selling price less taxes imposed in respect of the sale. The amount of the copyright payment due on a record sale based on a percentage of retail price is irrespective of the number of recorded tracks upon it, or the playing time of any track, or the playing time of the record as a whole. Where an album contains works with different music copyright owners, the mechanical royalty payable for the whole album is divided among the copyright owners in accordance with the number of tracks they each own.

**21.3** In the USA and Canada, for example, there is a minimum statutory mechanical fee per track, with a secondary calculation based on the playing time of the track, to be fair to very long tracks, and albums containing one continuous musical work. The amount of the mechanical royalty received by the owner of the copyright in the composition is irrespective of the royalty rate for the artiste and the selling price of the record.

## 22 Controlled compositions

**22.1** Some recording contracts impose conditions on the artiste in respect of musical compositions of which he is the writer, and over the publishing of which he has direct or indirect control. Other record companies will try to impose the conditions on songs written by the artiste, irrespective of whether or not he controls the publishing of them. In the USA and Canada there will also be a limitation on the number of tracks to be included in an album, and its total running time. This is to identify and limit the amount of the mechanical royalty to be paid on the album as a whole. Such compositions are generally referred to as "controlled compositions". This is because where the statutory payments are calculated on tracks and time, the record company wants to limit its payment liability. The intention of the record company may be to obtain a copyright licence at a reduced mechanical royalty rate from the writer/artiste and the publisher of the song (which would not otherwise be available or demanded) just because the artiste has some control over his publishing career. The intention of the clause should be to ensure that the record company is not charged in excess of the minimum rates by the publisher of the artiste/composer. A demand for a reduction would not be reasonable, but a sensible upper limit based on proper rates would be.

**22.2** The justification put forward by the record company for a reduced mechanical rate is that the artiste and the record company are engaged in a common venture, although they are not partners, and so the record company should be given the benefit of the reduced mechanical rate as a contribution by the artiste to the common cause. The major negotiable mechanical royalty is for the USA and Canada, the mechanical licence being issued by the American publisher in respect of North American record sales. Unless the artiste owns his own copyrights, such as through a wholly owned publishing company, he is not legally capable of giving the record company any assurance on the copyright royalty rate it will be charged.

Even if his publisher is receptive to the idea, no artiste should agree to such a clause unless in return he is getting an additional adequate financial benefit in some other way. The publisher cannot be compensated any other way under the recording deal. Why should an artiste/composer receive a lower copyright payment from his own record company than he would receive from any other record company whose artiste records a cover version of a controlled composition?

**22.3** Provided that the artiste/composer is otherwise compensated, there are categories of records where the record company which has to pay a fixed rate mechanical royalty could justify a reduced payment. These include promotional albums, and others disposed of at cost price or less to clear stocks, and any other record disposal on which the artiste does not get an artiste royalty. The reduction is not justified for budget label record sales, or mail order or record club sales, as the artiste has already substantially reduced his share of royalty in his capacity as an artiste. As no royalties at all are paid to the artiste on promotional and other "free" records distributed, if he is the composer of the recorded songs, the mechanical royalty is his only means of earning from those records, insofar as publishers make a charge for those categories of record sales.

**22.4** The artiste may not record only his own compositions, and as the record company has to pay the full minimum mechanical royalty rates for other composers' songs, there would be discrimination against the artiste if he were asked to procure a lower rate in respect of his controlled compositions. There is created a disincentive for him to record his own songs, and in any event the publisher (and copyright owner) of the controlled compositions may not wish to be bound to give the artiste's record company a reduced rate. What *quid pro quo* does it get for going so? A controlled composition clause does not commit the artiste to be in control of his publishing, or connected with it, so a side effect is that the artiste may rearrange his songwriting and publishing affairs legitimately to prevent his songs from coming within the controlled composition definition.

**22.5** Whether or not the song is a controlled composition, the following provisions will usually be included in a recording contract in which the company wishes to restrict the possibility of having an excessive liability to mechanical copyright payments:

(a) A limitation on the amount of the mechanical royalties to be paid by the record company on the sale of all records in North America. This is done either by agreeing a fixed monetary rate per record irrespective of the number of tracks it contains, or by agreeing the statutory minimum mechanical royalty rate per track with a specified limit to the number of tracks on each record for which the royalty will be paid. It will then be the artiste's responsibility to ensure that the album he records contains only the number of tracks, or the music playing time, which complies with the limits.

The limitation should apply to albums only. If an album delivered to the record company commits it to paying mechanical royalties in excess of the agreed maximum by reason of the playing time, or the number of copyrights recorded on it, the recording agreement will normally state that the excess will be recoverable from the artiste's royalties as a performer. The artiste will therefore ensure that the limits are achieved, as he receives the whole of the artiste's royalties, but perhaps only 60% of the ultimate mechanical royalty on record sales received by his publisher.

(b) An undertaking by the artiste to procure that mechanical licences will be granted to the record company in accordance with whatever is agreed in (a). Unless in fact he has absolute control over the music publishing company, or unless he is specifically authorised by it to do so, no such undertaking can be given by him, and he must ensure that the recording contract contains no such reference. If he is the composer, the requirement is reasonable. As it is a crucial point where it applies, the artiste should get confirmation from his USA publisher that only the applicable statutory minimum royalty will be charged.

(c) Clarification of what constitutes a musical work eligible for the mechanical royalty. For example, a track's worth of what could only be described as bland background music would not be acceptable to the record company, its safeguard is not to accept it under the "acceptable commercial quality" clauses. A totally unacceptable clause would be one stating that no mechanical royalty will be paid on any recorded musical work which is based on a composition in the public domain. If the recorded song is a copyright work in itself without question, even though based on a public domain work, and if it is accepted as such by all the copyright income collection societies, the mechanical royalty must be paid. Again, this would be a matter of dispute with the publisher, but the artiste should not be penalised. One purpose of the clause is to try to ensure that the record company only gets original songs recorded by the artiste on the album. Another purpose is to prevent the publisher and the artiste from claiming copyright royalties on what might be dubious grounds. Commercially, the record company's view should be "that which sells is good".

(d) Where a song has an interpolation of part of a separate copyright work, which is sufficiently substantial to require payment of the minimum statutory mechanical royalty, the amount paid for that interpolation will be part of the agreed maximum mechanical royalty payable for the whole album.

**22.6** Outside North America, when a record company controls territories which have different mechanical royalty rates, it is clear what is payable where the record is sold in the country of its manufacture. If the record company exports a record from a manufacturing country for the purpose of retail sale in another country:

(a) Even though the mechanical royalty rate may be the same, the retail price of the record is not likely to be the same in the two countries. So the choice of the country in respect of which the mechanical royalty is to be paid will decide the amount paid. It should be paid in the country in which the retail sale takes place.

(b) The local sub-publisher of a song in the country of importation of records containing that song, which are then sold, will never receive any mechanical royalties from sales of that record if the record company were to pay the mechanical royalty in the country of manufacture. The local sub-publisher of that song in the exporting country would then receive mechanical royalties on records not sold in his territory. There can be no incentive for the sub-publisher of the songs in the importing country to obtain local language cover records of the composition, as he has no means of earning from them, if those records are manufactured in another country, unless the mechanical royalty is paid in the country of retail sale.

**22.7** The mechanical royalty is payable irrespective of who performs the composition on the record sold, and regardless of the style of rendition, or the arrangement of the composition.

## 23 Other copyright fees

**23.2** Other potential copyright payments, which should be dealt with on a once-only fee basis are:

(a) Lyric sheets which may be included within the packaging of the album. The lyrics can be printed either on the album sleeve, or on a paper insert with the record in the sleeve. The publisher of the lyrics, as the copyright owner, must give permission for them to be used, and for which a fee is charged. It is impractical to charge a rate per record sold, as for a literary work, as the accounting problems (such as free records, returns etc) and the profit margins would not allow for such a payment.

(b) The album artwork, and any copyright photographs used in it, which were acquired independently of any specific front cover artwork commission. Whether a painting or a photograph is used for the front cover, and for any other photograph or copyright work included anywhere on the album sleeve, either the copyright must be assigned, or the limited use must be licensed, to the record company. Whichever it is should be confirmed in writing. The licence must be worldwide, and to use the material as an album cover, or for any other use to do with the recording, and for posters and advertising and promotional material for marketing the record without restrictions. If the front cover is a painting, the original of which is retained by the painter, the record company may want an option to purchase it.

**23.3** If the record company commissioned the photograph or the painting, it should ensure that it had the copyright assigned to it. An exclusive worldwide licence would be necessary where the painting is already in existence, and the painter or other owner of both the painting and the copyright in it does not wish to sell it, but will agree to its use as an album cover. A word of warning in respect of photographs and paintings. Ownership of the article itself is not evidence of ownership of the copyright in it. The purchaser of a painting does not automatically get the copyright, that has to be specifically assigned to him in writing by the painter, or whoever has obtained the copyright from the painter. The same will apply to the possession of a photograph, or a photographic negative. The record company must get reasonable proof that the person purporting to give the consent to make commercial use if the work is entitled to do so, ie, that he is the owner of the copyright in the item. Failure to get it right will result in an expensive claim for compensation. The usual credits contained on the album artwork should also give the owner of the painting his credit, and should set out his copyright notice in respect of the painting, although the copyright of the whole album sleeve (including the painting) will be credited to the owner of the recording.

## 24 Period of contract

**24.1** Most artistes try to renegotiate their recording contracts in their favour in times of success, but they would never voluntarily offer to reduce the royalty or advances payable by the record company because the artistes have hit a bad patch of unsuccessful records. Record companies would like to be able to terminate an unprofitable artiste's contract as soon as it is convenient to the record company, but would like to retain a successful artiste for as long as possible.

**24.2** As in any other form of contract, a recording agreement can be for a fixed number of years, or on an annual option basis up to a maximum period. The period can also be related to the delivery to the record company of a number of albums, either as a fixed number, or with options for further albums (up to a maximum number) following the delivery of an initial number of albums. Although there may be a time table in the recording agreement for the delivery of recordings, if the period of the contract is not conditional upon the number of albums delivered to the record company, the opportunity for the record company to make back its investment in the artiste, represented by advances and production and promotion costs, can be jeopardised by an artiste who never gets round to finishing his "hit album".

**24.3** Many recording contracts contain a clause entitled the record company to suspend the period of the agreement for lack of records delivered to it, for strikes preventing the manufacture of records, for breach of contract, for *force majeure*, and for whatever else seems relevant. The only commercially valid reason for suspension of the contract period is where the artiste agreed to deliver to the record company a certain number of albums, and the financial provisions of the deal both as to advances and royalty rates were negotiated on that basis, and the artiste has failed to deliver his minimum number of recordings. All other reasons, except for breach of contract, have nothing to do with the artiste and are beyond his control. Where the contract includes suspension provisions, there must be a longstop terminal date, whatever the circumstances, to prevent the contract being unenforceable for uncertainty of time. Where the artiste has split his worldwide recording rights between two companies, both starting at the same time, he will want them to end at the same time. If one contract contains suspension provisions which are activated, this will not happen.

**24.5** The right to suspend the period of the contract is only acceptable to give reasonable assurance to the record company of fulfilment by the artiste of his original obligations, ie, to provide properly recorded albums. Artistes are advised to delete any ill-defined or sweeping reference to rights of the record company to suspend the period of the recording contract. If such a clause is agreed to by the artiste, it must be specific and it must contain proper and reasonable safeguards for the artiste.

**24.6** If the recording contract includes suspension rights in favour of the record company and for example, if the record company suspends the current contract year for a *force majeure* reason unconnected with the artiste, and prior to or within the period of suspension the artiste has delivered his minimum recording commitment for that contract year, then the period of his recording contract is increased through no fault of his own. This is not acceptable. By way of comparison, the record company does not agree that each contract year will be deemed to have expired on delivery of the last of the records to be made in that year, so that the next contract year can start earlier, giving the artiste the ability to reduce legitimately his total exclusive contracted period. This can be achieved by not having contract years, but by relating the contract period to album delivery dates.

The wording of the *force majeure* suspension clause might enable the record company to suspend the period of the contract, if for example, its Antarctic factory froze and stopped manufacturing records. This incapacitating event in no way affects the other 99% of the record company's worldwide activities, and so should not be able to trigger any suspension rights. There must be a limitation on the severity of, or the territorial extent of, an incapacitating event upon the happening of which the record company can suspend the entire recording contract term, and it must relate to or affect the artiste's obligations. Even if, through some catastrophe, the record company was wholly inoperative for three months, if that did not affect the ability of the artiste to perform his own obligations, it is not material to his contract, and should not affect it. Where the period of the contract is directly linked to the delivery of the recordings, the determining factor must be the date of delivery by the artiste of each album, and not the date of release of the album by the record company. The delivery date should be the date upon which the record company receives all of a fully edited master tape and completion of all album artwork, including copyright credits.

**24.7** If there is an album delivery schedule whereby the next album shall not be delivered to the record company before a given date, or after a given date following delivery of the previous album (beyond which period suspension may apply), the artiste should never be in the position of being prevented by the record company from fulfilling those obligations, due to a contract period suspension for any event with which he is not connected. This form of scheduling applies where the contract period relates to the delivery of, say, five albums. The record company does not want all five delivered over a short period of time. This aspect is discussed in paragraph **8.6** of chapter five.

## 25 Minimum recordings

**25.1** An exclusive recording contract with an artiste should oblige the record company to make, or to afford the artiste the opportunity of making, say, not less than one album in each contract year. If that minimum recording obligation is not fulfilled due to the default of the record company, the artiste has a reduced ability to earn money under the contract, and in extreme circumstances he should be entitled to terminate it. Delay in recording an album may be because it was agreed that a number of singles would be released first, to get public reaction to the artiste before incurring the expense of recording an album. If that has been done with little success, and the record company does not wish to proceed to an album, it should release the artiste from its contract. "Default" would not include circumstances where the record company refuses to provide money or facilities to enable the artiste to make a recording until he complies with his own outstanding obligations, if they are material. An artiste's right of termination should apply whether or not the record company has a record release commitment, as without recordings being made, there is nothing to release. The artiste should not accept any compromise on this point, such as the record company being able to extinguish its obligation by making a nominal payment to him in lieu of each of the minimum recordings it has not allowed him to make.

**25.2** No record company will accept an obligation to actually release a minimum number of records made by the artiste during any contract year. A record company is only likely not to want to release an album if it fails to qualify as being of commercially acceptable quality, in which case it will not come within the definition of an accepted album. No record company will sit on an accepted album, not release it, and require the artiste to record a second album. He may be allowed to do some more recording in an effort to get the rejected album into an acceptable state.

**25.3** Some recording contracts entitle the record company to carry forward any recordings made in excess of the minimum commitment in any one year towards satisfaction of the minimum recording commitment in the next year. This would not apply to a contract based on only a specific number of albums to be delivered. If the minimum commitment is one album a year, two albums made in one year and none in the next year, would be bad planning, and a waste of resources in the barren year. Such a clause should be modified if the contract entitles the record company to call for more than the minimum recording commitment within the contract year, to ensure that there will be an accelerated recording schedule, and no unproductive contract year. If the clause is agreed, an alternative is that satisfaction of the next year's worth of recordings simply shortens the total period of the contract by substituting a number of recordings for a period of time. Where the minimum recording obligation is a modest number of single play records in each contract year, the making of an album's worth of recordings in the first year might cover the minimum recording obligation for the whole term of the contract, although that will not be intended. In such a case, an optional album should be treated as an additional recording, not being in substitution for existing commitments.

**25.4** The contract must also specify clearly what is meant by a "recording", which, unless it is properly defined, could mean a single recorded track, or a single record with A and B sides, or even an album. It should also specify that each recording must be newly recorded. If the minimum recording commitment is so many singles and so many albums, the contract should specify whether that means new recordings for the albums. Otherwise the record company can economise and help to fulfil its minimum album recording commitment by consolidating some of the already recorded (but not yet released) single records, together with some new tracks to be recorded. The recording commitment is satisfied by making the recordings, whether or not they are released.

**25.5** It is a common practice to make an album, and to release a single record from it prior to the album's release, to generate interest in it. If, shortly after the release of an album, the artiste records a hit single which becomes a hit, it is possible for the next pressing of that album to contain the "A" side of the hit single. Alternatively, if the album is found to have sold on the strength of one or two tracks, these can be issued as a single record at a later date, to revive the album sales when they have passed their peak. Duplicated releases of recorded tracks should not be counted towards the minimum recording commitment. The definition of minimum recordings will normally state that a live album will not count towards it. Because live albums usually contain mostly tracks previously recorded by the artiste on studio albums, record companies will restrict the number of live albums it is prepared to accept and release within the total contract period. There should also be some reference to acceptance or not of project albums, or soundtrack albums if the artiste is a composer in demand for film or TV music.

## 26 Promotion budgets

**26.1** Each record company has its own system of budgeting for the promotion of records by trade advertisements, merchandise such as "T" shirts and badges, window displays in shops, purchase incentives, through to expensive TV advertising. There will be a basic level of promotion which any record company will give any album. Above that level, the potential value of the album to the record company through expected sales will determine the advertising intensity, and the willingness of the record company to spend money on special projects.

**26.2** Greater promotional effort is required at the start of an artiste's recording career, so the record company is investing to create the rewards to come from the success of future recordings. Successful artistes still need promotion to make the public aware of the existence of their next album, as well as to persuade them to buy it. No part of a record company's promotional budget is recoverable from the artiste's royalties, except for any special item of an unusual nature the cost of which is first agreed to be shared with the artiste. A record company will monitor carefully what it spends on promotion, as that expenditure reduces the company's profit on the album. An album heavily promoted at great cost, but with unexpectedly low sales, may not earn for the record company what it has spent on promoting it. An example will be the cost of unsuccessfully promoting an album by TV advertising.

**26.3** As promotion costs do not affect the artiste, there is a challenge for him to make the record company commit to a substantial promotion budget for each album. The record company will ultimately spend only what it considers the album merits. As the record company will have a corporate annual promotion budget, excessive expenditure on a promotion obligation to an artiste can act to his detriment if the record company has to reduce its ordinary promotional expenditure on the artiste.

**26.4** Record companies are also requested by the artiste's manager for financial support towards an anticipated loss when the artiste is about to tour a foreign country to promote his first album. When the artiste is relatively unknown, and so cannot demand high concert fees, the cost of putting on the tour is likely to exceed the tour income. Wherever possible, a tour in a country should be timed to coincide with the release there of an album, so that the tour can promote it. Personal appearances, with the media promotion given to them, have a significant effect on local record sales. Tours are used by the record company as a focal point of specific advertising, to concentrate attention on the ability of the record buyer to see the artiste. Reasonable tour support from the record company by way of contribution to tour losses should be treated as a promotional expense, and not a recoupable advance, as the tour is also of benefit to the record company. It is for the record company to agree with its local distributor/subsidiary/licensee which of them contributes what to the support of the tour. The record company will normally require that:

(a) The tour support payment is not a previously agreed cash figure based on the artiste's forecast of expense, as that would be an incentive for the artiste to inflate his forecast and make a profit on the tour support payment—or simply to spend unnecessarily. It should be a commitment to pay for the tour finance shortfall, up to a maximum amount.

(b) Should the record company so request, all tour income and expense will be audited to ascertain the tour loss. Any contribution by the record company will be either up to a cash limit, or it will be the payment of specified expenses, such as air fares. If the tour support liability is substantial, the record company should ascertain in advance what payments and expenses in the course of the tour will be legitimate for the audit purpose, and so for the calculation of tour loss to be supported.

(c) Financial support will probably be limited to the first tour of one major market under the recording agreement and not, for example, extended to the first tour of every country.

(d) The management and agency commission payable by the artiste on gross tour income is not normally included as an expense for the purpose of calculating the overall tour loss which the record company has agreed to support. A valid record company view would be that, as they have no control over the level of those commissions, they should not subsidise them. Also they are not an inevitable expense which is essential to enable the tour to take place.

## 27 Advertising and promotion

**27.1** When a record has been released, for it to be successful, the public must be made aware that it exists, and they must be induced to buy it. Record companies regularly publish their new release list, so that the record retail trade is kept well informed. Further advertising may be undertaken in the popular weekly record and music publications, as well as through other media, such as local radio stations and posters. In such a competitive business so much of the advertising material uses startling and artistically original themes, which, if taken in isolation will catch the eye, but if presented as part only of a large display may only confuse. Advertising, as opposed to promotion, is a passive means of drawing the attention of the record buying public to a particular artiste or record. How this is done most effectively will depend upon the type of music of the artiste, and upon how his public image is being built up.

Promotion covers the more active areas of advertising and publicity, such as press reviews and receptions, shop window displays, and arranging for the record to be played on radio, and for the artiste to appear on television.

**27.2** The record company needs the full co-operation of the artiste in providing photographs, biographical material and anything else for use in advertising. If the artiste employs a press and publicity consultant, he must keep the record company well informed. Any artiste will be sensitive to some degree of his public image. The consent of the artiste should be sought for the use of specific biographical material or photos, which consent should not be unreasonably withheld. A significant proportion of album sales is influenced by the visual appeal of the sleeve, which has much value as an advertising medium by registering recognition in the minds of fans who scan the record racks, and by being the basis of posters and other visual forms of advertising.

**27.3** Because sophisticated recording studio equipment can enhance a mediocre voice, when the artiste appears live, the audience expects his performance to reach the standards set for him by his records and his promotion. A successful artiste must have personality or an appeal on stage. To some extent this can be manufactured in the minds of the fans through clever promotion, but it should not oversell the artiste so as to positively misrepresent his capability.

**27.4** With effective promotion and sufficient expenditure it is possible to generate enough sales to put an album into the lower regions of the record popularity charts. From then on it will only continue on its way up if it has the necessary individual quality or appeal. The payment of money, either as a fee or to provide funds for the purchase of records in quantity, so that the record can be bought into the popularity charts, is dishonest practice. It is a form of bribery and corruption, and the reputable people in the record business keep well clear of it and actively discourage it.

**27.5** The need for success is a vicious circle. With the exception of firmly established artistes, a record will not come to the attention of the public unless it is broadcast on radio record programmes. The record of an unknown artiste usually will not be selected for such a programme unless it reaches the record sales charts. As (obviously) no record reaches the comparative charts without achieving significant sales, the impression given by the initial promotion behind a new album or single is essential to get things moving. Selected wholesale or retail record shops spaced throughout the country make returns to the company publishing the charts of sales of records in each week. The combined lists give a reasonable indication of the relative popularity of records sold during that week. Each record company knows how its own artiste's records are selling, but it may not have accurate information for comparison of its record sales with those of other record companies. Promotion generally of the artiste in his career should emphasise his most recent successful record release. An artiste may become synonymous with one particular hit record, which becomes from then on his signature tune. Provided the tune remains popular and recognisable, it is a handy promotion vehicle.

## 28 Coupling and compilations

**28.1** The combination of recorded tracks contained on an album is known as "coupling", for want of a better description. A compilation album is one which is literally compiled, ie, it contains a variety of tracks by different artistes, or by the same artiste but chosen from different albums. For a top artiste it may be essential that his type of music is heard within a certain context, so his album track selections and choice of coupling are carefully thought out. Record companies are reluctant to accept any restriction on their absolute freedom to use each individual recording of an artiste in any compilation or combination. The restrictions normally are that the album will never be released in any other format different from that as delivered, without the consent of the artiste. Also, none of the artiste's recordings are to be put onto a compilation album with tracks by other artistes without his consent. In each case the consent should not be unreasonably withheld or delayed.

**28.2** Unless restrictions are imposed upon the record company by the artiste in the recording contract, once it has released the original album as recorded by the artiste, it will be entitled to make use of the individual tracks in its absolute discretion. It will not have to consult the artiste or the record producer or anyone else before doing so. It is important to a major artiste that the coupling of any of his recordings together with recordings by other artistes is not used in a derogatory manner, such as together with a collection of unpopular or inferior performances to tempt people to buy the record because of the major artiste's track. Such a clause would have to specify in detail what the record company would be entitled to do, and what it is restricted from doing.

**28.3** There are various ways of reviving tracks from an album which has had its day, and therefore of making the best use of an asset already paid for. A record company with many star artistes, subject to any contractual restrictions, can make a compilation album containing one or more tracks from records made for it by each of such artistes. Where a compilation album is produced in limited quantities for promotion purposes only, it is called a "sampler" record, but these should only be produced for new artistes. Unless there are strict limitations on the numbers of sampler records pressed, and on their destination and selling price, they should be treated as regular compilation records for royalty calculation purposes.

**28.4** A minor record company, with only one or two star artistes, and several unknown artistes, may promote the unknown artistes by releasing a compilation album, consisting of a selection of tracks by the lesser artistes together with one or more tracks by star artistes on it. The intention is to get some sales, in the hope that the minor artistes will be heard, like, and become known and popular in their own right.

**28.5** Selections of recordings from an artiste's album can be re-issued on extended play records, or a single record may contain an edited version of an album track, with the intention of promoting it into the charts on its own merit. The record track being promoted will be nominated as the "A" side, intended to be given prominence on radio programmes. Great thought is given to what should be the supporting "B" side track. If another potential hit composition is used, the value of it is unprofitably absorbed in needless competition with the "A" side track. Where a "token" or "filler" track is used for the "B" side merely to complete the single record, buyers may think that the price of a single record is too high for only one good track. A "token" track is one which is an acceptable "B" side composition, carefully chosen not to be competitive with the "A" side. Where no suitable material is available, an old favourite song, given a face lift by a new arrangement, is sometimes used as the "B" side.

**28.6** A major artiste will want to be consulted by the record company upon the couplings of his recordings in compiling any proposed record, whether or not containing wholly his own performances. Where an artiste becomes known through a series of successful singles, and the record company decides to release an album of the artiste's recordings, the choice of which established and which newly recorded and unreleased performances to use can be crucial to the success of the album. Many artistes assume that the record company has to keep to the format of the album as delivered, where negotiations on the recording contract terms never dealt with the point.

**28.7** Certain record companies specialise in putting together and releasing compilation albums. There is a pattern to the choice of tracks on each album, both as to the artiste and the song. Such compilations are not limited to the artistes of any particular record company. Each track is chosen for its selling power, whoever the artiste and whatever the song, there being no intention to create an opportunity to promote an unknown or mediocre product. The consent of the owner of the mechanical copyright in the recording is required. The compilation record company will negotiate a royalty with each participating record company, which will share that licence receipt with the artiste, in accordance with the terms of the recording contract.

## 29 Re-recording restrictions

**29.1** All recording contracts prohibit the artiste from recording for any other party, within a number of years after the end of the recording contract, any composition which has been recorded by him for the record company during the exclusive period of the agreement. The prohibition is intended to prevent an artiste from changing record companies, and immediately re-recording for the second record company all his previous hit songs, some of which may be still selling many records. This is in effect an extension of the exclusive rights of the record company over the content of those recordings beyond the expiry of the exclusive contract period. If the artiste does well with his new company, that can create a "second wind" demand for his previous recordings, to the benefit of the record company which owns or controls them.

**29.2** If the artiste could re-record successful songs for another company immediately after the expiry of his contract with a record company, there would be confusion in the minds of record buyers, and the value of the first record company of its rights in the original recordings of the artiste would be eliminated. As the provision is a protective measure for the first record company, it would not be logical to extend the restrictive period for re-recording compositions beyond the expiry of the period for which the first record company has exclusive rights in the original recording. If the first record company owns the rights in the recordings, an arbitrary but reasonable restricted period is used. The record company might be willing to consider limiting the restriction period to, for example, the period ending one year after the recording has been deleted from the record company's current catalogue, or, say, seven years from delivery of the recording to it, whichever is the longer.

**29.3** Where the record company owns the recordings made by the artiste which are not released during the exclusive period of the agreement, they can still be released by it at any time afterwards. Therefore the re-recording restriction must be for a time which runs from a known date, such as the date of delivery of the recording to the record company, or the termination date of the exclusive period of the recording agreement, whichever is the later. If it runs from the date of first release of the record, there must be a committed record release schedule, so that in the absence of a release date, the last date of the committed release period can be the starting date of the re-recording restriction period.

**29.4** It is difficult to evaluate the damage which the previous record company suffers if the artiste breaches his undertaking and re-records a song within the prohibited period. If the re-recording follows closely upon the release of the original record by the previous record company, which is selling well, inevitably the re-recorded record will be bought by people who would otherwise have bought the original record. If the record company becomes aware of the intention of the artiste to re-record a song in breach of his undertaking, it could get an injunction against him. If the record company only becomes aware of it after it has been released, what can it do? It can claim damages from the artiste for the breach, but could it injunct the other record company? The re-recording is not an infringement of copyright, it is just the result of a breach of contract by the artiste. The court may decide either way, depending on the cirumstances, and the "balance of convenience" commercially.

If the re-recording is released a substantial way into the period of prohibition, it could revive the declining sales of the original record, and the previous record company would suffer no loss. If the previous record has been deleted from the first record company's current catalogue, it will suffer no damage from sales of the re-recording. If the artiste releases a re-recorded song after the expiry of the restricted period, even though it may be proved to have been recorded within the restricted period, the previous record company may have difficulty in proving that it has been caused loss and damage. The wording of the restriction should specify whether it is the re-recording or the re-release which is to be the breach. It will normally be the re-recording.

**29.5** If the artiste changes from one group to another, which new group performs live during the prohibited period one of his previously recorded hits, and the concert is recorded, he would be in breach of his undertaking. If the second group is already successful in its own right, the performance by it of a cover version of the original song, which for the artiste (who is a new member) is a re-recording, it will sell records irrespective of the new member's presence. The real damage to the previous record company will be difficult to establish. The effect of the re-recording restriction will also depend on the artiste. If he is the lead singer of the group, and is the composer of the song, then breach of the restriction is a serious matter. If the artiste was the group's drummer, and was not the composer of the song, in this example the breach would be more of a technicality, than a real threat to the previous record company.

**29.6** To give them an additional selling period for their records without competition, some record companies include in their artiste's contracts a condition that the artiste will not release his first recording with a new record company until the expiry of so many months following the termination of his existing recording agreement. The reason given is that if the record company has released the last of the recordings made for it by the artiste only a short time before his exclusive contract expired, or even shortly afterwards, the additional period of no competition gives the record company a reasonable chance to promote the newly released record. That is reasonable, and in any event it may take some months before the artiste records and releases a new album. It would not be reasonable if the last recorded album for the record company was released a year previously, and its sales peaked even before the expiry of the recording agreement.

## 30 Accounts

**30.1** Record companies ought to account quarterly to the artiste, as computerised accounting is universal. Some will account half yearly, the only difference is one of cash flow for the artiste. Accounts ought to be deliverable within 30 or 45 days, after the just completed accounting period. The record company statement should contain details of record sales in each territory for which it has rights, whether at full price or not; all advances made or deemed to be made (such as recording costs) and their state of recoupment; all other material information, and the net amount (if any) due to the artiste—together with a cheque.

**30.2** As with other agreements, the artiste must have the right to audit the record company's accounts. If necessary where clearly something is wrong, the record company should authorise the artiste to get information and verification direct from licensees and others who have accounted to the record company, or it should exercise its own audit rights against them to clarify anything which seems not to be correct.

# CHAPTER 5

# *Independent Record Production Agreements*

## SECTION I: GENERAL COMMENTS

### 1 General

**1.1** An artiste either enters into a contract direct with a record company for his recording services, or he contracts with a production company, which records the artiste and sells or leases the master tapes of the recordings to the record company. There may be many reasons for using a production company. A successful artiste may want to own the mechanical copyright in all of his recordings, a potentially valuable asset. A new artiste may be unable to get a direct signing to a record company. A production company may be used by a music publisher for the benefit of a composer/artiste signed to it. The production company wants its product released commercially, and the record company wants to keep its risk under control.

**1.2** Historically production companies were a fruitful source of new talent for record companies. In recent years it has become very difficult to get any kind of deal with a major record company, because of the economics of the business, and the choice of available artistes, who normally sign direct deals. Nevertheless, it is useful to have production deals explained.

Even if the production company will be providing the record company with unknown artistes, or if it is not already a significant influence in the business of the record company, the record company will give it a credit for the production of the recordings it provides. The credits should appear on the record sleeve with the other credits, and also on the disc label. A production company which may have successful, or potentially successful, artistes needs an outlet for its recordings to the record buying public. At the other end of this scale the production company can also negotiate with a record company for the manufacture and distribution of records using the production company's name, label or logo.

**1.3** Each production agreement with a record company is different, because the requirements of the parties vary in each case. This chapter deals with those points which are most likely to be raised for discussion within the negotiations between a record company and a production company in connection with different kinds of production deals. In respect of full-blooded production deals as described in section III of this chapter, it also assumes that:

(a) The production company has overcome the first hurdle of persuading a record company to take its product.

(b) There is an umbrella agreement between the production company and the record company whereby the record company may choose to take artistes found by the production company, and may reject others. Those others are then not retained by the production company. Having chosen an artiste, there is an agreement between the companies dealing with that specific artiste, when there is a choice between the following:

(i) the production agreement setting out the royalty, advances, period and so forth which will appertain to all chosen artistes, who are all dealt with under the same agreement.

(ii) the contractual terms for each chosen artiste being agreed independently, and dealt with in separate agreements.

To avoid confusion, a (b)(i) deal will be called a "production deal", and a (b)(ii) deal will be called an "artiste deal". The contractual differences relate mainly to the recoupment of advances as between the record company and the production company, and product delivery.

**1.4** Section II of this chapter deals with the following types of production agreement:

(a) logo agreements (paragraph **3**);
(b) a pressing and distribution deal (paragraph **4**);
(c) label agreements (paragraph **5**).

Section III of this chapter deals with matters relevant mostly to a label deal, but as there is no set format for a production deal, their relevance ought to be considered for any deal.

## 2 Production company functions

**2.1** With the increasing cost to the record companies of launching and promoting artistes, the number of new artistes they are prepared to sign is controlled by their investment budgets. Therefore it can be difficult to place an unknown artiste as a direct signing with a record company. The artiste's chances can be increased by a production company undertaking the initial risk and effort which might be unacceptable to the record company.

**2.2** Where the production agreement is limited to an artiste deal, the record company can more easily assess its risk, and its negotiation of the financial terms is less defensive. If the agreement is a production deal, negotiation will include fairly stringent safeguards for the record company, both financially and on an artistic level. Record companies will not normally commit to "unseen" artistes, the present scrutiny system is too thorough.

**2.3** Because the production company normally acts as a principal when negotiating with the artiste, whether it is a production deal or an artiste deal, the obligations it has to the artiste in his recording agreement are its own responsibility, and the record company has no direct responsibility to the artiste. Nevertheless, to some extent the production company will have obligations to the artiste of honesty and good faith, and must act accordingly in its negotiations with a record company. Important aspects are:

(a) The difference in the royalty rate received by the production company from the record company, and that paid by the production company to the artiste.

(b) Defining what proportion (if any) of royalty advances received by the production company should be paid to the artiste. Payment could be when the advance is received by the production company, or when the artiste completes the relevant album recording, whichever is the later.

(c) Establishing the minimum commitment of album delivery in each contract year to which the record company will be entitled.

(d) The maximum period for which the artiste may be committed to the record company, if it takes up all of its options.

**2.4** A production company negotiating on an arms-length basis with the artiste can choose whether or not to disclose to him the proportion of royalty paid by it to the artiste out of the royalty rate received by it from the record company, and the value of the advances it receives, provided that the deal it offers the artiste is fair and reasonable. A production company which is connected with the artiste's manager must disclose to him what royalty and advance payments it is receiving, and they must agree the proportion to be retained by it. This applies to any other benefit receivable by the production company when it is not a genuine arms-length company. Any complaint by the artiste usually relates to money, or wanting an account of other benefits received by the production company, or the lack of promotion of his recordings.

**2.5** Record production costs are treated as an advance by the production company to the artiste on account of, and recoupable from, his royalty earnings. This is the same as a direct signing artiste's record company deal. It is the production company, and not the artiste, which receives the royalty advances from the record company, even though they are intended as a contribution to the costs of making the artiste's recordings. Contractually the artiste is due royalties only on record sales. In the absence of agreement to the contrary, he is not entitled as of right to a share of advances received by the production company, even if they are related only to delivery of his recordings to the record company. This point is even more important to the production company where the advance does not cover the whole of the costs of recording the artiste's album. The artiste may be concerned that if he does not secure a portion of the advances, the production company will not have available cash to pay his royalties as and when they become due.

**2.6** There is no obligation on the production company, by custom or otherwise, to offer to the artiste any specific proportion of the royalty rate it receives from the record company, the royalty rate agreed is a matter of negotiation. If the artiste is paid a ridiculously low rate of royalty by the production company, taking into account all other benefits it receives under its agreement with the record company, the agreement with the artiste might be considered to be unreasonable and unduly oppressive. To stand the test of time, any agreement with the artiste must be fair and reasonable.

**2.7** The terms of the agreement with the record company also affect the terms which the production company must have in its artiste's agreements. (See paragraph **14** onwards). The production company is in the middle of a deal which, for all parties, must be as commercially workable and contractually watertight as possible. Some of the points raised in this chapter have also been referred to in chapter four on direct signing artistes' agreements with record companies. The production company should first negotiate its deal with the record company, then it is able to set up its artistes' contracts with consistent terms and conditions. The production company's approach may be different, depending on whether it is an artistes deal or a production deal with the record company.

## SECTION II: TYPES OF AGREEMENT

### 3 Logo agreements

The production deals described in paragraphs **3** and **5** below are means whereby new talent is found for record companies. Paragraph **4** deals with the independent style of production over which the record company has no control, and in which it has no risk.

**3.1** The simplest form of agreement with a record company is for the production company to provide it exclusively with the recordings of such of the production company's artistes as the record company chooses to take. The record company wholly funds the cost of recording, and takes the whole of the financial risk. As this is the closest type of agreement to the direct signing of an artiste to a record company, in agreeing which of the production company's artistes to accept, the record company will apply much the same artistic and economic criteria as it would have applied to deciding upon a direct signing of that artiste. Recordings of the agreed artistes will be released on the label of the record company, and the production company remains in the background.

**3.2** The production company will be given credit through its logo on the record sleeve and disc label, but so far as the public is concerned, the artiste appears to record for the record company. There are advantages for the artiste and the production company in using the identity of the record company in this way, as it has an established name, substantial funds, an effective promotion department, and the means of releasing the artiste's records in other countries.

**3.3** A disadvantage to the production company in a logo production agreement is that, however successful its artistes become in the future, it does not get the benefit of having its name prominently linked with their recordings. If the production company becomes successful quickly, it may be able to negotiate with the record company for an individual label identity at the right time.

**3.4** Unless the record company places restrictions on the production company (see paragraph **9.1**), it need not enter into an exclusive production agreement with the record company for all of its artistes, the record company itself will want to pick and choose artistes submitted to it. If the production company has several artistes available, by remaining independent it can retain the advantage of being able to offer the other artistes to different companies. The choice will be influenced by the financial terms offered, and the willingness and ability of the chosen record company to do more for the artiste than any other interested record company. Whether this strategy can be successful depends on the economic law of supply and demand. There are more artistes wanting a recording deal than record companies willing to take them, so the record companies can and do choose carefully.

**3.5** Where an artiste is comparing different record company offers for a direct signing, the companies have all the scope they need to vary their usual terms in an effort to obtain the artiste's exclusive recording services. A production company, which has an exclusive production agreement with a record company which will cover any of its artistes which are accepted, can only negotiate with an artiste within those limits in respect of royalty rates, advance payments and a minimum recording commitment.

**3.6** One reason for a production company being prepared to commit all of its artistes through one record company exclusively is that, in return, the record company will assist the production company by taking over the financing of its artiste's recordings. The production company would otherwise need considerable financial resources to pay for an increasing number of recordings to be made during each year of the production agreement. New artistes found in each year, and which are accepted by the record company, must be recorded, while at the same time existing artistes will have their own schedules for recordings to be made during the year. As part of the overall production deal, the production company and the record company must agree a system of submitting artistes for approval by the record company. Possibly there will be no new artistes in a given year, it depends on available finance.

**3.7** As the record company deals with the record release administration, including the manufacture, distribution and promotion involved, the production company does not have the legal responsibility for the administration and payment of mechanical copyright royalties.

## 4 Pressing and distribution agreements

**4.1** A production company can have an independent operation, where it is in the place of, and has the same function as, a record company so far as the artiste is concerned. The main differences are that:

(a) it may not have the same financial capacity as a record company to deal with many artistes at the same time;

(b) it contracts with specialist record companies for the use of their record pressing and distribution facilities.

The production company's exclusive recording agreement with the artiste must enable the production company to act in its absolute discretion in the decisions on when, where, and by what means recordings made by the artiste will be released. But it must make a meaningful commercial effort to do so.

**4.2** Each record company has its own distribution arrangements whereby the wholesale centres, retail shops and other outlets are kept supplied adequately with records made by that company's artistes. The essence of a pressing and distribution agreement (a P & D deal) is that the production company makes use of the record manufacturing and distribution facilities offered by a record company operating in the P & D business, for a fee. The principal points to be negotiated are:

(a) The manufacture of records by the record company from master tapes supplied by the production company, with special reference to:
  (i) priority of pressing time on machines, particularly when there are pressure periods, such as at Christmas;
  (ii) the numbers of records to be pressed initially, and the arrangements for re-pressing when stocks are low,

(b) The printing of sleeves for albums. The quantities will be related to the number of records being pressed, and should include additional sleeves for use in window displays and other promotions. As P & D companies use independent contractors for sleeve printing, it may be wise to have an initial sleeve print run which will be adequate for one album re-pressing schedule, to fulfil any unforeseen demand for the records which arises at short notice.

(c) Distribution of records to shops. Either the production company will do its own distribution, or more likely it will use the distribution facilities of the P & D company. The P & D company will have a country-wide efficient distribution system, and its salesmen will have their contacts and credibility with the shops they service. The distribution may have to be on a sale or return basis.

(d) The storage of stocks of records, and the maintenance of stock levels. Records are only pressed when, and in quantities, decided by the production company, taking account of the cost, and so as not to create excessive stocks.

(e) Administering the music copyright royalty payments. The P & D company will want to be indemnified by the production company from claims by copyright owners if it has not obtained the necessary written consents, or if it has not given the correct credits to them. If the P & D deal includes the obligation of the record company to receive payment for records distributed which have been sold, it will usually pay the copyright royalty direct to the copyright owner, and account to the production company accordingly.

(f) The financial arrangements between the production company and the P & D company. The production company is paying for services rendered by the P & D company where the commercial risk, and all expense from manufacturing a record through to selling it, is carried by the production company. The charges made by the P & D company will be expressed as a cost per record manufactured, with a further cost per record distributed.

There may be other associated costs, such as copyright payment administration, all of which should be set out in the agreement between the parties. Record companies which have record pressing facilities in excess of their immediate requirements may make them available for the custom pressing of third party products. If the record company has no other participation in the records being pressed, it will require a warranty, covered by an indemnity, that the pressings are legitimate, and that there is no possible legal or third party liability for having pressed them which can fall on the record company.

**4.3** The major differences between a P & D deal and a production agreement with a record company are:

(a) In a production agreement the record company pays to the production company royalties on sales of the records. In a P & D deal, the P & D company is paid a fee for each record manufactured, and a further fee for each record distributed.

(b) After paying the pressing and distribution fees, the production company retains the balance of the income under a P & D deal. Out of this will be paid the record promotion costs, the mechanical copyright royalties (unless these have been retained and paid out by the P & D company), the artistes' royalties, any producer's royalty, and all other expenses of the production company relating to the recording. The balance is the income of the production company. The impact of VAT has not been referred to for simplicity.

(c) Under a production agreement, the record company pays the mechanical copyright royalty out of its share of money direct to the copyright owner of the recorded composition. These payments are not deducted by the record company from royalties due to the production company. In a P & D deal, copyright payments are the responsibility of the production company. The manufacturer of the records is responsible for the copyright payments so the P & D company is usually authorised to pay them direct to the copyright owners. Although the P & D company physically makes the records, it is employed to do so as a contractor, and the production company is the technical manufacturer. A production agreement gives the record company the exclusive right to manufacture the records, and it is not doing so as the agent or contractor of the production company.

(d) Under a production agreement the record company may have whatever territory is agreed. A P & D deal is a limited UK operation.

**4.4** One handicap in England of a P & D deal is that record shops will not purchase for retail sale more than a minimal quantity of records (if any) unless the artiste is well known, or the record is in the charts, or the production company's label has a consistent reputation for releasing successful records by new artistes. A sale or return basis is normally applied by record shops, as they will then have no financial loss if the records are not sold.

Under a P & D deal the record company makes its charges for each record made and distributed whether or not the records are ultimately sold by the record shop or returned to the P & D company, and irrespective of whether or not the production company is making a profit from them.

**4.5** The main legal obligations relating to the manufacture and sale of records are:

(a) that the requirements of the Copyright Designs and Patents Act 1988 are complied with by the production company, in respect of the performers, and of the copyright material performed;

(b) that the records do not infringe any third party rights, and are not defamatory, blasphemous or obscene;

(c) that all correct credits and copyright notices are set out on the album sleeve, and on the record label.

The volume of pirate and counterfeit record and tape sales is a serious threat to the record industry. Record companies with pressing plants and distribution facilities which they make available for a third party product must do their best to ensure that they are not dealing with illegal records. Manufacturers of blank tape cassettes should also be reasonably satisfied as to the *bona fides* of any new customer who orders cassettes in bulk quantity for the purpose of manufacturing records for commercial sale.

## 5 Label and logo agreements

**5.1** A label agreement means that the record company and the production company enter into an exclusive agreement whereby the production company provides all of its agreed artistes recordings exclusively to the record company, which manufactures and releases those records for sale within its territory under the label or trade name of the production company. This is the style of production agreement referred to in Section III of this chapter. Record companies release records by their own artistes under different record labels, each of which distinguishes the sort of music it identifies with, and the sector of the record buying public it is aimed at. The production company's record lable is treated commercially in the same way, but in accordance with the terms of the production agreement.

**5.2** A logo agreement is the halfway stage between a simple production agreement under paragraph **3**, and a label agreement. The production company has its graphic trademark or logo to identify it, which will be featured on the record sleeve, the disc label and all advertising and promotional material. In a logo agreement, although the records are still released under the record company's label, the trademark or logo of the production company is given equal prominence with that of the record company wherever it appears in connection with the record. A logo agreement is generally used by a production company which does not have enough artistes with record selling power to make a label agreement worthwhile. The production company still gains recognition for its individual identity, and has full use of all the record company facilities and departments.

**5.3** In both label and logo agreements, the production company will have to give assurances to the record company that the trademark, logo or label identification to be used does not infringe the rights of any third party. In both a label and a logo agreement the record company administers and undertakes almost every aspect of the production company's business other than the actual recording. In a pressing and distribution agreement the record company only acts as a manufacturing and clearing house for the production company's own records.

## SECTION III: TERMS OF PRODUCTION AGREEMENTS

The following terms will form the major part of negotiation of the agreement between a production company and a record company for an artiste's deal or a production deal, as described in paragraph 1.3. Not all the details may be necessary for any particular production agreement, but the principles are relevant when a production company is negotiating in general terms with a record company. Any item, which is usually contained in a recording contract (see chapter 4), and which has no unique significance to a production agreement, will not be discussed in this section.

## 6 Mechanical copyright of recordings

**6.1** The basis of the agreement between the production company and the record company will be either by an assignment or a licence of the mechanical copyright in the recordings. These are set out in more detail below. One of the objects of having a production company is to end up with the ownership of record masters, a potentially valuable asset.

(a) A mechanical copyright assignment. The record company will own the mechanical copyright in the recordings, and will be entitled to sell records for so long as copyright in those recordings exists. The period of copyright in a recording is for 50 years and after the end of the year of first publication (ie release for sale to the public) of the recording. As the period of copyright in a musical composition expires 50 years after the death of the composer, the copyright periods for the record itself and for the recorded composition will be different. The useful life of most records is short, so the different life periods are academic to them. It is important to records which become eternal classics.
are academic to them. It is important to records which become eternal classics.

(b) A mechanical copyright licence. The production company retains the mechanical copyright in the recordings, and the record company will be granted an exclusive licence to make and sell records derived from each recording for the licence period. This is the best method for a production company to promote its artistes because:
   (i) the licence reversion rights in successful recordings are valuable, as deleted records can be revived and repackaged;
   (ii) the mechanical copyrights are an asset to the production company, should the shareholders wish to sell it;
   (iii) the production company retains control over what happens to its recordings;
   (iv) the licence agreement is limited in time.

In practical terms if the exclusive licence period granted to the record company is long enough to cover the useful life of a normal record, there is no significant disadvantage in having a licence deal. Once the records have been deleted from its current catalogue, it takes no active marketing interest in them, and they have no earning power. If the record company is granted major territories in its licence, the period will have to be considered.

## 7 Territory

**7.1** If, under the production deal, the record company requires the mechanical copyright in the recordings to be assigned to it then it will automatically have worldwide rights in them, in the same way as for a directly signed artiste. If the record company is only granted an exclusive licence, it can be for such territories as the parties agree.

Deciding which record company should have the rights over which territory, or whether to give the worldwide rights to one record company, is more difficult for a production agreement involving many artistes, than for a production company offering only one artiste to the record company. It is not just a question of whether one record company with worldwide exclusive rights will be effective for all of the artistes throughout its territory; equally important will be the different financial possibilities which may be available by splitting the artistes between different companies for major territories. The main points to consider are:

(a) A record company with an exclusive worldwide agreement will have different royalty rates for its local territory, and for "abroad". "Abroad" may mean the rest of the world, or for royalty rates it may be split between a number of other major record selling markets at the same rate, and then a lower rate for the rest of the world. A production company with substantial artistes might obtain for each of the major territories a royalty within the top rate available from the record company. Unless the basic royalty rate is very low, the differential of royalty in respect of different territories is always there, whatever the top royalty rate may be. As a record company with worldwide rights will not disclose the royalty rates it receives from each of its foreign licensees, the production company cannot judge the justification for the specific differential offered to it.

The production company can allocate the major record selling territories to different record companies, when the reason for the royalty differential disappears, and the maximum available royalty rates will be received from each territory. While royalty rates are important, they are not the whole story. All other commercial factors should be examined relating to each record company choice. Due to the artistes and the market, splitting the major territories may not be a viable proposition, or even an available one. For example, in 1992 it will not be possible to divide up rights within different EEC countries.

(b) Advances on account of royalties offered by a record company with an exclusive worldwide agreement will usually be less than the total advances for the same recordings which can be obtained by splitting the major record selling markets between different record companies. One reason is that foreign licencees in a worldwide deal are not likely to contribute to advances, as they might not even release the artiste's records. Direct deals for those territories will produce some advance, and generally a better royalty rate.

(c) In a production deal (see paragraph **1.3**), advances received by a production company from a record company with a worldwide agreement will be in respect of all the recordings of each artiste for the world, and so will be recoupable from royalties due on worldwide sales of all the records, irrespective of which portion of advances is applicable to which recording. Therefore when the record company renders an account to the production company, unrecouped advances in respect of one artiste's albums will be offset against royalties due in excess of advances in respect of another artiste's albums. This is known as "cross- collateralisation".

By splitting the territories between different record companies, the advance paid by each record company is only recoupable from the royalties due from it. Therefore one record company's unrecouped advances are not set off against royalties due from another record company in excess of its own advances. This helps cash flow.

(d) The production company has greater flexibility when negotiating with different record companies within different territories in respect of the exclusive periods of their contracts for album delivery, and the continuing rights of each record company in the records delivered to it by the time their contract has expired.

**7.2** Limited territorial rights may be easier to place on good terms with a local record company. The local licensee, which is entitled to obtain the recordings from a record company through a worldwide production agreement, may not release them or promote them if it would have rejected the artiste had it been given a free choice. Unless the local record company is enthusiastic about the artiste, there is little point in giving it the rights to his recordings. A worldwide deal sounds great, but no record company guarantees to release a record anywhere. A copy will be sent to each licensee or local subsidiary, which will or will not release the record then, or at any other time, as it decides in its own discretion. The major territories are not likely to do so unless the record has first made the charts in the UK. If the production company is looking for a label agreement with substantial financial commitments from the record company, then the record company will require at least the major record selling territories, if not worldwide rights.

## 8 Period of agreement

**8.1** There is the period during which the production company provides its artistes exclusively to the record company, and there is the period for which the record company has the exclusive rights to the recordings which have been delivered to it by its chosen artistes. Termination of the production agreement will not affect the continuing period of exclusivity the record company has in the recordings already delivered to it. For example, the production agreement period may be three years, and the continuing period of rights in the product delivered in that time may be five years after termination.

Whether the rights of the record company in the recordings is perpetual or for a limited period of time depends on whether the production agreement is by way of mechanical copyright assignment, or licence (see paragraph **6.1**). As with the limitation of territory, there will normally only be a limitation of period where the record company is granted a licence.

**8.2** The record company will choose specific artistes found by the production company, and will then be entitled to take all of their recordings made under the production agreement. If the production company turns out to be a goldmine with a predominance of successful artistes, the record company wants to have a sufficient period of exclusivity so that it can benefit from having taken a gamble which paid off. When an artiste has been chosen, the record company will have an agreed maximum exclusive contract period for him, or a specified number of albums to be made by that artiste, irrespective of the production agreement period. There are practical reasons for not having too short a period of rights over the artiste, such as:

(a) the time it takes to record albums, manufacture the records, and release the albums in the record company's own territory;
(b) the time lapse between having a local release, and the album being released in any major foreign territory;
(c) the time between a record being broadcast, becoming known and liked, and being bought as a result;
(d) the considerable expenditure needed to promote an album

during its active selling life;

(e) the period between sales in foreign territories in any accounting period being notified, and the relevant royalties being paid to the record company, the accounts for such sales and receipts being prepared, and the royalty accounting and payment being made to the production company.

**8.3** The production agreement's exclusive period will be either a fixed term of years, or a number of option periods, covering all artistes accepted by the record company, and who become contracted to the production company during that period. Although an artiste may be contracted to the production company during the last year of the production agreement, the commitment to the record company will be to provide a minimum number of recordings to be delivered by each such artiste, even though later albums may be delivered after the expiry of the exclusive production agreement period.

**8.4** In a mechanical copyright licence deal it must be decided whether:

(a) The exclusive rights of the record company to each album last for a fixed period from the date of its delivery to the record company. In this case the rights to each album would revert to the production company as the exclusive period for each album expires.

(b) The exclusive rights of the record company under a production deal or an artiste deal in respect of all the albums delivered will terminate on the same date, irrespective of when the albums were delivered. This would be best if the production company wants to have available the whole catalogue of albums from the same date, as there is good demand for the rights to re-release successful "golden oldies". The record company will have the earlier albums for a longer period than the later albums. The exclusive rights in the last to be delivered albums must continue for a sufficient period to allow the record company adequate exclusive time within which to promote them, recoup any outstanding advances, and make a profit. If the overall exclusive period is fairly long, there can be agreed an alternative earlier date for termination, ie, when all of the albums have been deleted from the record company's current catalogue. As already stated, a limiting factor can be that the UK record company may delete the album from its current catalogue, but one or more foreign licensees may be in the course of releasing the album, or it may not have been out long. The licensees rights will have to be referred to.

**8.5** Where the production company is to deliver to the record company a given number of albums from each artiste:

(a) If the production agreement covers several artistes, each the subject of an artiste deal, the calculation of the number of albums to be recorded by each artiste should be based on a practical delivery schedule of recordings to the record company, the intervals of which may differ between the artistes. One album a year from each is the likely minimum.

(b) In a production deal what is to happen if an artiste either leaves the production company, or gets seriously behind in his recording delivery schedule? This will affect the extent to which royalty advance payments are to be made by the record company, when they were based upon the contracted album delivery schedule. It will be more serious to the record company where royalty advances are made periodically, and not on each album delivery. Periodic advances are not sensible for the record company, and do not create any incentive for the production company to get albums recorded and delivered. Where, for example, one of the production deal artiste's records are successful, and those of other artistes are not, the delay in delivery of the sucessful artiste's recordings reduces the ability of the record company to recoup its total advances to the production company. Not having to pay the advances on the recordings not yet delivered does not assist in the recoupment of the previous advances, which can only be achieved through record sales. In an artiste deal, only his recordings are relevant so that risk will not apply.

In either of (a) or (b), the record company will probably have yearly options to continue the agreement, so that if it simply is not working, it can cut its losses, or at least its future expenditure. It will then have some albums on which to recover the outstanding advances.

**8.6** Whatever may be the basis upon which the production company is providing the record company with the product, the following points should be considered:

(a) The production agreement should differentiate between studio recorded albums, live concert recorded albums, and double albums, for the purpose of calculating the minimum recording delivery commitment. There may also be a maximum commitment of album acceptance by the record company, ie, an artiste may be prohibited from exceeding his recording schedule. It should limit its risk on an unknown product by applying its usual "commercial quality" criteria, and the production company should not be able to deliver any old album just to get the royalty advances.

(b) For the record company to make the most of each album as it is released, there should be within the recording delivery schedule a minimum and a maximum period after the delivery of any album within which the next album must be recorded and delivered. This prevents the production company from spending all its time recording albums, and delivering them to the record company within the first few months, in satisfaction of the whole production agreement's contractual commitment of albums at once. The recording delivery schedule also gives the record company a reasonable time after releasing an album within which to promote it, establish it, and get the greatest selling power out of it before the next album is delivered. The reasons for the recording, as well as the delivery of albums, being included within the minimum and maximum dates are:

(i) the sales success of each album can only be measured at such a time after its release which has enabled the public to respond adequately to it;

(ii) whether or not an album has been successful may influence the musical style and content of the next recorded album, to follow success or to avoid a similar musical failure.

The recording delivery schedule is sensible for the artiste as well, because touring the major record selling markets should coincide where possible with the release of a new album to maximise its promotion.

(c) If there is a substantial period of time between the minimum and maximum dates within the recording delivery schedule, the artiste should be prohibited from recording an album more than a specified period of time prior to its delivery to the record company. Ie, an album must be delivered as and when completed. There might also be the refinement of stating that each album must be completed within, say, eight weeks of starting recording. This ensures that the artiste is recording in his contemporary musical style, to be consistent with his current image and his live act around the projected release date. The production agreement should also deal with what is to happen where any artiste gets ahead of his recording delivery schedule by reason of the adjustment of recording dates to fit around tours, or for any other good reason.

These time limits also prevent the production company from completing its recording commitment to the record company by putting together albums consisting of the excess recordings the artiste made at the time of recording his earlier albums, but which the production company did not deliver to the record company at that time. The record company should prohibit the production company from doing this as it is against the intention of the deal, and may be a means of getting album delivery advances which are not merited.

(d) Unless there is some limit on the total extension of a contract year (where that right exists) for non-delivery of a recording by an artiste, in the case of a production deal difficulty will arise when other artistes who are not in default must record in accordance with their own recording delivery schedule for the following year.

**8.7** If an artiste has to deliver to the record company a minimum number of albums in each contract year, as an album which is due could be delivered on the last day of the contract year, the deficiency will not become known until that date. Where the production agreement contains contract period suspension provisions, the next following contract year does not start until the suspension has been lifted, such as by the delivery of a late album. During the suspension period, the production company should not record artistes' albums to be delivered in the next contract year. To do so might breach the time limits set out in the recording delivery schedule for that year.

**8.8** The principle of suspension of an artiste's recording contract was discussed in the previous chapter. The production company has several factors to consider relating to suspension terms, such as:

(a) The production company must be safeguarded by having similar provisions in its artistes' contracts. This prevents the suspension of the production agreement extending the period of the record company's exclusivity in respect of the artiste beyond the time for which the artiste is contracted exclusively to the production company.

(b) The suspension of the whole production deal by the record company because of one defaulting artiste might create contractual difficulties for the production company when it consequently applies suspension rights to artistes who are not in default. Therefore the delivery of an up-to-date artiste's recordings should still continue, particularly if the production agreement states that all of the recordings by all of the artistes will revert to the production company on the same date. The suspension of an artiste deal is not a problem, because that is a back to back contract, and the production company suspends its artiste's contract accordingly.

(c) In the last contract year of a production deal, if by the date upon which the suspension starts, an artiste has fulfilled his recording delivery commitment, the obligation of the production company to the record company in respect of that artiste should cease on the date upon which the last contract year would otherwise have expired. The record company retains no advantage over the artiste by having his agreement suspended.

(d) Subject to paragraph **8.6**(c), if the production company provides the record company with more than the required number of recordings of an artiste in any contract year, the record company may decline to accept that the excess in that contract year shall be set against the minimum recording delivery requirements within the next contract year.

## 9 Acceptance of artistes

**9.1** Exclusivity in any production agreement must be a mutual obligation if it is to have any value. The record company will require the shareholders and directors of the production company to give written assurances which will prevent them from expecting the record company to take all the accepted artistes offered to it under the production agreement, while being able at the same time to choose whether any artiste they find should go through that production agreement, or through another competitive deal they set up with a second record company. This kind of prohibition would depend entirely upon the role the directors and shareholders play in the promotion of the artistes' careers.

**9.2** As the record company is the exclusive outlet for the recordings of accepted artistes, it must take delivery of each recording made by an accepted artiste during a contract year, and promote it to its full ability. Acceptance of an artiste by the record company will normally depend on hearing some demo recordings, and exercising the same criteria which it would apply to a potential direct artiste contract.

The record company must then take the good albums with the not so good albums. As the definition of a "not so good album" is one which does not sell well, it may not be identified as being one until some time after its release. Even if the production agreement has built in a guaranteed minimum record company promotion budget, the record company will insist that how it spends the money allotted will be in its sole discretion.

**9.3** The record company will want the right to release the first album of the artiste with the option of retaining him if the album is successful, and rejecting him if it is not successful. This will not be possible where the artiste is contracted for a three album deal. The same objective may be achieved where an artiste deal period is made up of a number of option years, but there may be an initial period in excess of one year. Even if the record company were to be given that right, the definition of success, and the time within which it is to be achieved, would need careful consideration.

**9.4** A concern of a production company may be (in its opinion) that not enough promotion expense is incurred by the record company in support of an album which is having difficulty in selling. The opinion of the production company may be that with sufficient expenditure the album would have been successful. The commercial element of the record company will say that there is little point in spending on promoting an album more money than can be earned from it. The artistic element of the record company may wish only to promote heavily an album which has every indication of prospective success. The decision has to be a reasonably judged commercial one made by the record company in good faith.

What is, and what is not, adequate promotional expense and effort can only be a matter of opinion. Each side inevitably adopts the view which suits it own purpose, and no record company will give a production company the right to remove an artiste from an exclusive production agreement for an alleged lack of promotion.

**9.5** In a hard economic climate it is possible that the record company will want an each way bet, ie to see how the first year or album goes for an artiste before committing itself to a longer perod. This is a more cautious approach to an artiste acceptance procedure, but a production company may have to accept it.

**9.6** The risk of rejection by the record company of an album recorded by a new artiste can be minimised by sample tracks being submitted to the record company for approval. If the record company is entitled to approve sample tracks, it must be clear whether the right extends to all of the tracks on the album, or only to a selection for the purpose of approving the musical concept of the album. If the musical style and quality of those sample tracks are acceptable to the record company, the album as a whole when recorded should be accepted. The relevant clause must clarify whether the album must contain the sample tracks which were approved. The record company runs the risk that any of the tracks on the album which were not among those submitted for approval might not be considered to have achieved a set standard. If the objection is serious and reasonably founded, the offending track will have to be substituted by another track which is acceptable to the record company. The production company would have to bear the cost of doing any further recording needed to make the album acceptable. (See paragraph **10.4**).

## 10 Record releases

**10.1** Subject to paragraph **8.6**(b) and (c) the recording delivery schedule should be based upon:

(a) The ability of each artiste to record a certain number of albums without detracting from their touring and other business commitments, and without creating inferior recordings due to the pressure of time.

(b) The ability of the record company to release and fully promote those recordings within its overall album release schedule.

(c) The record company paying to the production company royalty advances, which will be calculated as an annual financial commitment according to the number of albums to be delivered in each contract year by the production company. Some artistes will be worth a higher advance payment for each album than other artistes.

**10.2** The recording delivery schedule will represent either a fixed number of albums, with a realistic rate of delivery not likely to be exceeded; or it will be a minimum number of albums with delivery intervals which allow a reasonable opportunity for additional albums to be delivered if requested by the record company. For example, it would be not less than one album in each contract year, with the right of the record company to require one more album to be recorded in each two year period. With a minimum recording delivery schedule, the production agreement should:

(a) Impose a maximum number of recordings to be delivered under the production agreement, so that the number of additional albums requested does not become excessive.

(b) Make it clear whether any excess albums accepted by the record company will entitle the production company to receive additional royalty advances within that contract year. Whatever is the basis of the recording delivery schedule, the production agreement is likely to state that the royalty advance payments will be reduced or withheld if less than the minimum number of recordings is delivered in any contract year. The production company must include in each of its artiste's recording agreements the recording delivery schedule details appertaining to that artiste. The recording delivery schedule states the commitments the production company has to the record company. The record release clauses contain the obligations of the record company to the production company in respect of the recordings delivered to it under the production agreement.

**10.3** Each album delivered will be a significant cost to the record company in royalty advance payments and promotional expense, so it will include in the production agreement the right to reject an album on the grounds of poor content or inferior sound or technical quality. A justifiable rejection on these grounds should not bring the album within the category of rejection of the artiste. It will require additional work to be done on the album to get it right, or a new recording will be required. The record company will apply the same criteria of quality and acceptability as it does to directly signed artistes. In short, neither the artiste nor the production company should be able to rip off the record company.

Because the record company will have exclusive rights over the recordings delivered to it, the production agreement must contain all the "ifs and buts" of when, where, and through what medium the recordings will be released. Ordinarily record companies never undertake to release albums, but, under a production agreement, if it does not do so, there must be a contractual fall back position for the production company. The major requirements will be:

(a) That an album shall be released in its home territory (the UK) within a stated period of time after delivery to the record company of the master tape and complete artwork. Unjustified failure to release the album on time, plus perhaps reasonable evidence of there being no intention of ever doing so, should bring it within the context of a rejected album, and will represent a material breach of contract. The wording of any *force majeure* clause in the production agreement is important. For example, if the record company is prevented from releasing an album solely because of a strike at the factory of the sleeve printers, that reason should not entitle the production company to withdraw the album and the artiste from the production agreement.

(b) That each album shall first be released on a major full price label of the record company, unless the production agreement is itself a label deal. The details of record releases at other than full price, and through other than ordinary retail channels, will be the same as those in an ordinary artiste's recording contract.

(c) That (for a major artiste) first releases of an album will be contemporaneously in such of the major record selling territories as are set out in the production agreement, which might only be the UK and the USA. This is only likely in the case of a major artiste, who is already a steady international success. Although the production company is always anxious to have its recordings released as quickly as possible in as many countries as possible, the production agreement must take into account that the record company within each major committed territory has to fit the album into its own album release schedule. Also, each territory may not receive the copy master tape and artwork films at the same time, and they will each have their own priority problems of record pressing and sleeve printing. Therefore the definition of "contemporaneous" in the production agreement must be realistic.

Album releases in each of the minor territories will depend entirely on the decision of the local licensee. There will be some countries where the album, whether because of the artiste, the language or the style of music, will not sell, and therefore will not be released.

**10.4** Any album released by the record company which contains a selection of recorded tracks not being in accordance with the content or sequence of any master tape delivered by the production company, will be a compilation album or a recoupled album. The possibilities are:

(a) an album containing only recordings by the same artiste, chosen as a mixture from all of his recordings;

(b) an album consisting of recordings by different production agreement artists;

(c) an album consisting of a mixture of recordings by production agreement artistes together with a mixture of recordings by artistes outside the production agreement but contracted to the record company;

(d) the record company and the production company consenting to one or more recordings by a production agreement artiste being included on a compilation album issued by a third party consisting of recordings by artistes who are contracted to various record companies.

**10.5** The production agreement must contain the rights of, and restrictions upon, the record company in respect of compiled and recoupled recordings. Points to be raised will include the following:

(a) Under a mechanical copyright licence deal, the record company should not release any album containing wholly the performances of a production agreement artiste which has a recoupled selection of recordings unless the production company has consented both to the principle and to the choice of recordings.

If the royalty rates differ between the albums from which the various recordings are taken, a new royalty rate should be agreed for the compilation album. Alternatively each track on the compilation album will have the same royalty rate as that applicable to the album from which it was taken, and a composite royalty rate is calculated.

(b) The record company should not use the recordings of a production agreement artiste in compilation albums with the recordings of any other artistes without first obtaining the consent of the production company to the recording used, and its approval of the other artistes whose recordings will also be on the album. The production company should have the right to restrict the number of occasions this is done for any artiste, in any territory, in any year. This is only likely to happen for an album. An example would be "Chart hits of 1989" where one of the album tracks had been released as a single "A" side, and went to the top of the charts.

(c) No compilation album should include recent recordings by production agreement artistes, in the sense of a "best of" collection, as this implies the artiste is over the hill and is being given the recording equivalent of a memorial. This applies especially if there has been released, or there is about to be released, a live album containing some of the proposed compilation album tracks. Live albums are themselves compilations of recordings which usually are not included together, or in that sequence, on any previous studio album recorded by the artiste. The benefit of a live album is that, at a concert, the artiste will perform a mixture of tracks to publicise his new (or next) album, together with old past favourites to please the fans. A live album may not have the precise and clinical sound quality of a studio album, but it exudes atmosphere.

(d) The production company must ascertain whether the proposed compilation is on a full price or budget price label release, and in which countries it is intended to be released. The compilation album should complement the existing albums of the artistes whose recordings are on it. The difference in the production company's earning power between full price and budget price sales of the compilation album will depend on the likely record sales of the country in which it is to be released.

(e) The artwork for the album cover of a compilation album, if containing wholly the same artiste's tracks, should not mislead record buyers into thinking they are getting newly released recordings.

If the artiste is one of many on the compilation album, the others not being production agreement artistes, he should have a credit of equal prominence on the album sleeve and all advertising material where all the artistes are equally famous. If the artiste himself is famous, and the other artistes are relatively unknown, without his consent the production agreement artiste must not be given greater prominence than that given to any other artiste in the use of photographs, or in the credits and the structure of the album artwork. This is to prevent the album artwork from misleading people, who might not otherwise buy the album, into thinking that the production agreement artiste is the prime feature of it.

## 11 Royalty advances

**11.1** Royalty advance payments by the record company will be specifically recoupable from royalties due to the production company. They must not otherwise be returnable to the record company if the total royalties due to the production company do not exceed the advances. If the production company fundamentally and irretrievably breaches the production agreement (such as by delivering no recordings), the record company should be entitled to claim back all advances, and to make any other claim for compensation and damages which may be available to it.

In the case of a production deal (see paragraph **1.3**) the advances will be recoupable against all albums delivered by the production company irrespective of which artiste recorded them. In the case of an artiste deal, the recoupment will be against all of the albums of the relevant artiste; irrespective of which advances were made against which of his albums.

**11.2** The recoupment risk to the record company for an artiste deal is greater, so the advances may not be so significant. Higher royalty advances may be agreed for a production deal, where the record company has the safety of all advances being cross-collateralised against all royalties due to the production company irrespective of the artistes within the production deal whose record sales created those royalties. A production company needs to receive from the record company sufficient money as an advance on account of its royalties:

(a) To help to finance the making of recordings, and to cover ancillary expenditure, such as album artwork and photographs, and some promotion and advertising if required.

(b) To instil in the record company a sense of urgency to sell records, at least to recoup what it has spent in royalty advances.

(c) The production company will have to provide any balance required for recording costs in excess of the royalty advance contribution towards them, together with its own funds for overhead expenses not directly incurred in making and promoting recordings. The record company will not be prepared to finance the production company entirely; it will insist that the owners of the production company ensure that it has adequate funds to finance itself fully. The record company must be reasonably satisfied that the production company will stay in active business for the period of the production agreement.

**11.3** The financial arrangements between the record company and the production company on the one hand, and those between the production company and the artiste on thee other hand, are entirely separate, as are the two sets of accountings and all other obligations. The artiste is not entitled as of right to any part of the royalty advances received by the production company from the record company under the production agreement, even though they might be related to delivery of the artiste's albums. If the production company were to give the artiste a contractual entitlement to share in those royalty advances without having certain limitations imposed on that right, then:

(a) In the absence of agreement to the contrary, the artiste might claim to be entitled to the same proportion of the royalty advance received by the production company on his album deliveries as the proportion of his royalty rate from the production company is to the royalty rate received by the production company. This would have several implications:

(i) the production company would have to disclose to the artiste the production agreement royalty rates, which information the artiste might not otherwise be entitled to receive;

(ii) artistes' agreements with production companies would have to contain a clause negating the artiste's right to receive a proportion of the royalty advances received by the production company;

(iii) if the production company has already made royalty advances to the artiste (either actual or deemed), which remain unrecouped when the production company receives royalty advances from the record company, the artiste should not be entitled to receive any part for so long as his own advances remain unrecouped;

(iv) if the advance is payable on album delivery, the clause in the artiste's contract would have to make it clear that, as the advance is to go towards that album's cost, and as that cost is already a deemed advance to the artiste, in effect he would have no claim on the advance now being received.

(b) It would conflict with any other agreement for royalty advance payments contained in the artiste's contract with the production company; he could not have two advances from the same payment.

(c) The artiste would be sharing in the benefits of the business of the production company without participating in any risk, such as (in a production deal) the recoupment of cross-collateralised advances by the record company from the royalties due to the production company from the sales of records by all of its artistes.

(d) It would mean that if no records were ever sold of the artiste's recordings, in effect he would still have received royalties. That is not likely, but the advances may take some time to recoup.

**11.4** The royalty advances received by the production company will be either:

(a) In the case of a production deal in equal instalments periodically during each year of the production agreement, and:

(i) Royalty advances will be a fixed figure for each year based on a minimum recording delivery schedule. The advances will not usually be increased by delivery of recordings in excess of the minimum commitment.

(ii) The advantage to the production company is that, depending on the dates upon which it delivers recordings, and the dates upon which it receives royalty advances, some royalty advances can be available prior to the recording costs of some albums being incurred.

(iii) If the record company has no right to suspend the production agreement period, it will want to adjust the amount of royalty advances paid in the following contract year if the minimum recording delivery schedule is not achieved in the previous contract year. Either the royalty advance payments in the following contract year will be reduced proportionately to the shortfall in the number of recordings delivered, or (but less likely) the minimum recording delivery schedule in the following contract year will be increased to compensate for the shortfall in the previous contract year.

(b) In either a production deal or an artiste deal an agreed royalty advance for each album delivered to the recording company in accordance with the schedule. There will be a minimum and a maximum recording delivery commitment in respect of which royalty advances will be paid. The album advances will differ according to the popularity of each artiste, and the number of albums they are to deliver in a contract year. Advances may not be paid at all for live recordings of the artiste's concerts, and double albums will not qualify for any increased advances, because of the increase in the production costs, even if they are accepted as part of the agreed delivery commitment.

**11.5** A disadvantage to the production company is that the recording costs of each album have to be incurred first, which costs will only be recovered (or contributed to) from the royalty advance received on delivery of the recording. The cashflow can be assisted by having the album royalty advance split into two payments, the first of which is to be made a specified time prior to recording taking place, and the second to be made on delivery of the recording. The production company will give written notice to the record company that it has a firm booking of studio time to make the recording, and that the first half of the royalty advance is payable on a stated date. The record company should obtain independent verification of these facts from the studio before paying the first royalty advance instalment.

There must be some safeguard for the record company to prevent the production company from obtaining the first part of the royalty, and not recording the album within the specified time thereafter. That ruse may be used where short term finance is required by the production company for some other purpose.

Therefore there must be a provision to re-structure the royalty advance payments on subsequent albums, if the production company does not comply strictly with this clause. For example, unless there is a stated period within which the album must be made once recording has started, studio time could be booked for several days at a time with substantial intervals in between. One sanction might be the forefeiture of the second half of the royalty advance if the production company is significantly late on delivery.

**11.6** Where the production agreement is for a period of years consisting of annual options to be exercised by the record company, and if the production company receives low album delivery advances, it should try to negotiate a reasonable royalty advance as consideration for the exercise of each option. This gives the production company further working finance, and if the option advance is substantial, it tests the enthusiasm of the record company for the future prospects of the production agreement. If the earnings of the record company under the production agreement to that date have been disappointing, but success is in sight, the record company may exercise the option to have further time for recouping outstanding expenditure, and hopefully to make a profit.

A safeguard may be to state that the next year's option advance payment will be reduced according to a scale if the aggregate of all advances has not yet been recouped by the record company. This could apply equally well to both a production deal and an artiste deal.

## 12 Royalties

**12.1** Although a royalty is only paid on a record sale, in a production deal the royalty rate will apply to each of the production agreement artistes, irrespective of which artiste is successful, and which is not. A production company will only agree a different royalty rate for each artiste which contracts with the production company during the course of the production agreement, if he comes under an artiste deal.

If the royalty rate is increased at the beginning of each contract year, or upon the exercise of an option by the record company, the increased rate will apply to all records sold derived from recordings which are made during the period covered by the new rates of royalty. This benefits the production company, because in the absence of any limitation contained in the production agreement, recordings of relatively new artistes will receive the same increased royalty as the album sales of a highly successful artiste. All artistes have albums which do not do as well as expected, and some have albums which exceed all hopes. The record company judgement is based upon average success.

**12.2** The record company may prefer to reward high album sales with a high royalty rate, which can be done by escalating the royalty rate in steps according to the sales of individual albums. The escalation might apply whereby the combined sales of the existing albums of an artiste will make his future recordings eligible to start at the royalty rate, but there is no logic in including unsuccessful albums in any increased royalty structure.

**12.3** Royalty advance payments to the production company, even though based in amount on the potential album selling power of each production agreement artiste, are aggregated, and in a production deal all royalties due to the production company, irrespective of which artiste they relate to, are cross-collateralised by the record company for royalty advance recoupment purposes. When agreeing to a system of royalty rate escalation, the production company must investigate the practical results in varying hypothetical examples of comparative success as between its artistes, to ensure that it can finance the royalty payments it will have to make to successful artistes. For example, if the production deal has three artistes, all of whom have delivered one album, none of which have recouped their advances, there can be a massive recoupment commitment. They each then deliver one more album, and two do not sell, but one artiste has a monster hit. Luckily for the record company, the hit album sales royalties wipe out the entire aggregated outstanding advance recoupment. The artiste is lucky because he gets higher royalty rates on much of the later sales. However, the production company, because of the advances recoupment by the record company relating to the other two artistes, has received no further cash with which to pay the successful artiste the substantial royalties now due to him. This example shows the major defect of a production deal if cashflow is not carefully controlled.

**12.4** The calculations of royalties in a production agreement for full price, mid price and low price record sales do not differ materially from those contained in a direct artistes recording contract. The production company, when negotiating with the record company, should take into account its intended royalty commitments to its artistes, and how it can obtain the best available percentages in the major record selling territories.

There is no definition of what is the maximum possible royalty rate available from any record company. Many factors affect the monetary value of any quoted royalty percentage. A true comparison can only be made between the monetary value of, say, the sale of 50,000 albums at full price in the same territory, disregarding royalty advances. The comparative test should be extended to royalty differences according to different royalty territories, and to reduced royalty rate categories of record sales. Although this repeats to some extent points already made in chapter four, some of the factors affecting the monetary value of a royalty rate which is quoted as a percentage of selling price are:

(a) On what proportion of sales of records is the royalty paid?

(b) If the answer to (a) is less than 100%, is there also a royalty-free allowance for records which are sold but subsequently returned to the record company for credit, or as being defective? if so, is the royalty free allowance a percentage of sales, or is it actual returns? If it is actual returns, is it clear that any records returned, which are subsequently resold, are included for royalty calculations. Any allowance provision should only give the record company reasonable safety against paying a royalty on a record which is not sold. Any further leeway reduces the monetary value of the royalty percentage. This "loss" can be significant in the case of a high selling album.

(c) The definition of "sales" for royalty purposes may differ between record companies, and should be read carefully in conjunction with the credit and allowance provisions.
(d) Is the royalty based on retail price, or some other figure, such as the ex-warehouse cost or wholesale trade price? If so, what is the control over a variable element in the royalty rate calculation which is wholly within the record company corporate structure. Anything other than retail price has too great an adjustment possibility factor relevant only to internal costing structures. In this example, a comparative analysis of the monetary value of the quoted royalty rate per full price record sold is essential. An impressive sounding royalty rate may turn out to produce a lower monetary value than anticipated.
(e) The quantity of "free goods" allowed for promotional purposes. What is the definition of "free"? If it is a reduced price, how does that compare with the low price or budget sales on which some royalty is paid.
(f) The album and tape packaging allowance. Is it a percentage of retail price, or is it the amount it actually costs—and how is that computed?
(g) Reductions of both the royalty rate and the basis of calculation of the royalty on records sold at less than full retail price or through specialist distributors.
(h) For "controlled compositions", is a reduction made in the royalty rate to compensate for any excess over the minimum rates in the statutory mechanical copyright payments.

## 13 Termination provisions

**13.1** Where the production deal is by way of mechanical copyright assignment, termination means that the production company has no further obligation to provide the record company with artistes or recordings. The record company continues to manufacture and sell the records in the ordinary course of business, and to account to the production company accordingly. The production company accounts to the relevant artiste, until in the course of time records are deleted from the record company's catalogue. At no time do the rights in the recordings revert to the production company.

**13.2** On the termination of a production agreement with a record company which is by way of a mechanical copyright licence, the following points should be dealt with:
(1) The termination of the exclusive right of the record company to

manufacture records from recordings delivered to it, and which have been commercially released. Two common time limits are:

(a) In the case of an artiste deal, it can be a number of years after the delivery of the last album. All the album rights revert at the same time, and for earlier albums the record company will have had longer rights periods than for later ones. It can also be a fixed period of time for each individual recording, from normally the date of delivery to the record company of the recording, or the date of the first release. Therefore the rights in each recording will revert to the production company at a different date. If it is agreed that the album release date starts the rights period for it, there must be a maximum period of time after the date of delivery of the recording for its first release, and from which the time will begin to run even if the album has not been released.

(b) In a production deal it can be a number of years following the termination of the exclusive period of the production agreement. Different artistes will have been provided to the record company at different times, so the dates at which they each deliver their last album will be different. Some of these may not be released until just before, or some time after, the expiry date of the production agreement. Because of the cross-collateralised royalty advances, the overall rights expiry period needs to be a number of years following the last album delivered by the latest artiste to be provided to the record company. All of the albums of all of the artistes are retained, and the rights in them all will revert to the production company at the same time.

(2)(a) The continuing rights of the record company in recordings already delivered to it, but unreleased at the date of the expiry of the production agreement. The production agreement must specify a maximum period after delivery within which records must be released to entitle the record company to have any manufacturing rights to them. It is vital to the production company that records are released on schedule, as record sales are the only means of generating royalties so that advances can be recouped, and a profit can be made. If the album is not released by the cut-off date without a good reason acceptable to the production company, and if a release is not intended, the album should revert to the production company. Whether the record company would get back its advance payment depends on the production agreement.

The importance of a cut off date depends on whether the exclusive manufacturing period is related to individual albums, or whether there is a common terminal date for all albums, whenever delivered. Unless there is a cut-off date:

(i) It is possible for the record company to release albums not in the sequence of their delivery, although that is not likely. This would be of concern where the rights in the albums are held by different record companies in different territories, where the release sequence must be the same, even if the release dates are different.

(ii) An album which is released by the record company very late, and so with a minimal or inadequate exclusive manufacturing period, reduces the ability of the record company to make the most of its sales potential. There is no point in spending money on manufacturing costs and promotion if there is not a reasonable period in which to exhaust the sales potential of the album.

(iii) If the release is very late, especially after the production agreement has ended, the artiste may have made new recordings for another record company, which may also have been released. The late released album by the previous record company will interfere with the new album release.

(b) The rights of the production company in recordings still in its possession, and not delivered to the record company at the end of the production agreement, where the minimum recording commitment has already been satisfied. This will depend upon whether the record company is entitled to have delivered to it all records made by the production agreement artistes, even if in excess of the minimum, or if it is only entitled to the stated contractual number. If each artiste's recording commitment has been satisfied, what is to happen to any such excess recordings? If the record company wants them, what advances will be paid, and when will they be released? It is not likely that the production company will make excess albums for which there is no scheduled advance payment, due to the cost. If the delivery schedule has been properly calculated, there should never be such a gap that an unscheduled album is even contemplated.

(3) After the expiry of the exclusive manufacturing period, either the manufacturing parts for the records must be destroyed, or they must be handed back to the production company, together with all copy master tapes. The latter is not practical where many manufacturing countries are involved, in which case an affidavit made by an officer of the record company confirming such destruction will be acceptable.

(4) The record company will need a non exclusive period of time within which to sell off the residual stocks of records it may have at that date, which are still subject to royalty payments. Any excess stock of records held at the end of the non-exclusive sell-off period

will have to be destroyed. The record company should be prohibited from manufacturing excessive quantities of records in the last part of its exclusive manufacturing period, the purpose and consequence of which is to have substantial residual stocks. This would only be considered by the record company if, despite the end of its exclusive period, the sales of a specific album are still at a high commercial rate.

(5) If there are restrictions on the six year time limit within which the production company will be deemed to have accepted the accuracy of the record company's royalty accounting statements, it must decide whether or not to audit the final accounts of the record company shortly after receiving them for the period up to the expiry of the non-exclusive record stock sell-off period.

(6) Although upon the expiry of the record company's exclusive manufacturing period the rights to manufacture and sell records from those recordings revert to the production company, it will be restricted from re-marketing them in any combination for an agreed period following the expiry of the record company's non-exclusive residual stock sell-off period. This will only be of any consequence if the records are still in demand, such as by a specialist low price label company, or for inclusion on a compilation album.

(7) The winding up and accounting for any outstanding royalty reserves retained by the record company within a reasonable time after after the expiry of the non-exclusive stock sell-off period.

(8) The continuation of accounting by the record company for sales of records until the exclusive and non-exclusive manufacturing and selling rights of the record company have expired.

(9) Ensuring that there are no outstanding obligations on either side.

**13.3** If the production agreement is by way of assignment of mechanical copyrights, it should contain the right of the production company to call for a reassignment of those rights if the record company goes bust. They can then be properly promoted through another record company, so that neither the production company nor the artiste are unfairly prejudiced.

The same commercial position is created where the record company deletes the recordings from its current catalogue, so they stop being manufactured and sold in the major record selling territories. A practical solution would be for the production company to be entitled to reversion of the rights in consideration of paying the record company an over-ride royalty on all sales for a period of time. This proposal would not affect a foreign licensee who is still making and selling the records.

## SECTION IV: THE ARTISTE'S CONTRACT

The contract between each artiste and the production company will be similar to an ordinary artiste's recording contract, the principles of which were discussed in the previous chapter. Certain aspects may be different, as the terms of the production agreement will determine what the production company must agree with the artiste to keep within its warranties and obligations to the record company.

### 14 Royalty rates

**14.1** The artiste will negotiate for the highest royalty rate he can get, but the production company is limited in what it can pay to the artiste by what it receives as a royalty rate from the record company. The production company, when negotiating its royalty rate with the record company, must allow for the artiste's royalty, the record producer's royalty, and a reasonable royalty for itself.

**14.2** Where the production company has several artistes contracted to it, they may not all receive the same royalty rate. The production company must set itself a maximum royalty rate which it can afford to pay, and negotiate with each artiste a fair royalty rate within that limit. The production company must be prepared, if necessary, to exceed its usual limits where the artiste warrants a more favourable deal, such as:

(a) A composer/artiste who is already established and successful, and whose name and popularity is valuable to the production company in promotional terms. A top royalty rate may also be paid to him in return for a music publishing deal being given to a production company subsidiary. This is not normally recommended from the composer's point of view.

(b) An artiste who has great potential, but no proven success. A sliding scale can be used, relating an increasing royalty rate to an increased level of record sales on individual albums.

In a production deal, because advances are cross-collateralised against royalties by the record company, a higher royalty rate for one successful artiste, out of a number of unsuccessful artistes, can create a major cashflow problem for the production company.

**14.3** The detailed basis of royalty calculations by the record company, when accounting to the production company, will have to be followed by the production company in its artiste's contracts. So also will the accounting methods and dates, and all other financial terms contained in the production agreement which affect each of the artistes. This simplifies the accounting procedure, and ensures that, due to careless negotiation, the production company is not obliged to pay royalties to the artiste on a basis which it cannot maintain or administer. For example, if the production company is paid a royalty based upon 95% of the net sales of records, it has a calculation crisis if it contracts to pay the artiste his royalty on 100% of all records sold. The accounting dates in the artiste's contracts must allow sufficient time for the record company to account to the production company. For example, if the record company accounts within 45 days of each quarter, for the benefit of the artistes the production company should account (say) within 60 days of each quarter, for royalties which it has received. If it accounts within 30 days of each quarter, it will retain royalty payments from the record company for an extra quarter before paying them out. Properly timed accounting dates will:

(a) Maximise the amounts to be accounted for to the artiste each time by the production company. This would reduce the cashflow value to the production company of artistes' royalties which could be retained for longer.

(b) Give the production company enough time to prepare from the accounting statements it receives from the record company the statements to be given to the artiste.

(c) Ensure a smooth cash flow for the production company. This is crucial where cross-collateralised advances still exceed total royalties payable to the production company at the date of each accounting from the record company, but artistes who are in credit with the production company must be paid the royalties due to them.

**14.4** An artiste who signs a recording contract with a production company must check and understand the wording of the royalty calculation and payment clauses. The production company will only pay to the artiste his royalties as and when it receives its own royalties for his record sales from the record company. The principle is fair, but there are circumstances when that is not acceptable to the artiste, because he has no knowledge of, or control over, the financial arrangements set out in the production agreement. The artiste does not have contractual access to the record company to force direct payment of his share of the production company's royalties. The accounting obligations of the production company depend upon the definition of "received". On the relevant accounting date the production company may not actually receive cash from the record company, due to the level of unrecouped advances. However, within those advances, it will already have "received" the royalties in respect of the account now due to the artiste. If the production company means that if it receives no cash it pays no royalties, that is not acceptable. It would then be in financial difficulty, and in breach of the artiste's contract, if it is unable to pay the royalties due to him.

**14.5** The production company is liable as a principal in its agreement with the artiste, and must take all reasonable steps to ensure that the record company pays royalties due to it. In a production deal, where all royalty advances received by the production company are cross-collateralised against all royalties due to it on record sales of all albums, the artiste must ensure that contractually the royalties due to him on the sales of his albums will be accounted for to him by the production company, irrespective of its recoupment position in respect of any other artiste contracted to it. If the royalties are only payable to the artiste as and when received by the production company from the record company, due to cross collateralisation exercised by the record company, it is possible for the production company to receive substantial royalty advances, and never any subsequent royalty payments. If there is doubt as to the financial standing of the production company, the artiste should not contract with it. But if he does, the best safeguard for the artiste is to have secured a proportion of all advances received by the production company in respect of potential sales of the artiste's recordings. This can be done in the case of an artiste deal, but may not be practical for a production deal. Relevant points are:

(a) The production company receives a general advance, not calculated upon any specific album delivery schedule. It is not practical to have retained in a separate account a portion of the advance to cover the artiste's royalties on potential record sales. At the date of receipt of the royalty advance there is no means of ascertaining either the possible record sales of the artiste within the period covered by the general advance, or what proportion of the advance ought to be attributed to the artiste.

(b) The royalty advance is paid on the delivery of each album to the record company. That may be shared with the artiste on a pro rata basis, subject to any previous advances to the artiste from the production company, including all record production costs, having been recouped.

(c) The production company can pay out of its own resources a general advance to the artiste, or album delivery advances, on account of royalties due to him, irrespective of what it receives under the record company deal.

(d) The artistes recording costs are already a deemed advance from the production company, to be recouped out of royalties due to the artiste.

(e) All advances received from the record company will be needed to pay the costs of record production.

## 15 Key group member option

**15.1** It is fundamental to any production agreement with a record company that the recording services of the artistes are exclusive to the production company. The individuals of a group should be contracted exclusively to the production company, whether or not they remain with the group for the whole of the exclusive period of the production agreement. This would only be valid if that artiste's career will be promoted wholeheartedly and without delay, eg, if he is a key member. Within the production agreement, acceptance by the record company of the group may be conditional upon certain named members of the group remaining as part of it. The record company may consider that those key members constitute the musical nucleus of the group upon which the acceptance decision was made. The record company may also want to have an option to accept as a separate artiste under the production agreement any key member, such as the singer, who leaves the group. The option right must be contained in the relevant artiste's recording agreement with the production company, and should also be contained in each artiste's individual side letter. (See paragraph **19**.)

**15.2** The record company may also insist on approving replacement members of the group, whether or not the replacement is of a key member. Where the key member leaves the group, and the record company does not want to retain the group in its changed form, it must decide within a stated time, and give the production company written notice of that decision. The production company must have the right of termination on this ground contained in its artiste's agreements. As between the production company and the record company the main points of discussion will be:

(a) The exercise of an option to retain a key group member should not give the record company a greater exclusive period in respect of the key member's separate recording services than it would have had under the production agreement. The key member will have an artiste's deal, in the same way that a new artiste would be contracted through the production agreement. A key member may start a solo career with the approval of the group and of the production company, but nevertheless remain a member of the group for group activities and recordings. At the end of the exclusive period of the production agreement, the production company must not find itself with a group exclusively recording for one record company, and a key member as a solo performer exclusively recording for another record company.

(b) The royalty rate paid by the record company to the production company for a key member's solo recordings must not be less than the standard production agreement royalty rate if he is to become an accepted artiste under it. Similarly, the key member should be given not less than the royalty paid to the group he has left. This shows the difference of royalty per man between a solo artiste and the members of a group.

(c) If the key member solo performer becomes an accepted artiste, but no longer remains with the group, will the record company still have to retain the group under the production agreement?

(d) The decision by the record company upon whether the key member solo performer is an accepted artiste in replacement of the group, or whether both will continue to be production agreement artistes, will have an effect upon:

(i) the production company's minimum and maximum recording delivery commitment;

(ii) the calculation of royalty advances to the production company where they are periodic payments not related to album deliveries;

(iii) the recording delivery schedule of the key member solo performer within the remainder of the exclusive period of the production agreement.

**15.3** Guest artiste status by any production agreement artiste on recordings released by other record companies will require the consent of both the production company and the record company. In this context the "guest artiste" will be, for example, appearing as a celebrity fifth member of what is usually a four man group, to produce a one-off record for charity. Consent, and the conditions of consent, will depend, for example, on whether the guest appearance is on only one track, or on the whole album. Uncredited session work should be permitted without consent having to be obtained, but both the production agreement and the artiste's agreement would have to make that clear.

## 16 Period of agreement

**16.1** The production company must ensure that the artiste's recording agreement period is at least as long as the period for which the company could be required to provide the artiste to the record company. It must also include (where relevant) the right to suspend the period of the artiste's agreement where those rights are exercised by the record company in respect of the production agreement. Suspension rights are suspect in law, as being unduly onerous or oppressive, unless the wording and operation of the clause is only enough to be a reasonable and justifiable requirement for the protection of the relevant company's rights.

Where the production company's agreement wth the artiste is for successive option periods, it will be in breach of the production agreement with the record company if it neglects to exercise the options, where the artiste still has part of his production agreement time to run. It is therefore essential to ensure that if the record company has option rights, their exercise must be at the latest sometime before the option against the artiste has to be exercised.

## 17 Termination of agreement

**17.1** Specific provisions for termination by the artiste of his agreement with the production company depend on any limitations in that respect imposed on the production company by the record company. Outside the normal contract termination provisions, the production company must not grant to the artiste specific termination rights which are not compatible with the terms of the production agreement. The artiste should not accept restrictions on his termination rights which clearly exceed reasonable commercial requirements and safeguards for the production company. As the production company (so far as the artiste is concerned) bears all the commercial risk, and is financing the artiste whereby the artiste cannot lose but can gain from that investment, it is reasonable for it to have commensurate security of exclusivity to the artiste's recording services. The production company must anticipate and deal with any circumstances whereby the artiste may have a right to terminate his agreement, causing the production company to be liable to the record company for breach of contract. Record companies will not give any production company the right to terminate its artistes' agreements within its own discretion for so long as the record company wishes to retain them. Even if the production company has a right to terminate its agreement with any artiste, it should check with the record company before it does so. The record company may want the production company to retain the artiste for some reason, or the record company may prefer to exercise its rights under the artiste's side letter.

## 18 Assignment of artistes' contracts

**18.1** As (apart from a side letter) there is no direct contractual link between the artiste and the record company, the production company controls the artiste. There may be a side letter between the artiste and the record company, but this takes effect only when the artiste ceases to record for the production company during the record company's exclusive period. Apart from any limitation imposed by the artiste, the production company cannot assign the benefit of the artiste's contract otherwise than as set out in the production agreement.

**18.2** The record company must not be materially affected by any internal contractual re-arrangement between the artiste and the production company. Depending upon the purpose of the assignment the following points should be considered:

(1) The artiste should satisfy himself that where the production company wants to assign the benefit of the artiste's recording agreement to a third party:
  (a) It is not a device which would prejudice the flow of, or diminish the share of, money received by the production company which is ultimately payable to the artiste. The artiste would need some knowledge of the relevant terms of the production agreement and of the proposed assignment.
  (b) The assignee is of sufficient substance and reputation that it will be able to undertake all the obligations of the production company, and that the assignment will not prejudice his professional and personal standing.
  (c) That the assignment is authorised by the record company. This prevents legal action being brought by it against the artiste where an unauthorised assignment by the production company is in breach of the production agreement.
  (d) If the assignee has paid to the production company an advance on account of a royalty override consideration for the assignment, no part of the override royalty or of the advance shall be recoupable from, or collateralised against, the artiste's share of the royalties which will be paid by the record company to the assignee.

(2) In the production agreement the record company should:
  (a) Prohibit the production company from assigning the artiste from the production agreement without its prior consent, and which will only be given upon such terms as it may reasonably require to protect its rights.
  (b) Have a legally enforceable claim and compensation clause which becomes operative if the production company breaches its obligations to provide the artiste exclusively to the record company.
  (c) Impose reasonable restrictions upon the outside recording activities directly or indirectly carried on by the shareholders and

directors of the production company. Otherwise the promoters of the production company can bypass the exclusivity of the production agreement by placing new artistes they find with another production company with which they are connected.

(d) Deal with the adjustment of payment of royalties and recoupment of royalty advances, and any cross-collateralisation rights against royalties, which would be affected by an assignment of an artiste's contract. There may be a distinction between albums of the artiste which have already been delivered, and those yet to be recorded.

(e) Ensure that the production company guarantees the performance and observance by the assignee of the production agreement terms, or that some other acceptable guarantee is provided.

(3) The production company should ensure that:

(a) The assignment of an artiste's agreement is authorised by the record company in writing, to prevent the implementation of any financial deterrents in the production agreement for unauthorised assignments.

(b) The artiste's contract allows assignment by the production company. If an unauthorised assignment by the production company entitles the artiste to terminate his agreement, the production company will be in breach of any undertaking it has given to the record company to do nothing which prejudices the rights it has acquired.

(c) Its assignee is controlled by the production company, or that there are adequate safeguards to ensure that the production agreement in respect of that artiste will be honoured in all respects.

(d) The assignment is by a formal document because:

(i) if the production company and the assignee are connected, they may need to satisfy the Inland Revenue that the assignment is not a tax avoidance device, and is a *bona fide* commercial transaction;

(ii) a detailed assignment will enable the production company to sue upon it if necessary, or to enforce an indemnity given by the assignee.

**18.3** The record company can reduce the adverse consequences of an unauthorised assignment by a production company of any of its artiste's contracts by being entitled to retain royalties due to the production company against damages to be claimed by the record company. If an unauthorised assignee is in danger of not receiving the royalties payable by the record company in respect of the assigned artiste, the production company will be forced by it to obtain the consent of the record company, which may then consent to it but impose conditions upon the assignment.

To be enforceable, any royalty withholding provisions in both the artiste's contract and the production agreement must not constitute a penalty.

**18.4** If there is a dispute between the record company and the production company resulting in the record company withholding all royalties due to the production company, whether or not it was contractually entitled to do so, the artiste is likely to suffer, because cash will not be available for his own royalty payments, whatever his contract says.

**18.5** The production company should have the right in its artiste's agreements to assign the benefit of them to the record company at the record company's request, provided that:

(a) The assignment will in no way adversely affect the artiste.

(b) The record company undertakes to fulfil all of the outstanding and the future obligations of the production company to the artiste. Any outstanding obligations would have to be identified.

(c) Any financial transaction between the two companies in connection with the assignment does not delay the payment of, or lessen the amount of, the royalties to be accounted for to the artiste.

## 19 Side letters

**19.1** It will suit both the production company and the record company to have a side letter between the artiste and the record company. A side letter serves two functions:

(a) To have the artiste personally warrant to the record company that he is aware of the production agreement terms which affect him, and to undertake with the record company that he will observe and perform all of those terms as if he were a signatory to the production agreement.

(b) If the artiste has left a group which was contracted to the production company, he grants to the record company an option to take up his recording services on the same terms as those of his contract with the production company. The option should be exercisable by the record company within, say, 21 days after being notified in writing by either of the artiste or the production company of the termination of the artiste's membership of the group.

**19.2** The side letter must fulfil all the requirements necessary to form a binding contract as it stands, without relying upon the production agreement or the artiste's agreement with the production company. Therefore there must be some valid consideration contained in it to support the ability of the record company to enforce it at some uncertain time in the future. It's terms must be specific and unconditional, and any additional restrictions contained in it must not be unduly oppressive, nor must they invalidate the whole option by being in restraint of trade.

A side letter could be awkward for the artiste, for example if he terminates his agreement with the production company because in his opinion the record company had failed absolutely to promote him or to release his recordings. If the record company takes up its rights under the side letter, the artiste would then be able to sue the record company, or (if he is entitled to) he can terminate the agreement, as he will have the same terms as the production company.

**19.3** The terms of the side letter should cover:

(a) Delivery of recordings. This should only be the number of albums which the artiste, through the production company, has yet to deliver to the record company.

(b) Royalty advances. These will not be the same for each album as the royalty advances paid under the production agreement, which were calculated according to many other factors, including their cost of production. The record company is taking over the cost of record production, so the artiste will have to agree a normal advance.

(c) Royalty rates on future recordings. These must not be less than the royalty rates being paid to the artiste by the production company. The royalty cost to the record company is reduced, as it is not paying the "top up" royalty previously received by the production company.

(d) Recoupment of royalty advances. The artiste must ensure that the operation of the side letter creates a new agreement between the artiste and the record company entirely independent from the production agreement. All future royalty advances paid to the artiste by the record company should be recoverable only from royalties due on sales of future recordings made by the artiste for the record company. Recordings made by the artiste for the production company will stay within the structure of the production agreement. Royalties arising on sales of those records will be paid to the production company, subject to the royalty advance recoupment rights of the record company existing prior to the side letter being exercised.

Even if the production company has not itself recouped all advances it has paid to the artiste, the record company should not pay the artistes royalties on the new albums to the production company.

(e) Past recordings. For the benefit of the artiste, once the production company has recouped all of its advances to the artiste (whether in cash or as deemed advances, such as recording costs), the record company should be authorised by the production company to pay to the artiste direct his share of royalties arising from his production agreement record sales, and the production company's share would be paid to it as normal. This authority would have to be subject to any contractual right of the production company to withhold royalty payments to the artiste pending settlement of any claim it has against him, but only where such a right was being exercised at the date of transfer of payment obligations direct to the artiste. This would need the consent of the group, and would adversely affect the production company's cashflow.

**19.4** The artiste benefits from the existence of a side letter because, should the production company wind up, cease to trade, or become otherwise permanently inoperative, he has a potential contract with the record company which (if the side letter option is exercised), ensures continuity of future recording and payment of royalties from sales of those records.

The production company, being in the middle contractually, needs the device for two reasons. First, it can negotiate an absolute release from the record company in respect of future obligations including compensation in respect of that artiste commencing from when the side letter comes into effect. Secondly, through the operation of the side letter, the production company should ensure that it is free from further obligations to the artiste, except for continuing accounting provisions in respect of existing records.

**19.5** Where a production company loses the recording services of an artiste:

(a) The record company loses its own share of income created by the sale of records to be derived from the artiste's future recordings.

(b) The production company will not receive from the record company royalty advance payments attributable to that artiste's future albums. It will continue to receive royalties on sales of that artiste's existing albums.

(c) If all the advances received by the production company are cross-collateralised against all royalties due to the production company irrespective of the artiste, the overall royalty advance recoupment rate by the record company will be reduced. This adversely affects the cash flow of the production company, and its ability to pay the artistes who are in credit their due royalties.

(d) The exercise by the record company of a side letter in respect of an artiste who terminates his agreement with the production company cancels what would otherwise have been the adverse effects upon the record company. Furthermore, the record company will have increased its profitability on that artiste because any royalty advances paid to him direct will not be so great as those paid under the production agreement. The royalty rates paid to him on record sales will be less than those which would have been payable to the production company.

CHAPTER 6

# *Record Producers' Agreements*

## 1 General

**1.1** Where record producers are employed by a record company on the permanent staff at a salary, under the 1988 Copyright Act the rights in the creative and created products of their services will automatically belong to the company. The rights of the record company and the producer who is independent will depend on their contract. The role of a producer is different from that of a sound engineer, although they both use the electronic studio equipment in a creative manner. Many record producers are sound engineers who have developed their career.

**1.2** Independent record producers have to rely on their ability being proved with successful records. A successful record could be described as one which sells well, irrespective of genuine musical quality. It is an advantage to know the right people in the record companies who know of, appreciate, and use their services. Being an independent record producer is a job without any long term security, but the rewards of success will be far greater than the salary of the average "in-house" record producer.

Producing hit records is an art, and successful producers are in great demand. The financial attraction is that his source of income (the record produced) may sell for many years in the case of an established artiste. It may be "rediscovered" by every new generation of record buyers, and so become a pension as well. A record producer should always have an agreement to establish his rights in the product of his services.

**1.3** Apart from the financial potential open to an independent record producer, he is free to produce records for many artistes, depending only on his availability and the demand for his services. A producer who is an employee of a record company would usually be prohibited from acting as an independent record producer in his spare time. Studios operate on a 24 hour basis, and most recording is done when ordinary sane people have gone home from work.

## 2 Skill and experience

**2.1** Music depends for its commercial success upon its appeal to the record-buying public, although the performance embodied in a hit record need not be intelligible, musically tasteful, or perfect in its rendition. It is the quirk of musical beat, or the emotive prominence of an instrument, or perhaps an indefinable quality of arrangement which may distinguish one best-selling recorded performance from any number of unsuccessful performances, although the teams which produced them did their best.

**2.2** Cover records can be more successful than the original record released, presumably because there was an appeal in the second production which was lacking in the original recording. A lot also depends on the difference in the popularity of the respective artistes, but this chapter deals with the musical content of a recording.

**2.3** Among the skills required of a successful record producer are:

(a) He must be familiar and experienced with the use of all the intricate studio equipment made available to him, and he must be capable of creating the most attractive sound effect with it.

(b) He must have a feel for the current and the upcoming record buying public mood.

(c) The composition to be recorded must be translated creatively by making the musical arrangement and the artiste's performance original within his style of music, as well as being consistent with the current public taste and demand.

(d) He should know the capabilities and musical compatibility of all the musical instruments to be used on the recording. The alternative is to make the record sufficiently bizarre or original to attract public attention through outrage or amusement.

(e) He must be able to get on with record company executives and the artiste he is recording. They are putting financial and artistic trust in his judgement, he is in control of the creation of an investment.

**2.4** To be successful, any record must be broadcast on radio or TV sufficiently often for it to become noticed by the public. Of all the records released for sale each week, only a small proportion sell enough copies to warrant a place in the record popularity charts. Sheer musical and technical expertise, and the vivid imagination of the record producer, can never guarantee the success of the record, but without those ingredients any record starts at a disadvantage.

**2.5** The skills of the producer are wasted unless he has the personality to have a rapport with the performers in the studio, and to have them confident in his ability to make creative and practical directions or suggestions during the progress of the recording.

**2.6** It is only part of the record producer's job to attend to the actual recording of the song, and to obtain the best sound possible from each performer on tape. Great importance is placed on the knack of "mixing" the vocal track, the backing music tracks and any special effects tracks into one integrated master tape with the most effective combination of sound. A weak voice can be brought out by multi-tracking and increasing its comparative volume over the music; and an instrumental solo can be highlighted within the tune as a whole. The end result is an expression of the musical taste of the producer, who projects into a sound recording his interpretation of the musical ability and style of the performers.

**2.7** The recording equipment available is so sophisticated that the record producer can do justice to the most startling of inventive compositions. This includes the use of electronic music, multiple tracking by the same artiste, dubbing in any required noise or sound, and making a recording bearing little resemblance to what would be heard if the same work were to be performed live on stage. Technology will enable a machine to emulate any musical instrument, so relying upon human ability is no longer a limiting weakness. This may not please the Musicians Union, but it does allow the producer's imagination free rein.

## 3 Producers' royalties

**3.1** The remuneration of a record producer depends upon whether he is an independent producer, or whether he is an employee of the record company. A record company employee may be paid a fee for each record produced by him as well as a basic salary. A valued in-house producer may also be paid a royalty on the sales of records he produced, but this would have to come from the record company on its own account, or on behalf of the artiste. The studio charges time rates for use, or time booked even if not used. Some studios may become investors in a recording, by (for example) not charging the full or any rate for studio use, and taking a royalty on sales of the records.

**3.2** An independent producer is in a better position than a record company employee to earn a high income and to establish his reputation, because his time is his own and he controls what he does. His career is dependent upon getting the right people to have sufficient faith in his ability to risk financing the production of their artiste's records under his control. An independent producer will be paid a royalty which is usually calculated on the same basis as the artiste's royalties, whether he is paid by a record company or to an artiste out of his own royalties.

**3.3** The royalty rates available to a record producer are as negotiable as those of the artiste, up to around 4%, depending on his reputation. The royalty rate will also depend on who contracts with (and so pays) the producer. The choices are:

(a) The record company. The less the artiste is paid as a royalty, the greater will be the margin available for the producer. If the artiste receives a high royalty rate, the record company has a limited margin to contribute in paying the producer. At the high artiste royalty rate levels the record company may make the artiste pay part of the producer's royalty by deducting it from the artiste's royalty.

The benefit to the producer of contracting direct with the record company is that if it is a major company it will remain in business for as long as the producer is likely to be due his royalties. Also he will be accounted to earlier than if he is contracted to a production company.

(b) The production company. The combined royalty it can pay out in total to the artiste and the producer is limited by the royalty it receives from the record company. Production companies do not have the same survival rate as major record companies. The producer should try to get an irrevocable authority for direct payment from the record company (as the source of record royalties) if the production company goes bust or simply fails to pay. This would have to be done so as not to upset the recoupment by the record company of its advances to the production company. Adjustment will be needed so that direct payment to the producer does not affect the recoupment period beyond what it would otherwise have been.

(c) The artiste. Of all three choices of payer of the producer, the artiste will have the least available royalty margin. He is the most unreliable person to contract with in respect of ensuring prompt or accurate accounting to the producer for his royalties for so long as the records he produces are sold. Should the producer's contract be with the artiste personally, with the best of will between them, delays and difficulties will arise if the artiste is made bankrupt, or is involved in litigation in connection with the recordings, and when he dies. If the producer is paid by the artiste out of royalties he receives, there may be tax implications to be dealt with. Therefore the producer will insist his royalty is paid direct to him from source, ie, the record company, in the same manner as in (a) above.

Although the producer may be paid what is effectively a part of the artiste's royalty, in his agreement it should be expressed as a separate royalty independent of what is paid to the artiste. The reason is that if the artiste becomes bankrupt, and if contractually the producer is being paid part of the artiste's royalty entitlement, his trustee in bankruptcy may be able to treat the producer as a creditor of the artiste, and retain the royalty portion.

**3.4** An important factor in determining which of the above alternatives is contractually correct is who has the choice of producer. He who chooses should pay. Few record or production companies would risk wasting expensive studio time, or the quality of the final recording, by allowing the artiste either to record without the supervision of a competent producer, or to choose a producer who is not approved by the company. Whoever is the payer, the producer can still arrange for that royalty to be separately contracted for to ensure proper payment and accounting into the future.

**3.5** The producer's royalty rate can be either:

(a) A (probably low) fixed rate irrespective of the level of record sales and wherever they are sold, the price level of the records sold, or the medium through which the records are sold. The same rate will therefore apply to budget sales as well as full price sales, in the UK or Australia. This might not fit in with a record company's accounting structure, particularly if it licences products abroad.

(b) A rate which is reduced or increased proportionately wherever the artiste's royalty rate is reduced or increased, with the top rate being calculated on normal full price retail sales. If the artiste's royalty clauses are mirrored in the producer's agreement, he should check that any artificial reductions (such as under a controlled composition clause) are not included in his production contract.

**3.6** The pro-rated system is essential to a production company or to an artiste if they pay the producer, as they will have compared the producer's royalty rate with their own top royalty rate received from the record company. Without the pro-rated levels, the amount paid to the producer from the amount received by the artiste or the production company on, say, record club sales in a minor territory, will be uneconomic. To be consistent, the producer will not be paid his royalty on those categories of record sales where the artiste receives no royalty. If the producer's royalty is the record company's responsibility, it does not affect the artiste—possibly except for the setting of his own royalty rate.

There may be categories of record sales where the artiste's royalty is reduced for sound reasons, such as TV advertised albums. The producer has no choice in the manner of promoting a record he produces, so should he also have his royalty rate reduced? It depends upon his royalty rate, and (for example) whether he is contracted to produce the next few recordings by the artiste.

**3.7** The producer's royalty provisions must make clear the position on compilation albums, where his royalty will depend on the number of recordings he produced in relation to the total number of recordings on the album. This would apply, for example, where he produced a hit single for the artiste, which is subsequently included on an album of the artiste which he did not produce. The royalty rate in respect of the use of substantial extracts from records produced by the producer will have to be dealt with in his agreement, such as on a background music continuous track medley record which contains excerpts from recordings by various artistes.

**3.8** On a comparison of the relative royalty values of the producer and the artiste in respect of any recording, the producer has an advantage over the artiste. Subject only to recoupment of royalty advances paid to him, the producer will be paid his royalty on all sales of the record; but the artiste will have recording costs as well as his royalty advances deducted from royalties due to him. It is possible for the record producer to receive more money from the sale of a record than for example, a member of a five man group receives, depending upon the level of record sales, the comparative royalty rates, and the recording costs to be recouped. The producer is providing a service, he is not interested in promoting the recording in the same way an artiste does. The remuneration for those services will be commensurate with the success of the artistes and record company's investment, the only risk he has is that the record sales may be low.

**3.9** A royalty paid to the producer, as opposed to a flat fee, makes the producer reliant on record sales for his income, which creates an incentive for him to produce good quality commercial albums. If he produces a hit record he can earn a lot of money, as well as adding to his reputation. Although he has to wait for record company accounting dates before receiving his royalties, to have royalties payable to him in the future for work done in the past is a great benefit.

**3.10** The producer should make sure that if his producer's agreement is directly with a group, which subsequently either breaks up and ceases to record, or terminates its then existing recording contract, any such event will not adversely affect his right and ability to continue to receive his royalties on sales of their records which he produced. As in paragraph **3.3**(b), the only safeguard is to have direct payment from the record company.

**3.11** In any dispute between the artiste and either the record company or the producer in respect of the quality of the record or the royalties due to the producer, or his apparent inexperience or inability, the rights of the producer will depend upon with whom he made his contract. If the producer contracts with the record company, his position will not be affected by any tantrums between the artiste and the record company; as the record company is the source of the income of both the producer and the artiste.

## 4 Royalty advances

**4.1** A royalty advance should be paid to the producer when the production contract is signed. The amount of the royalty advance is negotiable, depending upon the reputation of the producer, the royalty rate he receives, and the ability of the artiste to sell records. The reasons for an advance are:

(a) The producer is setting aside time in the future for the record production, and will decline any other record production offers which affect his availability during that time. Through no fault of the producer, the recording may not take place, or may be started but abandoned after a lot of time spent on it, or the artiste may change his mind about employing the producer. The contract should treat the royalty advance as a non-returnable cancellation charge in all circumstances, other than the failure of the producer to complete the recording and mixing of the album wholly due to his own default or breach.

(b) Recordings which are produced may never be released for sale. In that case the royalty advance will be the only compensation the producer will receive for the work he has done, and the time he has spent on producing those recordings. It is possible that individual tracks may not be released immediately, or for a considerable time. As the income of the producer depends on record sales, his agreement could have a clause whereby if any of the recorded tracks which he has produced are not released within, say, 12 months after completion, the advance attributable to those tracks will be increased by an agreed amount at that time. As and when the tracks are released, the higher advance is recoupable in full as usual. That would depend on the level of the advance he has received already.

(c) Royalties due to the producer from sales of the records he produces will take a long time to come through. If the artiste's recording contract allows the record company to retain reserves out of his royalties against excess record returns in later accounting periods, the same system will be applied to the producer's royalty.

**4.2** If the producer's contract is still being negotiated at the start of recording, the royalty advance should be paid to him at that time on a non-returnable basis. Payment should not be delayed until his contract is signed, if he is doing his job. Payment gives him some protection if the record company fails to submit one to him for consideration. This will avoid the record production being completed without the producer having the security of either a payment or a contract. The artiste may otherwise use that fact unfairly in the final negotiations on royalty advance payments or royalty rates once the recording has been completed. Depending on the status of the record company, the producer should halt the production at some point until his contract is signed.

**4.3** If the producer is the regular producer of singles and albums made by the artiste, and as some will be more successful than others, recoupment of advances should be clarified. The advance received by the producer for a specific recording should only be recouped from royalties accruing on sales of that recording, and the producer's agreement should be worded accordingly. For example, if some tracks he produces are never released, as they were excess to requirements at the time, the advances he received for those tracks will never be recouped. They should not be aggregated with the advances received for successful recordings for recoupment.

## 5 Artistic control

**5.1** If there is a dispute between the producer and the artiste prior to recording taking place, it is likely to be on a business level. After recording starts, any dispute is likely to be on an artistic level. "Artistic" will cover the choice of material to be recorded, musical arrangements of it, all the way through to the final mix of the master tape.

**5.2** The producer's agreement will stipulate that the employer of the producer has ultimate artistic control over the recordings to be produced, which will mean the choice of compositions and the musical direction of the album. The producer should have the choice of session musicians, consultation on the choice of studio, and direction of or supervision over the final mixing of each recorded composition.

**5.3** There is a difference between the functions and skills of the producer, and those of the studio engineer. Every artiste has his personal views on what his recorded performance should sound like, but the objectivity which a producer brings by way of artistic criticism for the purpose of producing a good commercial sound is vital. Producers are generally also expert sound engineers, or know the workings of the studio and its equipment so well that to use an engineer would be a hindrance. If the producer is not familiar with the studio, the use of a competent sound engineer is valuable under his direction.

**5.4** The choice of songs may be made by the artiste, his manager or the record company. Although the producer will have his own opinion of the songs which the artiste will record, he must recognise that the choice has been made to represent the artiste to the record buying public in the best possible light, and to make his live personal appearances artistically consistent with his record releases. If the artiste is also a composer, the music or lyrics can be modified in the course of recording, depending on how the production is going. He may also be able to write for each album a different concept of his music, ie there is great flexibility in the choice of material. If he is not a composer it will be necessary to choose the songs to suit his style. Either way the purpose is to sell records, and the input of the producer is valuable as an expert on what is the musical trend at that time. It would be even better if he could accurately forecast the next trend—musical experimentation can create a trend.

**5.5** The musical direction and the arrangement of the songs to be recorded should have been worked out by the artiste in rehearsal first, to avoid wasting expensive time in the studio. Many rock bands put the musical ideas together at rehearsal, and work out the final version of the songs in the studio, depending heavily upon inspiration at the time.

The producer should not be concerned, unless he is responsible for calculating the recording cost budget, and making sure that it is not exceeded. He is there to help to create the best sound possible from what the artiste wishes to record. Efficient use and management of studios, musicians and the artiste will be necessary to reduce cost and to make the best of the available talent.

**5.6** To comply with the requirement in the artiste's recording contract to provide the record company with "commercially acceptable" recordings, the producer's agreement will oblige him to produce the fully mixed recording to the same quality. For the producer, acceptability should mean no more than good technical quality, he is not responsible for the choice of the material. If the producer does not produce a good technical quality recording, his agreement may enable the record company to reject the recording, and to terminate his contract. In such a case it must be made clear whether he is still entitled to retain any royalty advance paid to him, or whether the royalty advance (or part of it) is returnable.

The perceived quality also refers to the artiste's performance, in that if he is an awful singer, or the group are not competent musicians, the better the technical quality is, the more the performance deficiencies are displayed. Part of the producer's job in obtaining an acceptable recording is to perhaps fudge the technical quality in order to obtain an overall result which is commercial.

## 6 Third party liabilities

**6.1** Even though the producer may choose the studio, sound equipment, musicians, musical arrangers and other necessary items, it should be the producer's employer who is contractually liable to hire, pay and fire all third parties, and who is liable for studio costs, session fees, and the safety of and payments for all equipment which has to be acquired for the recording. This will normally be done through established "fixers", who will get together a complete backing package of musicians, do the musical arrangements and sheet music, and provide a professional service.

**6.2** The producer must make sure that if he does all the telephoning and written confirmations, it is specifically on behalf of his employer with no recourse to the producer, and that is made clear to all third parties. This is most important where the producer either personally or through a fixer:

(a) Books studio time.

(b) Hires equipment. Any dispute is likely to be over:
  (i) Hire charges, especially where the equipment breaks down, or is not returned promptly after use.
  (ii) Damage to or loss of equipment.
  (iii) Where a claim is made under (ii) and insurance cover was forgotten, if it is the hirer's responsibility.

(c) Books musicians. Care has to be taken that:
  (i) All the 1988 Copyright Act performers protection formalities are observed, and all necessary written consents are obtained. Without these any recording of a person's performance breaches their statutory rights, and can make the recording illegal.
  (ii) The correct session fees are paid promptly. Failure can mean the wrath of the Musicians Union. Essential travelling and subsistence expenses will need to be agreed.
  (iii) Any necessary musicians or other credits are agreed at the time of booking.

(d) All applicable Musicians Union agreements and recording regulations are observed.

## 7 Producers' time commitments

**7.1** The producer might have to attend rehearsals by the artiste prior to recording, to get the feel of the music. At that time he should make any suggestions which would help the artiste in the studio. Rehearsals are useful for reducing unnecessary studio time, and for assessing the songs to be recorded.

**7.2** The producer will have to attend the studio at such times as shall reasonably be required of him. In practice the studio will be booked for specific recording periods, or a block time booking will be made within which the recording should be completed. The time spent in the studio at each recording session will depend on the physical stamina of the artiste and the producer, and their reasonable personal requirements not connected with the recording. Musicians charge rates by the "session", which is a limited time period, and these rates will increase if they play more than one instrument. The booking of studio time should fit in with the session musicians requirements, to keep wasted studio cost to a minimum.

**7.3** If the location of the studio is not within easy every day reach of the producer, his reasonable expenses of travel and accommodation will be paid by his employer, and he will either be fed adequately or given a *per diem* allowance sufficient for that purpose. These terms are essential where the artiste records outside the United Kingdom for tax reasons. No part of the producer's royalty advance should be deemed to be on account of those expenses, nor should they be set against his royalties.

## 8 Recording cost budget

**8.1** The producer may be required either to provide his employer with a detailed budget of all costs to be incurred during the period of the recording, or he may be given a maximum expense figure within which to work. As a fixed maximum figure can only be accurately assessed by preparing a detailed budget, a fixed amount should not be accepted by the producer if failure to keep within it incurs him in a penalty. There are certain items which can be budgeted for, and others will only be estimates or noted requirements. If all is well prepared, and the number of tracks known, an outside limit with a generous contingency can be given on studio time. Simply giving an outside limit invites the temptation to spend up to that amount, even if it is not strictly necessary. For example, a group can go on mixing an album's worth of tracks for ever, trying to get the ultimate sound.

**8.2** If the producer prepares the budget, he must include every possible cost he knows will be incurred, together with a substantial allowance for unforeseen expenses which might be incurred through no fault of his. The producer's agreement must make it clear that:

(a) Such a budget is prepared by the producer on a "no liability" best estimate basis, being for information purposes only. There are so many factors outside his control which can make a budget over-run, some of which may be record company requirements.

(b) If the budget is exceeded otherwise than by breach of contract by the producer, he incurs no liability for the excess. The most common cause of exceeded budgets is waste of studio time, either by not using it to the full time capacity, or by using recording time for rehearsing unprepared material. Even if there is no budget, the producer should do his best to complete the recording as quickly and as efficiently as possible, which itself will reduce costs to the minimum. Part of the reputation of a good producer is his ability to prevent recording costs getting out of hand. All recording costs will be treated as an advance against royalties payable to the artiste, so he has a genuine interest in keeping costs to a minimum. Most artistes forget that aspect in the excitement of recording, or while enjoying looning about in the studio. If every hour the artiste had to go to the studio office and pay out cash for the hour's studio, musician, and incidental costs, the time taken to produce a record would be halved.

## 9 Re-recording restriction

**9.1** The producer's agreement should not restrict him from producing the recordings of any other artiste, however competitive the musical style of that other artiste may be. A restriction may be imposed on the producer from producing for any other artiste a cover version of the artiste's original recordings he has produced. The restriction should be limited to a reasonable period after the first release of the original recording. A successful cover version will damage the sales of the original recording, so there should be some effective method of compensating the first artiste if the producer breaches his restriction.

**9.2** If the producer breaks the re-recording restriction openly, or can be proved to have done so on the quiet when there is no producer's credit, the best contractual sanction is to withhold the producer's royalties pending settlement of a claim against him by the record company or the artiste through the courts. The retention right must be in the producer's contract, and it should only extend to an amount which could reasonably be anticipated as compensation if the claim is successful. A producer should not agree to a retention clause, as the record company should have adequate royalties in the pipeline to cover the claim. Any retention should be put on deposit so that any money returned to the producer will have attracted interest. A retention can act as a disincentive for the record company to pursue its action expeditiously. As any other artiste, using any other producer, could produce a cover record, with the same damaging results, the extent of damages which could be claimed if the producer breaches his restriction would be examined closely by the court.

**9.3** Arbitrary penalties of any kind should never be accepted by the producer, but there are circumstances when severe damage could be done to the original artiste's record sales arising from the deliberate breach of contract by the producer. There is no firm basis on which the extent of the damage caused to the artiste, and its compensation, can be calculated fairly in advance. For example, whatever may be the ultimate record sales of the original recording in the face of direct competition from a cover version, there is no means of certifying what the sales of the original recording would have been with no competition. If the cover version is recorded by a major artiste, it is also possible for the sales of the original recording to be greater than otherwise, due to the increased promotion of material recorded. The success of the cover version may also create airplay opportunity for the original record, which it might not have had due to its initial lack of success. If the artiste is also the composer of the song, he will benefit from copyright royalties on record sales and from increased PRS income on performance of the song, whichever version it may be.

## 10 Credits

**10.1** An independent producer's work must be given the correct credit, and an appropriate clause must be set out in his agreement, as it can only be a contractual right. Credit should be given on the record label and the record sleeve in a place and with a prominence to be agreed. The producer will not normally be given credit on advertising, promotion or publicity material, unless he is so well known and respected as to be a marketing asset in his own right. Some producers are consistently successful, and some are just trendy. The identity of the producer who is the flavour of the month is a valuable selling point.

A record company employee will not normally be given credit for producing the record as he was only doing his job, but this will depend upon his standing with the record company and the artiste.

**10.2** If, despite all his efforts with a talentless artiste and dreadful material, a top producer cannot obtain what he considers to be a satisfactory recording, he may well insist on the record company omitting his name altogether as the producer. He does not want his image to be tarnished by the release of a record which features in the list of all time "turkeys".

**10.3** A well known producer may want to be able to advertise the fact that he is the producer of the recordings, in his own promotional material or in the music media. He should be entitled to do so provided he maintains his confidentiality obligations, and does not misrepresent his role, or make any disparaging remarks about the artiste, even in jest.

**10.4** A record producer will not be entitled to the benefit of the "moral rights" referred to in section 77 of the 1988 Copyright Act. The rights of identity with the recorded work (section 77), and the rights to object to a derogatory treatment of the work are granted to the "author" of the work. By section 9 of the 1988 Act, the author of a sound recording is defined as "the person by whom the arrangements necessary for the making of the recording are undertaken". Furthermore, by section 11, the author (with certain exceptions) is the first owner of the copyright in the work. That could not be intended to be the producer of the record, however much he considers himself to be the creator of the sound (see paragraph **11.2**).

## 11 Rights in product

**11.1** Although every person has certain exclusive rights in his own performance and any product of it, under his agreement the rights in the recordings made by a record producer will be vested in the record company. The producer then has no control over what is done to that recording after he has completed his job. When and where the record is released is a record company marketing decision.

**11.2** As the producer of a record has a rather indefinable "performance" in the finished record, it is difficult to see what it is he could control. He does not perform in the normal meaning of the word, but the final sound embodied on the master tape represents an investment of original creative effort by the record producer.

**11.3** Where an independent producer is given credit for the record production, his income and reputation depend upon its being considered to be an artistic performance and a commercial success. Within his producer's agreement he should have the right to prevent either:

(a) The re-recording of part of, or the re-mixing of part or the whole, of the recording by someone else without him being given the opportunity to produce the recording or mixing. He should be contacted by the record company, and given a reasonable period within which to deal with the job. If he is not able to do so, the record company must be free to get on with it. Depending on the extent of the work required, and the time needed to do it, the producer could ask for a reasonable fee, not to be recoupable.

(b) Additional recorded tracks (ie, on a multitrack tape containing individual musicians' performances) being mixed with the tracks of a composition the producer has previously recorded and mixed, so as to obtain a new master tape of that song but with a different sound or quality. This is an extension of (a), and might be done where there is a change in the membership of a group between the recording of an album, and its release. The producer should ask for reasonable confirmation that such activity is not in breach of the group's recording contract, or any agreement between the group members.

This restriction on the record company is important where the producer of the new material is to be given a "co-producer's" credit together with the original producer without either his knowledge or consent.

**11.4** That attitude is understandable from an artistic viewpoint, but the record company will not allow its decisions on commercial and artistic matters to be unreasonably restricted where it owns the rights in the recording. To give the record producer those rights means a detailed clause in his contract to apply where he cannot be found, or refuses to reply to a notice, or arbitrarily refuses to agree with the record company. For an independent record producer to ensure that he has total control over the recordings he must own or control the production company through which the recordings he produces are licensed to the record company. This is seldom the case.

## 12 Breach by producer

**12.1** The artiste and the record company depend on the producer to supervise and control the progress of the recording. It can be serious to both the artiste and the record company if the producer, having started recording, fails to do his job. He can miss recording sessions, fail to book musicians, or arrive late or leave early, get drunk during recording, or deliberately produce a ridiculous sound. The record company should if necessary have "plan B" ready as a contingency, in case the producer is incapacitated or dies during the record production.

**12.2** By the time recording starts, he will have received his royalty advance, and will have committed his employer to the cost of studio time, musicians, and the hire of equipment. Apart from terminating the producer's agreement, demanding the return of the advance, and removing his authority to continue producing the recording, the employer can only sue the producer for breach of contract where that remedy may be applicable to the facts. This is not of immediate comfort where the recording of the album is seriously delayed, or the recording costs have become excessive half way through the job.

**12.3** The producer may not have already considered the potential consequences of breaching his contract, as so many adverse situations may arise. As well as the cost of settling the financial demands of all concerned with the disastrous recording, there is possibly the whole cost of doing the recording again, or postponing tours by the artiste which were set up to promote the release of the recording, re-scheduling the artiste's activities for months ahead, and dealing with the music press should it hear of the fiasco.

## 13 Termination and delegation

**13.1** By the nature of its creativity, the parameters of the job of a record producer are not clearly defined—it is to produce a recording of a song by an artiste economically and by an agreed date, and to be commercially acceptable to the record company. The producer will be prohibited from delegating his responsibilities, it is one of the few occupations which have to be a personal responsibility throughout. At the completion of the recording it can be assessed as to whether it will be commercially acceptable. But in what circumstances would the record company want to be able to terminate the production agreement while recording is in progress? Apart from the points set out in paragraph **12.1** they should relate to the refusal or total inability of the producer to manage the budget and personnel side of administration upon which the proper progress of the recording relies.

## 14 Further options

**14.1** A top producer will pick and choose artistes to produce. If he decides upon an artiste who is offered to him, due to current or upcoming success, it is because he believes the artiste will sell records. A well produced album will help achieve that success. The producer may ask for an option to be the producer of the artiste's next recording, so as to maintain the artiste's impetus, and to be able to participate in his record sales success. High record sales benefit the producer's reputation and his bank balance.

## 15 Cross-collateralised recoupment

**15.1** Following on the point made in paragraph **4.3**, if a producer is employed by a record company to produce the recordings of various artistes, royalties payable to him for each artiste's recordings should not be cross-collateralised against unrecouped advances received by the producer for recordings produced by him for other artistes. They should be accounted for independently. This situation is not likely to occur, and is not acceptable, but any producer should be aware of the possibility.

CHAPTER 7

# *Music Publishing*

## SECTION I: COPYRIGHT IN MUSIC

### 1 General aspects

**1.1** The copyright law has just been revised and updated by the Copyright, Designs and Patents Act 1988, and all references to "the Act" and sections of it refer to the 1988 Act. Chapter ten sets out a detailed analysis of the Act as it relates to music publishing, recording and artistes' rights and activities. The previous Copyright Act was passed in 1956, but many copyright aspects have developed beyond its scope. The legislation relevant to music has not changed dramatically, although the music business has developed commercially at a rapid rate. The Act only relates to the United Kingdom. This chapter deals with the broad aspects of copyright law as applied to music, as the whole of the music publishing business is based upon the existence of copyright as an asset to be protected and exploited commercially. It is not a highly technical and exhaustive analysis of the law, there are many admirable academic text books for that purpose.

**1.2** To avoid litigation over claims by other people alleging that a song is in breach of their own copyright, composers must write songs which are original. A composer should become familiar with the legal technicalities of copyright, so that he can understand the meaning and implications of the warranties he will have to give in a music publishing contract. These are dealt with in section II of this chapter.

### 2 Copyright in musical works

**2.1** Copyright is the basic proprietary right of an exclusive nature attaching to any original musical composition or lyrics created which is set down in some permanent form. The permanent form may be writing, musical notation, a sound recording, or some other means whereby it can be reproduced.

**2.2.1** For originality to exist there has to be some skill or creativity exercised in the collection of words and musical notes which makes the composition a protectable product of the composer's mind. The 1988 Act has no reference to the exercise of skill—the test is simply that of originality. Copyright does not depend on the musical quality of the composition, either in a technical sense, or whether it is pleasant to listen to. The composition must be of sufficient length to justify it being a musical work (see paragraph **2.3**).

The theory behind copyright protection is to prevent any other person from being able freely to appropriate the skill and effort exercised by a composer or lyric writer, resulting in an original creation which is distinct and different from any other. Whether skill or creativity exists may sometimes be questioned. If a piano player switches on a tape recorder, and for three minutes bangs away at the keys blindfold and totally at random, is the result created by skill? It might in fact be quite melodious, and who would know of the strange circumstances of its creation. The composition so created would be original.

**2.2.2** The "skill and effort" element is to prevent a person, for example a lyric writer, from having exclusive rights over a random collection of words, whereby he corners the market in the use of the English language. The existence of originality implies that the composer must have had some input of his own creation, which comes about through at least some exercise of skill or effort. The protection is in the whole of, or that substantial part embodying the whole meaning of, the lyric writer's thoughts. Individual phrases in common use will not of themselves be exclusive to the lyric writer, unless they form the "substance" of the whole lyric. Even then the protection is only within the context of the lyric. The same principles apply to the combination of musical notation.

**2.3** The following points are relevant:

(a) There is no copyright protection in a song title as such, as it is not sufficiently substantial to be treated as a literary work, (the *Exxon* case (see Appendix III)), even if the title is an invented word or a combination of invented words. If the title is long enough, it may have a copyright, but its author has no exclusivity to the combination of words outside any connection with the song. There is no definition of how many words are required to achieve copyright protection. The same applies to the extent of a musical copyright, there are not a number of notes, or playing time in seconds, beyond which the music is a work, and below which it is not. A good example is the short TV station or radio station identity call, which is only a few but very distinctively arranged notes. These are protected by copyright, and earn high performance fees for the composers.

(b) Whether the song title is made up of ordinary English words or invented words, the composer has the common law right to prevent their use by others in that combination in connection with a musical composition, whereby the use would pass off the other song as the composer's song. This would deprive him of an element of earnings and reputation, and is a misappropriation of goodwill, product identity and related rights. Nevertheless, an examination of the PRS database song titles on which it collects performance income will show that there are many instances of groups of song titles which are similar, or almost identical.

(c) Although there will be copyright in original works which contain passages of an obscene, libellous or immoral nature, publication and sale of records, or transcriptions of those elements, may be attacked if found to be unlawful or in breach of personal rights. The Court will not enforce the copyright exclusivity and right to reproduce defamatory or illegal works on behalf of the copyright owner.

**2.4** Under English law, copyright protection does not depend upon any form of registration of the original work, and the composition does not have to be first published, or offered for sale as a record, for copyright to arise, it is an automatic process at the time the original work is first set down. If the music is original, but is never set down in a permanent form, it will not have copyright protection, because it remains just an idea. In a single composition it is possible for the copyright in the words and the copyright in the music to belong to different persons, and in each of the words and the music the copyright may be held by two or more persons jointly.

**2.5** The technical requirements for the creation of copyright under the Act in respect of music, and lyrics, are as follows. The music itself comes under "musical work" and lyrics are a "literary work", and, while a more detailed reference will be found in chapter ten, set out below is a precis of some of the essential sections of the Act, limited to compositions:

(a) By section 1(1)(a) copyright is a property right in an original literary or musical work.

(b) By section 3(2) copyright does not subsist in a literary or musical work unless and until it is recorded in a permanent form, in writing or otherwise.

(c) By section 9(1) the author means the person who created the work. This is irrespective of who is, or who is deemed to be, the first or the subsequent owner of the copyright in the work (see (e) below).

(d) By section 10(1) a work of joint authorship means a work produced by the collaboration of two or more authors, in which the contribution of each author is not distinct from that of the other author or authors.

(e) By section 11 the author of a work is the first owner of any copyright in it. Where a literary or musical work is made by an employee in the course of his employment (ie, it is his job to write lyrics or to compose music), his employer is the first owner of any copyright in the work, subject to any agreement to the contrary.

(f) By section 12(1) copyright in a literary or musical work expires at the end of the period of 50 years from the end of the calendar year in which the author dies. For a work of joint authorship (see (d) above) the period will start on the death of the last of them to die. This section has to be read in conjunction with paragraphs 12(2)(a) and 12(4)(a) of Schedule I to the 1988 Act. This is because the 1956 Act gave a copyright life of 50 years from the date of first publication for works which had not been published by the date of the author's death. Paragraph 12(2)(a) says that if the 50 year period on posthumous publication has started, it will continue. Paragraph 12(4)(a) says that if the author died before the 1988 Act became effective, and a work had not been published by the date it did become effective, then the 50 years for that work will begin to run from that effective date, irrespective of its date of subsequent publication (see paragraph **14**).

(g) By section 151(2) a work qualifies for copyright protection in the UK if the author was at the material time ie, when he wrote the work, a "qualifying person". This definition includes a British citizen or an individual domiciled or resident in the United Kingdom. Under the various copyright conventions the UK recognises and protects the copyrights created under the laws of other convention member countries, but that is not the same as a copyright originating in the UK.

(h) By section 76(3) the author of a musical work, or lyrics, has the right to be identified wherever:

(i) the work is published commercially;

(ii) copies of a sound recording of the work are issued to the public;

(iii) a film is shown to the public, if its sound track includes the work.

This comes under the "moral rights" which have been introduced into the UK copyright legislation for the first time.

## 3 Copyright infringement

**3.1** Infringement of copyright is caused by the unauthorised use of the copyright work, or of a substantial part of it. The copyright owner does not have to prove that he has suffered loss or damage to support his claim, such as where there is no calculable deprivation of earnings of the composer, or no unjust enrichment of the wrongful user.

**3.1.2** By section 16(1) of the Act the owner of copyright in a work has the exclusive right:

(a) to copy the work (see **3.1.3** below);
(b) to issue copies of the work to the public (see **3.1.4** below);
(c) to perform, show or play the work in public;
(d) to broadcast the work or to include it in a cable programme service;
(e) to make an adaptation of the work (see **3.1.5** below);
(f) to do any of (a) to (d) in relation to an adaptation of the work.

By section 6(3) references to doing any of the above restricted acts are to the doing of it:

(a) in relation to the work as a whole, or as to any substantial part of it; and
(b) either directly or indirectly.

**3.1.3** By section 17(2) copying in relation to a literary or musical work means reproducing the work in any material form, including (by subsection (6)) the making of copies which are transient, (such as being projected onto a computer screen while not being permanently stored in a database), or incidental to some other use of the work.

**3.1.4** By section 18(2) the issue to the public of copies of the work means the act of first putting those copies into circulation, and not to:

(a) any subsequent distribution, sale, hiring or loan of those copies; or
(b) their subsequent importation into the United Kingdom.

**3.1.5** By section 21(3) an adaptation of lyrics will include a translation of them. In relation to music it means making an arrangement or transcription of the work.

**3.1.6** There are also "secondary" infringements of copyright, mainly being the possession or use of infringing material, as opposed to creating it.

**3.2** The meaning of "substantial" in section 16(3)(i) above, in the context of an infringement of music, is not necessarily just the extent to which the composition has been copied. It refers more to the essential element of the music which is distinctively recognisable as being the song, or an adaptation of it. Neither does the copying have to be precise. If the recognisable essence of the tune has been used as the central theme of another composition, so that a listener would readily assume that the two compositions are from the same source, that is strong evidence that the second tune may be an infringement of the first. The difficulty, as in all similar compositions, is to decide upon the degree of similarity, and sometimes which came first.

The meaning of "substantial" in the context of reproducing a literary copyright work, such as for quotation in a book, will refer to the extent of the work so reproduced. The Act authorises the reproduction of parts of copyright works in limited circumstances, which are not of a commercial nature.

## 4 Copyright in a sound recording

**4.1** Copyright exists in every sound recording of which the maker was a qualified person at the time when the recording was made. By section 13 of the 1988 Act, the period of copyright for a recording is fifty years from the end of the calendar year in which the recording is first made, except that if it is released within that fifty year period, the copyright period will be fifty years from the end of the calendar year in which it was first published. By paragraph 12(5)(a) of Schedule I of the 1988 Act, if a recording was made after 1 June 1957, but was unpublished when the Act became effective, the copyright period for such a recording will be 50 years from that effective date.

Publication of a record is effected by releasing it for sale to the public, ie, commercially. In a sound recording there are two possible copyrights; the recording itself, and the material which is recorded. The copyright contents will, in most cases, have a copyright which outlives the copyright in the recording of it, except where the recording is made after the death of the author of the contents. This chapter deals with the recorded material, not the physical record, the rights to which relate to the performances upon it. The acts reserved to the owner of the copyright in a sound recording (ie the mechanical copyright), mean that he has the exclusive right to:

(a) make a record embodying the recording;
(b) cause the recording to be heard in public;
(c) broadcast the recording.

These rights of the owner of one recording of the work do not inhibit the right of the owner of the copyright in the recorded material from having other recordings made of it. On the contrary it is his publisher's job to try to get other recordings made of it.

## 5 Originality

**5.1** Copyright in a composition depends essentially upon its originality. The number of songs which have been written, be they entirely original, reminiscent of earlier works, new original arrangements of existing copyright material, or based upon music in the public domain, makes it inevitable that some songs will have a recognisable similarity in whole or in part to other compositions.

**5.2** In every song there is likely to be some musical construction similar to parts of other compositions, to a greater or lesser degree, especially within a limited category of musical composition, such as a well defined dance rhythm. Most rock music and country and western music is based upon a very limited core rhythm. An instrumental beat, or a distinctive part of the backing music of a song, can suggest to a composer the basis of a completely new and otherwise original musical composition. Because of the high earnings which can be achieved by a composer from all the means of promotion of a hit song, he must be careful not to leave himself open to claims against him for breach of copyright. Occasionally legal actions are brought by unknown composers who allege that well known composers have "pinched" their music, either wholly or by using it as a central theme inspiration. The burden of proof is a heavy one.

**5.3** For an alleged infringement of copyright to succeed, it must be proved that one song was copied from another, or that it incorporates a "substantial" part of that other song. Therefore careful comparison must be made between the song complained of and the work it is claimed to infringe. The comparison is to see whether the two works are sufficiently alike, when analysed and performed, to conclude that the alleged infringement is a copy of the original work within those parameters. Comparison of the technical musical structure and the qualitative substance of each song should also be undertaken.

**5.4** Although specific sections, however small, of any new composition may be similar to sections from existing copyright compositions, before claiming a breach of copyright it must be decided whether the "infringing" composition as a whole bears a substantial resemblance to the composition alleged to be infringed. No infringer is going to make the equivalent of a facsimile copy of the music, the art of successful infringement is to make such modifications as may survive the comparative tests, while retaining as much as possible of the appeal of the song which has been copied. Investigation will try to ascertain whether the similarity has arisen by coincidence, or whether on balance the essence of the song has been copied.

**5.5** It is not so difficult to ensure that lyrics do not infringe existing copyright material, as the comparison of lyrics is more easily done. Any composer of music or writer of lyrics is physically not able to ensure that he does not unknowingly infringe any small part of the vast amount of worldwide existing copyright material. There is no means of comparing his composition with all others. It is only when the new composition sounds sufficiently like a well known piece of existing copyright music that the similarity is noticed, which makes it possible to identify where the comparisons should be made.

**5.6** For example, originality of lyrics can be separated into an originality of the concept of the song, so that the words convey a novel message; and an originality only in the structure of what is an otherwise unoriginal message. The difference can be understood where, for example, a poem may be original in its concept and structure, whereas the untold number of love songs will have a common theme, and in many cases similar rhyming lyrics.

## 6 Transfer of copyright

**6.1** Copyright can only be assigned in writing, which is why such care is taken in the assignment clauses in a music publishing contract. Where a composer delivers a manuscript or recorded tape of an original copyright song to a publisher with whom he has no written contractual commitments, even if the composer is paid for the song, he still retains the copyright in it. If both parties intended that he should assign to the publisher all of his rights in the song, including the copyright, the transaction may be sufficient to create an agreement to assign the copyright. The composer will retain the copyright until that agreement is completed by a written assignment of the copyright being executed by him. Until that is done, the publisher has no proprietary rights in the song, and cannot record it or publish it without the composer's consent.

The assignment can be made subsequently so that all prior acts of the publisher in dealing with the song can be ratified. If the composer refuses to complete the deal by signing an assignment, and if the publisher is legally entitled to have the copyright assigned to him, the publisher will have to take legal action claiming specific performance. The intentions of the parties at the time the song was written, or when it was delivered to the publisher, will be a matter of evidence (see paragraph 12).

By section 93 of the 1988 Act, where a beneficiary under a will is bequeathed a document or recording of an original music or literary work, of which the testator was the author and the copyright owner, and which was unpublished at his death, in the absence of any indication to the contrary in the will or any codicil to it, the bequest is deemed to include the copyright in the work. If the testator was the owner of the copyright in only the music, or if he was a joint author, the transfer of copyright is only to the extent of whatever copyright was owned by the testator immediately prior to his death. The testator can equally well bequeath the manuscript to one beneficiary, and the copyright in it to another beneficiary.

## 7 The effect of copyright

**7.1** The right of copyright is that of absolute and exclusive legal and beneficial ownership, although it is an intangible right. The copyright owner is entitled, in English law, to his rights in the composition in the UK, and elsewhere by copyright conventions. In some countries their own law may require compliance with certain formalities before acknowledging the existence of the composer's rights in the material he has created, and subject also to any copyright convention to which the UK and the other country are both signatories.

**7.2** The copyright in a composition can be assigned or licensed for any agreed period of time, whether throughout the world or limited to use in any country. Within the EEC there are regulations, eg, Article 85 of the Treaty of Rome, which prohibit the actual or artificial restriction of competitive activity. This includes granting limited territorial rights in intellectual property assets, such as patents or trademarks. In 1992 there will be a free market, but how this might affect restricted licensed copyright use in the customary manner of the established music publishing industry, is not yet known. It is the licensing of an intellectual property right. Certain limited uses of patents and trademarks come within the established block exemptions to Article 85, so why should licensed copyright be treated any differently?

**7.3** Upon an assignment of copyright, there will be no automatic right to a reassignment upon the happening of any event, such as a breach of contract by the assignee, unless the assignment specifically says so. The wording of the clause determines its effect. If it is just an agreement to re-assign the copyright, such as where the publisher goes bust, the composer will have to try to enforce that agreement by court action if the liquidator refuses to comply with it. This may be time consuming and expensive, and may not succeed. The re-assignment would need to be activated automatically by the happening of the relevant event, ie, the retention by the publisher would be conditional upon the event not happening.

**7.4** A copyright licence should set out the circumstances and the events upon the happening of which the licence can be terminated. This is easily done, as a licence is the granting of a temporary use, as opposed to an assignment of copyright, which is a permanent transfer. It is customary for the copyright in a composition to be assigned by the composer to the publisher of the composition. In return the composer receives an income from the publisher, consisting of royalties from the sale of sheet music, and a share of any other income received by the publisher from performance and exploitation of the composition. If the publisher persistently refuses or fails to account to the composer, the only really effective antidote is to have the right (and the right mechanism) to get the copyrights back from the publisher.

## 8 Copyright owner

**8.1** The possible categories of copyright owner are:

(a) the original author of the lyrics, or composer of the music;

(b) the employer of a songwriter under a service agreement (paragraph **12**);

(c) a person who commissions or purchases a musical composition together with an assignment of copyright (paragraph **10**);

(d) a beneficiary under a will to whom the copyright is expressly bequeathed;

(e) where the owner of the copyright in it dies and bequeaths the manuscript of an unpublished work, then in the absence of any specific bequest of the copyright, it will pass to the beneficiary together with the original manuscript (section 93 of the 1988 Act).

More detailed explanations of (a)–(c) are dealt with where applicable in this chapter.

**8.2** As a general rule, the copyright in a composition belongs to the originator of the set down work, but this is not always so. If a composer, who is not able himself to set down in music notation form what he composes, employs another person to do so for him, he should agree in writing before anything is done that the copyright in whatever is written down belongs to the composer. An exchange of letters confirming the terms of the employment will suffice. The composer is the originator of the song, and will be deemed to be the author of it, although he did not first set it down. The technical rules relating to copyright do not always follow commonsense, so the facts of each case should be studied, and the appropriate formality or application complied with (see paragraphs **9.4** and **12.1**).

## 9 No protection in an idea

**9.1** Copyright does not exist in an idea or concept. There must be a permanent record of the idea in its complete form, when it is transformed from an idea into an original work. Whatever original work has been so set down thereby becomes copyright material, provided that:

(a) It complies with all of the other requirements of the 1988 Act.

(b) It is not a copy of an existing copyright work whereby it breaches the rights in that existing copyright. The creation of the copyright, to whom it belongs at the moment of creation, and who is rightfully entitled to it, are different matters.

**9.2** If only the rough basis of a complex tune is set down, that does not necessarily give protection to the whole composition, the details of which remain only in the composer's mind. What is set down will have copyright protection. If the basis represents the "substantial" element of the tune, all else being incidental "fleshing out", the tune will be protected.

**9.3** If a distinctive, but not substantial, part of an expressive composition lends itself to providing ideas for the basis of further original works, the composer of the first work cannot always prevent creative composers from exercising their skill in using those ideas.

**9.4.1** Copyright is created by statute, and its technicalities must be observed. An example would be where at a party, a composer playing the piano has then and there an inspiration for an original tune, and he promptly plays whatever he has composed in his head. If an astute guest, on his own initiative, as he is listening, puts down on paper a full musical notation or a comprehensive top line based on the concept of that original inspiration, he may have a claim to the copyright in that tune.

**9.4.2** The reason is that, although the composer had an original idea, it had no legal protection in copyright until it was set down in a permanent form. In the absence of anything to the contrary, the author and first copyright owner of the work will be he who first sets it down, as it is that act which transforms an idea into a copyright. This will depend upon the interpretation of section 9(1) of the Act, which states that the author of a work is the person who creates it. The composer certainly creates, but does the recorder also create? The composer should be protected.

**9.4.3** In the absence of any prior communication or arrangement between the composer and the guest in connection with that tune, the guest who set down the composition would be in none of the categories of commissioned or employed persons whose work is done in a fiduciary capacity or for another's benefit, and so it may be possible for the apparently inequitable position to stand. If the guest is invited to listen to the tune in confidence, the composer can prevent the guest from breaching the terms of his audience.

## 10 Commission for selection

**10.1** Where a composer is specifically asked by a person (the commissioner) to compose a selection of songs for his consideration, one or more of which may be accepted, paid for and used by the commissioner, any songs not accepted by him will remain with the composer, who will retain the copyright in them. The composer will also retain the copyright of any work accepted by the commissioner, unless it is assigned by the composer to the commissioner in writing specifically in the letter of commission, or by any subsequent document.

**10.2** The selection of songs composed may be only variations of one central basic musical theme, and so those songs retained by the composer will have similarities to the songs accepted, but each song will have a copyright of its own. The commissioner, in accepting only one or some of the songs, may have no remedy if the rejected songs are published or recorded in competition with the songs accepted. The legal position of the two parties in respect of songs not accepted by the commissioner should be agreed when the arrangement is entered into, or when the choice of songs is made.

**10.3** Where a particular song is commissioned and accepted, the commissioner can by agreement prevent the composer from using that original inspiration of his to create further songs which are similar in sound, style and concept to the accepted songs, whilst not being in breach of their copyrights. This may be academic, except under **10.5** below, but should be considered in applicable circumstances.

**10.4** Either the composer agrees to assign to the commissioner the copyright in all the songs he composes within the context of his commission, or he agrees only to assign the copyrights in those songs which are accepted by the commissioner. Where the parties themselves are not certain where they stand in law, or if they had never considered the matter of copyright, an indication of their intentions will be the financial terms agreed upon. Intentions themselves may not be sufficient to prove the right of the commissioner to an assignment of the copyright in an accepted song, although it is reasonable to assume that nobody would purchase a song without wanting complete ownership which only comes with the copyright. It is a pity that the 1988 Act did not cure this anomaly, which is a considerable cause of confusion.

**10.5** An exception to the general custom is the thriving business of producing "jingles" for TV or radio advertisements. A manufacturer advertises its product on TV, and all TV ads have a catchy and (in most cases) original jingle comprising music with or without words, to give brand identity and an "image" to the product. The advertising agency which produces the TV advertisement will commission a "jingle" from a well-known jingle writer. Almost without exception the jingle writer will retain the copyright in the jingle, and grant the product manufacturer an exclusive licence limited to using the music on the TV advertisement. If there are any "knock-on" benefits, such as expansion of the jingle into a hit single record, in the absence of a written agreement to the contrary, only the jingle producer will benefit from all copyright related income.

## 11 Musical arrangements

**11.1** By section 21(3)(b) of the 1988 Act an arrangement of a musical work is an adaptation of it, and by section 21 that is a restricted act, ie it needs the consent of the copyright owner, or it will be an infringement. A different musical arrangement of an existing copyright song can itself acquire copyright protection if it is sufficiently original musically, and sufficiently distinctive in its sound, from the song which has been arranged. Therefore the owner of the copyright in a work should never authorise the making of an arrangement of it without ensuring that any copyright thereby created belongs to him. The new copyright will only arise in those parts of the arrangement which are original, provided that they are sufficiently substantial to "stand alone" as a musical work in their own right. An unauthorised arrangement is an infringement because it is a modified copy of the work, and simply calling it "an arrangement" does not validate the infringement, even if the arranger openly credits the source of his inspiration. The value of copyright protection would be negated if any composer could with impunity appropriate the skills and creativity of another composer simply by changing the emphasis of a sufficient number of notes on a musical score.

**11.2** It is common for musical arrangements or adaptations to be made of music which is in the public domain. For example, the classics are always a popular source of recording material. The musical arrangements will only acquire their own copyright to the extent of the skill exercised in creating them, and of their musical originality. A musical copyright which has become public domain material cannot be revived, even by re-arrangement, but the arrangement itself, if sufficiently new and different, can have a separate copyright. There can be many arrangements of one piece of famous and popular classical public domain music, and if they are each claimed as being copyright, they will need titles which will identify them individually for recognition by PRS on performances.

**11.3** The same comments can apply to all of the original songs which need a common basis, such as to be within any similar musical beat or rhythm, for example, that used for dancing. To maintain the musical qualities necessary to remain in any recognised dance category, all compositions used for the purpose will incorporate the central dance theme. Around this will be expanded the original composition, so arranged as to contain that theme. Yet there is no exclusivity in the use of the central dance beat or rhythm.

## 12 Where original copyright owner is not the composer

**12.1** There are circumstances in which the copyright in a composition will not automatically belong to the composer, or to the person who first set it down in a permanent form.

(a) If a composer is commissioned to write original music under an agreement which assigns the copyright in all of the songs to the commissioner, then whether or not the commissioner ever uses them, the composer's sole interest under the agreement will be the financial provisions. The effect of the commission agreement is that the commissioner is the first copyright owner of the compositions.

(b) If the composer is subject to an exclusive contract to compose music and write lyrics for a music publisher, (or any other employer on this basis) the copyrights in all the compositions created by him during the period of the agreement belong to the publisher. The wording of the agreement may be that the publisher will own the copyright in all songs composed and written by the composer during the period. The effect is the same. This is the basis of all agreements between composers and publishers, also known as songwriting agreements. Confirmatory assignments of the copyright of each song as and when written will be required from the composer to identify the existence and ownership of individual songs, so that they can be registered with PRS and notified to sub-publishers. Failure to do so does not mean the publisher does not own the relevant individual copyright, so refusal by the composer to provide a confirmatory assignment does not affect the legal ownership of the copyright by the publisher.

An exclusive songwriting agreement is also used where the composer owns his own publishing company, the sole assets of which are the composer's creative commitment and the copyrights he creates during the period of the contract. The composer's service contract with his company must state that "the course of his employment" will include all composing activities whenever they take place during the period of the contract, not just during office hours, otherwise the exclusive service contract has no value.

(c) If a company providing songwriting services to customers employs a composer to set his own music to lyrics provided by a customer, or a lyricist to set his own words to music provided to the company for that purpose by its customers, the copyright in the original work of the composer or lyricist will not belong to their creator, provided the documentation is correctly drafted, and the copyright assignment is direct between the composer and the customer. If this does not happen, the company's customer will have paid for something which he will not own. Where the copyright is assigned by the composer to the songwriting service company, which intends to assign the copyright to the customer once he has paid, the effectiveness will depend upon the terms of their agreement. But the service provided by the company is of little use to the customer if, after he has paid the fees, he does not own the copyright in the whole of the work returned to him by the company.

(d) If a musician is employed to set down for the first time in musical notation the composer's original creations from the live playing by the composer of an instrument, the agreement between them must state that the copyright in the notated music will belong to the employer composer. Where the music is on tape, it has already been set down for copyright purposes, so while an assignment in writing of the copyright from the notator is not legally required, it should be provided as a formality.

**12.2** The above examples may seem obvious, but if the composer does not understand and follow the requirements of the Act for copyright protection unnecessary problems can arise unexpectedly. Disputes are caused where there is no written agreement, or where the agreement does not specify what the composer is being paid for, or who owns the copyright in what he produces. In most cases the parties will not have thought about what needs to be done, and will have assumed the transaction to be complete, and copyright to be assigned, once the composer has handed over his tape or top line, and has been paid.

The practical elements of copyright assignments and music publishing agreements are dealt with in Section II.

## 13 Proof of prior existence

**13.1** Whenever there is an alleged infringement of copyright, the difficulty in respect of works which were not recorded or published shortly after being composed may be to establish the dates upon which they were first created, and written down. This is where a registration procedure for copyright in the UK would be useful. Reasonable proof must be provided that the allegedly infringed work existed and complied with the copyright formalities, prior to the other work which is claimed to be an unauthorised and infringing copy. In practice this can be difficult, so an aspiring composer (for example) may seal a tape into a parcel and deposit it with his bank, or send it to himself by recorded delivery and leave it unopened, as a means of establishing a known date by which it was created and set down.

**13.2** Proof of prior existence of a song does not of itself prove that the second similar song is a breach of its copyright. But whatever the circumstances surrounding the creation of the two similar works, there can be no infringement without prior existence of the allegedly infringed work, and the opportunity to hear what it sounds like. If, for example, the complainant's tune had been at the top of the Hit Parade for six months prior to the defendant's own composition being created, the defendant will have a harder task to prove independence of creativity than if the first tune had been composed but had never been commercially recorded or published.

For example, it is possible for a composer to provide his publisher with a tape recording of an original song, which remains on the shelf with no commercial recording being made from it, or sheet music printed of it, or of it being made available to the public in any other way (the first song). Another composer, not knowing of that shelved composition (and having no means of discovering it), writes a similar song which his own publisher gets recorded commercially, and which is highly successful (the second song). The second song could not have been copied from or based substantially upon, the first song, and so however similar it is to it, there can be no breach of copyright of the first song in those circumstances.

**13.3** What is the legal position if the first composer's publisher takes the first song from the shelf and records it for commercial release? Not being aware of the facts, the composer and publisher of the second song, which is an existing recorded work, will claim copyright infringement by the released record of the first song, and naturally will not believe that it was written and recorded prior to the creation of their own second song. Assuming that the first publisher proves the prior existence of the first song, and therefore that his composer did not copy or make use of any part of the second song, then:

(a) each song will have its own copyright;
(b) the subsequent recording of the first song is legitimate in copyright terms.

However, it will be subject to the practical problem of whether the marketing of two musically similar songs with different lyrics and different titles will confuse the public, and will be damaging to them both.

In this example, the owner of the copyright in the subsequently composed but first commercially recorded song may be able to prevent the late recorded release of the earlier composed song, under the principle of "passing off". That will depend upon the extent of the similarities between the two songs. Passing off is not dependent upon product ownership, it relates to confusion and damage caused by similarity of product, and marketing and product identification.

**13.4** A composer, when entering into a publishing agreement, will schedule to it the titles of any songs already composed and to be included in the agreement, the copyrights of which are then specifically assigned to the publisher. If that is the first commercial dealing with the songs, the composer should also state when they were composed.

The publisher will want a tape copy, and top lines of each song, to prove its copyright, and to confirm its lyrics and its musical notation. In an alleged infringement of copyright, which song preceded which chronologically is a matter of fact, which will have to be proved by supporting evidence.

*Deliberate similarity*

**13.5.1** An artiste who releases a successful record of a song written by one composer for him, may get another composer to deliberately write a similar composition for him to record to keep the attention of the public, while the successful first record is still in its mind.

**13.5.2** Although the second work bears a strong musical resemblance to the first, it will have different lyrics. The question is whether the music has sufficient distinction and originality to warrant a separate identity and copyright, or whether it constitutes an arrangement of the first song, and therefore is an infringement.

**13.5.3** If the second record is successful, and is strikingly similar to the first record, the second composer may be sued by the first composer for breach of copyright. Possibly no action will be taken by the first composer if the second record does not sell and makes no money, because only if it is a success can the measure of damages reasonably be quantified, and the financial risk of litigation be justified. Damages in a successful action for breach of copyright can be considerable in the case of a top hit record, but the cost of litigation is also high.

**13.5.4** Although the second song's recording may not have been successful, the composer of the first song should still act to protect his copyright. If he does not, although he is fully aware of the breach of his rights, and if the second song is revived successfully at a later date, the composer of the first song may have difficulty at that stage in preventing the revival. Where the revival occurs more than six years after the potential breach of copyright became known to the composer of the first song, he will be statute barred from making any claim at all. Prior to the expiry of the six years, the court may decide that, in all the circumstances, by the inactivity of the composer, notwithstanding having knowledge of the infringing work, he has waived his rights to prevent the second song from being promoted at any time in the future.

*Unconscious copying*

**13.6.1** Professional and prolific composers keep current musical tastes and commercial appeal in mind. The principal sources of income for a composer are record sales and performing fees; the latter being regulated to a great extent by the former. Similarity between songs can arise from what is oddly described as "unconscious copying", where a composer has in the back of his mind musical memories and ideas, which blend in with the tune or rhythm around which he is trying to compose something original, without consciously recognising that the source of such harmonies is influenced by existing tunes.

**13.6.2** The true product of unconscious copying, however hard that may be to prove, is not a breach of copyright. It follows that if the new work is proved to be not in breach of copyright, it must be entitled to a copyright of its own. The concept is based upon the principle that, to be in breach of copyright, the composer must have consciously or deliberately copied or made unauthorised use of the prior copyright, whether in whole or in substantial parts. The likelihood of a composer creating subconsciously, or independently from existing well known music, a composition which is nearly identical to it is so remote that the details of the defence of unconscious copying to a copyright infringement claim will be treated with some suspicion.

## 14 Copyright protection periods

**14.1** For musical compositions published during the life time of the composer, the period of copyright extends to the end of the fiftieth year from the end of the calendar year in which the composer died. For the transitional provisions appertaining under the 1956 Act for posthumously published works (see paragraph **2.5**(f)).

**14.2** If there are two or more joint composers, ie where their individual contributions to the composition do not have separate and identifiable copyrights, the copyright protection period is for the period of 50 years from the end of the calendar year in which the last surviving joint composer died.

**14.3** Where the copyright composition is anonymous, there being no known or credited composer, or where it has been written under an unidentified pseudonym, the copyright protection period will be for 50 years from the end of the calendar year of first publication. If, within that period, the identity of the composer is made known, the period of protection will be extended to the ordinary copyright protection period. If the identity of the composer becomes known after that period has expired, the work remains in the public domain.

**14.4** Where the copyright in the lyrics and the copyright in the music are separately owned, the copyright protection period in each separate copyright will follow the rules independently of the other separate copyright.

## 15 Joint copyright ownership

**15.1** Copyright in a musical composition can be held by one or more persons. If it is owned by more than one person, the rights between them depend upon the circumstances in which the composition was created, if there is no agreement between them upon it. In the absence of an agreement to the contrary, the following rules will apply:

(a) If the work is jointly produced whereby the individual contributions to it cannot be ascertained or separated, the copyright in the whole work will be held by them jointly in equal shares.

On the death of a joint copyright owner, whoever becomes entitled to his copyrights will receive his share of income for so long as there is any.

(b) Where the consent of the copyright owner has to be obtained, none of the joint copyright owners individually can exercise the copyright owners' rights in the work without the agreement of all of the others. There are no rules as to a majority decision, and there is no provision that consent of one stubborn joint copyright owner cannot be unreasonably withheld.

(c) If the collaboration of the composers results in distinct and identifiable contributions to the composition, each contribution being sufficiently substantial for it to be entitled to a separate copyright, the copyright in each of such parts will belong to the respective creators. Thus, the copyright in the music may belong to one person and the copyright in the lyrics may belong to another.

The contribution made by one distinct copyright within the composition may be significantly less than the contribution made by the other distinct copyright, such as where the lyric content is modest. In the absence of an agreement to the contrary, the copyright royalties due to the composers between them will be shared equally where the copyrights are used together.

(d) The owner of each separate copyright in the composition can exercise his own rights in his copyright part without requiring the consent of the owner of the copyright in the other part. This happens, for example, where someone wishes to publish only the words of a composition in a book without the music, or where the words are to be reproduced upon an insert to an album sleeve.

## 16 Performance of copyright works

**16.1** Ownership of the performing right includes the exclusive right to:

(a) perform the work in public;
(b) broadcast the work;
(c) authorise the work to be transmitted by means of a diffusion service.

**16.2** Control over, and the collection of money arising from, the performing right in a composition is vested in the Performing Right Society Limited within the UK (PRS) through the composer's and publisher's membership of PRS. PRS grants licences for the performance of the copyright works publicly within the UK, for which fees are paid to it. PRS then accounts to the composer and publisher for their respective shares of income collected by it, after deducting its administrative charge.

If the composer does not have a publisher, and is not a member of PRS, and owns the copyright in his music, he also owns the performing rights in it. He then has the impossible task of collecting money from those who perform his works, or of preventing them from doing so because they do not have his consent. If the composer is not a PRS member, but has a publisher who is, the publisher can protect his rights and collect his share of performing fees for him until he is eligible for membership. A word of warning—outside the UK most countries will not collect the composer's share if he is not a PRS member, his share goes into their "black box". It is therefore essential that a composer becomes a PRS member as soon as he is eligible to do so.

**16.3** PRS is affiliated to other worldwide performing right societies, and through them it collects performance income arising within their respective territories in respect of compositions owned by its members. The composer does not have to rely on the honesty or existence of the publisher of the composition for the collection and payment of the performance income. PRS accounting records can be a useful indication of the popularity of a record, although there can be "airplay hits" which for some reason do not sell well as records. If there is a significant discrepancy between the PRS figures for a country, and a local record company's sales accounting, it may be time to audit the record company if there is no reasonable explanation for the difference.

**16.4** PRS accounts half yearly, and there is a time lag between performance income being collected by the society situated in a foreign country; that society accounting to PRS, and then PRS accounting to the composer in the UK. If, for example, the major part of the composer's income arises in the USA by way of record sales and performances it would speed up the collection/payment process of the USA performance income for him to be a member of one of the two American collection societies, ASCAP and BMI. For an English composer this is not encouraged by PRS, as the publisher's share will be under PRS control, while the composer's share will be under ASCAP's control, which is not administratively tidy. The composer cannot belong to both societies at the same time. PRS would then receive from the USA only the publisher's share of performing income arising in the USA on that composer's work, except for the UK, when it would account to the USA for it.

**16.5** The collection of performance money is not an exact science, except where specific detailed returns are given to PRS setting out broadcast programme content by composition. The charges levied by PRS upon those who perform copyright music under a PRS licence will not always be allocated in detail to specific compositions. Examples are the "blanket" licences granted to most small users, such as shops and restaurants, in return for a fee in accordance with the appropriate tariff then applied by PRS.

## 17 Value of copyright

**17.1** Calculation of the value of the copyright in a musical composition is necessary for:

(a) The assessment of any inheritance tax or capital gains tax which may be imposed upon the transfer or sale of the copyright. Although copyright is a legal asset, its assignment by the original composer to a publisher in return for the payment to the composer of royalties arising from its exploitation is always treated so that the royalties are income, and not a capital receipt. The royalties are subject to income tax, and not any tax related to capital gains. Any further dealings with the copyright would be deemed to be a transfer for value, and the normal rules for taxation or *ad valorem* stamping on the transfer would apply.

(b) The assessment of damages in a successful action for breach of a songwriting contract, or an infringement of copyright.

**17.2** The precise potential value of the copyright in any composition is impossible to calculate. The value can only be related to the earning power of the composition. There may be an arbitrary basis for guessing a value where a new song has yet to be exploited, and where the composer is well known. An indication can be his ability to obtain high advances on account of his share of income from his publishers. An example is in a publishing agreement, where the copyright in future works is assigned by the composer to the publisher, but as they have not yet been created, calculation of their value in advance is impossible.

**17.3** Copyright in any composition will only have a value if the composition becomes popular, and earns money from record sales and public performances. Even then, at which point in time is the assessment of its value to take place? Upon the sale of an established catalogue of musical copyrights, the value placed on them is what someone will pay; the amount usually being based on the past history of the catalogue's income, and the likelihood of those compositions being recorded and performed publicly in the future. A catalogue value reduces the guesswork risk relating to specific works, as on balance some songs will earn more than others, and the overall price may be fair.

**17.4** The perceived value of a catalogue of only one composer's works may be different, depending on whether the purchaser is another publisher or the composer himself. Another publisher is only purchasing the selling publisher's own share of income. The composer is buying not only the publisher's share of income, but also the ownership of his products, and therefore the future freedom to deal with them as he sees best. If the composer has had several publishers, each of which owns copyrights in compositions created by him, and if he can acquire the copyrights in all his old songs, then, combined with his future songs, the whole enlarged catalogue can have an enhanced value.

## 18 Unauthorised recordings

**18.1** The recording of any performance of a copyright musical work without the prior consent of the owner of the copyright, or not being strictly in accordance with any "permitted use" exceptions set out in the 1988 Act, is a breach of copyright.

**18.2** The market for unauthorised recordings of live and otherwise unrecorded performances by successful artistes is an enormous source of illicit earnings. The position is especially serious for the owner of the copyright in the composition where unauthorised recordings are made from unobtainable material, such as where a famous composer/artiste has recorded privately his own original compositions which have never been commercially recorded and released.

**18.3** The recording and selling of unauthorised recordings damages the artiste, as, for example, the covert recording of a live performance is not likely to have been professionally produced, and will be of poor sound quality. The premature release to the public of an unauthorised version of a yet to be released song destroys the impact of the forthcoming commercial release of the authorised version. The rights of the owner of the copyright in the song, and the record company, will have been severely damaged.

**18.4** Re-recording of a copyright work, ie, duplicating from an existing recording, by an individual privately on his tape recorder for his own personal use and enjoyment is prohibited by section 17 of the 1988 Act. However, by sections 22 and 23 of the 1988 Act, it seems that possession of an infringing copy is not actionable, provided the copy is owned only for private and domestic use. The distinction seems rather fine. It is only where the re-recording is privately distributed, or sold to the public, or performed publicly, that the copyright infringement, known as a secondary infringement, becomes known and can be dealt with by the copyright owner.

**18.5** The illegal copying of popular readily available copyright records, and the manufacture of unauthorised records from them, is an enormous worldwide industry. The development of highly sophisticated recording equipment encourages this industry. Copyright owners and performers lose vast sums which should have been paid as royalties on the sales of unauthorised records.

## 19 Electronic music

**19.1** Prior to the 1988 Act, legislation relating to the copyright in music assumed that the originator of the copyright composition would be a human being. But technology through computer programming, or the manipulation of electronic devices, has the ability to create independently of any human being a series of sounds which it can put together in a harmonic continuous theme constituting a musical composition. Whatever the merits of the musical quality of such inanimate creations, they are original and they are musical, although the computer itself may not have exercised skill and creativity in composing the music.

**19.2** Should such compositions have the benefit of copyright protection, and if so, to whom should it belong? For the copyright in a musical composition to arise under the normal construction of English law, it must be original, and must be set down in a permanent form, and the composer must be a qualified person. Clearly a computer cannot be a qualified person.

**19.3.1** The 1988 Act sets out the rules for computer generated data, in this case relating to music. Section 3 of the Act includes a computer program within the definition of a "literary work", following the Copyright (Computer Software) Amendment Act 1985. A program is only a set of instructions in a computer language, and is not itself a form of musical notation or any recognisable music-related text. The music is produced by the computer hardware being activated by the program and either reproducing sound through the use of a music synthesiser, or (possibly) a print-out of a form of music notation.

**19.3.2** Section 9 of the 1988 Act defines the author of a computer generated literary work as being the person by whom the arrangements necessary for the creation of the work are undertaken. Ordinarily this will be the programmer, but the ordinary rules determining who legally is the first copyright owner will apply. For example, if he is an employee whose job is wholly software or computer related, which could include the creation of music through computer manipulation, his employer will own the copyright in it. If his employment relates solely to creating, for example, accounting and financial software packages, and he produces software for music generation in his spare time on his domestic PC, it has nothing to do with his employment, and he will own the copyright in it.

**19.3.3** If music is created and set down first, and then a computer program is devised to enable the sense of the music to be permanently stored on a data base, that will be an arrangement of the work. Running the program through a computer for its interpretation (such as by using a synthesiser), will be a performance of that work. If the creation of the program was not authorised by the copyright owner in the work, it will be an infringing adaptation of the work, and the data base will be an infringing recording of it.

**19.3.4** As the program itself is in a permanent form, if it is the electronic "notation" of an original work, it will have copyright protection as a literary work. Therefore there is the curious possibility that the means of creating the music is a copyright literary work, and the end product of "performing" the literary work will be protected as a copyright musical work.

**19.4** In the case of a computer generated work an interesting question is whether a different program, devised independently, and which produces the same or a similar musical composition, is breaching the musical copyright created by the first program. There is no element of copying of the first program involved in the creation of the second computer program. If this could be a breach of copyright, as the computer is hardly a fit party to defend legal proceedings, would it be equitable to sue the programmer who had no intention of breaching anybody's copyright? If the second programmer, being familiar with the music, has merely interpreted it electronically in his own style, or in a different computer language, he is making his own adaptation of it, and the relevant rules apply. Therefore it is possible for the second programmer to infringe the copyright in the music, but not to infringe the program which originally created that music. They are separate copyrights, and the copying test for infringement has to be applied to each of them independently.

## 20 Public domain

**20.1** Musical compositions for which the period of copyright protection has expired, fall into the public domain. Use of a public domain work needs no consent, and requires no credit or royalty payments.

**20.2** Public domain works, particularly the classics, can provide a worthwhile source of inspiration for composers. An original adaptation of a public domain work, or a new composition based on a public domain work theme, can acquire a copyright of its own if it is sufficiently original, and if it does not breach any other copyright, whether or not created previously from the same source of inspiration. There is no means of reviving the public domain work, the question is whether the new music based upon it is sufficiently original in its own right to be entitled to copyright protection.

**20.3** Where, in a song, the words are copyright but the music is in the public domain, the use of the music alone cannot be prevented, but the use of the lyrics, or the use of the combined words and music, can be controlled by the owner of the copyright in the words. Copyright royalties will only be payable for the use of the section of the composition which has copyright protection. The public domain music can be re-recorded with different lyrics. The arranger of the music for the re-recording would have to be careful not to use any existing third party arrangement of the music, which may have its own copyright. If there is only one copyright work among other public domain works contained on a record, the full copyright royalty will be received by that one copyright owner, if it is based on the unit price of the record irrespective of what copyrights are on it.

## 21 Grand rights

**21.1** Theatrical performance rights for the presentation of musical works live on stage as part of a dramatic or musical play are one of the many rights derived from copyright. They are most important to the composer of the songs contained in a live musical play. These musical rights are referred to as grand rights. The grand rights copyright owner (usually the music publisher) controls absolutely the use of the music in this manner, and can prevent a third party from performing the music theatrically or dramatically without his consent. The consent can be granted or withheld at his absolute discretion.

**21.2** The income from grand rights is the payment made to their owner in consideration for the granting of a licence to the theatrical production company of the grand rights in the work for the specific theatrical production as defined in the licence agreement. Key elements in the agreement will be the period of rights, the licensed territory (normally very local), exclusivity, and what precisely is the licensed production. There will be script approvals, and other relevant terms and conditions contained in the licence. The payment will be a percentage of box office gross receipts, as defined in the licence.

**21.3** A condition of granting grand rights should be that any significant adaptation of re-arrangement of the music or lyrics in the course of creating the licenced stage production must be first approved by the publisher, and if approved it must be given an assignment of any further copyright which may have been created by so doing.

**21.4** If the composer of the music and lyrics is not also the writer of the spoken script (if any) in between musical numbers, the composer should ascertain how the scriptwriter will be credited, and how the script and music/lyrics will be put together as a complete working stage script.

**21.5** As grand rights are a separate but related part of the performing rights portion of the copyright in the composition, unless the composer specifically reserves them for himself when assigning the whole copyright to his publisher, the grand rights will pass to the publisher. The public performance rights are assigned by the publisher and the composer to the Performing Right Society, but the publisher (not the PRS) will control the grand rights, and will collect all money arising from them. The grand rights fees are not the same as the public performance income to be collected by PRS.

## SECTION II: MUSIC PUBLISHING AGREEMENTS

### 22 In general

**22.1** The basis of a music publishing agreement is the ability of a composer to assign now, or to agree now to assign in the future, the copyright in compositions not yet created, but to be composed by him during the period of the publishing agreement. This may include the assignment of any existing copyrights which the composer owns. If a composer's copyrights are owned by his own company, which enters into a music publishing agreement with a publisher, that will be by way of an exclusive licence. A sub-publisher will be granted an exclusive licence to publish the compositions, in his own territory. For simplicity it is assumed in this chapter that the publisher will own the copyrights in the compositions.

*Identifying Publishers' Rights*

**22.2** A composer's creativity cannot be monitored, except where he informs the publisher of the original songs he has written, and when he delivers the written lyrics and lead sheets or a taped version, so that the song can be firmly identified. If during the publishers rights' period a composer sets down a new song to establish its copyright, it belongs to the publisher through the publishing agreement. But if the publisher is never made aware that the song exists, such as where it "comes to light" or is "composed" after the expiry of the publishing agreement, he has no evidence on which to base his claim to it. If the composer has been careless, and has left conclusive evidence or strongly indicative clues, which point to the composition having been created during the exclusive publishing period, the publisher should claim it under the agreement. If this does not work, the publisher may well ultimately challenge the composer by litigation.

If the composer keeps in his mind an original song, and never sets it down during the period of the publishing agreement, no copyright has been created to which the publisher has a right of assignment. Morally it would appear that the composer is in the wrong, but he may be legally in the clear. He would be caught if the wording of the copyright assignment clause covered songs created by the composer during the period of the agreement, although they may not be set down until afterwards, such as where he performs it live on stage, but never sets it down. This may be unlikely, but it is possible. This might happen if he has an inspiration shortly before his agreement period expires. It would then be a matter of proof, and of wording of the agreement, in deciding whether the publisher has a valid claim to the copyright in the inspiration.

**22.3** The assignment of the copyright in the composition is made by the composer direct to a music publisher, or to a publishing company either owned by the composer and managed by the music publisher, or jointly owned by the composer and the publisher.

**22.4** Copyrights of successful songs are valuable, as they are the rights from which arise various sources of income. A successful composer will try to maintain control over the publishing of his songs so that he can:

(a) negotiate for himself a high percentage of the income received by the publisher from the use of those copyrights;
(b) control the level of retention of foreign earnings received by sub-publishers, especially those connected with the publisher;
(c) protect the copyrights from not being promoted properly, and from being retained by a dishonest or defunct publisher.

**22.5** If the composer assigns the copyright in the compositions to the publisher, the composer ceases to control them. The publisher may be actively, but ineffectively, promoting the copyrights. Or he may have a burst of initial enthusiasm, followed by a lack of interest, because he says nobody wants to use the songs. Where the composer has good commercial and contractual reasons to regret the original assignment of the copyrights to the publisher, he may have to sue the publisher as a last resort to get back the copyrights in his unpromoted compositions. The publishing agreement should have proper termination provisions, and copyright re-assignment obligations, to guard against that event.

**22.6** By assigning the copyrights to the composer's own publishing company, he stays in control of the destiny of his songs, subject to any licence agreement that his publishing company has with a major music publisher for the promotion and administration of the copyrights, and the collection of income arising from them.

## 23 Trust and confidence

**23.1** The successful working of a publishing agreement depends largely on the personal relationship of trust and confidence between the composer and the publisher. A form of dishonesty which might be tried by composers who are disillusioned with their publishers is to "cease" to compose, when a reliable colleague of the composer suddenly finds the gift of "composing" hit material. Little can be done about such dishonest activity, as the burden of proof by the publisher of the composer's malpractice is almost impossible, unless the accomplice confesses, or the collaborators are sufficiently careless. Such a breach of contract is difficult to deal with effectively through the court without substantial evidence.

**23.2** A "ghost composer" in these circumstances would get the undeserved personal recognition and credit for composing the songs, which the genuine composer needs if he wants to maintain his reputation. This is not the same as a composer using a pseudonym to hide his identity, with the knowledge of his publisher. The difference is that in the case of the ghost composer, deception is intended against the publisher. Anonymity for the real composer in favour of a ghost composer is a great deterrent, as is the fact that the ghost composer is contractually entitled to receive the composer's share of all income, which he may "forget" to pay over to, or to share with, the real composer. The real composer would have great difficulty, both with the court and his publisher, if he tried to sue the ghost composer for his money, as he would have to reveal the true facts and his dishonesty. It is also possible that the court would not believe the composer's revelation, and would confirm the ghost composer to be the true composer of those songs, if the ghost composer maintained such a claim. As the agreement between the composer and the ghost composer would be a device fraudulently to deprive the publisher of its assets (the copyrights), if they were discovered, both the composer and the ghost composer would be open to both civil and criminal charges. If the composer decided subsequently to change his mind, and sued the ghost composer to get back his rights, the court might dismiss such a claim as a matter of public policy.

## 24 Future copyrights

*Example*

"In consideration of the obligations of the publisher set out in this Agreement the Composer hereby assigns to and vests in the publisher the worldwide copyright, right, title and interest in:

(a) the compositions the titles of which are set out in the Schedule hereto; and
(b) all of the compositions (being music and/or lyrics) written or composed by the Composer during the period of this Agreement

whether permanently set down or recorded before or after the expiry of the period of this Agreement."

**24.1** It is possible to have a legally enforceable agreement containing the present assignment of future copyright, although musical compositions are the product of personal services. As copyright can only be assigned in writing, a publishing agreement containing the assignment by the composer of his future copyrights grants to the publisher the copyright in them automatically upon their creation. The publisher has the right to call for a specific written confirmatory assignment of the copyright in each composition as and when it is written, so that the title, lyrics and musical content of the song is formally identified. Thus the agreement can be enforced by a court order requiring the composer to execute a confirmatory and identifying assignment of copyright in respect of works composed by the composer during the period of the publishing agreement.

**24.2** It might appear that this is an exception to the general principle that a composer cannot be forced to compose. The right of enforcement is not to make him compose, as it only arises in respect of a created product of the composer's services (the copyright work), where the title of the publisher to the copyright in it is to be identified in accordance with the publishing agreement.

If the publishing agreement contains an obligation upon the composer to compose and deliver to the publisher not less than a stated number of songs in each year of the agreement, the publisher cannot get a court order to force the composer to write the outstanding number of songs not delivered. Because the rights of the publisher are already created when the composer signed the agreement, what he does write he cannot withhold from the publisher.

As the copyright in the composition will have been assigned to the publisher by the operation of the publishing agreement and the 1988 Act, if the composer refuses to execute a confirmatory assignment of the copyright in a song he has written, he does not thereby deprive the publisher of its right to the copyright in that song. A confirmatory assignment is also a practical requirement for lodging with the PRS and the other copyright income collecting societies, as the document is their authority to collect and pay out the performance income of the song to the right persons in the right proportions. Failure by the composer to provide this written document will deprive him and the publisher of performance income if delayed indefinitely. An established and reputable publisher may persuade the PRS to collect the income, and make international notifications, pending the sorting out of the paperwork.

**24.3** Where the copyrights of existing compositions are to be included on the signing of the publishing agreement, their titles should be scheduled for identification. The PRS must be notified of the change in the publisher/income collector for its accounts records, and any further period during which the previous publisher is entitled to collect income on the compositions he used to publish.

**24.4** If a composer does not have a minimum song delivery commitment, what happens where he simply ceases to write songs? Ultimately the publishing agreement expires and that's that, subject to any right of the publisher to be repaid advances for which nothing has been produced by the composer. The composer has committed no breach whereby the publisher can claim damages for loss of earnings from songs not composed. If the composer terminates the agreement by breach, anything he writes for another publisher during the remaining contract period can be claimed by the publisher. Again, if he writes no more songs, there is no basis for a claim against him, even if he had a minimum commitment.

## 25 Joint and collaborative copyright

*Example*

"(a) Whenever the Composer composes any music or writes any lyrics in collaboration with any other person whether or not that person requires a credit therefor or will be entitled to a portion of the Composer's share of income therefrom the Composer will procure that such person also signs the confirmatory assignment of the copyright created by him in that composition to the Publisher on the same terms as the Composer together with an irrevocable authority in writing to the Publisher to split the Composer's share of income hereunder in whatever proportions they have agreed.

(b) If any proposed Collaborator is subject to an existing publishing agreement with a third party the Composer will consult with the Publisher before commencing any collaborative composing or writing so that the rights in the resulting co-written compositions can first be agreed with the Collaborator's Publisher."

**25.1** Complications can arise where a composer, who has an exclusive publishing agreement with a publisher, collaborates with one or more other writers or composers in the creation of a composition. The composer can only assign to his publisher that part of the copyright of the song which belongs to him. This could be the whole of, or only a part of, either or both of the words or the music.

**25.2** For this reason, a common term found in publishing agreements is that if the composer collaborates with anyone else, a condition of that collaboration must be that the collaborator also assigns the copyright in his contribution to the joint song to the composer's publisher. The other composer receives what is due to him, but the exploitation of the composition as a single unit by the publisher is administratively more efficient. This may not be possible when each collaborator is subject to an exclusive publishing agreement with a different publisher.

**25.3** The joint efforts of collaboration can result in a composition wherein no identifiable portion of the song belongs to any one collaborator, ie, it is a joint composition. The copyright in the whole composition will normally belong to the collaborators jointly in equal shares, although they can agree to different proportions of the income being received by each of them. In theory all that each composer can do in such a situation is to assign to his publisher his portion of the whole copyright. But as it cannot be identified, in practice one or other of the publishers will take the whole composition, and share the publisher's share of income.

The publishers will have to sort out what portion of the whole income is to be received by the composers and in what proportions; and how the publishers will share the balance. This may be difficult to work out where:

(a) the composers receive from their respective publishers different percentages of net receipts from the exploitation of their respective compositions, which means that the publisher's shares are similarly different;

(b) the position regarding the recoupment of advances is different as between each composer and his own publisher.

## 26 Re-assignment to composer

Example

"If the Publisher or any of its Sub-publishers fails to procure any *bona fide* commercial record release containing any composition delivered by the Composer to the Publisher within [two years] of such delivery then irrespective of the efforts made by the Publisher the Composer will be entitled to give the Publisher written notice that failing any such record release within [three] months after delivery of the notice the Publisher shall re-assign the copyright in that composition to the Composer unconditionally."

**26.1** In every publishing agreement the composer should have the right to a reassignment of the copyright of songs which the publisher does not get recorded commercially, within a reasonable time after their delivery to the publisher. The period should be specified, such as two years. This guards against the publisher never activating the song. If the publisher does nothing with the song, the composer will never have the chance to earn royalties from it. The same right should apply where even though the publisher does its best, there is still no success. Without a recording no song will be successful, and the composer should be entitled to try elsewhere with it. The right of the publisher to retain the song should not apply to where he gets it published only, ie, just printed sheet music, even if ostensibly for commercial distribution. If the song is never recorded, it will never be heard, and if it is totally unknown, the availability of sheet music is academic and of no commercial value.

**26.2** An interesting position would arise where, due to the inevitable time lag of effective communication between a publisher and its sub-publishers, the following happens. After the (two year) period the publisher re-assigned the copyright of an unrecorded composition to the composer, who promptly assigns or licenses it to another publisher. A month later, in the USA, a major artiste releases an album which contains the composition. It transpires that two months prior to the re-assignment, the USA sub-publisher gave the song to the artiste's manager, who, only after the re-assignment had taken place, went through the usual label credit clearance with the sub-publisher, up to which time neither the publisher nor the sub-publisher were aware the recording had taken place during the period prior to the reassignment. What are the publishers rights now with the benefit of that information? If a "record release" is the condition of retaining the copyright, the publisher is unlucky, and has no rights. If the condition is to "have the composition recorded", in fact he will have complied with it. The wording of the clause will determine the point in time when the right to retain the song crystalised. Can he sue the composer and his subsequent publisher to set the re-assignment aside, such as by pleading mistake? Probably not. To be an effective basis of claim, the mistake must be of law, not of fact. The publisher re-assigned the song to the composer in the belief that he was obliged to. The composer accepted the re-assignment in good faith, and entered into a legal agreement with the subsequent publisher in good faith. The prior publisher just did a bad deal. It would not make any difference if the composer had not yet found an alternative publisher for the song.

**26.3** The publisher should not be entitled to demand any financial payment or other consideration on reassignment of the copyrights to the composer in the circumstances of paragraph **5.1**. If the publisher paid the composer a specific advance for the song, that was in consideration of the assignment of its copyright to the publisher. The publisher has had his value for money, and his failure to get it recorded is his own problem. The unrecouped advance should not be repayable on reassignment of the copyright to the composer.

A reasonable exception would be where the publisher, at the composer's request, is re-assigning to the composer the copyright in all his works, although he is not contractually obliged to do so. The publisher is cutting short his exclusive rights period, and a fair condition would be repayment to the publisher of any outstanding balance of any unrecouped advance on account of income previously paid to the composer, and possibly repayment of specific promotional expense incurred by the publisher at the insistence of the composer. Alternatively the publisher could take an override percentage of the new publisher's share of income for a period of time to cover the advance reimbursement.

**26.4** The right of re-assignment of the copyrights to the composer should also apply if the publisher ceases to trade, winds up or goes into liquidation. This is not a common feature, but it is logical. If (as is more common) the publisher is given a relatively short term exclusive licence to publish the works, that will terminate upon such an event. If, for administrative reasons, the publisher is assigned the copyrights, for whatever period, the composer should be in no worse a position than if he had been a licensor.

This may seem hard on the creditors, but the composer is entitled to protect his own interests. Without such a reassignment, any future income received by the publisher from the promotion or performance of the song, would be treated as its assets for the benefit of its creditors, of which the composer would be one. The composer would not be a secured or preferential creditor, so he would not continue to receive any of his contractual entitlement until all creditors (including himself) have been paid.

Unless the publisher is one of the major companies which is unlikely to go bust, if the composer is a high earner, he should insist that the publisher put his share of earnings into a separate designated bank trust account, although that idea would probably not protect the composer's share of income arising after the event of liquidation. As the liquidator has considerable powers, he may be entitled to ignore the contractual right of reassignment. As already stated, the best protection for the composer is to grant the publisher a terminable licence.

If it is agreed that fundamental breaches of the publishing agreement by the publisher should entitle the composer to have re-assignment of all copyrights, as well as terminating it, then the right will have to be specifically stated in the agreement. For example, if the publisher persistently refuses to pay the composer, or if demonstrably the composer is being systematically cheated in breach of the publisher's obligations to the composer, why should the publisher be entitled to retain the rights in the compositions? The composer has the right to sue for the missing or incorrect accounting each time, but that is an expensive and time consuming process, which does not solve a continuing problem.

**26.5** Upon the reassignment by the publisher of any copyright to the composer, the following will have to be dealt with:

(a) The rights of sub-publishers in those copyrights. If the reassignment was due to non-promotion, the sub-publisher's rights should also terminate, as there will be no existing local sources of income. If the reassignment is due to the publisher going bust, or upon termination for fundamental breach of the publisher, the rights of sub-publishers will terminate unless the contrary is agreed, which it normally is. The wording of the termination or copyright reversion clause should make it clear that, from that point onwards, the rights of the sub-publisher are transferred directly to the composer, so that the sub-publisher accounts directly to him (or to his new publisher). Once the copyright has been reassigned to the composer, the publisher should not benefit from it. This has an immediate effect if termination and reassignment are due to the publisher's fundamental breach, or going bust. If it follows a normal agreement period expiry, in accordance with the contract it will contain a clause allowing the publisher a further period of time to collect income for his benefit.

The sub-publishers only get their rights from the publisher, and if it ceases to have any, technically they have no claim upon the composer. In most cases active sub-publishers are allowed to continue. Difficulty will arise where the sub-publishers paid the publisher significant advances on the composer's works, which are mainly unrecouped. These advances will have been only on account of the publisher's share of income, so the composer should continue to get his own share as usual. Although the composer did not receive the advances from sub-publishers, his right to receive the publisher's share direct from the sub-publishers after termination will be withheld towards recoupment of those advances.

(b) The validity of all consents given by the publisher as copyright owner to third parties, where the item consented to has not yet been put into operation. These consents will remain effective, but whether any payments to be made to the publisher after the date of reassignment could be claimed by the composer will depend on the clause. Future income from past dealings with the copyright would normally remain the publisher's property.

(c) Notifications to all relevant copyright income collection societies, performing right societies and record companies, so that copyright credits, and the flow of publishing money in the pipeline, are dealt with correctly in future.

(d) The rights (if any) of the publisher to participate in the income which is in the pipeline (ie, which has been generated but which has not yet been received by the publisher) at the date of reassignment of the copyrights. This will depend on the wording of the agreement. It would be safer for the composer to collect all money coming in, and to pay over to the publisher its contractual entitlement, thus ensuring that he does not have to sue for his share.

Most publishing agreements do not go into this kind of detail, but for a composer dealing with a smaller (even though honest) publisher, it would save a lot of problems should the worst happen to the publisher.

## 27 Types of agreement

**27.1** There are broadly three kinds of publishing agreements, depending on the style of commercial relationship between the composer and the publisher. Whilst in each case the publisher acquires the right and obligation to promote the copyrights and to collect and account for the resultant income, the wording of the agreements will differ in the rights clauses. A publishing agreement can:

(a) Encompass exclusively the copyrights of all of the composer's original works created during the term of the agreement, by way of an immediate assignment of future copyright. This can be by a songwriting agreement (where the composer is an independent contractor), or by a full service contract, such as where he owns his own company, and provides all of his entertainment services to it. The copyrights in all the composer's compositions belong to the publisher at the moment of creation, whether or not he can use them. The assignment can be for the life of copyright, or a limited period.

(b) Be by way of exclusive licence granted by a company which owns the copyrights in the compositions created during that period, together with any others it already owns and which are not committed to any other publisher. This will be for a limited period.

(c) Entitle the publisher only to an exclusive first option to call for an assignment to him of the copyright in any of the composer's works created during that time. This is a possibility for limited purposes only, and it is not used as a long term commitment.

**27.2** If the publishing agreement has a limited period of time, then at the expiry of that period either the publisher will re-assign the copyrights, or the exclusive licence will terminate, as the case may be. The publishing agreement will then deal with any continuation rights of the publisher in respect of the compositions which came within his agreement period (see paragraph **19**).

**27.3** Under paragraph **6.1**(b) the publisher only gets "use" rights, and does not get any ownership rights. If the agreement is worded correctly, the publisher still gets all of the rights he needs to enable him to promote the compositions effectively, and in all material respects as if he were the copyright owner. However, by using a licence as the means of granting the publisher his rights, the composer is able to protect himself much more effectively from the publisher's breaches, dishonesty or liquidation. The reason is that termination of a licence can be effected more easily and quickly than trying to get a copyright reassignment from a reluctant publisher, or his liquidator.

**27.4** Where, under paragraph **6.1**(c), the publisher does not exercise his option in respect of any composition offered to him, the copyright in it will remain with the composer. The publisher will have waived his rights to it, and the composer can place it wherever he wants. The option should be exercisable by notice in writing to be received by the composer within a stated reasonable time after submission of the manuscript or a tape of the new song by the composer to the publisher. An example will be in the specialised jingles market, where several original efforts are asked for, from which only one will be chosen for the TV or radio advert.

If the composer is not an artiste the option period should give the publisher a reasonable opportunity to assess the potential of the songs. Even successful and high earning songs may have been in the hands of their music publisher for some time prior to their success. An alternative is to require the publisher positively to reject in writing the songs he does not want. Psychologically the publisher is not likely to write a letter of rejection, and he must think positively about keeping his rights if he has to write a notice of acceptance to the composer.

## 28 Financial terms

**28.1** The publishing agreement must contain proper financial terms as part of its legal consideration for the assignment of the copyrights or the grant of an exclusive licence (as the case may be). The other part of the consideration is the stated obligation to promote the composition to the best of its ability. The financial terms are for the benefit of the composer in the event of commercial promotion by the publisher of any of the songs. The publisher's and the composer's shares of the various sources of income must also be set out in each individual copyright confirmatory assignment. For example, it will be the written authority to the PRS to divide performance income, and to make the correct payments direct to the composer and to the publisher.

**28.2** The publisher will pay the composer an agreed proportion of the money received by the publisher from the exploitation of the compositions. The composer must understand what are the potential sources of income, how his share is calculated, what is a fair share, what it represents out of the gross copyright income arising at source, and as received in the hands of the publisher. When negotiating with the composer for his publishing agreement, disclosure by the publisher of his "standard practices" (assuming he is asked the right questions) will enable the composer to obtain fair terms. The most important of these is how the income arising abroad is dealt with, and what deductions are made to it (and why) before it is received by the publisher.

If the terms offered are not found to be fair, he must negotiate with the publisher to get them. If the composer genuinely believes that the final terms offered are not fair, he should not do the deal. If, on looking around, he finds he cannot get a better deal elsewhere, then, whatever his aspirations are, he will have to accept reality. For example, if the major territory sub-publishers are connected with the publisher, or have the same shareholders as the shareholders in the publisher, look hard at the retentions allowed by the publisher to its related sub-publishers. Set out below are the principal sources of music publishing income and the proportions of receipts which the composer can expect to be paid are set out in paragraph **12**.

*Sales of sheet music*

**28.3.1** Sheet music can mean single song sheets, and songbooks (sometimes called albums or folios) containing a collection of songs in sheet music style. Songbooks can be expensive to compile, with photographs, possibly biographical material, and a glossy cover. The full royalty rate should still apply, and there should be no allowance for the cost of the production of the songbook. That will be taken into account when fixing the retail price, and therefore the trade price, which is what the publisher receives. If the songbook contains only some of the composer's works, his share of the royalty will be proportional to the number of his songs in the book against the total number of songs in it.

**28.3.2** Royalties are not paid on professional sheet music copies, and copies distributed free of charge by the publisher for the purpose of promoting the music. The composer must watch for any extension of royalty free copies which is unreasonable, such as a combination of professional copies and "the first so many copies sold". Either the composer is paid his royalty on all the copies sold, or the professional copies allowance is removed and substituted by "the first so many copies sold" being royalty free, to give the publisher flexibility.

**28.3.3** It must also be clear what is meant by "the first so many copies sold", as without an explanation it can mean any of:

(a) The first so many copies of single sheet music sold by the publisher only.
(b) The first so many copies of single sheet music by the publisher and by each sub-publisher.
(c) Either of (a) or (b) but to include the same number of folios (whether or not comprising wholly the composer's works) as copies of single sheet music; and either of (a) or (b) but in different editions. If editions are referred to, what constitutes an edition should be defined. A simple reprint, even with a different cover, should not be an edition for this purpose.

If these categories are aggregated, there won't be much left on which to pay any royalty. The sheet music clause should only allow the publisher sufficient freedom not to have to pay a royalty to the composer on sheet music actually distributed free in good faith for *bona fide* promotional purposes. When in doubt, the composer should get a clear explanation of what the publisher actually does.

**28.3.4** Common exclusions from sheet music distributions for royalty purposes are band copies, medley arrangements and printed music using only sections of the compositions, all of which are intended to be distributed free, or perhaps at cost—which should mean production cost. Royalties should be paid where these are sold commercially, whatever the price charged. If the publisher receives a once only fee for the inclusion of the printed music in a newspaper, music textbook or for similar use, the fee should be shared with the composer as "any other income" under paragraph **11** below.

## 29 Performance fees

**29.1** Performance fees received by the publisher are collected by the PRS and its international associated and affiliated societies. The publisher has to be a member of PRS, otherwise PRS will not collect its performance income. The same applies to a composer, although his publisher through PRS can collect his income arising in very few countries. The PRS in each country grants licences to authorise the public performance of copyright works for a fee, whether the performance is by records or by live performance. Unauthorised public performance of a copyright work, ie, without a PRS licence to do so, is a breach of the performing right section of its copyright, and can be prevented. This point is not always appreciated by shops, restaurants and other public places where background music is played. When discovered, apart from any other action taken by the PRS against the proprietor of the premises, he will be charged a fee for retrospective use of the music.

**29.2** The PRS will distribute the performance income it receives in respect of the composer's works separately to the publisher and to the composer in the proportions set out in the publishing agreement. This is repeated in the confirmatory assignment and in the PRS composition notification document. For the composer to receive his share direct he must be a member of PRS, otherwise with his express written authority, and so far as PRS is able to do so, the publisher may collect his share on his behalf. If the publisher collects the composer's share of performance income, that should be paid to the composer within, say, 14 days of the publisher receiving it, so that the composer, and not the publisher, has the use of the money. This would be an exception to the normal accounting provisions (see paragraphs **12.8** and **12.9**). The performance income collected by the publisher for the composer would be subject to being retained by the publisher towards recoupment of advances the publisher has paid to the composer, unless it is prohibited from doing so under the publishing agreement. As the composer would have received his share of performance money direct from PRS had he been a member, in which case it would not have been available to the publisher for recoupment purposes, the publisher should agree not to retain it, but should pay it over to the composer. If the level and structure of advances paid by the publisher to the composer are substantial, the publisher may require to receive his performance income as well towards recoupment. Membership of PRS should be applied for as soon as the composer is eligible.

**29.3** If the composer is a PRS member, but agrees that his share of performance income should be paid to the publisher, for example, to secure the recoupment of advances, PRS will only do so under an express written authority to PRS from the composer. When recoupment is complete, PRS should be directed to revert to paying the composer his share direct. The PRS may be reluctant in certain circumstances to pay the composer's share to the publisher at all, but ultimately the composer's wishes should be accepted and complied with.

**29.4.1** Where a substantial part of a successful composer's earnings consists of performance income, he should consider carefully the structure of the publishing of his songs so as to get the greatest benefit from that income. An efficient structure will not of itself increase the amount of the income at source, but it can make it worth more in the composer's hands, by accelerating the payments, and reducing the total cost to the composer of commissions taken by the various copyright collection societies. Ordinarily the PRS will receive from its overseas affiliates the performance income collected by them locally and attributable to a PRS contracted publisher and composer. The disadvantage to the composer is that if, for example, (as a major territory) his USA performance income is substantial, there is a considerable time lapse between it being collected in the USA, accounted for to PRS, and PRS accounting to the composer. There is also the administration charge, being a percentage of the amount collected by both PRS and foreign collection societies. PRS does not commission foreign remittances.

**29.4.2** Should the composer leave England and live permanently in America, it will be worthwhile for him to receive direct his share of American performance income collected by ASCAP, rather than having it travel from ASCAP to PRS, only to be remitted by PRS from the UK back to the composer in America. There will also be a benefit in minimising exchange rate losses in the transaction. ASCAP would then become his prime collection society, and he would resign from PRS. Where the composer owns his publishing company, which is UK based and which has the copyrights in his works, the composer resident in the USA might be able to receive his performance income direct from ASCAP, and the UK company would retain PRS membership to collect through its publisher all other performance income. Subject to tax and other matters, the composer might consider transferring the copyrights to the USA, as the USA is his home.

Whilst PRS and the other collection societies exist to benefit their members, they do not want collection and payment to be unnecessarily complicated, or even uneconomical, just to enable a composer to fine tune his cash flow. This is only worth contemplating if the performance income is substantial, and if the flow of it at that level is likely to continue for some years, and if the composer will remain resident in the USA.

## 30 Mechanical royalties

**30.1** Mechanical royalties are those royalties on record sales paid by the manufacturers of records (including tapes, laser discs etc) to the owner of the copyright in a musical composition which has been recorded, whether the recording is made by the composer or by any other performing artiste. If the composer is also the artiste, his royalties as a performer paid to him by the record company are not copyright payments, and are no concern of his publisher.

**30.2** Under section 8 of the Copyright Act 1956 there was a statutory right to record in the UK a composition which already had an authorised recording commercially available in the UK, on payment to the copyright owner of a royalty, and on completing the necessary reporting formalities. The statutory royalty had been set at 6¼% of retail selling price less VAT of the record, split 3⅛% to each side, then equally between the compositions on each side separately, irrespective of relative playing times. The 1988 Act contains no equivalent to section 8 of the 1956 Act, which is wholly repealed on the 1988 Act coming into force. There have for some time been rumblings within the UK publishing industry that the 6¼% was unrealistically low in comparison with other European rates. This will be the opportunity of the industry to establish an effective licensing system, under the provisions of the 1988 Act, with a rate and rules set out with 1992 in mind.

**30.3** Mechanical royalties can either be paid to the publisher direct by the record company under a specific licence, or the publisher can appoint the MCPS to collect the royalties from record companies on its behalf. All publishers belong to the MCPS, and sign an agreement which authorises MCPS to licence their catalogues for recording. In the USA statutory royalties are based on a minimum payment for each copyright composition recorded, with an increase in the rate depending upon the playing time of the recorded work. In the UK and other countries the statutory rate is a percentage of retail selling price of the record less the tax element of the price. At the date of publication of this book no new arrangements have been created under the 1988 Act to be in substitution for section 8 of the 1956 Act. No deductions, such as packaging costs, are made from the retail price in the calculation of mechanical royalties.

## 31 Synchronisation fees

**31.1** These are the fees paid to the publisher for the use of a composition in the sound track of a cinematograph or TV film or a video cassette which is released commercially. The consent of the copyright owner is required for such use, and a fee is negotiated, or consent is refused, in the absolute discretion of the publisher. The "synchronisation" is the combining of the recorded sound with visual images. The same principle applies to audiovisual records, whether for commercial home use, or for promotional broadcasting, although the fee structure may be modified for non-commercial use. A promotional video of good quality is expensive to produce, and is intended to boost the sales of the audio record, from which the publisher of the recorded composition will benefit.

**31.2** If the composition is also contained on a recording which is to be performed in the film or TV sound track, the consent of the owner of the copyright in the recording (normally the record company) is also necessary, independently of the consent of the publisher of the recorded composition.

**31.3** Where the composition is to be recorded especially for the soundtrack of a film, the payment to the publisher for the right to use the music is entirely separate from any fee the composer may receive from the film production company for orchestrating, arranging, conducting or performing the work for recording on the sound track. If the film production company pays the composer a commission fee, or any other form of payment related directly to the time he has to spend on the creation of the composition, that will belong wholly to him. As such a fee is paid in consideration of the composer doing that work, it is already a payment for value and should not be recoupable from any form of income created through the use of the work. If the publisher wants an advance for the use of the music, it must ask for one.

## 32 Any other income

**32.1** Where money is received by the publisher from any use of the composition which is not included in any of the above categories of income, the composer should receive his agreed proportion of it which is normally at the same level as that for mechanical royalties. There should be no limitation on this general income inclusion, as publication of the words or music of the composition may occur in unlikely circumstances. One example is the printing of the words of the lyrics of the recorded songs on an album, either onto the album sleeve itself, or on a separate lyric sheet included with the album. The consent of the publisher of the lyrics must be obtained, a fee agreed, and the correct copyright credits printed on the lyric sheet. Where the publishing company is connected with the record company, either directly or by having common shareholders, it must still charge the record company an arms-length appropriate fee. This is even more important where the composer is not the artiste performing on the recording.

**32.2** Within the UK it is not difficult to ascertain the money which is received by the publisher as incidental receipts. In many other countries, unless the English publisher or the composer is aware of them, there may be amounts received by the local sub-publishers, which are unallocated sums universally retained by the recipient, without either notifying the publisher or sharing the proceeds with it. These sums are generally know as "black box" payments, which are never declared by the sub-publisher in his accountings to the publisher. If they can be identified, the sub-publishing agreement should deal specifically with these sources of income.

**32.3.1** A levy may be collected by the local copyright society on the retail sale of blank tapes. The levy represents a copyright income, which is distributed to local publishers in a practical attempt to compensate them for the incalculable loss they suffer by the unauthorised private use of blank tapes for recording songs. This deprives the publishers of income by reason of the inevitable reduction in the sale of records and pre-recorded tapes, so the publisher and the composer both suffer. Within the EEC the advent of 1992 may see the harmonisation of any differences or anomalies in this and other copyright payment matters currently existing in individual countries.

**32.3.2** The local sub-publisher will claim that such arbitrary receipts, which are not treated as copyright income, and are not allocated among individual copyrights, represent money due to the sub-publisher in its own right, and which is not received by it on behalf of the copyright owners it represents.

## 33 Payments by a publisher

*Sheet music*

**33.1** The royalties payable will be either 10% or 12.5% of all income received by the publisher in respect of any sales of printed music of the compositions, or the royalties will be those percentages, but calculated upon the marked retail selling price of all copies or versions sold.

Obviously the calculation based on retail selling price will be greater than that based on net receipts, which means effectively the trade price. If the publisher prints and sells to the public all its own sheet music it should pay the royalties based upon the retail price. If it licences specialist publishers (in the sense of producers and distributors of sheet and folio music) to do so for them, then obviously if the royalty is based on a percentage of net receipts it will have a lower monetary value to the composer. The royalties will be based upon a net receipts basis in respect of sub-publishers' sales of sheet music.

*Performance fees*

**33.2** The composer should never receive less than 50% of the performance fees received by the publisher. A composer with reasonable prospects of significant earnings will receive more, a popular level being between 60% and 75%. If a cover record is procured by the publisher, then the royalty on performances of the song in the territory in which the cover record originates will be reduced.

*Mechanical royalties*

**33.3** Customarily the percentage paid to the composer is the same as that for performance fees. In neither case will the publisher be involved in substantial expenditure directly referable to promoting and improving those sources of income. The rate retained by the publisher in respect of the sale of cover records will be increased (see paragraph **18**).

*Synchronisation fees*

**33.4.1** Each fee is negotiated with the film production company, and so involves the publisher in some time and effort. There may also be a conflict of interest if the publisher is associated with the record company, where the consent is sought for performance in the sound track of the composer/artiste's recording of the composition. Each fee should be negotiated separately, on an arm's-length basis. The percentage paid to the composer should not be less than the percentage for mechanical royalties.

**33.4.2** The film production company may be associated with a music publisher for collaboration on film scores. In this case it may be a condition of a commissioned film score agreement with a composer that the copyright in it is assigned to the associated publisher. If the composer has an exclusive agreement with a publisher, the film production company would have to deal with the publisher for the associated publisher to have the rights. This will mean that either the composer receives his share of income but his usual publisher does not benefit, or that all of the payments from the associated publisher are paid to the composer's publisher, to be shared with the composer as agreed. In practice the two publishers will do a deal on the publisher's share of income. The film production company will also want the exclusive right to make or authorise the first commercial recording of the sound track music, and to receive a percentage of the record company income on sales of the record. A sound track album will benefit both the composer and his publisher, as they will share in the copyright income on such sales.

*Any other income*

**33.5** This covers unexpected payments not included in the specific categories of income, which will usually be once-only payments. The proportion paid to the composer should be at the highest level for any above category, as they are treated as windfall payments to the publisher.

*Income received by the publisher*

**33.6.1** The publishing agreement will usually state that the percentages paid to the composer will be of money which has actually been received in the UK by the publisher, or by some party on its behalf. Where the publisher has only UK rights, it receives the income gross from each source, so the composer's share has the maximum monetary value, and is easily accounted for. The position changes when the publisher with an exclusive world wide agreement sub-publishes the composer's works with local publishers in each foreign country.

**33.6.2** The sub-publisher will retain a proportion of gross earnings arising in his territory, in accordance with his sub-publishing agreement, and will remit the balance to the publisher. It is the amount received by the publisher which will be divided with the composer, so the composer will have to know the financial terms of the sub-publishing agreement to be able to calculate his share of gross earnings arising from that foreign territory. For example, a composer negotiates (in simple terms) a share of 75% of the publisher's receipts. He then finds that a sub-publisher retains 50% of local receipts, only remitting 50% to the publisher. The composer's 75% of 50% only represents 37.5% of income arising at source. This is not good news, especially if the sub-publisher is connected with the publisher. Information on all of the sub-publishing financial arrangements is also useful to the composer where the publisher has existing and fixed catalogue sub-publishing commitments throughout the world. With that knowledge the composer can negotiate higher percentages of UK receipts to even out the effects of any unusually disadvantageous (to the composer) sub-publishing agreements. The relevant points to take into account are set out in paragraph **12.7** below. If the publisher already has long term exclusive commitments to a sub-publisher, say, on a 50% of local income retention across the board, the composer may decide not to do a deal with that publisher, however good the publisher may be otherwise.

*Sub-publishing income*

**33.7.1** The value to the composer of his share of gross earnings abroad will depend upon the structure of the sub-publishing arrangements, such as:

(1) An independent sub-publisher might do no more than collect gross income and remit it for a small percentage, probably between 10% and 15% of the amount collected, depending on the anticipated annual value. The higher percentage would apply to lower amounts, to make the efforts of local copyright registration, and any other protective formalities, and accounting, worth while. A full sub-publishing agreement will entitle the sub-publisher to retain not less than 20% of all money collected. If the flow of money is not significant, it can be increased but it should not be more than 30%. This retention may go up to 50% of mechanical income from a locally produced *bona fide* commercially released cover recording of a composition. The performance fee retention may also go up to 50% of the local performance income from the covered composition, irrespective of whether the local cover version or the original recording is performed. Performance returns never differentiate between the individual recorded versions unless they have different titles. If the original version is a monster hit in the territory, with constant air play, the rush release of a local version is unlikely to make much impact on which of them is actually performed. To have immediately 50% of all performance income as a result is an excessive benefit to the local publisher in that example. The uplift may be less, or even eliminated, for the catalogue of a successful composer for that reason. The definition of what is a cover record for the purpose of increasing the percentage retained by the sub-publisher is discussed in paragraph **18**. A fairer means of getting the increased percentage for performance income is to state that, within each of the sub-publisher's accounting periods, the increase will be in the ratio of sales of the cover version of the record to the sales of the original version. This will represent their relative values in the market.

The percentages agreed with a sub-publisher will depend on the likely flow of money from which he will retain a percentage. The higher the money flow, the less his retained percentage will be. If he gets a catalogue of the composer's works, all of which are on actively promoted recordings, the fact that some works may earn much less, or much more, than others does not affect the overall percentage retention for the catalogue.

(2) The local sub-publisher's agreement with the publisher will state that his increased share of local mechanical royalties is on sales of local cover records. The agreement should differentiate between sales of those cover records and sales of imported or other recorded versions of the composition. Ie, if it is not recorded locally, it is not a cover record. For example, a USA sub-publisher obtains a cover record of a UK original recording, and as it will be sung in English, it will be marketable in all English speaking countries, and elsewhere if the performer is an international artiste. An instrumental version will be marketable throughout the world. The USA sub-publisher will have a higher retention of income on local sales of that local recording. As the USA sub-publisher is not entitled to share in any income arising outside his territory, the sub-publisher in each other territory in which that recording is sold will collect the mechanical copyright income arising from their local sales of that record. Because each of the other sub-publishers did not obtain the USA version, for retention level purposes, to them it is an original recording (ie not a cover record), and they should account to the publisher for income on the sales of it accordingly. The same will apply to any other non-local recording. Otherwise the full percentage rate will only be paid to the publisher on one version, and the earnings increase of the sub-publisher will not depend on him getting a local recording of the composition released in his territory. The wording of the cover record clause must be drafted accordingly.

(3) The percentages retained by all sub-publishers of the publisher should be researched carefully before the composer signs with the publisher, where the income from the composer's works will be substantial. Sub-publishers in different territories may have different terms. The sub-publisher should get a reasonable return for his efforts, but a successful composer should not be deprived of more of his gross local earnings than necessary. It is also in the publisher's interests to restrict the amounts to be retained by the sub-publisher, unless the sub-publisher is owned by the publisher. Specifically the composer must look out for any "creaming off" of income as an artificial device by having an intermediate company between the publisher and the sub-publisher.

**33.7.2** (1) Where the sub-publisher is owned or controlled by the publisher, it has a conflict of interest when negotiating with the sub-publisher for the percentage to be remitted to the UK from the gross income arising locally. This retention should be no more than the publisher would pay to an independent sub-publisher for that country. If the connected sub-publisher retains a higher than usual percentage with the knowledge of the composer, then the percentages paid to the composer out of the publisher's UK receipts should be higher than usual, to remedy the position in monetary terms. The local connected sub-publisher must do everything that an independent sub-publisher would do (ie, it must be a genuine operation with premises, staff, and all else needed for a commercial operation). It should retain no more than the level of income as would be given to an independent sub-publisher for the same level of representation. The publisher should satisfy the composer that the existence of the connected sub-publisher is a genuine commercial necessity, operating an active enterprise, and is not just an expedient device for filtering off an artificially high "sub-publisher share" of income. If the sub-published territory has exchange control problems, and as a one-off deal the sub-publisher has obtained for the publisher a large advance in hard currency, which might normally not be obtainable, it may deserve a higher than normal retention percentage as a *quid pro quo*, although it would increase the recoupment period. That would be a good commercial reason, but should be agreed with the composer.

(2) The composer should restrict the publisher from increasing any percentage to be retained by any sub-publisher without the composer's prior consent. The publishing agreement can also restrict the publisher from exceeding stated percentages in the amount to be retained locally by each sub-publisher who is appointed in the future, whether or not it is associated with the publisher. Where all of the sub-publishers are part of a worldwide group of publishers, the composer can be paid his percentage based on the actual local gross income, leaving it to the publisher to agree with each sub-publisher how they share the balance between them. This is called an "at source" deal, and is only likely to be acceptable where the overall publishing receipts are very significant. The same result can be achieved on an individual sub-publisher basis, by getting the wording of the contract right. It would not be commercially viable for small amounts, or where the composer does not yet have international success. The advantages are:

(a) The composer knows what proportion he is getting of source income from each territory.

(b) The amount retained by the sub-publisher comes off the publisher's share, and does not affect the composer.

(c) It helps the composer to audit local sources of income to ascertain correct accounting, as well as relying on statements produced by the publisher.

(d) It is easier to check on the cash flow, both as to time and amount, to ensure that all local money is included in the earliest possible accounting period, both from its source to the sub-publisher, and from the sub-publisher to the publisher. A major worldwide publishing group can also help the cashflow of an internationally successful composer by assessing "pipeline" income due to him, and giving him occasional advances on account of it when requested. Pipeline income is money already flowing through the system, but which has not yet been received by the publisher, or which has been received but is not to be accounted for in the near future.

(e) The true extent of local collection costs and other deductions and "shrinkages" can be ascertained more readily.

**33.7.3** A publisher must never be entitled to grant to any sub-publisher the rights for the sub-publisher itself to sub-publish any part of its territory with someone else. Any such contractual arrangement is highly suspect for many reasons, and can provide the publisher with great practical difficulty if the local gross income is not paid, or if it is incorrectly accounted for. Part of the reasoning is to prevent a publisher, which is given worldwide rights, from itself publishing in the UK, and granting the rest of the world to a foreign subsidiary, which then itself sub-publishes other individual territories to subsidiary companies. If a sub-subpublisher retains 50%, and remits 50% to the sub-publisher, which retains 50% of what it receives and remits the balance to the UK publisher, the composer's 75% of that is 18.75% of what arose at source.

**33.7.4** If the publishing company which owns the copyrights in the composer's works is owned jointly by the publisher and the composer, the calculation of the composer's percentages must take that into account. That company will use the services of the publisher in return for a percentage, which must be a proper commercial rate. If the composer gets 50% as a composer, and owns half the copyright owning company, one way or another he gets 75% of income attributable to those copyrights, plus half their value.

**33.7.5** (1) It is a matter for negotiation as to whether the composer should receive any proportion of advances received by the publisher from sub-publishers at the time they are paid. As the composer should have already negotiated a reasonable advance from the publisher, the question should not arise. If the composer received an initial advance, but with no further commitment from the publisher for advances, sub-publishers advances received by the publisher, for example, on the renewal of the sub-publishing deal, would be of interest to him.

The publisher's decision will depend upon whether the sub-publisher's advance was entirely related to the composer's works, or whether it was a general advance from the sub-publisher to the publisher covering a collection of catalogues of works by many composers.

(2) If the sub-publisher pays an advance related only to the composer, the publisher will receive no more income from the sub-publisher in respect of the composer's works until that advance has been recouped by the sub-publisher. The sub-publisher will still render accounts to the publisher showing what would have been paid to the publisher but for the advance, and will state the balance of the advance still to be recouped. At that point the publisher will be deemed to have received what is due to it, by reason of having had the advance. If he did not get his proportion of the sub-publishing advance, and if there are no unrecouped advances to him from the publisher, the composer must be accounted to by the publisher for what is due to him, and paid accordingly. If the composer's works represent a major catalogue, the total value of worldwide advances obtainable from sub-publishers can be substantial.

(3) The composer must ensure that his publishing agreement does not enable a publisher to receive sub-publishing advances on the composer's works and to try to delay paying the composer on an accounting from the sub-publisher simply because at that time he received no cheque from the sub-publisher. The definition of "money received" by the publisher must make it clear, as it is obviously intended, that advances, because they were received prior to the relevant accounting period for which a statement is delivered to the composer, included the money now due to him. This point may seem to be pedantic, but the wording of a contract is most important. No such problem of interpretation would arise with a reputable publisher. There is also the practical point that if the publisher has spent all his advances prior to having to account to the composer, it may not have the ready cash available to pay him. The composer may then have to sue the publisher. The publisher will then be in breach of contract, which may trigger termination rights by the composer.

**33.8** Publishers normally account to composers half yearly, but it should be questioned as to whether they could account on a quarterly basis. For some composers' works there may not be much to pay each time as the composer gets his share of performance income direct from PRS if he is a member, and if he is not a member his publisher can collect some of it for him. The major source of earnings for which the publisher will account will be mechanical royalties received from record companies (either direct or through MCPS). For income arising outside the UK, the sub-publishers will account to the publisher.

**33.9** The composer wants to receive as quickly as possible his share of earnings which are received by the publisher. If the publisher accounts 45 or 60 days after the close of an accounting period (standard accounting is 90 days), the publisher may have received money in July of one year, of which the composer does not get his share until the middle or end of February in the next year. This has two practical effects; the publisher is effectively getting an interest free loan of that share for that period, and the composer does not have the use of the money. Computerised accounting systems make 60 days anachronistic, but the publisher may need, say, 30 days within which to process all accountings for all of its composers. It depends on whether the half yearly accounting is for the June and December periods, or March and September.

## 34 Warranties and indemnities

**34.1** In a copyright assignment publishing deal, the publisher will rely on the validity of, and his ownership of, the copyright when he promotes the composition. Where he gets his rights under an exclusive licence, he will need assurance that it is valid. For his protection, the publisher will require the composer to enter into the following warranties:

(a) That the composition is original copyright material, and that the composer is the sole composer/lyric writer of it, and that it does not breach any third party rights. If he is not the sole composer, the details of the other composers must be provided (see paragraph **4**). The originality point is also relevant where the copyright work is an arrangement based on a work in the public domain.

(b) That the composer is entitled to assign the copyright to the publisher unconditionally free from any lien or encumbrance, and that he has not assigned the copyright elsewhere or otherwise dealt with it in any way. Alternatively, that the composer is free to grant the exclusive licence, and that in doing so he is not in breach of any third party rights. This assurance is needed by a publisher when his agreement with the composer follows an expired or terminated agreement between the composer and another publisher. The publisher should try to check whether any composition presented to it shortly after the termination of a prior publishing deal could possibly have come within the prior publisher's rights.

(c) That none of the lyrics will be defamatory, obscene, or otherwise objectionable. The publisher will see the lyrics well before any publication takes place, and should raise any query immediately. If the composer is an artiste who generally composes as he goes along in the studio, it is possible that the lyrics will be recorded before the publisher is given the final version of the composition.

(d) That without first notifying the publisher in writing, the composer will not compose under a pseudonym, or use a name not being his legal name or one by which he is professionally known. The composer must also agree to sign any document needed to identify him as the composer, for the correct copyright credits and for PRS registration purposes. There is only a problem where the use of another name is intended to deceive or defraud the publisher.

(e) That he will give details to the publisher of every composition he creates during the term of the agreement, together with top lines and lyric sheets, or a tape recording. "Creates" should specifically include any composition which can clearly be shown to have come into existence during the period of the agreement, but which is not set down permanently until after its termination.

The purpose of the delay would be to have the date of its first setting down to be after the expiry of the publisher's agreement. The theory is that, as the work only then becomes a copyright, it is not within the publisher's rights.

**34.2** These warranties will be supported by an indemnity from the composer to the publisher, agreeing to compensate him for the consequences of any breach by the composer of the warranties. The terms of the indemnity, and the composer's potential liabilities should they be invoked, must be fully understood by the composer. The publisher knows that any indemnity from the composer is only as effective as his ability to raise the amount of compensation he may owe to the publisher. There will be some security for a publisher with a successful composer, as the publisher will continue to receive the composer's share of money (except for performance income), which he can retain towards his loss. For the publisher's protection, the composer should not give his warranties "to the best of his knowledge and belief", as the publisher relies absolutely upon the warranties being correct, and the subject matter is solely within the knowledge of the composer. The statements are either correct or they are not.

**34.3** For the protection of the composer, an indemnity on a copyright warranty should be reasonable, and the following should be taken into account:

(a) Losses, damages and expenses incurred by the publisher must be reasonably directly attributable to the breach of the warranty. Deciding what is, and what is not, sufficiently directly attributable to the breach can be difficult.

(b) The loss or damage incurred by a breach of a warranty cannot be forecast at the time of the assignment of the copyright to the publisher. There may be technical breaches, which do not cause any monetary loss or expense, and which are easily cured when discovered. Such a breach may be inadvertent, and not discovered by either party for some time.

If the agreement sets out in advance of any breach by the composer a specified sum to be paid to the publisher as compensation should a breach occur, that precludes the proper calculation of loss, and ignores the possibility of no loss being incurred by the publisher. It would be hard to prove that the estimate is not a penalty, which would make the indemnity unenforceable, particularly if it was clearly excessive and oppressive.

## 35 Joint publishing

**35.1** There can be joint publishers of a composition, each of them being given equal prominence in the copyright credit. This will happen where two or more co-composers are individually signed to different publishers exclusively. This can happen when one composer writes the music, and the other writes the lyrics. Both co-publishers have to sign documents which require the copyright owner's consent for use of the joint material. Each composer will still receive his proportion of the composer's share of receipts of the joint publishers from the work, which leaves the publisher's share of income to be divided as they agree. The whole of the income may be split 50/50 between the two publishers, each then paying to his own composer whatever share he may be due.

If, under his publishing agreement, one composer receives 75% of receipts, and the other composer under his publishing agreement receives 60%, a compromise may be agreed for the composers' share of the joint composition. One compromise is what will be the share on this composition for the composers; and the other compromise will be whether the composers split that 50/50 or 60/75? It will normally be on a 50/50 basis. Other examples of disparities which may need to be resolved are that one publisher may own the copyrights of his composer, and the other only has an exclusive licence: and one publisher may have worldwide rights, and the other only the European territories. For the protection of all of them, a satisfactory compromise has to be reached.

**35.2** Where there are many compositions created by the same co-composers to be jointly published, such as for a musical play, the joint publishers may form a company owned by them in their agreed proportions to cover all of the works for the whole of the relevant territory. This would ensure parity in all respects over the shares of income, and will simplify the credits and copyright society registrations.

**35.3** Where two otherwise independent music publishing companies become the joint publishers of a catalogue of copyrights, such as where one of them publishes the lyric writer's works, and the other publishes the composer's works, points for discussion will be:

(a) In what proportions will they own the copyrights, and what will be the copyright credit?

(b) How will the publishers share of income be divided, and how will the expenses of each joint publisher be dealt with?

(c) What element of control is to be exercised by each of them in any negotiation where the copyright owner's consent is required?

(d) Who will decide what sub-publishing deals should be done, with whom, and upon what terms?

(e) What happens in the event of one of the publishers going out of business in respect of:

(i) Who will own the copyrights? The defunct business will still be entitled to its share of income, but the active publisher will have to be able to give the whole copyright owners consents, sue infringers in the name of the copyright owner, and soforth. The active copyright owner should have the right to buy the other half of the copyright at a proper value. If the joint publishers are sued by a third party for copyright infringement, the active publisher may end up with the whole liability. Its right of compensation for half of it from the bust company will be valueless, except perhaps as against the copyright value, or its share of income.

(ii) Who will administer the business of the catalogue? The active publisher will, but there may have to be an adjustment of income shares to offset the fact that it carries the whole cost of doing so.

(iii) For how long will the publisher's share of the income be divided between them, and will the proportions vary? Subject to (ii) above, for so long as the defunct company (or its successor in title) owns half the copyrights.

(iv) Who will take the benefits of long-term publishing agreements with composers? The active publisher should, after the other publisher went bust.

(v) How will all future copyright credits be dealt with? That will depend on what happens to the other half of the copyright, and who owns it.

(f) The effects of one of the co-publishers going bust will depend on the co-publishing structure. The lyric writer or the composer (as the case may be) contracted to the bust publisher, may be entitled to reversion of his rights on termination of his publishing agreement. If not, the receiver for the company will consider what is best for its creditors.

## 36 Publisher's activities

The composer grants the publisher its rights, and assigns to it the copyrights in his compositions, in consideration of the royalties to be paid to him, and of the publisher agreeing to use its best endeavours to promote the compositions. The agreement should describe what is intended to be a satisfactory promotion, although anything other than spending a budgetted sum of money will be subjective.

**36.1** The publisher's main functions are:

(a) to print, sell and promote the composer's works, and to get them commercially recorded, used and exploited, by all available means to the best of their advantage and earning capacity;

(b) to collect all copyright income arising within his territory in respect of those works;

(c) to protect the copyright of the compositions, and to prevent their unauthorised use, and to take action on any breach of the copyright.

**36.2** The key word is "promotion", but that does not describe adequately what a publisher has to do. A well organised publishing company has many departments dealing with administration, protection and promotion of all the compositions within the publisher's catalogue. For obvious commercial reasons, the most active element of the publisher's entire catalogue will be those songs which have been recorded. The general areas of promotion of a song will include:

(a) Completing copyright registration formalities with all the relevant copyright income collection societies, and complying with any legal formalities required to protect the copyright itself in any foreign country for which the publisher has rights. This may well be done through sub-publishers. The publisher must also ensure that the correct copyright credits are given wherever any use is made of any of the copyrights.

(b) Printing and selling sheet music and books.

(c) Trying to get the song recorded for the first time if the composer is not an artiste, or trying to obtain cover recordings if he is an artiste.

(d) Obtaining the most advantageous sub-publishing deals, and keeping sub-publishers up to date on all of the compositions created by the composer

(e) Watching out for, and dealing with, infringements of the copyrights.

(f) Obtaining airplay, and helping to promote the sales of recordings of the compositions.

(g) Negotiating fees for the use of the compositions where the copyright owner's consent is required.

(h) Ensuring that all sources of income are correctly and promptly collected and accounted for.

**36.3** The publishing agreement may not set all these points out, but at least there must be an obligation upon the publisher to use its best endeavours to promote the songs. If challenged on this point, the publisher should have some evidence on file that it has been genuinely active in the promotion of the songs, such as correspondence, telexes, and anything else which would show what it has been doing. If the publisher has poor results despite strenuous efforts, it is fulfilling its obligations, but should examine the methods used.

## 37 Sub-publishing

**37.1** An established music publishing company, which has an active business within its own territory, must expand internationally. The best method will depend upon the size of its earning catalogue, its financial strength, and within which countries it will lose income if it is not represented. Methods of international representation include:

(a) Associated or subsidiary company of the publisher. The local sub-publishing company will have its own administration, and the publisher will normally have a controlling shareholding. The agreement between the publisher and its subsidiary or associated sub-publisher will deal with such matters as local taxation, running costs, financial control, and what proportion of all income arising within the territory will be retained by the sub-publisher. Notwithstanding the relationship, the publisher must deal with the sub-publisher as firmly as if it were an independent company. There must be a genuine trading relationship on an arm's-length basis, and the retentions from income by the sub-publisher must not exceed what it would have been allowed if it had been independent of the publisher.

(b) Independent sub-publisher. If the volume of business abroad is insufficient to warrant the cost of a subsidiary company, or if there is no genuine commercial reason for having one, an independent publisher based in a country within the publisher's territory can be appointed either:

(i) As an active sub-publisher, promoting the works and building up the business of the publisher within that territory, for a reasonable share of the sub-publisher's gross receipts.

(ii) As a passive sub-publisher, keeping the works alive with minimal expense and effort. This means supervising the collection of earnings and the maintenance of copyright notices, and watching for obvious breaches of copyright. This is a "collection deal", the sub-publisher retaining only a modest percentage of all money collected by him. Such a system will not suit the composer whose works need active promotion, but may suit the owner of a catalogue of "standard" compositions.

(c) Collection society deal, ie, not having a sub-publisher at all, and relying on the local performing right society to collect performance income, and any local mechanical copyright income collection society to collect record sales royalties.

A catalogue of "standard" works, which are self promoting by being universally known, and so which are constantly being performed and recorded, may not require active promotion, and the cost even of passive representation may not be justified financially. In minor territories little will be lost by way of income or opportunity if the publisher keeps an eye on things and allows the local collection societies to receive all money arising in the territory, and to account for it to the publisher. The commission charged by each collection society is the only expense to be anticipated. For standard compositions there comes a saturation point of promotion expenditure, after which the cost of the effort exceeds the additional income which is generated.

The disadvantages of leaving everything in the hands of a collection society are that the publisher must accept their accounting methods and dates, and that it is not their job to spot or remedy any unauthorised use of the copyrights, or enforce the publisher's rights over a breach of copyright. There may also be missed many opportunities for the compositions to be used, if only someone had been there to deal with them.

## 38 Sub-publishing agreements.

**38.1** Sub-publishing agreements are by way of a licence to publish, not by an assignment to the sub-publisher of copyright for that territory. It is possible to sub-publish by way of limited copyright assignment if that is beneficial for some reason. The licence will entitle the sub-publisher to do all things within the territory which the publisher would have been able to do itself. If a publisher can establish its overseas sub-publishing on the same basis for the whole world, its own administration and accounting can be more efficient in dealing with:

(a) which territories are sub-published on a copyright licence basis, and which (if any) are sub-published on a territorial assignment of copyright;
(b) which of the licensed territories are due for option renewal, and when each option must be exercised by the sub-publisher;
(c) the proportions of income to be retained by the sub-publishers, particularly if the composer has an "at source" deal;
(d) in the case of copyright licensed territories, what requirements are needed to give the succeeding sub-publisher title to act after the preceding sub-publisher's catalogue rights, and run-on period, have terminated;
(e) when accountings are to be made to the publisher;
(f) what needs to be done upon the termination of any sub-publishing agreement.

**38.2** The publisher will notify the sub-publisher of all new compositions coming under the agreement, and, if it is an overall catalogue deal, together with details of the composer, royalty terms and date of first publication. Each sub-publisher must be provided with enough information to ensure that collection societies are notified in time to collect all of the mechanical royalties and performance fees, and that all local copyright formalities are dealt with.

**38.3** Where the territory does not have English as a major language, the sub-publisher must supervise all foreign language lyric rights, and must collect the copyright income arising from cover records in the local language. The sub-publisher should be committed to trying to obtain a local language cover record, and must ensure that the copyright in the local lyric is assigned to the publisher where that is possible (see paragraph **20**).

**38.4** If the sub-publisher refuses to account to the publisher for money due to it, or where the sub-publisher's accounts are incorrect or deficient, the liabilities of the publisher to the composer will depend upon their agreement. The composer has no privity of contract with a sub-publisher, so the responsibility of ensuring collection of income should be accepted by the publisher. Where the accounting to the composer is to be made only from money actually received by the publisher, if it never receives the money because of local currency regulations or other good cause, it should ensure that the sub-publisher deposits the composer's share in a bank in the foreign country in the composer's name.

If the sub-publisher simply refuses to account to the publisher, the publisher must inform the composer promptly, so that remedial action can be decided upon. Otherwise the composer will receive nothing. The publisher should be contractually obliged to collect all the income due from sub-publishers, or, (such as where the sub-publisher is a subsidiary) if there is any difficulty in getting payment, in any event it should pay the composer his share of money which should be received. This compulsion will not generally be acceptable to a publisher, as both it and the composer are subject to normal commercial risks with independent sub-publishers. A subsidiary can be controlled, the only external hazard being exchange control restrictions, when the publisher should not be penalised.

**38.5** The publisher with worldwide rights should be committed to paying the composer even though the publisher has to sue his sub-publisher. The publisher appoints a sub-publisher as its local agent or representative, so why should it not have the same level of responsibility as any other territorial principal? Alternatively the publisher might re-assign its rights in the defaulting territory to the composer, in which case the publisher should not be entitled to receive any further income from that territory.

## 39 A cover record

**39.1** A cover recording should be defined as one which is recorded locally by a local artiste, and released in the local territory. But what would happen if an American performer, while on tour in Australia, recorded there a locally composed song provided by a local publisher, but the first release of the record was some months later in the UK and USA simultaneously to benefit those sectors of his worldwide tour? While he would not be a local artiste, all the other "local" requirements are complied with, except for local release. Presumably the Australian publisher would have to wait until the record was released in Australia before he becomes eligible to share in any income arising from his original efforts.

**39.2** Where the composer is an artiste who records his own material, any other recorded version of one of his songs is treated as a cover recording, ie not the original recording, but only in the territory where it is recorded. In practice there is no inquest over whether the local publisher procured the local recording or not; if it is recorded and released in his territory the sub-publisher retains the higher rate.

**39.3** There are some interesting points on cover records which are worth looking at. It depends on what is meant by a cover record. To some it means the second or subsequent recording available after the release of the original, ie, a local artiste "covering" a hit record. For sub-publishing purposes it means a local recording, whether or not there is already any other version available in the territory.

(a) If a local recording is released before the release there of the original recorded version by the composer/artiste, should that be treated as the original recording for that country? It is in one sense, but as the local sub-publisher will be deemed to have procured that local recording, it is a cover record and he should benefit from the higher rate.

(b) Where the composer is not an artiste, it could be said that any locally procured recording is a cover record, even though it may be the first and only version of that song released in that country. There must be exceptions to that rule. Where an English composer has a UK publisher, its job is to get his song recorded. Therefore any recording in the UK satisfies the "cover record" formula. But, if that were the case, the composer would never be paid the top income percentage on mechanical royalties or on performances. The cover record principles should therefore only apply to sub-publishers.

(c) For example, if a worldwide publishing deal originates in England, the following alternatives can apply:

(i) The song is first recorded in England by an artiste, released in England, and is not released anywhere else. The release in

England of another recording of the song by another UK artiste is a cover version in England subject to (a) and (b) above. If that second recording is released worldwide, is it treated as an original recording for each other territory where it is released, as it was not a local recording. This emphasises the principle that the sub-publisher should only get a higher percentage on recordings made and released locally, no matter how many other non-local versions are released locally for sale.

(ii) The composer gives a demo tape of a song to his UK publisher. The publisher, while looking for an artiste in England who is prepared to record the song, as part of his duties sends copies of the demo tapes to each of his sub-publishers. One of them gets a local artiste to record it, there being no other recorded version in existence anywhere at that time. That will still be treated as a local cover version for that territory, although it is an original recording.

(d) To recapitulate, in any sub-publishing territory, an original recording is any recording which is not recorded locally, and the publisher retains the lower rate no matter how many "original" recordings there are. A cover record in any country is one which is recorded and released locally, only in respect of which the higher rates will apply.

## 40 Post-termination collection of income

**40.1** A publisher or sub-publisher (as the case may be) is entitled to retain his share of gross income arising in his territory within the period of his agreement. His agreement will have two periods to consider. The first is the exclusive period during which he gets the rights to whatever compositions are created by the composer. The second is the period thereafter, during which he continues to have exclusive publishing rights, but only to the compositions acquired during the first period. This paragraph deals with what happens after the expiry of the second period. Payment of the income attributable to the last year of the second period may not be made by record companies and collection societies for anything up to twelve months after the end of that year, depending upon how the termination date fits in with their accounting dates, and how efficient their accounting systems are. If the run-on period referred to in **19.2** is, say, five years, it can be agreed that any accounting thereafter is not attributable to the publisher, ie, the expiry date of the run-on period is also an absolute cut off date for income collection as well. This is the neatest and simplest way of solving the problem. However long the run on period is, there will always be income arising in its last year which is not received until after that year has expired. If the catalogue is fixed, ie, no new material is provided to the publisher during this period, and if that period is, say, five years or more, he may not be granted any run-on period. In which case alternative methods of compensating the publisher for this time lag are:

(a) To let the publisher collect the publishing money paid within the year (or whatever period is agreed) following the termination of the sub-publishing agreement. Disadvantages are that:
   (i) some of the money collected in that year may be in respect of the three or six months following the publishing agreement termination date;
   (ii) the next publisher of that catalogue for that territory does not receive any money during his first year, so he would have to make up for it by having the right to collect income during the year following the termination of his own publishing agreement.

(b) To let the publisher collect the income arising from the date of his appointment, and not to let him collect any money arising following the termination of his agreement. The disadvantage to the publisher is that he is collecting the rewards of the efforts of his predecessor's last year, and not collecting the rewards of his own last year's effort, which may have been much greater. Also the first publisher to be granted the rights for the territory will lose one year's worth of income as he will not get the first year's income until some time in the second year. That could be compensated for by giving him one year more than subsequent sub-publishers get.

**40.2** Normally a publisher will want not less than five years as a run-on period for the promotion of the sub-published works and for the continued collection of income, but may settle for three years. The new publisher will start to deal with all new material of the composer with effect from his appointment. If he is still the composer's publisher when the previous publisher's rights in the old catalogue revert, the new publisher would include them in his rights.

## 41 Foreign language lyrics

**41.1** The main points which concern both the writers of foreign language lyrics and the publishers or sub-publishers who commission or authorise the lyrics are:

(a) Who owns the copyright in the lyric.
(b) Agreeing royalty terms with the lyric writer for the use of foreign lyrics.

(c) Where there are local recordings of the same tune in both the original and the local languages, the local collection society might attribute public performances of the composition only to the local language version, regardless of which language version was actually played. This protects local enterprise producing cover records in the local language, and it is impractical to ascertain on each occasion which language version was performed, unless they have different titles. That would prevent the composer or the original lyric writer (if different from the composer) from getting performance fees, so the local performing right society should be notified that all of the performance fees are to be split between the original composer and the local lyric writer. This split will be agreed at the time the local language lyric is authorised.

**41.2** In the contractual restrictions on the sub-publisher, and the calculations of its increased share of income on local language cover recordings, the sub-publishing agreement must take into account the ease with which a tame lyric writer (such as an employee of the sub-publisher) can be used to create a situation where the sub-publisher and his lyric writer gain on performance income, and the composer loses, through a legal device which may never be commercial. The more successful the original version is, the greater is the reward for malpractice in respect of local lyric versions. A sub-publishing deal for a major composer's catalogue should control this area strictly.

**41.3** Where a sub-publisher commissions a lyric in the local language, the rights of the lyric writer depend entirely upon the terms of the assignment of his copyright in the lyric to that sub-publisher:

(a) If the assignment of the copyright in the local lyric to the sub-publisher is limited to its own sub-publishing territory, the sub-publisher can protect the lyric writer's interests and the collection of his royalties within that territory. The sub-publisher has no rights in the lyric outside the territory, and (assuming that the local version is capable of selling well outside the territory) it is for the lyric writer to negotiate his terms for the rest of the world with the original publisher, or its various other sub-publishers. This is not a problem where the local language record is not likely to be sold or played anywhere else.

(b) If the lyric writer assigned the copyright in the lyric to the sub-publisher for the world, it is not able to protect the lyric writer's interest, or the copyright, outside its own sub-publishing territory. The sub-publisher has no right to use or control or collect money from use of the original composition, or any variation of it, outside his own territory. As the lyric writer will have divested himself of the whole of the worldwide copyright in the lyric, he is not able to approach the original publisher, or any other sub-publisher. The local sub-publisher should rectify the situation by reassigning the copyright for the rest of the world to the lyric writer, as he is not giving anything back to the lyric writer which he could use himself.

Use of the foreign lyric anywhere in the world without the consent of the lyric writer, while be remains the owner of the copyright in the lyric, is unauthorised, and subject to the local copyright laws, is in breach of his copyright.

CHAPTER 8

# Group Administration

## 1 General

**1.1** Artistes tend to form a group, hinging their future fortune or disaster on people they may not know well, without having an agreement between themselves to govern their individual rights and liabilities.

**1.2** All promoters such as managers, record companies and publishers, entering into a legal relationship with a group will require the members to sign a contract, especially where large sums of money are being spent on the group. Both parties should have agreed terms of reference by which their rights and liabilities can be ascertained in the event of a dispute between them.

**1.3** The value of a contract for personal services is often questioned because of the risk of it not being enforceable. The contract will not make the artiste sing, perform or write, but it will confirm the business relationship between the artiste and the other party. It is also used to settle a basis of calculating what compensation should be paid upon the failure of either party to fulfil his contractual obligations.

**1.4** Frequently the members of a group will commit themselves to a manager or to a record company without considering how that contract affects them each as individuals. They tend not to be aware of their own individual liability to the manager or record company if any of the other members default on their own part of the agreement; or if they personally do anything which adversely affects the ability of the other members of the group to fulfil the group obligations.

**1.5** Seldom does a prospective manager engage artistes individually and form them into a group, although there have been instances of successful manufactured groups. Generally the group is already formed, and a manager negotiates the terms of his agreement with the group as a whole. Many unknown groups consist of amateur musicians, who retain their ordinary jobs to ensure a regular income until they are sufficiently well known to earn enough from their musical activities to support them on a full time basis.

## 2 Promotion agreements

**2.1** A management, recording or other promotion agreement for the group may be entered into separately between each member of the group and the promoter, or it may be contained in a single document with all the members jointly and severally contracting with the promoter. The effect of the phrase "jointly and severally" is to make each member individually liable for all or any part of the group obligations and liabilities. These must be considered carefully by any member who has substantial personal assets, before he enters into any joint commitment with the other group members.

**2.2** Individual forms of the same agreement for each member can help changes in the membership of the group to be documented more easily. If the leader, or any other member of the group, agrees special terms with the promoter, it will be more convenient to set these out in a separate document. This also avoids any complications which may arise from having a document which deals simultaneously with the release of a member of the group, and the admission of a new member. If legal action arises between the promoter and a single member, or a section of members not being the whole group, the other members of the group are not brought into the action unnecessarily.

**2.3** Music business agreements are more searchingly scrutinised by the parties when they are breached, or circumvented, than when they are entered into. This is due to the way success, or the lack of it, highlights any flaws in the details of the original negotiations with the benefit of hindsight.

## 3 Agreement between members of a group

**3.1** Before any business venture is considered, the members of a group should have an agreement between themselves. The agreement should be drawn up when the group forms, to cover all forseeable enterprises with which it intends to become involved. The agreement can be entered into at any stage of a group's career, as long as they all agree with what it contains. There are two ways of doing it: either the group members can sign a partnership agreement, or they can become the shareholders in a limited liability company. If nothing is done, the members will be deemed to be a partnership in respect of their musical career. See paragraph **30** for a summary of relevant rules applied by the Partnership Act 1890.

**3.2** The principle of partnership will still exist where each member of the group appoints the manager separately to manage his personal career, without contractual reference to any of the other members. If the group enters into contracts with third parties as an apparently consolidated entity, each member may be held fully liable as a partner for the defaults of the group as a whole within the context of those contracts.

**3.3** The terms of an agreement between a promoter and all the members of the group together are of little use for reference when the group has an internal dispute which is limited to matters relating to the members' rights and obligations as between themselves under that promoter's agreement. Internal matters of the group, which were not considered or dealt with when the group was formed, will have to be decided by the group members from time to time. In any agreement it is difficult to cover every conceivable business aspect of such a personal relationship, as circumstances constantly change.

**3.4** This chapter sets out the more important points to be included in an agreement between the members of a group. As these are seldom thought of by groups at the time, it is for their professional advisers to prompt their consideration at the earliest possible opportunity.

## 4 Consequences of partnership

**4.1** The principal element of a partnership is that there exists a relationship between persons carrying on a business in common with the intention of making a profit. There are certain exclusions and limitations to that general statement, but most groups of musicians who are not employees of a company are partnerships, whether or not they are aware of that fact.

**4.2** In the absence of an agreement between the partners setting out all the terms governing their business relationship, the Partnership Act 1890 will determine the rights and liabilities of each partner in respect of the other partners, and unconnected third parties. Only some of the sections of the Partnership Act 1890 can be excluded or varied by agreement, and those relate mostly to dealings between the partners themselves. Those aspects of the Act which tend to be a surprise to group members, who are not aware of its existence, include the following: (but see paragraph **30** for a more detailed reference.)

(a) Where any member of the group commits the group in the ordinary course of the group's business to a liability, eg studio time, the group as a whole is liable for the cost if the studio is not used. If the member did not have the authority to so act, within the group he may be liable personally for the cost, but the studio can still look to each member of the group for settlement of the bill.

Where the member of the group who created the liability was not a partner, but only a salaried employee member of the group, (such as one of the paid but independent backing band), if the studio reasonably assumed that he was a partner, or that he had the group's authority, the bill will still have to be paid by the group.

If the studio knew that the employee did not have the authority to make the booking, and they did not get confirmation from a partner member, or somebody who did have authority, the studio may be limited to getting its money from the employee who made the booking. By reason of the way in which most groups work, it is likely that the group would have the liability.

(b) Each member is responsible jointly and severally for any liability arising from the acts or omissions of any other members in the ordinary course of the group's business, and :

(i) a new member is not responsible for liabilities arising prior to his joining the group;

(ii) a member who leaves the group is still responsible for liabilities arising while he was a member of the group.

In this context the most likely claim is for income tax on group earnings, which, because it is not collected immdiately on the PAYE system, is calculated and claimed by the Inland Revenue, sometimes years afterwards. The claim will be against all of the members who received, or who were entitled to receive, the income on which the tax is levied, and if all but one of the members have disappeared, that one will be liable for the whole tax claim. The fact that he has the right to a contribution from the other ex-members does not relieve him of the liability to the tax man for the whole amount.

Another liability from the past can be damages in compensation for a breach of contract by the group, whether or not the amount of damages has been settled at the date of a change in the membership of the group. The recoupment of outstanding advances is a continuing liability, but as it is covered only by retention from continuing income, it tends not to be a problem.

(c) No majority of the members can expel any member unless there is a specific agreement between the members to that effect. The agreement can be written or oral, but an oral agreement is harder to prove.

(d) Where there is no limit on the time for which the group is to remain together as a partnership, any member can leave the group at any time by giving notice to the other members. This could be most inconvenient, especially if there is an imminent tour or recording, so the agreement between the members should have a minimum notice period.

(e) If a member, without the consent of the other members, carries on any business of the same nature as, and competing with, that of the group, he must account for and pay over to the group all profits made by him in that business. Strictly, session work and solo projects could come within that section of the Act, but it is customary for such outside activities to be carried on by a member without having to account to the group for the proceeds. Where the withholding of consent by the group is considered to be unreasonable by the affected member, he has no remedy other than personal persuasion.

## 5 Sharing of profits

**5.1** The agreement between the members should state the proportions in which the profits should be shared, and how the expenses are to be dealt with. In the absence of anything agreed to the contrary, it will be assumed that the net profits from group activities will be shared between the members equally, and that all group expenses (including individual's expenses incurred wholly for the benefit of the group) also will be shared equally. There may be reasons for an unequal distribution of profits, which may relate to a period of time, or to a specific event such as a tour or recording. This might apply when a new member has joined the group just before the event. The method of calculating who gets what should be set out clearly in the agreement.

**5.2** The members must also agree upon what is to happen to the income derived where individuals want to do deals for solo projects. As a fundamental condition the solo projects must not breach any third party rights granted by the group, or any restrictions placed upon the group in any contracts they are bound by, such as for recording or publishing. For example, will the other members of the group together receive an override royalty on record sales of the solo project? They would not normally expect to do so, any more than they would want to share the expense in doing it (see paragraph **18.2**).

**5.3** If there is to be an unequal distribution of profits in the early period of the group's existence, such as where a new member is effectively recognising his purchase of a share of goodwill, among the considerations may be :

(a) Who paid for what part of the instruments and the public address system. Members may have owned their instruments before joining the group, or the individuals may be buying their own instruments on hire purchase, having joined the group. If the HP agreement is with that individual, he will be responsible for paying all of the instalments. What happens when the HP payments are to be treated as a group debt—especially where the individual's own instrument went in part exchange ?

(b) Who is the "life and soul" of the group. The founder member may be the driving force behind the group's success, and he may have gathered the group together to act originally in a supporting role. The group name may be that of the founder member, who may also be the personality of the group known best to the public. The other members may be included on a salaried probationary basis before becoming profit sharing members of the group.

(c) The personal circumstances of the members. Although the relative personal fortunes of the members will not normally be taken into account, the tax liabilities, assets, and personal or family commitments of a member may influence his views on the sharing of group income and expense. His personal circumstances may also influence the willingness of the member to accept joint responsibility for group liabilities. In theory the risk is spread equally among the members, but in practice the member with substantial assets has the most to lose in a crisis or disaster situation.

## 6 Sharing of expenses

**6.1** Any expense incurred will be either a group expense, or one for which the individual member is personally responsible. When in doubt, any member about to spend money should check with the other members or the group's manager whether the expense will be a group liability. As between the members, liability for expense will depend on whether it is for the benefit of the group, and whether it is authorised. For example, a member who owns his own instrument may be responsible for its repairs, or for hiring a replacement while it is being repaired.

**6.2** Group expense should be shared in the proportions in which group income is shared. Normally the whole of the group expense is deducted from the whole of the group income from whatever source. Group income normally excludes music publishing income, which belongs only to those members who are the composers or writers, and who are contracted to the music publisher (see paragraph 7). If specific expenditure is to be deducted only from specific income, before incurring the expense the group should first check upon the potential consequences financially. If not all the members are affected, or if they are all affected but in different proportions, or if the expenditure may exceed the income, what might appear to be a good idea may prove in fact to be impractical or unfair.

**6.3** The group should also agree upon who is to be liable for grey areas of expense, such as :

(a) Where the group is working away from home base, hotel charges and *per diem* payments are a group expense. If a member chooses to stay with a friend or relative living locally, rather than at the group's hotel, can he claim, as a group expense, his part of the hotel expense he would have incurred, and/or his *per diem* payments ? These payments are to cover actual expense, they are not intended as extra pocket money if the expense is not incurred. As hotel and *per diem* payments will be at the same level for each group member, if a member takes his wife or girl friend on tour, any additional cost to him is his personal responsibility. For example, some hotels charge for the room whether one or two people use it; and some have a supplementary charge for a second person.

(b) The reasonable cost of one or more individual members occasionally entertaining promoters, record company executives, and other similar expenses directly related to the group's business affairs. As the cost of entertaining can easily get out of hand, there must be limits and guidelines. An experienced artiste will never pay the bill anyway.

(c) If the group travels by air first class as a group expense, can an impoverished member change his ticket to tourist class and keep the difference ? If that philosophy is agreed by the group, it will lead to all sorts of ingenious chicanery, and inevitably to arguments.

**6.4** In theory, the group should only pay for actual expense, and if a member chooses to do it more cheaply, it has cost the group so much less. In practice the group may allow such perks if every member has the same freedom of choice, and if the perk element of the expense charged is allowable against tax, or ultimately becomes set against part of that member's share of income in the group accounts. The device in (c) above may not be possible where the promoter is paying the group's air fares as part of their tour fee—when such a ticket switch should be disclosed. At that level the promoter will not get excited over the difference.

**6.5** Expenses attributable to certain members only, or to certain activities not involving all members, should be dealt with separately from group accountings.

Allowances must be made in all internal group financial arrangements for what happens to outgoing and incoming members. The accounting principles must also be such that on final dissolution of the group as an entity, its assets and liabilities, and the right of all present and previous members to receive future royalties, can be dealt with fairly.

## 7 Composer members

**7.1** A composer member of a group is entitled as of right to receive the composer's share of publishing royalties from songs he has written, even if the royalties arise through those songs being recorded and performed on stage by the group. If it has been agreed between the composer and the rest of the group that copyright royalties due to the composer from songs recorded by the group are to be included within the broad definition of group income, there can be an agreement either:

(a) for the composer to assign the composer's share of income to the group for distribution between the members in the agreed proportions; or

(b) to attribute all of the members of the group as the joint composers of the song, so that each will receive his share of income direct without having to rely on an agreement with the actual composer.

**7.2.1** No group would be advised to use alternative (a) above, because of its disadvantages, which include:

(a) The tax liabilities on the right of the composer to receive the income, and upon his voluntarily giving some of it away, which would have to be clarified.

(b) The other members relying on contractual rights which may not be honoured by the composer member after he leaves the group. If the income split is intended as a permanent deal for any given songs, then there is no reason why it should not be put on a permanent legal footing.

(c) The effort and cost of detailed accounting by the composer indefinitely for an isolated source of income.

**7.2.2** The agreement must be carefully worded to ensure that the group gets no greater benefit than that intended by the composer. Any song composed after the composer/member leaves the group should not be included in such an arrangement, even if the first recording of the song is made and released by the group.

**7.2.3** While the sharing of the composer's income exists, the other members of the group are participating in a source of income which would not otherwise have been available to them, so the arrangement is a concession by the composer. On leaving the group, the composer ceases to share in the group income arising from future recordings or events in which he does not perform. The group members will be able to participate indefinitely in the copyright income arising from compositions recorded by the group while the composer was a member.

If the composer leaves the group after completing a recording containing his songs, but prior to its release the group erases the composer's performance and substitutes it with that of his replacement, the composer's income sharing agreement for that recording should terminate. As the group is thereby depriving the composer ex-member of his part of the group's royalty on the sales of that record, it should be deprived of its share of the composer's income from the recorded songs (see paragraph **15.8**).

**7.3** Alternative **7.1** (b) above is the ideal practical method of putting the principle into effect. A disadvantage for the composer is that he does not get the sole credit. For all legal purposes each member of the group owns his part of the copyright, so the publisher of the songs must have an assignment of the copyright from them all.

If each member of the group contributes genuinely to the creation of each composition to such an extent that the group becomes the joint composers in any event, the device is not necessary.

**7.4** The group members may not be all contracted to the same publisher. This can happen where there has been a change in the original group membership, and a new member already has a publishing contract. A composer/member who has a different publisher to the rest of the group will be wrongfully depriving his own publisher of advance recoupment rights, and the full publisher's share of income, if he attributes his sole compositions to all the group members.

## 8 Transport

**8.1** Transport is essential for the mobility of any group. Vehicles bought with group money will need to be registered in the name of a member of the group, or of a nominee of the group such as the manager, or the company which has service contracts with the group members. A nominee (except the group's employment company) would hold the beneficial ownership of the vehicle in trust for the group as a whole, subject to:

(a) his statutory obligations, and his liabilities as the legal owner of the vehicle;
(b) the rights of any HP company or any other party with a lien over the vehicle, and any guarantor of a financing agreement.

**8.2** The nominee will be the legal owner of the vehicle and his name will be on the log book. To make clear the rights of the group to the vehicle, there should be an agreement with the nominee covering the beneficial ownership, insurance and HP or other obligations. Road tax and insurance for any vehicle would be technically the liability of the nominee legal owner, as would be any road traffic offence relating to the construction and use of the vehicle, and any other offence which imposes liability upon the legal owner of the vehicle. Examples are the ultimate responsibility for traffic tickets and unclamping charges. If the vehicle is bought on hire purchase, the nominee is responsible personally to the finance company, both for the payments and for observing the conditions imposed upon him by the hire purchase agreement.

All such expenses paid by the nominee should be group expenses, and the nominee must safeguard himself from the consequences of any inability of the group to reimburse him his proper expenditure.

**8.3** An argument against the vehicle being bought and owned by the manager of a new group which is weak financially is that he then has a strong practical means of influence over it. The total vehicle, travelling, running and maintenance costs will be recoupable from the group, under the terms of the management agreement. Although he may own the vehicle, a manager who would withhold its use without a justifiable reason would be in breach of his obligation to act in the best interests of the group. He would be restricting their earning capacity, and may cause breaches of venue contracts, thereby damaging the group's reputation and making it liable to compensation claims. If the group is in substantial breach of contract with the manager, or has wrongfully terminated the management agreement, there is no reason why the group should be entitled to use the manager's vehicle as one of the benefits of the agreement, while refusing to fulfil its obligations to him under it.

## 9 Instruments and PA system

**9.1** Either the instruments are all owned by the group as a whole, or each member is the owner of his own. Instruments and the PA system owned by the group are general group assets, which can be dealt with as all the members together see fit. The selection or disposal of group owned instruments should be a joint decision, and should be subject to consultation with the member who plays the relevant instrument. The best equipment is expensive, and an artiste may not be able to afford it. A good part of the dazzle of entertainment is the display provided by the group on stage, and tatty or obviously inferior equipment can be an acute embarrassment both visually and musically.

**9.2** Where the equipment is jointly owned by all the members of the group, a member may be dissuaded from leaving without giving the others any warning, and thereby prejudicing the livelihood of the group, as he would leave his equipment behind. Group-owned equipment helps an unknown and impecunious group to ensure reasonable continuity of membership, as it may be easier to find a musician to suit the group equipment than to find one who has his own complete set of equipment.

**9.3** If instruments which are intended to be owned by the group are bought on hire purchase by one member with his own money, they are legally his until fully paid for, so he can leave the group taking the equipment with him. The only recourse by the other members is either to pay off the outstanding balance and reimburse him his proportion, or to recover from that departed member's share of future earnings any portion of the HP payment with which they may have been debited. If the departed member is not entitled to a share of future earnings, such as where no records have been made by the group while he was a member, their portion of the HP payments will be a debt due from the departed member. The group should not act arbitrarily or unfairly so as to prejudice any departed member's financial obligations to the HP company, such as by retaining the equipment and refusing to settle the HP debt.

**9.4.1** The HP company will usually require a guarantor of adequate means to guarantee performance of the obligations contained in any HP agreement with an artiste, as entertainers generally are considered bad credit risks. The initial depreciation of the equipment is such that, during the first part of the hire purchase term, the HP company will lose money if the equipment has to be repossessed for non payment and sold. Should such a loss occur, the HP company is entitled to obtain payment of the outstanding balance from the artiste who signed the HP agreement. Settlement of the outstanding debt is not likely if the artiste could not pay the instalments in the first place, hence the insistence upon a guarantor.

**9.4.2** The HP company which repossesses the equipment is not bound to dispose of it for its full market value. As the artiste will be responsible for any outstanding balance not covered by the proceeds of the sale, he might reduce his liability by arranging with the HP company for him to do the selling, to get the best price obtainable.

## 10 Breach of copyright and defamation

**10.1** A composer member of a group must not involve the group in litigation relating to alleged breach of copyright, or to alleged passing off of his compositions in breach of third party rights in existing copyright works. The composer will be liable on his own account, but the group will also be liable for having recorded the infringing composition, and for having issued it for sale to the public. Where there is one real composer in the group, but by agreement all of the group members are the attributed joint composers, they must rely on the actual composer's assurances that they have not breached their warranties to the music publisher for originality and non-infringement.

**10.2** There is a risk in making a record, or in giving a live performance, for gimmick or publicity purposes which unfairly or untruthfully parodies or criticises other people in a malicious fashion. The danger is that the bounds of permitted tolerance of satire or criticism will be broken, bringing the acts complained of into the realm of defamation. The performance would have to be not factually true, malicious and unjustified ridicule or scorn and which leads to loss of business, or to damage to reputation or professional standing. Deliberate lampooning would have to be intentionally virulent to bring it within the risk.

**10.3** Records have been banned from time to time from performance over radio or television as they were considered by the broadcasters to be in bad taste, or to be unduly provocative from a religious, political, or moral point of view. This is a form of legitimate and justifiable censorship, aimed at recorded material which is blasphemous, defamatory, obscene, or which in legal terms has a tendency to corrupt. Outcry and indignation expressed by a minority in respect of a record can have the unintended effect of boosting its sales, as any resulting ban on sales or performances is usually given publicity. The public may be curious to hear what is being withheld from them that can be considered so shocking. In the music business, any type of material which makes money will be promoted by someone for so long as it is profitable.

## 11 Bank accounts

**11.1** Within most management agreements, the group will irrevocably authorise the manager to receive all group earnings and to supervise group expenditure, and either to account to the group as a whole, or to each member of the group separately. The system of accounting as between the members themselves for the group expenses, advances and shares of income will be agreed, so the manager can account accurately to the group.

**11.2** Successful artistes may have considerable tax problems, due to the fluctuation in the amounts earned in each year, and the uncertainty of differentiating between when income is earned and when it is received over a period of tax years, and the relation of deductible expenditure to it.

**11.3** The financial circumstances of each group member may differ considerably from the others, so that one system of accounting may not suit all the members all the time. For a group whose income and expenses are low, initially the whole of the group's income could be received into a single bank account in the joint names of all the members, where they do not have a manager or accountant. The group must decide who will be signatories to the account, and how many signatures would be needed for withdrawal of money. If they are not all required to sign cheques, this would involve a substantial element of trust between signatories and non signatories. A possible disadvantage of a single group bank account for all of the members is that it can be blocked arbitrarily by any member. Where only some members are signatories, there is a risk of any combination of signatories being dishonest. These are ordinary business risks, which are not unique to the music industry.

**11.4** A lot of hard work, and most of the financial difficulties caused by reckless spending and disregard for income tax liabilities, will be avoided by the appointment by the group of an experienced and able accountant to advise upon the financial side of the group's affairs, and to keep proper accounts for it. Financial planning seems to be low on the list of priorities of most artistes. Artistes who have had unpleasant experiences in the music business want to keep the control over their earnings away from their manager, and from fellow group members. Many trust their manager implicitly, and have never been let down.

**11.5** In a position of success each member will have his own personal bank account, and group income and expense will be dealt with through the books of its manager or employment company. The maintenance of proper accounts is essential, so that the group obtains all the available tax concessions, deductions and allowances. Without proper accounts, present and past group members will not be satisfied that the group is receiving all that is due to it, or that each membr is receiving his correct share of group earnings, or that group and personal expenses have been correctly allocated. Financial planning will help the group to avoid unprofitable or potentially disastrous projects or contracts, and will help to reserve adequately for tax and other liabilities.

## 12 Group name

**12.1** The group name will be a joint asset of the members, together with whatever value and goodwill goes with it, unless by specific agreement:

(a) The group name is that of the prominent member who formed the group, and who registered himself as the sole proprietor of the name as a trademark prior to the group formation. If the name of the group is also the legal name of the group leader, or is the pseudonym by which he is widely professionally known, naturally he would like to retain absolute control over its ownership.

(b) The name is fictitious and belongs to a third party (such as the group's employment company), which allows the group to use it by agreement. Any goodwill value will be enjoyed by whoever are the group members from time to time.

From the outset the group should settle the ownership and use of the group name, to avoid dispute in the future. The name alone of a successful group can make a tremendous contribution to its earning power and popularity, even though the individual members may not have the same distinction, and may change over the years.

**12.2** If the group name is an original made up word, or is connected with a logo, or is in any other way eligible for registration as a trade mark, registration will strengthen the ability of the owner of the name to control its use within the UK. That use will extend to merchandising, and other commercial uses of the name. Where the name has become firmly identified with the group throughout the world, what happens when the owner of the group name (such as under paragraph **12.1** (a)) leaves the group? Irrespective of any agreement with the other members of the group entitling him to retain the group name for his own use :

(a) It may be practically impossible to dissociate the name from that group in the minds of the public, and what should they call themselves in the future ?

(b) The owner of the group name may be forced to allow the group to continue to use the name by reason of an undertaking in that respect in the group's recording agreement.

(c) Any new group formed by the group name owner, using that name, or something very similar to it, may be sued for passing off by the first group despite the group name owner's rights, especially if there is still a substantial number of the original group's records being sold internationally.

**12.3** The rights of the owner of the group name can be protected by him licensing the use of the name to the group. One condition of the licence would be the continuance of the group name owner as a member of the group. Even then, termination of the licence will not necessarily remove the problems described above.

**12.4** If the name is a general group asset, and if the group is a partnership, this should be stated in the group agreement. If the business of the group is run through a limited liability company, the name of which is the group name, it is a company asset. If the company name is that of one of the members, he must have an agreement with the company whereby if he leaves the group, the company and the group will change its name, and he will be allowed to trade using his name without opposition by the company or the group. Again, the problems described in **12.2** above will apply. To have such an agreement gives a considerable bargaining power to the group name owner, who (if he does not get what he wants) may threaten to leave the group, and so deprive them of their identity.

**12.5** The members should agree that when any of them leaves the group, unless the name is his personal name, the sole rights to the name, and any goodwill vested in it, remain with the group. If there is a fundamental splitting of a group with a fictitious name into two rival continuing groups, only one section should be entitled to use the name, to avoid the confusion of two competing groups each with the same name. Something positive should be agreed, such as the section containing the greater number of members retaining the name. If the group is equally split—well, toss a coin.

**12.6** Any member leaving the group should be prohibited in the group agreement from passing himself off as still being a member, and from devising and using another name so similar to the group name as to cause confusion in the minds of the record-buying public. A passing off action could still be brought by the group against the departed member's new group, notwithstanding the absence of specific agreement, if the deliberate imitation of the group name is sufficiently blatant, confusing and damaging.

**12.7** The group may disband on a permanent basis, so that the members each join new groups, or each form their own new group, or concentrate, for example, on producing records, or being a song writer. Some years later one or two of the old group members decide to re-form the group with other musicians who were never members of it, and they do so using the old group name. What is the legal position? Records made by the original group may still be selling well, and the name would still be recognised, ie, it still retains a substantial goodwill value. Even worse, the two ex-group members may not even have been within the group at the time it ceased to exist. The position will depend on whether there is still a valuable goodwill and reputation alive in the old group name, owned by those who were members when it broke up. Other points are checking upon the existence of an enforceable group membership agreement, and whether there is a valid trademark throughout the major territories, and to some extent upon the intentions of the last constituted group to get together again, despite the passage of time. In the absence of a group agreement or a trademark, will a passing off action succeed? Can some of the old group members legally object to the proposed use of the group name ? For a period of time there will be a protectable interest in the group name as a property right. But at some point in time, if it can be shown conclusively that it has effectively been abandoned, and there is no intention to revive it, the original name could, for example, be used as the basis for "The New [ ]". Alternatively some other means could be found of differentiating sufficiently between the original group and its supposed reincarnation.

**12.8** Prior to granting merchandising licences, if there is any doubt, the group should check that it has the exclusive legal rights to use the name for that purpose. The group name may be so similar to the name of a product or service that, although the group may be entitled to use it in the context of its musical career, it will not be able to use it commercially. "Who gets what" should be agreed for departing and incoming members in respect of income derived from the use of the group name in commercial promotions. For example, where the group enters into a long term merchandising contract, during which period one member leaves the group, and a new member joins it, what are their respective rights in the future group income from that contract? The leaving member should only participate in accountings for income attributable to the period prior to his departure. Points to consider are:

(a) The merchandising agreement will have been signed by the then current group members, and the royalties will be group income. This will be dealt with as general group income on a change of membership, and in the absence of anything to the contrary they are due to the people comprising the group from time to time.

(b) If the group agreement specifies that a departing group member is entitled to continue to receive his share of royalties derived from long term contracts, that is usually intended to cover such items as future record sales of recordings on which he performed, or publishing income where he was a co-writer. This is because those sales or exploitations are of products containing his performance or creativity. For merchandising, after he leaves the group he has no further input to the group. As merchandising is the commercial exploitation of current goodwill image and identity, he would not continue to participate in future income.

(c) If the merchandising agreement and the group membership agreement are contradictory, the decision may depend upon which agreement came into existence first. As the merchandising agreement will not refer to the point, and as a group agreement is a rarity, **12.8** (a) above will normally apply.

## 13 Dismissal and substitution of group members

**13.1** Although a group may start its career happily, in the course of time a member may become personally incompatible with the other members of the group, or he may develop his own talents in such a way as to outgrow the group, or he may diverge from its way of music. The reasons for this happening may be an inability to adapt to the musical progression of the group, either in skill or style; or it may be an unwillingness to experiment with creative musical ideas; or it may be an attitude expressed in public which is embarrassing or damaging to the reputation or image of the group as a whole.

**13.2** The decision of all of the members should be required to dismiss a member from the group, for whatever reason. The group may wish to specify in the group agreement the reasons in principle which would enable a majority of the members to make such a decision, or they may wish to leave it open to a straight majority decision for any reason. In the absence of any reference, it will have to be a unanimous decision under the Partnership Act 1890. It may be difficult to define what is to be considered fair and reasonable in reaching a decision, as the causes tend to be personal or emotive, but the rule will apply equally to all members. When deciding whether dismissal of a member from the group is justified, it may be difficult to distinguish between serious complaints against a member, an irreconcilable clash of personalities between members, or an internal political intrigue with questionable motives.

**13.3** Dismissal must be subject to the right of the departing member to continue to receive his share of future income from past events in which he participated, such as records and published compositions. If the member's departure was a breach of the agreement, or if he committed other breaches which caused the group any loss, expense or liability, that income will be available to satisfy any compensation agreed or ordered by the court. There are other rights which should remain with the departed member, such as the right to audit group accounts. Release of the group member must also be subject to the fulfilment of all existing contractual obligations of the group to third parties, where the presence of the departing member is essential. Any member who wishes to leave the group voluntarily does not want to have unnecessary hindrances or penalties for doing so, assuming that he gives proper notice and deals correctly with all of the outstanding items when he leaves.

**13.4** Should a majority of group members have the power to bring in a substitute or additional member, if they consider that decision is in the best interests of the group as a whole? Any dissenting member must then either accept the situation, retire from the group, or negotiate with the majority for a mutually acceptable basis for remaining in the group. The decision should be made unanimously, or not at all, to minimise such problems.

**13.5** The manner in which any major group decision is taken and inplemented should be open, fair and democratic. A member who believes he is being hard done by, and fails to persuade the other members to agree, should be given an opportunity to ascertain his rights within the group structure according to the group agreement. He should be allowed to speak to the group manager and other group advisers in an effort to dispel any misunderstanding which he considers might have caused the rift.

**13.6** In practice it may well be that rules, and the concept of fair dealing, do not exist in spirit within the group, other than the simple principle that each man looks after himself. This situation indicates a total lack of mutual trust and confidence between group members. The chances are that any group existing on that basis in that context will be broken up by greed and double dealing between the members at the first sign of real success.

## 14 Rights and liabilities of new members

**14.1** Before a new member joins the group he must find out his rights and obligations from the date of joining. He should also enquire about, and investigate, any of the business affairs of the group existing at the date of his joining which could adversely affect him. As he is unlikly to be aware of the group's financial and commercial dealings which are current at that time, he should ask if there are any, and what they are. These enquiries are seldom made. Whatever the terms of his engagement, and however friendly the negotiations may be, he is entering into a business venture, and should treat it as such.

**14.2** The simplest way of dealing with any existing group liabilities is for the other members of the group to disclose them and indemnify the new member from them. Most groups change their membership without having either the time or the inclination to document the event properly, or at all.

**14.3** Without realising the consequences of what he is doing, an incoming member might agree to take over a liability left outstanding by his predecessor. Legally, and in the absence of anything to the contrary, he would have no such liability. However, this can happen where there is an unresolved dispute with a third party in progress when he joins the group, and subsequently he becomes a joint party as a member of the group at that time to a settlement agreement which, after the date of his joining, requires the provision of services or the payment of money by the group to the third party. Any warranties, undertakings and indemnities in respect of past matters which he gives as a signatory to the settlement agreement may be impossible for him to fulfil, as he was not connected with the event being settled. He should insist upon not being financially involved, and upon the previous group member being a signatory to the settlement agreement if compensation is to be paid to the other party. For example, where this is to be an override royalty on the sales of future albums the ex-member's share of income from his past records can be debited by his share of the amounts due under the settlement agreement.

**14.4** Depending upon the circumstances in which he agreed to accept his share of the future liability for the past event, the new member might be able to claim that there was sufficient misrepresentation or non-disclosure by the other members of the group, or that there was such a mistake by him as to the fundamental purpose and meaning of the settlement, that in law he is not bound by it. This argument would be more in his favour if he received no *quid pro quo* for accepting the liability. Where there is doubt in the future as to what was the agreed extent of liability of the new member, the absence of a written contract will provoke arguments around the reconstruction of the original deal, relying upon memory alone. As people tend to remember only those things which favour them, such a dependence is unreliable. In the above example, as the new member was not connected with the event which caused the liability, even if he is a signatory to the settlement agreement, the liability should only be deducted from the shares of group income receivable by the other remaining members, and the ex-member.

**14.5** The new member must look after his own interests, and what he does not ask about is not likely to be volunteered or discussed. Any unknown artiste who is offered an opportunity to join a successful group is not likely to demand disclosure of all possible liabilities, or to appear fussy in his negotiations, for fear of the opportunity being withdrawn. Until the new member has settled into the group, and has become familiar with the way in which it works, he will not know whether his choice was wise.

## 15 Rights of a departing or dead member

**15.1** Where a member leaves a group, or dies, he (or his estate) should get confirmation of, or should ascertain, his continuing rights to share in future group income arising from events occurring or records made while he was a member. His continuing liabilities should also be ascertained, such as outstanding and future income tax payments. The group agreement will determine which parts of future income are to be shared, and how the share is to be calculated. Royalty statements provided by publishers, collection societies and record companies are usually sufficiently detailed to enable accurate apportionments to be made.

**15.2** Upon departure, the member's account with the group for his proportion of outstanding recoupable loans and advances due from him, and income due to him, should be brought up to date, verified, and agreed by all members. Any settlement payment of what is due up to date should be made, or the right to such a payment should be acknowledged if there are no funds available at that time to meet it. This protects either party from the other raising protests at a later date on all accounts prior to leaving—unless there has been a genuine mutual mistake, or unilateral misrepresentation or fraud which is only discovered subsequently. If a record royalty or publishing advance is made just before he leaves, of which he would have received a share had he stayed, it will have to be agreed whether he should still get it. It will be recouped from future income from the relevant source of income, but is normally paid on account of future activity, such as recordings to be made, or compositions to be written. On that basis he should not receive a proportion of the advance, as he will not be connected with any such future activity.

**15.3** The departing member is entitled to a release from all further contractual liabilities as between himself and the other members of the group, subject to full disclosure by each side of anything which has been done putting the other party at any potential risk. If all the group members are joint and several guarantors of their group bank account, leaving the group does not automatically terminate the ex-member's liability under that guarantee. The situation must be dealt with at the time the guarantee is given, or the departed member can only ask for a release. If the group is heavily overdrawn, this might not be given by the bank. A possibility would be to substitute the new group member for the old one.

If the departing member is a nominee for the group on any hire purchase agreement or other contract, he should be relieved by the group of all such obligations, as he will cease to derive any benefit from them. For an HP agreement, this would mean paying the outstanding balance, or the HP company agreeing to a substitution agreement entered into with another member of the group in replacement of the departing member.

**15.4** Whether the departing member remains committed to third parties which are entitled to the group's personal services for recording, publishing or otherwise, will depend upon whether he is contractually committed as an individual irrespective of his group membership. If the agreement specifies that it is the group however composed from time to time which matters, members who leave the group will be free of the contract. A leaving member should obtain written confirmation of that fact from the other contracting party. If the departing member is not released from the agreement by leaving the group, he will have to negotiate his release separately with the record company or publisher, as the case may be.

**15.5** A third party, whose contract does not automatically release a departing member of a group, might consider a release to be misplaced "generosity" depriving him of the opportunity to obtain a financial settlement for the release. Whether this is fair in any case depends upon the reason for the settlement. The departing group member may owe the third party money personally, apart from recoupable group debts. No artiste should assume that all third parties are charitable organisations which do not mind losing money, or the rights to potentially profitable business opportunities. The third party's point of view is that an obvious loophole would be opened by the assumption of an automatic right of release, where contracts might become ineffective through clever juggling with group membership which the third party cannot control.

**15.6** If the group is constituted within a limited liability company, the formal aspects of directorships, share holdings and other matters will have to be dealt with. If the group is a partnership, a change of partnership agreement will have to be signed. If the musical instruments a departing member uses are group assets, they must be handed over to the group, or bought for an agreed value.

**15.7** A departing member, who is entitled to a share of future group income, should have the right to audit the acccounts of the group from time to time to confirm whether his accountings are accurate. This would not be necessary if he is able to receive his share of income direct from source, usually a record company or a music publisher, or copies of their statements.

**15.8** Where a member, who is entitled to a share of record royalties, leaves the group after the completion of a recording, but before it is released by the record company, the remaining members of the group should not be entitled to remove the departed member's performance from the recording, and substitute the performance of his successor in the group. To do so would deprive the departed member of the right to receive his share of royalties from the sales of the record, and to be associated with its success. The same point arose in paragraph **7.2.3** in respect of a composer group member.

**15.9** But if the group finds a successor for the departed member immediately, and the release date of the record will follow closely upon the date of change of group membership, together with the publicity surrounding the change, it would give the reconstituted group a good start if its first record after the change can be released containing the new member's performance. Therefore it would benefit the new group to have the right to substitute the new member's performance on the recording, should it wish to do so. The alternatives are not to release that record for the time being and to get into the studio as soon as possible to record an entirely new album by the new group line up. It would not be good for the new group to promote a recording made by the old group. They might decide not to release that recording at that time, but to archive it for possible future release because:

(a) The musical style of the new group may be different.
(b) The new member may be a great song writer, who wants to put his musical influence on the new group's first record, and of course to get the composer's income from those songs.
(c) The group's record company may object, and refuse to pay advances for the unreleased old group album. If that were to happen, would the record company also not want to pay for the recording cost of the shelved album? It would normally have to, as the only normal contractual right not to do so would relate to delivery of an album which is not of satisfactory commercial quality.
(d) The unreleased record may be more valuable to the record company as a mystery item to be "discovered" when every gimmick is required to maintain interest in the group in the future.
(e) Future compilation albums of old group recordings would have an added attraction by including hitherto unreleased tracks.

## 16 Group representation

**16.1** If it is difficult to get all the members of the group together for meetings, a spokesman member should be delegated to represent the group in talks with its record company, management or agency. Basic policy decisions should be taken by the members together. The spokesman should put forward group opinion or policy as decided by the group, and not his own idea of what should be decided. Most group members like to be wholly involved in group development or deals, and meetings should be able to be fixed to suit them all.

**16.2** In more formal matters such as major contracts, each member to be bound by it will have to sign the document. If the same document affects the whole group, a meeting of all the members and the group's advisers should be called, when its meaning and consequences can be explained, and any questions asked by the group can be answered. This procedure should start at the preliminary stages of negotiating any major long term contract, such as for recording, and should continue until it is signed. The manager should attend to all such matters for the group in consultation with it, but a group spokesman is still needed to maintain an adequate exchange of opinions and ideas between the group and those connected with its promotion.

**16.3** Many of the problems which arise between a group and its manager or record company are caused by lack of communication. It is better for the group to be over-informed rather than kept in the dark. Trouble starts to brew once any management acts independently on the assumption that the group "wouldn't want to know" or "wouldn't understand" the details of a proposed deal.

## 17 Group decisions

**17.1** For the success and internal well being of the group all of the members should agree upon everything which materially affects the group's career. Sometimes the interests of the group do not coincide with the hopes or intentions of one of the members. Decisions are normally taken on a majority vote basis, which is satisfactory until a clash of personalities between the members breaks the group into two or more irreconcilable points of view. If a group reaches that point, the members will not perform efficiently together, as the enthusiasm and mutual creative reaction on stage or in the studio will have been lost.

**17.2** Failure, and the subsequent disintegration of a group, is often found to result from such an internal showdown. Despite the different artistic temperaments of the members, the group must decide whether the commercial objectives of achieving fame and fortune are sufficiently important to make the effort to achieve a peaceful personal existence worthwhile. Otherwise the principle of each member having the freedom of unhindered personal expression may prevent them from remaining together as a working unit for business purposes.

**17.3** A group frequently fights its way into the limelight of public acclaim on the strength of its musical appeal as a unit, or the talent or the personality of one prominent member, such as the lead singer. Until such recognition is obtained for the group, each member needs the others to work and to think as a team. Success and recognition tend to give a greater prominence to the star member than to the others, who may be relegated to acting as a backing group for the star. The star then faces the temptation of offers from elsewhere, or he may wish to go solo within his existing contractual arrangements.

**17.4** The prospect of continuing success for each member of an already successful group which has split due to artistic differences is small. What is overlooked in the heat of the moment is that the split so often destroys whatever was the indefinable magic ingredient which gave the original group its popularity. There is also a usually groundless belief that fans of a group will remain loyal to individual members who break away from the group. In the rare cases where such a loyalty survives, it is mostly due to those fans being equally keen on the aura and music which that member continues to create when developing his new career.

## 18 Outside activities

**18.1** The group does not hold its members body and soul; the bond is only a limited commercial arrangement within the music business. Friends who band together to form a group might think initially that friendship is the main basis of their venture. Sad to say money and success will almost always change that idealistic state of affairs.

**18.2** Every member of the group must be allowed to have personal and business activities and interests entirely separate from his group commitments. Those activities, and the time spent on them, should not interfere with his obligations to the other members of the group, or with any contract to which he is a party as a member of the group. Also, such personal activities should not be in competition with his group activities, or raise a conflict of interest between himself and the other group members. Even within the music business there will be limits upon the construction of what is, or what may be, competitive as between his personal and his business affairs.

**18.3** Subject to a group member having the time to devote to both careers, performing as a straight dramatic stage or screen actor might not compete with his personal appearances as a member of a group.

The major problem will be finding the time to do justice to both careers, and one of them may have to be treated as part time. If the stage career is concentrated on musical plays, from which may result films and cast albums, there is bound to be an element of competition, and time will become even more of a problem. Being the producer of recordings made by other artistes will not compete with being a member of a recording group, providing that the time commitments for the group activities have absolute priority. The final decision rests with the interpretation of the terms of any agreement referring to his personal services as a member of the group.

## 19 Loans, advances, liens

**19.1** The group may operate within itself a system of allowances to individual members by way of loans or advances in anticipation of future income. If so, on each accounting date there must be an arrangement for the recoupment of all outstanding advances from the earnings then due to the borrower/member. This must be on a business-like basis, with proper written evidence and records of payment and receipt, and with a note of any conditions placed upon the loan. The group should have an irrevocable written authority and consent from the borrowing member to retain his share of income, or a portion thereof, until the total loan is repaid. All of those transactions will be dealt with through the group's manager or accountant, for convenience and to keep the books straight.

## 20 Personal disputes

**20.1** As the group formation is a calculated commercial enterprise, personal disputes between members which are not connected with group activities must be settled outside the scope of the purely business relationship. It is impossible in practice for the members to be completely impersonal, and forebearance is required between quarrelling members to keep the group sufficiently united to perform to the standard expected of it by its fans and promoters.

**20.2** Few groups are as close in their private lives as they might appear to be in their public lives. The main sources of discontent are personality conflicts, money, musical presentation, and the general administration of the group. A group which discusses its problems freely within itself, and with its manager, will reduce the risk of internal friction to the benefit of all concerned.

## 21 Professional advisers

**21.1** The music business is a potential paradise for those whose hobby it is to indulge in litigation as a threat to back up their demands, whether or not they are reasonable. The key element involved is almost always money; whether it is money which could have been earned, or money earned which has disappeared, or money paid in advance which has never been recouped, or even the speculative value placed upon the ability to control the services of an artiste through a contract.

**21.2** Generally the alleged infringement of rights arises directly from breach of contract, or from thoughtlessness, or dishonest disposition of rights or of income. When this happens the group should consult without delay competent legal and financial advisers who are familiar with the complexities of the music business. Some artistes view advisers with suspicion, others would consult them if they could afford to. It is a free choice, but a prudent record company, publisher or manager will insist, for their own protection, on the individual members seeking advice on their respective contracts.

**21.3** Advice should be sought before entering into a transaction, and, if necessary, afterwards to ensure that the artiste's interpretation of that advice is correct and is being observed properly by the other party to the contract. Prior to agreeing to the terms of any agreement of significance to the group, among the items on which it should seek advice will be:

(a) Is the concept of the agreement one which is beneficial to the group, and is there any method better than that proposed to it of achieving the same objectives?
(b) Are the warranties and undertakings asked of the group reasonable, what do they mean, and what are the possible consequences of not being able to fulfil them?
(c) Are the financial terms fair, is the group properly safeguarded against failure by the other party, and can the specific remedies available to the group provide reasonable compensation, assuming that the other party is financially sound?
(d) Are there any unreasonable restrictions upon the group, both as to its involvement in the deal, and as to matters connected with it, and which could possibly affect it?
(e) What are the comparative risks taken by the group and the other party, and are the comparative rewards potentially due to each of them disproportionately in the other party's favour?
(f) What further rights and safeguards for the group, and what

further obligations on the other party, should be included within the agreement? Do they affect what is already set out—and if so, how should the existing terms be modified to make the agreement a fair one?

(g) In the case of a long term contract, or one which requires significant investment of time and money by the other party, can any company search, credit search or any other normal cautious business investigation give the group some comfort as to the ability of the other party to fulfil all of its commitments?

**21.4** It will be more effective, and probably less expensive, if the group's advisers are consulted prior to any negotiations taking place. Their job can be made more difficult if, prior to seeking advice, the group has hastily and without proper thought committed itself to a course of action, or to contractual terms which it subsequently regrets in the light of the advice it receives. Even if the negotiations have not progressed that far, the group may have given the other side certain firm impressions which are hard to retract from, or it may have placed limitations on the negotiating freedom the advisers would prefer to have.

**21.5** Even if the group has always dealt with its own business affairs, advisers may be able to suggest courses of action which are beneficial to the group, and which may not have occurred to it before. The cost of obtaining advice usually will be less than the cost of sorting out a legal or financial tangle which could have been avoided in the first place. Advisers are not perfect, but they do have more experience than the group, and they do look at a problem or proposal objectively.

## 22 Insurance

**22.1** There are certain risks, however remote they may seem, which should be insured against because the potential liabilities would cripple any group financially. For that reason the premiums charged are expensive, and few people can afford to insure against every eventuality. Set out below are some of the risks which should be insured against. If the group cannot afford the premiums, how much less can it afford a total loss, or a substantial claim, arising because that risk becomes a reality?

(1) Injury to, or death of, a member. The loss of a member of the group through injury or death may cause financial loss to the group. Examples are where that event causes the scrapping of a half-finished album recording, or the cancellation of a half-completed tour. The

loss may be two-fold in the case of a tour—not being paid for unfulfilled date contracts, and a liability to compensate the promoter for his losses and expenses. The tour contract should contain a *force majeure* clause which should be worded sufficiently widely to cover this kind of event. The group will also lose potential earnings during the time taken to replace a dead member, or while waiting for the full recovery of an injured member.

There is a distinction between:

(a) A policy the benefits of which go to the group, to compensate it for the loss or expense incurred.

(b) A policy the benefits of which go to the injured member, or to the estate of a dead member. If the injury terminates the ability of the member to persue his musical career, the policy benefit in his favour will help to compensate him for his loss of earning power.

A policy in favour of the remaining group is common sense, and the premium will be a group expense. Any individual member wishing to insure for his own benefit will have to pay his own premium. Other parties, such as the group's manager or record company, also have an insurable interest in the group.

(2) Equipment. All equipment should be insured for the replacement value, not for the market value at the time of loss. As the cost of new equipment increases, the value of second hand equipment decreases, and the differences between these two figures when the equipment is replaced can be substantial. The depreciation on musical equipment can be dramatic, and the cost of the different types of insurance will need to be compared.

Insurance against damage should include the repair costs, and freight charges from the place of damage to the repairer's factory or local representative and back to the group, as the equipment may be damaged while the group is on tour at the other side of the world. Damage insurance should also cover the cost of hiring or otherwise temporarily replacing the damaged equipment while it is being repaired. Equipment which the group has hired for a period of time, or which is being bought on hire purchase, will usually have to be insured for full value for all risks as a condition of its hire and use. If the equipment is being provided by an independent contractor, such as a PA system or a complete lights rig hired for a tour, and it is operated by his employees and he transports it, it is for him to insure it, and his contract with the group must make that clear. The fee for the equipment contracted for will have taken the cost of insurance into account, so there should be no extra charge.

(3) Third party liability and employer's liability. The group should insure itself against third party liability caused by, eg damage to or

loss of other people's equipment or property or the death of or injury to any person incurred through the group's faulty equipment, or through the negligence of any group member, or any of its employees or others for whom the group is responsible. Personal injuries, or claims for lost earnings through injury, can result in heavy compensation claims.

The group should be insured as an employer from the consequences of the acts, defaults and negligence of employees. If independent contractors are used by the group, such as for the stage lighting, a condition of the deal should be that they are fully insured, and that they will indemnify the group from claims which may arise because their equipment is defective or dangerous, or is used or set up negligently.

(4) Concert tours. The additional areas of risk for which insurance cover should be considered are :

(a) Comprehensive medical attention, including the cost of travel home for treatment in the most serious of cases.

(b) Failure to collect guaranteed minimum fees due to cancellation of a concert by reason of accident to, or ill-health or death of, members of the group, or due to bad weather in the case of an outdoor concert. There are many *bona fide* and justifiable reasons why concerts are cancelled, such as the death or genuine incapacity of a group member, or failure of scheduled air lines, weather, and so on. Concert contracts may preclude liability to the promoter arising from non-performance of a concert for *force majeure* or other good reason beyond the group's control. Any insurance should relate to the direct losses and expenses incurred by the group, ie what would have been the net profit. On balance most groups consider that the risk is not economically insurable, both because the risk is small enough to take, and the premium would be prohibitive. There are specialist insurers in the market who well understand the problems of artistes, and who are willing to advise upon any potential risk. Any insurer will apply strict conditions upon the cause and proof of the incapacitating event, especially the areas of:

(i) Could or should the incapacitating event have been reasonably foreseeable?

(ii) Could the event have been prevented, or cured in time to perform the concert?

(iii) Is the event truly incapacitating of the group's ability to perform the concert, or is it just a great inconvenience? Was the avoidance or cure of the event possible, but judged by the group to be too expensive, or otherwise not commercially practical?

(iv) To what extent was the event caused by the act or default of the group, or by anyone under its supervision or control?

(c) Theft of money while on tour, where large cash sums are held to pay expenses, or where concert fees are collected in cash or by certified cheque after the performance. There will be strict conditions as to the limit of money to be held, both as to amount and as to time—such as over a week-end or bank holiday when banks are not open. A condition would be the prompt deposit of the money somewhere secure, such as a hotel safe, and that it is banked at the earliest opportunity. Reasonable safeguard precautions would be required while the money is in transit prior to deposit.

(d) Contingent liability cover when travelling by chartered aircraft not owned by a national airline. This will only be necessary if there are any risk areas excluded by the charter agreement.

(5) Loss of, or damage to, original multitrack recorded tapes. Such tapes are unique in that they are the original recording from which master tapes are taken, which contain the sound reproduced by the manufactured records. The multitrack tapes are the only source from which the individual recorded tracks of the song can be re-mixed. Although the song can be re-recorded, by that time the group may have changed members, or their style of playing may be different. There is no means of valuing an original multitrack tape, so the premium will be guesswork, and the conditions imposed may not be practical or worth the cost. It may cover the cost of re-recording the album, but up to a maximum figure.

**22.2** Contracts of insurance are based upon the essential element of good faith, which must be exercised when :

(a) Completing the proposal form. Not only must all the answers be truthful, but they must disclose the whole truth, even if it means expanding an answer beyond the scope of the question, or revealing relevant facts not enquired about.

(b) If the group is aware of any factor which the insurance company could not reasonably be expected to know or discover, but which might affect their decision to accept the risk, or affect the premium charged or the conditions placed upon the policy, the group must disclose that factor fully, even though it anticipates an adverse reaction from the insurance company.

(c) Giving a full and accurate value for any identifiable object which is being individually insured. Where it is an intangible liability, or an asset not capable of precise valuation, the cover will be to an agreed level. Where the object has no obvious value, an arbitrary value will be agreed by the insurers.

If the object is deliberately and substantially under insured, upon a claim being made the insurers may be entitled to pro rate the insured value against the actual value, and pay only that proportion of the loss. In a sufficiently serious case the insurance company might believe the under value is so gross that it represents a fundamental misrepresentation to the extent that it refuses a claim, and repudiates the policy as having been made by the group in bad faith. If the object is substantially over-insured, the insurers will only pay out the agreed value, ie the replacement value or market value, depending on the policy wording. The over-insurance may have been only too optimistic a valuation although made in good faith. A blatantly serious over valuation might in certain circumstances be suspected as an attempt to defraud the insurance company.

Insurance proposal forms will ask whether the same item is insured for the same risks with any other insurer. If so, the motive might be questioned. The principle is that insurance is a contract of indemnity, ie, limited to covering a loss, it is not a method of investing for the purpose of making a profit. The party insured must not have an incentive to encourage or to permit the happening of the event insured against.

(d) Making a claim. The insurers will need to be satisfied that the claim is genuine, and that the insured has complied with all of the terms of the insurance contract, including any specific security measures which were imposed. If the claim is for loss, such as theft, the insurers will also need to be satisfied that the loss is permanent. For example, is the claim actually covered by the policy; did the cause of the claim arise prior to the date the policy was taken out; or is the claim excessive for the loss? The policy terms must be read carefully.

## LIMITED COMPANIES

### 23 In general

**23.1** The professional advisers of the group may suggest the formation of a limited liability company with the name of the group. This would be instead of the group being a partnership. Provided that the membership of the group remains stable, it would give them greater security as between themselves. The security will be not only as a member of the group, in that if they each become a shareholder in the company, it makes arbitrary dismissal less likely and more complicated. The legal requirements of accounts and other matters relating to the administration and formalities of a company make unauthorised behind the scenes activities harder to conceal. They may be advised not to be the shareholders or directors, in which case the choice of who will fill those capacities would have to be made very carefully.

**23.2** If the group is reconstituted, it would be possible for any new member to be on trial for a period of time before being made a full member of the group and acquiring shares in the company. The company may be formed for a limited purpose, such as for publishing the group's music, and does not have to control the whole of its activities. Whether or not a company should be formed in the first place will depend upon the strategy the group is advised to adopt to limit personal liabilities, or to reduce its global tax bill, or to deal with certain rights and the flow of income from them to their best advantage.

## 24 Service contracts

**24.1** Each member of the group should be given a service contract with the company, the contents of which would depend upon the purpose for which the company was formed. A service contract would serve to strengthen the individual security of the members, as it should set out in detail what is to be done in the event of the premature termination of the agreement, whether by breach or by mutual consent. Compensation can more easily be dealt with, and a service contract can ensure continuity of payment in the future of each member's share of income from past compositions and records. A company is of a more permanent nature than a partnership, where, after several changes in partners, the situation can become confused if it is not dealt with properly.

## 25 Shareholders and directors

**25.1** The shareholders and directors of the company must be agreed upon. Subject to the tax implications, and the best way of achieving the purpose for which the company is formed, the group members can hold the issued shares in agreed proportions, and each can be a director. The members of the group may decide upon different proportions of shareholding between them, such as in the ratio in which they would have shared income and expense had there been no company.

**25.2** This could lead to a complicated set of Articles of Association for the company to deal with the regulation of the transfer and transmission of shares. Where the members are not equal shareholders, the system of administration and decision making must be dealt with in reasonable detail when the company is set up. Some of the questions to be answered are:

(a) In what proportions will the shares be held by the members of the group at the time the company is formed?

(b) Is the manager of the group, or anyone else outside the group membership, to have a shareholding in the company?

(c) If the number of members of the group is increased in the future, will all the shareholders give up enough shares *pro rata* for the new member to have his agreed shareholding?

(d) In the case of, for example, a music publishing company, without transferring any shares, a new member who is a composer can still be given his correct composer's share of the copyright income. Increasing the composer's share to the appropriate level can make it represent in money terms the same value as having a shareholding. The new member would not have a share in the copyrights, and would not receive a proportion of the publisher's share of income. However, in money terms that will have been equalised in the greater composer's share of income.

(e) Will any shareholder be able to transfer his shares to his wife or children, either when he is alive, or through his estate when he dies? If not, the other members will have to buy the shares for full value, otherwise they are worth nothing in the hands of the shareholder. In the case of a valuable company this can be expensive, and is another circumstance in which the benefits of insurance can be desirable.

(f) When a shareholder member leaves the group, will he have to transfer the shares to the other shareholders? If so, what safeguard does he have against an arbitrary or political decision made for the sole purpose of depriving him of his shares?

(g) What happens where a shareholder offers his shares to the other shareholders :

(i) By doing so, does he have to leave the group?

(ii) Can he offer only some, or does he have to offer all of the shares?

(iii) Do the other shareholders have the right to take them up *pro rata* to their existing shareholdings, or is there a differential discriminating against new members?

(iv) What happens if the shares are worth far more than the cash available between the other shareholders for their purchase?

(h) what are the tax implications for the members on selling or buying the shares once they have a value greater than face value, and how can any tax liabilities in the future be minimised?

## 26 Formalities

**26.1** There are strict legal and accounting requirements of running a company, and where the directors and shareholders are the members of the group, they tend to have little knowledge of them, and do not take much interest in them. Company directors can be made personally liable for debts of an insolvent company in certain circumstances, and the group members must be made fully aware of their responsibilities when acting in that capacity.

## 27 Taxation

**27.1** Taxation is one of the most important considerations in deciding whether a company would be an advantageous business vehicle for the group. The decision will depend upon how the group is constituted and managed, and how the company can be used for the benefit of the group in the future. The combination of the effects of both company and personal taxation must be reviewed to see how the eventual overall tax liabilities of each of the members can be minimised. For example, a company can put into a pension plan for key employees a higher proportion of his income than he could as an individual, and still get the full tax relief.

**27.2** Not many artistes have sufficient knowledge and experience of commercial and financial matters to be able to deal with their business affairs with any substantial degree of skill. In the music business there may be high earnings today, and reliance upon social security tomorrow—by which time the artiste finds he has acquired the handicap of champagne tastes and a beer income. The greatest hazard is the failure to reserve from income as it is received the full amount required to provide sufficient funds for income tax, which will be charged at a later date. This is caused by not resisting the urge to live now and pay later. In the short term that philosophy can work where next year's income always significantly exceeds this year's income. This should not be relied upon. An accountant with expertise in the music business is essential to the peace of mind and pocket of every successful artiste.

## 28 Contracts for the group's services

**28.1** The company will enter into all contracts with third parties on behalf of the group for the provision of its services. As it will be acting as a principal in its own right and not as an agent for the group, the company itself will be liable to third parties if such contracts are not fulfilled by the group as its employees.

**28.2** A promoter contracting with the company for it to provide the services of the group will normally require the separate personal guarantees of all of the members to ensure the fulfilment of the contract. The manager of the group, and every other promoter who has a long term contract with the group through its company, will normally require a side agreement with the members of the group individually.

**28.3** All such agreements given by the members of the group are dormant personal guarantees which become effective only when the company fails to perform its obligations. Guarantees may be required where the company has no substantial assets available to meet any liabilities which might be incurred. The existence of guarantees helps to strengthen the contractual rights of the promoter should any member of the group leave the company (and therefore the group), or refuse to perform group commitments for the company. An explanation of such a side letter is set out at the end of chapter four, on artiste's agreements with record companies.

**28.4** The difficulty of enforcing contracts for personal services are not removed by the use of a corporate intermediary, although a strong personal interest and responsibility within the company is an incentive to each of the group members to work for its success. The members of the group will also think twice before breaching their obligations to the company, if that would have the effect of damaging their own property, or if a proportion of their own share of income is paid towards the costs of the company when it sues the breaching member. A disadvantage of a company through which the group operates is that promoters and record and publishing companies dislike dealing contractually with any artiste through a third party with limited liability.

**28.5** There are circumstances where the arrangements between the group and the employing company are truly commercial contracts negotiated on a genuine arm's-length basis. Other group/company contracts are superficially commercial, but are not treated or intended internally to be truly arm's-length. Where a corporate arrangement is intended to minimise personal taxation, the reality behind the apparent commercial entity will be strongly scrutinised by the Inland Revenue. A relevant point in this context is that in a truly commercial transaction no employee of the company guarantees the company's performance of third party contracts.

## 29 Advance payments

**29.1** Major artistes negotiate considerable advance payments to them on account of anticipated income on the signing of any recording or publishing contract, or any other contract where the income will be generated well into the future. For a recording contract the advance payments may also be related to album deliveries, and for a publishing contract the advance may depend upon a minimum number of compositions being assigned by the composer. The amounts negotiated will depend on whether the contract is long term, the other party's assessment of the likelihood of recoupment within a reasonable time from the possible income to be derived, and upon the level of any other expenditure by the promoter to benefit the group.

**29.2** Artistes who are contracted personally are less inclined to risk costly litigation by taking the advance money and breaking such contracts, especially before the advance has been recouped. If an artiste's company, which contracts with the promoter, is sued because the artiste breaches his service contract with the company, the artiste himself cannot be joined in legal proceedings unless he has signed an enforceable guarantee of his own performance in favour of the promoter.

## 30 Partnership Act 1890

**30.1** Assuming the group is a partnership, in the absence of a written partnership agreement, the above Act will apply as a set of established rules to govern the following matters:

(a) Each group member will legally commit the others when dealing with third parties on group business, unless the third party knows the group member has no such authority.

(b) Each group member is liable for *all* of the group debts, not just his share of them.

(c) A new group member is not liable for anything done before he joined the group.

(d) A group member remains liable after he leaves the group for all matters occurring while he was a member.

(e) A member who leaves the group will not be responsible for anything occurring after he leaves.

(f) Rights and obligations as between group members can only be created and changed by unanimous consent, or they can be inferred by a course of dealing. The course of dealing would have to be consistent and well established to provide a set pattern which is clearly identifiable.

(g) Unless otherwise agreed, equipment bought with group funds belongs to the group, not to any individual. With the agreement of all the members it can be transferred to an individual member if his account within the group is debited with that cost, or if he pays for it.

(h) The members will share equally in the group income and the group expenses.

(i) No new member may be brought in unless all of the group members agree.

(j) Any disagreement on ordinary business matters may be decided by a majority of the members, but no change may be made to the nature of the business unless they all agree.

(k) A majority of the members cannot expel a group member, it has to be a unanimous decision (except, of course, by the member in question).

(l) If no period has been set for the duration of the partnership, any member can at any time give notice of leaving, preferably in writing. Termination of his membership takes effect on the date the notice is given. There is no implied obligation to give a minimum notice period.

**30.2** From the above statutory rules it will be seen that a written agreement covering these elementary business and contractual matters would be useful. Most artistes have never heard of the Partnership Act, and simply run the group and its affairs as they think best. Sometimes things are done fairly, but occasionally rough justice prevails.

CHAPTER 9

# *Merchandising and Endorsement Agreements*

## SECTION I: MERCHANDISING

### 1 General

**1.1** When an artiste becomes successful, there can be great potential in linking the promotion of his name and image with the sale of suitable merchandise. The merchandise will appeal to a wider range of consumers if it has a practical or decorative use. To get the best out of any merchandising scheme, the artiste must be reasonably well established. Most merchandising for artistes is dealt with on a simple basis for "T" shirts, posters, badges and concert programmes. The agreement is probably a one page letter telling the licensee to get on with it, fixing an advance payment, and agreeing a royalty or fee. That might not change for most artistes, but if serious long term merchandising is contemplated, a more carefully constructed agreement is desirable. This chapter deals with matters which should be considered, although they may not all be relevant or appropriate for every deal.

**1.2** Merchandising at its best is a highly organised business which can be very profitable. Considerable finance may be necessary for the licensee to set up the deal, depending on the type of merchandise to be manufactured and sold, and the media used for promotion and publicity to make the public aware of its existence. Sufficient stocks must also be readily available to fulfil the demand which is created.

**1.3** A detailed preliminary market research need not be necessary where the right to use the artiste's name is in connection with articles in every day use. More careful planning may be necessary where the project is novel in its concept, or where the form of merchandise is unique, unusually expensive, or with limited specialised appeal.

**1.4** The merchandise agreement will be by way of a licence to produce and sell specified articles using the name and/or image of the artiste. A licensed right is held by the licensee subject to the licence terms, which should include the right of the licensor to control the manner in which the licensee represents the artiste, and termination provisions with reversion of the licensed rights.

**1.5** Pirating of merchandising rights, or their unauthorised use, is a hazard facing someone with a hot property who has a high investment in his stock of merchandise, and a substantial artiste's royalty liability under an exclusive agreement. If a licence has not yet been granted by the artiste in that pirated area, or for that pirated product, the potential sales market can be either saturated to the extent of extinguishing its potential demand for the product, or spoilt to prevent effective and economical authorised marketing. In either case the artiste loses potential income and has no control over the quality of the unauthorised products being sold. If the goods are shoddy, they will reflect adversely upon the artiste's reputation. The purchasers have no way of knowing that the artiste is not involved in the unauthorised activity unless warnings are extensively advertised.

**1.6** If an exclusive merchandising licence is already in existence, the licensor can get into expensive legal difficulties if he has undertaken to prevent pirating by court action. Taking legal action against all infringers would be expensive, time consuming and not always effective. It is not practical for all territories, and no licensor should take on such a liability. The more popular the merchandised rights, the more likely will be the unauthorised use of them. The extent of the legal difficulty, and the commercial embarrassment, will depend upon the wording and intent of the warranties and undertakings by which the licensor is bound. Any assurance the licensor gives for policing unfair competition through the sale of unauthorised products must be subject to his own opinion in good faith upon the chance of success, and the economics of trying to do so.

**1.7** There are so many artistes with imaginative names that, unless the artiste is a star of worldwide, or at least of "western world" status, the impact of merchandise promotion based upon him can be lost in the mass of original, startling and creative publicity at present in vogue in the music business.

**1.8** Any merchandise promotion will benefit if the artiste has a strong personal association with what is being promoted, such as a musical instrument. Otherwise the promoter must use the popularity of the artiste as a performer to establish a demand for what he intends to market. Although merchandising can have an enormous turnover, as a business for an artiste it is influenced substantially by the ebb and flow of the devotion of his fans.

**1.9** If an artiste has a value for merchandise promotions, it may not be in his best interests to grant all the available rights exclusively to one party within any territory, unless that party shows that all of the potential outlets have been explored and that he undertakes to promote actively all of the rights granted to him. Some areas of promotion will be more valuable than others. By negotiation with different interested parties, the value of those rights, and the ability of the parties to deal with them effectively, can be assessed more accurately.

**1.10** From the artiste's point of view, merchandising is a means of making money and consolidating his identity with the public. The merchandise manufacturer depends on the "brand loyalty" of the artiste's fans to induce them to purchase the goods. That the artiste may thereby become more famous is incidental to the merchandiser, although the more popular the artiste becomes the stronger will be the merchandiser's selling ability.

**1.11** Many well planned merchandise promotion schemes for artistes do not come up to expectation, both as to sales potential, and the royalty income. This can happen where the products are not right, or the reasons for the artiste being successful have not been used to promote the projects. The reason can also be bad business methods, or selling over priced poor quality goods. A mystique or scarcity value, or blatant eccentricity surrounding an artiste, may be what attracts public attention to the artiste and his antics. Many styles of advertising build in these features deliberately to create a demand to hear the artiste and to see him, as by arousing a personal curiosity the unexplained can have more interest than the obvious. By removing the cause of the curiosity, and laying the artiste open to public gaze, the attraction which made the artiste popular in the first place can be destroyed.

**1.12** Any merchandising licence should give the licensee the freedom he needs to do a good job, but at the same time it must not either give him exclusivity where he cannot use it, or unreasonably restrict the artiste from promoting his career generally.

## 2 Identity of licensor

**2.1** The artiste, his management and his agency must clearly define between themselves who is to have the right to place merchandising licences. This will determine which of them will be entitled to share in the licence royalties and to what extent. There are some very experienced merchandising companies which provide a full service of licensing the character, monitoring licences, inspecting sample products, receiving licence fees and generally running the business side of the licensor's activities.

**2.2** The artiste should recognise that he will not have the expertise, contacts, or sources of finance to go it alone in the initiation, negotiation, promotion and fulfilment of merchandise deals. Even if this side of the artiste's promotion has been excluded from the management contract, the manager, or a separate commercial manager or agent, should be appointed to deal with it when it becomes a viable commercial proposition.

**2.3** It may be in the artiste's best interests for all of the merchandise rights to be kept separate from the record and personal appearance sides of his musical career. The artiste may incur heavy financial liabilities as an entertainer, such as in damages for breach of contract or breach of copyright, when it will be an advantage to him, if it is possible, to prevent attachment of the income arising through his merchandise activities. If the merchandise licensor is a limited company, the proposed licensee must satisfy himself that the company is entitled to act as it purports to, and that it can do so for the whole of the term of the proposed licence agreement.

**2.4** The artiste's professional advisers will guide him upon the corporate set-up for the merchandise rights, to minimise his personal tax liabilities, and to get the best advantage from his merchandising income. For administering the merchandise company, the artiste's manager will require his management commission, but excluding exceptional circumstances, the manager should have no more control or commission than he would have received under his normal management agreement.

**2.5** An agent, who only acts for the artiste to obtain employment for him, will not normally be involved with the granting and negotiation of merchandise contracts. Whether an agent should participate in earnings from merchandise deals depends upon whether they were procured by him, or whether he was otherwise instrumental in obtaining them. For this reason it has already been pointed out in the chapter on agency contracts (chapter two) that great care must be taken in defining upon which earnings of the artiste the agent will be entitled to receive commission.

**2.6** If the value of the proposed merchandise promotions stems from the artiste participating actively as a sponsor or advertiser, he should assign to the merchandise company such of his personal rights as will be legally required to enable the company to give and fulfil the usual warranties and undertakings contained in merchandise agreements. The assignment can be contained in a service contract with the company, entitling it to call upon the artiste to do all things reasonably required by it to ensure the success of all of the merchandise promotion projects entered into.

Because merchandising is also a specialised method of representing and promoting the artiste as an individual, whereby licensees spend the money and do the work to create the income from which a royalty is paid to him, the responsibilities involved should be taken seriously by him and the merchandising promoter for their mutual benefit.

## 3 Prior agreements

**3.1** Before any firm offers are made to a licensee, or negotiations with a prospective licensee are concluded, the merchandise company must ensure that there are no existing conflicting agreements, or outstanding options, relating to any current merchandise deals involving the artiste. The merchandise company should maintain a register of current licence agreements, setting out what products they cover, the licensed territories and the periods of each agreement, including option periods. Any passive and non-profitable conflicting agreements should be terminated if possible. Previous options over merchandise rights which have yet to be exercised must be left to lapse, unless they can be revoked or bought back. Prior licence agreements which have terminated must nevertheless be checked to ensure that there are no outstanding items to be dealt with.

**3.2** Most merchandise agreements contain a non-exclusive right for stocks existing at the date of termination of the agreement to be disposed of within a specified time thereafter. Whether this clause has been complied with correctly will depend upon confirming the stocks existing at the date the licensee's right to manufacture ended, and comparing that figure with the shipments of stock and confirmed sales accounted for within the stock sell-off period, and the declared terminal stock held by the licensee. If a subsequent licensee will not be manufacturing and selling the same range of products, it would not affect him if the artiste authorised the previous licensee to sell and account for his terminal stock of merchandise for a short time after the expiry of the non-exclusive sell-off period. The decision to do so will depend on the original sell-off period, the stocks held at termination, the efforts already made to sell stock, and whether an extension would be genuinely beneficial. In practice, the licensee will dispose of his terminal stock one way or another, so it might as well be on an authorised, royalty paying basis.

**3.3** Any technical or legal requirements needed to complete the reversion of merchandise rights after the termination of each licence agreement must be complied with. Depending on the type of merchandise, and the form of the licence, included among those formalities may be:

(a) Changing the registered user details in the local trademarks registry or completing or assigning any registered design or trademark applications arising from the effects of (b) below.

(b) Confirming the artiste's rights in the copyright and other proprietary rights of any original item of merchandise specifically designed by the licensee and permanently associated with the artiste. This will only occur when the merchandise is incapable of being put to any other use beyond its close association with the artiste.

**3.4** All sub-licences entered into by the licensee must be checked, to make sure they have also terminated, and that they were authorised in accordance with the original licence terms. Unless a licence agreement covers a wide territory, it will usually prohibit the original licensee from assigning any of his rights without the licensor's prior written consent. Each sub-licence can only grant to the sub-licensee rights which the original licensee himself is entitled to, and it must also be subject to any conditions (including termination provisions) by which the original licensee is bound. If the original licensee has contracted to give the sub-licensee more rights than the licensee himself has, the sub-licensee may be able to sue the original licensee for misrepresentation, but the termination of the merchandising licence by the licensor effectively terminates any sub-licence as well.

**3.5** If the original licensee itself does not manufacture the goods it merchandises, it must ensure that its agreement with the manufacturer is consistent with the rights granted by the licence. This will apply mainly to quantities and the quality of the finished article, and the satisfactory use of the artiste's name or image. The licensor should have the right to inspect samples of the goods and to refuse the sale of those not reaching the agreed specifications. If the goods are consumer goods which come within manufacturing or materials regulations for safety or otherwise, they must be complied with.

## 4 Rights granted to a licensee

**4.1** As the merchandising rights in respect of a successful artiste are valuable, and as the quality and presentation of the products will reflect on the artiste's reputation, the licence agreement must be sufficiently detailed and clear to protect the artiste, while giving the licensee a fair deal. Set out below are the major items which should be dealt with when negotiating what the licensee is entitled to.

## 5 Name and likeness

**5.1** The licensee will be given the exclusive right to use the name and likeness of the artiste, and any logo or device with which he is associated, in connection with the manufacture and sale of specified categories of goods within a specified territory for a specified length of time. A merchandising licence, like any other commercial contract, can have a period of time and termination provisions in accordance with the ordinary principles, and so these items are not dealt with individually in this chapter.

**5.2** An artiste can make famous a caricature, image or invented person, with characteristics identified only with the artiste. The licensee should be prevented from using or depicting that personification in any way uncharacteristically, or in such a manner as to alter materially the impression or qualities which attract that representation of the artiste to the public.

**5.3** Where the artiste is a group of musicians, a long term licence for the exclusive use of their professional name and likeness is of use to the licensee only for so long as the unit comprising the same individuals continues to exist. An exception is where the group name, rather than the identities of the individuals, is the selling factor, or where the group is identified universally by the founding member only. The following points are relevant:

(1) If the group name is the principal significant focus of the licensee's operation, he should ensure that his rights will continue for the rest of his agreement if the group changes members in the meantime. The licensee should ask for confirmation of the name ownership, and, where the licensor is an intermediary, confirmation of the relationship between the owner of the name and the licensor.

(2) Where the group has certain central characters whose presence in the group has caused its success, the licensee will want to be able to use the identity of those individuals if their prominence in any aspect of the group merchandising campaign is essential. The following

practical areas must also be covered:

(a) To what extent can such a member be given prominence in advertising, both in group-orientated advertising, and as an individual in advertising products related to that member's speciality, such as guitars? There may be two possible means of an ace guitarist being merchandised; as a member of the group and as an individual. The same can apply to the lead singer, or any other group member who is a character in his own right. In such a case the licensee should make sure his agreement covers both possibilities. For the individuals, care should be taken not to breach any separate endorsement deal he is contracted for. Endorsement is dealt with in section II of this chapter.

(b) What happens to the rights of the licensee if such a star group member leaves the group? The licensee may wish to retain his rights, but:

(i) The group will find a replacement member, and the merchandising agreement with the group must not conflict with any potential rights of the licensee over the similar use of the personal name of the departed member.

(ii) The departed member may want to be free of all previous group commitments, including merchandising.

(iii) Any new group the departed member may join will want to have his merchandising activities related to the name of the new group, rather than as an individual who will be identified still with his previous group.

(iv) The licensee may have stocks of merchandise referring to the group, including the departed member. He ought to be allowed to dispose of this stock, but that should not prevent him from preparing new products referring to the new group constitution. The turnover of stock is such that this should not be a problem, especially if there is a reasonable period before the new group records or tours.

(3) The group members must agree whether the licence income is to be treated as group income irrespective of the group membership at the time the money comes in; or whether the licence income is due to those persons who comprised the group when the licence was signed, irrespective of when the income from that licence comes in. That will depend on whether only the name of the group is being used, and upon the ability to identify which royalty payments to the group are in respect of which particular group membership's merchandising activities.

(4) Whether the artiste is a group or a solo performer, any exclusive merchandising rights granted to a licensee must be subject to any

rights which are contained in the artiste's recording contract. Record companies usually require the right to use the name and likeness of the artiste to sell and promote his records. The clause will be wide enough to cover merchandise, such as "T" shirts, badges, posters, and other promotional items on a limited scale, which are used only for localised promotion and are not usually sold to the public. The rights may be exclusive insofar as promoting records are concerned, and will be in respect of only directly related advertising and publicity.

## 6 The product

**6.1** Unless the artiste is licensing his worldwide merchandising rights without product category limitation to one licensee (which is most unlikely), the range of products to be included in the scope of the licence must be clearly defined. Vague descriptions, such as "clothes and clothing accessories" will create confusion when there is a dispute as to what is meant by "accessories".

**6.2** The artiste should decide the broad categories of merchandise which can usefully be promoted with his image. This will depend on whether the artiste is a male or female, and what sectors of the public identify themselves with the artiste. Usually a prospective licensee will approach the artiste, and propose his requirements by way of product and any other concepts. If it sounds sensible and will be profitable, there is no reason to reject the proposal.

**6.3** As the artiste has no connection with the design or manufacture of the merchandised products, he should have no liability to consumers if the product is defective or dangerous. Nevertheless the licence agreement should contain a suitable warranty and indemnity from the licensee to the artiste covering this aspect. (See paragraph **17.11**).

## 7 Exclusivity and territory

**7.1** To have any value, the licence must be exclusive to the licensee for his products within the licensed territory. Exclusivity eliminates authorised competition with the licensee by others in the rights he has acquired. Where different licensees are given different markets or territories on an exclusive basis, the licensor has to be very careful not to infringe the UK or EEC legislation, or Directives or Regulations aimed at what they consider to be anti-competitive practices. Infringement can have serious consequences, and can make the licence agreements defective. There is also now the prospect of a European free market in 1992, which will affect any exclusive European territory deals which are currently not illegal.

**7.2** For the protection of the artiste there should be either a rewarding incentive, or a negative disincentive, to the licensee to ensure, so far as is commercially possible, that he does his best to promote the merchandise. Otherwise there is a temptation for the licensee to remain inactive until he feels that the market will be most receptive. The positive incentive can relate to royalty rates and possible additional rights in a situation of great success. The disincentives can relate to termination provisions or minimum royalty payments to protect against inefficiency.

**7.3** Where the professional name and reputation of the artiste are both recognised worldwide, and clearly there is no possibility of another artiste using that professional name, it can be licensed exclusively throughout the world. The artiste will have to warrant to the licensee that he is entitled himself to the exclusive use of that professional name in the licensed territory, and so that he is entitled to grant the licence to use it. An artiste who is popular only locally may discover that, in all good faith and unknown to each other, there is another artiste elsewhere in the world with the same or a similar professional name with his own local reputation and popularity. Neither artiste could warrant safely to a licensee that he has the exclusive use of his professional name in the other artiste's home territory, in case he could be prevented from doing so by legal proceedings. This risk is not likely in the case of an internationally promoted artiste.

**7.4** The description of the territory must be clear and precise. It must not be described, for example, as "the Commonwealth", or with any other general identification which may change geographically or politically during the period of the licence. Without a precise definition "the Commonwealth" could mean the Commonwealth as constituted at the start of the licence, or whichever countries make up the Commonwealth from time to time.

**7.5** If the warranty by the artiste in the licence as to his exclusive rights over the professional name is breached, the licensee will expect to be compensated for his loss of profit, reimbursed his expenses, and indemnified against any consequences of acting in reliance on the warranty being correct. The artiste will be required to warrant that he has granted no other rights to third parties which would be breached by, or conflict with, the exclusive licence. Any such prior existing rights must be disclosed to the licensee, and the licence modified accordingly if necessary. Any warranty must be subject to the overriding provisions of the legal system governing commercial transactions in and between different licensed territories. For example, despite a licence being subject to English law, the country in which it is to be effective may have local laws protecting a licensee upon termination by having compensation payable to the licensee (see paragraph **16**). As warranties are representations in absolute terms, they should only be given if the artiste is confident that there is no risk of them being wrong or misleading.

**7.6** The licensee will be entitled to take legal action against third parties who infringe his enforceable exclusive rights, such as the production of unauthorised versions of the merchandise. The artiste should assist the licensee in any reasonable manner at the licensee's expense. The artiste should not commit himself to the risk of time and expense in being responsible for taking legal action against any infringer. He should be prepared to take any action needed to preserve his warranties.

## 8 Infringement

The following courses of action can be used to identify and stop infringements of the licensed rights and products.

*Passing off*

**8.1** If the infringing goods also use the artiste's name or likeness in a manner similar to that used for the products manufactured by the licensee, whether or not being visibly attributed to the licensee, there will be a claim against the infringer for passing off his goods as those of the licensee. The infringer's intention is to cause confusion in the minds of purchasers who would assume that the infringing merchandise is the product of the licensee, or that the licensee has authorised its production. The licensee has established his business and created the market for the goods. Each infringing item sold will wrongfully deprive the licensee of what would have been his profit, and the artiste of what would have been his royalty on the sale. The sale of an infringing item may also have absorbed what would have been the purchase of an authorised item, on which the licensee would have made a profit and the artiste would have received a royalty.

*Breach of copyright, privacy, defamation*

**8.2.1** Where the infringing item is a breach of copyright in the original item, an action for breach of copyright will be available to the artiste, or whoever else owns the copyright in the original item. Examples are photographs used for posters, and artwork used for "T" shirts. There is no copyright in a slogan or album title, but unauthorised use may be an infringement of a commercial right which has attached to it a valuable goodwill and business activity. It is immaterial for copyright whether or not the authorised item has been licensed in the territory where the infringement is made and sold.

**8.2.2** There is no law of privacy in the United Kingdom, for legal action to be successful a recognised legal right must have been broken. If the artiste did not own the copyright in the photograph of himself being sold on "T" shirts or as posters, he would have to establish another legal right to determine whether that has been breached. Whoever else is the owner of the copyright in the photographs will have a right of action against the infringer. Professional photographers always retain the copyright in their work, and receive fees for its reproduction in magazines and elsewhere. The licensee or the artiste would have to get a specific clearance from the photographer, even if the artiste has previously used the photograph, for example, for an album sleeve.

**8.2.3** Famous people in the public eye have a marketable property in their identity, so the unauthorised use of that identity is actionable as depriving the person of his marketable reputation and goodwill. This is a form of intangible personal asset (see paragraph **17** for endorsement). In such an example, if the artiste has already granted similar rights exclusively to a licensee, who at the time of the infringement had established his market, a passing off action might also be available.

## 9 Registered design and trademarks

**9.1** Where the artiste grants a licensee rights over a graphic mark or name which is the property of the artiste, and which is registered as a trademark in the licensed territory, legal action is also available against infringers in that territory for breach of that registered right. The action can also be brought by the licensee who is a registered user of the device or logo, which may be more convenient to the artiste. For a unique and original device or logo which is not registered, the action for breach of copyright and passing off will still be available.

**9.2** There is a significant difference between the ease of taking infringement action where there is the statutory protection of registration, and having to produce the proof of confusion and damage necessary for a successful passing off action. If the registration protection is infringed, then without having to prove damages, a writ can be issued for an injunction and compensation. By contrast, in a passing off action it is well established that all of the following tests or conditions need to be satisfied to succeed:

(a) there must be a misrepresentation;
(b) made by a trader in the course of his trade;
(c) to customers or consumers;
(d) which is calculated to injure the business and goodwill of another trader;
(e) and which actually causes such damage.

[The Warnick Advocaat case 1980 RPC 31.]

## 10 Rights of the licensor

The details of the merchandising licence will depend on what is involved in the deal, so this chapter can only set out the major matters likely to be considered.

*The merchandised product*

**10.1** The merchandise which is promoted through the use of the artiste's name and attraction must meet high standards of manufacture and presentation. Shoddy goods, although not part of the artiste's business activities, will nevertheless be connected with his reputation in the minds of dissatisfied customers. Similarly, high quality goods will reflect well on the artiste, although his only connection with them is in a marketing capacity. Marketed merchandise does not hold out to the purchaser the same form of recommendation as is implied where the artiste endorses the goods, but he does suffer to the same extent from the adverse effects of justified consumer dissatisfaction.

**10.2** The following should be included in the artiste's rights under the merchandising licence:

(a) The right to inspect samples of the goods from time to time to ensure their manufacturing quality, if necessary in accordance with agreed specifications. This will also enable the artiste to check that any photograph or logo is being used in the correct style, and with the right quality of presentation. This is normally achieved by the licensee having to submit a sample of each product for approval prior to committing to manufacture. Approval should be required to be given in writing within (say) 14 days after submission. For the licensee's protection, the clause should state that if no response is received within (say) 21 days, approval will be deemed to have been given. Subsequent inspection may be undertaken from time to time to ensure that the article as produced consistently conforms with the approved sample.

(b) The right to control the format of the combined presentation of the product and the artiste to the public by way of advertising and promotion. The licensee should not be able to advertise the product in such a way that it looks like an endorsement by the artiste of the products. For example, how and in what context will the identification of the artiste with the product be projected, and what representations and claims does the licensee make for the product which by implication are supported by the artiste, eg, as to the quality or performance of the goods? The artiste must not be involved in false or misleading representations, or those which otherwise bring the product and the artiste into disrepute.

**10.3** The right to be able to intervene if the price structure of the merchandise is excessive, even allowing for adequate margins to cover the cost of the artiste's participation. This is not a case of illegal resale price maintenance, but establishing a fair price for the merchandised product. The ultimate sanction is termination of the licence agreement. Reasonable pricing depends on the product's comparative manufacturing and marketing costs, and the primary target sector of the public. If the main appeal is to the young teenage group, the artiste should avoid the risk of being charged by his fans with callous exploitation of their loyalty to him with the sole motive of profit.

**10.4** Unless the licensee is an established merchandiser with a fair reputation, he might think that it is in his interests to make the most out of his products by charging high prices and using the artiste's selling influence for so long as the market is there. Although the artiste can earn high royalties over that short period of time, they may not compensate him for loss of prestige and professional reputation for having been involved in what is perceived as a rip-off situation.

**10.5** If the item licensed is a registered design, or logo or trademark, or where the artiste is the owner of the copyright in what is being represented or marketed, the correct copyright and registration credits must be placed, wherever required for the protection of such rights, under international and local laws. This will be on the product itself, its packaging and in all publicity and promotional material, and advertising.

## 11 Royalties

**11.1** The financial return to the artiste is a royalty paid by the licensee upon sales of licensed merchandise. Normally either a fixed sum of money is payable upon the sale of each article irrespective of the selling price, or a royalty is paid on the sale of each article based upon a percentage of its retail selling price, or its net invoice value if not retailed by the licensee, excluding VAT in each case.

**11.2** Fixed sum payments do not benefit the artiste, as the licensee can make a bigger profit by raising his price, and by doing so he is not obliged to pay a share of the increase to the artiste. The decline in the value of money is a good reason for the artiste not using the fixed sum system, except possibly where the fixed sum is so calculated that impressive sales have to be achieved to enable the licensee to reach the point of making a profit for himself.

**11.3** The percentage royalty on the retail selling price or net invoice value ensures that the profit of the licensee arising from the sale of merchandise is proportional to the income of the artiste. This minimises the risk of the licensee finding some ingenious method of legitimately reducing the amounts to be paid to the artiste. This can happen where the base price is a wholesale price, or any other figure which is within the control of the licensee. Trade discounts or incentives deducted from the base price can lead to the licensee being dishonest, such as by wholesaling to his own retail company at an unrealistic price. If the licensee sells direct to consumers, where he is not the manufacturer of the licensed products, the royalty should be on retail price. If there would be a bit of each, the two bases of calculation can be agreed to apply in each case as appropriate, and at the higher of the two possibilities. The rising prices of the items of merchandise, and the consequent increase in the amount of the royalty to the artiste, will keep the artiste in pace with inflation.

**11.4** If the percentage is of recommended retail selling price, that is easily ascertainable, but there is a distinction between the recommended retail selling price and the price which may actually be charged. As the amount of discounts or other forms of price reduction are not permanent, and are not the same over the whole territory, it may not always be practical to base the royalty on actual price. For example, if a discount is considered not to be a commercial arms-length deal, it should be disregarded and the royalty should be on the original invoice price.

**11.5** Agreement upon rates of currency exchange in relation to royalty payments is not so easy where, for example, the licensor is a Bahamian company, the licensee is an American corporation, and the royalties are to be paid in Switzerland. A UK licensor will normally want to be paid in sterling, or US dollars. A great deal will depend upon what tax problems are involved, and upon which system is most advantageous to the artiste where he is not the licensor. The rate of exchange can be determined as being the same rate at which the licensee exchanges his foreign royalty currency into sterling, or the due date of payment to the artiste of his royalties.

If the relevant currencies are not stable, and a licensee deliberately delays payment past his contractual date so as to take advantage of currency variations at that time, there can be a clause giving the artiste the option to treat the contractual date of payment as the date of the exchange rate calculation, to discourage such practices.

**11.6** A sliding scale can be used to calculate royalty rates. One method is to impose a high royalty rate on marginal sales, and thereafter the greater the volume of sales the lower the royalty rate per item, in case the sales never become significant. Alternatively the reverse can be applied, where the royalty rate increases in accordance with increased sales levels. Once sales increase, the licensee's costs are lower per item, his profit margin is higher, and that is the time for the artiste to participate fully in the profits available. If the licensee has a range of goods under the agreement, will they all have the same royalty rate? If the rates are different, due to different profitability levels or projected sales levels, any applicable escalating royalty rate can be across the board, or more likely, related to individual lines of merchandise. The purpose is to have overall a fair royalty to the artiste, and a reasonable profitability to the licensee.

## 12 Royalty advances

**12.1** Upon the execution of the licence agreement the licensee should pay a non-returnable advance on account of royalties to be earned. The artiste receives an immediate income, and the licensee has to work to generate the profit to cover the advance, because until then he is out of pocket. Subject to any minimum royalty commitments, the licensee has no obligation to make further payments to the artiste until sales of the merchandise have reached the volume at which royalties payable to the artiste exceed the total of advances already made. The advance royalty payment must be specified to be "non-returnable", so that if the promotion of the merchandise fails, the artiste will not have to repay the advance to the licensee. Any advance royalty payment must be recoupable only from the artiste's earnings in connection with the agreement.

If there are different product ranges with different royalty rates, the artiste should consider whether the attribution and recoupment of advances should not also be separated accordingly.

## 13 Minimum royalty

**13.1** To reduce the risk of a licensee doing nothing to promote his rights, and thereby earning nothing for the artiste, the licence agreement should contain a minimum royalty clause. The amount of the minimum royalty can be in addition to royalty advance payments, although it would normally be a top up at the end of a licence year if the total accounting falls short of the balance between the advance and the minimum royalty commitment. A minimum royalty clause is only necessary where it is important for the actual products to be sold, as opposed to the licensee simply acquiring the rights by agreeing to pay an advance. This is treated by the artiste as a positive inducement for the licensee to trade actively, rather than as a penalty for not doing so.

**13.2** The licensee will have to pay to the artiste a minimum royalty in each annual accounting period, which can be based upon the estimated volume of sales the licensee should be able to maintain with a reasonable effort. This will ensure that the artiste has a minimum earning from the venture. The higher the minimum royalty required, the more serious are likely to be the intentions of the licensee, because he would need to be confident of being able to recoup his outlay and of making a profit. Subject to the recoupment of advances, the minimum royalty payments should be paid at the end of the relevant accounting period. If there is any concern that the licensee may not pay, or may not survive, the minimum royalty should be guaranteed by a bank or should be paid as the equivalent of an annual advance. Even better, that party should not be appointed as a licensee.

**13.3** The licence agreement must state whether a licensee, who has not achieved enough sales to cover the minimum royalty payments, can nevertheless maintain his rights by making up the difference in each accounting period out of his own pocket. The decision will depend upon whether the artiste is more interested in increased sales, rather than a minimum income only.

**13.4** It may suit the licensee not to exercise his rights energetically, and to treat the minimum royalty payments as an unavoidable business expense. This is possible where, for some reason, that expense is worthwhile to the licensee whose intention is to block off from competitors that particular section of the artiste's merchandise value. In such a case a substantial minimum commitment and a right for the artiste to terminate the agreement for lack of activity will be essential. What would constitute a lack of activity may be difficult to define precisely.

## 14 Accounting

**14.1** Merchandise agreements should contain accounting dates and procedures to suit the capability of the licensee, its own accounting arrangements with third parties, and the requirements of the artiste. The accounting dates will be half yearly or quarterly, depending on the likely flow of income hoped to be generated. The licensee should undertake to produce his statement and payment within a reasonable specified time thereafter, eg 21 days after each quarter day. If the licensee has a large territory and (with consent) sub-licenses some of the rights, or if he has regular major outlets for his products, the artiste should establish the dates by which the licensee expects to be accounted to by these third parties. He should make sure that the accounting dates to him from the licensee "catch" the most recent receipts by the licensee, otherwise that money will fall into the next accounting period. This is a question of cash flow efficiency. The statements rendered to the artiste by the licensee should set out in detail all sources of income and sales by category of product and when the sale was made.

**14.2** The licensee must keep separate accounts for his activities under the agreement, and the artiste should have rights of inspection and audit upon giving reasonable prior notice of his intention to do so. If there is doubt as to the accuracy of the accounting the artiste's auditor should verify the figures independently by contacting sales outlets, and any manufacturers used by the licensee for the products. The audit clause should give such right of access, and the licensee should undertake to provide the necessary authority to such parties to disclose information to the artiste's auditor.

The licensee should account to the artiste's country in its legal tender, except where for tax or other reasons the artiste legitimately requires payment to be made by the licensee in another country or in another currency.

## 15 Guarantor

**15.1** It is unlikely that an artiste with a valuable product will give exclusivity to a licensee who does not have the ability, finance or organisation to promote it properly. Where a smaller company is given exclusive merchandising rights, the artiste should consider requiring the licensee to provide a guarantor of the performance of its obligations. A guarantor can be either one or more of the directors of the company, or some independent third party. A director ought to be someone who is financially sound enough to be worth attaching as guarantor to indemnify the artiste against loss or expense. A guarantor stands in the place of the licensee if he cannot meet his commitments, so there is little point in having a guarantor who is financially worthless.

### 16 Law of licence

**16.1** The licence agreement should specify which legal system will govern its interpretation and enforcement. If it is not specified, confusion can arise where, for example, the artiste and the licensee are resident in different countries, and the licensee's territory covers more than one country. In the absence of a specified legal jurisdiction, the possibilities are the licensor's legal system, or the licensee's legal system. The decision will be influenced by where the agreement is signed, and where the operation of the rights granted will take place, and on balance the licensee may have the advantage over the licensor.

**16.2** The artiste has the right to decide by which system of law he would like the contract to be governed. The laws relating to commercial contracts differ throughout the world; both as to the formalities necessary to constitute a binding contract, and what can and cannot be contained in a contract as enforceable obligations, limitations and incentives. Although two parties can agree on any matter to be contained in their contract, whether any unusual term of the agreement is enforceable will depend upon the principles of the relevant law of the contract.

## SECTION II: ENDORSEMENT

### 17 General concept

**17.1** A successful artiste has a valuable asset in his name and reputation, which is marketable in connection with products, and sometimes with services. Merchandising is the generalised cashing in of this asset to promote and sell almost anything, subject to approval by the artiste. Consumers do not believe that the artiste is in anyway connected with the products, which tend to be subject to the impulse purchase trend.

**17.2** The artiste may go a major step further by endorsing products. These products tend to be serious, more expensive consumer products, in contrast to the inexpensive merchandised everyday items. The purpose is to persuade consumers to buy these products by association with the artiste, and with the consumer believing and possibly relying on the express or implied recommendation of the product by the artiste. Endorsed products are heavily advertised and promoted to give the association with, and recommendation of, the artiste maximum exposure.

**17.3** The enhancement of, or risk to, the career of the artiste will be influenced by the description, quality and reputation of endorsed products to a far greater extent than by the sale of general merchandise. Unless the artiste is a household name outside his musical career, it is not likely that he will be asked to endorse something unless his name is connected with it, such as a musical instrument. But if the opportunity does arise, an endorsement agreement will be drafted for submission to the artiste, and this section deals with the more usual matters for negotiation.

**17.4** The monetary value to both the artiste and the manufacturer of an endorsed product within the music business is limited to the extent that there is a market for it, and by the sales competition it faces from other makes of similar product. For that reason the artiste should not be restricted unduly from endorsing general products not competing with any music business product. During the period of promotion for the endorsed product, eg, one year to catch regular trade, the Christmas market and to mop up in the spring, the artiste will normally be restricted from endorsing any other product, whether or not it is competitive. It is a matter of marketing impact, to give the product a promotional hook for advertising which its competitors will not have. There will also be a restriction on his endorsing any product within, say, three years, which is competitive or which is made by a competing manufacturer.

**17.5** Endorsement will be of one particular item, usually identified by the brand name and the manufacturer, rather than of a general specification of goods. Endorsement is a much more personal and direct appeal from the artiste, who is assumed to have good grounds for recommending the purchase of the goods he endorses. Endorsement carries in the mind of the person thereby influenced to purchase the goods an assurance of quality and success in its use or application, implied by the assumption that the artiste would not otherwise use or recommend such a product. Therefore the artiste must be careful in his choice of endorsement, especially if he does not have personal experience of the product he is asked to promote.

**17.6** The artiste's rights may be infringed if, without his authority, he is depicted as a product endorser. This is also misleading, by purporting to be an authorised specific recommendation or endorsement of products. There can also be an implied endorsement where, for example, a picture of the artiste using the goods is contained within an advertisement for those goods, which gives the firm impression that the artiste is making a silent recommendation. Apart from legal principles, anyone who promotes or advertises consumer products is subject to the codes of practice laid out by the Advertising Standards Authority. The codes are voluntary, and are not legally enforceable, but they are taken seriously.

**17.7** If the artiste, who, for example, is famous for always using a known guitar, is photographed unwittingly playing a guitar of another make, the manufacturer of the other guitar would use that photograph as an endorsement of his product at his peril. Using a guitar and recommending it are two different things, especially if the artiste is already contracted to endorse the guitar with which he is professionally associated. Publication of the photograph as a news item, where that is clearly no endorsement or advertisement, but simply a general comment of public interest, could not be prevented by the artiste.

**17.8** An endorsement which is not authorised could be defamatory if it is contrary to the known attributes of the artiste, so that his personal standing and integrity, and his professional reputation, would be substantially damaged in the eyes of those who assumed the endorsement to be genuine. An example might be an implied endorsement of some hell's brew liquor by a teetotal artiste, or an implied approval of hard drugs by a dedicated anti-drug artiste. The circumstances would have to be dramatic, untrue and professionally damaging to be considered defamatory. Most successful actions for defamation relate to the artiste's private life.

## 18 Fees

**18.1** While the product is promoted in association with the artiste's recommendation, individual items of the product do not contain any reference to the artiste, except perhaps on the packaging. If the product manufacturer has a one year endorsement agreement with the artiste, it would not, as a business decision, saturate its advertising of the product using his name, as the impact wears off by becoming stale. There would be periods during the year, such as at Christmas and for special sales periods, when the promotional material will be changed to emphasise the endorsement.

**18.2** The products will be established in their own right within their market, and the endorsement is one of many methods of maintaining consumer awareness. They are not wholly dependent on featuring the artiste, as merchandised products are.

**18.3** Therefore the remuneration of the artiste in consideration of endorsing a product will not be a royalty on sales, but a fee to be negotiated. It may be a flat fee, or it may have a potential increase structure calculated upon a greater than normally anticipated sales level of the endorsed product. The fee will also take into account any restriction accepted by the artiste as part of the deal, thus reducing the potential market within which he might be in demand as a shining example of godliness and cleanliness.

**18.4** The fee level would depend on whether the agreement extends beyond endorsement promotion within the UK. A factor to be taken into account on territorial exposure is the advertising/promotion budget being allocated to the endorsed product. Media advertising on a regional or national basis will have different costs, and the greater the budget the less the impact upon it of a fixed fee. There comes a time where the fee level will be influenced by the budget figure, depending on the anticipated exposure the endorsement will be given.

## 19 Territorial limits

**19.1** The endorsement agreement should state whether the rights granted are in respect of the UK only, or whether they are, for example, European or even worldwide. If the rights are to be exercisable outside the UK, the following will need to be dealt with:

(a) how is the fee level to be calculated, and who is to be responsible for paying it?

(b) will more than a year be needed as a contract period to enable the other territory to fit in their own promotion plans?

(c) will agreed photos and quotations need to be modified to cater for different consumer tastes and markets?

(d) how can the artiste approvals system be simplified for promotional material?

(e) are there any regulations outside the UK relating to endorsement which need to be considered?

**19.2** Any "UK only" rights must be considered within the broader EEC market, particularly with the implementation of abolishing trade barriers, and the effect of anti-competitive and trade restriction laws and regulations. If the product packaging contains the endorsement, limitations on distribution and sale within EEC countries are illegal unless one of the specific exemptions apply.

## 20 Approval of material

**20.1** The artiste should approve all basic promotional and advertising material, to ensure that it is reasonable, accurate and truthful. If the material infringes any legal prohibition or requirement, or contravenes any relevant code of practice, the artiste may come in for criticism as well. The precise wording of any quotation, direct or indirect, must be checked and agreed, and photos to be used will also be agreed.

## 21 Product liability

**21.1** Unlike a merchandise licence agreement, the role of the artiste in endorsing a product is active in the sense of positively promoting it by recommendation. The manufacturer's hope is that the endorsement will influence consumers to purchase their product. While in this case the artiste is not connected with the design and manufacture of the endorsed product, with the trend of consumer protection legislation, it might be possible that a consumer who has been injured by a defective or dangerous endorsed product to have a claim against the artiste for recommending it.

**21.2** If the wording of the quoted endorsement is careless, and can be interpreted as positive assurance by the artiste as to the safety, structure, quality, and benefit of the product, and the injured consumer relied on that representation, it would be worth joining the artiste as a co-defendant to an action against the product manufacturer for damages. The endorsement would have to be a statement of facts, not opinions, and the claimant would have to show that it was reasonable for him to rely on the statement. As the statement could not be a contractual representation, the claimant would have to prove it to have been a tortious representation. The artiste's defence would be that the representation was made in good faith based upon the facts as he believed them to be after making reasonable enquiries. He will have to show that he did take care in asking about the products, and that the information he was given should have been reliable.

The endorsement agreement should contain a warranty and indemnity from the manufacturer in respect of the legality of all promotional projects and material, and of the product being endorsed, to enable the artiste to join the manufacturer in any legal action as a third party.

*Termination*

**21.3** Once the product manufacturer has signed the endorsement agreement and paid his fee or advance, apart from the usual termination reasons, two specific reasons to be included for the benefit of the artiste should be failure of the manufacturer to make any further agreed payments, and failure to comply with the agreed format of presenting the artiste and the agreed wording of any specific nature by way of recommendation.

CHAPTER 10

# The Copyright Designs and Patents Act 1988

On 15 November 1988 the Copyright Designs and Patents Act 1988 was passed by Parliament, although it did not become effective until mid 1989. In this chapter it is called the 1988 Act. It repealed entirely the Copyright Act 1956, the Performers Protection Acts of 1958 and 1972, the Copyright Amendment Act 1983, and a considerable amount of other intellectual property related legislation.

This chapter is a summary of the significant elements of the new relevant legislation which is set out in the 1988 Act in connection with music, sound recordings and artistes. For convenience, references to a "work" mean a literary or musical work, and references to the "author" relate to the creator of such a work.

The 1988 Act is well set out, and the sections are clearly stated. For the purposes of this chapter the relevant sections are either quoted from the 1988 Act or are paraphrased, to simplify the wording or to remove any duplication. There is also a commentary where an expansion or explanation would be useful. In most cases it is necessary to see how the facts of a case fit in with the relevant sections, so it becomes a matter of interpretation and application.

Section I of chapter seven explains in some detail the technical and practical requirements for the creation and protection of copyright. To some extent parts of this chapter will cover the same ground, but with a specific reference to sections of the 1988 Act.

## SECTION I: MUSIC AND RECORDS

### 1 Creation of copyright

**1.1** By section 1, provided the qualification provisions referred to below (see paragraph 2) are satisfied, copyright will exist in any sound recording, or any original musical or literary work created by any person within the United Kingdom. Lyrics come within the definition of a literary work. The Act does not define what is "original", but it is well established that for a work to be original, there must be some skill or labour exercised by the author in the creation of the work.

**1.2** By section 3, copyright does not subsist in an original musical or literary work unless and until it is recorded in writing or otherwise. A work is "made" when it is recorded, ie, that is the point in time when it comes into existence as a proprietary right. There is no copyright in a musical concept or idea, even if it is performed live, unless and until it is set down in some permanent form, such as on a tape. Storing a work in a computer data base or memory will be sufficient for the purposes of constituting a recording, provided that it is a permanent storage, so that it remains capable of reproducing the material at any time. If the storage is transient, ie it is a record but only for a short space of time, after which it is wiped out, that is not a sufficient recording. It is advisable to have a print out of the stored material made as soon as possible after its creation, which can be the visible permanent set down record. Otherwise, if the data base "crashes" and is wiped out, the record of the existence of the original material is lost. A print out from a transient data base will become the permanent, record of the material, in which case the date of the print out will be the date upon which copyright protection is created. At that time the transient data base can be disregarded for copyright purposes.

**1.3** The setting down does not have to be with the author's consent, ie the person who originates the song. The fact that a composer has a bright new concept, and plays it on the piano down at the pub, but has never put it on tape or done a top line musical score for it, does not give him the exclusive right to be the first person to set it down permanently—and thus to be the author. (See paragraph **9** of chapter seven.) Technically, whoever first sets it down, the author of it, subject to specific exceptions (see paragraph **2.1**). Whose copyright it will then be is another matter. Is it essential that at all times there must exist a permanent record of the work? For example, having established it as a copyright work beyond question, what happens if the only tape recording of the composition, or the only copy of the top line are accidentally destroyed? Neither the previous legislation, nor the 1988 Act, refer to the maintaining of a permanent record as being a pre-requisite of continued copyright protection. The author or publisher will simply re-record it or re-print it. Where there are conflicting copyright claims, the date of priority of copyright existence may be crucial, but how do you prove it where there is no corroborative evidence. This is where copyright registration would be useful.

**1.4** By section 5, a sound recording means a recording of sounds, or the recording of the whole or any part of a literary, dramatic or musical work, from which the sounds may be reproduced. This is regardless of the medium on which the recording is made, or the method by which the sounds may be reproduced. There must be a device, be it a tape, disc, or some other technological gadget which, when activated whenever called upon to do so, will reproduce the sound, ie, it is a permanent storage of a means of reproducing it faithfully.

**1.5** The copyright in the recording is not to be confused with the copyright in the work recorded. For example, if a recording is made of a public domain work, the material is not protected by copyright, but the recording of it is. Anyone can make their own recording of that material, but they cannot reproduce any other recording without the consent of the owner of the copyright in it.

## 2 Qualification for copyright protection

**2.1** It is generally assumed that any original work coming into existence in the UK will have UK copyright protection, whoever the author may be, whatever his nationality, and even if he is only here on holiday. This is not necessarily so. Set out below under sections 154 and 155 of the 1988 Act are the necessary criteria which must be complied with first. Any person who does not fit the criteria will not necessarily find his works initially in the public domain, just because he has not created them originally in his own country. He will be protected by his own country's copyright law, and within the UK through the reciprocity of legal protection given by the 1988 Act, or by the copyright conventions to which the UK and most other countries are a signatory.

**2.2** By section 154 a work qualifies for copyright protection in the UK if the author was at the material time a qualified person. This can broadly be defined as:

(a) A British citizen. British nationality is defined by statute, the simplest check is to look at your passport. There is no requirement for the British citizen (or the person domiciled or resident in the UK) to have been in the UK at the time of creating the work. If a composer/artiste is making a recording outside the UK, and at the same time outside the UK composes the material which he is recording, its copyright protection is not affected.

(b) An individual domiciled or resident in the UK. The individual need not be a British citizen if he complies with either status. Neither "domiciled" nor "resident" is defined in the 1988 Act, and so will have the normal meaning attributed to them. Domicile is a rather hazy concept. A person's first domicile is that of the place where they are born, and thereafter it means the country they consider to be their permanent home, whether or not they live there much over the years. Residence is a state of being present in a country for long enough for it to be considered to be the person's current fixed base for living.

(c) A UK corporation, ie, a limited company incorporated in the UK. This will apply where, such as under section 11 (see paragraph **3.4**), the 1988 Act deems an employer to be the first owner of the copyright. A corporation is inanimate, and so cannot be the author of the work in the creative sense. There is no reference as to what would happen where, for example, the UK corporation employs an author who would not have been a qualifying person had he been the first owner of the copyright. It does not matter that the UK corporation is a wholly owned subsidiary of an American publishing company, even though both its ownership and its effective control are outside the UK.

**2.3** A work of joint authorship will qualify for copyright if at the material time any of the authors is a qualifying person. If one of the joint authors does not so qualify, only the qualifying ones will count for copyright ownership, and for calculating the copyright period applicable to the work. If the work is a joint work, where the contributions of all of the authors is indistinguishable as between them, the copyright in the whole composition will not be affected, as whatever bit might not have protection cannot be identified. For a joint work where the words are by one author and the music is by another, whichever distinct part is created by a non-qualifying person will not be protected. As already stated, while the protection may not be present as a UK originating work, it is likely to be present through the operation of an international copyright convention. The distinction is that, under a convention, the UK is recognising protection granted to the work by the copyright laws of the author's own country.

**2.4** The "material time" for assessing the qualification of the author of a work is:

(a) For an unpublished work, when it was made, ie, when it was first set down in a permanent form. If the work was written over a period of time, then the material time will have to cover a substantial part of that period. It is not likely that an author who was a qualifying person when he first started to create the work would have ceased to be one halfway through doing so, unless there was a substantial intervening period between bouts of creativity, and his status changed in the meantime. For example, someone who was not originally a qualifying person could in the meantime become a UK resident. If the question ever arose, it would be a matter of fact, depending on all of the circumstances.

(b) For a published work, when it was first published. If the author had died before publication, his qualifying status at the time immediately before his death would be the applicable test.

It is possible for the author not to have been a qualifying person at the time he wrote the work, but to have become one prior to his death. If the work is not first published prior to his death, in that case he will be deemed to have been a qualifying person when it is first published.

(c) For a sound recording, when it was made. This is not always certain. Artistes have been known to put down an instrumental track or two (on a 24 track studio tape) over a period, and then at sometime in the future put the final vocal track down. Each individual track may not have much meaning until the whole (say) 12 tracks are transferred onto a two track master tape, although the 24 track tape can be played in the studio, such as when mixing the individual tracks. Strictly speaking, the first instrumental track is a recording in its own right. Each time another track is put on the tape, it might be considered as a new individual recording, as the sounds are on separate sound channels, although set out on the same physical medium. The complete mixed recording is first created as an amalgamated unit of all the separate tracks when it is transferred to a single master tape, and that is probably the first date that, the work as a whole is set down or made. If the multitrack tape is taken as the evidence of the recording having been made, then a different recording will be "made" every time a new track is put down on the tape, and the complete recording is "made" when the last track is put down.

In the case of a sound recording, there is a distinction between the date it was made, and the date when it is first released to the public, ie, not releasing it commercially does not increase its potential copyright protection period.

**2.5** By section 155 either a work or a sound recording qualifies for UK copyright protection if it is first published in the UK, or in any other country to which the 1988 Act extends. "Published" means the issue of copies to the public, and includes making it available to the public by means of an electronic retrieval system. Simultaneous publication in the UK and in any other country does not affect the UK qualification. For this purpose publication elsewhere within 30 days prior to the UK publication is deemed to be simultaneous. This section is independent of the operation of section 154, which does not specifically require the first publication of the work or the recording to be in the UK. Section 155 extends copyright protection to material first published in the UK. First publication is treated as a qualification giving the same rights to a work as if it were protected under section 154. If a work or recording is first published in the UK, the qualification criteria set out in section 154 do not have to apply.

## 3 Identity of author

*Author*

**3.1** By section 9 the author of an original work means the person who creates it. In this context "creates" means to first make or set down the work; it does not necessarily mean to have the original idea. In the case of a sound recording, the author will be the person by whom the arrangements necessary for the making of the recording are undertaken. It is not clear whether this is to be taken literally, as different people may "make arrangements". The MD of a record company may agree that a recording can be made; the A & R department may book the studios; or the producer may organise the precise arrangements and control the transition of the artiste's performance onto a multitrack tape ready for mixing. It would be reasonable to assume that, in this example, the author would be treated as the record company, under the direction and control of which these people will be working. It may also be the first owner of the copyright in the recording.

Where a work is computer generated, the author will be the person who makes the arrangements necessary for the creation of the work. Ordinarily this will mean the programmer, who is creating the music through his instructions, comprising the computer program, which, when run through the computer and being attached to the right music electronic synthesiser, plays music. Electronically created music must still follow the ordinary rules for the creation of copyright, ie, it must be set down in a permanent form. The program itself will be in a permanent form, but it has no visible relationship to music. However, if by "playing" the program, music will be produced, it complies with the requirements. This will apply to a digital recording, where the components of sound are captured electronically, developed and can be reproduced through the use of first rate equipment without any discernible sound quality loss.

By section 178 "computer generated" means that the work is generated by computer in circumstances such that there is no human author of the work. "Computer" is not defined. To not have a human author must mean that the process of human input or effort goes through some intermediary process which does not itself produce music as a natural consequence, such as through a program. A music synthesiser is a computer, but if by touching a series of keys music is thereby instantly generated, it is not functioning any differently from a piano or guitar in essence. The copyright result would be the same, and the author would be easier to identify.

If the work is already recorded or written down in musical notation, and the use of the computer is to arrange the music, copyright will already exist in the work, and it will not be originated as such yet again by the computer—it will simply be a different version. Following the normal rules, if the new version is sufficiently different from the original work, it can have an independent copyright of its own.

As the author of a work is not necessarily the first owner of the copyright in it (see paragraph **3.4**) it may be necessary to establish who is the author for determining who is the first copyright owner.

*Joint authors*

**3.2** By section 10 a work of joint authorship means a work produced by the collaboration of two or more authors, in which the contribution of each author is not distinct from that of the other author or authors. An example would be "music by A and B", or where it is "music and lyrics by A and B". In either case the copyright in the whole composition is owned by them in equal shares, in the absence of any agreement to the contrary. If it is "music by A and lyrics by B", that credit implies that each is the author of the whole of his distinct and identifiable contribution, and in that case separate copyrights have been created. The fact that they are intended to be one composition does not affect the issue. They are each capable of being independently reproduced or performed as works in their own right.

In that example, as the music and the lyrics are independent copyrights, the rights in each can be dealt with separately for licensing, such as for authorising the reproduction of the lyrics in a book of poems, and where only the music might be put on a film sound track as background music. Where the example is "music by A and B and words by B", then each of them will be treated independently for crediting the relevant copyright ownership.

*Unknown author*

**3.3** The identity of the author is only considered to be unknown if it cannot be ascertained by reasonable enquiry. Even if the author of a work is not known, logically the work must be in a permanent form, otherwise nobody would know of its existence. That may be a top line or a tape, so reasonable enquiries can be made as to its origin, or who performed the work on the tape, or where the possessor of the tape got it from. If there is no known author, how can it be shown that the work is in fact protected by copyright? Copyright cannot be claimed by assumption, in the sense of: "Here's a work with no known author or copyright owner, I'll claim it until he comes along". There is nobody to claim it, to protect it, to pay copyright royalties to, to licence its use, and if the unknown author never appears, for all practical purposes the work may as well have been in the public domain. All of this might apply, for example, to a tape of songs which is received by a publisher with no covering letter, no identity on the tape label, and no means of identifying the sender—who never thereafter contacts the publisher. If it is good commercial material, the publisher should publish it and get it recorded, claim the copyright, and hold it in trust for the rightful owner should he ever turn up. It would be a pity to waste it, and it is reasonable to assume that the author wanted it to be exploited, or he would not have sent it in to the publisher. Advertising for him after achieving success would produce a host of "authors", all willing to participate in the composer's share of earnings, and apologising profusely for not having contacted the publisher sooner. If his identity is unknown, but subsequently the author is discovered, and his claim is validated to the satisfaction of the publisher, from then on his authorship is recognised in the usual way (see paragraph **4.2**).

*First owner of copyright*

**3.4** By section 11 the author of a work is the first owner of the copyright in it, except that where a literary or musical work is made by an employee in the course of his employment, his employer is the first owner of any copyright in the work. There is a distinction between legally being deemed to be the first owner of the copyright in the work, and having the right to have the copyright assigned from the author, who is the first owner. In the first case the author has never had any legal rights in the work, not even at the moment of creation. In the second case, the author owns all of the copyright in the work, until it is assigned by him. An assignment is not needed from an author in the first case to vest the copyright in the employer; in the second case the person entitled to the copyright does not have any legal rights in it without the assignment. Meanwhile he would have beneficial rights in it. A practical aspect is that if, for any reason, the purported assignment by an author in the second case category is invalid, despite the intention that the assignee should acquire the copyright, he does not do so in law, until that invalidity is rectified. This can arise through sloppy drafting where, whatever else may be stated, there is no specific reference to the copyright being assigned.

Examples of what are commonly believed to be within the employee relationship are where A commissions B to write an original song for him; and where A who cannot write musical notation, asks B to do so for him as he plays the music live. The first example creates the status of an independent contractor, not that of an employment, so a specific assignment of copyright would be required. In the second example, if he were to do that from a tape recording of the song, then copyright would already have been created before notation, as the tape would be the first "making" of the work in a permanent form. If properly established in a letter, the second example should come within the definition of employment.

For the employee to be caught under this section, his specific job must entail the creation of the copyright material. For example, if the copyright manager of a publishing company writes songs in his spare time, they will belong to him. If he is employed as a song writer and musical arranger, the company will own any copyrights he creates in doing his job. That will be the case whether he creates it during office hours, or whether he does so while soaking in the bath at home.

Even experienced composers, or even publishing companies, do not always follow the correct procedures. The essential thing in any case is to have a written agreement specifically referring to the copyright, and stating that it will belong to A, even though technically B may be the author, and even if this is a duplication of a right arising under the 1988 Act. Whatever the circumstances, an oral agreement will not suffice. For an employee the copyright assignments can be referred to in his service contract, although the 1988 Act is clear. But it draws the parties' attention to the point, and any queries or misunderstandings can be resolved at the time the contract is signed.

## 4 Duration of copyright

*Normal rule*

**4.1** By section 12 copyright in a literary or musical work expires at the end of the period of 50 years from the end of the calendar year in which the author dies, except as set out below. In contrast to section 2(3) of the 1956 Act, this will apply whether or not the author's works have been published prior to his death. Thus, the copyright period for a work published posthumously will expire 50 years after the author's death. For this purpose "author" ordinarily refers to the first copyright owner, ie normally the composer or lyric writer. Where the author himself is not the first owner of the copyright (such as where his publisher is), nevertheless his date of death is the relevant one for calculating the 50 year period. If that were not the case, and if his employer were a company, there could be a perpetual copyright period, as a company does not "die". Copyright may be owned by a company, but its author will have been a person. Where the composition seems to be a perpetual "golden oldie", the publisher must make a note of the date of the death of the author. For many ordinary songs the total copyright period may be academic, as they are sunk without trace after a few years.

Section 2(3) of the 1956 Act stated that if a work had not been published by the date of the death of the author, the copyright period would be for 50 years from the date of first publication. This is not the case under the 1988 Act, if a work is now first published thirty years after the author's death, it has a copyright life of only 20 years. Schedule 1 of the 1988 Act contains transitional provisions for posthumous works. By paragraph 12(2)(a), if time is currently running for a posthumously published work, copyright in it will expire when it would have expired under the 1956 Act. By paragraph 12(4)(a), if the author has died prior to the 1988 Act coming into force, and if there are works of his still unpublished, they will have a copyright life of 50 years from the end of 1989, whenever they are published.

*Unknown author*

**4.2** If the work is of unknown authorship, copyright expires at the end of the period of 50 years from the end of the calendar year in which it is first made available to the public, whatever form that publishing may take. "Making available to the public" includes performance in public and being broadcast, or being included in a cable programme service. The practical difficulties of administering the copyright are referred to in paragraph **3.3**. If within that 50 years the author's identity becomes known, this rule will revert to the normal 50 years from death. However, if the author's identity only becomes known after the expiry of 50 years from the year in which the work was first made publicly available, there is no reversion to the normal rule so as to revive the copyright, ie, it remains in the public domain.

If the author was known, but having written his only eternal hit song he sank back into obscurity and disappeared without trace, what happens if the publisher, despite all reasonable efforts, cannot establish whether he is alive or dead? The 50 year period is triggered by the composer's death. He is not an "unknown author", so the 50 year period does not start to run until the author's death has occurred. The copyright cannot be perpetual, and there must come a time when his death must be presumed. The principle does not appear to have been tested.

*Computer generated work*
**4.3** If the work is computer generated, copyright expires at the end of the period of 50 years from the end of the calendar year in which the work was made. This refers to where the work is first made by computer generation, ie, when it first attains copyright protection. If an existing work, which has fallen into the public domain, is re-created by computer generation to make it multi-channel, or to produce a sound quality for it which it had never previously enjoyed, that technological intervention will not revive the original copyright in the work. It may create a new copyright arrangement of it. There is an interesting point here. There will be two potential "makings" of the computer generating "device", the source code (the blue print) of the program, and the program itself, being the working environment of the source code. This has an analogy in the 24 track studio tape being the source code for a recording, and the fully mixed two track master tape being the program which can be run to reproduce the music. It is likely to be assumed that the final program itself as archived onto a data base or other permanent storage form, will be the "making" for calculating the 50 year period, as the source code is only the technical instruction of how the program is assembled.

*Joint authors*
**4.4** If the identity of all of the joint authors is known, the 50 year period will start on the death of the last of them to die. If they are not all known, it will start on the death of the last of the known authors to die. In this case "joint" means, for example, "music and words by A and B" in indistinguishable portions. Where it is "music by A and words by B", as each of the words and the music have separate copyrights, the normal rules will apply to each of them in connection with their individual authors. If A outlives B by ten years, the copyright in his section of the work (the music) will be protected for ten years longer than the section created by B (the words). It is also possible to have "music by A and B with words by B". In this case the period of copyright in the music follows the above rules, and the period of copyright in the words follows the rule in paragraph **4.1**.

*Sound recordings*
**4.5** By section 13 copyright in a sound recording expires at the end of the period of 50 years from the end of the calendar year in which it is made, or 50 years from the end of the year in which the sound recording first became available to the public, provided that first release is made within 50 years from the date the record was made. In respect of recordings made between 1 June 1957 and the date the 1988 Act

became effective, and which by that time had not yet been published, the copyright period will be 50 years from that effective date. If it is published during that time, the 50 years will run from the date of publication. The copyright in the recording itself is not connected with the copyright in the work performed on the recording. Therefore, when the copyright in a recording expires, that does not mean that anybody can do anything with it as they see fit, such as where the consent of the owner of the copyright in the recorded work must be obtained. An example would be where it is proposed to reproduce the public domain recording containing a copyright work on the sound track of a new film.

## 5 Rights of copyright owner

By section 16 the owner of the copyright in a work has the exclusive right to do the following acts in the United Kingdom. The copyright in a work is infringed by a person who, without the licence of the copyright owner, does or authorises another to do any of the restricted acts referred to below, directly or indirectly, in relation to the whole or to any substantial part of the work.

*To copy the work*

**5.1** By section 17 copying means reproducing the work in any material form, including storage in a computer data base. There is no exception which states that copying for private use only will not be an infringement. Contrast this with paragraph **6.2**, where the secondary infringement is not incurred by having an infringing copy only for private and domestic use. There seems to be no legal implication that possession of an infringing copy within that exception must be because the possessor made it. Under section 182 of the 1988 Act, making an unauthorised recording of a performance "for private or domestic use" is not an infringement of the performer's rights. Why can a person make a copy of a copyright work in the same circumstances and not be an infringer? This is not a suggestion, but the differences are not consistent, although they are an attempt to live with the realities of life.

The unauthorised recording of video programmes for private viewing is a primary purpose for having the machine. The same principle was taken up in the *Amstrad* case (see Appendix III), where CBS and others sought a declaration against Amstrad that selling double deck tape recorders, which enable the high speed transfer of recorded tape material onto a clean tape encouraged and facilitated the breaching of the Copyright Act 1956, and should therefore be unlawful. The claim went to the House of Lords, who found in favour of Amstrad.

A material form is not necessarily one which is instantly readable, it is a permanent form from which reproductions of the work can be made. Copying also includes making copies which are transient; an example would be retrieving information in a data base onto a screen. Although what is visible on the screen is not itself permanent (it is erased when the screen is switched off), it will remain "permanently" on the screen until removed. Once it has been removed, it can only be shown again by calling it up from the data base, and therefore it is a separate copy.

The relevance of the data base aspect is that one data base held in the basement of a building in London (or anywhere else) can be accessed by terminals in any part of the world, in any number, at any time, and for any length of time, limited only by access channels and the hardware sophistication controlling the data base. If a terminal in Tokyo accesses the data base and puts the material on screen, a printer in Tokyo can then be used to make a hard copy of the screen display. Transmission by fax is also the making of a copy, ie, literally a facsimile. A data base means of storage and retrieval is not likely to be a common form of breaching the copyright in music, unless the notation is set out in the data base as well as the lyrics.

There are limited and controlled circumstances in which a copyright work may be reproduced (see paragraph 7).

*To issue copies of the work to the public*

**5.2** By section 18 this means putting into circulation in the United Kingdom or elsewhere copies of the work not previously put into circulation. The restricted right is the right of being entitled to be the first to issue copies to the public. Once that has been done by or with the consent of the copyright owner, he cannot stop any subsequent importation, distribution or sale of copies of the work. As audio and audio visual items are dealt with in the same section, and as the restricted right relates to copies "not previously put into circulation", the authorised issue to the public of sheet music would not mean that a recording could be issued by other parties, as that would not be such a copy.

In respect of sound recordings, this also means the rental of copies to the public. This is not limited to the first rental, it means any rental at any time. Any party wishing to rent copies of audio or audio visual recordings to the public needs a licence from the owners of the copyrights in them, but if a licensing scheme is established under section 65, it will be deemed upon the appropriate licence payment. As video rental, for example, is such big business, the licensing of the rights is strictly administered.

*To perform show or play the work in public*

**5.3** By section 19 this includes any means of visual or acoustic presentation, and "public" includes for example, lectures or speeches. There is no reference to the public having to pay to trigger the offence. "Public" is not defined, but will include invited audiences as well as random attendance, whatever the size. It need not be performed in a public place, eg, a restricted membership club's inner sanctum may not be considered by the club to be a public place, but for the purpose of this section it could be. A small gathering of friends at a private house will not be a "public" gathering. Application of the definition will depend on the circumstances (see paragraph **6.5**).

*To broadcast the work or to include it in a cable programme service*

**5.4** It is possible to broadcast a work in limited circumstances, such as through a factory-wide public address system.

*To make an adaptation of the work or to do any of the above in relation to an adaptation of a work*

**5.5** By section 21 an adaptation includes the translation of a lyric, and an arrangement or transcription of music. An adaptation of lyrics can also be a version of the story told or illustrated mainly by means of pictures in a form suitable for reproduction in a book, paper or magazine.

## 6 Secondary infringement of copyright

**6.1** Secondary infringement occurs where the infringer has not himself done the infringing, eg by copying the work, but has or uses infringing copies or articles. The following sections define different activities which will constitute secondary infringement. The most common form in the context of secondary infringement will relate to sound and audio visual recordings, although that could include secondary infringement of the copyright composition contained in it.

**6.2** By section 22 the copyright in a work is infringed by a person who, without the licence of the copyright owner, imports into the UK otherwise than for his private and domestic use, an article which is, and which he knows or has reason to believe is, an infringing copy of the work. Where the importer or possessor has only the one copy, the defence is available, if it can be proved. But if that one copy is not an ordinary cassette, but a clean master copy of the recording in professional tape format universally used to originate duplication of commercial copies, the defence should fail. There is a curious anomaly between section 17 (unauthorised copying) and this section. It is not legal under section 17 to record copyright works for private and domestic use, but it is legal to possess such an infringing article in those circumstances. Private and domestic use implies that no further copying or distribution will take place.

**6.3** By section 23 the copyright in a work is infringed by a person who, without the licence of the copyright owner:

(a) possesses in the course of a business;
(b) sells or lets for hire;
(c) exhibits in public or distributes in the course of a business;
(d) distributes, otherwise than in the course of a business, to such an extent as to affect prejudicially the owner of the copyright

an article which is, and which he knows or has reason to believe is, an infringing copy of the work.

This is a clear statement that any public dealing in an infringing copy is illegal. The inclusion of (d) is to catch the entrepreneurial part timer, who has a sideline in dealing in illegal tapes, or other copyright works. It is a logical extension of section 22, where possession for private and domestic use may be accepted for one infringing copy, but not for a garage full of them, even if they were all different. The "extent" element in (d) makes the offence completely flexible to the disadvantage of the entrepreneur, as even one infringing copy affects the copyright owner prejudicially, ie, the loss of revenue or royalty on the sale of the item. The ordinary definition of what constitutes a business is wide, and would extend to an habitual course of action. If the entrepreneur only once ever "stores them for a friend", he would not be in breach of (a) above, as it would not be in the course of a business. In this case section 22 would apply, because a garageful of infringing material would not constitute private use. Either way the entrepreneur would be liable to legal action.

**6.4** By section 24 copyright in a work is infringed by a person who without the licence of the copyright owner:

(a) makes;
(b) imports into the UK;
(c) possesses in the course of a business;
(d) sells or lets for hire, or offers or exposes for hire

an article specifically designed or adapted for making copies of that work, knowing or having reason to believe that it is to be used to make infringing copies. There is a legitimate business in making copies of, for example, personal videotapes of an individual's holidays, or a business's internal executive training videotapes, which are its own property. This copying is likely to be in single or very small number units. If 1,000 copies are required, it must put the copying company on notice that they are likely to be used for a wide public distribution. In that case, if there is any suspicion as to whether the tapes are legitimate, the copying company should make reasonable enquiries. Companies which provide pressing and distribution facilities to third party producers of recordings could come within this section (under (a)) if they turn a blind eye to reproducing what has every sign of being infringing material. It is the knowledge of intent of the copying company which changes a legitimate business into a means of commercial production of illegal copies of copyright tapes, whether they are audio or audio visual recordings.

**6.5** By section 25 where the copyright in a work is infringed at a place of public entertainment, any person who gave permission for that place to be used for the performance is also liable for the infringement, unless when he gave permission he believed on reasonable grounds that the performance would not infringe copyright. That might include the committee of a club, or a hall manager. This section puts the onus on a hall proprietor to check positively that any material to be performed will not result in a secondary infringement of third party copyrights. This is not likely to be done, and in most cases is not practical. Would assurance from the person hiring the place of entertainment be sufficient? How could it possibly be checked?

This is to catch people and premises where the intended use is illegal, and when challenged, those who put on the show disappear, and the only person in sight is the hall proprietor who denies all knowledge of the intended and actual illegal performance. Assuming that proprietors become aware of the effect of this section, they should ensure that all contracts for the hire of the premises have appropriate clauses for their safety, and clear notices should be put up in dressing rooms, or elsewhere backstage, prohibiting the performance of infringing material.

**6.6** By section 26 where a copyright work is infringed by public performance by means of any apparatus:

(a) the person who supplied the apparatus is liable if he knew or had reason to believe that the apparatus was likely to be used to infringe copyright;

(b) an occupier of the premises where the performance took place is liable if he knew or had reason to believe that the apparatus was likely to be used to infringe copyright;

(c) a person who supplied a copy of a sound recording used to infringe copyright is liable if he knew or had reason to believe that it was likely to be used to infringe copyright.

Section 26 tidies up the other possibilities of who should have liability for the showing of infringing material. Without the "knowledge", or the "having reason to believe", a person would not contravene this section. The proprietor of any business that rents equipment out which might be used for this kind of purpose ought also to ensure that his terms and conditions cover the position.

## 7 Permitted acts

*Fair dealing*

**7.1.1** It is recognised that there must be certain permitted uses of copyright material which are not for commercial purposes, or which are not intended to deprive the copyright owner of any privilege or income, and therefore should not constitute infringement. There is no definition in the 1988 Act of "fair dealing", the facts of each case will have to be considered on their own merits.

**7.1.2** By section 29 fair dealing with a work for the purpose of research or private study does not infringe the copyright in the work. This section refers to the ability of a *bona fide* student to make copies of relevant parts of copyright works which he needs for the purposes of his study. If his need extends to a whole work, it may be cheaper to buy it. This relaxation would not give him the right to put together a students' "Acme Exam Passing" compendium of copyright material for the purposes of wider distribution.

**7.1.3** By section 30 fair dealing with a work for the purpose of criticism or review does not infringe its copyright, provided that it is accompanied by a sufficient acknowledgement. A reviewer may feel the need to reproduce passages from a copyright work in the course of preparing a review or artistic criticism, to point out the best or the worst of it, and to illustrate the rationale behind his conclusions. This might, for example, refer to a song's lyrics. The review should only reproduce pertinent parts of the work. The reviewer should also ensure that there is also printed next to it the correct copyright notice, and any other ownership details.

**7.1.4** By section 31 copyright in a work is not infringed by its incidental inclusion in an artistic work, sound recording, film, broadcast or cable programme. A musical work shall not be regarded as incidental inclusion in an artistic work, sound recording, film, reporter, recording interviews with members of the public, was standing by chance outside a clothes boutique, and copyright music being played in the shop could be heard in the background, that would be incidental, and not a breach of copyright. If a TV programme is being recorded, and the script calls for an actor to switch on the radio, out of which comes a recognisable part of a copyright musical work, that is not incidental use of it for the purposes of the 1988 Act. It may be incidental in the context of the TV programme, so interpretation of "incidental" is important.

*Educational purposes*

**7.2.1** By section 32 copyright in a sound recording or work is not infringed by its being copied in the course of instruction provided the copying:

(a) Is done by a person giving or receiving instruction. It would not be an offence if the class wrote out all of the music as part of its educational training, provided it could be shown that was genuinely the case, and not a means of avoiding the purchase of it, such as for a concert performance.

(b) In the case of a literary or musical work, the copying is not by means of a reprographic process, ie, it must not be a facsimile copy, and it must not involve the use of an appliance for making copies (see paragraph **7.2.3**). The inference in this section is that it refers to the reproduction of the whole of the work. Section 36 applies to passages from works.

The printed music side of all publishers' businesses has suffered considerably by the mass reproduction of, for example, sheet music for a choir or a class, as it wrongfully deprives the publisher and the composer of their rightful income. Short of using a reprographic system, any copying by the person giving the tuition will be by word processor or by hand. Even a word processor will be illegal, as it is an appliance used for making multiple copies. If a "fair use" copy under this section is subsequently dealt with in a manner which is an infringement, the "fair use" defence will not apply in respect of that infringing dealing. It is not a defence if the copy of the work used in the photo copier was not an infringement when it was made, therefore further copies of an initially non-infringing copy will themselves be infringements.

**7.2.2** By section 34 the performance of a sound recording or a work before an audience consisting of teachers and pupils at an educational establishment for instruction, or in the course of the activities of the establishment, is not a public performance for the purposes of infringement of copyright.

**7.2.3** By section 36 reprographic copies of passages from literary or musical published works may be made by an educational establishment for instruction, provided that no more than 1% of the work may be copied in any calendar quarter. This section can be differentiated from section 32, because it has two limiting factors. The first is that only "passages" may be reproduced in this way. The second is that only 1% of the work may be copied in any quarter. Whether this is a practical limitation remains to be seen. A passage constituting 1% of probably all musical works will not be worth reproducing. The need is for copies of the whole work, in which case the section 32 relaxation will be the only means of doing so. Copying is not authorised if licences are available for that purpose from the copyright owners, and the person making the copies knew, or ought to have known, that fact. Any educational establishment will be aware that consent must be obtained, and by experience should know whether it will be granted. It may be granted upon the payment of a per copy licence fee, which would still be less than the purchase cost of the same number of copies from a retail source.

*Libraries*

**7.3** By section 39 the librarian of a prescribed library may make and supply a copy of a part of a published edition of a work provided that:

(a) the persons only require them for research or study;
(b) only one copy is made;
(c) the copy is charged for at not less than the cost attributable to the production of the copy.

How much is a "part" to be copied will depend on the individual circumstances. It may be a page, or even a chapter. From experience the librarian will know when the request sounds odd.

## 8 Moral rights

For the first time in UK copyright law there is now included a "moral right" concept to protect copyright works from mistreatment, and to give the author the right to be identified with it. This provision enables an author to have statutory rights of certain controls which, until now, have been a grey area. Most European copyright legislation contains similar concepts, and the 1988 Act is the opportunity to update the whole UK copyright law into line with EC laws for the wider European market, and with the intended 1992 unification in mind.

*Author's identity*

**8.1.1** By section 77 the author of a work has a right to be identified as its author (providing the right has been "asserted" under section 78) whenever:

(a) the work is published commercially;
(b) copies of a sound recording of the work are issued to the public;
(c) a film of which the sound track includes the work is shown in public, or copies of the film are issued to the public.

The identification must be clear and reasonably prominent. Authors are normally given the proper credit for works, as part of negotiating the relevant contract. Section 77 is to cover the position where, for some reason, that does not happen.

**8.1.2** By section 78 a person does not infringe the rights of an author under section 77 to be identified with his work, unless the author has asserted his right to be so identified. He can do that in general terms, but may also do so in connection with any transaction:

(a) On an assignment of copyright in the work, by including a statement that he asserts his right to be identified. The assignee and anyone claiming through him will be bound by the assertion.
(b) In respect of anything else, by giving written notice to the same effect. Anyone to whose notice the assertion is brought will be bound by it.

**8.1.3** If the author makes no written assertion, he does not have the statutory right to be identified with the work. The author of a work is normally given proper credit in connection with it, so the statutory right is reinforcing common practice, to cover situations where the author is not so identified, with the result that he is in some way prejudiced. The right of assertion exists continuously, it is not compulsory, and it is not waived if not exercised. In an action for infringement of the right, the court will take into account any delay which may have been incurred in making an assertion. Although the section does not refer to it, it must be possible to be too late in certain circumstances to make an assertion. If a number of works are printed, or recorded, inadvertently omitting the identity of the author (who has not previously asserted), if he then does so, the party should not have to scrap the copies already printed or pressed and distributed. The matter would be rectified next time round, or perhaps by a sticker if that is feasible and economical.

*Derogatory treatment*

**8.2.1** By section 80 the author of a work has the right to not have his work subjected to derogatory treatment. "Treatment" means any addition to, deduction from, alteration to or adaptation of the work, not being a translation of an arrangement or transcription involving more than a change of key or register. This section may affect the public distortion of the work which is sometimes excused by stating "in the style of" the author whose work is imitated. The treatment of a work is "derogatory" if it amounts to a distortion or mutilation of the work, or if it is otherwise prejudicial to the honour or reputation of the author. This may be a matter of degree, or of opinion, but the section gives the author the right to prevent his work from being plagiarised, or so presented as to demean the intended interpretation of the work. This would not apply to authorised versions or adaptations.

The right is infringed by a person who publishes commercially, performs in public, broadcasts or includes in a cable programme service a derogatory treatment of the work, or issues to the public copies of a film or sound recording of, or including, a derogatory treatment of the work.

**8.2.2** By section 83 the right granted by section 80 is also infringed by a person who:

(a) possesses in the course of a business;
(b) sells or lets for hire, or offers or exposes for sale or hire;
(c) in the course of a business exhibits in public or distributes;
(d) distributes otherwise than in the course of a business so as to affect prejudicially the honour or reputation of the author.

An article which is, and which he knows or has reason to believe is, an infringing article. An infringing article is a work, or a copy of a work, which has been subjected to derogatory treatment, and has been, or is likely to be, published commercially, broadcast or performed in public.

*False attribution*

**8.3** If a person has attributed to him a song he did not write, or music he did not compose, it is either an error or a deliberate ploy to give the work a credibility and value to which it is not entitled. In common law terms this would come under "passing off", and the attributed author would claim an injunction and damages. The 1988 Act has, within the limited copyright area, given a statutory framework to deal with false attribution.

By section 84 a person has the right not to have a work falsely attributed to him as its author. In this context "attribution" means a statement, express or implied, as to who is the author. The attribution can be made in respect of issuing copies of the work to the public, or broadcasting it with such a false attribution being made. This section also applies where, contrary to the facts, a work is falsely represented as being an adaptation of the work of a person.

This section would not apply where the author is the author of the work, but does not want to be known as its author, or to be associated with it. It would not be a false attribution, it would only be an unwanted one.

Infringers are those people who issue to the public, broadcast or perform any item with a false attribution.

## 9 Dealings with rights in copyright works

*Transmission of a copyright*

**9.1.1** By section 90 copyright is transmissable by assignment, testamentary disposition, or by operation of law, as personal or moveable property. Any transmission may be partial, ie as to one or more of the rights which are contained within the overall right of copyright, and as to part only of the copyright period. An assignment of copyright is not effective unless it is in writing, signed by or on behalf of the assignor.

**9.2** A licence granted by a copyright owner is binding on every successor in title to his interest in the copyright, except a purchaser in good faith for valuable consideration and without notice (actual or constructive) of the licence. This will also apply where he is the prospective owner of copyright under section 91. A substantial part of the music publishing industry is based upon copyright licensing, and all principal publishing agreements specify that any sub-publishing licence is not to be affected on any dealing with the copyrights in the compositions. Where any compositions are already published and sub-published, there should never be a situation where there are any silent unknown licences which could be prejudiced under this section. A copyright licence should always oblige the copyright owner to inform any other relevant party of the existence of the licence.

By section 91 where, by a valid written assignment, a person is legally and beneficially entitled to the ownership of future copyrights, he may validly assign those future copyrights to another person. When those copyrights come into existence, that assignee will be able to enforce his rights accordingly. For his own safety the assignee should try to short circuit the intervening agreements, and get an assignment direct from the author, or whoever was the original contracting party.

**9.3** By section 93 where, under a bequest in a will, a person is entitled to an original document or other material thing embodying a copyright work which was not published before the death of the testator, then unless the will specifies otherwise, the bequest shall be construed as including any copyright in the work owned by the testator. For that to be the case, either the testator would need to be the author of the work, or he would have to show that the copyright in the work had been assigned to him while he was alive. If the testator did not own the copyright in the unpublished work, the ordinary rule would apply. If there is no means of establishing whether or not the copyright had been assigned to the testator, any commercial or proprietary use would create the risk of the author of the work, or his literary heirs, raising an objection.

There has always been a separation between ownership of, say, a musical manuscript, and the copyright in the music set out on that manuscript. Prior to the 1988 Act acquisition of the manuscript as a bequest did not also transfer the copyright in its contents. It remedies what has often been an injustice, where the testator (who was not aware of the technicalities of copyright law) assumed that a bequest of the manuscript would transfer also the copyright of its contents. The section still allows the testator to make the distinction, such as where he may want the ownership of invaluable manuscripts to go to a museum, but wants his heirs to own and benefit from the copyright in the contents of the manuscript. In such examples the museum would have to obtain the consent of the copyright owner before any commercial use of the manuscript could be made.

**9.4** By section 94 moral rights are not assignable. By section 95 on the death of a person entitled to moral rights, under sections 77 and 80, the right passes as he directs in his will. If there is no such direction, but the copyright in the work forms part of his estate, the right passes to whom the copyright passes. Whoever then becomes the owner of the rights can assert them in their own name. The identity of the author would not change, but the right to prevent derogatory treatment of the work would be to the same extent as the author would have been able to do.

## 10 Remedies for infringement

**10.1** By section 96 an infringement of copyright is actionable by the copyright owner, who can claim injunctions, damages, accounts and any other relief available to a property right claim. This right is not available to a licensee, who only has the limited use of the rights, not their ownership. A licensee can be authorised to take all actions that would have been available to the copyright owner, but the copyright owner may nevertheless have to be a party to the legal proceedings.

**10.2** By section 97 where, in an action for infringement of copyright, it is shown that at the time of infringement the defendant did not know, and had no reason to believe, that the work was copyright, the plaintiff is not entitled to damages, but can make any other claim. Proving no knowledge of copyright may be difficult, particularly if the breach is made in the course of a commercial use of the work. In the case of a musical composition, whether it is in printed form, or in the form of an audio or audio visual device, any user must have at least a suspicion that it is copyright material, and owned by somebody. The only music available will have been published or recorded, and in most cases the infringement will be high volume unauthorised reproduction for commercial distribution.

**10.3** In a copyright infringement claim, where the infringer is well aware that the material being infringed is copyright the court may award additional damages to the copyright owner having regard to:

(a) the flagrancy of the infringement;

(b) any benefit received by the defendant by reason of the infringement.

Copyright infringers, particularly the illegal manufacturing ones, have taken the view that the risk they run is, at worst, that they would be ordered by the court to pay to the rightful recipients what it would have cost them in copyright royalties and any other payments due on the sale of a recording. These would include a licence royalty per unit in the case of a normal authorised territorial manufacturing deal. Legal costs are an occupational hazard. Under section 97 the court now has a statutory guideline whereby the copyright owner can not only be recompensed for what he has lost in revenue (compensatory damages), he can claim punitive damages to such a level as will effectively deprive the infringer of any benefit he may have gained, not necessarily just at the expense of the copyright owner. A claim under this section may have a greater effect than the present claim for "an account of profits". The damages can now also be influenced by the flagrancy of the breach, ie, the more brazen the infringer, the greater can be the damages awarded against him.

**10.4** By section 99 where a person:

(a) has an infringing copy of work in his possession custody or control in the course of a business;

(b) has in his possession, custody or control an article specifically designed or adapted for making copies of a copyright work knowing, or having reason to believe, that it has been or is to be used to make infringing copies the copyright owner may apply to the court for an order that the infringing article or copy be delivered up to him. By the time a court order has been obtained, even under the Anton Pillar system, the infringing goods may have disappeared. This is the usual means whereby discovered infringements are seized, and presumably ultimately destroyed. The fact that the infringer has incurred considerable expense in buying cassettes, or making the copy records, is not material—he cannot ask that they be wiped off and sent back to him. That is one of the risks of infringing. By section 114 an application may be made to the court for an order that an infringing copy delivered up by an infringer under section 99, or seized under section 100 (see **10.5** below) shall be forfeited to the copyright owner, or destroyed or otherwise dealt with as the court thinks fit.

**10.5** By section 100 an infringing copy of a work which is immediately available for sale or hire, and in respect of which the copyright owner would be entitled to apply for an order under section 99, may be seized and detained by him (subject to any court order under section 114) provided that:

(a) before anything is seized, notice of the time and place of the proposed seizure must be given to a local police station;

(b) a person may enter premises to which the public has access, but may not seize anything in the possession or custody or control of a person at a permanent or regular place of business of his, and may not use any force;

(c) when anything is seized, there shall be left at the place of seizure a notice in the prescribed form containing the prescribed particulars as to the person by whom the seizure was made, and the grounds on which it is made.

Because of the restrictions placed on this right of action, it is not an effective alternative to the section 99 or any other "search and seize" orders available from the court. It might be of use against street traders, but without any court order it would be advisable to have police in attendance, assuming the street traders skilled look out system can be beaten.

**10.6** By section 104 where a name purporting to be that of the author appears in copies of the work as published, or when it was made, he shall be presumed to be the author, and that the work was not made in circumstances whereby he would not own or retain the copyright in the work (see paragraph **8.3**).

**10.7** By section 105 in respect of copies of a sound recording issued to the public with a label stating that:

(a) a named person is the copyright owner;
(b) the recording was first published in a specified year or in a specified country

the label will be presumed correct until the contrary is proved. These are presumptions in legal proceedings, to form a base from which proper investigations can be undertaken. The information on the products would be relevant for examining any claim that the defendant had no reason to believe that the products were infringements.

## SECTION II: RIGHTS IN PERFORMANCES

### 11 Performers' rights

This Part of the 1988 Act is in substitution for the Dramatic and Musical Performers' Protection Act 1958, and the Performers' Protection Act 1972. The purpose of these statutory provisions is to protect a performer from the unauthorised misappropriation of rights in the product of his performances.

The right to make a recording of a performance, and the right to exploit that recording are not necessarily the same. If the recording is an infringement due to lack of the performer's consent, any dealing with it is also an infringement, whoever owns the recording. If consent is given, and the recording is authorised, thereafter the performer has no control over what happens to the recording.

**11.1** By section 180 "performance" includes a live performance given by one or more individuals being a musical performance, or the performance of a variety act or any similar presentation. Any professional performance by an artiste will come within this definition. It does not have to be before an audience, it can be in the studio or anywhere else. "Performance" will cover rehearsals, it does not have to be the final polished version. It may not even be planned; if an artiste does an impromptu song with a busker in Leicester Square, that is a performance. A performance is a qualifying performance if it is given by a qualifying individual, or takes place in a qualifying country.

"Recording" in relation to a performance means a film or sound recording:

(a) made directly from the live performance;
(b) made from a broadcast of, or cable programme including, the performance;
(c) made directly or indirectly from another recording of the performance.

**11.2** By section 181 a performance is a qualifying performance if it is given in a qualifying country.

(a) "Qualifying country" means the UK, or another EEC member state, or a country which is a party to a convention relating to performers' rights to which the UK is also a party.

(b) "Qualifying individual" means a citizen or subject or, or an individual resident in, a qualifying country.

(c) "Qualifying person" is a qualifying individual or a corporation formed in the UK or another qualifying country which has a place of business in the qualifying country at which substantial business activity is carried on.

**11.3** By section 182 a performer's rights are infringed by a person who, without his consent:

(a) makes, otherwise than for his private or domestic use, a recording of the whole or any substantial part, of a qualifying performance;

(b) broadcasts live the whole, or any substantial part, of a qualifying performance.

However, damages will not be awarded if a defendant shows that, at the time of the infringement, he believed on reasonable grounds that consent had been given. Reasonable grounds would include, for example, where an artiste allows the defendant to book studios for a recording to be made for the defendant, the artiste performs, allows the defendant to have the master tape, and then when the recording has been completed, refuses to give his consent under the provisions of these sections. The purpose of these sections is to protect a performer from unauthorised recording and exploitation of his performances. In this example everything was authorised. To attempt to withhold technical consent may not work. Nothing in this part of the 1988 Act refers to the consent having to be in writing, whereas under the old Performers' Protection Acts it had to be in writing. So a clear course of conduct could amount to consent, as in this last example. Here again the concept is introduced of an exception being made where the otherwise illegal recording was made for "private and domestic use".

**11.4** By section 183 a performer's rights are infringed by a person who without his consent:

(a) shows or plays in public the whole or any substantial part of a qualifying performance;

(b) broadcasts or includes in a cable programme service the whole or any substantial part of a qualifying performance;

by means of a recording which was, and which that person had reason to believe was, made without the performer's consent. Performance in public of an audio or audio visual recording which contravenes the performer's rights is illegal. The question will be whether the person performing the recording knows it was illegal. The wording of the section seems to give a presumption of innocence in favour of that person, ie, it must be proved that he knew the recording was illegal.

**11.5** By section 184 a performer's rights are infringed by a person who, without his consent:

(a) imports into the UK otherwise than for his private and domestic use;

(b) in the course of a business, sells or lets for hire or distributes

a recording of a qualifying performance which is, and which that person knows or has reason to believe is, an illicit recording. If the illicit recording was innocently acquired by that person or his predecessor in title, the only remedy against him will be damages not exceeding a reasonable payment in respect of the act complained of. Innocently acquired means that the person did not know, and had no reason to believe, that it was an illicit recording.

## 12 Rights of person having recording rights

*The rights*

**12.1** By section 185 an "exclusive recording contract" means a contract between a performer and another person under which that person is entitled exclusively to make recordings of the artiste's performances for commercial exploitation.

A "person having recording rights" is a person with the benefit of an exclusive recording contract, and who is also a qualifying person.

**12.2** By section 186 a person infringes the rights of a person having recording rights to a performance if, without his consent or that of the performer, he makes a recording of the whole or any substantial part of the performance, otherwise than for his private and domestic use. What is not clear from this section is that, should the consent of the owner of the recording rights be refused, but for some reason the performer consents, the recording of the performer's performance by a third party should still be an infringement of the owner's rights. The words "or that of the performer" cause the confusion. This is a contractual reinforcement of a record company's contractual rights. Damages will not be awarded against a defendant who shows that at the time of the infringement he believed on reasonable grounds that consent had been given.

**12.3** By section 187 a person infringes the rights of a person having recording rights to a performance if, without his consent or the consent of the performer, he:

(a) shows or plays in public the whole or a substantial part of the performance;

(b) broadcasts or includes in a cable programme service the whole or any substantial part of the performance by means of a recording which was, and which the person knows or has reason to believe, was made without the appropriate consent.

**12.4** By section 188 a person infringes the rights of a person having recording rights to a performance if without his consent or the consent of the performer he:

(a) imports into the UK otherwise than for his private and domestic use;

(b) in the course of a business possesses, sells, hires or distributes

a recording the performance of which is, and which that person knows or has reason to believe is, an illicit recording. Where a defendant shows that the illicit recording was innocently acquired by him or his predecessor in title, he will only be liable for damages not exceeding a reasonable payment in respect of the act complained of. "Innocently acquires" means that the person did not know and had no reason to believe, that it was an illicit recording.

## 13 Remedies for infringement

**13.1** By section 197 an illicit recording is a recording of the whole or a substantial part of a performance without the consent of the performer, except if made for private purposes.

**13.2** By section 195 where a person has in his possession custody or control in the course of a business an illicit recording, a person having performer's rights or recording rights to the performance, may apply to the court for an Order for delivery in the same way as under section 99. The same conditions apply as for section 114.

By section 196 an illicit recording which is immediately available for sale or hire, may be seized by him in the same way as under section 110. The same conditions apply as for section 114.

## 14 Offences

**14.1** As well as the performer, or the person having recording rights, being able to sue in the civil courts manufacturers of and dealers in illicit recordings, they are able to get further relief under the criminal law. These twin sanctions make the task of protecting the rights easier, and the penalties for being discovered are now much greater.

**14.2** Section 198 sets out the following offences:

(1) A person commits an offence who without consent:

(a) makes for sale or hire;

(b) imports into the UK except for private and domestic use;

(c) possesses in the course of a business with a view to committing an infringing act;

(d) in the course of a business sells, lets for hire or distributes

a recording which is, and which he knows or has reason to believe is, an illicit recording.

(2) A person commits an offence who causes a recording of a performance made without consent to be:

(a) shown or played in public;

(b) broadcast or included in a cable programme service

thereby infringing performances or recording if he knows, or has reason to believe, that those rights are infringed.

CHAPTER 11

# *Basic Legal Points Relating to Music Contracts*

This book is intended to be a practical commentary upon contracts relating to the important areas of the music industry. This chapter describes some of the relevant basic aspects of English contract law, and the chapters on specialised forms of contract should be read accordingly.

This is not a definitive treatise on those matters which are discussed; it is designed as a general indication to the layman of their nature, and of the reasons why they ought to be considered. When in doubt, there is no substitute for expert advice.

## SECTION I: PRELIMINARY CONSIDERATIONS

### 1. Basic idea

**1.1** There should be no mystery about a contract, which is a document containing the terms governing the agreement between the parties, ie a set of commercial rules. To be binding in law a contract need not necessarily be in writing. A written contract may confirm the terms of a previous oral agreement, which itself can be legally binding, but it is usually the result of completed negotiations.

**1.2** There is a difference between an oral agreement, which is intended to be legally binding on both parties without a written document between them; and an agreement which has been negotiated, but which will not become legally effective until there is a document signed by both parties. In the second case, if no agreement is signed, neither party is committed. If there was no such distinction, the ordinary commercial process of negotiation would become technical and complicated.

**1.3** If, in anticipation of the formal document being drawn up, an artiste records for the record company, or a composer assigns copyrights to a publisher, or an artiste signs a personal appearance contract, if all else has been agreed but no document has yet been signed, there would be sufficient part performance of the negotiated agreement to create some obligations between the parties. A written agreement avoids having to rely on memory in the event of subsequent disagreement upon what was originally negotiated. An oral agreement still needs to contain the essential formalities necessary for a binding contract, which are:

(a) a specific unconditional offer;
(b) a specific unconditional acceptance of that offer; and
(c) the passing of consideration, such as money, or an undertaking to do some act or perform some service, or to forego some right.

**1.4** If the terms of an agreement are not put in writing, a plaintiff in a court action may have difficulty in proving his case where a disputed term of an oral agreement is to be identified, interpreted or enforced.

**1.5** The contract as set out should represent accurately and completely what is agreed. To agree something in conversation, and to put that agreement into writing effectively to represent precisely and unambiguously what is meant, are two different matters. The parties should consider all the likely consequences and effects of the terms of their deal. These can then be dealt with specifically in the agreement to avoid future problems. A hurriedly and inadequately prepared written contract may be more dangerous than not having one at all, if it does not reflect the true agreement between the parties.

## 2 Private arrangements

**2.1** The reason for having a clear definition of what should constitute a legally binding contract is because the parties may only want to come to a private arrangement. An informal or private arrangement, whether oral or written, sometimes called a "gentleman's agreement", is one which the parties never intended to be legally enforceable, but to be binding upon them in honour only.

**2.2** If a private arrangement is entered into, it is assumed that none of the parties intend to create a legal business-like relationship. It is no more than a statement of intent between them. However, there will always be people who habitually do their business on the basis of a handshake, considering the deal to be legally binding. They do not realise that such an arrangement may be inadequate in law if the essential elements for a binding contract do not exist. To avoid any misunderstanding, the parties should make the basis of the deal clear, even by confirming it in a letter without delay. Another benefit of doing so is that if there has been any misunderstanding, that may be discovered when the letter is received (see paragraph **1.3**).

**2.3** Mutual intention to create a legal relationship between the parties is the crux of an enforceable agreement. If no such intention is present, such as in a private arrangement, there is a presumption that no legal contract arises—the matter rests as one of trust and honour. If the trust in the honour is broken, the disappointed party must put it down to experience. Where a contract comes into existence through negotiation with professional advice, and is incorporated in a formal document, it is presumed to be intended to be legally binding in law.

**2.4** A private arrangement, notwithstanding its informality, may have been intended by one or both of the parties to be legally binding. Consternation will follow if, when clinically put to the test of whether or not it was a contract in law, it fails. If one party intended to be legally bound, but the other did not, that other party would have difficulty in pleading mistake, or that it was intended by him to be only a private arrangement, if the contract appears to be legal and binding on the face of it. Ignorance of the law is no defence, even where unforeseen hardship arises through it. If it were a defence, the legal system would break down, and the security of properly drawn up commercial agreements would be at risk.

**2.5** Where the friendly deal is in fact a firm business transaction, as evidenced by the details of the deal and the manner in which it was negotiated, and how it is being operated, it is more difficult to prove that no legal contract was intended by both parties. In these circumstances "gentleman's agreements" are most unsatisfactory, especially where the details of the deal are complex. Even if both parties regard the deal as a firm legal contract, although entered into on an informal basis, there is the hazard of relying upon memory for vital details. The human memory is often unreliable, and selective in the clarity of its recollection.

## 3 Previous contracts

**3.1** Before being committed irrevocably to any agreement, the first thing to check is whether there are any prior commitments, or options, or any other claims which may affect the agreement, or the right of either party to execute it and fulfil their obligations under it. Any prior agreement must be investigated to ascertain whether it is still in force, or whether it is dormant but still with potentially enforceable rights, such as where it contains an option for renewal.

**3.2** An agreement which is time expired, or which has lapsed through non-renewal of an option, or which has been properly terminated, will not affect the issue. Nevertheless it should be checked for any outstanding reassignment of rights, or whether, as a result of the termination, any notices still have to be given to third parties.

**3.3** An exception to the presumption of safety is an agreement which, although technically expired or lapsed, has in fact been extended by the same parties continuing in business within the same activity upon the same terms as if the agreement had not ended. In that case reasonable prior notice of termination may have to be given in writing. The same applies where an agreement for an unspecified length of time contains no termination clause. What would constitute a reasonable period of notice depends upon the facts of each case.

## 4 Series of agreements

**4.1** In an agreement which is one of a series of agreements, each dependent upon the other, the warranties, undertakings and grants of rights specified in it must be consistent with those contained in the prior agreement from which it obtains its title.

**4.2** A party who acquires rights under a prior contract, and who intends to pass on those rights under a new agreement, cannot grant any more than he is entitled to himself. In a series of contracts the most common hazard is to grant rights over a period which can ultimately exceed that during which the grantor himself has control over those rights. The new agreement either should be made subject to the continuance of the prior agreement, or there should be some device to ensure that continuity of the rights is guaranteed despite failure of the prior contract. This can only safely be done by having a side agreement directly with the party which owns the rights.

**4.3** An agreement may contain indemnities whereby the grantee (the person granted the rights) is made liable to keep the grantor (the person granting the rights) indemnified against any loss, damage or expense which may be incurred by the grantor if the grantee commits a breach of contract. If the grantor has delegated all of his own rights and responsibilities to the grantee, he must rely on the grantee not to incur any liabilities which will adversely affect the grantor in the future.

**4.4** If a prior contract in the series is terminated, thereby depriving a party of his rights under that contract, then as grantor of those rights in the subsequent contract, he will be in involuntary breach of contract. The result is that he may be liable for compensation if he cannot fulfil his own obligations under the subsequent contract. This may sound complicated, so the safest thing is to go back to the original source of all rights wherever possible, and get a direct contract cutting out all those in between. It can be dangerous to rely on intermediate contracts.

**4.5** A practical precaution is for the grantor to have a clause in his agreement to the effect that, should the prior agreement terminate or become unenforceable by him through no fault of his own, the subsequent agreement under which he has liabilities will cease to be effective without any financial penalty being incurred. This will not normally be acceptable to the party at the end of the contract sequence. This limitation is unsatisfactory for record companies and other promoters, which in reliance on the agreement may expend large sums of money on promotion of an artiste, as there is no certainty of the continuation of their rights. For this reason record companies insist on having the artiste either contract with them direct, or sign a "side agreement", whereby the record company is granted the exclusive recording rights of the artiste in reversion immediately upon the termination howsoever of the present intermediary agreement, such as with the artiste's employment company.

## 5 Personal services

**5.1** The court will not order specific performance by an artiste of a contract for the provision of his personal services. It is not practical to insist that an artiste sings, plays an instrument or writes music if he refuses to do so. Neither will the court grant an injunction which effectively prevents an artiste from performing elsewhere or for someone else in order to make a living, even though that performance is a breach of the contract in dispute.

**5.2** Such an injunction would amount to official pressure exerted to make the artiste either perform his original contract or starve. An injunction would be tantamount to obtaining an order for specific performance. The court generally considers that the appropriate remedy for the promoter is damages awarded against the artiste for breach of contract, and to compensate the promoter for any loss incurred.

**5.3** An injunction may be granted to prevent unauthorised dealings in recordings, or of music copyrights or other impersonal assets or rights. This is irrespective of the fact that they have been created by the personal services rendered by the artiste to third parties in breach of his contract. For example, if a composer assigns the copyright in future works to one music publisher, but when those future works are created he assigns them to another music publisher in breach of his contract, the first music publisher still has a valid claim on those copyrights. The first music publisher cannot force the composer to compose, but should he do so, the right of the publisher is in the product of the services, as opposed to the services themselves. He can get a court order to have those copyrights assigned to him under the terms of the breached agreement, and can get an injunction to prevent them from being assigned elsewhere.

## 6 Infants

**6.1** Infants are in a special category when it comes to entering into contracts. Legally an infant is a person still under eighteen years old, and it is difficult to hold infants to agreements they sign unless certain elements protective to them are present. This emphasis is even greater when the artiste is still under age at the time he disputes the contract. An artiste who signed an agreement while under age, and who has recently attained his majority, still has a reasonable chance of terminating his contract lawfully if it is one which he could have terminated while he was an infant. But the chance is diminished if:

(a) He has positively affirmed the contract in a substantial manner since attaining eighteen. Where he has continued to record, perform or compose, it is presumed that he has decided to comply with the agreement as if he had signed it after reaching eighteen. If, as an afterthought, rather than from desperate hardship, the artiste wants to terminate the agreement by using the technicality of having signed it whilst an infant, his subsequent actions will be significant in determining his right to do so.

(b) He has not terminated the contract within a reasonable time after attaining eighteen. What is reasonable depends on the circumstances, the reason why termination was not sooner, the reason for the termination being considered, and whether that reason arose prior to or after the artiste reached eighteen.

(c) The artiste has obtained a proper benefit under the contract, to an extent which would make termination inequitable. The law is designed to protect infants from the folly of their own inexperienced actions. It is not a charter to enable any contract, however favourable to the infant, to be terminated solely by reason of age. For example, if the agreement is one of which the court would have approved had it been consulted, it has the ability to confirm that the artiste remains bound by it.

(d) If the artiste has acted upon the contract after attaining eighteen so as to prevent the other contracting party from being returned to the state appertaining immediately prior to the signing of the contract. This point is related to point (f) below, although there may not have been such an intention originally. If the promoter has done all that could reasonably be required of him within a commercial transaction to benefit and safeguard the infant, and in good faith he has committed himself to third parties in reliance upon his agreement with the infant, the court is reluctant to make the promoter liable for obligations he could not fulfil if the artiste terminates his agreement purely on the question of age.

(e) The artiste obtained independent legal and financial advice prior to signing the contract, and can be presumed to have known exactly what he was doing. The quality of the advice will determine whether the infant knew fully what he was about to do, and the disadvantages, consequences and rewards of doing it. There is also the question of what is right where the artiste, despite having been legally and properly advised not to do so, entered into the agreement notwithstanding that advice. If the promoter knew of that advice, and the reasons on which it was based, by entering into the agreement he would take a calculated risk.

(f) It can be proved that the artiste signed the contract with every intention of taking the benefit, and of repudiating his liabilities subsequently in a deceptive or fraudulent manner.

**6.2** The court has considerable powers of discretion in deciding what is equitable, taking all the circumstances into account. The glitter of potential fame and fortune draws to the music industry a large number of youngsters. The potential earnings for promoters, and the attraction of a young artiste to a young audience, put exciting young stars in a vulnerable position, due to their age and inexperience. However, artistes under age have entered into contracts and accepted large sums of money in advance with every intention of terminating the contract when the time is right.

**6.3** A guarantor of the artiste's performance of his obligations does not reduce the hazards of infant's contracts. If the contract is held by the court to be unenforceable against the infant, the guarantor will not be forced to fulfil an unenforceable contract, but he may be ordered to compensate the other party for loss even though the infant himself would not have been liable to do so.

**6.4** The simplest way of getting a sympathetic hearing from the court is to ensure that a contract with an infant has the following basic qualities:

(a) It must be genuinely for his benefit, whether by giving him a proper training, or by giving him proper opportunities of advancement in his career. These requirements are not appropriate to the average hopeful artiste, so the manager or record company must make every visible effort to help him within the context of their own activities. If the potential benefits were there, but notwithstanding all reasonable efforts, they subsequently never materialised, the mere lack of receipt of benefit does not automatically give the infant the right to terminate the contract. If the lack of success or development was due to the culpable fault or neglect of the promoter, that is exactly what the law favourable to infants is intended to protect them from.

(b) The terms of the contract must be reasonable to the infant. The liabilities, obligations and restrictions affecting him must not be of any greater severity or extent than is necessary or reasonable:
  (i) to ensure the due performance by him of his part of the agreement;
  (ii) to give reasonable protection to the promoter;
  (iii) to give the promoter a reasonable return for his investment of time, money and risk.

(c) The financial return to the infant under the contract must be a reasonable proportion of the earnings arising from his efforts, and of any secondary sources of income from commercial promotion based upon him. Account will be taken of the commissions or royalties payable to the promoter, or through him to third parties; and of the manner, scope and extent in which expenses incurred by the promoter are set off against the share of income due to the infant.

(d) The infant must have clearly explained to him the meaning of the terms of the agreement, his responsibilities and obligations under it, and the possible consequences of failure or refusal to comply with them. For this purpose, and also to prevent the infant from saying subsequently that he did not read or understand the contract, it is essential that he is given every opportunity and encouragement to seek competent independent legal and financial advice. It would be worth the promoter, or his solicitor, getting an independent adviser for him, at the cost of the promoter. This cost should not be recoupable from any earnings due to the infant if the deal goes ahead, nor should it be repayable if it does not go ahead.

(e) Depending upon the age of the infant, and the sensitivity of the contract, the parents or legal guardian of the infant should also be informed of and consulted upon the contract, or they should be a party to it. They should be satisfied that the infant is being treated properly and fairly, and may themselves wish to take advice on the proposed contract. Although they would be unwise to do so, they can be asked to guarantee the performance by the infant of his proper obligations, and to compensate the promoter if the infant breaches his contract.

**6.5** Any guarantor (who may or may not be a parent) should also seek legal advice on his potential obligations. In the case of a contract which has been breached, damages can be high where losses are computed in respect of an artiste who is successful. The guarantee should cease to be effective on the infant's eighteenth birthday. For his safety, the guarantor should stipulate that, after that date he will have no liability for the past unless a claim emerges, and is made, say, within six months (see paragraph **8**).

**6.6** What happens if an infant, for example, successfully terminates his recording or publishing contract, but in the meantime has made a record or created compositions? This comes within paragraph **6.1**(d), ie, is everything reversed, and does he get back the rights to the recording or to the song? If the commercial and financial terms of the deal are fair and reasonable, and the infant has received a benefit (such as advances), and/or will receive a proper benefit on the sale of the records or the promotion of the copyrights, on balance the court will leave existing arrangements as they are, if it is satisfied that all is well. The effect is that the artiste terminates his contract, and is released from all future commitments, if the record company or publisher has acted reasonably and in good faith. The validity of the artiste's written consents required under the 1988 Copyright Act (or the 1956 Act where relevant) may need to be confirmed by the court.

## 7 Termination of agreements

**7.1** Agreements can be terminated in the following ways:

**7.1.1** By effluxion of time. Where an agreement is stated to run for a specified time only, when that time has expired the agreement ends. If the parties to that agreement disregard that date, and continue in business as if that date had not been reached, the agreement becomes an agreement at will, terminable by reasonable notice in writing at any time by either party.

**7.1.2** Upon completion of purpose. Whatever may be the intended period of the agreement, it may contain a provision for termination by either party giving to the other notice of intention to terminate the agreement on a certain date, or upon the happening of a certain event. The event may be, for example, delivery of an agreed number of copyrights or recordings; or it may be the conclusion of a certain transaction. The event need not be a breach of contract. The notice should be in writing, and where possible should be given not less than a specified minimum period of time before the termination is to take effect. Notice provisions should always be contained in agreements which do not have a fixed terminal date.

**7.1.3** By notice upon breach. A substantial or irreparable breach of a fundamental term or condition in an agreement may entitle the injured party to terminate the agreement for that reason, whether or not that right is contained in the agreement (see paragraph **23**).

In the absence of specific notice provisions, notice of termination can be given by one party where the other party has so acted in bad faith, or is in such default of his obligations that the injured party is entitled to deem the agreement at an end on the basis that the other party has totally repudiated his rights under it. That might precipitate a legal argument over whether the termination is lawful, questioning whether the grounds are genuinely fundamental. The purported grounds of termination, and the surrounding actions of the parties, will be significant in deciding the issue. If the court decides that the termination was not proper, the consequences of the purported act of termination may cause the terminating party himself to be in breach of contract.

Any agreement should specify a procedure to be followed should a breach of contract occur. For example, written notice of the breach should be given by the complaining party to the breaching party, with a requirement that it must be remedied within a specific time. Failure to comply with the notice creates the right to terminate. Non-compliance may be either a total disregard of the notice, or it may be because, despite all reasonable efforts of the breaching party, the remedy will happen, but not in the specified time. The time stated in the clause should be sufficient to enable the party to remedy the matter if he gets down to it promptly. There is no point in having an unrealistically short time period.

Depending on the nature and purpose of the contract, it may also be agreed that a breach of certain fundamental terms, specified to be "of the essence" of the agreement, will give rise to a right of termination. This avoids a dispute as to whether the breach is sufficiently substantial, or whether the term breached is sufficiently fundamental, to create a right of termination under the general law. This will normally be where an event is crucial to the deal, without which it is not intended that the deal will proceed, but which ordinarily would not be considered to be fundamental. An example would be where something has to be done by a specified time. The clause must state clearly that the event is "of the essence of the agreement".

**7.1.4.** Automatically upon the happening of specified events such as:
(a) liquidation of a company;
(b) a company or business ceasing permanently to trade;
(c) bankruptcy of an individual;
(d) attempted assignment of the benefit of a contract, or of a right connected with it, which is specifically prohibited;

Each example will depend upon the wording and intention of the clause invoked. It is the happening of the event which is crucial, not just the threat or the possibility of it.

**7.1.5** *Force majeure* deals with all those possible but unexpected events which are outside the control of the parties, and which by their nature or effect prevent the fulfilment of a contract. The law recognises that if certain intervening events, which could not have been reasonably foreseen, either nullify the entire objective of the contract, or make it impossible to achieve, the contract can be ended without liability for either party arising from that event. The termination does not "wipe out" other obligations or rights already existing under the contract, and which are not affected by the *force majeure* event.

The *force majeure* event may only cause a delay in fulfilling the contract, and it may not be a total frustration of it. Where the time lost due to a *force majeure* event only deprives the injured party temporarily of what he has contracted for, and provided that performance of the prevented event on the due date was not of the essence of the contract, one alternative is to agree to extend the term of the agreement for the period of lost time.

**7.1.6** By mutual agreement any agreement can be terminated or amended in any way at any time with the consent of all parties. The unanimous consent relates to rights and obligations between the parties themselves, but will not affect any continuing rights of or obligations to, independent third parties, contained in or arising from the agreement.

**7.1.7** By substitution of agreements. Where a subsequent agreement is made between the same parties, which effectively takes over all of the rights and obligations contained in a prior agreement between them, the prior one should be specifically terminated. If it is not terminated, but thereafter is totally ignored in favour of the new agreement, the previous agreement will be deemed to have been terminated.

It is more likely that a subsequent agreement will only amend certain aspects of the original agreement, which then remains in force subject only to the alterations.

**7.1.8** By the actions of the parties. It is possible for an agreement to be terminated by the person entitled to all of the rights under it, if he so behaves with reference to it as to indicate clearly and unequivocally that he no longer requires the other party to be bound to fulfil any of his obligations under it. It may be difficult to decide whether termination is intended, or whether the agreement has only become temporarily dormant.

The interpretation of what a course of behaviour means, and what the consequences are, is usually a matter of opinion. The party believing himself to be released should obtain written confirmation from the other party that the agreement has ended. He will then find out whether his view is correct. Because the termination has simply evolved, there is unlikely to be any clear date upon which it occurred. If written termination is forthcoming, a specific date should be agreed, so that dealings with the rights in the agreement prior to and after that date can be separated, if necessary.

The termination of most contracts will still leave outstanding matters between the parties which need to be cleared up. The termination document should deal with the details of who does what and who gets what.

## 8 Guarantors

**8.1** Each party should take reasonable steps to minimise their personal risk of liability to third parties in respect of loss, damage or expense which may be caused by any default of the other party. If the risk is inherent in the circumstances of the agreement, where appropriate, references should be obtained from the other party as a means of checking upon the ability of that other party to honour his obligations.

**8.2** Depending on the type of liability, such as the payment of money, a guarantor may be required from the party giving the indemnity. In the event of loss, damage or expense being incurred through the breach by that party of any of his obligations, the guarantor is available to satisfy any financial claim to the extent that the defaulting party is not able to do so himself.

**8.3** Any prospective guarantor must ascertain the full possible extent of his contingent liabilities under his guarantee. He must also calculate the risk he is running, and the likelihood of his guarantee being called upon. In the absence of express agreement, a guarantor has no right to interfere with the business transaction which he is guaranteeing, even though he can foresee the happening of whatever will cause his liability to arise.

**8.4** Unless there is a specific right to do so set out in the agreement, the guarantor is unable to withdraw from his guarantee unilaterally. He may be clear of liability if the agreement is unenforceable upon the party he has guaranteed, or if it is an illegal contract.

**8.5** A guarantee can be limited in amount or in time. If a guarantor dies, his estate continues to be liable in his place. If a guarantor becomes bankrupt, the trustee in bankruptcy may disclaim the liability. If the liability which is guaranteed ceases to exist, so effectively does the guarantee of it.

## SECTION II: IMPORTANT FEATURES OF CONTRACTS

### 9 Difference between deed and agreement under hand

**9.1** There are legal and practical differences between a deed (a formal document with a seal), and an agreement under hand (an ordinary agreement signed by all parties). An agreement under hand must have adequate consideration to be enforceable, whereas it is not necessary to specify a consideration in a deed. The consideration is usually the exchange of money, or the fulfilment of an obligation, or the disposal of rights in products such as recording rights or musical compositions (see paragraph **14**). The consideration must be present or future, it cannot be past consideration. In a recording or publishing agreement it will be the company's promise to make and promote records, or to promote compositions, and to pay royalties. The question of proper consideration can get very technical in complicated cases.

**9.2** If an agreement under hand contains no consideration at all, or only refers to past consideration, it is treated as a voluntary unilateral agreement. This means that it may not be specifically enforced unless it has been so acted upon by the parties as to estop the party granting the rights from revoking it. Otherwise it may be revoked by him at any time prior to completion of its purpose. Once the agreement has been completed,it cannot be revoked so as to unravel the whole transaction retrospectively.

**9.3** Specific performance may be ordered by the court where both the parties have so acted upon the terms of a unilateral revocable agreement that it would be impossible or inequitable to return them to their respective positions appertaining prior to the agreement being signed.

**9.4** Unless it is otherwise specified in an agreement under hand, its terms can be varied orally by mutual consent. Oral variations can be as binding as the original agreement, but a memorandum in writing should be made to evidence the precise terms of the variation. A deed can only be varied by another deed.

## 10 Recitals to an agreement

**10.1** Recitals are the preamble of an agreement—the "whereas" part at the beginning. These describe briefly the context in which the agreement is entered into. They should not contain any grant of rights or obligations unless they are also fully set out in the main part of the agreement. Recitals can be useful if there is a dispute at a later date, as the legal advisers (who may not be those who negotiated the agreement), will have some explanatory background to the deal.

**10.2** Recitals become necessary to avoid confusion where the same parties enter into an agreement which is supplemental to the principal agreement, or if they enter into different agreements dependent upon or related to each other. The risk of errors in drafting associated agreements will be reduced, and each agreement will have an easily recognisable identity of its own.

## 11 Contents of an agreement

**11.1** An agreement should contain in sufficient detail all the fundamental points agreed upon, together with all the necessary ancillary matters to make anything work, and the usual clauses which are relevant to commercial agreements. It is dangerous to rely upon unwritten understandings which form part of the deal, but which are not thought worthy of inclusion in the formal document. To the contrary, there should be a clause stating that only the terms stated in the written agreement will apply. It may not always be possible to keep the agreement simple, but it is a false economy to leave relevant details out only for the sake of brevity.

**11.2** Litigation frequently is caused either by ambiguity in the drafting of clauses, or by a dispute as to whether or not a specific point should be deemed to be included as having formed part of the negotiations upon which a party claims to have placed reliance. Terms can sometimes be implied into an agreement from a relevant unwritten universal commercial understanding, or an established trade custom and usage. Any representation, warranty or undertaking offered as a substantial inducement to a party to enter into the agreement should be recorded in it, if it is to be relied upon.

**11.3** Even if there is a clause in the agreement to the effect that the written terms are the only ones binding the parties, which can only be amended by a document in writing signed by both parties, it may be possible for a written term to be varied effectively by the unrecorded but accepted actions of expedience or custom of either party. These would have to be known by the other party and positively approved, ratified or acted upon by him. An exchange of correspondence would be adequate to confirm the variation in writing, it does not have to be another formal agreement. If the parties get along well, and both believe they fully understand the variation, it may not occur to them that its details should be confirmed in writing. The point will only be raised if there is a subsequent dispute on the variation.

## 12 Options

**12.1** An option which is granted to one party to enable him to extend the period of an agreement, or for any other purpose, must be supported by consideration to be specifically enforceable, unless it is contained in a deed. If an option is not specifically enforceable, it can only be revoked prior to its exercise; but if it has been properly exercised, it will remain binding upon all parties. If the option to extend the period of a principal agreement is contained in a supplementary agreement, it should have a consideration independent of any expressed in the principal agreement. Past consideration is not legally effective.

**12.2** The clause containing an option should set out all of the conditions affecting its exercise. For example, it is useful to make the exercise of an extension option limited in time to not after, say, 30 days prior to the date of expiry of the agreement. This gives the grantor of the option adequate time to decide what to do if the option is not exercised. Exercise of an option should be in writing, and should be actually received by the grantor, rather than being effective if posted to him by a given date. An option should be irrevocable during the period within which it is exercisable. If an irrevocable option has no specified period, it may be revoked at any time by written notice; it cannot be perpetual.

**12.3** Upon assignment of the benefit of an agreement containing an option which has been granted to a third party to it, written notice of the assignment should be given to the third party to make him aware that any exercise of the option will be against the assignee of the benefit of the agreement.

## 13 Signature

**13.1** The proper completion of the legal formalities relating to the signing and dating of agreements is important. These are the first things to check when considering their validity. All the parties should have signed the agreement, and should have initialled all alterations made to its text. This prevents a signed agreement subsequently being amended or added to in a prejudicial or fraudulent manner without the knowledge and consent of the party affected by the amendment. If alterations are not initialled, that does not invalidate the contract, but the alterations can be challenged by the party affected by them.

**13.2** All signatures should be witnessed, and the witness should also state his address and occupation. Lack of a witness does not invalidate the document, but where it was signed with nobody present it is possible for a party to claim that it is not his signature at all. A witness to a signature can give evidence that it is genuine. To maintain impartiality, none of the witnesses should be a party to the agreement.

**13.3** A signatory to an agreement on behalf of a company or partnership should be prepared to provide reasonable evidence that he is entitled and authorised to commit the party, and to sign the agreement for it. For a company, a verified copy of a resolution of the board of directors authorising the signatory to execute the agreement would be best. If the signatory is a director of the company, or is well established as having signatory powers, his signature will bind the company. The partnership is likely to be a group of artistes, and group member authorities have been discussed in chapter eight.

## 14 Date

**14.1** Strictly the date should be the date of signing of the agreement. Where necessary there can be a clause stating that the agreement is to take effect from a specified date before or after the actual date of signature. The same result is obtained by merely pre-dating the agreement to its genuine starting date, unless the intended effect of pre-dating is to deceive, or to obtain a fraudulent benefit, or to deprive others of rights which they would otherwise not have, or to preserve rights which would otherwise have been lost. Pre-dating an agreement is not recommended.

## 15 Under hand or seal

**15.1** Each signing party should check whether his signature should be under seal. The seal denotes the document to be a deed, otherwise the document is said to be under hand. If the signature is under seal, the hallowed sentence "I deliver this as my act and deed" should be recited while the forefinger rests on the wafer seal affixed beside the signature, although seldom is that done except on ceremonial occasions. The signature to a deed must be witnessed.

**15.2** In the case of a limited liability company, its seal should be affixed to a deed (or any other document where the seal is used) in the presence of the persons authorised by the Articles of Association to witness the impression of the seal. If the document is under hand, the signature by an authorised person for and on behalf of the company will be sufficient.

**15.3** Where there is doubt as to the validity of the sealing, or the authority of the signatory, the party relying on the agreement should require a sight of the minutes of the meeting of the board of directors of the company which authorised such seal or signature to the agreement.

## 16 Original and counterpart documents

**16.1** Although it is not necessary, it is preferable for an agreement to have all its original copies signed by all parties. Each party then has a completely executed original copy of the agreement. If there are only two parties, it is as easy to have each party sign one of the copies, and exchange it for that signed by the other party. The one signed by the grantor of the rights will be known as the original copy, and the other will be known as the counterpart.

**16.2** In the case of a group with many members, they can all sign the same original document together with the promoter, everyone receiving a photocopy of the completed agreement. Alternatively, each can sign a separate document with the promoter, provided that where the agreement is the same for each artiste, each document is identical with the others in all respects. The latter course is more convenient if this membership of the group is likely to change constantly, or if there is a likelihood of different dealings between the promoter and certain members only.

## 17 Stamping

**17.1** All agreements, whether under seal or under hand, need to comply with the Inland Revenue regulations in force at the time of signing as to stamping, before they are admissible as evidence in court for the purpose of enforcement. When in doubt, executed documents should be submitted to the Inland Revenue for adjudication as to whether an impressed stamp is necessary. The most common stamping requirement is "*ad valorem*", where a transfer or assignment of valuable assets (such as copyrights) is made. The *ad valorem* stamp is a percentage of the value of the asset transferred. Failure to stamp does not invalidate the document, but it may be unenforceable in a court action until it has been stamped. Stamping out of time normally incurs a penalty of an additional amount payable.

# SECTION III: POTENTIAL DEFECTS

## 18 In general

**18.1** A party to a contract who regrets not having considered fully the meaning and effect of its terms before entering into it, or who is dissatisfied with the way the promotion of his career is going, and having no valid contractual ground for doing so, may wish to terminate the agreement prematurely but in no way wrongfully. The following are among the technical points which ought to be considered in such circumstances.

## 19 Unenforceable contracts

**19.1** No court will enforce a contract the principal purpose of which is illegal. Where the contract as a whole is enforceable, but it contains an illegal section which is not important to the agreement, it may be deleted from the agreement without affecting the rest of it.

**19.2** Examples of illegality or unenforceability are:

(a) a harsh and punitive penalty clause dressed up as a genuine pre-estimate of proper compensation;

(b) a contract which relates to an illegal payment (however dressed up) representing nothing other than a bribe or other inducement for rewarding corruption;

(c) an agreement between several people representing a conspiracy to defraud a promoter, or to obtain a benefit through deception;

(d) agreements which do not comply with legal requirements relating to artistes' services, such as the written consents required under the 1988 Copyright Act;

(e) an agreement the purpose of which is contrary to public policy.

**19.3** If the substance of an illegal contract has been performed, but the payment of the money or the delivery of any other consideration has been withheld, a claim for it through the court will fail.

## 20 Mistake

**20.1** It is possible for a party to terminate an agreement on the basis that he signed it by mistake. This may be difficult to explain satisfactorily. Mistake must be of fact, not of law, and must be either as to the fundamental basis of the agreement, or as to a fundamental term of it. In this context "mistake" is not just an error of judgment or the result of carelessness. It means that the document which was signed bears no legal relationship to what was agreed.

**20.2** The mistake must be that of both parties, except where the mistake by one party is such as to indicate clearly that the agreement as a whole is completely different in content and purpose from that intended to be entered into. Two guide lines are that:

(a) an agreement will not be enforceable if the party claiming mistake signed it under the genuine misapprehension that it was another document of a totally different legal nature and intent;

(b) mistake cannot be pleaded if the general purpose of the agreement as set out was intended, but the party pleading mistake merely had not read the document carefully, or at all, or had not enquired sufficiently into what he did not understand, though given adequate opportunity to do so.

**20.3** The burden of proving that a genuine mistake as defined above has occurred is high. Negotiation, however inadequate, must have preceded the drafting of the agreement, and had the person read the document before signing it, he should have realised something was wrong.

**20.4** A common form of mistake (in the form of an error) arises where an artiste has failed to obtain his release from a prior existing agreement in respect of the rights purported to be granted by him in a new agreement. The cause of the error may have been ignorance or carelessness, or it may have been intentional, in the hope that no problem would arise. This type of mistake will not nullify any liability of the artiste under the new contract. He can find himself in breach of two contracts, each with a different party, for the same thing at the same time.

**20.5** Although the mistake may make the operation of the new agreement ineffective in practice, it may still be effective legally. If that is so, the artiste will be liable to the other party to the new contract in damages for breach of any relevant warranty; as well as to the other party to the old agreement in compensation for loss or unrecouped expense. One answer would be for the new promoter to negotiate an assignment to him of the benefit of the prior existing contract. An interesting situation arises, as he now has two different contracts with the artiste for the same services, and each contract will have different terms. These should be rationalised to be in line with the second agreement.

## 21 Misrepresentation

**21.1** To affect the validity of a contract, a representation must be a statement of fact, and not just of an opinion. The representation may be inferred by conduct, which leads the other party reasonably to assume the fact tacitly being represented. A representation which is clearly not intended to form part of the contract, or which is not used to procure or induce the signing of the contract, does not of itself affect its validity or enforceability.

**21.2** For the claim of misrepresentation to be successful, the claimant must act promptly on discovering it. The claimant should also make it clear that further negotiation to deal with the misrepresentation after it has been discovered will be without prejudice to his rights in respect of it if the negotiations fail. If the misrepresentation was not a fundamental one leading to a claim of repudiation of the agreement, the claimant will need to show he has suffered some loss or disadvantage which can be quantified for compensation.

**21.3** There are two categories of misrepresentation:

(a) innocent misrepresentation—misleading statements, but free from fraudulent intent. The representee can repudiate the contract if the misrepresentation is substantial, fundamental and strikes at the essence of the contract. He cannot obtain damages unless the representation was in connection with a right or obligation under the contract.

(b) fraudulent misrepresentation—the representee can repudiate the contract and claim damages as well, whether or not the representation was in connection with an essential term of the contract.

**21.4** There are two further points to consider:

(a) Where third parties have innocently acquired rights under the contract, which will be prejudiced by its repudiation, the court will not necessarily grant it, to protect the third party's interests.

(b) Where misrepresentation induces in one of the parties to the contract a fundamental mistake as to the nature of the contract, ie, where the entire basis of the contract is mistaken, the contract can be treated as void *ab initio*. This means it is treated as never having been entered into in the first place, and therefore as never having had any legal effect. Where that happens, whatever has been produced in the meantime has to be unscrambled, so that the parties can be put back to square one. A composer would get his copyrights back, depending on how that would affect *bona fide* third parties who would be damaged as a result. In other circumstances it is simply terminated, so that the artiste has no future obligations.

**21.5** A third party may not be able to protect rights purported to have been granted by the "non existent" contract, because all rights ceased to exist when it was repudiated. If the third party is damaged it would have a claim against the party from which it got its rights, eg for breach of warranty.

## 22 Duress

**22.1** A contract will not be binding in law upon someone who was a party to it against his will, either:

(a) by the use or the threat of the use of physical force where there is a real fear for personal safety; or

(b) by the exertion of an overriding or undue influence by a person who is in a fiduciary capacity to the signing party. An example is where a trusted manager or adviser is relied upon absolutely by the artiste when he proposes the agreement, or when he pressures the artiste to sign the contract, against his own judgement.

**22.2** Where there is a fiduciary capacity between the artiste and, eg, his manager, the concept of undue influence also extends to the "bargaining power" type of influence, where the artiste has no chance of negotiating, and is given a "take it or leave it" offer for the terms of the agreement. This may not apply where the artiste still accepts the deal after taking legal advice. Duress does not extend to the use of proper and reasonable commercial pressure within any arm's-length transaction between negotiating persons of comparable status or size.

**22.3** The question is whether the contract would have been entered into but for the strong fiduciary pressure or the genuine and substantial fear of personal safety. Where the parties are independent of each other, duress will not apply where there is simply an anxiety in the artiste's mind that the contract will have to be signed at all costs, in order to retain or obtain the benefits claimed to be available through it. Duress will apply where the artiste did not want to sign the contract, and would not have signed but for that overriding pressure or genuine fear. The burden of proof is high, and the risk of such a claim can be minimised by the artiste receiving competent independent professional advice before signing.

## 23 Bad faith and breach of contract

**23.1** If one party to a contract has acted in bad faith in the substantive areas of the deal, or is in breach of any fundamental term of the agreement, then subject to any clause in the agreement setting out a procedure to be followed in the circumstances, the aggrieved party may well have a right to terminate the contract forthwith. What is "fundamental"? A fundamental term can broadly be described as either:

(a) Something by its nature essential to the agreement, eg, an artiste's warranty that he is free to sign a recording agreement.

(b) Something made essential by mutual agreement, eg, a management company providing the personal supervision of the artiste by a nominated executive. To make sure that such a condition is to be treated as fundamental, it should be stated as being "of the essence" of the agreement, and should be referred to in the termination clause.

What is bad faith? It is broadly where one party covertly acts deliberately and dishonestly so as to materially mislead, or so as to substantially damage, the other party, generally while pretending otherwise. The bad faith may relate to something trivial or serious, but either way it is implicit in contracts that each party will act in good faith towards the other.

**23.2** If the term breached is not fundamental to the agreement, but nevertheless seriously affects it and is incapable of effective remedy, there might still be the right to terminate. It is a matter of degree, and depends on the wording of the termination clause.

**23.3** If the breach is unintended and insignificant, and is capable of effective remedy, or if proper compensation in all the circumstances would be damages, the court may well refuse the termination claim, and give the defaulting party the opportunity to remedy the breach or to accept an assessment of damages.

**23.4** The party seeking to terminate the contract must do so promptly after becoming aware of the breach. Otherwise he runs the risk of being deemed to have accepted or waived the breach, so as to estop him from the right of termination. There is a statutory limitation period of six years within which an injured party can sue for reparation or compensation, but this is normally applied to circumstances where that party does not become aware of his right to make a claim until long after the event complained of. There is also the equitable principle of laches (delay), where if the injured party becomes aware of his right to make a claim or to take legal action, but does nothing about it for long enough, he is deemed to have accepted the breach, and waived his right of action. Waiver is more clearly applicable where the aggrieved party, after the breach (and in the full knowledge of it), does any act or thing or accepts any act or thing from the breaching party, which indicates that the breach is forgiven.

**23.5** Termination of the contract and damages for the breach may both be available, they are not necessarily only alternative remedies. Acceptance of an offer of compensation in full and final settlement of a breach of contract prior to giving notice of termination for that same breach negates the right to terminate. The drafting of the compensation settlement agreement must make it clear whether prior breaches of a similar nature or any other breaches are also waived and taken account of within the compensation payment.

## 24 Options

**24.1** If the promoter is entitled to extend the period of the agreement by the exercise of an option, check whether the option is revocable, and whether it is still valid. If it has already been exercised, make sure the exercise was in accordance with its conditions; such as, was it in due time, and was it properly served on the right party? An option which is exercised but not in accordance with its terms, and which is nevertheless accepted by the other party and acted upon by all concerned, will be binding.

## SECTION IV: GENERAL CONSIDERATIONS

### 25 Rectification

**25.1** An agreement is construed and enforced by the court in accordance with its clear and unambiguous language setting out the intentions of the parties to it. If the principal terms of the document are incomprehensible or contradictory, the court will not attempt to create an agreement by deciding what might have been intended. The court may use common sense and the evidence of the context in which the agreement was entered into to interpret its meaning, where the lack of clarity is caused only by inadequate use of the English language. If the document is so vague as to be meaningless, there may well be no agreement enforceable in law. The same rules apply to oral agreements as well as to written ones. The main difficulty in oral agreements is to prove the existence of the terms which have to be relied upon to support a claim.

**25.2** Evidence of prior representations claimed to be relevant to the meaning or operation of the agreement, which ought to have been, and which are not, contained in the formal document, will only be allowed if it is to prove fraud or mutual mistake. When one party later alleges that previously agreed oral terms have been omitted entirely from, or are only partially set out in the written agreement, if both parties agree to the omission, there is no problem. Further documentation can be signed to bring those oral terms into the written agreement. Otherwise the aggrieved party must issue proceedings to attempt to rectify the error. That is why it is useful to have a clause which makes it clear that any item not in the document will not be part of the agreement.

**25.3** If the court accepts the plaintiff's claim, and can be satisfied that a typist's error, or some other genuine reason, resulted in the omission; or that the error was on both sides; or there was unilateral fraud, it can order the agreement to be amended accordingly. The remedy of rectification will not be available where one party subsequently thinks of something which he would have liked to include in the agreement if only he had thought of it at the time. That is not an omission, it is hindsight.

**25.4** Where alterations to an agreement are negotiated after its execution, the parties should either enter into a supplemental agreement if the subsequent variations are minor, or they should sign an entirely new agreement in substitution for the previous one if the variations are extensive. Applying to the court for rectification is not a procedure to be used where the entire agreement is to be attacked; it is only to amend or complete the text of an agreement in special circumstances.

## 26 Undertakings

**26.1** Where there are services to be performed, either to create a product such as a recording, or from which there should result a secondary service such as an introduction or booking, even the best of efforts in good faith may fail to achieve the objective required. For this reason the wording of the obligation in the contract determining its legal effect upon the party who has to fulfil it must be considered carefully. To agree to do something is itself enforceable if the obligation is not conditional on some uncertain factor yet to occur.

**26.2** It is more positive and absolute to require an undertaking from a party to a contract to perform or to procure the performance of an obligation, rather than for him just to agree to do it. To undertake to do something where it is not certain that such an objective can be fulfilled is a hazard which beats a well worn path to the court. The belated explanation that fulfilment had become impossible or inconvenient for whatever reason will not necessarily remove the obligation for that party to compensate the other for loss arising from the breach of the undertaking. A record company may agree to make records, but it never undertakes to procure their release for sale to the public. Managers and agents cannot undertake with confidence to obtain and maintain for the artiste a certain minimum level of earnings or employment.

**26.3** It would become unnecessarily complicated for the party to give conditional undertakings, because the conditions would have to be specified, and interpreted strictly. If ordinary commercial prerequisites are the conditions, then the force of an undertaking is lost. For these reasons obligations in the music business are normally made subject to the exercise of "the best endeavours" of the person being bound to perform. If best endeavours are used, but even then the obligation is not fulfilled, the person bound has discharged his duty, providing he used good faith. What is the difference between "best endeavours" and "reasonable endeavours"? There is no absolute bench mark below which an effort is only reasonable, and above which it becomes best. "Reasonable" implies a lesser effort required than for "best", but it is a personal judgement on the relevant circumstances whenever the efforts have failed.

**26.4** Where an artiste wants to get out of a contract, but has no genuine ground for complaint, the first things he attacks are the "best endeavours" clauses, claiming that they were not exercised properly, or sufficiently strenuously, or in good faith. The inevitable question is who is to judge what is represented by "best endeavours"—the answer is that each case must be considered on its own merit through the eyes of a reasonable independent observer.

## 27 Warranties

**27.1** Warranties in contracts are statements or representations concerning the truth of facts, or the existence of circumstances, which have particular relevance to the contract, and upon which fundamental issues to the contract are based. Most warranties are the subject of indemnities by the warrantor, where breach of the warranty might involve loss, damage or expense to the party relying upon the warranty. Many warranties are intended to replace the necessity for the other party to ascertain facts independently, and they are used also where the facts or circumstances are only within the knowledge or responsibility of the warrantor.

**27.2** Breach of a warranty will entitle the other party to claim damages, and to invoke any indemnity he may have from the warrantor to cover losses he has sustained by the breach. If the validity of a warranty is specified to be "of the essence" of the agreement, breach of the warranty will entitle the other party to terminate the agreement. As an indemnity is in essence an insurance policy, the warrantor is only liable for losses which have actually been incurred. In many cases the loss cannot be quantified, but appropriate factors will be taken into account if damages are awarded by the court. In an extreme case of misrepresentation, the aggrieved party may be entitled to rescind the contract altogether. To "rescind" means to nullify the contract, ie, to treat it as never having been entered into. Rescission will not be an available remedy if the parties have so acted or progressed during the period of the contract that they cannot be put back at square one.

**27.3** Warranties are representations required to confirm to other parties to the contract facts they can rely on, as the same warranties may be passed on by them to third parties in subsequent contracts. For example, a composer will warrant that he is the original author of the composition he is assigning to the music publisher, who will deal with rights in the composition on that basis. The financial aspects, guarantees, or the passing of title to property dealt with in a contract may be subject to warranties being proved correct, which is why they should not be treated casually or drafted carelessly.

## 28 Conditions

**28.1** Conditions are terms in a contract which have to be fulfilled either before the contract becomes binding, or before certain aspects of it come into effect. The intention is that if a condition is not fulfilled, the event dependent upon that condition will not occur. Conditions normally relate either to statements to be relied upon but not yet proved ("I will sign the management agreement if you guarantee me a recording contract within three months"), or to future events the outcome of which will determine the action of the parties ("If you provide me with a studio free, I will deliver ten recorded tracks to you by 1 June").

**28.2** Conditions can either be precedent to, or subsequent to, the event in question. If a condition precedent, upon which the whole contract depends, fails, the contract does not come into effect. Where an existing contract contains a condition subsequent which fails, the agreed effect of the failure should be set out in the agreement.

## 29 Legal versus moral rights

**29.1** There are two kinds of legal rights—those contained in the written law and decided cases, all of which can be referred to; and those not written, but which through the ages have become enforceable as "acting upon the conscience". In a sense, the latter are moral rights which have been opted into the legal system under the heading of equitable rights, which represent a flexibility in the written law.

**29.2** In the music business there is a tendency to confuse equitable rights with moral rights more related to emotion and the concept of fair play. Unfortunately the two do not always concur, where unfairness (which is a very subjective viewpoint) can operate harshly in a moral sense upon an artiste, notwithstanding that the "oppressor" may be strictly within his legal rights.

**29.3** A sense of moral injustice does not mean that an agreement can be terminated, if there are no contractual or legally founded grounds for doing so. The best protection for an artiste is to be represented by a reputable and trustworthy agent and manager, as well as having good professional advisers.

**29.4** To many artistes the act of signing an agreement has no more significance than that of obtaining a receipt for money paid in advance for services to be rendered. What they cannot understand is how a piece of paper can cause them so much expense and trouble if they subsequently decline to do what they had agreed to do. For whatever reason they may feel no longer morally bound to comply with their obligations, but legal remedies are available to the other party should they dispense with their agreements in an unauthorised manner.

## 30 Damages and penalties

**30.1** If there are provisions in a contract setting out what is to be paid to an injured party in the event of a breach of contract, to be enforceable they must be a genuine and reasonable pre-estimate of damage or loss. If those provisions are deliberately unduly oppressive with the purpose of dissuading a party from defaulting, or if they have no reasonable basis of calculation, they may be considered by the court to be a penalty, and will therefore not be enforceable. A penalty is a form of threat, a crude means of attempting to obtain punitive damages far in excess of proper compensation. It is intended to intimidate the other party. The party claiming the benefit of the penalty will not be allowed to modify the claim to whatever level the court considers would be justified. The penalty provision stands or falls absolutely, the court will not allow an each way bet on compensation.

**30.2** Calculation of potential or foreseeable damages in advance upon the non-fulfilment of any term of the contract must be upon fair and reasonable principles where the precise damages are not readily ascertainable from the facts. Whether or not any properly calculated sums are greater or less, within reasonable bounds, than the court might award is not the test, as what would be awarded cannot be forecast accurately. If the parties wish to have a pre-estimated compensation provision, they should set out in the contract a fair and reasonable basis of calculation, or some reference whereby it can be proved that proper pre-estimation of a fixed amount took place.

**30.3** A penalty clause is not the same as a clause allowing an aggrieved party to withhold further payments, pending settlement of compensation by negotiation or by the court. Any excess held above the final compensation figure must be paid over. Whether or not such a provision is fair to the alleged defaulter depends upon the circumstances in which the withhold can be applied; if there is a limit to the amount withheld; the terms of its release, and whether interest is paid on the repaid amount for the period during which it was withheld. It could in practical terms act as a penalty if the withholder is extremely dilatory in proceeding with his claim. Legal actions can take years to come to court so an indefinite withhold may well be considered to be a penalty.

## 31 Proper law of the contract

**31.1** Where the artiste signs an agreement with a foreign record company, publisher or manager, the contract should state which country's laws will govern its interpretation and enforcement. For an English artiste, or other party, it should be English law. The clause should also state that the English high court will be the court of competent jurisdiction. This will prevent the other party instituting legal proceedings in his country's courts, but following the principles of English law. The applicable law is generally specified to be that of the country of the party granting the rights. The principles of commercial dealings and contract law in each country differ, and if there is any advantage or benefit to be gained through familiarity with the law, or having any legal action heard locally, it ought to go to the party giving the rights. There is also greatly increased cost and inconvenience in having to take or defend legal proceedings in a foreign country.

**31.2** If the contract is silent on the point, the two alternatives of choice of legal system are first where the contract was made, and secondly where it is to be performed. The parties may choose to have any legal system they wish applied to the agreement, even one completely independent of the countries involved in the deal. As the terms of the contract must be considered within the framework of the chosen legal system, the legal adviser to the party giving the rights must be familiar with it, or he would be at a considerable disadvantage.

**31.3** A contract made in England and intended to be subject to English law sometimes has been taken from, eg, an American form of contract. This may contain terms and conditions which are inapplicable, inappropriate or unenforceable in English law, or which may be considered by an English court to be unduly onerous. Little harm is done if the offending term is not essential to the contract as a whole; but if it is, the purpose of the contract may be defeated entirely.

**31.4** Arbitration is an alternative means of resolving disputes relating to an agreement. It can be quicker in the sense that an arbitration award can be obtained long before a legal action comes to trial in the courts. It would not be quicker if the court remedy is, for example, an injunction to cover an urgent matter. Another difference is that arbitration is private, whereas the contents of a writ, and the details of the judgement, are publicly available. The choice will be either arbitration or access to the court, and on balance access to the court is preferred by almost everybody active in the music business.

## 32 Standard agreements

**32.1** The phrase "standard agreement" is a misnomer which tends to mislead those who are new to the music business. With the exception of printed forms of agreement issued by societies or associations for their members to use, there is no such thing as a strictly standard agreement within the music industry for recording, publishing, management or otherwise.

**32.2** The major record and publishing companies have their individual settled basic forms of contract, which are treated as "standard" for their own use. This is to make their contract departments more efficient, and because their operational departments, accounts and administration are geared accordingly. Therefore no alteration of substance is allowed to its basic format unless absolutely necessary. There are many "standard" customary terms within each of the branches of the music industry; some laid down by law or a governing body, society or organisation, and others by common experience. Though the concept of such standard clauses may be the same, the wording and effect of each company's clauses will differ.

**32.3** Inexperienced or desperate artistes, when negotiating their own deals without advice, have signed away their services for a pittance and upon onerous or unfair terms on the insistence that the agreement is "standard". This is not to say that all "standard" clauses are harsh—that depends entirely on the integrity of the company the artiste is dealing with, and the negotiating power of the artiste. If recording, management, agency or music publishing agreements from different companies are compared, there will only be similarity on the theme, but not necessarily in their wording or layout, or the extent of their obligations.

**32.4** Because the main offices of many recording and publishing companies are situated in the USA, there has been a tendency for the UK subsidiaries to use the American style of layout and expression in contracts, although some of the terms are neither appropriate nor suitable under English law. American agreements tend to be much more detailed, and so seem to be unduly complicated. Perhaps American Lawyers are paid by the word for drafting them.

**32.5** Standard forms of agreement are used because it would be too time consuming and uneconomic for a large busy company to draft a new agreement in similar terms for each individual artiste. The basic variable terms are negotiated with the artiste, and may be incorporated as a schedule into the framework of the standard agreement. Any printed form offered to the artiste must be perused carefully by him to ensure that terms already stated in it, but not altered, do not conflict with those additional terms which are being separately negotiated. They may be new terms, or they may modify existing terms.

**32.6** The system of standard contracts saves time and energy by restricting the day to day negotiating to merely agreeing with the artiste what is to be set out in the blank spaces of the contract. However, a major artiste will warrant individual attention, as he is in a much more advantageous negotiating position. When negotiations have been concluded, failure to complete a standard form of contract properly is a potential cause of errors. The parties must not be able to repudiate the agreement for uncertainty, or as not representing at all what was agreed. Where there is substantial commercial risk and financial potential in the deal, it is safer to draft the agreement from scratch, even if it has to be based upon the standard terms.

**32.7** A common error is not drafting the agreement as a whole around its basic object. A rambling unstructured form of standard contract makes it vulnerable to expert analysis for discrepancies. Some draftsmen follow the Alice in Wonderland statement "What I tell you three times must be true". A complicated deal may have a long contract, but its language should be simple, and its meaning should be clear.

## 33 Changes in circumstances

**33.1** If a contract was fair, reasonable, fully understood and agreed to at the time it was signed, the fact that circumstances may have changed, ie, the artiste is now much more successful, does not make the contract unenforceable. If, with the benefit of hindsight, it seems that there may have been undue influence, non-disclosure or misrepresentation, which caused or mainly contributed to the apparent disparity of value or benefit to the artiste under the contract, he may have a claim for modification or termination of it.

Unless a contracting party is under one of the legal disabilities such as infancy, lunacy or bankruptcy, on the face of it and until proven otherwise, he is deemed to have considered and agreed to all his obligations contained in the agreement, and to be competent legally to enter into it. Applying the same reasoning, if a well-known artiste negotiates a very favourable contract based on continued anticipated success, would he be prepared to negotiate downwards if, to the surprise of everyone his career takes a spectacular dive?

**33.2** In the music business it is common for the course of progress of an artiste's career, or the promotion of certain sides of it, to alter original financial aims and forecasts. In hindsight the artiste may feel that what was originally agreed to be paid to a manager, or to be received from a record company or music publisher, in the context of the circumstances at the time, does not now suit his status or requirements. This enhanced vision is a common cause of dispute. Success by an artiste tends to dim in his memory any recognition (where that is deserved) that (for example) the record company may have risked large sums of money, and made a great promotional effort for some years to achieve success for the artiste, but for all of which the artiste may never have attained such popularity.

**33.3** As success for the artiste also means success for his manager, it is clear that the manager is not in business only for the benefit of the artiste—a point which some artistes resent. A realistic manager will have his agreement with the artiste drafted to allow for financial adjustment and flexibility during the progress of the career of the artiste, to keep up with changing circumstances.

## 34 Bounced cheques

**34.1** A cheque is an authority by the drawer of it to his bank to pay the stated sum to the person named on the cheque. Receipt of a cheque does not mean the money will be paid, so when large sums are involved, or where the money to be received is also to be paid away contemporaneously, either cash or a banker's draft should be required. This precaution may not be necessary in practice where the paying party is of such financial and business standing and repute that their cheque is obviously acceptable, such as major record and publishing companies. Asking for a banker's draft is not considered to be an insult or a sign of mistrust by major companies. As a banker's draft is the same as cash, to be able to deposit a high value draft and get the interest for the days it might take for a cheque to clear has merit.

**34.2** Where an agreement is for the transfer of rights in consideration of the payment by one party to the other of a sum of money by cheque, the contract should be specifically held in escrow, ie not binding in law, until written notification of clearance of the cheque has been received through the payee's bank. Clearance of the cheque should be a condition precedent to the effectiveness of the contract. This is one example of where it is essential everytime to get a banker's draft, there is no point in having a conditional transfer.

**34.3** If the agreement becomes binding in law at the time when the parties sign it and the cheque is handed over, and the cheque then bounces, that will not necessarily re-open the contract if it contains other valid and adequate consideration for the transaction. The remedy is to sue for the payment of the amount due as a breach of contract, or to sue on the dishonoured cheque itself as a separate issue.

**34.4** The question is has there been sufficient consideration at the time of signing the contract to make it binding? If payment of the money represented by the cheque is the only legal consideration in the contract, it can be argued that if the cheque is not honoured, no consideration has passed, as it was to be a sum of money which was never received. Alternatively, as the cheque is only a means of transferring money, the obligation to pay is still outstanding and the contract remains in existence. The wording of the relevant clause in the contract must be considered. Most agreements which have the payment of money on signing as part of the consideration, also contain an acknowledgement of its receipt.

**34.5** An undertaking to pay money in the future is good consideration, and that promise is not necessarily broken by the cheque not being met. An example would be where the payment date is deferred by acceptance of a post-dated cheque, which is presented for payment well before that date, and which therefore is not paid. If the purpose of the agreement has yet to be concluded, and if the payment of money is the only outstanding condition, the position would be one of stalemate.

A claim for specific performance will be met by a claim for payment of the consideration.

## 35 Bankruptcy and liquidation

**35.1** An agreement for personal services should be terminable forthwith upon the bankruptcy of either the personal manager or the artiste. The following are among the practical restrictions which will apply to a bankrupt:

(a) no personal bank account can be opened or maintained by him;
(b) all money due to the bankrupt is payable to his trustee in bankruptcy;
(c) he cannot contract to pay money otherwise than through his trustee;
(d) he cannot obtain credit without disclosing his bankruptcy;
(e) he cannot become or remain a director of a company;
(f) any business of which he is a proprietor at the bankruptcy date comes under the control of the trustee;
(g) he cannot enter into commercial relationships with other parties.

**35.2** Bankruptcy severely restricts a successful artiste, as, until he obtains his discharge from bankruptcy, all royalties and fees due to him are directed to his trustee. However successful an artiste is, he can face bankruptcy if he runs up vast unpaid tax bills. Whether bankruptcy of an artiste will adversely affect contracts between him and third parties depends upon when they were entered into and for what real purpose, and upon whether the artiste obtains a reasonable benefit from them.

**35.3** Certain types of contracts entered into within the previous two years can be rescinded by the artiste's trustee. This will usually occur where the contracts were entered into shortly before the bankruptcy intentionally to defraud creditors by diverting funds otherwise receivable by the artiste, or by transferring assets, for the purpose of minimising the drastic effects of bankruptcy where it was likely or inevitable. The transferred assets can be repossessed by the trustee, except where several transactions later there is an independent *bona fide* third party purchaser for value.

**35.4** Bankruptcy of a member of a group of artistes trading as a partnership can create difficulties for the working activities of the group. Where the bankrupt artiste stays with the group, a deal will have to be done with the trustee to enable the group to fulfil its contractual commitments, and to spend and receive money without having to clear every transaction or decision with the trustee. The bankrupt artiste will probably leave the group, which can then continue in business unhindered. The trustee of the bankrupt artiste would be paid all future income due to him from all of his past activities.

**35.5** The same right of termination should apply where the company with which the artiste signs a contract ceases permanently to trade, or goes bust. Practical matters, which have been dealt with in other chapters are:

(a) should the artiste be entitled to claim back musical copyrights from a liquidated publisher?
(b) the artiste should, where appropriate, ensure that royalties due to him are not retained by the liquidated company's receiver for the benefit of all unsecured creditors.

**35.6** An interesting position would arise where the bankrupt member of a group is also its only composer, but where as part of the group membership agreement, all of the members of the group are attributed as joint composers. It is not likely that the composer member gets any additional benefit for agreeing to the deal, and if his trustee ever became aware of it, could he set it aside? The point never seems to have arisen.

## 36 Power of attorney

**36.1** Contracts should be drafted with reference to what safeguards can be applied when things go wrong. Where rights in the products of personal services are created, such as mechanical copyrights and musical copyrights, some contracts include an authority from the artiste to enable the other party to complete and sign assignment documents under a power of attorney given by the artiste. An example is where a composer has an exclusive songwriting agreement with a publisher, and he refuses to complete the confirmatory assignment of the copyright of a specific composition which has been composed under the agreement. Apart from its rights under the 1988 Copyright Act, by the composer giving it a power of attorney, the publisher is protected, and the artiste's estate is not deprived of anything. A power of attorney becomes invalid upon the death of the person giving it, even if it is stated to be irrevocable.

**36.2** There are clear rules which have to be complied with to enable a power of attorney to be valid under English law, and casually drafted clauses may be invalid. The exercise of the power must be strictly in accordance with its terms. If the artiste has no alternative, at least he must ensure that the terms of the power of attorney are clearly defined, and restricted in use to the proper purpose of the agreement.

## SECTION V: LICENCES AND ASSIGNMENTS

All contracts, whether for recording, publishing, merchandising or otherwise, where the artiste disposes of the rights in the products of his personal services, will be in the form either of a licence or of an assignment. The contracting parties should have a basic understanding of their respective major differences, advantages and disadvantages.

### 37 Broad definitions

**37.1** A licence grants a restricted legal right for a specified period of time. The restrictions are reservations by the licensor of all matters to be excluded from the licence, the terms governing the exercise of the rights, and the specific right of termination of the licence on the happening of certain events. Meanwhile, the underlying beneficial ownership of the rights remain with the licensor. As a guide, the outright sale of a right will be by assignment, while the granting of a temporary use of a right will be by licence.

**37.2** In an unconditional assignment, the legal and beneficial ownership of the subject passes absolutely out of the hands of the assignor to the assignee with no right of recall. If the assignment is conditional upon, for example, the completion of instalment payments, it will not be effective until all the payments have been made. In that example, care must be taken in drafting the assignment to ensure that it is not complete on payment of the first instalment, leaving the assignor only the right to sue for the balance of unpaid instalments.

**37.3** An assignment may contain an option in favour of the assignor to repurchase the rights, should the assignee wish to sell them at a later date. It may also contain a right for the assignor to call for reassignment of the rights upon the happening of any specified event, eg bankruptcy or liquidation of the assignee. Where there is an assignment with no conditions, and if the assignee breaches future obligations, the assignor is limited to a claim for damages only, and not to a claim for reassignment of the rights. Where the assignor of the rights has a right to call for a reassignment of them, their value at that time will be different to the value at the date of the original assignment. Does the assignor have to pay for the added value, or does he get it as a windfall? For example, the reassignment of copyrights at the end of a publishing deal will be for no payment. If the assignee originally purchased for value, such as where one publisher sells a catalogue to another, if he repurchases that catalogue at a later date he will pay the going market value at that time.

**37.4** There cannot be licensed or assigned any rights which are not either owned by the licensor or assignor, or which are not his to call for from a third party. If there is any difficulty on the part of the licensor or assignor in giving warranties of title to the rights, and if time is of the essence of concluding the deal, an unsatisfactory compromise is to give a conditional contract. That means if the condition is fulfilled the contract comes into operation, but if it is not fulfilled, it does not. The condition would be the ascertaining of the title to the rights in question, and there should be a time limit on doing so.

## 38 Distinction between licences and assignments

**38.1** The main use of licenses is in respect of merchandise agreements relating to the name or likeness of the artiste, and in record company contracts where the mechanical copyright in the recording is licensed from an independent production company. Musical copyrights are usually assigned by a composer to the music publisher, and sub-publishing agreements are usually by way of licence. A publishing agreement between a composer's company and a publisher will also be by a licence.

**38.2** It is unlikely that either party will warn the other of what to investigate before signing the contract, or what safeguards to require in it. In the negotiation of music business contracts, only a little knowledge of law and of the business practice is a dangerous thing. Expensive, and possibly irretrievable, errors can occur if proper advice is not obtained in the first place. One of the few things which can be forecast as a certainty in the music business is that the only two times any contract is looked at are when it is signed and when it is disputed. It is then analysed in a wholly different context.

**38.3** Music business contracts can be placed in two basic categories; those for the rendering of personal services, and those for the creation of products through the performance of personal services. Once the contract is terminated, in the former case the promoter has nothing further with which to deal, but in the latter case the two likely products to survive termination will be either recordings or musical copyrights. If, on the termination of the contract, the rights in the products are to remain with the other party, there will be an assignment. If the rights are to be returned to the original owner, there will be a licence.

## 39 Party executing the document

**39.1** The person executing a licence or assignment must be the person owning the rights, or the person who has the unquestionable authority of the owner of the rights to do so. There are two points to consider. First, the licensee or assignee must be satisfied that he acquires legal title to the recording or the copyrights as stated in the contract. Secondly, where an agent signs for and on behalf of the owner, both the agent and the licensee or assignee need to be satisfied that the authority is valid. A manager or agent may have the right under the terms of his contract to bind the artiste by signing an agreement "on his behalf". Nevertheless he will be at risk in so doing, unless the terms of the contract have first been agreed to by the artiste. If the artiste's authority is in vague or ambiguous terms, the artiste might deny later the validity of the authority of the manager or agent to commit him.

## 40 Minimum royalty provisions

**40.1** For the protection of the licensor, the liability of a licensee to fulfil his obligations, or to do a good job, can be safeguarded to some extent by having a "minimum royalty" clause. As record companies will never guarantee any level of sales of records (advances on account of royalties only represent a figure they hope they can recover), minimum royalty provisions apply mainly to merchandise agreements (see chapter **9**). Failure to reach the minimum stated payments by not having done enough to generate the necessary income should entitle the licensor to terminate the licence. What may not always be fully covered by this clause is the incapable licensee who has not been successful, but who wishes to continue representing the licensor, and so makes up the deficit in the necessary minimum payments out of his pocket in order to keep the rights.

**40.2** To counter this in relation to products, the requirement could be minimum certified sales. This system will also discourage the speculative investor who would like to tie up an artiste with a comprehensive contract in recognition of future potential, but without any immediate intention of acting positively for his benefit.

## 41 Sublicences

**41.1** A sublicence is a delegation by a licensee of his own rights to a third party. When a licensee grants a sublicence, he must receive from his sublicensee a return which will cover at least his obligation to account to his own licensor. The more "middle men" there are, the greater is the progressive deduction from gross income needed to satisfy the commission requirements of each sublicensee in his turn.

**41.2** A licensee must pass on to his sublicensee all of his obligations under the original licence. He should also require from the sublicensee indemnities in respect of breaches by him of any term of the licence. Some major obligations are the observation of territorial limits; to maintain quality and service; to account for business done and income arising; to preserve the head licensor's rights, and to deal with termination of sublicences when the main licence ends.

**41.3** It would be acting in bad faith to ask the sublicensee to take over any outstanding obligations of the sublicensor without first disclosing them in full, and allowing the sublicensee to ascertain whether they affect his decision to take the sublicence.

**41.4** Whether a licence is granted to an individual or to a company, for the protection of the licensor the right of the licensee to assign the benefit of the licence or any part of it should be restricted to either a re-assignment to the licensor, or to an assignment only to a reputable assignee with the licensor's prior written consent.

**41.5** The consent may either be given at the absolute discretion of the licensor, or it may be "not to be unreasonably withheld". What is reasonable depends on the reasons for the assignment, the financial standing of the assignee, and the likelihood of the assignment being detrimental to the licensor. A relaxation would be to enable an individual to assign the benefit of the licence to a company of which he remains both a director and the controlling shareholder. In all cases the licensor would be entitled to ask the licensee to enter into a specific guarantee of the performance by the sublicensee of its obligations.

**41.6** The first sublicensor, ie the original licensee, will remain liable to the licensor for the acts and defaults of any sublicensee, as he is the original contracting party. His sublicence is only treated as a form of delegation of his own rights and obligations. For this reason indemnities, prior references and guarantors of good standing may be required from the sublicensee to protect the sublicensor from being held liable by the licensor for the consequences of breaches by the sublicensee.

## 42 Continuity for sublicensee

**42.1** A sublicensee will lose his rights upon the termination of the main licence. To avoid the potential complications of sublicences, and to protect the continuity of the rights to be acquired by a prospective sublicensee, the licensee can approach the licensor to see whether he will accept a surrender of the existing licence. If the licensor will do so, he can release the original licensee, and transfer the licence directly to the sublicensee.

**42.2** The benefit to the original licensee is that he no longer has potential liabilities under a licence in which he is not active. The main advantage to the new licensee is he is dealing direct with the licensor. A possible disadvantage to the original licensee may be that he was going to make a profit on the difference between what he would have received from the sublicensee, and what he was obliged to pay his licensor.

APPENDIX I

# *Questions and Answers*

This Appendix consists of a number of questions and answers which may well be asked by artistes who are not yet familiar with dealing with managers, record companies, publishers and agents. It is assumed that readers of the chapters on the relevant contracts will have an elementary understanding of how the business works, and it is hoped that these answers will be useful. They are the writer's views, and are intended to be a guideline only, not an absolute bench mark.

## MANAGEMENT QUESTIONS

**Q1** What do I look for in a manager?

**A1** Someone who is established, experienced and with a good reputation. Find out if he really is interested enough to sustain an effort until things develop.

**Q2** Do I give worldwide or European representation?

**A2** A major management will want worldwide representation. If the manager is not active internationally and if you are in an early stage in touring and recording, give him UK or European rights.

**Q3** What is a fair management commission?

**A3** This depends on what the manager will do for you, and sometimes on whether he actually gets you recording and publishing deals, or only inherits them. The top rate is 20%, but it is not likely to be less than 15%.

**Q4** What management expenses should I pay for?

**A4** You should only pay for expenses which are not the manager's ordinary business costs and which you are first consulted on, and approve. You will of course be responsible for payments he makes on your behalf as a convenience for your benefit, and which are not his own expenditure.

**Q5** What are the manager's responsibilities?

**A5** To do his best to get you work, and long term contracts for recording and publishing. All these activities will be part of his overall obligation to promote you and your career, and make you money.

**Q6** How long should the management agreement be for?

**A6** Normally between three and five years, but preferably three. It might be extendable if specified targets are achieved. Alternatively, have a one year trial period with a specified target (such as a recording contract) which would then extend for a further period of two or three years.

**Q7** How should I be able to terminate the management agreement?

**A7** Apart from the standard termination reasons, you will want to terminate the agreement if the manager and you fall out seriously, or if he does not exert himself sufficiently and reasonably for you.

**Q8** Must the agreement be exclusive?

**A8** Yes, for the benefit of both of you. It is the exclusivity which makes sensible termination provisions an essential safeguard.

**Q9** What are fair manager's commission rates after termination?

**A9** In fairness the manager should be entitled to commission for a reasonable period after termination, for two reasons. The first is that due to the time lag in the creation of and accounting for income, there will be commissionable income arriving after termination. The second is that if the manager has built you up during the lean years, he should have some on-going benefit from the success so developed. An exception may be if you have terminated the agreement for good reason, such as dishonesty of the manager.

**Q10** Do I have to do what my manager wants?

**A10** No. He is there to advise, direct and manage, but you as his employer have the final decision on all things. You should not be penalised for not agreeing to do something proposed.

**Q11** Should my manager receive all my income?

**A11** In the early years he will, as it will be needed for expenses and promotion. If your income becomes significant you will need an accountant, and he or your bank can receive it. So can the manager, if you trust him and he is not likely to go bust.

**Q12** Can I insist on personal management?

**A12** Generally only if the manager is already an individual, or if an individual in the management company was the only reason you appointed it.

**Q13** Can I be involved in planning my career?

**A13** You must be involved. Managers are advisers; accept their guidance, but the responsibility of decision making is yours.

**Q14** What happens if I leave my band and join another one?

**A14** If you are a group member and you leave it, you will remain subject to the management agreement if you signed it in an individual capacity.

## AGENCY QUESTIONS

**Q1** Where do I find an agent?

**A1** An agent will only be interested when you have a record out or have some other platform from which you can justify being given a support act status. The decision will be that of the main act, who may not want to risk an unknown "warm up".

**Q2** Do I give worldwide or European representation?

**A2** For an unknown artiste UK and Europe will be adequate, otherwise it is a matter of commercial judgment.

**Q3** What is a fair agency commission?

**A3** Anywhere between 10% and 15% in the normal circumstances. There may be a good reason why in specific circumstances a higher rate is agreed, but an agent does not have the same responsibility or role as a manager. A combined management and agency commission of 35% is already a substantial expense out of gross income.

**Q4** What agency expenses should I pay for?

**A4** The principles relating to management expenses apply also to agents.

**Q5** What are the agent's responsibilities?

**A5** To get you live appearance dates, and to promote your reputation and career by so doing. An agent is not involved in other activities.

**Q6** How long should the agency agreement be for?

**A6** An annual renewable contract will be sufficient for a new artiste. A fixed period will not normally exceed two or at most three years.

**Q7** Will my agent and manager work together?

**A7** Yes. The agent will present all proposals to your manager, who will consult you upon them. Any appearance offers obtained by the agent must fit in with your record release schedule and other business activities.

## RECORDING QUESTIONS

**Q1** What does a record company look for?

**A1** It is difficult to get a record deal. To take an artiste for recording requires a high investment of time, effort and money; so is the artiste likely to be profitable? The assessment is almost like any other venture—is the product (ie, artiste plus material) commercially attractive, is it able financially to support record company effort (such as by touring), and does it have effective management?

**Q2** How do I get a record company's attention?

**A2** Sending tapes in to the A & R department is useless. You can have a show case appearance and invite record companies, but they won't attend unless there is a compelling reason. Record company executives are very pressed for time, if there is any between lunch and meetings. A personal introduction at the highest level through a respected manager is the best approach.

**Q3** How long will a record deal be for?

**A3** That depends. For a new artiste there may be a series of option years, each successive option only being exercised if the previous year was successful. For a successful artiste the choice is between, say, a three year period or, say five albums, however long it takes to record them.

**Q4** Will I be committed to making a minimum number of records?

**A4** You may be committed to making a minimum number of records at the request of the record company. It will not itself commit to making any, except for the first contract period. It is an each way bet to enable the record company to develop success, and to drop failure, as theirs is the financial risk. If the record company accepts a minimum commitment (say one album) per year, the agreement will normally say that if it does not enable you to make the record you have no claim for damages for potential lost earnings, reputation and career development.

**Q5** Will the record company control the choice of what I record?

**A5** It will include that right in its contract, but only to stop you recording junk just to complete your album commitment. On the basis that both you and your company will want successful records, the choice will be agreed between you.

**Q6** What is a "commercially acceptable" recording?

**A6** The best that can be reasonably achieved by way of artistic interpretations and technical quality. This will be the producer's responsibility.

**Q7** Will the record company pay for making the recording?

**A7** Yes, but the cost will be treated as an advance to you on account of royalties. If the advance is not recouped, you do not have to pay it back. Hence the importance of keeping recording costs to a minimum. This applies to all recoupable advances.

**Q8** Who will choose and pay for the record producer?

**A8** For a new artiste the record company will choose the producer, a successful artiste will choose his own. The producer gets a royalty on record sales, which should be the responsibility of the record company if the artiste gets an average royalty.

**Q9** What is a fair royalty rate on record sales?

**A9** What is fair depends on the artiste's expected record sales level. An average royalty would be between 10% and 12% of sales price (less VAT and packaging costs) on full price records. The royalty will be reduced for budget and other types of lower price sales.

**Q10** Do I get paid on all records sold?

**A10** You should be paid on all records sold and not returned, for which the income has been received by the record company. You might be paid on 95% of all records sold, the 5% being to cover returns. In some countries record returns can be high, so they will be deducted.

**Q11** What is the purpose of a royalty reserve?

**A11** A royalty reserve retained by the record company is to cover the likelihood that returns in the next accounting period will be from sales in the prior period. It is a means of ensuring that the record company is covered in advance for returns deductions.

**Q12** What royalty advances can I expect?

**A12** Apart from recoupment of recording costs, the record company should agree to make a cash advance as well. The amount will depend on projected recoupment risk. Advances can be paid on any of the contract signature, yearly option renewals and album deliveries. All advances are normally recoupable. A non-recoupable advance is effectively a gift from the record company.

**Q13** Do record companies guarantee to release records I make?

**A13** Even if you make a record the record company will not undertake to release it. It will normally release it in your own territory, the UK. It will only be released elsewhere if the local record company likes it, but that is not your record company's decision.

**Q14** What can I do if the record company does not release a record everywhere?

**A14** Nothing, if it has no commitment. A successful artiste can negotiate a clause which states that if his records are not released in specified territories within (say) nine months after its UK release, the territory and the album and all future albums for that territory will revert to the artiste.

The territory would have to be isolated, such as Australia, and not an individual European country.

**Q15** Will the record company want worldwide rights?

**A15** Yes, unless the artiste is so strong internationally that, for example, separate territories can be profitable—such as Australia; North America and Japan; Europe and Scandinavia.

**Q16** Do I still get paid if my record company goes bust?

**A16** Only to the same extent as all other unsecured creditors, however well your records sell.

## PUBLISHING QUESTIONS

**Q1** Do I need a publisher, are they worthwhile?

**A1** If your compositions are never recorded you don't need a publisher, and there is nothing from which either of you could make any money. If you have compositions on internationally sold records, you need someone to collect the copyright royalties for you. The greater the exposure of your songs commercially, the more economically justified is the cost of having an effective publisher, who has a vested interest in collecting everything due to you.

**Q2** What is a fair proportion of my song's earnings for me to receive?

**A2** Years ago 50% was the norm for starters. The norm now is between 60% for a new composer, up to 75% or 80% if the composer is very successful with high and constant earnings from his songs.

**Q3** What does the publisher do for its share?

**A3** The publisher should use its publishing network in its territory to register your song with the local PRs, collect all mechanical and other income arising, try to get a cover record locally, and generally promote the songs. In practice all songs cannot get individual attention. But have you got the time, experience and energy to do better?

**Q4** Will my share of income ever increase?

**A4** When you renew your agreement or switch your publisher at the expiry of its agreement you can negotiate an increased share of income if you started at a relatively low level and have been successful. There is normally a ceiling of 80%

**Q5** How do advance payments work, and should I ask for them?

**A5** Advances are on account of royalties, to be recouped in full before you receive royalty payments. They are an inducement, and effectively an interest free loan. Publishers will pay advances, so ask for one. The amount will depend on whether the publisher is getting an existing active recorded catalogue of your songs, or if you have just signed your first record deal. It is simply a risk assessment.

**Q6** Do I have any control over my publisher?

**A6** Influence yes, control no. Most publishers welcome constructive suggestions. Provided they use their reasonable endeavours they can act at their discretion. Without record sales there is nothing to publish.

**Q7** Can I ever get my songs back?

**A7** Your publishing agreement should state that if a song is not recorded or does not have other substantial commercial use within, say, two years, you can ask for that copyright back free of charge.

**Q8** What period should I be committed for?

**A8** Anywhere between three and five years, depending on the status of your recording career. After expiry the publisher will retain the rights in those songs written during the period of your agreement, but you can publish new songs elsewhere.

**Q9** What territory should I give my publisher?

**A9** A publisher will want worldwide rights for a new composer. A successful established composer will probably grant territorial rights to get the most out of his catalogue. The right choice of publisher is important.

**Q10** What are my responsibilities to my publisher?

**A10** To act in good faith, pursue an active writing career, and assign to him the copyright in all material written during his agreement period, whether or not recorded. You earn more from your songs than he does, so help him where you can.

**Q11** Can I co-write songs with other composers?

**A11** Yes, but check your agreement. If the co-writer is free for publishing, you must get him to publish his share of the joint composition with your publisher.

**Q12** How do I know I am being accounted to properly?

**A12** If you have strong justifiable suspicion of fraud or dishonesty, then audit the publisher. Major publishers will account correctly, but all are subject to arithmetical error or incorrect percentage attribution. If in doubt, ask. You can have a rough check by comparing the publisher's accounting against record sales and your own PRS returns.

**Q13** Can I write music for other people, such as for a film soundtrack, where the film company want to own it?

**A13** Only if your agreement excludes that from the publisher's rights, or if your publisher does a deal with the film company.

**Q14** Do I have to provide a minimum number of songs to the publisher?

**A14** Steer clear of such a commitment. Just a minimum number of songs is meaningless without some qualitative benchmark. Short of owning a record production company you cannot guarantee releasing a significant number of recorded compositions in the relevant period. This idea usually relates to high advances, which can only be recouped if there is a sufficient volume of recorded compositions which sell well.

**Q15** What happens if my publisher goes bust?

**A15** Ordinarily, you are just an unsecured creditor, so your money in his bank account goes into the "pot" from which all his debts are cleared before all creditors receive the balance *pro rata*.

# APPENDIX II

# *Example agreements*

This Appendix contains examples of agreements relating to each of the chapters, with the exception of chapter five. Recording agreements differ widely from company to company so the example given is only a basic format for illustration.

There is no perfect agreement which deals with everything, and which is an industry-wide standard. Each manager, record company or publisher has its own form of agreement which is designed to suit its business requirements. These examples are intended to give an idea of what should be dealt with, but they are not put forward as being the all-embracing last word.

Some of the concept clauses may be considered revolutionary or over the top, but they are worth looking at. They are influenced by the reasons given by the judges in the cases set out in Appendix III for granting relief to artistes and composers when setting agreements aside. A brief analysis of those reasons is set out at the end of Appendix III, and it would be useful for the reader to look at that analysis before going through these example agreements.

The major features within each category of agreement tend to be common to all of the relevant companies, but each company has a different approach to commitments.

There are common "boiler plate" clauses which have been set out from clause 10 onwards of the management agreement, and which are not repeated in each agreement. Where different example agreements contain similar clauses, they are not always worded the same, so a variety of approaches can be seen. When drafting any agreement, choose the appropriate clauses, and modify them where necessary. Individual deals may need additional clauses to cater for specific agreed terms.

At the end of each example agreement there are some notes on clauses which need some explanation or comment. The numbers refer to the clause numbers of the relevant agreement.

## MANAGEMENT AGREEMENT

THIS AGREEMENT is made the day of 19
BETWEEN of
(hereinafter called the Artiste) of the one part and
of
(hereinafter called the Manager) of the other part

WHEREAS at the request of the Artiste the Manager has been advising him on his entertainment career since on or about [ ] and the Artiste now wishes to make the appointment permanent.

NOW IT IS AGREED as follows:

*Appointment*

1 (a) Subject to and upon the terms and conditions herein set out the Artiste hereby appoints the Manager as his sole and exclusive manager and agent throughout [the World] hereinafter called the Territory.

(b) It is of the essence of this Agreement that the Manager provides the personal services of Mr [ ] at all times to manage and supervise the career of the Artiste [or such other person as may be approved by the Artiste and such approval may be given or withheld in his absolute discretion].

(c) The Artiste agrees to refer to the Manager all enquiries for his services hereunder received by him and also agrees in conformity with Clause 5(a) not to sign any agreement coming within the terms of this Agreement without first taking the Manager's advice thereon.

(d) During the period of this Agreement the Artiste undertakes not to appoint any other person firm or corporation as his manager in breach of any terms contained herein.

*Managed activities*

2 The appointment of the Manager shall be in respect of all the activities of the Artiste within the [popular music] entertainment industry including but not limited to the following:

(a) Personal appearances whether or not before an audience and whether or not live and/or recorded for exhibition or broadcast.

(b) The making and commercial distribution and sale of audio and audio/visual recordings of performances of the Artiste in any mechanical, tape, laser, electronic or other format.

(c) The writing of musical compositions with or without lyrics and the writing of lyrics whether or not the Artiste composed the music and the making of any musical arrangements adaptations or versions thereof.

(d) Exploiting his name reputation and image by merchandising sponsorship endorsement or any other advertising or promotional means.

(e) Producing engineering and supervising recordings to be made by any other Artiste.

(f) The Artiste appearing in television programmes cinematograph films or in live theatre productions as an artiste or as a serious actor.

*Period of Agreement*

3 (a) This Agreement shall be deemed to have commenced on the [ ] and (subject to clauses 3(b) and 10 hereof) shall continue for a period of [three] years.

(b) If the Manager has not procured for the Artiste the signing of a long term recording contract (with reasonably acceptable terms) with a major commercial record company within [six] months after the date of signing this Agreement then the Artiste shall be entitled during the [four week] period thereafter to terminate this Agreement forthwith by giving the Manager written notice.

*Artiste's warranties*

4 The Artiste warrants to the Manager that he is entitled to enter into this Agreement and that (save as disclosed in the Schedule hereto) there is no

existing written or oral agreement commitment or understanding with any third party which is contrary to or which inhibits the rights herein granted to the Manager and that during the period hereof he will not enter into any such agreement commitment or understanding.

*Manager's obligations*

5 The Manager agrees with the Artiste that it will undertake the following matters to the best of its ability in good faith:

(a) It will plan the career of the Artiste and advise him on all matters which arise for consideration and on matters which the Manager believes should be investigated for the purpose of obtaining employment or generally developing his career and enhancing his reputation.

(b) Where necessary it will appoint such agents as shall be agreed after consultation with the Artiste upon such terms as shall be appropriate for the purpose of the appointment and the agency commission and its recoupable expenses will be the liability of the Artiste.

(c) It will negotiate (or supervise the negotiation by the agent of) all personal appearance contracts and other contracts for his personal services or otherwise arising within the activities referred to in Clause 2 provided that in all cases:

(i) The Artiste will first be consulted for his approval upon the advisability and potential benefits of entering into any such contract and the commitments relating to the contract will be explained to him.

(ii) Except as otherwise authorised by the Artiste in writing all contracts in respect of which he has any obligation will be signed by him.

(d) It will take all reasonable steps to ensure that any payment to be made to the Artiste under any contract is collected and that where advisable suitable arrangements are made in advance to secure such payment.

(e) It will arrange that all substantial income for the Artiste from his recording or music publishing contracts are paid directly to his accountant (or such other party he nominates) who will be authorised by the Artiste to make the payments due to the Manager under Clause 7 hereof.

(f) It will receive all personal performance and (subject to (e) above) other income due to the Artiste and will open a trust account at its bank in the name of the Artiste for all income and expense relating to the Artiste and in respect thereof the Manager will:

(i) Maintain complete and accurate [monthly] accounts and cash flow requirement forecasts in consultation with the Artiste.

(ii) Pay to the Artiste all excess funds not required in the near future after deducting all commission and other money properly due to the Manager under (f)(iv) and subject to Clause 6(d).

(iii) Give copies of all such [monthly] accounts to the Artiste's accountant so that (*inter alia*) the Artiste's tax liabilities can be reserved for in full.

(iv) Reimburse itself the management commission due to it on all such income together with all authorised expenditure incurred for the benefit of the Artiste in accordance with Clauses 6(b), 6(c) and 7(d).

(g) It will do all other things necessary to deal with or to fulfil all of the above obligations and will provide all management related services customarily expected from a manager.

(h) In the event of the Manager becoming aware at any time of a potential conflict of interest as between itself and the Artiste in any matter it will promptly and fully disclose such conflict in writing to the Artiste with a view to resolving it in good faith and to enable the Artiste to take independent legal advice thereon.

*Management expenses*

6 (a) The Manager will be responsible for all of its ordinary business expenses and all other expenses incurred by it in undertaking its activities hereunder for the benefit of the Artiste except as set out in (b) below.

(b) The Artiste will be responsible for any extraordinary expense incurred by the Manager at the specific request of the Artiste and which shall be approved by the Artiste prior to being incurred if it exceeds (£250) as well as any expense incurred by the Manager on behalf of the Artiste and which is not a management expense and in this regard if the Manager in good faith and for the benefit of the Artiste pays any outstanding account or liability of the Artiste he will be entitled to be reimbursed.

(c) Recoupable expenses incurred by the Manager for the Artiste will include but will not be limited to:

(i) All travel accommodation *per diem* and incidental expenses for the Artiste and any group member or other person connected with the Artiste or for whom the Artiste is responsible.

(ii) Promotional and advertising expenses including reasonable entertaining costs (but not to exceed [ ] in any month without approval).

(iii) Agreed equipment or vehicle purchase lease or rental costs.

(d) The Manager is hereby authorised to reimburse itself all reasonable expenditure due to it under (b) and (c) above but the Manager will ensure that the cash flow forecast and retention of income referred to in Clause 5(f) takes reimbursements into account when calculating forthcoming cash requirements and payments to the Artiste under clause 5(f)(ii) will be subject to all such retentions from money received by the Manager.

(e) The Artiste acknowledges that it has approved the account submitted by the Manager in respect of expenses for which the Artiste is liable from the effective date in Clause 3(a) to the date of execution hereof and that the agreed sum of [ ] shall be recoupable by the Manager under (d) above.

*Management commission*

7 (a)(i) In consideration of the Manager fulfilling all of its obligations hereunder the Artiste agrees to pay the Manager [ ] percent of the gross earnings of the Artiste received during the period of this Agreement by the Artiste or by any party on his behalf from activities of the Artiste as set out in Clause 2 within the Territory arising from contracts procured by the Manager during the period of this Agreement provided that in respect of tours undertaken by the Artiste outside the UK the commission shall be [ ] percent of net profit where "net profit" means gross tour income less the direct costs of running the tour (but excluding agency commission on tour income and excluding third party tour support value or payments).

(ii) In respect of income received from the Artiste's existing recording and music publishing agreements the management commission shall commence upon accountings made by each of those companies on or after the [ ] [and the commission rate payable in respect of such income shall be [ ] percent]. If during the period of this Agreement the Manager procures or negotiates a new contract with a different recording or publishing company the commission on the income arising therefrom shall be at the rate set out in (a)(i) above.

(b) Subject to (c) below commission will be payable to the Manager on income received by the Artiste after the expiry of this Agreement as follows:

(i) In respect of the Artiste's then existing recording contract upon royalties paid in the (two) half yearly accountings after expiry in respect of recordings made and released prior to expiry and in respect of any recordings made during the period of this Agreement but not released until after its expiry (but only if it is released within [4] months thereof) upon royalties paid in the (two) first half yearly accountings in respect of sales of that recording.

(ii) In respect of the Artiste's publishing contract upon royalties paid in the [two] half yearly accountings after expiry in respect of compositions written during the period of this Agreement.

(iii) In respect of any tour or extensive booking at one venue in being at the date of termination upon the income arising for the whole of such tour or booking including any uninterrupted extension thereof.

(c) No commission will be payable on record royalties retained in recoupment of recording costs or on promotion video recoupable costs or upon support provided by any party to reduce a tour loss or cost in whatever form that support may take.

(d) All travelling accommodation and other expenses incurred by the Manager will be its own liability except as set out in Clause 6(b) and also where the Artiste agrees that reasonable costs for travel on tour or to check on recording being undertaken abroad will be chargeable to the Artiste.

(e) The Manager will not be entitled to receive any commission on income paid (whenever arising) after the date of termination under subclauses (b)(i) (ii) and (iii) of this Clause if this Agreement is properly terminated by the Artiste under Clause 10(a) below.

*Manager's accounts*

8 (a) The Manager shall maintain complete and accurate books of account in respect of all income of the Artiste received by it and of all expenditure made by it which is recoupable from the Artiste and will maintain complete copies of all contracts under which fees or royalties are payable to the Artiste and all documents under which payments are made on behalf of the Artiste or otherwise for his account and the Manager will account to the Artiste accurately and fully in respect thereof.

(b) The Artiste or his authorised representative will be entitled to inspect and take copies of all accounts maintained by the Manager not more than once in each year upon giving it not less than 14 days prior notice in writing.

*Management of other artistes*

9 The Manager shall be entitled to manage any other artistes provided that the ability of the Manager to provide the Artiste with the same level of attention and expertise is not impaired and that no conflict of interest arises

between the Artiste and any other new artiste taken on for management by the Manager and subject to Clause 1(b).

*Termination*

10 (a) Either party shall be entitled to terminate this Agreement by written notice upon the happening of any of the following events:

(i) The other party failing to remedy a material breach of this Agreement within [21] days after receiving a written notice specifying the breach and requiring its remedy.

(ii) The other party persistently being in material breach of this Agreement and for this purpose "persistently" means the [third] occasion upon which the other party has received a written notice under (i) above not withstanding that it or he has on the previous [two] occasions remedied the relevant breach in time.

(iii) The Manager failing to provide the Artiste with the personal services of [ ] or such other approved person in accordance with Clause 1(b) otherwise than for reasons of holiday temporary ill-health or any other reasonable explanation of temporary absence and for this purpose "temporary" shall mean a continuous period not exceeding [one] month.

(iv) The Manager winding up ceasing to trade or compounding with its creditors.

(b) Termination of this Agreement will be without prejudice to any rights of either party existing at that time.

(c) If a party waives any breach by the other party that will not be deemed to be a waiver of any other breach whether or not of a similar nature. For the purposes of this subclause a party will be deemed to have waived a breach if in the full knowledge thereof no action is taken in respect thereof within [ ] weeks after becoming aware of the breach.

*Confidentiality*

11 Each party agrees with the other that it will maintain as confidential and will not make any unauthorised use of any private or confidential information about the other party and its business or its private and financial affairs as the case may be.

*Assignment*

12 The Manager shall not be entitled to assign the benefit of this Agreement or any of its obligations hereunder to any other party without the prior written consent of the Artiste which shall not be unreasonably withheld provided that the obligation set out in Clause 1(b) remains fulfilled and that the proposed assignee has no less a name reputation and commercial and financial status as the Manager.

*Notices*

13 Any notice to be given under this Agreement shall be in writing and to be effective shall be delivered or sent by recorded delivery to the Manager at its registered office and shall be delivered personally to the Artiste or sent by recorded delivery to his last known permanent address provided that if the Artiste is outside the UK on tour or recording or otherwise the notice must be delivered to him personally to be effective.

*Entire agreement*

14 (a) This document contains the entire agreement between the parties and any prior representation statement or assurance which is not set out herein will not be effective.

(b) Each party agrees and confirms that there is no representation or statement upon which they have relied in entering into this Agreement and which is not set out herein.

(c) This Agreement may only be modified by a written instrument signed by both parties.

*Force majeure*

15 Neither party will be deemed to be in breach of any of its obligations if prevented from carrying them out due to circumstances beyond their control provided that:

(a) if it is possible to achieve the purpose of the obligation in any other reasonably expedient manner the breaching party will do so; and

(b) as soon as the preventing circumstances cease to apply the breaching party will promptly fulfil any outstanding part of the obligation;

(c) the parties will co-operate to minimise any adverse consequences during the period of the intervening *force majeure* circumstances.

*Unauthorised commitment*

16 The Manager has no authority to (and undertakes not to) pledge the credit of the Artiste or to purport to enter into any commitment on his behalf which is not within the express authority granted to him hereunder.

*Schedules*

17 Any Schedule or attachment hereto shall be deemed to be incorporated herein provided that if there shall be any conflict between the terms of this Agreement and any schedule or attachment then this Agreement shall prevail.

*Applicable law*

18 This Agreement shall be construed and enforced in accordance with the Laws of England and the English High Court will be the court of competent jurisdiction.

*Invalidity*

19 If any part of this Agreement is found to be invalid due to the application of any UK or EEC law or legal principle then that invalid part will be deemed removed from this Agreement and the parties agree to use their best endeavours in good faith to achieve the same objective by a lawful means.

*Legal advice*

20 Both parties confirm they have taken legal advice on the construction obligations and consequences of the terms of this Agreement which affect them and that they are fully understood and agreed.

*Clause headings*

21 The headings to the clauses are for convenience only and are not to be taken into account in the interpretation of any part of this Agreement.

IN WITNESS whereof the hands of the parties have been hereunto affixed the day and year first above written.

SIGNED by the said
[the Artiste]
in the presence of:

SIGNED FOR AND ON BEHALF OF
[The Manager] Limited
in the presence of:

**Comments on this agreement**

Whereas—delete or modify according to the facts.

1(b) This is not needed if the manager is an individual.

2(b) and (c) These are needed even if long term recording and publishing agreements already exist, in case they terminate and new ones will be negotiated.

3(b) When the period expires the artiste should decide promptly whether to terminate or continue the contract.

4 All potential problems or contract claims must be disclosed.

5 If the manager is expected to do any specific matters as part of his appointment, they should be set out.

7(a)(ii) If the artiste has just terminated a management agreement, where the ex-manager is entitled to his commission on recording and publishing royalties for a period after termination, the artiste should not pay two commissions on the same income. If the artiste/composer is already highly successful, he may want a lower commission to be payable on those existing sources of income.

7(b)(i) and (ii) Whatever extra collection time is allowed to the manager must be clear. This affects the financial ability of the artiste to give his new manager commission on that income. Two full commission rates would be wholly uneconomical.

10(a)(iv) Add "if bankruptcy proceedings are instituted against him" if the manager is an individual.

AGENCY AGREEMENT

THIS AGREEMENT is made the day of 19
BETWEEN of
(hereinafter called the Artiste) of the one part and
of
(hereinafter called the Agent) of the other part

WHEREBY it is agreed as follows:

*Appointment*

1 The Artiste hereby appoints the Agent to be his exclusive agent [throughout the world] [for the countries set out in the Schedule hereto] (hereinafter called the Territory) in respect of live concert and touring appearances of the Artiste.

*Period*

2 This Agreement shall be for an initial period of one year and shall be renewable by mutual agreement on an annual basis thereafter.

*Agent's obligations*

3 (a) The Agent shall use its best endeavours to obtain offers of employment for the Artiste from Promoters within the Territory and shall communicate all such offers to the Artiste's Manager (the Manager) and shall discuss the same with the Manager (and the Artiste if the Artiste wishes to do so).

(b) If the offer of employment is acceptable in principle the Agent will promptly negotiate with the Promoter suitable terms for the appearance contract in accordance with the instructions or directions of the Manager.

(c) The final terms available from the Promoter will be submitted to the Manager for approval and if approval is given the Agent will submit to the Manager the Contract with the Promoter which has already been signed by the Promoter and when the Artiste signs the appearance contract the Agent will effect an exchange of signed contracts with the Promoter.

(d) The Agent is not authorised or entitled to make any assurance or commitment on behalf of the Artiste to any third party which has not been specifically approved by the Artiste.

4 (a) Upon exchange of any appearance contract where a percentage of the fee is payable in advance the Agent will ensure that it is paid on or before such exchange and that it will be held on deposit for the benefit of the Artiste pending completion by him of the contracted engagement.

(b) If terms of a tour contract include the provision by the Promoter of goods and/or services such as equipment or airfares the Agent will use reasonable endeavours to ensure that the Promoter will fulfil his obligations but it is acknowledged by the Artiste that such supervision is not an absolute obligation of the Agent under this Agreement.

(c) Unless other specific arrangements have been made with the Promoter the Agent will ensure the collection of the balance of the fee together with any other payments which may be due to the Artiste under the appearance contract promptly after its completion and the Agent will account to the Artiste for the whole of the fee plus any interest on the advance fee deposit less the commission due to the Agent within [ten] working days after the completion by the Artiste of the contracted event.

*Agent's commission*

5 (a) In consideration of the performance by the Agent of its obligations hereunder the Artiste agrees to pay to it a commission of [ ] percent of the gross fees received by the Artiste or by any party on his behalf from the personal appearance engagements performed by the Artiste procured or negotiated by the Agent or by any other party on behalf of the Artiste during the period of this Agreement and to be performed either during or after the exclusive period of this Agreement.

(b) A commissionable event under this Agreement will include any uninterrupted extension of such event where that extension goes beyond the termination date of this Agreement.

(c) This Agreement will not extend to any personal live appearance of the Artiste the primary purpose of which is to record in sound or audio-visually such performance for promotional or commercial use except that if it is performed before a paying audience and the Artiste receives a separate and distinct fee for the appearance itself and not related to or being on account of any fee royalty or other payment to be made to the Artiste in respect of such recording then the Agent will be entitled to receive commission on that appearance fee.

(d) The Agent will not be entitled to be paid any commission on the following:

(i) Any form of tour support in money paid by the Artiste's record company publisher or any other party whether or not it will be recouped by that party from royalties or other payments due to the Artiste under the relevant contract.

(ii) Any form of tour support received by the Artiste in kind such as airline tickets or equipment or services discount facilities.

(iii) Any fee royalty or other payment received by the Artiste from radio stations record companies and other parties (except the Promoter of the event) in consideration of enabling any recording (audio or audio-visual) to be made of the live performance by the Artiste such as under (c) above.

*Appointment of sub-agent*

6 (a) If in respect of any appearance contract for an event to be performed outside the UK the Agent has utilised the services of any other party to secure or negotiate such event the Agent will be wholly responsible for the fee charged by that other party and in dealing with that other party the Agent shall be acting on its own behalf and shall not purport to do so on behalf of the Artiste and shall not act in any manner so as to commit the Artiste to any liability to that third party.

(b) If the Agent fails to pay such party or if the Agent is in breach of its agreement with such party whereby that party is successful in making a claim against the Artiste or in obtaining legal restraint on any part of the fee to be received by the Artiste from the promoter of the relevant event the Artiste shall be entitled to be paid on demand by the Agent that payment together with all legal and other costs incurred in defending the claim or to withhold all of it from the Agent's commission without prejudice to any other rights the Artiste may have against the Agent.

(c) If the Artiste agrees to be responsible for any part of the sub-agent's fee or commission that must be confirmed by him in writing to be effective.

(d) The Agent will not appoint any sub-agent within the UK without the prior written consent of the Artiste.

*Agent's expenses*

7 The Artiste will not be responsible for any expenses incurred by the Agent in connection with any activity it undertakes for the benefit of the Artiste unless they have been previously authorised and approved by the Artiste.

*Termination of exclusivity*

8 The Artiste will be entitled to terminate the exclusivity of this Agreement by giving the Agent not less than [one] month's written notice if the Agent in the reasonable opinion of the Artiste in good faith substantially fails to obtain the quality and amount of employment reasonably expected to be available to him within the Territory within the first [six] months of this Agreement.

[STANDARD CLAUSES]

IN WITNESS whereof the parties hereto have set their hands the day and year first above written.

**Comments on this Agreement**

8 As the agreement is exclusive, if the agent does little for the artiste, that can prevent him from earning a living. It will be in breach of its best endeavours obligation under clause 3(a), and the standard termination clause will enable the artiste to give a breach notice. As reasonable endeavours may be difficult to define, clause 8 is suggested as a possibility. It could of course be exercised harshly by the artiste, so should only apply to a "high risk" agent from the artiste's point of view.

## ARTISTE'S AGREEMENT WITH A PROMOTER

THIS AGREEMENT is made the day of 19
BETWEEN of
(hereinafter called the Promoter) of the one part and
(hereinafter called the Artiste) of the other part.

WHEREBY IT IS AGREED as follows:

*Definitions*

1 'The Venue" shall mean [hall, town, country]

"The Date" shall mean the [ ] of [ ]

"The Concert" shall mean the professional performance of the Artiste on the Date

"The Performance" shall mean the start time on the Date at or about [ ] with the performance of the Artiste continuing for not less than [90] minutes excluding encores

"The Fee" shall mean the sum of $[ ] [on account of [ ] percent of the value of all seated and standing ticket sales]

"The Deposit" shall mean [ ] percent of the Fee.

"The Artiste" shall mean the Artiste as constituted as at the date of this Agreement.

"The Agent" shall mean the duly appointed agent of the Artiste for the purposes of this Agreement being [ ]

| | |
|---|---|
| "The Equipment" | shall mean all of the equipment of the Artiste to be installed in or used at the Venue including (but not limited to) sound amplification equipment, lighting rig, sound mixing desk sound monitor system and any special effects. |

*Obligations of Artiste*

2 (a) The Artiste undertakes that it will appear at the Venue on the Date and will give a public performance before a live audience in its customary presentation to the best of its ability.

(b) The Artiste will install its Equipment within the Venue at such reasonable times prior to the Concert as shall be agreed with the Promoter and will conduct a satisfactory sound check thereof upon the completion of installation.

(c) The Artiste will no less than [ ] days prior to the Date give the Promoter written notification of any sound lighting or other equipment which the Artiste requires the Promoter to provide for the Performance.

3 (a) The Artiste warrants that all of its Equipment will be in accordance with its manufacturer's specifications of safety of construction and use or will otherwise be safe and in good working order and that the installation and use of the Equipment in the Venue will not cause any safety hazard.

(b) If any of the Equipment is of an unusual nature shape or size or requires a different or greater power supply than normal or if the construction of any stand or support of any of the Equipment requires unusual space or stability connection with the Venue structure or if the use of any special effects requires specific safety features or if there is any other matter in connection with the Equipment which should be notified to the Promoter the Artiste will do so within [ ] days prior to the Date.

4 (a) If required by the Promoter the Artiste will provide the Promoter with a list of all of the Artistes personnel (including management and other representatives) who should have access to the Venue at any time so that security check-lists and back-stage and on-stage and general Venue passes can be produced as required for them and the list of personnel will indicate what category of passes any individual should be given.

(b) The Artiste will be responsible for all acts and defaults of its personnel and for any damage caused to the Venue or committed within the Venue by them and the Artiste warrants that it is fully insured for any consequences which may arise therefrom and that it will indemnify and keep the Promoter harmless from (and will pay it forthwith on demand) any loss damage cost or liability incurred by the Promoter arising therefrom.

5 (a) Where applicable it will be the responsibility of the Artiste to obtain in good time any travel visas and work permits required for the Artiste and all personnel accompanying the Artiste.

(b) The Artiste will ensure that any Carnet requirements for the Equipment are complied with and that such Carnet is issued in good time to enable the Equipment to be transported to the Venue.

*Representations of Artiste*

6 The Artiste warrants that it is entitled to sign this Agreement and that it has no personal touring recording or other commitments which might interfere with the ability of the Artiste to perform at the Venue on the Date as herein set out.

7 The Artiste hereby authorises the Promoter to use the name and likeness of the Artiste solely in connection with the advertising and promotion of the Concert.

8 No part of the Artiste's live performance (including the material to be performed by the Artiste) shall be in breach of any third party right.

9 That the Artiste as constituted as at the date hereof shall be the same as at the Date and if for any reason prior to the Date there is any change in the membership of the Artiste (specifically due to any member or members leaving the Artiste) the Promoter shall be entitled to terminate this Agreement forthwith by written notice if the revised Artiste has a substantially different line-up and does not have the same commercial attraction as the present line-up in the reasonable opinion of the Promoter made in good faith.

10 This Agreement has been negotiated by the Promoter with the Agent and the Artiste irrevocably confirms to the Promoter that the Agent:

(a) has the full authority of the Artiste to negotiate and agree the terms of this Agreement with the Promoter for and on behalf of the Artiste and the Artiste confirms its acceptance of them;

(b) has the full authority of the Artiste to receive both the Deposit and the Fee on behalf of the Artiste and such payment in full by the Promoter shall be deemed to be the fulfilment of its obligation in that respect to the Artiste.

*Obligations of Promoter*

11 (a) In consideration of the Artiste performing its obligations hereunder the Promoter agrees to pay the Artiste the Fee which shall be paid:

(i) as to the Deposit on the signing of this Agreement by or on behalf of the Artiste;

(ii) as to the balance thereof [within 2 days after the Concert] [on the night after completion of the concert] by certified cheque or bankers draft.

(b) It is agreed that the Promoter will also provide or pay for the provision of the following:
[List additional items].

(c) In the event that the promoter is obliged by its Inland Revenue authority to deduct any withholding tax or any other tax from the Fee it shall be entitled to do so provided that:

(i) the Inland Revenue is promptly and fully paid all such tax;

(ii) a tax deduction certificate is issued to the Artiste without delay.

12 Attached hereto as Schedule "A" is a list of the agreed requirements of the Artiste as to Equipment siting personnel accommodation security and other administrative matters which shall be deemed incorporated herein and all of which the Promoter agrees to provide or deal with as the case may be.

13 (a) The Promoter confirms that the Venue is fully licensed for entertainment and that all certificates or consents required from the local authorities in respect of the Venue have been obtained with special reference to fire and safety regulations and that all its facilities including the power supply are in good safe working order.

(b) The Promoter warrants that adequate and complete accident and personal injury and all other pertinent insurance cover is in place for the Concert and that the Artiste is also covered thereby for public liability.

14 The Promoter agrees to do the following or to ensure the provision of the

following:

(a) To provide proper and adequate security staff both backstage and in the auditorium at all times before, during and after the Concert.

(b) To notify the Agent of any special requirements relating to the Venue which are to be observed or performed by the Artiste or their personnel.

(c) To provide such Venue and back-stage passes as shall be agreed with the tour manager of the Artiste in accordance with Clause 4(a).

(d) To enable the Artiste's road crew access to the Venue as agreed but in good time to enable the Equipment to be installed and a sound check to be undertaken.

15 (a) The Promoter will ensure that no unauthorised recording (whether audio or audiovisual) will be undertaken in the Venue during the Concert.

(b) If the Artiste wishes to record or film the concert the Promoter will be notified in writing and the Promoter agrees that such recording may be undertaken provided that the filming or recording is done in accordance with all relevant local Musicians Union rules or other appropriate regulations which will be notified by the Promoter to the Artiste on request.

16 The Promoter will only have one other artiste performing on the Date and the Promoter:

(a) will first agree the identity of the first act with the Artiste;

(b) the first act performance will last for no longer than [45] minutes and will terminate no less than [30] minutes prior to the performance time of the Artiste;

(c) will agree with the Agent the status size and billing of the first act upon all promotional and advertising material issued by the Promoter.

17 The Promoter will not be entitled to change the Venue without the prior written consent of the Artiste which may be withheld in its absolute discretion.

18 The Promoter shall not be entitled to assign the benefit of this Agreement to any other party without the prior written consent of the Artiste which may be withheld in its absolute discretion.

19 At the request of the Artiste the Promoter will provide it with no more than [ ] free tickets for seats within the top price seating.

20 Adjacent to the Artiste's dressing rooms the Promoter will provide a hospitality room of reasonable size both before and after the Concert for the use of the Artistes and their guests.

*Termination and postponement*

21 (a) The Artiste will be entitled to terminate this Agreement forthwith by giving written notice to the Promoter if the Artiste is prevented from performing the concert due to accident illness or other incapacity of a serious nature which circumstances shall be deemed to come within the definition of *force majeure*.

[(b) If the notice of termination is given to the Promoter under (a) above within [14] days prior to the Concert by which time the Promoter will have incurred considerable irrecoverable cost and expense the Artiste agrees to perform a substitute Concert for the Promoter [within [4] months thereafter] [during the next tour of the Promoter's country] upon the same terms as herein stated].

(c) If required by the Promoter for submission to its insurers or for any other valid reason the Artiste will provide promptly a doctor's report on the extent of the incapacity and his recommendations on not performing the Concert on health grounds.

(d) In the event of termination of this Agreement under this Clause the Artiste shall give the Agent prompt instructions to return the Deposit to the Promoter.

[STANDARD CLAUSES]

IN WITNESS

**Comments on this agreement**

Most concert or tour bookings are made on the Artiste's agency standard form of booking, plus a rider containing all the Artiste's detailed requirements for equipment, stage configuration, and another couple of pages of needs. An agreement of this nature would be unusual, but it highlights some of the more important matters to consider on a major tour or foreign concert.

1 Outside the UK the fee will be in US dollars. It may be a flat fee, or a percentage of gross ticket sales.

If there is a dramatic change in the group line-up so that the star lead singer leaves, the promoter may not be getting what he contracted for, or what the audience expect to see.

2(b) This will usually be done early in the day of the concert.

2(c) and 3(b) This depends on the hall and the artiste's equipment. Any unusual requirements may need preliminary work at the hall to accommodate them.

4(a) Security passes are important to ensure that only authorised personnel are allowed in the hall.

(b) If any fittings or fixtures are needed to be moved, either do it gently or get the promoter to organise it.

5 Failure to arrive on time for the concert for these reasons will not come within a normal *force majeure* clause.

9 See comments under clause 1.

11(a)(ii) This should state whatever has been agreed.

11(c) Withholding tax has to be dealt with.

12 The most important item (after the money) in the rider, which deals with all of the logistic, technical and personal needs of the artiste, which are treated as part of the contract.

21 This is only likely to be invoked if it is reasonably suspected that the illness or incapacity is suspicious, vague or exaggerated, and is only being given as a plausible reason for cancelling the concert.

## ARTISTE'S DIRECT SIGNING RECORDING CONTRACT

THIS AGREEMENT is made the day of 19

BETWEEN LIMITED of

(hereinafter called the Company) of the one part and

of

(hereinafter called the Artiste) of the other part.

WHEREBY IT IS AGREED as follows:

*Definitions*

1 "The Term" shall mean the period commencing on the date hereof and terminating on the [ ] day of [ ] 19[ ].

[ALTERNATIVELY] shall mean an initial period of one year from the date hereof and the Company shall be entitled to extend the Term for no more than [three] additional years by giving to the Artiste written notice not less than [30] days prior to the expiry of the relevant year provided that the Company is not in breach of any of its obligations (particularly album release and royalty accounting) at the date such written notice is given.

"The Territory" shall mean [the World]

"A Single Record" shall mean a 7 inch vinyl disc record or the CD or other configuration equivalent containing one recorded composition on each side containing the Artiste's performances and whether being an audio or audio visual record.

"An Album" shall mean any disc or tape or other play back device in vinyl or CD or other configuration containing no less than [eight] and no more than [ten] recorded performances of the Artiste with a total playing time of no more than [ ] minutes and whether being an audio or audiovisual record.

"A Master" shall be the fully mixed two track master tape of a single record or an album (as the case may be) which shall contain recordings performed by the Artiste and which are of a commercial and technical quality satisfactory to the Company in its reasonable opinion.

"A Record" shall mean any recording made for the Company by the Artiste in accordance with this Agreement.

"The Producer" shall mean the record producer chosen by the Company in consultation with the Artiste.

"Full Price Record" shall mean a Record sold at the recognised top retail price in its country of sale based upon the Company's recommended full retail price.

"Budget Price Record" shall mean any Record which is promoted on a budget line label or otherwise at a recommended retail price (or its local equivalent) being [two thirds] or less of the Company's full retail price for records.

"Low Price Record" shall mean a Record sold at a price being less than [one half] of the Company's full retail price.

| | |
|---|---|
| "Net Sales" | shall mean for royalty calculation purposes the number of records sold in an accounting period for which the Company has received the proceeds of sale less the number of records returned to the Company in that accounting period as being defective or for exchange and for which full value credit has been given. |
| "Royalty" | shall mean for clause 19 hereof the percentage referred to of the Full Price or Budget Price or Low Price (as the case may be) Sales of Records after deducting all sales taxes applicable thereto and the relevant packaging charges levied by the Company from time to time against all of its Artistes for the relevant format of the recording (ie, an album cover or double album cover or tape CD or other audio visual recording container). |
| "A Qualifying Performance" | shall have the meaning attributed to it in Section 181 of the Copyright Designs and Patents Act 1988 (hereinafter called "the Act"). |
| "The Artiste's Consent" | shall have the meaning attributed to it in Section 182 of the Act. |
| "A Track" | shall mean a recorded composition contained on any Record. |

*Grant of rights to the Company*

2 The Artiste hereby undertakes to perform exclusively for the Company for the purpose of making Records as herein set out during the Term and in respect of all such performances the Artiste:

(a) confirms that in each case his performance will be a qualifying performance.

(b) assigns to the Company the copyright and all other rights of a like nature in and to his recorded performances.

(c) recognises that this Agreement is an exclusive recording contract in accordance with Section 185 of the Act.

3 The mechanical copyright in and to all Records made by the Artiste hereunder will be the absolute property of the Company.

4 The Artiste grants to the Company the right to use his name and likeness in any reasonable manner as the Company considers best in connection with the distribution promotion advertising and sale of the Records provided that the Artiste will first be given the opportunity to approve of photos and biographical material to be included on any Record sleeve or other packaging such consent not to be unreasonably withheld or delayed.

5 (a) The Artiste hereby irrevocably authorises the Company to make Records of his performances and to distribute and sell them in any configuration and whether audio or audiovisual throughout the Territory in accordance with the policy of the Company from time to time.

(b) If the Company licences any other party to make, distribute and sell the Records in any part of the Territory the terms of such licence shall contain all the relevant obligations of and restrictions upon the Company as set out herein and the Company shall be responsible to the Artiste for any default or breach of this Agreement caused by a licensee of the Company.

6 (a) The Artiste warrants to the Company that he is entitled to enter into this Agreement and to grant the rights as herein contained and that in so doing and in the Company exercising its rights hereby granted neither the Artiste nor the Company are or will be in breach of any third party contractual right nor will they infringe any third party proprietary right.

(b) The Artiste undertakes with the Company that he will not do anything or execute any document which will result in the derogation from or breach of the rights he has granted to the Company hereunder.

(c) The Artiste undertakes that during the Term he will not make any performance which to his knowledge will be recorded by any party other than the Company without having obtained the prior consent of the Company in writing.

7 The Artiste undertakes to indemnify the Company from any claim cost damage or expense (including reasonable legal costs) incurred by the Company as a direct result of the breach by the Artiste of any of his grants of rights or warranties set out herein.

*Artiste's obligations*

8 As and when reasonably required to do so hereunder the Artiste will:

(a) Attend meetings with the Company to discuss and agree when any recording is to be made and also who will be the producer of it and what is to be the likely material to be recorded and to approve a recording budget.

(b) (i) (if he is a composer) compose and write suitable commercial compositions in accordance with his normal professional style for all recordings and that (except as may be agreed by the Company) he will record only his own compositions;

(ii) the Artiste will procure that his publisher will issue the Company with the necessary consents to make and publicly release within the Territory the first recording of any of the Artiste's own compositions and that no mechanical royalty will be required for any part of the Territory in excess of the set or customary minimum rate applied [on an industry-wide basis].

(c) Attend adequate rehearsals of the performance of compositions to be recorded so as to make proper use of studio time when it is being recorded.

(d) Co-operate fully with any musical arranger and with the Producer to ensure that the compositions to be recorded will be of the best commercial quality and musical appeal reasonably obtainable when recorded.

(e) Attend the recording studio on time and to perform to the best of his ability under the direction of and in consultation with the Producer and where necessary repeating or re-recording material so that the final version is of the best technical quality reasonably obtainable for each Record.

(f) Attend all mixing sessions with the Producer if requested by the Company so as to ensure that the final Master is acceptable to the Artiste and to the Company as representing a Record fit to be released for sale to the public.

(g) Provide to the Company all credits and other information required for the Record sleeve and label and will be available at all reasonable times to discuss and approve packaging or sleeve artwork and other promotional material to be used in respect of the release and promotion of the Record.

(h) Discuss and agree with the Company the format of any recording to be made of a visual promotional video or any other audiovisual recording of any composition and to make himself available for any such recording to be undertaken.

9 The Artiste will ensure that at all times he will remain a fully paid up member of the Musicians Union and of any other union of which membership may be required to enable the Artiste to perform or record in accordance with this Agreement.

10 The Artiste agrees that when giving live concerts or when on tour:

(a) He will promote his latest recording and will perform a reasonable proportion of his recorded material.

(b) When requested he will agree to the Company televising or filming any concert if the recording is done for the purpose of creating a "live album" recording for issue as an audiovisual recording hereunder it being the responsibility of the Company to obtain all other necessary consents and also provided that:

(i) the cost of recording and filming the event will not be recouped by the Company from any royalties due hereunder to the Artiste until the accounting period after the release of the audiovisual recording and if it is not released for commercial sale by the Company within [18] months after the recording and filming has been completed then without prejudice to any other right of the Company the cost of recording and production will be the liability of the Company and will not be deemed to be an advance recoupable by the Company from the Artiste; and

(ii) the cost of such a production and recording will not be cross collateralised against the royalties paid by the Company to the Artiste on the sales of any other Record it being agreed that all costs thereof will only be set against and recouped from the royalties due on sales of the commercially released recording of the production.

*The Company's obligations*

11 (a) The Company agrees to request the Artiste to make in each year of the Term [one Album] to be recorded no later than [six] months from the commencement date of the relevant year and the Company may ask the Artiste to record any number of single records not containing any material on the Album (subject to (e) below) provided that the dates for recording will be agreed to fit in with the touring and other work schedule of the Artiste.

(b) The Company may request the Artiste to make any further Albums at any time during the Term provided that if two Albums are recorded during one year that additional Album shall not be deemed to be in satisfaction of the minimum of one Album to be recorded in the next or any subsequent year.

(c) The making and release of an audiovisual live album under clause 9(b) shall not be deemed to be in satisfaction of the minimum of one Album to be recorded in any year of the term.

(d) Unless the Artiste first agrees in writing (and subject to (e) below) the Company will not be entitled to satisfy the minimum commitment of one Album in any year by putting together an Album constituted of either or a combination of:

(i) excess recorded tracks made at the time any previous Album was recorded but which were not used on that Album;

(ii) any recordings made from time to time specifically for inclusion on single records but which have not yet been commercially released on such records.

(e) (i) If it is clear that a track on any Album is or may be a hit in its own right the Company may release it together with a suitable "B" side not being a track on the Album as a single record.

(ii) If immediately prior to the making or the commercial release of an Album the Artiste has had a hit single the Company shall be entitled to include it on that next album.

(f) The Company agrees that for the first foreign tour the Artiste makes within either of Europe or the USA which will exceed [ten] concerts the Company will provide tour support by the payment of money provided that:

(i) If the audited cost of the tour exceeds the gross income of the tour the Company will pay the tour loss or [£ ] which ever shall be the less (or such other sum as the parties shall agree) within [14] days after being satisfied as to the accuracy of the tour loss.

(ii) Management and agency commissions are not to be treated as a tour cost.

(iii) The Company has sight of the tour budget prior to the tour taking place and provided that controllable costs (such as flight tickets and hotel bookings) are at an economical rate reasonably applicable to the needs of the Artiste and all of those who are travelling with him on the tour.

12 The Company undertakes that each Record made by the Artiste at its request (subject to it being of commercially acceptable quality) will be released commercially within the UK within [4] months after the Company has received the Master and complete agreed package artwork track listing copyright credits and all such information normally contained thereon and that the Company will promote distribute and sell copies of the Record using its reasonable endeavours.

13 (a) The Company undertakes to inform such of its subsidiaries or licensees which it reasonably considers may be interested in the Albums outside the UK and within its Territory of the existence of the Albums and with sample copies thereof and will use its reasonable endeavours to promote the Album to such parties.

(b) The Artiste accepts that (subject to clauses 11 and 13):

(i) The Company is not able to insist that any such subsidiary or licensee can be forced to release the Album within a reasonable time after its UK release or at any other time.

(ii) The reasonable endeavours of the Company under Clause 11 and 12(a) above will be within the normal Company levels of promotional time and expense and that its marketing policies will be applied in good faith and that subject thereto all decisions are made at the discretion of the Company.

14 The Company agrees that in any part of the Territory in which is released any Album its first release will be on the Company's (or a subsidiary's or licensees) Full Price Record label and that its subsequent release on any Budget Price or other Low Price label will not be undertaken within [12] months after such first Full Price release.

*Financial terms*

15 (a) The Company agrees to pay to the Artiste the following sums by way of advances on account of royalties due to the Artiste under this Agreement:

(i) The sum of [ ] on the execution of this Agreement (receipt whereof is hereby acknowledged).

(ii) [IF APPLICABLE] the sum of [ ] on the exercise of each option by the Company to extend the Term.

(iii) [IF APPLICABLE] the sum of [ ] upon the delivery of the Master of the first Album to be recorded in each contract year during the Term.

(b) Any advance payment becoming due under (a) above will be paid whether or not at that time the Company will have recouped all previous advance payments to the Artiste.

16 The royalties and any royalty advances paid by the Company to the producer of any recording made by the Artiste hereunder [will be the responsibility and liability of the Company and no part thereof will be recoupable from the Artiste] OR [will be at the cost of the Artiste and the Company shall be entitled to recoup the whole of such payments from any royalties due to the Artiste hereunder].

17 (a) Before the production of any Record is commenced the Company the Producer and the Artiste will agree a budget and the Company and the Artiste agree to use their reasonable endeavours to ensure that the budget will not be exceeded it being accepted by each of them that the budget is only a forecast and guideline.

(b) The whole cost of making any Record (including but not limited to studio and tape charges arrangers fees and musicians costs and any other direct cost) will be paid by the Company and will be deemed to be an advance to the Artiste which together with all advances made under clause 15 or otherwise by the Company to the Artiste shall be recoupable by the Company as a first charge from any royalties due to the Artiste hereunder.

18 Any payment made to the Artiste as tour support under the provisions of Clause 11(f) will not be recoupable from the Artiste's royalties.

19 With the exception of the recording and production costs referred to in Clause 10(b) (if they are recoupable from the Artiste) any and all advances made by the Company to the Artiste (or to third parties for the Artiste's account) shall be recoupable from any and all royalties due to the Artiste in respect of the sales of any and all Records made by the Artiste hereunder to the intent that the aggregated advances on any accounting date will be recouped from the aggregated royalties due to the Artiste on that date and that only the excess balance of royalties over advances will be paid to him.

20 The Company agrees to pay to the Artiste the following royalties upon sales of single records audio albums CD records and audiovisual recordings for home use:

[INSERT COMPANY'S ROYALTY RATE STRUCTURE]

*Accounting provisions*

21 The Company will maintain accurate and up to date accounts for all Recordings made and sold by it and of all accountings received by it from foreign subsidiaries or licensees and will render accounts to the Artiste within

[60] days after the 30th June and 31st December in each year in respect of all monies received by it from record sales within the UK and of all monies received by it from subsidiaries and licensees within the previous six months in respect of record sales within their licensed territories.

[ADD STANDARD AUDIT CLAUSE]

22 (a) If the Company or (as the case may be) the Company's subsidiary or licensee in the USA and Canada retains reserves from each royalty accounting for record sales in those territories against returns to be made to it in respect of record sales in previous accounting periods then the reserves in respect of each accounting will be in accordance with the overall policy of the licensee but shall not exceed [ ] percent on Album royalties and [ ] percent on singles royalties due upon each accounting from that licensee to the Company.

(b) The royalty reserve retained in any accounting period will be liquidated within the [third] accounting thereafter.

(c) The amount of liquidated reserves added into any accounting to the Company or to the Artiste (as the case may be) will not be included in the figure upon which the royalty reserve percentage is calculated under (a) above for that accounting.

23 The Company will notify the Artiste in writing within a reasonable time after any Album released by the Company or a subsidiary or licensee in [the UK, USA, Japan] is permanently deleted from its current catalogue of available product within those territories.

24 If any country within the Territory:

(a) Imposes a sales tax or other tax upon the royalties ultimately to be received by the Artiste the Company shall promptly notify the Artiste thereof and shall take any reasonable steps to prevent that deduction (where it is legally possible) and shall provide the Artiste with any tax deduction certificate applicable thereto.

(b) Imposes a foreign exchange transfer restriction then the Company will ensure that an interest-bearing account will be opened with a reputable bank in the name of the Artiste into which will be paid his portion of royalties during such period of restriction.

*Re-recording restriction*

25 The Artiste undertakes that he will not re-record for any other party within [5] years from the date of the termination of this Agreement or [1] year from the deletion of the Record from the Company's UK current catalogue of available product (whichever period is the shorter) any composition recorded by the Artiste hereunder except that if any such recorded composition has not been commercially released for the first time at least in the UK by the Company within [12] months after the termination of this Agreement then this prohibition shall not apply thereafter to any such composition.

*Termination*

26 [Add to a standard clause where the Artiste is a group]

(a) In the event that any of the members of the Artiste contracted hereunder leave the Artiste and if any other person becomes a member of the Artiste written notice thereof with all details will be given promptly to the Company and where it is possible the Company will be given advance notice of the change in membership.

(b) The Artiste undertakes to procure that any new member signs an agreement with the Company in identical terms as those applying to the Artiste at that date failing which (or if the new member will be in breach of any third party rights in doing so) the Artiste undertakes not to make him a member of the Artiste until he does sign the Company's agreement with the full legal entitlement to do so.

(c) (i) If upon any member leaving the Artiste the Company reasonably considers in good faith that the constitution or marketability of the Artiste after taking account of his replacement has so fundamentally changed that it does not have the same status or quality as the Artiste it contracted with the Company may terminate this Agreement by written notice.

(ii) The Company will be entitled (but will not be obliged) to ask the newly constituted Artiste to make test recordings upon which the Company can judge its decision.

[STANDARD CLAUSES]

IN WITNESS whereof

**Comments on this agreement**

This agreement assumes a solo artiste, it would need modification for a group.

1 Different companies will have different definitions of much the same items.

2 Part II of the 1988 Act relates to rights in performances, and it may become standard practice to refer to the relevant sections.

3 The rights in the recordings belong absolutely to the record company.

6(a) The artiste must ensure he has no existing commitments. If he has just left a group, he should get a written confirmation from its record company that its recording contract does not continue to apply to him.

6(b) The old section 8 (1956 Act) statutory notice arrangements will no longer apply when a copyright tribunal is set up.

11(a) There should be a one album minimum recording commitment. If the artiste is new in the first year it may only be, say, two single records, to test the market. There must be some absolute commitment to enable the artiste to make records if the relevant cases set out in Appendix III are taken seriously.

12 There must also be a release commitment at least in the UK. The 4 month period allows enough time from recording, and is to fit in with the option exercise provisions of the alternative definition of "the Term" in clause 1.

13(a) Nothing is guaranteed, but an effort should be seen to be made.

14 It is reasonable to have the first release of an album on a full price label. After that the marketing strategy will depend on the sales progress of the album.

15(a) The artiste should get cash advances somehow.

16 Who is responsible for the producer's royalty will be agreed in advance, it may even be shared.

17 This is why it benefits the artiste to reduce these costs to a minimum.

19 Successful albums pay for unsuccessful ones.

20 All companies differ, there is no point in speculating.
22 Even if the company's contract does not refer to royalty reserves, they will be applied by its USA licensee. The terms should be identified and agreed.
23 Not usual, but it would be useful information when touring those places. With a major tour set up far enough ahead, deleted records might be revived for the tour.
25 This is to protect the company's investment, and the period should be set accordingly. If it is not still in the company's current catalogue, a re-recording cannot be in competition. As the artiste cannot control when any foreign licensee may release a record, he cannot cater for all timing possibilities. His contract is with the record company. If a record is not released within 12 months of its being recorded it is questionable whether the company will ever release it, so this element will encourage such a release, or risk a re-recording of the song by the artiste.
26 If the band is Mr X (it tends to be the lead singer), with a group in support, then if he leaves the band it normally loses its commercial appeal and justification of investment. The record company really contracted with Mr X. Where that is obviously the case, the clause can say so, making the position clear, and Mr X will become a key man in the group.

## RECORD PRODUCER'S AGREEMENT

THIS AGREEMENT is made the day of 19
BETWEEN of
(hereinafter called the Company) of the first part and
of
(hereinafter called the Producer) of the second part and
of
(hereinafter called the Artiste) of the third part.

WHEREAS

(A) The Company has an exclusive recording agreement with the Artiste and proposes to record a long playing album (hereinafter called the Album) to be performed by the Artiste and comprising the Musical Compositions set out in the Schedule hereto or such alternative compositions as shall be agreed between the Artiste and the Company (hereinafter called the Compositions).
(B) The Producer is a well known Producer of records.

NOW IT IS AGREED as follows:

*Definitions*
1 In this Agreement the following words will have the following meanings:

"Record" shall mean gramophone records, recorded tape video disc laser disc or any other configuration or device representing the Album (including any audio-visual device having the same purpose and effect) wholly consisting of the Compositions.

"Territory" shall mean the world.

| | |
|---|---|
| "Net Sales" | shall mean all sales of Records for which the Company actually receives payment in the UK. |
| "Full Price Sales" | shall mean sales of the Records at the top recommended consumer Sales Price for the Records. |
| "Budget Sales" | shall mean sales of Records at a Price being less than [two thirds] of the recommended Full Sales Price. Sales of Records through extensive TV advertising in any country will be deemed to be Budget sales in that country for the calculation of the Producer's royalty thereon. |
| "Other Sales" | shall mean sales of Records licensed for a flat fee or sold at any price lower than the Budget Sales Price including mail order merchandise, promotion and other sales channels not being on a regular retail basis. |
| "Sales Price" | shall mean the recommended sales price in any category applicable in the country of sale or the country of manufacture at the choice of the Company (but in the same manner as the Artiste is accounted to for royalties on sales of the Album) less all Sales Tax and other statutory or other governmental deductions from the price. |

*Engagement of producer*

2 The Company hereby engages the Producer to produce the Album and the Producer agrees to do so upon the terms and conditions herein set out it being intended that the recording of the Album will commence on or about [ ] and shall be completed on or about [ ].

*Producer's obligations*

3 The Producer agrees to render to the best of his skill and ability all services usually rendered by a top reputable record Producer in accordance with the directions given to him from time to time by the Company and in collaboration with such persons as the Company may designate in order to create and provide to the Company a recording of each of the Compositions to a technical and artistic quality satisfactory to the Company.

4 The obligations of the Producer will include the following:

(a) Advising the Company or the Artiste upon any proposed additional requirements by way of instruments orchestration and appointing any arranger of the Compositions and any "fixer" required for backing musicians.

(b) If requested by the Company to submit a budget of the costs likely to be incurred by the Company in producing and recording the complete Album through to the fully edited and mixed two track master tape (the Budget).

(c) To listen to the Artiste in rehearsal if requested to enable the Producer to get a preliminary concept of the contents of the Compositions so that he can plan the production of the Album.

(d) To attend the recording studios in accordance with a time schedule which will be agreed so as to be convenient for the Producer and the Artiste and to make the best use of studio time.

(e) To direct and supervise the musical arrangement of the Compositions the sound engineering and artistic direction of the Artiste in his performance in the studio and to get him to record and (if necessary) re-record each Composition until the Producer and the Company are satisfied that the quality of the Album will be in accordance with Clause 3.

(f) To ensure that he will be available during the whole period of his engagement hereunder and that he will not take on any other engagement which may prevent him from doing so.

(g) In the event that for any reason the production of the Album is not completed within its estimated production time the Producer agrees to make himself available at such other times as shall be reasonably agreed by the Company in consultation with him to complete the Production and at no extra charge to the Company unless otherwise agreed in writing.

(h) Not to incur any unapproved liability or expense on behalf of the Company on the Artiste in connection with the production of the Album.

(i) Not to make any statement or disclosure to the press or any other party of any confidential information relating to this Agreement or the business of the Company or the professional activities or the private life of the Artiste.

*Obligation of the Company*

5 (a) The Company will provide the Producer with such assistance and facilities as he may require to produce the Album as set out within the Budget including the following:

(i) Paying for the arrangement of the Compositions and all additional musicians and musical instrumentation.

(ii) Paying for all recording and other costs set out in the Budget and any other costs which may be incurred provided that they are agreed by the Company.

(iii) Using its reasonable endeavours to ensure that the Artiste will be available for rehearsal recording and mixing the recording of each Composition.

(b) Except where this Agreement has been terminated under Clause 11 if the recording of any of the Composition at any time after its completion is to be re-mixed or re-edited or have additional material inserted into it then the Company will request the Producer to do so and if the Producer is not able to do the work as and when reasonably required by the Company it shall be entitled to have it done by any other person of its choice.

(c) The Company will ensure that if the Album constitutes the first recording of the Compositions it will have obtained the necessary consents of the owners of the copyrights therein and in any other case that all licensing formalities will have been complied with.

*Producer's proprietary rights*

6 The Producer hereby assigns to the Company any and all copyright and any other proprietary rights which may exist in or be created by the original performance of the Producer in producing the Album.

*Producer's remuneration*

7 In consideration of the Producer fulfilling his obligations set out herein the Company agrees to pay him:

(a) An advance on account of royalties payable hereunder of [£ ] payable as to one half on the signing hereof and one half on the completion of production of the Album to the reasonable satisfaction of the Company under clause 3 and the whole of such advance (together with any other advance the Company may pay to the Producer in respect of the Album) shall be recovered by the Company as a first charge on all royalties payable to the Producer hereunder.

(b) Subject to sub-clause (d) a royalty on [100% of Net Sales] of Records as set out in clause 9 below:
 (i) [ ] percent upon Full Price Sales.
 (ii) [ ] percent upon Budget Sales.
 (iii) [ ] percent upon Other Sales.

[Alternative (b) The royalty payable to the Producer will be [ ] percent of the Full Price Sales and shall be pro-rated in respect of all other sales in accordance with the royalty payment terms contained in the recording agreement between the Company and the Artiste which are set out in the Schedule hereto].

(c) In respect of any Record which does not wholly consist of the Compositions the relevant royalty rate will be pro-rated as to the number of Compositions within the total number of recorded tracks on the Record.

(d) In each case within (b) above the royalty is calculated upon the [established retail] price of the records less packaging costs and VAT. [Insert formula consistent with the Artiste's royalty calculation Clauses].

*Producer's credit*

8 The Company will give the Producer a credit as the producer of the Album on the record label and the record sleeve and whenever else in advertising and promotional material credits are given to persons or parties other than the Artiste the credit being "Produced by [ ]" with a typography and position no less favourable than other major third party credits.

*Accounting for royalties*

9 The Company agrees to account to the Producer for his royalties as set out below:

(a) All royalties shall be computed in the national currency [of the place of sale] and if the proceeds of a foreign sale are exchanged into sterling the royalties shall be paid at the same rate of exchange as that at which the exchange into sterling took place.

(b) The Company shall render written accounts of all sales of the Album which are notified to the Company and in respect of which it receives full payment in the United Kingdom such accounts being submitted to the Producer within [45] days after the [30th June and 31st December] in each year in respect of royalties received by the Company within the preceding half year.

(c) The accounts shall set out in reasonable detail the countries in which the sales have been reported and in which sales category (see clause 1 definitions of Record Sales).

(d) If in any country there is any restriction upon the remittance to the UK of money due to the Company this will be identified by the Company in the appropriate accounting and at the request of the Producer the Company will request the Company's local Licensee to open a bank account in that country in the name of the Producer and pay into it all blocked money due to the Producer from these royalties.

(e) The Company agrees to maintain full and accurate accounting records in connection with the Sales of Records of the Album and all royalties and sales receipts received by it.

(f) The Producer or his qualified representative shall be entitled to examine and take copies of the accounts relating to the Album not more than once in each year during reasonable business hours upon giving the Company not less than [14] days prior written notice.

(g) For the purposes of this Clause references to "Album" will include reference to any track on the Album which is released separately from it on any other Record released for sale.

*Company's manufacturing obligations*

10 The Company shall be entitled to (or not to) manufacture promote and sell Records of the Album throughout the world as it sees fit and to decide whether or not to continue to do so as a commercial decision for which it is solely responsible there being no express or implied obligation upon the Company to do so.

*Termination*

11 (a) The Company shall be entitled to terminate this Agreement forthwith at any time by giving the Producer written notice upon the happening of any of the following:

(i) The Producer failing persistently to attend to and deal with any material matters requiring his attention during the production of the Album whereby the production is delayed or the Budget is being or will be materially exceeded without the consent of the Company or the artistic and commercial quality of the recording is not or is not likely to be of acceptable quality in the reasonable opinion of the Company it being agreed by the Producer that the point at which this Agreement becomes terminable for those reasons is to be decided at the absolute discretion of the Company in good faith.

(ii) Without prejudice to the rights of the Company under (i) above if the Producer fails to remedy any specific material breach of his obligations within [3] days after receiving written notice from the Company stating the breach and requiring its remedy.

(iii) The Producer compounding with his creditors becoming bankrupt or being convicted of any criminal act or suffering any accident or incapacity which effectively prevents him from carrying out his obligations hereunder.

(b) The Producer shall be entitled to terminate this Agreement forthwith by giving written notice to the Company if:

(i) The Company fails to remedy any material breach of its obligations within [7] days after receiving written notice from the Producer stating the breach and requiring its remedy.

(ii) The Company winding up (except for amalgamation or reconstruction) ceasing to trade or compounding with its creditors.

(c) Upon termination of this Agreement by either party:

(i) If the recording of any Composition is substantially incomplete (as determined by the Company in its discretion upon a reasonable assessment of progress) the Company shall be entitled to have it completed by another producer and to give that other producer the production credit.

(ii) If the recording of a Composition is completed or substantially completed but it is not yet mixed the Company shall be entitled to have it mixed (or completed and mixed) by another producer in which case they will each have a co-producing credit.

(iii) If only some of the Compositions have been recorded and the rest of the Compositions are produced by another producer then each producer will be given credit accordingly for all the compositions which he produced.

(iv) The Producer will remain entitled to receive his royalties on the Compositions for which recording and mixing to the full status of a master tape has been completed subject to recoupment by the Company of any advance or any established compensation which may be due from the Producer to the Company.

(v) If any Composition has co-producers under (iii) above the Producer's royalty will be pro-rated between them as the Company shall determine in good faith upon an assessment of the overall contribution and time spent by each of them upon the production of it.

(vi) Any other outstanding rights or obligations between the parties shall remain including Clause 4(i).

*Assignment of obligations*

12 (a) The Company shall be entitled to assign its obligations hereunder to any party to whom it assigns the rights to manufacture and sells Records containing the Artiste's performance and the right to receive the royalties arising from the sale of the Records provided that the assignee undertakes in writing with the Producer to continue to pay him his royalty entitlement as set out herein.

(b) In no circumstances will the Producer be entitled to assign any of his obligations hereunder to any other party.

[STANDARD CLAUSES]

IN WITNESS whereof the parties hereto have set their hands the day and year first above written.

**Comments on this agreement**

If the agreement is for the production of a single record it can be modified accordingly.

1 This clause and all royalty and sales clauses should apply according to the record company's own accounting structure as set out in the artiste's agreement.

3 What is "acceptable" is a personal judgment.

4 Add in any other responsibilities the producer is taking on.

6 If the producer creates any original material, or helps with arrangements of the music, the publisher will want an assignment from him of the copyright in such additional work.

7 If the royalties and advance are ultimately being paid by the artiste he should agree to the producer's royalty rate.

8 The credibility of the first album by a new artiste can be influenced by the identity of the producer.

11(a)(i) If the producer is playing up, it can be difficult to pinpoint a time or event for which the ordinary rules for termination for breach could safely be applied.

11(c) These can be difficult to assess, in the end common sense has to be applied.

## SONG WRITING AGREEMENT (ASSIGNMENT OF COPYRIGHT)

THIS AGREEMENT is made the day of 19
BETWEEN of
(hereinafter called the Publisher) of the one part and
of
(hereinafter called the Composer) of the other part.

WHEREAS

(A) The Composer is the sole composer of the compositions set out in Schedule A hereto which are exclusively licensed to [ ] whose rights therein terminate on no later than [ ] (hereinafter called the Old Catalogue).

(B) The Composer is the sole composer of the Compositions set out in Schedule B hereto which are assigned to the Publisher hereunder which together with all future compositions composed by the Composer during the period of this Agreement are hereinafter called the Compositions.

(C) For avoidance of doubt herein the expression "composed" shall mean the composing of the music together with lyrics and/or the writing of any lyric for the music in respect of any Composition.

NOW IT IS AGREED as follows:

*Definitions*

1 "The Contract Period" shall mean the period commencing on the date hereof and terminating on the [third] anniversary date subject to earlier termination in accordance with clause 15 hereof.

"The Rights Period" shall mean the period of [five] years from the date of this Agreement.

"The Rights Extension Period" shall mean the period of [eight] years from the date of this Agreement which shall apply to any Composition for which the Publisher obtains a *bona fide* commercially released Cover Record during the Contract Period.

"to Publish" shall mean to promote the Compositions commercially throughout the Territory by means of publishing sheet music in folio or album form or procuring original or cover records of the Compositions or including the Composition in TV or film soundtracks and generally encouraging the use and performance of the Compositions in any commercial manner reasonably available now or by future means not yet known.

"The Territory" shall mean [the world].

"at Source" (as referred to in Clause 10) in connection with income shall mean the income arising to be paid gross in any country of the Territory whether it is to be collected by the Publisher or by any sub-publisher but (where applicable) after any recognised copyright income collection society shall have made any charge thereon in accordance with its rules.

"Cover Recording" shall only refer to a sub-published territory and shall mean only a recording made by a local artiste during the Contract Period and released by a local record company (including a local affiliate or subsidiary of an international record company) within that sub-published territory but excluding the UK unless the Composer is also an artiste who has released a record containing that Composition.

*Assignment of copyright*

2 (a) (i) Subject to and upon the terms and conditions and for the consideration herein set out the Composer hereby assigns to the Publisher the [worldwide] copyright title and interest and any other proprietary rights therein created nationally or internationally in and to the Compositions including all subsidiary rights arising from copyright or being the property of a copyright owner as defined and described in the Copyright Designs and Trademarks Act 1988 all of which rights shall be assigned and the Compositions shall be Published by the Publisher during the Rights Period or the Rights Extension Period as the case may be and the assignment of Copyright in respect thereof shall be limited to such periods and shall revert to the Composer on the expiry of such periods subject to clause 16 hereof.

(ii) This copyright assignment also applies to wherever the Composer has composed only part of a Composition where the other parts have been composed by one or more other composers and the notifications to be given by the Composer to the Publisher under (c) below shall identify clearly which part or parts of the relevant Composition are original to him and shall also give the Publisher the details of the Composers of the other parts of the Composition.

(iii) The Composer hereby asserts his right to be identified with each of the Compositions in accordance with Sections 77 and 78 of the Copyright Designs and Patents Act 1988.

(b) (i) If the rights in the Old Catalogue revert to the Composer during the Contract Period the Composer hereby grants to the Publisher for the remainder of the Rights Period the same rights as appertain to the Compositions except that such rights in the Old Catalogue shall be by way of exclusive licence.

(ii) In respect of any Composition within the Old Catalogue which has not previously been recorded if the Publisher obtains a Cover Record during the Contract Period then the Rights Extension Period will apply to that Composition.

(c) As and when the Composer writes any Composition he undertakes to:

(i) Provide to the Publisher top lines of the music and written down lyrics promptly after such creation or to provide the Publisher with a demo tape of the Composition of sufficient quality to enable the Publisher to top line the Composition and write down the lyrics.

(ii) Execute any confirmatory assignment or other document or do any act or thing reasonably required by the Publisher to confirm the Publisher's title thereto and to comply with any copyright income collection society regulations.

*Obligations of Composer*

3 The Composer warrants to the Publisher that:

(a) He is entitled to enter into this Agreement and that there is no (and the Composer undertakes not to enter into any) oral or written agreement or commitment to which he is a party which would cause him to be in breach of this Agreement or which would cause the Publisher to be in breach of any third party rights or which would inhibit the exercise by the Publisher of any of its rights set out herein.

(b) All of the Compositions are or will be original to him and that he has not or will not in composing them make any use of third party material and that no Composition will be defamatory or commercially or religiously objectionable or otherwise prejudicial to the name reputation and business of the Composer or the Publisher.

(c) He will not compose any Composition which he will attribute to any other person as the author thereof or in respect of which he will use a pseudonym which he does not notify to the Publisher and that he will not claim to be the author of any Composition of which he is not the author.

(d) He will use his reasonable endeavours to pursue his composing career and compose songs and with lyrics either for his own use or for the use of others which are of reasonable commercial appeal and of sufficient substance to merit being promoted by the Publisher but this does not create any express or implied obligation upon the Composer to compose any minimum number of Compositions during the Contract Period.

(e) If during the Contract period the Composer is an artiste being contracted to a reputable or major record company which records his performances and releases them commercially the Composer will use his best endeavours to include on all such records exclusively his Compositions unless there is a good reason for including the compositions of another composer in which case only [one] of such compositions will be so recorded it being accepted and understood by the Composer that the Compositions assigned to the Publisher hereunder will only have the opportunity of being successful if contained on commercially released records.

(f) As and when the opportunity arises he will use reasonable endeavours to promote his composing activities and cooperate with the Publisher in any reasonable ideas it has for doing so.

(g) That except for the Old Catalogue and the Compositions set out in Schedule B hereto there are no other compositions as at the date hereof of which the Composer is the author.

(h) That he is a member of the Performing Rights Society Ltd and if not that he will become a member as soon as he is eligible to do so under its membership rules.

4 The Composer agrees to indemnify the Publisher from any and all claims costs damages and liabilities (but excluding any prospective loss of profits)

incurred by the Publisher directly from the consequences of breach by the Composer of any warranty or representation made by him to the Publisher.

*Obligations and rights of Publisher*

5 (a) The Publisher will be entitled to collect all of the income royalties and fees arising within the Territory at any time during the Rights Period and within the period of [six] months thereafter.

(b) In respect of Compositions contained in Cover Records the Publisher will be entitled to collect all of such income paid during the Rights Extension Period.

(c) (i) Any income received by the Publisher arising in the UK or wherever else the Publisher does not use a sub-publisher after the expiry of the relevant [six] month period will be paid forthwith to the Composer without deduction.

(ii) The publisher will be entitled to receive and to retain its share of income paid by a sub-publisher by the end of the [six] month period although it is received by the Publisher after the expiry of that period but any subsequent payments by any sub-publisher to the Publisher will be paid forthwith to the Composer without deduction.

(iii) The six month extension referred to in (a) and (b) above will not apply if this Agreement is terminated under Clause 15 and all income received by the Publisher after the termination date with the sole exception of the first accounting after termination made by each sub-publisher will be paid forthwith to the Composer.

6 (a) The Publisher will use its best endeavours to:

(i) Promote and publish and obtain recordings of the Compositions throughout the Territory either itself or through sub-publishing representatives.

(ii) Ensure the prompt and correct accounting to it of all income arising from exploitation of the Compositions.

(iii) Ensure that the Compositions are registered with all appropriate copyright income collection societies.

(iv) (Where applicable) make all copyright registrations to protect the legal status of the Compositions.

(v) Take all reasonable steps to protect the copyright in the Compositions and to identify and (in consultation with the Composer) to pursue infringers of such copyrights where that is practical and economical.

(b) It is recognised by the Composer that until such time as Compositions become publicly available through any commercial means of exploitation the Publisher may not be able to perform some of its obligations under (a) but such recognition does not reduce the obligations of the Publisher hereunder.

(c) The obligations of the Publisher will not be modified or reduced by the extent of success achieved by the Composer his record company or any other party in promoting any of the Compositions.

(d) The Publisher will maintain a file of correspondence memoranda and other evidence of significant communications it has had with all of its sub-publishers and with any other third party within the Territory concerning the promotion publishing and recording of the Compositions which evidence shall be made available to the Composer for inspection at his request (but which shall not be more than once in each year) so the

Composer can be reasonably satisfied as to the Publisher's efforts on his behalf.

(e) For the purposes of this Clause reference to the Compositions will include the Old Catalogue when relevant.

7 Subject to the Composer's prior written consent and also his agreement upon sharing of performance income with the arranger or translator the Publisher will be entitled to make or authorise the making of arrangements of the music of any Composition or the translation of the lyrics of any Composition provided that the copyright and all other rights in the arrangement of the music of a Composition is assigned to the Publisher as an expansion of the copyright and all other rights in the original Composition and all credits and copyright collection society registrations will be made accordingly.

*Payments to Composer*

8 In consideration of the assignment by the Composer to the Publisher of the copyrights in the Compositions and the performance by him of his other obligations hereunder the Publisher agrees to pay the Composer the following royalties in respect of income arising within the United Kingdom or (as the case may be) received by the Publisher from its sub-publishers outside the UK (as set out in Clause 10) from exploitation of the Compositions and (where relevant) the Old Catalogue.

*Sheet Music*

(a) (i) Ten percent of the marked retail selling price of all folios or albums containing wholly the Compositions and *pro rata* where a printed album also contains third party copyrights.

(ii) [75%] of all income received by the Publisher from licensing the printing of any Composition by a third party.

(iii) No royalties will be paid on all copies of sheet music distributed free of charge for promotional purposes.

*Mechanical Royalties*

(b) [75%] of all royalties and other income received by the Publisher from licensing the use of any Composition in connection with the making of records tapes and other devices whether audio or audio-visual for sale to the public as "records".

*Synchronisation fees*

(c) [75%] of all income of the Publisher from licensing the inclusion of any Copyright in the sound track of a television film or cinematograph film or any other means or device of a like nature for public performance or exhibition or otherwise.

*Other use income*

(d) [75%] of all other income received by the Publisher not included above being for use of any of the Compositions in any manner.

*Performing fees*

(e) (i) [75%] of all money collected by the PRS in respect of the Compositions if the Composer is not a member of PRS and if he is a member the Composer will receive [9/12] and the Publisher [3/12].

(ii) This Agreement will be the certificate required for the PRS Rule 1(0) that the Publisher is entitled to exploit the Compositions.

*Advances*

(f) The Publisher agrees to pay the Composer the following advance payments on account of fees royalties and other income due to him hereunder and which will only be recoupable by the Publisher as a first charge from any and all of the Composer's share of income received by the Publisher:

(i) £ on the signing of this Agreement.

(ii) £ on each anniversary date of this Agreement provided that all previous advances have been fully recouped.

(iii) £ on the commercial release in the United Kingdom of the first long playing record performed by the Composer in each year of this Agreement containing all or all but [one] of his Compositions.

9 If a Cover Record is released in any part of the Territory the Publisher will notify the Composer in writing of the details thereof reasonably promptly.

*Sub-publishers*

10 (a) The Publisher will be entitled to appoint as sub-publishers outside the United Kingdom any reputable publisher provided that such delegation shall be without prejudice to the obligations of the Publisher itself within that Territory and provided that the sub-publisher retains not more than the following shares of "at source" income arising within its Territory:

(i) [25%] of mechanical royalties except for Cover Records when the proportion will be [40%] on Sales of the local recording only.

(ii) 3/12 of performance fees except that where it has procured a Cover Record when the proportion will be [5/12].

(iii) [25%] of all other income arising from any source within its territory.

(b) The Publisher will be entitled to appoint as a sub-publisher any subsidiary or associated company provided that it first informs the Composer thereof in writing and provided that the sub-publisher's retentions of "at source" income are no more than as set out in (a) above and that the terms of the sub-publishing agreement are the same as those the Publisher imposes upon other independent sub-publishers appointed by it elsewhere within the Territory.

(c) Upon request by the Composer the Publisher agrees to provide him with copies of all agreements with its sub-publishers in respect of the Compositions or the Old Catalogue but it will be entitled to delete private information such as advances received which are no concern of the Composer under this Agreement.

(d) No sub-publisher will be authorised to appoint any sub-subpublisher for any part of its territory.

*Publisher's Accounts*

11 The Publisher will maintain (and will require any such sub-publisher to maintain) complete and accurate books of account in respect of all exploitation and uses of the Compositions showing clearly the relevant use of the Composition and source of income the amount received and date of receipt and all other information relating thereto customarily required for accurate and timely accounting to the Composer and to enable auditing to

be undertaken.

12 (a) The Publisher will account to the Composer half yearly within [45] days after each 30th June and 31st December in respect of all receipts of the Publisher within the UK within the previous half year.

(b) The Publisher will use reasonable endeavours to ensure that income due to it from sub-publishers is remitted without delay and the Publisher will ensure that each sub-publisher accounts to it accurately in accordance with Clause 13(e).

(c) If a country within the Territory has exchange control foreign remittance restrictions the Publisher will procure that the Composer's share is deposited in a bank account on interest in his name except where the Publisher is still recouping any outstanding advances to the Composer when the amount due to the Composer shall be set against the advance by way of recoupment.

13 (a) The Composer or his authorised representative (who shall be a chartered accountant) shall be entitled to inspect and take copies of the accounts of the Publisher relating to the Compositions not more than once each year and within 12 months after the expiry of the [six] month periods referred to in Clause 5 or after the date of prior termination (as the case may be) by appointment and upon giving the Publisher not less than [14] days prior written notice.

(b) If there shall be any discrepancy in the Publisher's accounts in favour of the Publisher the Publisher shall be entitled to recoup any excess payment from the next accounting to the Composer without interest thereon.

(c) If there shall be any discrepancy in the Publisher's accounts in favour of the Composer:

(i) The discrepancy will be paid immediately.

(ii) Interest at [2] percent over the base rate applied by [ ] bank from time to time shall be payable thereon from its due date up to the date of payment.

(iii) If the discrepancy exceeds [5%] of the amount properly due over the period being audited then the reasonable costs incurred by the Composer in connection with the audit will be paid by the Publisher.

(d) The accounting by the Publisher from foreign source earnings shall be calculated in sterling at the same exchange rate as applied when the Publisher converted its relevant foreign receipts into sterling.

(e) (i) If there are reasonable grounds for believing that the accounting from any sub-publisher is incorrect the Publisher will request the sub-publisher in writing to satisfy the publisher on the error or to make the appropriate payment.

(ii) If the sub-publisher fails to do so and if the error is substantial the Publisher agrees promptly to undertake an audit of the sub-publisher's accounts and income reporting procedures at its own cost and to ensure that if any such discrepancy is found it will be collected by the Publisher and included within its next accounting to the Composer.

(iii) If a discrepancy is established and the sub-publisher fails at its next accounting to make it good the publisher will terminate its agreement with that sub-publisher forthwith.

*Copyright breach procedure*

14 If the Publisher receives any claim that any of the Compositions is in

breach of a third party copyright or other rights:

(a) It will promptly notify the Composer together with such details as may be available.

(b) The Publisher and the Composer will consult promptly to establish whether or not the claim has a good foundation.

(c) (i) If they are both satisfied that the claim is invalid the Publisher is entitled to defend the claim as it thinks best and the Composer will give the Publisher all assistance reasonably required of him and if ultimately the Publisher is advised to settle the claim by its legal advisers on economic or legal grounds which are accepted by the Composer it may so settle.

(ii) If notwithstanding any advice given to the Publisher under (i) above to settle the claim the Composer is advised by his legal advisers to maintain the defence the Publisher agrees to do so subject to the Composer taking full responsibility for the financial risk of costs and compensation and providing the Publisher with acceptable security in that respect.

*Termination*

15 The Composer will be entitled to terminate this Agreement at any time from the date hereof to the expiry of the Rights Extension Period forthwith upon giving the Publisher written notice upon the happening of any of the following events:

(a) The Publisher failing to remedy a material breach of this Agreement within [21] days after receiving a written notice from the Composer specifying the breach and requiring its remedy.

(b) The Publisher ceasing permanently to trade or compounding with its creditors or winding up except for amalgamation or reconstruction.

16 (a) Upon termination of this Agreement by expiry of the Rights Period or the Rights Extension Period (as the case may be) or under clause 15 above then subject to clause 5 all of the rights herein granted to the Publisher shall terminate forthwith and shall revert to the Composer including the copyrights in the Compositions and the Publisher hereby reassigns such copyright of existing and future Compositions to take effect on the happening of any such termination date.

(b) If the Composer lawfully terminates this Agreement under Clause 15(a) or under clause 15(b) then it is also agreed that the benefit of all agreements between the Publisher and all sub-publishers shall revert to and be assigned to the Composer from the effective date of termination who will be entitled to notify all sub-publishers accordingly and be paid all income arising thereafter and which would otherwise have been payable to the Publisher.

[STANDARD CLAUSES]

SCHEDULE A: [OLD CATALOGUE]

SCHEDULE B: [LICENSED COMPOSITIONS]

IN WITNESS

**Comments on this Agreement**

1 Definitions of the different Rights Periods and the Compositions will

depend on the deal. Also, as an alternative to the definition of "to publish", see the definition of "the Rights" in the sample catalogue publishing agreement.

2(a)(i) The grant of rights can also be by exclusive licence, and the other clauses would be modified accordingly.

2(a)(iii) This moral right assertion is due to the new Copyright Act.

2(b) If there is an Old Catalogue the rights of its present publisher may extend beyond the contract period.

6(d) A novel idea, worth trying. The composer is entitled to know what (if anything) is being done by the publisher.

8(f) These are the alternative possibilities, the composer should not expect them all to apply.

10(b) This is to help the publisher avoid what has been a publisher's problem in litigation.

16 Also a novel idea, to protect the composer. The same effect would be achieved by granting a non-exclusive licence.

**NB** If the agreement assigns the composer's copyrights to the publisher for the life of copyright, and not for a limited period, the following clause should be included:

"If within [24] months after the notification by the Composer to the Publisher of the details of a Composition the Composer has not recorded it or the Publisher has not procured a Cover Record [within the UK or the USA] then the Composer shall be entitled to serve on the Publisher a written notice requiring the reassignment to the Composer of the copyright in that Composition and the Publisher shall forthwith execute such an assignment."

## CATALOGUE PUBLISHING AGREEMENT (BY EXCLUSIVE LICENCE)

THIS AGREEMENT is made the day of 19
BETWEEN of
(hereinafter called the Publisher) of the first part and
of
(hereinafter called the Company) of the second part and
of
(hereinafter called the Composer) of the third part.

WHEREAS the Company has the benefit of a sole and exclusive song writing and composing agreement with the Composer dated the [ ] and which has an expiry date of [ ].

NOW IT IS AGREED as follows:

*Definitions*

1 "The Compositions" shall mean the compositions set out in the Schedule hereto together with all of the compositions written and composed by the Composer during the Contract Period.

"The Contract Period" shall mean the period commencing on the date hereof and terminating on the [third] anniversary date [terminating on

| | |
|---|---|
| | the [ ] day of [ ] subject to earlier termination in accordance with clause 16 hereof]. |
| "The Rights Period" | shall mean the period of [five] years from the date of this Agreement. |
| "The Rights Extension Period" | shall mean the period of [eight] years from the date of this Agreement which shall apply to any Composition for which the Publisher obtains a *bona fide* commercially released Cover Record during the Contract Period. |
| "The Rights" | shall mean the exclusive rights within the Territory to do the following things:<br>(i) To print publish and sell copies of the Compositions in sheet or book form.<br>(ii) To use the name likeness and biographical material of the Composer solely in connection with the exploitation of the Compositions.<br>(iii) To grant non-exclusive worldwide mechanical licences for the reproduction of the Compositions by any means for audio or audiovisual records commercially released for home consumption as "records" and to collect all royalties and fees arising therefrom.<br>(iv) To grant non-exclusive worldwide licences for the use of the Compositions in the sound tracks of cinematograph films TV films and all other audiovisual devices.<br>(v) Subject to Clause 7 the right to make or authorise arrangements and adaptations of the Compositions [provided that the Publisher obtains the prior written consent of the Company]. |
| "The Territory" | shall mean [the world]. |
| "at Source" | (as referred to in Clause 11) in connection with income shall mean the income arising to be paid gross in any country of the Territory whether it is to be collected by the Publisher or by any sub-publisher but (where applicable) after any recognised copyright income collection society shall have made any charge thereon in accordance with its rules. |
| "Cover Recording" | Shall mean only a recording made by a local artiste during the Contract Period and released by a local record company (including a local affiliate or subsidiary of an international record company) within any country of the Territory but excluding the UK unless the Composer is also an artiste who has released a record containing that composition. |

*Grant of rights*

2 (a) Subject to and upon the terms and conditions and for the consideration herein set out the Company hereby grants to the Publisher within the Territory the sole and exclusive licence to exercise the Rights in respect of the Compositions and the copyright and all other rights not hereby licensed to the Publisher in respect of the Compositions shall be reserved to the Company which shall be entitled to exercise them as it sees fit in its

absolute discretion within the Territory.

(b) Subject to clauses 8 and 16 hereof the Publisher shall be entitled to exercise the Rights in respect of all of the Compositions during the Rights Period and in respect of any Composition for which the Publisher procures a Cover Record it shall be entitled to exercise the Rights relating thereto for the Rights Extension Period.

3 As and when the Composer writes any Composition the Company undertakes to provide to the Publisher top lines of the music and written down lyrics promptly after such creation or to provide the Publisher with a demo tape of the Composition of sufficient quality to enable the Publisher to top line the Composition and write down the lyrics.

*Obligations of Company*

4 The Company warrants to the Publisher that:

(a) It is or (subject to Clause 18) will be the legal and beneficial owner of the copyright and all other rights in and to the Compositions within the Territory for a period which will exceed the Rights Extension Period.

(b) It is entitled to enter into this Agreement and that there is no (and the Company undertakes not to enter into any) agreement or commitment nor will it grant any assignment licence or other right in respect of any Composition which would cause it to be in breach of this Agreement or which would cause the Publisher to be in breach of any third party rights or which would inhibit the exercise by the Publisher of any of its Rights set out herein.

(c) All of the Compositions will be original to the Composer and that he will not in composing them make any use of third party material and that no Composition will be defamatory or commercially or religiously objectionable or otherwise prejudicial to the name, reputation and business of the Composer the Company or the Publisher.

(d) The Composer will not compose any Composition which he will attribute to any other person as the author thereof or in respect of which he will use a pseudonym which is not notified to the Publisher and that he will not claim to be the author of any Composition of which he is not the author.

(e) The Composer will use his reasonable endeavours to pursue his composing career and compose songs and write lyrics either for his own use or for the use of others which are of reasonable commercial appeal and of sufficient substance to merit being promoted by the Publisher but this does not create any express or implied obligation upon the Composer to compose any minimum number of Compositions during the Contract Period.

(f) If during the Contract Period the Composer is an artiste being contracted to a reputable or major record company which records his performances and releases them commercially the Composer will use his best endeavours to include on all such records exclusively his Compositions unless there is a good reason for including the compositions of another composer.

(g) That the Company and the Composer are members of the Performing Rights Society Ltd.

5 The Company agrees to indemnify the Publisher from any and all claims costs damages and liabilities (but excluding any prospective loss of profits) incurred by the Publisher directly from the consequences of breach by the Company of any warranty or representation made to the Publisher.

*Obligations and rights of Publisher*

6 (a) The Publisher will use its best endeavours to:

(i) promote and publish and obtain recordings of the Compositions throughout the Territory either itself or through sub-publishing representatives;

(ii) ensure the prompt and correct accounting to it of all income arising from exploitation of the Compositions;

(iii) ensure that the Compositions are registered with all appropriate copyright income collection societies;

(iv) (where applicable) make all copyright registrations to protect the legal status of the Compositions;

(v) take all reasonable steps to protect the copyright in the Compositions and to identify and (in consultation with the Company) to pursue infringers of such copyrights where that is practical and economic.

(b) It is recognised by the Company that until such time as the Compositions become publicly available through any commercial means of exploitation the Publisher may not be able to perform some of its obligations under (a) but such recognition does not reduce the obligations of the Publisher hereunder.

(c) The obligations of the Publisher will not be modified or reduced by the extent of success achieved by the Composer his record company or any other party in promoting any of the Compositions.

(d) The Publisher will maintain a file of correspondence memoranda and other evidence of significant communications it has had with all of its sub-publishers and with any other third party within the Territory concerning the promotion publishing and recording of the Compositions which evidence shall be made available to the Company for inspection at its request (but which shall not be more than once in each year) so the Company can be reasonably satisfied as to the Publisher's efforts on its behalf.

(e) The Company confirms to the Publisher that the Composer has asserted his rights under section 78 of the Copyright Designs and Patents Act 1988 and the Publisher undertakes to ensure that such rights are observed.

7 Subject to the Company's prior written consent and also its agreement upon the sharing of performance income with the arranger or translator the Publisher will be entitled to make or authorise the making of arrangements of the music of any Composition or the translation of the lyrics of any Composition provided that the copyright and all other rights in the arrangement of the music of a composition is assigned to the Publisher as an expansion of the copyright and all other rights in the original Composition and all credits and copyright collection society registrations will be made accordingly.

*Payments to Company*

8 (a) The Publisher (and each sub-publisher for its own part of the Territory) will be entitled to collect all of the income royalties and fees arising within the Territory and paid at any time during the Rights Period and within the period of [six] months thereafter.

(b) In respect of Compositions contained in Cover Records the Publisher will be entitled to collect all of such income paid during the Rights Extension Period and within the Period of [six] months thereafter.

(c) (i) Any income received by the Publisher arising in the UK or wherever else the Publisher does not use a sub-publisher after the expiry of the relevant [six] month period will be paid forthwith to the Company without deduction.

(ii) The Publisher will be entitled to receive and to retain its share of income paid by a sub-publisher by the end of the [six] month period although it is received by the Publisher after the expiry of that period but any subsequent payments by any sub-publisher to the publisher will be paid forthwith to the Company without deduction.

(iii) The [six] month extension referred to in (a) and (b) above will not apply if this Agreement is terminated under Clause 16 and all income received by the Publisher after the termination date with the sole exception of the first accounting after termination made by each sub-publisher will be paid forthwith to the Company.

9 In consideration of the grant of the Rights by the Company to the Publisher and the performance of the Company's other obligations hereunder the Publisher agrees to pay the Company the following royalties in respect of income arising within the United Kingdom or (as the case may be) received by the Publisher from its sub-publishers outside the UK (as set out in Clause 11) from exploitation of the Compositions.

*Sheet Music*

(a) (i) Ten percent of the marked retail selling price of all folios or albums containing wholly the Compositions and *pro rata* where a printed album also contains third party copyrights.

(ii) [75%] of all income received by the Publisher from licensing the printing of any Composition by a third party.

(iii) No royalties will be paid on all copies of sheet music distributed free of charge for promotional purposes.

*Mechanical Royalties*

(b) [75%] of all royalties and other income received by the Publisher from licensing the use of any Composition in connection with the making of records tapes and other devices whether audio or audio-visual for sale to the public as "records".

*Synchronisation fees*

(c) [75%] of all income of the Publisher from licensing the inclusion of any Copyright in the sound track of a television film or cinematograph film or any other means or device of a like nature for public performance or exhibition or otherwise.

*Other use income*

(d) [75%] of all other income received by the Publisher not included above being for use of any of the Compositions in any manner.

*Performing fees*

(e) (i) The Composer through his membership of PRS shall be entitled to 6/12 of the performance fees collected by PRS and of the remaining 6/12 the Company will receive [3/12] and the Publisher will receive [3/12].

(ii) This Agreement will be the certificate required for the PRS Rule 1(0) that the Publisher is entitled to exploit the Compositions.

*Advances*

(f) The Publisher agrees to pay the Company the following advance payments on account of fees royalties and other income due to it hereunder and which will only be recoupable by the Publisher as a first charge from any and all of the Company's share of income received by the Publisher:

(i) £ on the signing of this Agreement.

(ii) £ on each anniversary date of this Agreement provided that all previous advances have been fully recouped.

(iii) £ on the commercial release in the United Kingdom of the first long playing record performed by the Composer in each year of this Agreement containing all or all but [one] of his Compositions.

10 If a Cover Record is released in any part of the Territory the Publisher will notify the Company in writing of the details thereof reasonably promptly.

*Sub-publishers*

11 (a) The Publisher will be entitled to appoint as sub-publishers outside the United Kingdom any reputable publisher provided that such delegation shall be without prejudice to the obligations of the Publisher itself within that Territory and provided that the sub-publisher retains not more than the following shares of "at source" income arising within its Territory:

(i) [25%] of mechanical royalties except for Cover Records when the proportion will be [40%] on Sales of the local Recording only.

(ii) 3/12 of performance fees except that where it has procured a Cover Record when the proportion will be [5/12].

(iii) [25%] of all other income arising from any source within its territory.

(b) The Publisher will be entitled to appoint as a sub-publisher any subsidiary or associated company provided that it first informs the Company thereof in writing and provided that the sub-publisher's retentions of "at source" income are no more than as set out in (a) above and that the terms of the sub-publishing agreement are the same as those the Publisher imposes upon other independent sub-publishers appointed by it elsewhere within the Territory.

(c) Upon request by the Company the Publisher agrees to provide it with copies of all agreements with its sub-publishers in respect of the Compositions but it will be entitled to delete private information such as the amount of advances received which are no concern of the Company under this Agreement.

(d) No sub-publisher shall be authorised to appoint any sub-sub-publisher for any part of its territory.

*Publisher's Accounts*

12 The Publisher will maintain (and will require any sub-publisher to maintain) complete and accurate books of account in respect of all exploitation and uses of the Compositions showing clearly the relevant use of the Composition the source of income the amount received and the date of receipt and all other information relating thereto customarily required for accurate and timely accounting to the Company and to enable auditing to be undertaken.

13 (a) The Publisher will account to the Company half yearly within [45] days after each 30th June and 31st December in respect of all receipts of the Publisher within the previous half year.

(b) The Publisher will use reasonable endeavours to ensure that income due to it from sub-publishers is remitted without delay and the Publisher will ensure that each sub-publisher accounts to it accurately in accordance with clause 14(e).

(c) If a country within the Territory has exchange control foreign remittance restrictions the Publisher will procure that the Company's share is deposited in a bank account on interest in its name except where the Publisher is still recouping any outstanding advances to the Company when the amount due to the Company shall be set against the advance by way of recoupment.

14 (a) The Company or its authorised representative (who shall be a chartered accountant) shall be entitled to inspect and take copies of the accounts of the Publisher relating to the Compositions not more than once each year and within 12 months after the expiry of the [six] month periods referred to in Clause 8 or after the date of prior termination (as the case may be) by appointment and upon giving the Publisher not less than [14] days prior written notice.

(b) If there shall be any discrepancy in the Publisher's accounts in favour of the Publisher the Publisher shall be entitled to recoup any excess payment from the next accounting to the Composer without interest thereon.

(c) If there shall be any discrepancy in the Publisher's accounts in favour of the Company:

(i) the discrepancy will be paid immediately;

(ii) interest at [2] percent over the basic rate applied by [ ] bank from time to time shall be payable thereon from its due date up to the date of payment;

(iii) if the discrepancy exceeds [5%] of the amount properly due for the period being audited then the reasonable costs incurred by the Company in connection with the audit will be paid by the Publisher.

(d) The accounting by the Publisher from foreign source earnings shall be calculated in sterling at the same exchange rate as applied when the Publisher converts its relevant foreign receipts into sterling.

(e) If there are reasonable grounds for believing that the accounting from any sub-publisher is incorrect the Publisher will request the sub-publisher in writing to satisfy the Publisher on the error or to make the appropriate payment.

(ii) If the sub-publisher fails to do so and if the error is substantial the Publisher agrees promptly to undertake an audit of the sub-publisher's accounts and income reporting procedures at its own cost and to ensure that if any such discrepancy is found it will be collected by the Publisher and included within its next accounting to the Company.

(iii) If a discrepancy is established and the sub-publisher fails at its next accounting to make it good the Publisher will terminate its agreement with that sub-publisher forthwith.

*Copyright breach procedure*

15 If the Publisher receives any claim that any of the Compositions is in breach of a third party copyright or other rights:

(a) It will promptly notify the Company in writing together with such details as may be available.

(b) The Publisher and the Company will consult promptly to establish whether or not the claim has a good foundation:

(c) (i) If they are both satisfied that the claim is invalid the Publisher is entitled to defend the claim as it thinks best and the Company and the Composer will give the Publisher all assistance reasonably required by it and if ultimately the Publisher is advised to settle the claim by its legal advisers on economic or legal grounds which are accepted by the Company it may so settle.

(ii) If notwithstanding any advice given to the Publisher under (i) above to settle the claim the Company is advised by its legal advisers to maintain the defence the Publisher agrees to do so subject to the Company taking full responsibility for the financial risk of costs and compensation and providing the Publisher with acceptable security in that respect.

*Termination*

16 The Company will be entitled to terminate this Agreement at any time from the date hereof to the expiry of the Rights Extension Period forthwith upon giving the Publisher written notice upon the happening of any of the following events:

(a) The Publisher failing to remedy a material breach of this Agreement within [21] days after receiving a written notice from the Company specifying the breach and requiring its remedy.

(b) The Publisher ceasing permanently to trade or compounding with its creditors or winding up except for amalgamation or reconstruction.

17 Upon termination of this Agreement by expiry of the Rights Period or the Rights Extension Period (as the case may be) or upon earlier termination under clause 16 all of the rights herein granted to the Publisher shall terminate forthwith and shall revert to the Company including (where this Agreement is terminated under Clause 16) the benefit the Publisher has of all of the sub-publishing agreements entered into by it with effect from the termination date and the Company will promptly notify each sub-publisher accordingly which (as the Publisher hereby agrees) will from the date of termination make all accountings and payments to the Company wholly for its own benefit instead of to the Publisher.

18 (a) The Composer is a party hereto to give assurance to the Publisher that the Company is fully entitled to enter into this Agreement and the Composer has contemporaneously herewith signed a side letter addressed to the Publisher which has placed reliance thereon as a condition of entering into this Agreement.

(b) The Publisher agrees that in the event of the Composer ceasing to provide his composing and songwriting services to the Company or acting in any other way during the Contract Period whereby the Company is in breach of this Agreement then the Publisher will be entitled to exercise its rights under the attached side letter and whether or not it does so the Company will not be deemed to be in breach of this Agreement for the purposes of the Publisher having any monetary claim of any nature and howsoever arising against the Company from such breach.

[STANDARD CLAUSES]

IN WITNESS

## SIDE LETTER FROM COMPOSER TO PUBLISHER

Dear Sirs,

Pursuant to an exclusive contract dated the [ ] and expiring on [ ] between the undersigned and [ ] (the Company), the Company is entitled to my exclusive services as a Composer and songwriter. I have been advised that the Company is entering into a written agreement with you (the Publishing Agreement) whereby you are granted Licence rights for the Territory in and to the Compositions as defined therein. In consideration of your executing the Publishing Agreement, I hereby agree as follows:

1 I warrant that the Company has the right to enter into the Publishing Agreement and that the Company shall continue to have such rights during the whole of the period of the Publishing Agreement. I confirm all of the Company's obligations and Warranties in connection with me and with the Compositions and I shall duly and to the best of my ability perform and discharge them.

2 If during the period of the Publishing Agreement, the Company shall for any reason cease to be entitled to my songwriting services, or if the Company shall be in breach of the Publishing Agreement then I will at your request do all such acts and things as shall give to you the same rights and benefits as you may have at that date under the Publishing Agreement. In such event, I shall be entitled to the payment by you direct of all income which I would have received under my agreement with the Company.

3 You have the right to use and publish my name (both legal and professional), likeness and/or biographical material but only in connection with the exploitation of the Compositions, pursuant to the Publishing Agreement.

4 No termination of the Publishing Agreement shall operate to diminish any of my liabilities or obligations hereunder without your written consent.

5 Subject to Clause 2 I understand and agree that (with the exception of performance income) all income which may be due to me from the exploitation of the Compositions in the Territory prior to your exercise of this letter shall be paid to me by the Company and I shall look solely to the Company for such payment. Any such royalties and other monies which may become due to me directly from you under Clause 2 shall be available for the recoupment of any and all then outstanding advances paid by you to the Company under the Publishing Agreement.

Yours faithfully,

### Comments on this agreement

This agreement is based upon the composer's agreement, but grants a limited licence, and, for familiarity, it assumes the company is owned by the composer.

1 The alternative termination date can be used where the agreement is signed in a month which may be inconvenient for collection society or record company accounting dates. The termination date can be made to fall on a date which neatly covers a convenient PRS or other third party accounting date soon after the agreement's natural anniversary date.

2(a) The rights are granted by an exclusive licence, so many of the matters pertinent to a copyright assignment are not relevant.

9(f) Not all of those may be applicable.

11(a)(ii) If the composition is already highly successful as an existing recording, whether or not by the composer, there may be no justification in offering the sub-publisher any increase in his share of performance income. Alternatively it should get only a small increase in overall performance fees. Alternatively, pro rate them in the ratio of local cover record sales to sales of all other versions of the record on a six monthly basis, with a stated maximum percentage.

11(c) This will enable the company to pick up a retention or other obvious breach at an early stage.

14(e) A novel concept, but why not? The sub-publisher is the representative of the publisher, and as the company does not have any privity of contract with the sub-publisher, it has no direct right of action against it.

17 The licence expires, or is terminated under clause 16, and the rights granted to the publisher cease to exist. There is nothing to assign back to the company. On early termination the purpose is to take everything back from the publisher, so overseas deals should not be treated any differently from the publishers UK position.

18 The composer signs a side letter in favour of the publisher, in case he breaks up with the company.

**Side Letter:** This is a collateral guarantee from the composer to the publisher to safeguard it against the company ceasing to have the benefit of the composer's services.

## GROUP MEMBERSHIP AGREEMENT

THIS AGREEMENT is made the day of 19
BETWEEN of
and of
and of
(hereinafter individually called the Members)

WHEREAS on or about the [ ] the Members agreed to form a musical group (hereinafter called the Group) for the purpose of carrying on business together as musicians for their mutual benefit and by this Agreement they wish to establish the terms upon which Group business will be conducted.

NOW IT IS AGREED as follows:

*Constitution*

1 (a) The Group shall be constituted as a Partnership and this Agreement and any valid modification shall be the only terms which will apply to the Members within the context of the Group.

(b) In respect of any Member this Agreement will subsist until such time as he shall cease to be a Member except for those clauses which are stated to remain in force thereafter.

(c) The Members agree that they will act in good faith in connection with any matter relating to the constitution of the Group and any of the activities of the Group and any obligations entered into by the Group with third parties.

*Group decisions*

2 The following decisions shall be made and acted upon only with the unanimous consent of all the Members:

(a) the decision to appoint and the terms of the appointment of a manager of the Group or an agent to represent the Group;

(b) the admission of a new permanent Member of the Group;

(c) any change in the professional name of the Group;

(d) the choice of record company and publishing company and the negotiation of the terms of all long term agreements relating to the professional services of the Group or any promotion or exploitation of any product of or rights in the goodwill and reputation of the Group;

(e) the undertaking of any significant Group activity such as international touring or the recording of a TV special;

(f) forming a limited liability company for the purpose of transforming the present partnership into a corporate entity whether for tax or liability or any other financial or commercial reason;

(g) the making of any request for or commitment to any significant loan or other Group financial liability to any party (including any guarantee of third party obligations) and for any purpose and in this context "significant" shall mean a transaction or series of related transactions or a facility exceeding [£ ] whether or not the whole amount thereof is intended to be drawn down at any time;

(h) jointly investing or lending any excess Group Income in any venture outside Group activities in the normal course of business.

3 (a) Any decision not being within clause 2 or which is otherwise stated to require the unanimous consent of all Members will be decided upon by a majority of votes on a show of hands each Member having one vote.

(b) In the event of an equality of votes either side the matter proposed and voted upon shall be deemed to have been rejected.

(c) If the Group appoints its manager or any other party to adjudicate on any matter which cannot be resolved by voting then a condition of that appointment is that the decision of the adjudicator will be accepted by the Group.

## Change of Membership of Group

*Voluntary retirement*

4 If a Member wants to leave the Group for whatever reason he may do so by giving not less than [three] months written notice to the other Members subject to Clause 6(h).

*Expulsion of a member*

5 (a) (i) A Member may only be expelled from the Group by the unanimous decision of all of the other Members giving written notice to the expelled Member.

(ii) In the case of any ground for expulsion other than fundamental disagreement on Group policy or development the expelled Member must first (if appropriate) have been given a reasonable opportunity to remedy the complaint or to have been warned about his activity complained of and the written notice of expulsion must state the reason for the expulsion.

(b) If the unanimous decision is given without reasonable cause such as (but not limited to) a material breach of this Agreement or permanent incapacity or a serious criminal conviction or a fundamental disagreement with the Member over Group internal matters then the expulsion shall be without prejudice to any right or claim the expelled Member may have against the other Members as a consequence thereof.

(c) If the expulsion is for good cause as described in (b) above the only claim the expelled Member will have against the other Members is for a continued accounting to him of royalties and other income arising from records made songs written or events undertaken while he was a Member.

*Consequences of Membership change*

6 Whatever the cause of a Member leaving the Group the following matters will be dealt with:

(a) Subject to (b) below no single Member or minority of Members whether being expelled or leaving voluntarily will have any right in title to or claim upon the name of the Group or any goodwill attached thereto and the remaining majority of the Members together with any future Members (for so long as they are Members) shall have between them the sole right to the use of the Group name.

(b) (i) If the Group name is synonymous with or is substantially based upon the real name or the established professional name of an expelled or leaving Member nothing shall prevent the expelled or leaving Member from utilising his name as his solo professional name or from forming another Group using his professional name but not precisely in the wording or the logo design of the Group name and the Group shall have no claim for passing off or otherwise against that departed Member it being agreed that the Group will promptly change its name to one having no connection with or similarity to the name of that departed Member.

(ii) If the synonymous Group name has been applied for or registered as a trademark or service mark by the Group then the remaining Members undertake forthwith upon the departure of the Member to either assign the trademark or the benefit of the application to him.

(c) The share of continuing royalties due to any leaving Member from any recording or publishing agreement will be paid to him promptly subject only to the recoupment of his share of outstanding advances as at the date of his departure and the remaining Members will procure that no future advances made to them will be recouped from his future royalties.

(d) If the Member leaves the Group voluntarily it will be his responsibility to procure his release from all third party contracts relating to the Group activities.

(e) If the Member is expelled the remaining Members will procure that he is released from:

(i) all such third party contracts with the exception of any publishing agreement to which he is signed as an individual;

(ii) all bank guarantees hire purchase credit leasing or other commitments which are contracted for or committed to by the Group.

(f) His proportion of the net Group assets by way of equipment vehicles or otherwise will be credited to the departed Member and he will be paid (or his account with the Group will be credited with) the value thereof when the next Group accounts are prepared and in the event of disagreement upon the value all of the Members agree to accept a valuation given by the Group's accountants.

(g) The leaving or expelled Member may take free of any lien any musical instrument or other equipment which is generally recognised as his and which is not owned by the Group and if it is being leased or bought on hire purchase by the Group as a matter of convenience then before he takes possession of the instrument or equipment the Member will take over (and fully document the substitution of) all such commitments to the Group's satisfaction and will indemnify the Group from them.

(h) No Member may leave voluntarily or may be expelled until the completion of any forthcoming commitment for personal appearances which cannot be safely cancelled or which could not proceed if the leaving or expelled Member were not a Member for that appearance and:

(i) if a Member leaves the Group in disregard of any such obligation he will be wholly liable for the adverse financial consequences arising from any third party claim related to a breach of such commitments caused by his departure;

(ii) if a Member is expelled in disregard of any such obligations the remaining Members will be wholly liable for the adverse consequences arising from any third party claim relating to a breach of such commitments caused by their action.

7 (a) If the Group terminates this Agreement as between all the Members and ceases permanently to operate as a Group then all the Members will have equal responsibility for resolving or terminating all outstanding third party Group contracts and liabilities and they will have an equal share of net Group assets or will be equally responsible for net group liabilities.

(b) Subject to clause 6(b) none of the Members will be entitled to use the Group name without the written consent of all of the then living current Members as at the date of cessation provided that if any such Member cannot be found after reasonably diligent research (which shall be documented for proof) the consent of such missing Member will not be required.

*Non-Group activities*

8 (a) Any Member who composes the music or writes the lyrics for any composition which is recorded by the Group will be entitled to the copyright in and the whole of the income from his work.

(b) If two or more of the Members jointly compose and write any of the compositions it is agreed that they will own the copyright jointly (subject to the rights of the publisher of the members' compositions) and will share all of the composer's share of all earnings from that composition in equal proportions.

9 Without having to seek the consent of the other Members a Member will be entitled to be involved in any musical activity which does not directly compete or conflict with the Group activities and which does not put the Member or the other Members in breach of any agreement to which they are

a party or which does not otherwise infringe any third party rights including the following activties:

(a) Performing as a session musician with other artistes for live performances provided that no audio or audio/visual recording is made of the performance unless:
   (i) the Group's record company has agreed in writing; and
   (ii) the Member has signed a properly negotiated agreement to protect his interests and the interests of the Group (where applicable).

(b) Producing recordings being made by other artistes.

(c) Appearing in TV or films in any capacity except as a musical performer when this clause will apply.

10 If a Member (such as the lead singer) wishes to carry on a solo career as a performer as well as being a Member of the Group the consent of all of the Members must be obtained.

11 Any income arising to a Member from any non-Group activity will be entirely his and no part of the expense incurred in so doing will be a liability of any other Member.

12 The Members agree that they will not indulge in dangerous sports or activities without notifying the other Members so that any Group insurance may be taken out reviewed or increased and so that the Member can ascertain which (if any) sports or activities nullify the insurance or cause additional premiums to be payable.

*Financial Matters*

13 (a) Group equipment will be acquired as and when needed and equipment or instruments needed by individual Members may also be bought as Group equipment or by the Member personally as they may decide.

(b) when a Member leaves the Group he may take with him his personally bought equipment and will be credited with the value of his share of equipment retained by the Group.

14 The Group will be responsible for employing and paying for road crew or other permanent employees or independent contractors used for Group business but any Member shall be free to employ any person at his own expense to look after him and his equipment and he shall be wholly responsible for that person.

15 In the absence of anything to the contrary the Group will share all expense and all income from all sources in connection with Group activities equally between the Members.

16 (a) Each Member will be personally responsible for all income tax due on his share of Group income and all of the Members agree that they will instruct the Group's accountant to:
   (i) receive and to retain so much of the Group income as will be required as a reserve against the payment of income tax as and when demanded by the Inland Revenue and to maintain a complete accurate and up to date accounting system for its financial affairs;
   (ii) advise the Group on VAT registration and where applicable to maintain accurate and up to date VAT invoices and payments and to make all VAT returns on time.

(b) Each Member agrees to indemnify all of the others from any Income Tax or other fiscal liability on his personal income and they each agree to notify fully and promptly any taxable income to the tax authorities to reduce the risk of any unnecessary Inland Revenue investigation into the affairs of the Group.

17 (a) Each Member shall be responsible for all of his personal expenses incurred while being involved in Group activities such as flight and other costs for companions on foreign tours.

(b) If for any reason any Member is required to pay towards the satisfaction of any liability of the Group more than his proper proportionate share thereof he will be entitled to claim from all of the other Members their contribution to such excess payments.

*General Matters*

18 The Members acknowledge that each of them has an insurable interest in each other and that the Group should pay for permanent health life and accident insurance for the benefit of both the Group and or the benefit of individual Members to a similar agreed level.

19 None of the Members is authorised and each of them agrees not to make any commitment on behalf of the Group which has not been agreed between all of them except for ordinary every day business matters in consultation with the Group's Manager.

20 Each of the Members agrees to keep confidential and not to disclose to any unauthorised parties any private information relating to the Group its business affairs and any other matter private to the Members as individuals. This obligation will remain in force after a Member has ceased to be a Member of the Group.

21 The Members will at all times maintain their membership of the Performing Right Society and of the Musicians Union and any other trade union or organisation necessary to enable the Group to carry on its business effectively.

22 The members acknowledge that they have each been strongly recommended to seek Legal and accounting advice upon the terms of this Agreement in respect of their individual rights and obligations as a Member and that they have done so.

[APPROPRIATE STANDARD CLAUSES]

IN WITNESS etc

**Comments on this agreement**

There is no generally used format, so this example sets out those matters which ought to be considered.

2 An important practical exercise is to identify those decisions which should have unanimous consent, and those which will be accepted by a majority of members.

5 As partners should act in good faith (see 1(c)) this clause will reduce the risks inherent in arbitrary dismissal.

6 When a group splits up, the most common disagreement is on who can continue to use the name.

6(e) A leaving member should be free of contractual commitments which may be inpractical when he ceases to be a member.

6(b)(i) There will always be the risk of confusion, so the remaining members of the group should change its name on the change of membership.
6(h) Financial damage can be caused by a change in membership in the middle of a tour.
7 "Resurrecting" a group can be big business, but badly done it can ruin its old image. There is no implied right, except perhaps for the last version of the group.
16 Outstanding tax arrears with no funds to pay them is a common problem.
22 The time spent, and the cost, tend to inhibit the seeking of advice. In all other agreements the group members have a common interest as a unit against a manager, record company or whatever, and one adviser can act for the group. Here it is potentially member against member, so one adviser may have a conflict of interest in advising all the members. Discuss the problem with the group's adviser, who can recommend other solicitors who can give each member his own independent advice on the agreement. Without independent advice members can be too embarrassed to ask what might be considered to be awkward questions.

## MERCHANDISE AGREEMENT

THIS MERCHANDISE LICENCE AGREEMENT is made the
day of
BETWEEN of
(hereinafter called the Licensor) of the one part and
of
(hereinafter called the Licensee) of the other part.

[WHEREAS the licensor is the proprietor of the marketing and merchandising rights in the name and image of [ ] (hereinafter called the Artiste)]

WHEREBY IT IS AGREED as follows:

*Definitions*

1 In this Agreement the following words will have the following meanings:

| | |
|---|---|
| "The Territory" | shall mean [ ]. |
| "The Products" | shall mean [ ]. |
| "The Rights" | shall mean the right to manufacture distribute promote and sell within the Territory the Products which contain or upon which are exhibited the logo. |
| "The Logo" | shall mean the name and/or likeness of the Licensor [the Artiste] as set out in the schedule hereto. |
| "The Term" | shall mean the period commencing on the date hereof and terminating on the [ ] unless previously terminated as set out herein. |

*Grant of Rights*

2 (a) In consideration of the Licensee paying the royalties to the Licensor and observing and performing all of its other obligations hereunder the Licensor hereby grants to the Licensee exclusively the Rights within the Territory during the Term.

(b) The Licensor undertakes not to grant to any other party any exercise of the Rights within the Territory during the Term.

*Intellectual Property*

3 (a) The Licensor warrants that the Logo is the sole property of the Licensor and that so far as he is aware the Logo does not infringe the rights of any third party.

(b) The Licensor confirms that the Logo is not the subject of a trademark registration or application within the Territory.

**Obligations of the Licensee**

*Use of Logo*

4 (a) All uses of the Logo upon the Products will be in accordance with the terms of this Agreement and no modification may be made to any part of the Logo which shall always be used in the format set out in the schedule hereto.

(b) The Licensee undertakes not to make any challenge against the rights of the Licensor in the Logo or its validity in any way but so as not to prevent any claim being made by the Licensee against the Licensor if the Licensor shall be in breach of any of its warranties in relation to the Logo.

(c) If the Licensee becomes aware of any unauthorised use of the Logo within the Territory it will promptly notify the Licensor with appropriate details.

(d) No other logo device or wording will be used on any of the Products together with the Logo except with the approval of the Licensee.

*Approval of Products*

5 (a) The Licensee will submit to the Licensor samples of all of the Products and (where applicable) their packaging and any intended advertising and promotion material which will contain or refer to the Logo such samples to be of the same quality of the Product which is intended to be sold.

(b) The Licensor will use reasonable endeavours to notify the Licensee within [21] days whether approval is given and any modifications which may reasonably be required to ensure the proper depiction of the Logo and the quality of the Products.

(c) If any new Products are to be made or produced by the Licensee during the Term or if the design of Products will be changed significantly whereby the use of the Logo or the quality of the Product is modified then new samples must be submitted as in (a).

(d) Failure by the Licensor to notify the Licensee of approval in time will not be deemed to be approval.

*Quality Control*

6 The Licensee undertakes that all items of the Products:

(a) Will conform in all respects to the quality of the samples submitted to the

Licensor for approval and which are approved by the Licensor and (where applicable) will conform to any statutory or other regulation on safety or design within the Territory and the Licensee will supply the Licensor with [2] samples of each of the finished Products to check their standards of quality.

(b) Will not breach third party copyright design rights or any other rights in any respect.

(c) Will not be defective in workmanship or materials or will not be constructed of dangerous materials or those which are not suitable for the Product in relation to its intended or reasonably anticipated use.

7 If the Licensee intends to produce any consumer products which may if defective be subject to product liability claims it shall take out adequate product liability insurance and shall indemnify the Licensor from any claim loss damage expense or liability arising therefrom or from any other obligation of the Licensee set out in clause 6 or elsewhere in this Licence Agreement.

*Sales*

8 (a) The Licensee will use its reasonable endeavours to promote and sell the Products within the Territory throughout the whole of the Term.

(b) If the Licensee has not commenced sale of commercial quantities of the Products within [ ] months after the date hereof then the Licensor shall be entitled to terminate this Agreement forthwith by written notice.

(c) The Licensee will not distribute or sell the Products outside the Territory nor will it sell them to a third party within the Territory who the licensee is aware (or ought to be aware) intends to distribute or sell those Products outside the Territory.

(d) The Licensee shall ensure that all Products shall retain at all times the same quality as the samples approved by the Licensor and shall promptly take all steps to remedy any failure to achieve such level of quality and shall not distribute or sell any articles of the Products which are not in accordance with the approved quality standards.

9 (a) The Licensee at the time of submitting the Products to the Licensor for approval will notify it of the proposed wholesale price thereof from the Licensee to third parties or the retail price direct to consumers (as the case may be) and the Licensee undertakes to notify the Licensor of any significant changes therein.

(b) Subject as set out herein the Licensee shall be entitled to sell the Products howsoever he decides provided that the Licensor is accurately accounted to for royalties on sales.

10 If the Licensor requires reasonable quantities of the Products for its own purpose and not for onward sale the Licensee agrees to supply such Products on a cost basis royalty free.

*Royalties*

11 The Licensee will pay to the Licensor royalties at the rate of [ ] percent calculated on the net invoice value from the Licensee of sales of the Products subject to Clause 9(a) and excluding sales tax. If any cash discount is given by the Licensee otherwise than in the normal and proper course of business on an arms length basis to a party unconnected with the Licensee or

the Licensee's shareholders or directors the royalty will still be calculated upon the proper full invoice price which should have applied before the discount.

*Advances*

12 On the execution of this Agreement the Licensee will pay to the Licensor the sum of [ ] US Dollars as an advance against the royalties to be paid by the Licensee hereunder.

*Accounts*

13 (a) The Licensee will render accounts of sales of the Product to the Licensor within 30 days after the 30th June and 31st December in each year and within 30 days after the termination of the period referred to in clause 19(b) together with payment by banker's draft or certified cheque for the amount due to the Licensor after recoupment of outstanding advances.

(b) All accounting statements will show the number of items sold the invoice price and any other material details to enable the Licensor to check the validity of the accounts.

(c) All payments of royalty will be in US dollars if the Territory is outside the UK.

14 The Licensee undertakes to:

(a) Maintain accurate books of account in respect of all quantities of the Products which have been manufactured and all sales of the Products and to keep the accounts available for a further period expiring 12 months after the termination of this Agreement to take account of the sell-off period referred to in clause 19(b) and of the rights of the Licensor under clause 14(b) below.

(b) Permit a representative of the Licensor to examine the accounts of the Licensee not more than once each year and within 12 months after the termination of this Agreement. The Licensor will give the Licensee not less than 14 days prior written notice of its intention to make such an inspection. If such an inspection indicates that the Licensee has under accounted by [five] percent or more overall up to the inspection date then it will pay the Licensor the balance due and any interest thereon and for the cost of the inspection.

15 (a) If there are currency transfer restrictions in the Territory the Licensee shall notify the Licensor promptly in writing and will open a separate bank account in the name of the Licensor and will pay into it all sums due to him.

(b) If the Licensee is obliged by law to deduct a withholding tax on royalty remittances abroad it will provide the Licensor with a valid tax deduction certificate to enable the Licensor to obtain the benefit of any relevant double tax convention.

16 Interest at the rate of [ ] pa calculated on a daily basis will be charged on all overdue royalty accounts from the date due to the date of payment.

*Termination*

17 The Licensor will be entitled to terminate this Agreement by written notice immediately if:

(a) The Licensee remains in breach of any term of this Agreement for more than [21] days after receiving a written notice specifying the breach and requiring its remedy.

(b) The Licensee:

(i) ceases to trade;

(ii) winds up otherwise than for amalgamation;

(iii) has a receiver appointed over its assets;

(iv) compounds with its creditors.

*Effects of termination*

18 (a) Upon termination of or the expiry of this Agreement the Licensee shall forthwith cease manufacturing the Products and within [21] days thereafter the Licensee shall notify the Licensor in writing of the level of all existing stocks of Products in its possession and under its control.

(b) The Licensee shall be entitled for [90] days after termination on a non-exclusive basis to sell off existing stocks which sales shall be accounted for to the Licensor. Any stocks then remaining will be destroyed unless the sell-off period is extended by the Licensor.

19 The Licensee is an independent contractor and this Agreement does not constitute a partnership or joint venture between the parties.

[STANDARD CLAUSES]

THE SCHEDULE

[LOGO]

IN WITNESS

**Comments on this Agreement**

The Licensor may be a company to which the artiste is contracted, so the agreement would have to be modified accordingly.

1 The logo will probably only be the name of the artiste or group. If that is in a specific style, a copy should be scheduled as the format to be followed precisely.

2 If the product category includes "T" shirts, insert a subclause entitling the artiste's record company to produce a limited quantity for its own staff when, eg, launching a new album, provided they are not for general distribution or commercial sale.

3(b) If there are registrations within the territory they should be described and this subclause modified.

4 Approval may not always be practical or necessary, but the right should be there.

8(c) This subclause could not be included for any UK or EEC licensee due to the Treaty of Rome and UK anti-restrictive legislation.

11 If there are different products with different rates of royalty then set them out in a schedule.

12 For "dodgy" territories or licensees take as high an advance as possible, as future accountings may leave a lot to be desired.

12 and 13(c) Outside the UK the usual currency for accounting is US Dollars, but it can be whatever is agreed.

18 The likelihood of being accounted to accurately if the agreement has been terminated for good cause is not great.

# APPENDIX III

# *Cases*

Set out in this Appendix is a selection of cases which are relevant to different areas of music business, but this is not a definitive list. The explanation of each case is very simplified to demonstrate what it was about, the basis of the legal decisions, and the lessons which can be learned from them. Each judgment is very detailed and is interesting reading, and only a small part of the context can be included in the following summaries.

The impression that comes through from all of the cases is that they were instigated by a composer or artiste who became disillusioned with his lot, considered he had been treated unfairly, and felt so strongly about it that he decided to test it by court action.

How to judge what is "fair" can be difficult, as what might seem to be a sensible approach at the time may not be considered to be so when looked at retrospectively, if challenged in the future. The bigger the deal, the more important it is to get it as right and as fair as possible from both parties' points of view, and with reciprocally effective safeguards against the normal commercial risks relevant to the type of deal.

The circumstances of the contentious issues in these cases will be familiar to advisers. It can be difficult to make a manager, record company or publisher understand that common sense advice against tough or restrictive proposals is not a sign of weakness. If the artiste becomes sufficiently successful to make injustice (as he sees it) morally and financially worth fighting against, he will be able to afford the cost of testing it in the courts. The cost of forced retrospective financial adjustments can be ruinous. So all long term contracts should be reviewed occasionally, and, if necessary, adjusted in favour of the artiste, to reflect the revised value of his then current status.

## EXXON CORPORATION v EXXON INSURANCE CONSULTANTS LIMITED (1980)

(Copyright point)

**Legal point**

Could a single word have copyright protection?

**The facts**

Exxon Corporation is the international name of Esso Petroleum Co Ltd. Exxon Insurance Consultants had no connection with Exxon Corporation, which sued Exxon Insurance Consultants for breach of copyright in the word "Exxon", and for passing off. Exxon was a wholly original name created by Esso with great care.

**The decision**

"EXXON" did not qualify as an "original work" under the Copyright Act 1956 s2. The reason given in the judgement was that the word "EXXON", although invented and therefore original, did not have any meaning or substance in itself, and therefore did not constitute a literary work.

**The conclusion**

To be a literary work, and therefore protected by copyright, a collection of words must have some meaning and substance in their own right. A single word song title, or a song title with a very few words, will not be deemed to be a literary work. How many words a literary work needs has not been established, and there is no guidance in either the 1956 Act or the 1988 Act.

Exxon Corporation succeeded in getting a passing-off injunction.

## PAGE ONE RECORDS LTD and DICK JAMES MUSIC LTD v BRITTON (and other Trogg Members) and HARVEY BLOCK ASSOCIATES LTD (1967)

(The Troggs Case)

**Legal Point**

Could a manager get an injuction to prevent the group from appointing another manager in breach of their existing management agreement?

**The facts**

In February 1966 the group appointed Page One to be their exclusive manager for five years. In April 1966 Page One was also appointed their agent, and in May 1966 the group signed a recording agreement with the manager. In January 1967 they signed a publishing agreement with Dick James Music. The group became successful, due greatly to the manager's efforts. In June 1967 the group by a letter gave notice of termination of the management agreement claiming material breach, and made a claim for a return of all commission received. Page One sued the group claiming an injunction to prevent them from appointing another manager, ie, Harvey Block Associates. An injunction and damages were also claimed by Page One against Harvey Block. There was no evidence that the agreements were not fair or reasonable, or that better terms could have been obtained from any other company. Harvey Block had been approached by the group to see if they would manage it instead of Page One, for reasons which do not appear to have been specific or convincing.

**The decision**

The court found that Page One was not in breach of the three agreements, and that the other claims made by the Troggs would probably not succeed in a court hearing, but nevertheless the court would not grant Page One an injunction against the group. That would amount to enforcing a contract for personal services, which the courts will not do. In this case, and the same applies to the following cases where injunctions are sought against an artiste who has breached or repudiated his contract, two criteria are applied by the courts:

(a) an injunction is never granted at the request of a party against whom the party to be restrained could not have obtained specific performance;

(b) where a contract of personal service contains negative covenants, the enforcement of which will amount either to a decree of specific performance of the positive covenants of the contract, or to the giving of an order under which the defendant must either remain idle or perform those positive covenants, the court will not enforce the negative covenants (*Warner Brothers Pictures Inc v Nelson* (1936)).

**The conclusion**

This case illustrates the principle that it is not possible to enforce the performance of personal service contracts. Page One would have been entitled to claim damages against the group, as it clearly repudiated the management agreement without good reason.

## DENMARK PRODUCTIONS LTD v BOSCOBEL PRODUCTIONS LTD (1968)

(The Kinks Case)

**Legal points**

There were two interesting technical points. The major one was that the relationship requires a high degree of mutual confidence between a group and its manager. The manager should do nothing which he could reasonably foresee would destroy that confidence, and he should take all reasonable steps to preserve the confidence of the group. The other was could Denmark get an injunction to restrain Boscobel, its co-manager of the group, from placing the group's publishing with a third party? Although Denmark had been granted by Boscobel in the co-management agreement the right to place the copyrights, Denmark did not have any beneficial interest in them.

**The facts**

In 1964 the Kinks appointed Boscobel to be their manager, at 40% commission with the manager paying all agent's commission. Denmark was owned as to half by Larry Page, who agreed with Boscobel to co-manage the Kinks for 10% out of the 40% commission. The other 50% of Denmark was owned by Edward Kassner Music Publishing Corporation. Page took a close personal interest in the group, and was effectively its personal manager for promotional activities. Clause 6 of the agreement between Boscobel and Denmark gave Denmark the right to place all of the Kinks' music publishing, which they did to Kassner. Denmark itself took no benefit from the publishing arrangements.

In 1965 a USA tour was proposed for the group. Ray Davies of the Kinks was reluctant to go, although it was very important, but agreed in the end on the condition that Page would go on the tour representing the management as personal manager of the group. The tour was from 28 June to 10 July. On 3 July Page told all the group, except Davies, that he needed to return to

England, and went on 4 July. Davies was most upset when he heard of Page's departure. The group held a meeting on 4 July and decided to get rid of Page. The group did not have a direct contract with Denmark, the connection was through the co-management agreement. The group was legally advised that the way to get rid of Denmark and Page was to terminate its management agreement with Boscobel, so that the co-management agreement between Boscobel and Denmark would then cease to be effective. They would then negotiate a new management agreement with Boscobel alone.

The group terminated the agreement with Boscobel on the basis that Page, representing the Boscobel management, was in material breach of its managerial obligations by leaving the group "in the lurch" during their USA tour. This act caused the group to have a total loss of confidence in Page, who was therefore in breach of a manager's basic obligation to maintain the group's confidence. In September 1965 Boscobel wrote a letter to Denmark stating that the co-management agreement would terminate. Denmark sued Boscobel for an account of money under the co-management deal, and for an injunction to prevent Boscobel from placing the publishing of the group's compositions elsewhere.

### The decision

Upon the facts the group was entitled to terminate their agreement with Boscobel by reason of the serious breach by Page of his management obligations, causing a total loss of confidence in him (and therefore the management). The claim for an injunction on the publishing failed, because it was only to benefit a third party (ie Kassner), and not Denmark.

### Conclusion

Even if the manager is contractually a company, people do the actual managing. The artiste's business-life is in the hands of the manager, and there has to be a significant level of trust and confidence in the manager. If the confidence goes, so does the relationship. In a sufficient and serious proven case, an act or default which justifiably causes that confidence of the artiste to be broken can represent a fundamental breach of the management agreement.

## A SCHROEDER MUSIC PUBLISHING CO LTD v MACAULAY (INSTONE) (1974)

### Legal point

The publishing agreement could be terminated because:

(a) the agreement was held to be unfair, restrictive and in unreasonable restraint of trade, and there had been an inequality of bargaining power.

(b) Schroeder was in breach of an implied obligation not to unfairly or artificially diminish the income it received of which Macaulay was entitled to a share.

## The facts

In 1966 Macaulay signed a five year publishing agreement with Schroeder. This would automatically be extended to ten years if the receipts of Macaulay in the first five years exceeded £5,000. The relevant contractual points were:

(a) the total potential ten year period during which Schroeder would be entitled to have assigned to it the copyrights of the Macaulay compositions, for the life of copyright;

(b) there was no specific obligation in the agreement upon Schroeder to promote the copyrights;

(c) the agreement was exclusive, Macaulay could not assign any copyrights elsewhere during the contract period, Schroeder could assign any or all of the copyrights to any other party;

(d) Schroeder could terminate the agreement on one month's notice, Macaulay had no termination rights.

The agreement offered to Macaulay was in "standard" form (for Schroeder), and Macaulay was not able to negotiate its terms. In these circumstances there is no legal presumption that the terms are fair and reasonable. The whole agreement must be considered to see whether the restrictions are reasonably necessary for the protection of the legitimate interests of the company, and commensurate with the benefits accruing to the composer.

Schroeder UK was a subsidiary of Schroeder USA, (January Music), and Schroeder USA had subsidiary sub-publishers in other countries. It was an implied term of the publishing agreement that Macaulay would get effectively 25% of "at source" income being 50% of Schroeder UK receipts on the basis that a sub-publisher wherever would keep 50%. What happened was that the subsidiary sub-publisher retained, say 30%, and remitted 70% to January Music. Instead of remitting 50% of "at source" income to Schroeder UK, January remitted 50% of what it received, ie, 37.5% of earnings at source. Schroeder UK paid Macaulay 50% of what it received from January, so Macaulay got 17.25% of at source income, and not 25%. Schroeder contended that this was an accounting error only.

## The decision

The contract was considered not to be fair, and to be in unreasonable restraint of trade, for the following reasons:

(a) Primarily, Macaulay was committed for possibly ten years to assign all of his copyrights to Schroeder, and Schroeder had no specific obligation to do anything with them. The length of time was a crucial factor. If Schroeder did nothing, Macaulay had no right to terminate the contract, and so could be prevented from earning a living. The court did not accept the Schroeder suggestion that such an obligation to promote the copyrights might be deemed to be implied in such a contract.

(b) In any contract for personal services any restrictions on the composer have to be justified as being only to the extent reasonably necessary to protect the proper interests of the publisher, and must be commensurate with the benefits to be received by the composer. The whole agreement was considered to be too one-sided in favour of Schroeder.

(c) It had been argued by Schroeder that his contract was "standard". Macaulay had wanted to negotiate an agreement, but basically was not allowed to, Schroeder "enjoyed superior bargaining power". The terms of the contract were held not to be fair, it combined a lack of obligation on the part of Schroeder, with a total commitment on the part of Macaulay.

(d) The accounting for royalties through January Music was an unfair diminution of what Macaulay should have received, and was a breach of an implied term of the agreement that no unreasonable or artificial reduction should be made in the money of which Macaulay was entitled to a share when it was received in the UK. The defence of it having been an accounting error was not accepted by the court.

### The conclusion

A publishing agreement (or any agreement for personal services) must be fair and reasonable in all the circumstances, as to the period of the agreement, the obligations of the publisher, the obligations of the composer, and the restrictions on the composer. This does not mean that a publisher has to give in to all a composer's demands, the reasonableness is a market place value judgement. The distinction is that if the agreement had come about through equal power negotiation, that part of the decision may have been different. It is the apparent "take it or leave it" attitude which creates the presumption of unfair advantage, especially where there is an inequality of bargaining power. The publisher must not, by an artificial device, unfairly reduce what the composer would expect to receive under his contract. It was accepted that a sub-publisher, even though connected with the publisher, could retain 50% of income provided it is commercially active and making a charge for effort, if that was at the time the normal going rate. The breach was the further filtering of money through January Music, where there was no commercial justification for making any charge at all.

## FLEETWOOD MAC PROMOTIONS LTD v CLIFFORD DAVIS MANAGEMENT CO LTD (1974)

### Legal point

Ownership and use of a group name can be protected from a duplicated use which constitutes "passing off", and which causes professional confusion. A group name has a reputation and value, even if temporarily not in use. The question is to whom does the value attach?

### The facts

Fleetwood Mac had been formed in 1967, and between 1971 and 1974 it had the same members. The group name was made up from the names of Mick Fleetwood and John McVie. FMP Ltd was the company owned by the group, and CDM Ltd was its manager. In 1973 the group was touring in America, but the tour was cut short due to internal group problems. The group appeared to split up in late 1973, although in late 1974 they got together again. In early 1974 Clifford Davis put together a band, and called it Fleetwood Mac, for the purpose of completing the interrupted American tour, although there were none of the original group members in it. Davis had written to Mick Fleetwood and Mrs McVie, telling them of his plan to form a new group with the name, and inviting them to join it. They did not do so. Neither at that time did they, or any other of the original group members, complain about the proposed use of the name.

The "new" Fleetwood Mac started its American tour. Fans of Fleetwood Mac had bought concert tickets expecting to see the established original group, and what they actually saw was the new group. There was a level of complaints which, it was alleged, was damaging to the reputation of the original group. The original group then complained that obviously there was confusion in the minds of the public, and that the value and image of the group name was being usurped and damaged. The association of the identities and personalities of each of the original group members was what created the success of the group. The original group sued for an injunction to stop CDM Ltd and the new group from using the name.

**The decision**

The judge had to consider four points:

(a) was there a reputation in "Fleetwood Mac" as applied to the original group?

(b) if the second group uses the name, will there be confusion?

(c) will the original group suffer damage from use of the name by the second group?

(d) does the "balance of convenience" favour the original group or the second group? The court looks at the commercial practicalities, not just the purely legal point. The "balance" is judging beween the damage to the plaintiff if the injunction is refused, and the commercial loss to the defendant if it is granted. It also relates to what is fair as between the parties.

The judge, in all the circumstances, found that on balance the original group had shown enough evidence to justify the granting of an injunction against CDM Ltd and the second group to prevent them from forming and performing as a group called "Fleetwood Mac".

**Conclusion**

The name of a group is like any other trading name, ie, it identifies specific people, and the value of the name comes from the reputation attaching to those people. In this case the second group was made up of artistes none of whom had ever been in Fleetwood Mac, so the confusion for the fans, and the misappropriation of the reputation, was clear.

This case will not act as a precedent where, say, a five artiste group, all equally well known, splits into two separate groups, each wanting to use the original group name. The circumstances would have to be examined in detail; perhaps neither rival splinter group could use the name.

CLIFFORD DAVIS MANAGEMENT LTD v WEA RECORDS LTD (1974)

(The Fleetwood Mac case)

**Legal points**

CDM had obtained an interlocutory injunction against WEA and CBS to prevent them distributing in the UK an album with compositions written by Welch and McVie of Fleetwood Mac after the group left CDM Ltd. This case was an appeal from that injunction.

### The facts

This case follows from the previous case when Fleetwood Mac was managed by the plaintiff (CDM Ltd). The two composers (Mrs McVie in 1971 and Mr Welch in 1972) signed music publishing agreements with CDM for five years, extendable to ten years. They were "standard" agreements which clearly had not been the subject of negotiation. Neither composer had independent legal advice upon the publishing agreements. In 1974 the group split from CDM Ltd, which from that time had nothing to do with the group. The composers then wrote the songs for "Heroes are Hard to Find" and WEA (USA) made and released the album in the USA. WEA (UK) and CBS then wanted to release it in the UK. CDM Ltd applied for an injuction to prevent them from doing so, claiming that the copyrights of the compositions on the album belonged to CDM Ltd by reason of the publishing agreements, and that WEA and CBS would be infringing the CDM Ltd copyrights by issuing and releasing the album in the UK. The court initially granted an interlocutory injunction.

The Court of Appeal considered the matter, and examined the publishing agreements' terms, and the circumstances in which they were signed. Lord Denning said that the agreements gave the publisher, who was also the manager, a strangle hold over the composers, by means of the copyrights. The points he made were:

(a) the length of the period of the agreements—potentially ten years, was unfair, and that the benefits of the composers were minimal;
(b) the composer was bound to assign the worldwide copyright in each composition to the publisher, but the publisher had no obligation to do anything with them;
(c) the publisher had the right for six months to reject any new composition without payment;
(d) the publisher had the right to assign the agreement to anyone, and the composer had no say in it. The composer had no similar right.

The Judge considered the agreements to be restrictive of trade. Reference was made to the *Schroeder* case, and the same two principles were applied:

(a) contractual restrictions which appear to be unnecessary or to be reasonably capable of enforcement in an oppressive manner, must be justified before they can be enforced;
(b) if one party uses his superior bargaining power to exact terms that are unfairly onerous, or to drive an unconscionable bargain, the courts will relieve the other party of his legal duty to fulfil it.

### The decision

The court decided that there was a *prima facie* case that at a later trial the terms of each contract would be found to be unfair, that the consideration given for the copyrights was inadequate, that CDM Ltd exerted unfair bargaining power over the composers when signing the publishing agreements, and the composers did not have independent legal advice. The balance of convenience was in favour of WEA and CBS, because the sales of the record would be damaged if it was not released, and if in a subsequent trial CDM Ltd won its claim, it could be properly satisfied by the payment of damages. The injunction was discharged.

### Conclusion

The case was based upon the now familiar scenario of long term contracts with no reciprocity of benefit or safeguard. At this time the *Schroeder* case had just been decided by the House of Lords, and influenced the decision. The result was that a later trial would determine the rights of CDM Ltd in the album copyrights, and as it would not be damaged in the meantime, the injunction was lifted.

## GILBERT O'SULLIVAN v MANAGEMENT AGENCY AND MUSIC LTD

(Original decision in 1982, Court of Appeal 1984)

### Legal points

The manager (Gordon Mills), using an inequality of bargaining power, and in breach of his fiduciary duty, persuaded O'Sullivan to sign disadvantageous contracts for publishing and recording. The agreements were set aside, he got back his copyrights and record master tapes containing his performances, and got a retrospective adjusted accounting.

### The facts

In 1970 O'Sullivan signed management, publishing and recording agreements with companies controlled by Gordon Mills, who was his manager. At that time O'Sullivan was commercially naive, and trusted Mills implicitly. Mills never suggested that O'Sullivan should get independent legal advice, and he didn't. O'Sullivan was very successful but around 1977 became disillusioned with Mills. He questioned his contracts, and all business dealings by the Mills companies in connection with his records and copyrights. The terms of the agreements he had signed with the Mills companies were not as good as he would have received if the companies had been independent, with arm's-length transactions. The judge at the original hearing found the agreements to be void and unenforceable based on the *Schroeder v Macaulay* case, and because Mills had used undue influence over O'Sullivan arising from the special fiduciary relationship between them. The agreements were in restraint of trade, it having been held that the companies also were in a fiduciary relationship with O'Sullivan. There was considerable argument over whether the copyrights and master tapes should revert to O'Sullivan.

### The decision

The combination of breach of fiduciary duty, the lack of independent advice, the fact that the Mills owned companies received a greater benefit than they should have, the exercise of undue influence, and the fact that O'Sullivan did not receive royalty rates and income at a proper level as a result, made the agreements void and unenforceable. He got back his copyrights, his master tapes, and was awarded damages, based on an account of profits plus interest. The rationale for the delivery of the master tapes was that, although the maker of them (not O'Sullivan) owned the copyright in them, that copyright is subordinate to the copyright in the compositions themselves. As the musical copyrights were being assigned to O'Sullivan, and as the consent of O'Sullivan would be required for the use of those copyrights on the tapes, the defendant would have no right to use them. The damages took account of reasonable remuneration to the Mills Companies for the time and effort spent in promoting O'Sullivan.

Normally the court will not order a complete nullity of agreements where the parties to them cannot be put back into the positions they had enjoyed prior to the agreements being signed. However, the fundamental breach of the fiduciary relationship removed this argument, the judge took the view that the need was to achieve what was practically just between the parties.

### Conclusion

This case demonstrates the fundamental point that all dealings and contracts have to be fair if they are to pass the test of litigation. A person in a fiduciary position (such as a manager) has an even greater responsibility to the artiste. In any circumstances which might result in there being a conflict of interest, he should not advise the artiste at all, and should ensure that he actually gets competent independent legal advice. A useful rule of thumb might be that if the manager, if he were to be put in the artiste's position, would not be fully satisfied with what he (as a manager) is proposing, it may not be fair. An unfair advantage in negotiating power should be exercised with caution. The distinction between the *Schroeder* case and the *O'Sullivan* case is that Macaulay's agreement was held to be in restraint of trade and so only unenforceable with effect from a given date. The O'Sullivan agreements were induced through a high level of undue influence, by parties in a fiduciary capacity to him, and so could be set aside as though they had never been entered into.

## ARMATRADING v STONE (1984)

(Joan Armatrading)

### Legal Points

(a) Where an existing manager gets an artiste to sign a new management agreement with him, there is a fiduciary relationship, and a presumption of the exercise of undue influence, and superiority of bargaining power, where independent legal advice was not given to the artiste.
(b) A management agreement remuneration following termination must be reasonable, and restrictions on the artiste in the agreement must also be reasonable.

### The facts

In 1973 Armatrading entered into a management agreement with the Copeland Sherry Agency, in which Stone was a partner. The agreement would expire in March 1976. Stone effectively acted as her manager, representing the agency. In late 1975 they discussed the possibility of Stone becoming her personal manager when the existing management agreement expired. In January 1976 they both saw the same solicitor, when the main elements of the agreement were discussed, including the post-termination management commission on subsequent earnings of Armatrading. In February 1976 the solicitor prepared a draft agreement and they both had a meeting with him to discuss the terms. The next day the agreement was signed. The legal bill was sent to Stone, and as part of the evidence it was considered that the solicitor was effectively acting for Stone. At no time did Stone suggest that Armatrading should get independent legal advice. An important term of the new agreement was that the management commission was perpetual for contracts negotiated or signed during the period of the agreement, on the basis that Armatrading might not be successful until towards the end of the management period, and therefore only afterwards would the manager get a fair return for his efforts. The agreement was to be for five years, and the management commission was 20% on all earnings, even on gross tour income, except for where a new publishing or recording agreement might be negotiated for Armatrading, when the income from which would have a management commission rate of 25%.

The judge said that Armatrading had a trust and confidence in Stone because he had a duty to act in her best interests, and that Stone was aware that his and her interests when discussing the terms of the agreement were conflicting. Armatrading understood from Stone and the solicitor that the contract was a good standard one.

The commission was also to be paid upon agreements in substitution, extension or renewal of any already commissionable agreements, without time limits. This would restrict her ability to appoint another manager, and so would be a restriction on her ability to have her career properly managed.

In mid 1980 they discussed a new management agreement, but Armatrading was not keen on proceeding. In late 1980 she took independent legal advice, when it became clear that she had not understood the post-termination commission clause. In 1981 Armatrading informed Stone of her decision not to sign a new agreement.

The claim by Armatrading was to set aside the 1976 management agreement.

## The decision

Armatrading succeeded, upon the undue influence ground. This was described as a duty to ensure that the person liable to be influenced has formed an independent judgment after full, free and informed thought. She also succeeded on the ground of unequal bargaining power, and the judgment that the contractual restrictions placed upon her were unreasonable and onerous. An important ground was also that, in effect, the post-termination continuing remuneration was unreasonably onerous, and not reasonably required for the protection of Stone's interests in being remunerated for services he provided during the agreement. The judge decided that Armatrading had not been aware of the effect of that clause in the agreement. The benefit to her of Stone's management services was not commensurate with the financial restrictions placed on her ability to employ a new manager, by reason of the continuation of Stone's full commission rates. The judge said that, taken as a whole, the agreement was loaded unfairly in Stone's favour.

**Conclusion**

As in all management cases, the undue influence presumption must be rebutted to safeguard the contract. It also demonstrates how important it is to resist the urge to get commission for a significant period after the management period has expired.

## BARRY McKAY INTERNATIONAL MUSIC (UK) LTD AND L R JACKSON v EMI RECORDS LTD (1985)

(The Ray Jackson Case)

**Legal point**

The recording contract between Jackson and EMI had yearly renewal options, and a minimum recorded product commitment on the artiste and EMI. EMI had no release commitment for any recording made by Jackson. The minimum product in the first year was not fully recorded. Could damages be awarded to Jackson for loss of prospective earnings from records which were not made?

**The facts**

Ray Jackson was a member of Lindisfarne, which broke up in 1973. In October 1975 Mackay was appointed Jackson's manager. In March 1976 Mackay signed an agreement with EMI for the provision to EMI of Jackson's recording services. In the first year three singles were to be recorded, and if the options were exercised for years two and three, an album would be recorded in each year. If the option was exercised, an advance of £10,000 would be paid. One single was released in 1976, and although some recording was done in late 1977, nothing further was released. At the end of 1977 EMI made it clear that they were not going to release any more recordings by Jackson.

The claims made by McKay and Jackson were:

(a) As EMI did not make the two other singles in year one, Jackson lost the opportunity of earning artiste's royalties from them, and of enhancing his career as a performing and recording artiste.
(b) Jackson also lost the opportunity to receive publishing income.
(c) The option for year two had been exercised, and so £10,000 was payable, and (a) and (b) applied to the album which should have been made.

The defences put up by EMI were that:

(a) Jackson did not provide suitable material of adequate satisfactory quality in the opinion of EMI.
(b) Because of Jackson's alleged failure under (a) above, their obligation to record the minimum commitment did not become effective.
(c) Jackson had not suffered any loss or damage.
(d) The option for the second year had not been exercised. EMI considered that the first contract year had simply been extended by EMI orally to enable the two missing singles due in the first year to be recorded.
(e) In the opinion of EMI the material supplied by Jackson, if recorded and released, would have been a commercial failure.

(f) A clause in the agreement said that if Jackson could not fulfil his obligations due to reasons beyond his control, EMI could terminate the agreement or extend the then current year pending such fulfilment. EMI argued that providing unsuitable material came within this clause, so the contract year had been extended, as opposed to an option to continue into the second year having been exercised.

**The decision**

The court found that:

(a) There was no contractual obligation for Jackson to provide his own composed material, and performance by EMI by making the records was not conditional on him so doing. If EMI did not like his material, it should have found alternative suitable material itself.
(b) Despite contradictory evidence, the option for the second year had not been exercised and therefore the £10,000 was not payable.
(c) EMI was in breach of its agreement by not fulfilling the minimum recording commitment in the first year.
(d) Mackay and Jackson were entitled to claim for loss of potential earning, loss of opportunity of success, and loss of publicity to help Jackson's live performances. EMI submitted that because the calculation of damages would be difficult, it would not be right to attempt to do so. This proposal was not accepted. The court recognised that any award would be arbitrary, and awarded £12,500.

**Conclusion**

Standard record contract clauses on minimum recording commitment need to be fair, and should make clear the circumstances in which the record company would be justified in not recording that minimum commitment. The matter of release of records should be considered, as without a release, any minimum recording fulfilment has no value to the artiste. As, meanwhile, the artiste has granted exclusive rights to the record company, there may come a point at which such inactivity might be considered to be unduly onerous on him. There is the possibility of an artiste arguing successfully that no minimal release commitment (such as in the UK) may be considered a "one way ticket" and in restraint of trade.

McLELLAND v CARLIN MUSIC CORPORATION (1986)

(Sandy McLelland)

**Legal points**

(a) Carlin were contractually obliged to use their best endeavours to exploit McLelland's works. The claim by McLelland was that they procrastinated unreasonably in issuing first recording licences to the record company in breach of their best endeavours obligation, but only for the purpose of avoiding a recording being released by a given date. If the recording had been released by that date, a £15,000 advance would have been payable by Carlin to McLelland. Could Carlin reasonably refuse to issue or to delay the issue of such a licence?

(b) Exactly when is a record "released"?

(c) What are the strict rules on a first recording licence?

**NOTE** There were two actions, the first related to an album released in April 1981, and the second related to an album released in April 1982. For convenience these actions are separated. The legal points in connection with each are similar.

## First action

### The facts

In June 1979 McLelland signed a publishing agreement with Carlin for three years with an effective date of 1 May 1979. He was paid an advance of £15,000 on signature, and he would be paid further advances of £15,000 on the release of the first album of his songs performed by him as an artiste released at least in the UK in each of years two and three of the publishing contract. The following clauses in the publishing agreement were relevant to the case. By clause 6(b) he agreed not to grant any rights in the assigned copyrights to any other party. By clause 7(a) Carlin agreed to use their best endeavours to exploit McLelland's works. As the judge said, the clear purpose was for McLelland to record his songs, so that Carlin and he would receive their shares of the royalties arising from sales and performances of records. By clause 8(b) the £15,000 advance was not payable if McLelland was in material breach of the publishing agreement.

In December 1980 McLelland signed a recording agreement for an initial period of 17 months and thereafter annually with a record production company, with a minimum recording commitment of one album in the initial period and in each year.

The date of 30 April 1981 was crucial. On this date the first recording agreement period and the second publishing agreement contract year expired. McLelland had to perform his minimum recording commitment by that date, and for McLelland to get the £15,000 advance from Carlin, an album containing his compositions had to be released by that date. If the album was not released, he would be in breach of his recording agreement, and he would not receive the publishing advance. The recording of an album of his songs was made in late 1980 and early in 1981. Carlin had been aware of McLelland's recording contract, and they helped exploit a single which was released by the record company, having been taken off the album.

In February 1981 McLelland had a meeting with Carlin, at which it asked for a reduction of the forthcoming payment of £15,000. The proposal was rejected. A postponed date for the purpose of putting out another single was proposed by McLelland, which was not accepted. On 16 April McLelland's manager sent Carlin a cassette tape of the album, stating that it would be released on 24 April. He wrote again to Carlin on 22 April, stating that the letter was formal notice of the 24 April release, and that the £15,000 would become due. Carlin responded on 1 May, expressing doubt as to the 24 April release date, and stating that it had not received any composition copyright assignments from McLelland, or any statutory notices in respect of those songs from the record company.

McLelland's claim was that as the album had been released on 24 April, ie within the second publishing contract year, he was due the £15,000 advance. Carlin denied this on the following grounds:

(a) There was no proof of "release" on 24 April, or on any other date before 1 May.

(b) The £15,000 advance was only payable on the release of an album licenced by Carlin as the first recording of the compositions. As they had not given any licence the advance was not payable.

(c) McLelland was in breach of clause 6(b), as by authorising the production and release of the album, he purported to grant an interest in the copyright to a third party.

Carlin also responded by claiming an injunction, damages and other remedies.

## The decision

(a) As to the release date. The release date is taken to be the date upon which the record company gives an irrevocable instruction to its distributors to release the record to retailers against orders. The trade press was informed, and the album was listed as a new release in the edition of Music and Video Week of 25 April. Enough records were at the distributors by 30 April to satisfy initial demand. Therefore the album had been released by 30 April.

(b) As to the necessity for a prior licence. There was nothing in the publishing agreement that required a licence to be granted in advance of the album release to qualify it for the payment of the £15,000 advance. Ordinarily such licensing is treated as a formality. There was no legal requirement for a formal licence, the consent of the copyright owner could be given in writing, or orally, or by a course of conduct. By its conduct Carlin had given its consent, it had acquiesced in the recording and release of the album. They had not previously queried the licence, they had only concentrated on whether or not the £15,000 advance was payable.

(c) As to the breach of clause 6(b). The decision had two limbs:

(i) Carlin were the copyright owners and McLelland had no power to give the record company any interest therein, and the record company was well aware of the correct position and acknowledged it on the record label.

(ii) Even if McLelland were in breach of 6(b), it would not be a material breach. He had no reason to believe a licence would not be granted, and he was not knowingly or intentionally involved in any copyright infringement.

## Second action

## The facts

Neither party had terminated the publishing agreement, so if McLelland made a second album and released it prior to 1 May 1982 he could collect another £15,000 advance.

To ensure that none of the previous confusion and contention relating to the first album would apply to the second album, on 24 February 1982 McLelland's solicitors wrote to Carlin's solicitors referring to the new album, and requesting clearance procedures. Carlin asked for a significant amount of information during the correspondence, which McLelland's solicitors considered to be delaying tactics, and largely unnecessary and/or pedantic. McLelland pointed out that such procrastination was in conflict with the willingness and ability of McLelland to release a record containing his songs, from which Carlin would benefit as their publisher. It was also in conflict with Carlin's obligation under clause 7(a) of the publishing agreement to use its best endeavours to promote McLelland's compositions.

As at 19 April Carlin maintained that they would not grant the first recording licence on the basis that the record company did not appear to be a "*bona fide*" and responsible record company. On 26 April McLelland protested at the procrastination and stated that the album release would proceed. In telexes on 26 and 30 April Carlin confirmed its position.

The second album was released on 30 April 1982, within the contractual deadline. The legal arguments, and the judges decision, were the same as for the first action, with one exception. This was the question of whether Carlin had the right to refuse to issue the mechanical licence, as the copyright owner, as in this case the claims of acquiescence and consent did not apply. If they were so entitled, McLelland would claim that Carlin was in breach of clause 7(a), and consequently would be entitled to claim damages set at £15,000.

**The decision**

The judge said that from the correspondence it was clear that Carlin had procrastinated, and refused to grant a licence, in the hope of not having to pay out another £15,000. Carlin was in breach of their obligations under clause 7(a), and so lost.

**The conclusion**

This is an example of where the form of the argument was inconsistent with the substance of the facts. The publisher had an obligation to use its best endeavours to promote the artiste's material, and it was refusing to grant the licence necessary to release an album of his material. An influence on the judgement was the fact that McLelland was a singer/songwriter, and the only way to get his material recorded was to do so himself. Carlin had regretted doing the deal, and unsuccessfully argued technicalities to try to minimise its expenditure.

## ELTON JOHN v DICK JAMES MUSIC (1986)

**Legal points**

It was claimed that when EJ originally signed agreements with DJM for publishing, management and recording, there was an unequal bargaining power. Because EJ believed in Dick James, and not having had independent legal advice at the time, it was also claimed that there was a presumption of the exercise of undue influence over EJ by Dick James. The two claims were for the return of all EJ's copyrights, and for an account of money where EJ claimed he had been wrongfully deprived of a proper share of certain earnings.

**The facts**

These are complicated (the judgment is 127 pages long) so the following is a very simplified version. In 1967 Elton John entered into publishing, management and recording contracts with DJM related companies. They were not the subject of negotiation, they were explained to Elton John by Dick James, but he did not have independent legal advice on them. The agreements were changed from time to time, and Elton John was given a greater share of income received in the UK on the exploitation of his songs.

Where DJM had independent sub-publishers, generally mechanical royalties were retained by them as to 25% of source income for original recordings, and 50% for local cover versions. Where DJM had subsidiary or related sub-publishers, they retained 50% of mechanical income irrespective of whether there was an original or a cover record on sale locally. The USA had an active office with expenses and staff. In Australasia and France the companies had no expenses, no staff, and appointed local publishers to administer the DJM catalogues through the local subsidiary. In the mid 1970's further DJM subsidiaries were set up in Germany, Holland, Scandinavia, Japan and Italy, modifying the previous sub-publishing financial deals for those countries, escalating from a 25% to a 50% retention.

On a couple of occasions Elton John took advice on the contracts, and had been told that they could be better. At those times he chose not to act on the advice, and either challenge the agreements or try to get them modified. Overall he received a very considerable income under the agreements, but the claims he made ultimately were that:

(a) At the time he signed the original agreements he was under age (but his parents were signatories). Because Dick James was his trusted manager, and as the agreements were with companies owned and controlled by Dick James, there was a presumption that he had used undue influence in obtaining his signature. Elton John did not take independent advice, and was not advised by Dick James to do so, therefore the agreements should be set aside, and he should have all his copyrights back (following the *Gilbert O'Sullivan* case).

(b) Because of the relative importance and standing of Dick James to Elton John, and because the agreements were signed as presented to him, there was a presumption of unequal bargaining power as between them. It was therefore implicit that Elton John had no choice of what terms he would be committed to.

(c) There is an implied condition in his publishing agreement that the publisher would not enter into any arrangement which would unfairly, unjustifiably or artificially diminish the receipts of the publisher in respect of which the composer is contractually entitled to receive a share.

**The decision**

(a) DJM had breached its fiduciary obligations to Elton John relating to some of the sub-publishing deals for subsidiary companies.

(b) The mechanical royalty rate retentions by the DJM subsidiaries were excessive, and DJM had failed to inform Elton John of these provisions as a deliberate decision, which the court considered unconscionable. Therefore Elton John was entitled to an account for excess retained income.

(c) In respect of the recording contract, the "net share of income" provision did not apply where the company itself manufactured and sold records. On those sales, the company had to account to Elton John for an element of profit. The inter-company relationships were concealed.

(d) On the reversion of copyrights, the court said there were two necessary ingredients—a relationship in which one person has a dominating influence over the other; and a manifestly disadvantageous transaction resulting from the exercise of that influence. The court found there had been the exercise of undue influence, and that some of the contractual arrangements had been unfair transactions. However Elton John over the years had so accepted matters, and DJM had spent money and had worked to promote Elton John, that on the balance of justice the reversion claim would not succeed.

**Conclusion**

This case shows that artistes' or composers' agreements must be fair. It confirms that managers, publishers and record companies will, in relevant circumstances, be considered in law to be in a fiduciary relationship with an artiste. It also demonstrates that if an artiste or composer believes he has a genuine grievance, or that the contracts are unfair, he should promptly try to get matters rectified, failing which he should promptly take legal action. The practical difficulty is that taking legal action is expensive, time consuming, and instantly destroys what may otherwise be a good relationship with the other party.

## CBS SONGS LTD v AMSTRAD CONSUMER ELECTRONICS PLC (1988)

(Copyright point)

**Legal point**

Was it an offence under the Copyright Act 1956 to make and sell a double deck high speed tape to tape recorder? Did Amstrad authorise the infringement of copyright?

**The facts**

Amstrad makes, as part of a hi-fi system high speed, tape to tape recorders, so that the user can rapidly copy onto a blank tape copyright music which is on a pre-recorded tape. The high speed facility made it quicker and easier for illicit tape re-recording to be undertaken. It is an accepted fact that almost everyone who has a radio/tape player, or an ordinary cassette recorder, at some time records their favourite records for their own use, although wholesale recording is limited by the scope of the recording equipment available. This was a test case for an injunction and other remedies on the basis that Amstrad was inciting the breach of copyright by providing the facilities necessary to do so. Part of the Amstrad advertisement said "now features high speed dubbing, enabling you to make duplicate recording from one cassette to another, record directly from any source, and then make a copy, and you can even make a copy of your favourite cassette". A footnote to the advertisement said "the recording and playback of certain material may only be possible by permission. Please refer to the Copyright Act 1956, the Performers Protection Acts 1958–1972". Despite the footnote, the advertisement was considered by the plaintiffs to incite the infringement of the copyright law.

**The decision**

The court dismissed the claim, and the other technical claims made, including a claim that Amstrad owed copyright owners a duty not to infringe or authorise the infringement of copyright.

**Conclusion**

It was a curious claim, but worth a try. If it had succeeded, the same legal ruling would be applied to any tape recorder, to any photocopier, and any other device capable of making unauthorised recordings or copies of copyright works. The judge said that "home copying cannot be prevented, is widely practised, and brings the law into disrepute". Parliament did not grasp this nettle when drafting the 1988 Act, thus creating an odd anomaly. By section 17 it is an offence to copy copyright material without the consent of the copyright owner. There is no express latitude or exception for home taping for private and domestic use. However, under section 22 (within the secondary infringement sections) a person does not infringe copyright by importing into the UK an infringing copy, provided it is "for private and domestic use". You can possess an infringing copy, but you must not make one.

## ZANG TUMB TUUM RECORDS LTD and PERFECT SONGS LTD v JOHNSON (1988)

(The Holly Johnson/Frankie Goes to Hollywood Case)

**Legal points**

(a) Could ZTT and Perfect obtain injunctions against Johnson to prevent him from breaking his exclusive recording and publishing agreements?
(b) Were the agreements unenforceable, or had they been repudiated by the companies activities?
(c) Could excessive recording costs be the basis of a claim for damages by the artiste?

**The facts**

Johnson was the lead singer of Frankie Goes to Hollywood. Trevor Horn, the successful and respected record producer, saw the group on TV and, thinking they had potential, approached them with proposed recording and publishing deals with ZTT and Perfect respectively. Both of these companies were owned and run by Mr Horn and his wife, who was also active in the business. The recording contract was signed in September 1983, and the publishing agreement was signed in May 1984. Johnson and the group had independent legal advice prior to signing each of the agreements.

The group then made records for ZTT and their recorded songs were assigned to Perfect.

The first single "Relax" went to No 1 in the charts, as did the second single "Two Tribes". The first album "Welcome to the Pleasure Dome" was made in 1984. A second album "Liverpool" was made in 1985. A crucial element in the case was the question of recording costs, as, under the recording agreement, the recording costs were deemed to be an advance of royalties, and recoupable from them. The first album cost nearly £400,000, and after a considerable period of recording and mixing, the second album costs came to about £750,000. Johnson then left the group, and ZTT and Perfect issued proceedings on the basis that the agreements continued to be binding upon him as an individual artiste and composer.

The basis of Johnson's defence was that:

(a) the recording and publishing agreements were in restraint of trade;

(b) unequal bargaining power had been exercised by ZTT and Perfect when the agreements were signed, despite the fact that both sides were advised by solicitors.

Johnson also counterclaimed for damages, because the recording costs were excessive, which restricted his right to receive royalties.

The group's solicitor had tried to negotiate upon the terms of the recording agreement, to get better terms than the "standard" ones offered to the group. But, as the judge said "this was a take it or leave it contract", and ZTT were not prepared to get into negotiations. The same applied to the publishing agreement. It was the prospect of Mr Horn producing their records which influenced the decision of the group to sign the contracts, whatever advice they had received. It also became clear that the group would only get a recording contract if they signed the publishing agreement.

The recording agreement was for a six month initial period with seven potential option years. The minimum recording commitment on the group was a single for the initial period and for each of the first two option years, and then an album for each of the remaining option years. ZTT had the right, but not the obligation, to make the records, and it also had the right, but not the obligation, to release whatever was recorded. The judge rejected the submission that there was an implied term that records would be made within a reasonable time of the exercise of an option, failing which the group could give written notice making time "of the essence".

All recording costs were recoupable from royalties, and because of the costs of recording the singles and the first album, despite high sales, the royalties actually received by the group were low. Before the second album was to be recorded, the group and ZTT discussed the question of recording costs. The estimates given varied between £250,000 and £350,000. No specific budget was ever agreed. It appears that the recording in Holland cost about £250,000, but about £500,000 was spent in the UK on mixing the tapes of those recordings.

The recording agreement had a "leaving member" clause, which stated that if a member left the group, ZTT could require him to enter into a separate agreement "on all of the same terms and conditions as are set out in this agreement". The injunction claimed against Johnson was to restrain him from recording elsewhere, and to enforce his solo artiste career through ZTT.

The publishing agreement is between Perfect and "the Composer", which was defined as the named group members. The definition did not refer to it being applicable to any of them as separate individuals. The question was whether it should apply "jointly and severally" or whether it should be limited only to the group as a unit. So far, under this agreement the group had been credited as being joint composers of all of the songs which they had composed and recorded.

**The decision**

The judge found that ZTT and Perfect could not have their injuctions on the grounds that:

(a) In respect of the recording agreement:
   (i) The recording contract was not a fair bargain and was in restraint of trade. There was also an inequality of bargaining power between the parties. The fact that solicitors were involved did not change the issue, it was an unknown group negotiating with a major producer and his companies.
   (ii) The "leaving member" provision, according to the judge, was "a wholly nonsensical provision" which could not be applied to Johnson. He would also have found it to be void for uncertainty.
   (iii) There was no longer any degree of trust and confidence between ZTT and Mr Johnson.

(b) In respect of the publishing agreement, the definition of "Composer" as set out in the agreement limited the agreement to the copyrights written by the group members together, and did not extend to those written by any individual member by himself.

(c) In respect of the excessive recording costs claim by Johnson, the record company has an implied obligation to keep recording costs within reasonable bounds. ZTT had not done so, therefore Johnson was entitled to an enquiry for damages, so as to calculate the amount due.

**Conclusion**

In two respects the case shows that contracts have to be drafted carefully. The "leaving member" clause in the recording agreement, and the definition of "composer" in the publishing agreement, were strictly construed, and the judge would not allow any implied modification of interpretation to suit the company's claim.

Despite the group being advised by solicitors, the elements of unequal bargaining power and the unreasonable restrictions creating a restraint of trade still existed.

## CASE ANALYSIS

From this selection of cases it can be seen clearly that there are common factors which are the main reasons why the artistes or composers were successful in their court actions. These are set out below.

### 1 Fiduciary relationship

This applies primarily to management agreements. The basis is one of trust by the artiste that the manager will look after the artiste's interests, and that all things done by the manager will be to the artiste's best advantage—that is the manager's prime duty. The fiduciary obligation is broken where the manager has, for example, an undisclosed conflict of interest between the artiste's benefit, and his own. If the manager also has a recording or publishing company, and wants the artiste to sign contracts with them, there is a serious conflict of interest. To reduce the risk of breach of the fiduciary duty, the manager should:

(a) disclose and explain to the artiste the existence and ramifications of the conflict;
(b) ensure that he gets good independent legal advice;
(c) not make signing the contracts a condition of management;
(d) fully negotiate an agreement with the artiste's solicitor, and not try to push through "standard terms" under pressure;
(e) give the artiste not less than the same financial and safeguard terms than he would have obtained for him, or would have insisted upon for his benefit, if he had been negotiating with a third party at arm's-length on the artiste's behalf;
(f) accept obligations of a positive nature and reduce restrictions on the artiste to a minimum, commensurate only with the reasonable need to protect his fair rights.

Even then, there is still a real risk that a conflict will arise during the course of the operation of the agreement.

## 2 Undue influence

Undue influence is a separate head referred to in most of the cases, but it arises mainly from the existence of a fiduciary duty. Because of that duty, the law presumes that any proposal, guidance or requirement made by, say, the manager or publisher, in relation to a commitment to be undertaken, restriction to be accepted or benefit to accrue to the artiste, will have been achieved by wrongful pressure, or in circumstances where the artiste is not fully aware of the terms and consequences of the proposal. Undue influence is not limited to where the manager actually advises the artiste to accept contractual terms. It will also exist where the artiste feels morally obliged to accept the agreement for fear of the anger or disapproval of the manager, or where not to do what the manager proposes may be considered by the manager to be an insult or a questioning of his judgment. Influence is very much a psychological matter, and it becomes undue when mentally the artiste believes he does not have a free choice.

The question only arises where, on examination, the deal is suspect or deficient to the detriment or disadvantage of the artiste, resulting in the direct or indirect benefit of the manager or publisher. The best way to reduce this risk is to ensure that the artiste has separate advice, and that the proposed terms are fair and reasonable.

## 3 Unequal bargaining power

It is not safe to believe that if an artiste willingly signs an agreement he will be stuck with it, if the terms are found to be unconscionable. A significant factor in the decisions has been that "unequal bargaining power" has been held against the more powerful party as representing a form of unreasonable pressure. This is taken into account when other factors are also present, such as unduly onerous terms or unreasonable restrictions. A properly negotiated agreement does not have to give the artiste the best deal ever, but it should give him a fair deal.

The unequal bargaining cases mostly involve "standard agreements", where there are a few blanks for the contract period, the territory, the commission or royalty rate to be inserted, and after that simple exercise it is a "take it or leave it" position for the artiste. Because standard agreements are designed to cover all cases, the extent of the obligations and restrictions relating to the artiste are usually stringent. Standard agreements are applied to those artistes who do not have sufficient negotiating "muscle" to warrant individual attention.

To minimise the risk of exercising unequal bargaining power, a standard form of contract must be the subject of genuine "level power" negotiation, with a schedule setting out the modifications agreed. If the company believes the artiste is being greedy or unrealistic, it does not have to sign any contract with him.

## 4 Unequal obligations

The existence of unequal obligations generally arises from a combination of the exercise of unequal bargaining power, and the failure by the artiste to take independent legal advice. The courts treat a significant disparity of benefit or obligation as related to onerous terms and unfair restrictions, where these also exist. Examples of unequal obligations are:

(a) in a publishing agreement, where the composer has to assign all his copyrights to the publisher for their lifetime, but the publisher has no positive obligation to promote them in a proper commercial manner, or to reassign the copyrights if he does not promote them;

(b) in a recording agreement where the artiste has to record a minimum commitment at the company's request, but the company has no obligation either to record or to release any of them;

(c) an artiste or composer having no contractual right to give notice of termination, whereas the company can terminate by notice at any time.

A balance has to be struck between offensive unequal obligations, and a fair protection for the company for its effort and investment. The perspective depends on the overall impression of the agreement.

## 5 Restraint of trade

This appears in the context of exclusive agreements. An exclusive agreement which has an inequality in the sense that the artiste is committed exclusively to the company, but the company does not have a commensurate obligation to the artiste to release, publish or exploit the recordings or songs of the artiste, is suspect. If the publisher never gets the compositions recorded, or if the record company never records the minimum commitment or never releases what it has recorded, the artiste receives no income. At the same time, due to the exclusivity of the agreement, during its existence he cannot go to another publisher or record company to try to earn a living.

Restraint of trade is the concept of being prevented from earning a living. So, if a company in fact does little for the artiste, or produces little income (irrespective of contractual commitments to do so), the artiste has the choice of staying with the company with that risk, or of breaking away to protect his career and earning power. If the court considers that the exclusive agreement is a serious hindrance to the career and earning power of the artiste, and not a genuine mutual benefit with the company whatever the agreement says, it can set aside the agreement as being in restraint of trade.

To limit the risk, it is acceptable to have exclusivity, provided that the company is contractually obliged to make good commercial use of the artiste's product, ie, so that he can make a living. The contract period within which that must be done has to be reasonably short, because, for example, of the periods between making a record and getting it released, and releasing a record and paying the artiste any royalties on sales. If, the company fails to do these things for long enough, the artiste will have to be released from the agreement. The artiste must also be able to demonstrate that he is not the cause of any such failure or delay by the company.

## 6 Artiste's trust and confidence

This applies primarily to management agreements, because of the personal and fiduciary elements, and the trust the artiste must have in the manager to guide him professionally and to protect him commercially. The manager negotiates the sources of the artiste's earnings, ie, recording and publishing agreements, takes care of financial matters, and plans and promotes his career. There has to be a personal rapport with the manager, and a high level of faith in him.

Confidence is a personal matter, and the manager has some obligation to do nothing which would destroy it. In serious circumstances an act or default by the manager which causes a reasonably founded total failure of confidence can be one of the grounds for claiming breach of contract by the manager, or repudiation by it of the management agreement.

## 7 Independent advice

Independent advice is essential for the artiste whenever he is discussing or negotiating any agreement with any third party, such as a manager, record company or publisher. The purpose is to ensure that the artiste is given an unbiased, experienced and professional view, and has the meaning and consequences of the agreement fully explained to him. This reduces the risk of undue influence being exerted, but does not eliminate it, as the artiste can still be influenced in making his decision.

Independent advice does not necessarily validate and sanitise the position, such as where negotiations attempted by the artiste's solicitor are restricted or refused by the company, resulting in the existence of unequal bargaining power, onerous terms, and restraint on trade.

# Index